"The revised edition of *The Psychology of Perfectionism in Sport, Dance, and Exercise* is a timely and valuable contribution to the understanding of the rise of perfectionism in diverse physical activity settings. Professor Andrew Hill has done an excellent job in this second edition by providing new conceptual and methodological insights, updating the evidence base, as well as offering important practical suggestions to develop interventions that address the negative consequences of perfectionism for physical and mental functioning. I highly recommend this book to students, researchers, and practitioners."

Professor Nikos Ntoumanis, *University of Southern Denmark, Denmark*

"This second edition of *The Psychology of Perfectionism in Sport, Dance, and Exercise* by Professor Andrew Hill and his team of contributors is an essential read for researchers, coaches, exercise enthusiasts, as well as psychology practitioners. The book skilfully maps out the latest evidence related to the nature, development, and consequences of perfectionism in its various guises. It also thoughtfully presents evidence-informed recommendations for those working with athletes, exercisers, and dancers who exhibit perfectionism. A highly recommended read!"

Professor Mark Beauchamp, *University of British Columbia, Canada*

"Edited by one of the world-leading researchers on perfectionism in performance domains, and comprising a variety of insightful, critical, and novel chapters written by leaders in the field, this book should be a go-to resource for any academics or practitioners interested in understanding this complex and important topic. Taking a critical and reflective approach to the field, the text provokes you to reconsider perceptions pertaining to perfectionism and re-evaluate your understanding of both research and practice as it pertains to perfectionism."

Professor Camilla Knight, *Swansea University, United Kingdom*

The Psychology of Perfectionism in Sport, Dance, and Exercise

This extensively revised and updated edition offers a comprehensive account of the latest research and practice issues relating to perfectionism in sport, dance, and exercise.

The new edition of *The Psychology of Perfectionism in Sport, Dance, and Exercise* includes the latest understanding of perfectionism, its benefits and costs, and support that can be given to those at risk to the perils of perfectionism. The book features contributions from leading researchers and practitioners. With nine new chapters and six updated chapters, the book provides an exhaustive account of research, novel approaches to studying and working with perfectionism, along with critical reflections on key issues and controversies. The book includes a new section on emerging approaches and concepts, as well as a revised section on applied issues and practitioner perspectives offering three new approaches to working with perfectionism. With chapters featuring returning authors and new contributors with novel perspectives, this edition will be invaluable to individuals familiar and unfamiliar with this area of work.

This book will be an essential resource and vital guide for students and researchers, as well as practitioners, coaches and instructors in sport, dance, and exercise.

Andrew P. Hill is a Professor of Sport and Exercise Psychology at York St John University, UK. He has published over 80 studies of perfectionism in sport, dance, and exercise, and is one of the leading experts on the topic. He is an Associate Editor of *Sport, Exercise, and Performance Psychology* and an editorial board member of the *Journal of Sport and Exercise Psychology* and *Scandinavian Journal of Medicine and Science in Sport*.

The Psychology of Perfectionism in Sport, Dance, and Exercise

Second edition

Edited by
Andrew P. Hill

Routledge
Taylor & Francis Group

LONDON AND NEW YORK

Designed cover image: Getty Images

Second edition published 2023
by Routledge
4 Park Square, Milton Park, Abingdon, Oxon OX14 4RN

and by Routledge
605 Third Avenue, New York, NY 10158

Routledge is an imprint of the Taylor & Francis Group, an informa business

© 2023 Andrew P. Hill

British Library Cataloguing in Publication Data
A catalogue record for this book is available from the British Library

ISBN: 978-1-032-26378-6 (hbk)
ISBN: 978-1-032-25590-3 (pbk)
ISBN: 978-1-003-28801-5 (ebk)

DOI: 10.4324/9781003288015

Typeset in Bembo
by Taylor & Francis Books

This book is dedicated to Samuel Tomasz Hill, who was born on 28 February 2019

Contents

Illustrations

Figures

Tables

Contributors

Paul R. Appleton, PhD, School of Sport, Exercise and Rehabilitation Sciences, Manchester Metropolitan University, Manchester, UK.

Antoine Benoit, BA, School of Psychology, University of Ottawa, Ottawa, Canada.

Laurence Boileau, BA, School of Psychology, University of Ottawa, Ottawa, Canada.

Danielle L. Cormier, MA, College of Kinesiology, University of Saskatchewan, Saskatchewan, Canada.

Thomas Curran, PhD, Department of Psychological and Behavioural Science, London School of Economics and Political Science, London, UK.

Tracy Donachie, PhD, School of Psychology, Newcastle University, Newcastle, UK.

John G. H. Dunn, PhD, Faculty of Kinesiology, Sport, and Recreation at the University of Alberta, Edmonton, Canada.

Abimbola O. Eke, MSc, College of Kinesiology, University of Saskatchewan, Saskatchewan, Canada.

Marianne E. Etherson, PhD, School of Health and Wellbeing, University of Glasgow, Glasgow, UK.

Laura C. Fenwick, MSc, School of Science Technology, and Health, York St John University, York, UK.

Leah J. Ferguson, PhD, College of Kinesiology, University of Saskatchewan, Saskatchewan, Canada.

Gordon L. Flett, PhD, Department of Psychology, York University, Toronto, Canada.

Patrick Gaudreau, PhD, School of Psychology, University of Ottawa, Ottawa, Canada.

John K. Gotwals, PhD, School of Kinesiology, Lakehead University, Thunder Bay, Canada.

Michael C. Grugan, PhD, Department of Psychology, Northumbria University, Newcastle, UK.

Henrik Gustafsson, PhD, Department of Educational Studies, Karlstad University, Karlstad, Sweden, and Department of Sport and Social Sciences, Norwegian School of Sport Sciences, Norway.

Paul L. Hewitt, PhD, Department of Psychology, University of British Columbia, Vancouver, Canada.

Andrew P. Hill, PhD, School of Science Technology, and Health, York St John University, York, UK.

Anna Jordana, PhD, Department of Basic Psychology and Sport Research Institute, Autonomous University of Barcelona, Barcelona, Spain.

Gareth E. Jowett, PhD, Carnegie School of Sport, Leeds Beckett University, Leeds, UK.

Kent C. Kowalski, PhD, College of Kinesiology, University of Saskatchewan, Saskatchewan, Canada.

Michael R. Lizmore, PhD, National Wheelchair Curling Program, Curling Canada, Orleans, Canada.

Carolina Lundqvist, PhD, Department of Behavioural Sciences and Learning, Linköping University, Linköping, Sweden, and Athletics Research Center, Department of Health, Medicine and Caring Sciences, Linköping University, Linköping, Sweden.

Daniel J. Madigan, PhD, School of Science Technology, and Health, York St John University, York, UK.

Sarah H. Mallinson-Howard, PhD, School of Science Technology, and Health, York St John University, York, UK.

Luke F. Olsson, PhD, School of Sport, Rehabilitation and Exercise Sciences, University of Essex, Colchester, UK.

Martin J. Turner, PhD, Department of Psychology, Manchester Metropolitan University, Manchester, UK.

Dean R. Watson, MSc, School of Education and Psychology, University of Bolton, Bolton, UK.

Preface

It has been seven years since the first edition of this book was published. Research examining perfectionism in sport, dance, and exercise has changed considerably over this period. Notably, there are now more longitudinal, experimental, intervention, and meta-analytical studies, all of which offer additional insight into perfectionism and its consequences. Ensuring that researchers and practitioners have an up-to-date account of this new research was one of the main reasons for proposing this second edition.

Other impetus was provided by major changes in the leading protagonists in this area of research. Since the first edition, Professors Howard Hall and John Dunn have both retired, and Professor Joachim Stoeber has moved into a different area of research. Those familiar with perfectionism research will be aware of the significance of these individuals to our understanding of perfectionism. Many of the key ideas and debates regarding perfectionism can be traced to their seminal work. Those of us who continue in this area have a tough act to follow. I hoped we could use a second edition of this book to begin to chart new ways forward.

While eminent colleagues have left, several of the debates that characterize this area of research remain, of course; appropriate labels and measures, the perils of particular analyses, and, ultimately, the consequences of being perfectionistic. However, consensus is beginning to emerge on some of these issues. This consensus has been made possible due to recent conceptual, analytical, and empirical advancements that are organized and presented alongside each other in this edition for the first time. It will continue to be made possible, too, by the discussion, stock-taking, and reflection that inevitably takes place when collaborating to produce work such as this book.

With these things in mind, as with the previous edition of this book, the aim of this edition is to give readers a comprehensive, and updated, account of scientific research examining perfectionism in sport, dance, and exercise. However, more so than for the previous edition, the aim is also to be instructive of future empirical work and applied practice. New bones of contention, concepts, analytical approaches, and applied perspectives are emphasized throughout. Those who have kindly contributed to this book have been generous in sharing their insights and expertise, and collegial in their willingness to engage with each other even when debating opposing views. Thanks to these qualities, we continue to make strong progress in this area of research, and readers can benefit from the invaluable update that this second edition provides.

Organization of the Book

In curating and editing this second edition, my intention has been to serve readers who are familiar and unfamiliar with the first edition. Six of the original 11 chapters have been retained and updated. It was not necessary to revise all of the content of these chapters – as the history of perfectionism has not changed, neither has the account of that history, for example. However, readers will find significant new content in all of the retained chapters and a thorough account of research that has taken place since the first edition. There are also nine completely new chapters that include three dedicated to novel approaches and concepts, three new chapters focused on applied issues and practitioner perspectives, and three new reflections and future directions chapters.

Part I: Conceptual, Measurement, and Development Issues

Part I of the book opens with a chapter I provide that focuses on the conceptualization of perfectionism. In this chapter, I trace the modern study of multidimensional perfectionism to its historical roots. Recent developments are accounted for and include the formalization of the Comprehensive Model of Perfectionistic Behaviour (Hewitt et al., 2017), additional measurement tools, and consideration of evidence for, and against, the way we have come to understand perfectionism using a two-factor hierarchical model. In revising the chapter, I have rewritten the "issues, debates, and controversies" section. I now discuss three new issues that will shape how we study perfectionism in the future – (1) whether the tripartite model of perfectionism is obsolete, (2) whether perceptions of external pressure should be considered a quality of the athlete, dancer, or exerciser or a quality of the social environment (or climate), and (3) the viable alternatives to "healthy" perfectionism in sport, dance, and exercise.

Chapter 2 is authored by Daniel Madigan and provides an updated description and critique of the most common instruments used to measure perfectionism in sport, dance, and exercise. The chapter is more narrowly focused than its predecessor and includes only those instruments that, on the basis of their validity and reliability, are considered the best means of assessing perfectionism in these domains. From within those instruments, the best proxies for the two main dimensions of perfectionism – perfectionistic strivings and perfectionistic concerns – are also identified, along with sub-optimal and inadequate proxies. In this regard, it is a very useful and practical chapter that will help guide measurement decisions and encourage more consistency in the way perfectionism is operationalized.

The final chapter of Part I revisits the development of perfectionism and is, again, provided by Paul Appleton and Thomas Curran. The authors have updated the chapter so to account for new research inside and outside sport, dance, and exercise domains. More evidence has accrued that shows, as is the case generally, parents can instil perfectionism in their sporting children. In addition, among the different routes to its development, social expectation is emerging as perhaps the most prominent pathway. In sport, there is now also further evidence that coaches/instructors are instrumental and, even, that their influence can surpass that of parents. Unique to the study of perfectionism in sport, dance, and exercise, is the focus on motivational climates. The authors highlight recent insights that have been gained from adopting this approach and advocate for its continued inclusion in models of perfectionism development.

Part II: Established Approaches and Models

Part II of the book includes three chapters that provide a comprehensive and updated account of the three main approaches to studying perfectionism in sport, dance, and exercise. These are led by authors of the previous chapters from the first edition, but also include new contributors. Chapter 4 is provided by Gareth Jowett, Sarah Mallinson-Howard, myself, and Daniel Madigan, and offers an updated account of research adopting an independent effects approach. With its catalogue of research studies, this chapter remains an essential reference point for researchers and practitioners. In this version of the chapter, *total unique effects* are also now discussed and illustrated. The total unique effect of perfectionism is a recent innovation that allows us to determine the overall effects of perfectionism based on the opposing forces of perfectionistic strivings and perfectionistic concerns. The use of this approach suggests perfectionism is likely to have small net gains and large net costs in sport, dance, and exercise.

Chapter 5 is provided by John Gotwals and Mick Lizmore, and revisits research examining the tripartite model of perfectionism. Using the previous chapter, and subsequent reviews of others as touchstones, they update their account of research that has tested this model and now include a growing number of qualitative studies. In this chapter they also provide thoughtful responses to suggestions that the tripartite model may be obsolete (e.g. Hill & Madigan, 2017). The result is a reenvisaged tripartite model with underpinnings more closely aligned with the 2 × 2 model of perfectionism and a sharpened focus on how the two differ. The merits of the reenvisaged model and how well it fairs in future research, particularly in comparison to the 2 × 2 model, will be a key issue for debate and discussion in sport, dance, and exercise.

Chapter 6 is provided by Patrick Gaudreau and focuses on the 2 × 2 model of perfectionism. As with the other chapters in Part II, his chapter provides an update on research that has tested this particular model. Since the publication of the first edition, the popularity and standing of this model has increased and it is from this new vantage point that he argues that a focus on moderating factors and better measurement of personal standards perfectionism (or perfectionistic strivings) will further advance our understanding of multi-dimensional perfectionism and address misconceptions regarding the benefits of pursuing perfection versus pursuing excellence. He also calls for the 2 × 2 model to be used as a hub to integrate perfectionism research that has used different approaches. The argument for doing so is laid out convincingly in this chapter.

Part III: New Approaches and Concepts

Part III of the book is entirely new and includes chapters that introduce novel approaches and concepts. The first chapter in this part (Chapter 7) introduces *perfectionistic tipping points*. I have written this chapter and positioned it immediately after the 2 × 2 model perfectionism as it builds on the model by proposing a new way of conceptualizing the interaction between dimensions of perfectionism. I believe the approach represents an advancement in perfectionism research in that it will help us identify, based on levels of perfectionism, and perfectionistic concerns, in particular, for which athletes, dancers, and exercisers, perfectionism is problematic and less problematic. From the studies we have so far, it appears to take surprising little perfectionistic concerns to alter the effects of perfectionistic strivings. The chapter is very practical and includes instructions and an example of how to identify perfectionistic tipping points.

Chapter 8 focuses on *perfectionism cognitions* and is provided by Tracy Donachie, myself, and Marianne Etherson. This is the first departure in the book from a focus on trait perfectionism. The importance of perfectionism cognitions has so far been underappreciated in research in sport, dance, and exercise. In studying perfectionism cognitions, we are better able to access the inner experience of perfectionism. This is something that is especially valuable as we know the behaviours associated with perfectionism can sometimes be deceptive. Research in sport, dance, and exercise on perfectionism cognitions is currently limited to only a handful of studies. I envisage that perfectionism cognitions will become a much greater focus of research in these domains in the future. The useful overview and review presented in this chapter provides an excellent starting point for that research.

Chapter 9 introduces the concept of *perfectionistic climate*. I first pitched the idea of perfectionistic climates to Howard Hall and colleagues soon after the first edition of this book was published. One of the motives for this idea was the opportunity to challenge the notion that perfectionism was solely an individual issue or problem. It is quite evident that many athletes, dancers, and exercisers suffer the consequences of perfectionism not necessarily because they are perfectionistic themselves but because they find themselves in social environments where there is a strong emphasis on the need for perfect performance or bodily perfection. In this chapter, Michael Grugan, Luke Olsson, and Laura Fenwick present our initial conceptual framework for perfectionistic climate and the work Michael has led in developing an instrument to measure it in sport. While empirical work is in its infancy, they show how we already know a great deal about the likely effects of perfectionistic climates in sport through research examining perceptions of coach pressure.

Part IV: Applied Issues and Practitioner Perspectives

Part IV of the book includes three new chapters that introduce different interventions for working with perfectionism. Chapter 10 is provided by Dean Watson and two returning authors, Henrik Gustafsson and Carolina Lundqvist. The chapter illustrates how Acceptance-Commitment Therapy (ACT) can be used to work with perfectionism in sport. Intervention studies have only recently begun to emerge using this approach for perfectionism. However, it is evident from the chapter that this approach may be especially useful for perfectionistic athletes whose ways of thinking may be so deeply entrenched that accepting their perfectionistic thinking may provide more effective respite than trying to eradicate the thoughts altogether. The illustrative schedule of work and examples are a strength of this chapter, and will be useful for researchers in designing intervention studies and practitioners in their work with clients.

In Chapter 11, Leah Ferguson, Kent Kowalski, Danielle Cormier, and Abimbola Eke draw on their research to show how perfectionism, and self-critical tendencies, deny athletes self-compassion and, in doing so, diminish a vital resource for dealing with setbacks and maintaining motivation and wellbeing. The first intervention addressing perfectionism in sport that used a rigorous randomized controlled design was self-compassion-based, and took place ten years ago (Mosewich et al, 2013). There has been little work examining self-compassion and perfectionism in sport since. This is surprising given that the "compassionate self" is the antithesis of the "inner critic" that arises from perfectionism. The chapter illustrates a self-compassion-based approach in an applied context and is another excellent resource for researchers and practitioners.

The third chapter in this part (Chapter 12) is provided by Anna Jordana and Martin Turner, and adopts a Rational Emotive Behaviour Therapy-based (REBT) perspective to working with perfectionism. Modern approaches to perfectionism can be traced directly to Albert Ellis' work on irrational beliefs, who was the originator of REBT. As a result, perfectionism is enmeshed with irrational beliefs in a way that it can be difficult to disentangle. This chapter shows how they are different, the role of irrational beliefs in determining the effects of pursuing perfection, and proposes that, if irrational beliefs can be altered, so can the propensity for perfectionism to be problematic. Practitioners will find the example formulations and reformulations of perfectionism and beliefs extremely useful in understanding perfectionism and supporting their own athletes.

Part V: Reflections and Future Directions

The final part of the book again invites eminent experts on perfectionism to reflect on the current state-of knowledge in this area. The first of the three chapters (Chapter 13) is provided by Professor John Dunn – the developer of one of the most widely used measures of perfectionism in sport (Sport-Multi-dimensional Perfectionism Scale) and a distinguished researcher and practitioner in the area of perfectionism in sport. He provides a personal account of his career, his views on perfectionism, and highlights some of the key questions that remain unanswered about perfectionism. His reflections are essential reading for anyone interested in his approach. His account is also an excellent illustration of how researchers and practitioners take inspiration from each other's work, are driven by curiosity and good questions, and how behind every publication list and career there are interesting stories about the people doing the work and the connections they make.

Readers may be struck by the differences between John's position on some key issues surrounding perfectionism and those offered by others in this book, including my own. I expected this would be the case and it is one of the reasons I invited him to contribute to the book. To his credit, throughout the process John has been mindful and respectful of any potential awkwardness that might follow any disagreements. And, for my part, I have tried to do the same and adhere to the adage that editorship is not the same as censorship. For all these reasons, the chapter is both thoughtful and thought-provoking. It is noteworthy, too, that we actually agree on plenty of issues – perfectionism is complex and multidimensional, using the word "perfection" is important when measuring perfectionism, and the term "perfectionist" can be problematic. Regardless of any continuing areas of disagreement, I am grateful to John for writing the chapter and the book is undoubtably stronger as a result of its inclusion.

The second chapter in this part (Chapter 14) is provided by Professor Patrick Gaudreau, Antoine Benoit, and Laurence Boileau. In this interesting chapter they lay a foundation for a new approach to studying perfectionism. Key to this new approach is separating core features of perfectionism from its signature expressions. In addition, the authors argue that we must distinguish between excellence strivers and perfection strivers and that conflating the two, conceptually and operationally, may have unintentionally fuelled notions of healthy perfectionism. They also show that decreasing perfectionism need not come at the expense of decreasing excellencism, and how to tell the difference. Having explained their approach, the authors chart a number of interesting avenues for future research. There are many features of the chapter that are innovative and novel. It could potentially have a major impact on the way we study and understand perfectionism in sport, dance, and exercise in years to come.

As in the first edition, the book closes with a reflection chapter provided by Professors Gordon Flett and Paul Hewitt (Chapter 15) who remain the two most eminent authorities on perfectionism. In their previous chapter they introduced the concept of perfectionistic reactivity to illustrate the problematic ways perfectionistic athletes respond to adversity. In their new chapter they revisit the theme of reactivity and introduce the concept of *adaptability*. In doing so, they juxtapose this essential quality of successful athletes with rigid perfectionism, a profile of perfectionism characterized by extreme scores of all dimensions of trait perfectionism combined with other rigidities. They show how athletes, dancers, and exercisers exhibiting rigid perfectionism will typically be ill-equipped to successfully respond to the adversities they face. The chapter reinforces another important point that I believe we may have lost sight of in this area. Given the costs of perfectionism, athletes are likely to have been successful not because of perfectionism, per se, but because they have acquired other skills, such as greater adaptability, that may have allowed them to avoid succumbing to perfectionism. If we can identify other factors, we will be in a better position to support athletes, their development, performance, and wellbeing.

References

Hewitt, P. L., Flett, G. L., & Mikail, S. F. (2017). *Perfectionism: A relational approach to conceptualization, assessment, and treatment*. New York: The Guilford Press.

Hill, A. P., & Madigan, D. J. (2017). A short review of perfectionism in sport, dance and exercise: out with the old, in with the 2 × 2. *Current Opinion in Psychology*, 16, 72–77. https://doi.org/10.1016/j.copsyc.2017.04.021.

Mosewich, A. D., Crocker, P. R. E., Kowalski, K. C., & DeLongis, A. (2013). Applying self-compassion in sport: An intervention with women athletes. *Journal of Sport and Exercise Psychology*, 35(5), 514–524. https://doi.org/10.1123/jsep.35.5.514.

Part I

Conceptual, Measurement, and Development Issues

1 Conceptualizing Perfectionism
Resolving Old Quarrels and Starting New Ones

Andrew P. Hill

This chapter provides a historical overview of the concept of perfectionism. The first section details descriptions of perfectionism provided by early clinicians and theorists. The second section outlines common models of perfectionism adopted in sport, dance, and exercise. The third section discusses old and new debates in this area. These include whether the tripartite model of perfectionism is obsolete or can be re-envisaged, whether perceptions of external pressure should be considered a quality of the athlete, dancer, or exerciser or a quality of the social environment, and viable alternatives to "healthy" perfectionism and the pursuit of perfection in sport, dance, and exercise. It is argued that a re-envisaged model of the tripartite has merit, but it remains in a precarious position. In addition, relocating parental pressure and coach pressure is necessary to advance our understanding of perfectionism and the study of perfectionistic climates. Finally, following the publication of meta-analytical evidence that perfectionism likely has few benefits, and many costs, researchers and practitioners need to now consider the merits of its alternatives – pursuing high standards, imperfectionism, and excellencism.

A Historical Overview of the Conceptualization of Perfectionism

The historical roots of perfectionism lie in counselling and clinical literature. Indeed, in some form or another, perfectionism has featured in the work of a number of eminent psychotherapists including Adler (Ansbacher & Ansbacher, 1956), Freud (2015), and Horney (1946). However, Ellis (1957, 1962) was among the first to describe perfectionism in terms that can be more readily recognized in contemporary models. As noted by Ellis (2002), when he initially described the principles and practice of rational-emotive behaviour theory (REBT), a form of psychotherapy aimed at addressing illogical thinking and irrational ideas, he identified perfectionism as a major irrational idea associated with neurosis. In his view, perfectionism was reflected in the idea that "one should be thoroughly competent, adequate, intelligent, and achieving in all possible respects – instead of the idea that one … should accept oneself as a quite imperfect creature, who has general human limitations and specific

DOI: 10.4324/9781003288015-2

fallibilities" (Ellis, 1958, p. 41). When he later expanded the number of irrational beliefs associated with REBT, this particular idea was elaborated upon so to make clear that the competence, adequacy, and achievement to which he initially referred were tied to self-worth (Ellis, 1962). He also introduced a further irrational idea that he considered to reflect perfectionism. Specifically, that "there is invariably a right, precise, and perfect solution to human problems and that it is catastrophic if this perfect solution is not found" (Ellis, 1962, pp. 86–87). In REBT, these particular beliefs imbued individuals with an unrealistic and rigid perspective on the world and placed them under considerable stress, denied them potentially enjoyable and rewarding experiences, and invariably contributed to emotional disturbances.

At a similar time, based on his experiences as a psychiatrist Missildine (1963) considered perfectionists to be individuals who demand perfection of themselves, and sometimes others, and who "work methodically, systematically, and strenuously, with meticulous attention to detail, often to the point of exhaustion" (p. 75). He considered that perfectionists may typically be very successful in their respective fields. However, as normal standards of effort and achievement were simply not considered to apply, Missildine observed that perfectionists often came to consider themselves to be a "successful failure" (Missildine, 1963, p. 76). For Missildine, herein was the difference between true masters of any field and their perfectionist counterparts. Regardless of any objective accomplishments, perfectionists were unable to derive any lasting satisfaction from their accomplishments, were beleaguered by a sense that they must strive for "still better", and were beset by continual self-belittlement. In addition, it was continual self-belittlement, not a desire for mastery of other more virtuous goals, which underpinned the extraordinary efforts of perfectionists.

Many of the same observations were made by Hollender (1965, 1978). Citing a definition provided in a dictionary of psychological and psychoanalytical terms, Hollender defined perfectionism as "the practice of demanding of oneself or others a higher quality of performance than is required by the situation" (English & English, 1958, p. 379). Again, drawing on his experience as a psychiatrist, he described perfectionists as the "painstaking worker" who tended to focus on minutiae and who was intent on identifying defects and flaws (Hollender, 1965, p. 94). Unlike Missildine, Hollender argued that the efforts of perfectionists were not underpinned by self-belittlement alone. Rather, in his view, it was a continued pursuit of parental acceptance, carried into adulthood, which was responsible. From his experience, perfectionists came to believe that it was not who they were that was important but what they did or achieved. He argued that in the absence of a stable sense of self-worth, perfectionists came to depend on performance as a means of gaining acceptability and approval from others. Because of this dependency, and an intense emphasis on shortcomings, he noted that perfectionists rarely experienced complete satisfaction with their performance and were prone to bouts of severe psychological difficulties.

The theme of overvaluing achievement to the detriment of other things was also central to the description of perfectionism provided by Burns (1980, 1981). Burns described perfectionists as individuals who "strain compulsively and unremittingly toward impossible goals and who measure their own worth entirely in terms of productivity and accomplishment" (Burns, 1980, p. 34). Like the aforementioned views, Burns emphasized illogical and distorted thoughts. In particular, he emphasized all-or-nothing thinking, overgeneralizations, and rumination focused on personal imperatives ("should", "ought", and "must"). Collectively, this "perfectionizing" encapsulated what Burns (1980, p. 308) considered to be a cognitive style responsible for much of the psychological difficulties he found perfectionists to report. These difficulties included mood swings, low self-esteem, and severe anxiety and depression. Unfortunately, in his experience, many perfectionists came to view their perfectionism as a painful but necessary price for success despite the difficulties they experienced.

The work of Burns is especially noteworthy as he provided the first instrument to measure perfectionism. This was a self-report questionnaire adapted from the Dysfunctional Attitudes Scale (DAS; Burns, 1980), an instrument designed to measure attitudes associated with anxiety and depression. The development of Burns's instrument was shortly followed by the inclusion of a separate perfectionism subscale in an instrument designed to measure psychological and behavioural traits associated with eating disorders (Eating Disorder Inventory, EDI; Garner et al., 1983).[1] The description of perfectionism in the EDI closely matches Burns's view of perfectionism as encompassing excessive standards and distorted, dichotomous thinking. The development of instruments to measure perfectionism marked an important change in this area as they allowed those interested in perfectionism to move beyond descriptive accounts of the characteristic to scientific, measurement-based, enquiry.

As can be seen from the descriptions of perfectionism summarized here, no uniform perspective or definition was evident in the initial stages of research. Rather, those interested in perfectionism relied largely on the professional insights of clinicians and theorists to understand what the features of perfectionism were and what its likely effects might be. However, there were a number of common themes and, over time, perfectionism came to be understood as including exceedingly high personal standards and accompanying irrational beliefs or attitudes. Clinicians and theorists also rounded on the notion that perfectionism was largely a debilitating personality characteristic that held few benefits beyond, in some cases, a possible increase in productivity and success. In considering the overlap among these and other similar perspectives, they have described as unidimensional (Hewitt & Flett, 1991; Flett & Hewitt, 2002). That is, these perspectives mainly focused on cognitive factors (i.e. beliefs and attitudes) and emphasized self-focused or intrapersonal dimensions of perfectionism (as opposed to other-focused or interpersonal dimensions). These perspectives can also be considered unidimensional in that the pursuit of high personal standards was not considered conceptually distinct from the irrational beliefs or attitudes they were thought to serve.

Contemporary Multidimensional Models

Contemporary understanding of perfectionism has progressed from a uni-dimensional perspective to a multidimensional perspective. Multidimensional models began to emerge in the early 1990s and are characterized by the inclusion of multiple separate dimensions of perfectionism. Currently, there are a number of multidimensional models and psychometric instruments to measure perfectionism and these vary in content. In some cases, models and measures include interpersonal dimensions of perfectionism that focus on beliefs and perceptions about others, including specific others such as parents (e.g. Frost et al., 1990) and others in general (e.g. Hewitt & Flett, 1991). In other cases, high standards have been separated from other features evident in the accounts of early clinicians and theorists (e.g. Stoeber et al., 2006). A full description and critique of the instruments used to measurement perfectionism in sport, dance, and exercise is provided by Madigan in Chapter 2 of this book. Here, a briefer description is provided so to aid the reader in understanding research and other issues discussed in this and subsequent chapters.

One of the first multidimensional models to be developed and used in sport, dance, and exercise was proposed by Frost and colleagues (Frost Multi-dimensional Perfectionism Scale, FMPS; Frost et al., 1990). This model involves the assessment of perfectionism across six dimensions. The first dimension is the setting of excessively high personal standards for performance (personal standards). The second two dimensions are related to overly critical evaluative tendencies. These are a concern and fear of making mistakes in performance (concern over mistakes) and a vague sense of uncertainty with the quality of one's performance (doubts about actions). The next two dimensions reflect the conditional parental approval that is thought to give rise to perfectionism, high expectations (parental expectations) and a tendency to be overly critical (parental criticism). The final dimension is a desire for precision, neatness, and organization (organization). Though, due to its weak association with other dimensions and total perfectionism score, organization was not considered to be central to perfectionism by Frost and colleagues.

The model proposed by Frost et al. (1990) was subsequently adapted and applied to sport by Dunn and Gotwals (Sport-Multidimensional Perfectionism Scale, Sport-MPS and Sport-MPS-2; Dunn et al., 2006; Gotwals & Dunn, 2009; Gotwals et al., 2010). Their initial version entailed the removal of doubts about actions and organization dimensions because of concerns regarding the validity of the original items in the sport domain. In addition, two further dimensions were created to capture unrealistic expectations and criticism from coaches – a highly relevant other in the sport domain. Based on subsequent assessment of the psychometric properties of the adapted instrument, the two coach dimensions were merged and the two parental dimensions were merged to capture a sense that coaches (perceived coach pressure) and parents (perceived parental pressure) wanted athletes to be perfect. In the latest iteration of the instrument, new versions of the doubts about actions and organization dimensions have been added which focus on training/preparation and planning/routines, respectively. Chapter 13 by Dunn provides interesting reflections on the development of the S-MPS so I encourage readers to consult that chapter for more information on the instrument.

Another popular multidimensional model of perfectionism that has been used by researchers in sport, dance, and exercise was developed by Hewitt and Flett (Multidimensional Perfectionism Scale, HF-MPS; Hewitt & Flett, 1991). According to their model, perfectionism has self-oriented, socially prescribed, and other-oriented dimensions. These dimensions differ in the underlying motivation and target of perfectionistic standards, including an intrapersonal or interpersonal focus. As described by Hewitt and Flett (1991), self-oriented perfectionism is the tendency to set exacting high personal standards and to evaluate one's own behaviour stringently. By contrast, socially prescribed perfectionism is the belief that significant others expect unrealistic standards to be met, are harsh critics, and withhold approval based on performance. The final dimension, other-oriented perfectionism, is the tendency to impose unrealistic standards on others and evaluate others stringently.

A sport version of Hewitt and Flett's (1991) was developed by Hill et al. (2016). The Performance Perfectionism Scale for Sport (PPS-S) includes three dimensions of perfectionism that applies the concepts included in the HF-MPS to sport performance: self-oriented performance perfectionism (e.g. "I put pressure on myself to perform perfectly"), socially prescribed performance perfectionism (e.g. "People always expect my performances to be perfect") and other-oriented performance perfectionism (e.g. "I criticize people if they do not perform perfectly"). The instrument was intended to provide a domain-specific measure of dimensions of perfectionism that were analogous but also subordinate to Hewitt and Flett's trait dimensions. Of note, too, socially prescribed performance perfectionism does not make reference to specific others but is intended to capture pressure from a "generalized other". This was something that was considered important as other measures of pressure from specific others were available in sport (e.g. coaches) and the notion of the generalized other is prominent in the original concept (Hewitt & Flett, 2004).

Much of the work of my research group has adopted Hewitt and Flett's (1991) model. This is because we feel that it offers a more complete theoretical framework that explains the development of the three dimensions, the psychological mechanisms they are associated with, and their likely effects. In addition, these traits are now part of an encompassing model – The Comprehensive Model of Perfectionistic Behaviour (CMPB; Hewitt et al., 2017) – that provides a multi-level, multi-faceted, understanding of perfectionism. This model includes perfectionism traits, perfectionism cognitions (Flett et al., 1998) and perfectionistic self-presentational styles (Hewitt et al., 2003) in one integrated framework. The formalization of the CMPB is a milestone for contemporary multidimensional study of perfectionism and is sure to be included as a key development in future historical accounts of the study of perfectionism. Readers can consult Chapter 8 of this book for an introduction to the CMPB and how it has begun to shape research in sport, dance, and exercise.

A number of other multidimensional models and measures of perfectionism now exist that sit alongside those developed by Frost et al. (1990) and Hewitt and Flett (1991). One final model and measure of note, due to its popularity in sport research, is the Multidimensional Inventory of Perfectionism in Sport (MIPS; Stoeber et al., 2006). This approach was developed by Stoeber and colleagues. Originally the instrument included nine subscales that included, among others, personal "perfectionistic aspirations" and negative reactions to nonperfect performance, as well as pressure from coaches and parents, and pressure on teammates. In developing and revising the instrument, the two main subscales that are used are striving for perfection and negative reactions to imperfection (Stoeber et al., 2007; Stoeber et al., 2008). Both relate to personal standards and personal reactions (rather than others) and are assessed in relation to training or performance or both (i.e. "training/performance").

All of the measures discussed so far have, to varying degrees, been integrated into a hierarchical two-factor model of perfectionism. In the same way that the CMPB can be considered a major development for the study of multidimensional perfectionism, so too can the emergence of a hierarchical two-factor model of perfectionism. The model was created as a consequence of attempts to better understand commonality among different instruments and their underlying structure (e.g. Bieling et al., 2004; Cox et al., 2002; Frost et al., 1993). What consistently emerged from these studies is two higher-order dimensions of perfectionism. Some of these studies even suggest that the two-factor model offers a better representation of the structure of these instruments than separate models (i.e. dimensions loading on their respective instruments). Therefore, there is strong indication that, even though developed independently, and varying in content, quite often measures of perfectionism are tapping into the same two broad dimensions.[2]

For the models and measures in sport, dance, and exercise, the first higher-order dimension is manifest by combinations of personal standards, self-oriented perfectionism, and striving for perfection. Organization and other-oriented perfectionism can also be included but whether to do so is more contentious. Based on these manifest variables, the first higher-order dimension has been suggested to capture "aspects of perfectionism associated with self-oriented striving for perfection and the setting of very high personal performance standards" (Gotwals et al., 2012, p. 264). The second higher-order dimension is manifest by combinations of concern over mistakes, doubts about actions, and negative reactions to imperfection. Others subscales such as parental pressure (or parental criticism and parental expectations), coach pressure, and socially prescribed perfectionism have also been included but, again, this is somewhat that has been debated. Based on these manifest variables, the second higher-order dimension has been suggested to capture "aspects associated with concerns over making mistakes, fear of negative social evaluation, feelings of discrepancy between one's expectations and performance, and negative reactions to imperfection" (Gotwals et al., 2012, p. 264).

The two higher-order dimensions have been given different labels. In the initial factor-analytical studies themselves, these were "positive striving" and "adaptive perfectionism" and "maladaptive evaluative concerns" and "maladaptive perfectionism" (Bieling et al., 2004; Cox et al., 2002; Frost et al., 1993). Here, the labels suggested by Stoeber and Otto (2006) are adopted – perfectionistic strivings and perfectionistic concerns. These labels are more desirable because they better convey the notion that these are dimensions of perfectionism, rather than forms or types of perfectionism. In addition, these labels do not presuppose the effects of these dimensions ("adaptive perfectionism" suggests it might always be adaptive). Labelling them in a manner that presumes their effects is an ill-advised practice, in my view. In addition, disagreement over such labelling continues to be, at best, a distraction for researchers in this area and, at worst, has impended progress on understanding *when* and for *whom* perfectionism is adaptive or maladaptive.

There are a number of advantages of adopting the hierarchical model of perfectionism. In particular, it allows multiple models of perfectionism to be integrated and represented in a single unified model. In an area with a large number of models and measures, this is a particularly attractive feature. The hierarchical model also capitalizes on the conceptual and statistical overlap between different measures. Consequently, any peculiarities of individual models and measures are marginalized in favour of an emphasis on the commonality among them. These advantages have led to the hierarchical model establishing itself as a common approach to studying perfectionism in sport, dance, and exercise (e.g. Lizmore et al., 2019; Madigan et al., 2017; Watson et al., 2021) and the main way in which systematic reviews and meta-analyses of perfectionism research in these and other domains are organized (e.g. Hill et al., 2018; Smith et al., 2018; Stricker et al., 2022).

Despite its popularity and use, there have been very few formal tests of the hierarchal two-factor model in sport. The tests that do exist have normally been provided in measurement models or structural models that include other variables (e.g. Jowett et al., 2013). Two studies are particularly noteworthy with regard to testing the model, though. The first study was provided by Dunn et al. (2016) who tested the model using the S-MPS-2 and the MIPS in three independent samples of youth and university athletes. They found strong support for the two-factor model. This was the case using the S-MPS-2 alone and a combination of the S-MPS-2 and the MIPS, as well as when using confirmatory and exploratory-confirmatory analyses. The second study was provided by Hill et al. (2022) who tested the model using the S-MPS-2, MIPS, and PPS-S in university athletes. They also found support for the two-factor model but mainly from exploratory-confirmatory analyses and with some additional caveats regarding the inclusion of other-oriented perfectionism and perceived coach and parental pressure. These latter issues aside, though, generally, research so far is supportive of the two-factor model in sport.

In addition to factor analytical studies, evidence to support the hierarchical model is also provided in what Gaudreau and Verner-Filion (2012) have described as "functional homogeneity". That is, most dimensions indicative of perfectionistic strivings or perfectionistic concerns tend to display similar patterns of relationships with other variables. This is evident in research in sport, dance, and exercise as well as other domains. Much of this research is described in detail in subsequent chapters, particularly in Chapter 4. Therefore, it is not reviewed here. Readers need simply to note that a pattern of findings whereby perfectionistic strivings typically contribute to a mix of adaptive and a maladaptive characteristics, processes, and outcomes, and perfectionistic concerns typically contribute to maladaptive characteristics, processes, and outcomes is typical for research in this area.

It is noteworthy that evidence has recently begun to emerge that suggests that not all subscales of perfectionistic strivings and perfectionistic concerns behave the same. For example, different subscales have been found to have different associations with athlete engagement (e.g. Hill, Madigan, & Jowett, 2020) and athlete burnout (e.g. Waleriańczyk et al., 2022) in the same samples. In addition, meta-analytical evidence suggests that in some instances instruments may act as moderators of other observed effects. This includes, for example, the relationship between perfectionistic strivings and ego orientation and fear of failure, and perfectionistic concerns and anxiety (Hill et al., 2018). Therefore, some subscales appear demonstratable different even though they are constituting of the same higher order dimension. However, assuming similar effects for constitutes of the two-factor model, though not the same effects, appears to be a reasonable position for now given available evidence.

In describing the hierarchical two-factor model, the term heuristic is perhaps the most apt. This is because while it is a very useful way of integrating different models and interpreting findings from different studies, it is ultimately a simplification of a complex state-of-affairs. It is a suitable starting point and organizing framework for both research and practice. However, it is not a substitute for the more detailed and formalized theory offered by other approaches such as the CMPB. The CMPB provides the basis for hypotheses to be constructed and tested, identification of moderating factors (i.e. factors that alter the effects of perfectionism) and mediating factors (i.e. factors that explain the effects of perfectionism), and permits a level of scrutiny essential to careful development of our understanding of perfectionism. Some of the various disagreements in this area can be traced to the absence of clear definitions and sound theory. Therefore, it is important to retain firm theorical footing when testing the higher-order model of perfectionism, or any other model of perfectionism.

In providing a historical overview of the study of perfectionism and how researchers and practitioners have come to understand it as a complex and multidimensional personality characteristic, I hope to brace the reader for what comes next in this chapter and this book. The historical roots of perfectionism in clinical and counselling psychology, key advances in both theory and measurement, and current trends in how perfectionism research is being summated are all part of the backdrop for the study of perfectionism in sport, dance, and exercise. Some of the more contentious issues, such as whether perfectionism can be "healthy", for example, can be traced to the some of the historical decisions made in labelling, measuring, and statistically analysing perfectionism. In the same way, and in an effort to resolve areas of disagreement, so too can some of the exciting research and innovations that have begun to emerge in this area and are evidenced in this book.

Issues, Debates, and Controversies Revisited

In the first edition of this book a number of unresolved issues were introduced and discussed. The issues were (1) the value of perfectionism in non-clinical settings, (2) whether perfectionism is best studied as unidimensional or multi-dimensional, (3) whether perfectionism is a trait or disposition, and (4) if per-fectionism exists in healthy, adaptive, or positive types and forms. Seven years on, some of these issues now appear uncontentious. For instance, perfectionism has never been a more popular focus for researchers in sport, dance, and exer-cise, most of this research focuses on non-clinical groups, and continues to attest to its predictive ability for various outcomes in these groups. Similarly, despite some infrequent aberrations (e.g. A. Hill et al., 2018), researchers con-tinue to be committed to a multidimensional, rather than unidimensional, perspective on perfectionism in sport, dance, and exercise. With a shifted landscape in mind, in this next section two new issues are discussed – (1) whether the tripartite model of perfectionism is obsolete and (2) whether per-ceptions of external pressure should be removed from measures of trait (or dispositional) perfectionism and added to a measure of perfectionistic climate. I also revisit to the notion of (3) "health perfectionism" to consider the progress that has been on this issue and to consider the alternatives to perfectionism.

Is the Tripartite Model Obsolete or Can it Be Re-envisaged?

Following the publication of the first edition of this book, colleagues and I took a very critical stance on the merits of the tripartite model and the approaches used to test it (see Hill & Madigan, 2017). We argued that the model was most likely obsolete and encouraged researchers and practitioners to abandon it in favour of the 2 × 2 model of perfectionism (Gaudreau & Thompson, 2010). Our position was based on several key issues. First, a detailed review of research revealed mixed sup-port for the tripartite model. Notably, at the time, less than half of the studies sup-ported the hypothesized three-group structure of the model with other studies supporting a continuum-based structure (low, moderate, and high perfectionism groups) or alternative four-group structures. Second, we argued that the assumption that a typology of perfectionism exists, and the labels used ("heal-thy" and "unhealthy" perfectionists), were ill-founded and ill-advised with the only study examining the underlying structure of perfectionism concluding it was most likely continuum based (Broman-Fulks et al., 2008). Thirdly, research testing the 2 × 2 model of perfectionism had so far found consistent empirical support for distinguishing between four-groups rather than three-groups.

Gotwals and Lizmore (Chapter 5) have revisited research on the tripartite model and in doing so have provided an even-handed response to our arguments which may provide new impetus for use of a re-envisaged tripartite model in sport, dance, and exercise. Therefore, I thought it valuable to discuss the future of the tripartite model again here. Although we still disagree on some points – notably the utility of canonical correlation analysis as means of testing the tripartite model – we now agree on many key issues. The "healthy perfectionism" and "unhealthy" labels have been a source of contention for some time. We now agree that these are best abandoned. A re-envisaged tripartite model of perfectionism is best without them. Gotwals and Lizmore also argue that the assumption of a typology of perfectionism that has historically underpinned the tripartite model should be abandoned in favour of the view that perfectionism exists in the form of latent continuous entities. I agree with this suggestion. This approach has served the 2 × 2 model of perfectionism well and will likely do the same for a re-envisaged tripartite model. Certainly, too, statistical analyses that rely on or presume the presence of discontinuities (as opposed to studying perfectionism across the range of continuous scores) should be avoided (Hill & Madigan, 2017).

With agreement in place for these issues, the last remaining bone of contention is the existence of four versus three subtypes. Notably, the tripartite model does not include a group that has low perfectionistic strivings and high perfectionistic concerns ("pure evaluative concerns perfectionism" in the 2 × 2 model). This makes the existence of this subtype and hypothesis two of the 2 × 2 model (pure evaluative concerns perfectionism versus non-perfectionism) key to the survival of the re-envisaged tripartite model. This is a view previously espoused by Stoeber (2014) and Hill and Madigan (2017). If this subtype of perfectionism does not exist or there are no differences between this subtype and non-perfectionism, the tripartite model could retain its value and usefulness. If not, it may have been bettered by the 2 × 2 model.

On this key issue, Gotwals and Lizmore highlight that the evaluative concerns perfectionism subtype has rarely emerged in tests of the tripartite model (only once in 22 tests). This is a noteworthy finding. They also highlight moderating factors could explain the absence of the group and null effects. This is also an important possibility that will need to be explored further. However, I would highlight that when we first suggested that the tripartite model may be obsolete, there were few empirical studies to draw upon. Since, we have completed a retrospective reanalysis of 63 studies in sport where we found that the two subtypes in question differed on 416 of 443 occasions (94% of the time; see Hill, Mallinson-Howard, Madigan, & Jowett, 2020). In our analyses, large effect sizes were found when comparing the two subtypes for a range of motivation (e.g. fear of failure), wellbeing (e.g. depressive symptoms) and performance (e.g. performance satisfaction) outcomes. As such, the weight of evidence now appears even more in favour of abandoning the tripartite model. The identification of moderating factors in future work, then, is going to be extremely important to the continued use of the tripartite model.

Inclusion or Exclusion of Parental Pressure and Coach Pressure

One new contentious issue is whether perceived coach pressure and perceived parental pressure should be included on measures of trait (or dispositional) perfectionism in sport, dance, and exercise. Based on our work developing the concept of perfectionistic climates, colleagues and I have recently argued these particular dimensions of perfectionism are best considered markers of the social environment (Hill & Grugan, 2020; Grugan et al., 2021). In the first response to our call to change approach, Dunn (Chapter 13) has defended their inclusion on the S-MPS-2 and argued that perceived coach pressure and perceived parental pressure are facets of socially prescribed perfectionism. The issue is therefore worthy of some consideration here.

I agree that perceptions of pressure from coaches and parents could be reflective of socially prescribed perfectionism. However, there are some note-worthy differences between socially prescribed perfectionism and these other dimensions. In terms of their conceptualizations, socially prescribed perfectionism is a much broader concept that captures an oppressive worldview. By contrast, as something more discreet, perceived coach pressure and perceived parental pressure reflect particular others and more tangible behaviours. In my view, because this is the case, perceived coach pressure and perceived parental pressure are more likely to be veridical. That is, perceptions of parental and coach behaviours are more likely to reflect actual behaviours. This is less likely to be the case for socially prescribed perfectionism which does not necessarily reflect the behaviours of any particular other and develops at the marked point at which perceptions of external pressure have been internalized. On this point, Hewitt, Flett, and Mikail state:

> Socially prescribed perfectionists are people who have incorporated imposed expectations into their broader sense of self. They have come to believe that people in general, or society as a whole, has placed on them an unrelenting pressure to be perfect. These individuals should be distinguished from those who have the sheer misfortune of encountering a particular person who is impossible to please.
>
> (Hewitt, Flett, & Mikail, 2017, pp. 44–45)

Our conceptualization of perfectionistic climate, and new intended home of perceived coach pressure and perceived parental pressure, aims to capture the experiences of the very people who are misfortunate enough to be in environments where the goal structures, language, and behaviours of others, make them believe they need to perform perfectly. We propose to assess this subjectively (perceptions) and objectively (observation) and this necessitates a reconsideration of where best to locate perceived coach pressure and perceived parental pressure. In revisiting Frost et al. (1990), the developers of the original instrument from which the subscales come from, they justify the inclusion of parental pressure (criticism and expectations) on the basis of their value as etiological factors. However, in addition to creating conceptual confusion regarding the core features of perfectionism, it is also unclear what the presence or absence of these factors can tell us about their previous presence or absence. In all, following the emergence of a promising alternative approach, the value of the inclusion of these subscales is now questionable.

As Dunn points out, though, perceived coach pressure and perceived parental pressure do load well in higher-order models of perfectionism on perfectionistic concerns which supports their inclusion. As a counter argument, in recent work exploring the two-factor model of perfectionism in sport, we have found that the best fitting model is one that does not include these two subscales (Hill et al., 2022). Coach expectations and coach criticism also seem to load well on our climate measure with other coach behaviours (see Grugan et al., 2021). Hopefully researchers and practitioners will eventually find these findings comforting in regards to repositioning measures of perceptions and coaches and parents. However, ultimately, this is a conceptual issue for which we need to decide if relocating these dimensions of perfectionism helps clarify the core features of trait (or dispositional) perfectionism, and therefore strengthens or weakens its construct validity, and whether relocating them will help advance our understanding of perfectionism in sport, dance, and exercise.

In regards to advancing understanding, much of what we have learned so far regarding perfectionistic pressure in sport is owed to Dunn and colleagues and the inclusion of the parental pressure and coach pressure subscales in the S-MPS-2. However, if the effects of perfectionistic pressure are to be fully understood, I believe they will need to be untethered from trait (or dispositional) measures of perfectionism. We are beginning to see the possible insights offered of doing so in work examining perfectionistic climates (e.g. Grugan et al., 2022) and in other work on the development of perfectionism (e.g. Fleming et al., 2023). I anticipate that work of this kind will justify this change in approach and reveal how athletes, dancers, and exercisers might suffer the effects of perfectionism without necessarily being perfectionistic themselves.

Researchers and practitioners may quite rightly wait for more research to be provided before deciding on the merits of the change we are proposing. In the meantime, I highlight the steady emergence of evidence of perfectionistic climates in sport. Take, for example, findings of the independent investigation into the high-performance culture at Rowing Canada Aviron (Thomlinson, 2022a). The review provided participants with the opportunity to share their experiences of the high-performance environment and evidenced a culture in which maltreatment and disrespect behaviours from coaches was common. Staggeringly, 87% of respondents to the survey included as part of the investigation reported that they had "witnessed, been subjected to, or heard of maltreatment occurring ..." (Thomlinson, 2022b). In this instance, maltreatment referred to a range of conduct that results in, or has the potential to result in, psychological or physical harm, and included acts such as unwarranted personal criticism, punishing athletes for poor performance, and inattention to wellbeing and care (Rowing Canada, n.d.). These particular behaviours feature heavily in our conceptualization of perfectionistic climate.

A further example is provided by the Whyte Review (Whyte, 2022), an independent review into allegations of abuse in gymnastics commissioned by UK Sport. The review describes a culture where gymnast welfare was at the periphery of British Gymnastics World Class Programme and development pathways. Of the 400 submissions provided as part of the call for evidence in the review, 50% of the reports from gymnasts, parents, coaches, and other adults included elements of emotional abuse that included belittling language, excessively controlling behaviour, and instances of isolation and humiliation in front of others. The drive for "resilience" and "perfection" were identified among the factors that had contributed to this environment. The accounts of this environment are consistent with findings of recent qualitative research on the long-term effects of gymnasts' maltreatment experiences that also implicate the pressure to be perfect in enduring feelings of "not being good enough" (Salim & Winter, 2022).

One of the more staggering findings in research that has taken place on perfectionistic pressure since the first edition of this book is from a study by Nixdorf et al. (2016). They found that perceived perfectionistic pressure from coaches was positively related to depressive symptoms in adolescent athletes. This finding has not received the attention it deserves and I would think would be jarring for researchers and practitioners. By locating perceived perfectionistic pressure as part of the trait, there is a danger that the difficulties athletes are experiencing are too easily attributed to the athletes themselves rather than the environments that are being creating in these domains. Greater scrutiny of these environments is required and more purposeful attempts to maximize athletic potential while safeguarding mental health is needed. Relocating perceived coach pressure and perceived parental pressure to the climate has the potential to help with that endeavour.

A further reason I believe it is important to relocate coach pressure to a climate measure are the general benefits of building a line of research that studies perfectionistic climate and the insights this might offer. We have only begun to undertake this work but, drawing on general climate research, we can start to see the possibilities of where it may take us. For example, there will surely be value in studying state perfectionism (or "perfectionistic involvement" analogous to the Achievement Goal Theory notion of "goal-involvement"; Nicholls, 1989) and observing how athletes, dancers, and exercisers are predisposed towards perfectionistic involvement through an interactionist perspective including their personality (viz. trait perfectionism) and the context (viz. perfectionistic climate). Doing so will allow us to study the effects of thinking that you need to be perfect or perform perfectly "right now". This is something that could be more insightful than assessing either trait perfectionism or the climate alone (see Gershgoren et al., 2011, as an example)

At least two studies have begun to broach this issue. Both are provided by Boone and colleagues (Boone et al., 2012; Boone & Soenens, 2015) when examining the relationship between perfectionism and eating disorder symptoms. In the first study, they showed that a simple experimental inducement that encouraged university students to have the "highest possible standards" and "thereby avoiding to fail or to disappoint yourself or others" increased agreement with measures of both perfectionistic strivings (personal standards) and perfectionistic concerns (concern over mistakes and doubts about action) during the next 24hrs. In addition, students in the perfectionism experimental conditions reported higher subsequent eating disorder symptoms (restraint and binge eating) versus a non-perfectionism control condition, with analyses also suggesting that state perfectionistic concerns mediated these effects. In the second study, they found the same manipulation again increased levels of perfectionistic strivings (personal standards) during the next 24hrs and that, when body dissatisfaction was high, the inducement predicted subsequent eating disorder symptoms.

In their first study, Boone et al. (2012, p. 531) posed the interesting question "Is there a perfectionist in each of us?" I think the answer is yes and when we find ourselves in perfectionistic climates our more perfectionistic self is more likely to emerge. In order to test this and other proposals, we will need to relocate perceptions of external perfectionistic pressures from being a quality of the athlete, dancer, and exerciser, to being a reflection of the social environment.

Revisiting "Healthy Perfectionism" and its Alternatives in Sport, Dance, and Exercise

The final issue worth discussing featured in the first edition of this book – whether perfectionism exists in a healthy, positive, or adaptive type or form. It is an issue that researchers and practitioners have wrestled with and debated. Readers will find some evidence of progress towards consensus in this book with prominent researchers in this area supporting the proposal to abandon the terms "healthy perfectionist" (and "unhealthy perfectionist") (see Chapter 5) and warning against the possibility that performers, coaches, and parents could come to view perfectionism as desirable, by conflating striving for perfection with striving for excellence (see Chapter 6). For those interested in a fuller understanding of this debate and its history in sport, dance, and exercise, I encourage readers to consult the writings of Hall (2006; Hall et al., 2013; Hall et al., 2014) and Flett and Hewitt (2005, 2014, 2016). Readers can also find the issue discussed in my work with colleagues (Hill, 2021; Hill, Mallinson-Howard, Madigan, & Jowett, 2020; Hill, Madigan, Smith, Mallinson, & Donachie, 2020).

With other sources available, I do not want to dwell on this debate. However, I would like to offer a brief update on how the literature in this area has changed and why, I believe, we can at least begin to think about focusing on other matters, like viable alternatives to healthy perfectionism. Since the first edition of this book a series of major meta-analyses have been published and provide convincing evidence that, at least typically, perfectionism – both perfectionistic strivings and perfectionistic concerns – are likely to be unhealthy. These meta-analyses include examination of burnout (Hill & Curran, 2016), depressive symptoms (Smith et al., 2016), anxiety symptoms (Smith et al., 2017), bulimic symptoms (Kehayes et al., 2019), suicidality (Smith et al., 2018), and other psychopathologies (Limburg et al., 2017). The idea of a healthy dimension or form of perfectionism has been all but dispelled by this work.

Replicating this research in sport, dance, and exercise, though, particularly among more elite groups, may be necessary to fully extinguish the idea of healthy perfectionism in these domains. This is because some researchers and practitioners appear to remain unconvinced by this evidence and continue to justify the healthy moniker, and similar labels, on other grounds. Take, as examples, the proposal that "perfectionists ... who succeed (i.e. win) can be said to possess a somewhat adaptive form of perfectionism – they have successfully adapted their perfectionism to the demands of the environment" (Rees et al., 2017, p. 239) or that "Behaviours considered dysfunctional in one context may be considered functional in another. For example, perfectionism may be considered functional in some elite sport settings but less so in life" (Henriksen et al., 2020, p. 555). These positions are dubious, in my view, and are not supported by robust empirical research.

In reflecting on these positions, I have come to the realization that where I previously believed that it was research examining perfectionism and mental health in sport, dance, and exercise that was key to debunking myths regarding healthy, positive, and adaptive perfectionism, it is not the case. Rather, it is research examining perfectionism and performance in these domains that is more important in this regard. This is because the last outpost for healthy perfectionism appears to be the idea that perfectionism, regardless of its other costs, might contribute to superior athletic performance. At the moment, there is indeed support for a positive relationship between perfectionistic strivings and athlete performance (see Hill et al., 2018). However, in actuality, there are very few studies of this relationship and most have notable limitations that include the lack of measures of "real world" performance and reliance on student-athlete samples. Even fewer studies have been designed to test notions of perfectionistic vulnerability and perfectionistic reactivity that will be important to performance (see Chapter 15). More research is required in order to better understand this relationship.

In the meantime, what, then, are the possible alternatives to perfectionism and the pursuit of perfection? Some of the alternatives are discussed in this book. One interesting possibility is to pursue perfection more compassionately and less irrationally. Adopting an REBT perspective, Jordana and Turner (Chapter 12) argue that while perfectionism is extreme, rigid and illogical, it is not synonymous with being irrational. Rather, in their view, perfection is a goal that can be underpinned by irrational beliefs ("My performance must be perfect") and rational beliefs ("I would like my performance to be perfect, but it doesn't need to be"). A similar position is offered by Dunn (Chapter 13) who also believes that differentiating between *striving* for perfection versus *demanding* or *expecting* perfection is possible and necessary. Opinions will differ with regard to whether perfectionism, a personality trait that is enmeshed with problematic goals and irrational beliefs, can be managed in this way. However, it is an interesting position and, as an initial practical step, practitioners may find it useful.

Many might consider the absence of irrationality to mark a notable conceptual demarcation from perfectionism (see Greenspon, 2000, 2008, 2014). In reconciling these two views, perhaps we have arrived at something that might be termed *imperfectionism*. That is, the pursuit of perfection combined with acceptance that mistakes and failures are normal and have no bearing on personal value or self-worth (viz. a form of unconditional self-acceptance). This concept is aligned with the aforementioned approaches but offers a concept distinct from perfectionism. Notably, it does not merely include low or minimal evaluative concerns. Rather, instead, it includes the presence of an additional psychological resource (akin to unconditional or resilient self-acceptance) that buffers the negative effects of pursuing perfection. The usefulness of the concept of *imperfectionism* will be worth exploring in future applied practice and research.

A further alternative is to not pursue perfection at all. In most circumstances high standards are likely to be enough. Research has shown, at least in regards to emotional effects, differentiating between high standards versus perfection is important. This was illustrated nicely by Blasberg et al. (2016) who distributed two different versions of the same perfectionism questionnaire. One version referred to "high standards" (e.g. "I have high standards for my performance …") and the other version referred to perfectionistic standards (e.g. "I have perfectionistic standards for my performance …"). They found that whereas perfectionistic standards predicted greater depressive symptoms, lower self-esteem and lower life satisfaction, high standards predicted lower depressive symptoms (or did not predict them), higher self-esteem, and higher life satisfaction. We have yet to see this type of research in sport, dance, and exercise, but we might assume that the benefits of having high standards, rather than perfectionistic standards, will be similar.

A final alternative to striving for perfection is excellencism. Gaudreau (2018; Gaudreau et al., 2022) distinguishes between excellence strivers and perfection strivers. The latter pursue standards that are more extreme and less realistic, inadvertently pursuing excellence when doing so. In his view, "perfectionism starts when excellencism ends" (Chapter 14, this volume). This is a description that aligns well with views that perfectionism entails a form of "overstriving" (Covington, 1992). As such, encouraging athletes and others to stop at excellence may provide a better basis for success and satisfaction. Many questions remain about excellencsim – how it develops and its differences from conscientiousness. However, Gaudreau (2018; Chapter 14, this volume) has begun to lay the theoretical foundations for the approach and, in time, more empirical work will be available to determine its merits and utility in sport, dance, and exercise.

Perfectionism is not simply the act of goal pursuit or striving, of course. It is a way of viewing the world, oneself, and the relationship between success and personal value. If perfectionism was just about goal setting it would be easier to offer alternatives and advice to athletes. For most people, goals that are realistic and optimally challenging (given the circumstances and their ability) are likely to be the most beneficial for their performance, athletic development, and wellbeing. If so, it would also be easier to understand positions that imply it may be "functional" in sport. However, "perfectionism is a self-esteem issue" (Greenspon, 2014, p. 986), not a "goals issue". It is borne out of relational contexts in which acceptance and rejection from others has embedded a deep sense of inadequacy. Extreme achievement striving is an act of reparation. Alternatives to perfectionism, then, require alternative relational contexts and alternative energizing factors to underpin behaviour that are less perilous and based on a secure sense of self – a desire to challenge oneself, personal mastery, a sense of belonging, and sporting tradition. These motives need not be perfectionistic or compromise performance and wellbeing, and will likely make for more resilient athletes.

Concluding Comments

The current chapter places modern study of multidimensional perfectionism in context of its historical development and the ways it has previously been viewed and conceptualized. In considering the most pressing issues that need to be resolved in order to advance our understanding of perfectionism further I argue that a tripartite model, even a re-envisaged version, remains precariously positioned as an inferior alternative to the 2 × 2 model of perfectionism. In addition, it is now timely to relocate perceptions of external pressure from others from being a quality of the athlete, dancer, or exerciser, to being a quality of the social environment. Finally, after revisiting the issue of "healthy perfectionism", I argue that more research is required in order to substantiate the claim that, despite its costs, perfectionism may still, in some ways, be adaptive or functional in sport. As alternatives, I advocate for consideration of imperfectionism, high standards, and excellencism.

Notes

1 The perfectionism subscale has now been included in two further iterations of the Eating Disorder Inventory (EDI-2 and EDI-3; Garner, 1991, 2004).
2 I have limited discussion here to the subscales/dimensions of the two models presented in the chapter (Frost et al., 1990, and Hewitt & Flett, 1991). However, the subscales/dimensions of other models and corresponding instruments, such as the Almost Perfect Scale-Revised (APS-R; Slaney, Rice, Mobley, Trippi, & Ashby, 2001) or the Multidimensional Inventory of Perfectionism in Sport (MIPS; Stoeber et al., 2007), can also be considered to align conceptually with one of the two higher-order dimensions.

References

Ansbacher, H. L., & Ansbacher, R. R. (eds). (1956). *The individual psychology of Alfred Adler*. Basic Books.

Antal, F. (1962). *Reason and emotion in psychotherapy*. Lyle Stuart.

Bieling, P. J., Israeli, A. L., & Antony, M. M. (2004). Is perfectionism good, bad, or both? Examining models of the perfectionism construct. *Personality and Individual Differences*, 36 (6), 1373–1385. https://doi.org/10.1016/s0191-8869(03)00235–00236.

Blasberg, J. S., Hewitt, P. L., Flett, G. L., Sherry, S. B., & Chen, C. (2016). The importance of item wording. *Journal of Psychoeducational Assessment*, 34(7), 702–717. https://doi.org/10.1177/0734282916653701.

Boone, L., & Soenens, B. (2015). In double trouble for eating pathology? An experimental study on the combined role of perfectionism and body dissatisfaction. *Journal of Behavior Therapy and Experimental Psychiatry*, 47, 77–83. https://doi.org/10.1016/j.jbtep.2014.11.005

Boone, L., Soenens, B., Vansteenkiste, M., & Braet, C. (2012). Is there a perfectionist in each of us? An experimental study on perfectionism and eating disorder symptoms. *Appetite*, 59, 531–540. http://dx.doi.org/10.1016/j.appet.2012.06.015.

Broman-Fulks, J. J., Hill, R. W., & Green, B. A. (2008). Is perfectionism categorical or dimensional? A taxometric analysis. *Journal of Personality Assessment*, 90(5), 481–490. https://doi.org/10.1080/00223890802248802.

Burns, D. (1980). *Feeling good the new mood therapy*. New York: Ny Morrow.

Burns, D. D. (1980). The perfectionist's script for self-defeat. *Psychology Today*, 14, 34–52.

Covington, M. V. (1992). *Making the grade: A self-worth perspective on motivation and school reform*. Cambridge University Press.

Cox, B. J., Enns, M. W., & Clara, I. P. (2002). The multidimensional structure of perfectionism in clinically distressed and college student samples. *Psychological Assessment*, 14(3), 365–373. https://doi.org/10.1037/1040-3590.14.3.365.

Dunn, J. G. H., Dunn, J. C., Gotwals, J. K., Vallance, J. K. H., Craft, J. M., & Syrotuik, D. G. (2006). Establishing construct validity evidence for the sport multidimensional perfectionism scale. *Psychology of Sport and Exercise*, 7(1), 57–79. https://doi.org/10.1016/j.psychsport.2005.04.003.

Dunn, J. G. H., Gotwals, J. K., Causgrove Dunn, J., Selzler, A.-M., Lizmore, M. R., Vaartstra, M., Sapieja, K. M., & Gamache, V. E. (2016). A multi-sample investigation of the higher-order latent dimensionality of the Sport-Multidimensional Perfectionism Scale-2. *Psychology of Sport and Exercise*, 27, 150–156. https://doi.org/10.1016/j.psychsport.2016.08.006.

Ellis, A. (1957). *How to live with a neurotic: At home and at work*. Crown.

Ellis, A. (1958). Rational psychotherapy. *The Journal of General Psychology*, 59, 35–49.

Ellis, A. (1962). Reason and emotion in psychotherapy. Ontario; Citadel Press.

Ellis, A. (2002). The role of irrational beliefs in perfectionism. In G. L. Flett & P. L. Hewitt (eds), *Perfectionism: Theory, research and practice* (pp. 217–229). American Psychological Association.

English, H. B., & English, A. C. (1958). *A comprehensive dictionary of psychological and psychoanalytical terms: A guide to usage*. Longmans.

Fleming, D. J. M., Mallinson-Howard, S. H., Madigan, D. J. & Hill, A. P. (2023). A test of the 2 x 2 model of perfectionistic pressure in youth sport. *Psychology of Sport and Exercise*, 66, 102391. https://doi.org/10.1016/j.psychsport.2023.102391

Flett, G. L., & Hewitt, P. L. (2002). Perfectionism and maladjustment: An overview of theoretical, definitional, and treatment issues. In G. L. Flett & P. L. Hewitt (eds), *Perfectionism: Theory, Research and Practice* (pp. 33–62). American Psychological Association.

Flett, G. L., & Hewitt, P. L. (2005). The perils of perfectionism in sports and exercise. *Current Directions in Psychological Science*, 14(1), 14–18. https://doi.org/10.1111/j.0963-7214.2005.00326.x.

Flett, G. L., & Hewitt, P. L. (2014). "The perils of perfectionism in sport" revisited: Toward a broader understanding of the pressure to be perfect and its impact on athletes and dancers. *International Journal of Sport Psychology*, 45, 395–407.

Flett, G. L., Hewitt, P. L., Blankstein, K. R., & Gray, L. (1998). Psychological distress and the frequency of perfectionistic thinking. *Journal of Personality and Social Psychology*, 75(5), 1363–1381. https://doi.org/10.1037/0022-3514.75.5.1363.

Freud, S. (2015). *Beyond the pleasure principle*. Dover. (Original work published 1920).

Frost, R. O., Heimberg, R. G., Holt, C. S., Mattia, J. I., & Neubauer, A. L. (1993). A comparison of two measures of perfectionism. *Personality and Individual Differences*, 14(1), 119–126. https://doi.org/10.1016/0191-8869(93)90181–90182.

Frost, R. O., Marten, P., Lahart, C., & Rosenblate, R. (1990). The Dimensions of Perfectionism. *Cognitive Therapy and Research*, 14(5), 449–468. https://doi.org/10.1007/bf01172967.

Garner, D. M. (1991). *EDI-2: Eating Disorder Inventory-2 – professional manual*. Psychological Assessment Resources.

Garner, D. M. (2004). *EDI 3: Eating Disorder Inventory-3 – professional manual*. Psychological Assessment Resources.

Garner, D. M., Olmstead, M. P., & Polivy, J. (1983). Development and validation of a multidimensional eating disorder inventory for anorexia nervosa and bulimia. *International Journal of Eating Disorders*, 2(2), 15–34. https://doi.org/3.0.co;2-6">10.1002/1098–1108x(198321)2:2<15:aid-eat2260020203>3.0.co;2–6.

Gaudreau, P. (2018). On the distinction between personal standards perfectionism and excellencism: A theory elaboration and research agenda. *Perspectives on Psychological Science*, 14(2), 197–215. https://doi.org/10.1177/1745691618797940.

Gaudreau, P., & Verner-Filion, J. (2012). Dispositional perfectionism and well-being: A test of the 2×2 model of perfectionism in the sport domain. *Sport, Exercise, and Performance Psychology*, 1(1), 29–43. https://doi.org/10.1037/a0025747.

Gaudreau, P., Schellenberg, B. J. I., Gareau, A., Kljajic, K., & Manoni-Millar, S. (2022). Because excellencism is more than good enough: On the need to distinguish the pursuit of excellence from the pursuit of perfection. *Journal of Personality and Social Psychology*, 122(6), 1117–1145. https://doi.org/10.1037/pspp0000411.

Gaudreau, P., & Thompson, A. (2010). Testing a 2× 2 model of dispositional perfectionism. *Personality and Individual Differences*, 48(5), 532–537. https://doi.org/10.1016/j.paid.2009.11.031

Gershgoren, L., Tenenbaum, G., Gershgoren, A., & Eklund, R. C. (2011). The effect of parental feedback on young athletes' perceived motivational climate, goal involvement, goal orientation, and performance. *Psychology of Sport and Exercise*, 12(5), 481–489. https://doi.org/10.1016/j.psychsport.2011.05.003.

Gotwals, J. K., & Dunn, J. G. (2009). A multi-method multi-analytic approach to establishing internal construct validity evidence: The Sport Multidimensional Perfectionism Scale 2. *Measurement in Physical Education and Exercise Science*, 13(2), 71–92. https://doi.org/10.1080/10913670902812663

Gotwals, J. K., Dunn, J. G. H., Causgrove Dunn, J., & Gamache, V. (2010). Establishing validity evidence for the sport multidimensional perfectionism scale-2 in intercollegiate sport. *Psychology of Sport and Exercise*, 11(6), 423–432. https://doi.org/10.1016/j.psychsport.2010.04.013.

Gotwals, J. K., Stoeber, J., Dunn, J. G. H., & Stoll, O. (2012). Are perfectionistic strivings in sport adaptive? A systematic review of confirmatory, contradictory, and mixed evidence. *Canadian Psychology/Psychologie Canadienne*, 53(4), 263–279. https://doi.org/10.1037/a0030288.

Greenspon, T. S. (2000). "Healthy perfectionism" is an oxymoron! Reflections on the psychology of perfectionism and the sociology of science. *Journal of Secondary Gifted Education*, 11(4), 197–208. https://doi.org/10.4219/jsge-2000-631.

Greenspon, T. S. (2008). Making sense of error: A view of the origins and treatment of perfectionism. *American Journal of Psychotherapy*, 62(3), 263–282. https://doi.org/10.1176/appi.psychotherapy.2008.62.3.263.

Greenspon, T. S. (2014). Is there an antidote to perfectionism? *Psychology in the Schools*, 51(9), 986–998. https://doi.org/10.1002/pits.21797.

Grugan, M. C., Hill, A. P., Mallinson-Howard, S. H., Donachie, T. C., Olsson, L. F., Madigan, D. J., & Vaughan, R. S. (2021). Development and initial validation of the perfectionistic climate questionnaire-sport (PCQ-S). *Psychology of Sport and Exercise*, 56, 101997. https://doi.org/10.1016/j.psychsport.2021.101997.

Grugan, M. C., Hill, A. P., Mallinson-Howard, S. H., Donachie, T. C., Olsson, L. F., Madigan, D. J., & Vaughan, R. S. (2022). *When performances must be perfect: Introducing perfectionistic climate*. Department of Sport and Exercise Science Research Seminar Series, Manchester Metropolitan University, April.

Hall, H. K. (2006). Perfectionism: A hallmark quality of world class performers, or a psychological impediment to athletic development? In D. Hackfort & G. Tenenbaum (eds), *Perspectives in sport and exercise psychology: Essential processes for attaining peak performance* (pp. 178–211). Meyer & Meyer Publishers.

Hall, H. K., Hill, A. P., & Appleton, P. R. (2013). Perfectionism: Its development and influence on emerging talent in youth sport. In R. Lidor & J. Cote (eds), *Conditions of children's talent development in sport* (pp. 117–137). Fitness Information Technology.

Hall, H. K., Jowett, G. E., & Hill, A. P. (2014). Perfectionism: The role of personality in shaping an athlete's sporting experience. In A. Papaioannou & D. Hackfort (eds), *Routledge companion to sport and exercise psychology: Global perspectives and fundamental concepts* (pp. 152–168). Routledge.

Henriksen, K., Schinke, R., McCann, S., Durand-Bush, N., Moesch, K., Parham, W. D., Larsen, C. H., Cogan, K., Donaldson, A., Poczwardowski, A., Noce, F., & Hunziker, J. (2020). Athlete mental health in the Olympic/Paralympic quadrennium: a multi-societal consensus statement. *International Journal of Sport and Exercise Psychology*, 18(3), 391–408. https://doi.org/10.1080/1612197x.2020.1746379.

Hewitt, P. L., & Flett, G. L. (1991). Perfectionism in the self and social contexts: Conceptualization, assessment, and association with psychopathology. *Journal of Personality and Social Psychology*, 60(3), 456–470. https://doi.org/10.1037/0022-3514.60.3.456.

Hewitt, P. L., & Flett, G. L. (2004). *Multidimensional Perfectionism Scale (MPS): Technical Manual*. Multi-Health Systems.

Hewitt, P. L., Flett, G. L., & Mikail, S. F. (2017). *Perfectionism: a relational approach to conceptualization, assessment, and treatment*. The Guilford Press.

Hewitt, P. L., Flett, G. L., Sherry, S. B., Habke, M., Parkin, M., Lam, R. W., McMurtry, B., Ediger, E., Fairlie, P., & Stein, M. B. (2003). The interpersonal expression of perfection: Perfectionistic self-presentation and psychological distress. *Journal of Personality and Social Psychology*, 84(6), 1303–1325. https://doi.org/10.1037/0022-3514.84.6.1303.

Hill, A., MacNamara, Á., & Collins, D. (2018). Development and initial validation of the psychological characteristics of developing excellence questionnaire version 2 (PCDEQ2). *European Journal of Sport Science*, 19(4), 517–528. https://doi.org/10.1080/17461391.2018.1535627.

Hill, A. P. (2021). Perfectionism myths. In C. Englert & I. Taylor (eds), *Motivation and self-regulation in sport and exercise* (pp. 78–86). Routledge.

Hill, A. P., & Curran, T. (2016). Multidimensional perfectionism and burnout. *Personality and Social Psychology Review*, 20(3), 269–288. https://doi.org/10.1177/1088868315596286.

Hill, A. P., & Grugan, M. (2020). Introducing perfectionistic climate. *Perspectives on Early Childhood Psychology and Education*, 4(2), 263–276.

Hill, A. P., & Madigan, D. J. (2017). A short review of perfectionism in sport, dance and exercise: out with the old, in with the 2×2. *Current Opinion in Psychology*, 16, 72–77. https://doi.org/10.1016/j.copsyc.2017.04.021.

Hill, A. P., Appleton, P. R., & Mallinson, S. H. (2016). Development and initial validation of the performance perfectionism scale for sport (PPS-S). *Journal of Psychoeducational Assessment*, 34(7), 653–669. https://doi.org/10.1177/0734282916651354.

Hill, A. P., Madigan, D. J., Curran, T., Jowett, G. J., & Rumbold, J. (2022). Exploring the two-factor model of perfectionism in sport. Manuscript submitted for publication.

Hill, A. P., Madigan, D. J., & Jowett, G. E. (2020). Perfectionism and athlete engagement: A multi-sample test of the 2 × 2 model of perfectionism. *Psychology of Sport and Exercise*, 101664. https://doi.org/10.1016/j.psychsport.2020.101664.

Hill, A. P., Madigan, D. J., Smith, M. M., Mallinson, S. H., & Donachie, T. C. (2020). Perfectionism. In *The Routledge international encyclopedia of sport and exercise psychology* (pp. 405–412). Routledge.

Hill, A. P., Mallinson-Howard, S. H., & Jowett, G. E. (2018). Multidimensional perfectionism in sport: A meta-analytical review. *Sport, Exercise, and Performance Psychology*, 7(3), 235–270. https://doi.org/10.1037/spy0000125.

Hill, A. P., Mallinson-Howard, S. H., Madigan, D. J., & Jowett, G. E. (2020). Perfectionism in sport, dance, and exercise. In G. Tenenbaum & R. C. Eklund (eds), *Handbook of sport psychology* (pp. 121–157). Wiley. https://doi.org/10.1002/9781119568124.ch7.

Hollender, M. H. (1965). Perfectionism. *Comprehensive Psychiatry*, 6, 94–103.

Hollender, M. H. (1978). Perfectionism, a neglected personality trait. *Journal of Clinical Psychiatry*, 39, 384.

Horney, K. (1946). *Our inner conflicts: A constructive theory of neurosis*. Kegan Paul, Trench, Trubner & Co.

Jowett, G. E., Hill, A. P., Hall, H. K., & Curran, T. (2013). Perfectionism and junior athlete burnout: The mediating role of autonomous and controlled motivation. *Sport, Exercise, and Performance Psychology*, 2(1), 48–61. https://doi.org/10.1037/a0029770.

Kehayes, I.-L.L., Smith, M. M., Sherry, S. B., Vidovic, V., & Saklofske, D. H. (2019). Are perfectionism dimensions risk factors for bulimic symptoms? A meta-analysis of longitudinal studies. *Personality and Individual Differences*, 138, 117–125. https://doi.org/10.1016/j.paid.2018.09.022.

Limburg, K., Watson, H. J., Hagger, M. S., & Egan, S. J. (2017). The relationship between perfectionism and psychopathology: A meta-analysis. *Journal of Clinical Psychology*, 73(10), 1301–1326. https://doi.org/10.1002/jclp.22435.

Lizmore, M. R., Dunn, J. G. H., Causgrove Dunn, J., & Hill, A. P. (2019). Perfectionism and performance following failure in a competitive golf-putting task. *Psychology of Sport and Exercise*, 45, 101582. https://doi.org/10.1016/j.psychsport.2019.101582.

Madigan, D. J., Stoeber, J., Forsdyke, D., Dayson, M., & Passfield, L. (2017). Perfectionism predicts injury in junior athletes: Preliminary evidence from a prospective study. *Journal of Sports Sciences*, 36(5), 545–550. https://doi.org/10.1080/02640414.2017.1322709.

Missildine W. H. (1963). *Your inner child of the past.* Simon & Schuster.

Nicholls, J. G. (1989). *The competitive ethos and democratic education.* Harvard University Press.

Nixdorf, I., Frank, R., & Beckmann, J. (2016). Comparison of athletes' proneness to depressive symptoms in individual and team sports: Research on psychological mediators in junior elite athletes. *Frontiers in Psychology*, 7, 893. https://doi.org/10.3389/fpsyg.2016.00893

Pacht, A. R. (1984). Reflections on perfection. *American Psychologist*, 39, 386.

Rees, T., Hardy, L., & Woodman, T. (2017). Authors' Reply to Hill: Comment on "The Great British Medalists Project: A Review of Current Knowledge on the Development of the World's Best Sporting Talent. *Sports Medicine*, 48(1), 239–240. https://doi.org/10.1007/s40279-017-0802-3.

Rowing Canada. (n.d.). Rowing Canada Aviron safe sport policy manual. Retrieved from https://rowingcanada.org/uploads/2021/04/RCA-Safe-Sport-Policy-Manual_FINAL.pdf.

Salim, J., & Winter, S. (2022). "I still wake up with nightmares" … The long-term psychological impacts from gymnasts' maltreatment experiences. *Sport, Exercise, and Performance Psychology*. https://doi.org/10.1037/spy0000302.

Smith, M. M., Sherry, S. B., Chen, S., Saklofske, D. H., Mushquash, C., Flett, G. L., & Hewitt, P. L. (2018). The perniciousness of perfectionism: A meta-analytic review of the perfectionism-suicide relationship. *Journal of Personality*, 86(3), 522–542. https://doi.org/10.1111/jopy.12333.

Smith, M. M., Sherry, S. B., Rnic, K., Saklofske, D. H., Enns, M., & Gralnick, T. (2016). Are Perfectionism Dimensions Vulnerability Factors for Depressive Symptoms After Controlling for Neuroticism? A Meta-analysis of 10 Longitudinal Studies. *European Journal of Personality*, 30(2), 201–212. https://doi.org/10.1002/per.2053.

Smith, M. M., Sherry, S. B., Vidovic, V., Hewitt, P. L., & Flett, G. L. (2020). Why does perfectionism confer risk for depressive symptoms? A meta-analytic test of the mediating role of stress and social disconnection. *Journal of Research in Personality*, 86, 103954. https://doi.org/10.1016/j.jrp.2020.103954.

Smith, M. M., Vidovic, V., Sherry, S. B., Stewart, S. H., & Saklofske, D. H. (2017). Are perfectionism dimensions risk factors for anxiety symptoms? A meta-analysis of 11 longitudinal studies. *Anxiety, Stress, & Coping*, 31(1), 4–20. https://doi.org/10.1080/10615806.2017.1384466.

Stoeber, J. (2012). The 2×2 model of perfectionism: A critical comment and some suggestions. *Personality and Individual Differences*, 53(5), 541–545. https://doi.org/10.1016/j.paid.2012.04.029.

Slaney, R. B., Rice, K. G., Mobley, M., Trippi, J., & Ashby, J. S. (2001). The revised almost perfect scale. *Measurement and Evaluation in Counseling and Development*, 34(3), 130–145.

Stoeber, J., & Otto, K. (2006). Positive conceptions of perfectionism: Approaches, evidence, challenges. *Personality and Social Psychology Review*, 10(4), 295–319. http://doi.org//10.1207/s15327957pspr1004_2

Stoeber, J., Otto, K., & Stoll, O. (2006). MIPS: Multidimensional Inventory of Perfectionism in Sport. Retrieved from https://kar.kent.ac.uk/41560/.

Stoeber, J., Otto, K., Pescheck, E., Becker, C., & Stoll, O. (2007). Perfectionism and competitive anxiety in athletes: Differentiating striving for perfection and negative reactions to imperfection. *Personality and Individual Differences*, 42(6), 959–969. https://doi.org/10.1016/j.paid.2006.09.006.

Stoeber, J., Stoll, O., Pescheck, E., & Otto, K. (2008). Perfectionism and achievement goals in athletes: Relations with approach and avoidance orientations in mastery and performance goals. *Psychology of Sport and Exercise*, 9(2), 102–121. https://doi.org/10.1016/j.psychsport.2007.02.002.

Stricker, J., Kröger, L., Johann, A. F., Küskens, A., Gieselmann, A., & Pietrowsky, R. (2022). Multidimensional perfectionism and poor sleep: A meta-analysis of bivariate associations. *Sleep Health*. https://doi.org/10.1016/j.sleh.2022.09.015.

Thomlinson, R. (2022a). Independent high performance review – Appendix. Retrieved from https://rowingcanada.org/uploads/2022/10/RCA-Independent-HP-Review_Appendix.pdf.

Thomlinson, R. (2022b). Independent high performance review. Retrieved from https://rowingcanada.org/uploads/2022/10/RCA-Independent-HP-Review_Report.pdf.

Walerianczyk, W., Hill, A. P., & Stolarski, M. (2022). A re-examination of the 2 × 2 model of perfectionism, burnout, and engagement in sports. *Psychology of Sport and Exercise*, 61, 102190. https://doi.org/10.1016/j.psychsport.2022.102190.

Watson, D. R., Hill, A. P., & Madigan, D. J. (2021). Perfectionism and attitudes toward sport psychology support and mental health support in athletes. *Journal of Clinical Sport Psychology*, 1–16. https://doi.org/10.1123/jcsp.2020-0052.

Whyte, A. (2022). The Whyte review. Retrieved from www.whytereview.org.

2 Advances in the Measurement of Perfectionism in Sport, Dance, and Exercise

Daniel J. Madigan

There are currently many measures of perfectionism. These measures contain a different number of subscales and, most of the time, the subscales have different names. This presents a confusing situation to researchers unfamiliar with the perfectionism literature who want to conduct research on perfectionism in sport, dance, and exercise. The aim of the present chapter, then, is to provide clear recommendations for how to measure perfectionism in these domains. To do so, I first introduce readers to the conceptual foundations for these recommendations – the two-factor model and sub-domain-specific models of perfectionism. I then review general and sport-specific measures of perfectionism. In each case I note key features, offer critique, and recommendations in regards to their general use. I close the chapter by discussing which subscales offer best, sub-optimal, and inappropriate proxies of the two-factor higher-order model of perfectionism in sport, dance, and exercise.

Overview

In the first edition of this chapter all extant measures of multidimensional perfectionism were reviewed (Stoeber & Madigan, 2016). In this revised, second edition, my goal is somewhat different. While I again provide an overview of measures and measurement issues in this area, the focus is now only on the measures that are the most common, valid and reliable for assessing perfectionism in sport, dance, and exercise. In changing this approach, I have also updated the information provided based on new evidence and have added details of translated versions of measures now available in non-English languages. As a result of changing evidence, some of the recommendations have now also changed. I begin the chapter with a brief discussion of three important conceptual and practical issues that form the backdrop to my review, critique, and proposed recommendations.

The Two-Factor Model of Perfectionism

Perfectionism is multidimensional. This is because it has various interrelated defining features. Research has shown that these different features – when

DOI: 10.4324/9781003288015-3

examined together using factor analytic procedures – form two higher-order factors (Stoeber & Otto, 2006): Perfectionistic strivings and perfectionistic concerns. Differentiating perfectionistic strivings and perfectionistic concerns is central to understanding perfectionism. This is because this approach acts as a means to translate research adopting different measures, dimensions, and subscales into the same comparable language. Importantly, when we do so, perfectionistic strivings and perfectionistic concerns are found to show differing relationships with various outcomes, with only perfectionistic concerns consistently related to maladaptive outcomes (such as depressive symptoms), and perfectionistic strivings more mixed and sometimes related to more adaptive outcomes (such as performance; Hill et al., 2018). This approach, then, is integral to understanding perfectionism and its measurement in sport, dance, and exercise domains.

Proxies of Perfectionistic Strivings and Perfectionistic Concerns

The two-factor model necessitates the use of the best "proxies" of perfectionistic strivings and perfectionistic concerns. This is because perfectionistic strivings and perfectionistic concerns are broad, higher-order, dimensions that cannot be fully captured with single indicators. Combining two or more subscales allows for greater confidence in capturing the higher-order dimensions, rather than model-specific aspects of perfectionistic strivings and perfectionistic concerns. It also has the advantage of minimizing idiosyncrasies in individual subscales. As such, the recommendations that follow are based on the idea that multiple measures of perfectionistic strivings and perfectionistic concerns are required, or at least preferable, and that researchers should seek to use the best available proxy measures of the two higher-order dimensions of perfectionism when doing so.

(Sub-)Domain-Specificity of Perfectionism

One final issue taken into account as part of the present chapter is the importance of domain-specificity and the emergence of sub-domain measures of perfectionism. Few people are perfectionistic in all domains of life and, if you ask people about perfectionism in general, most will mention specific domains of functioning (such as work, school, or sport; Stoeber & Stoeber, 2009). Consequently, it is important to view perfectionism as a domain-specific characteristic (e.g. Dunn, Gotwals, & Causgrove Dunn, 2005). Researchers have therefore begun to measure perfectionism in this way. When doing so in sport, this approach shows greater predictive utility of sport-specific characteristics, processes, and outcomes than general measures of perfectionism (e.g. Dunn et al., 2011). Hence it is important to differentiate between general measures of perfectionism and domain-specific measures of perfectionism. More recently, it has also become apparent that it is important to differentiate sub-domains – that is, particular aspects of a domain. As such, global (e.g. life generally), domain-specific (e.g. sport), and sub-domain-specific (e.g. performance) measures are differentiated when considering the merits of particular approaches to measuring perfectionism in sport, dance, and exercise.

The next part of the chapter is a review of general measures of perfectionism that are recommended, to varying degrees, to measure perfectionism in sport, dance, and exercise, but were not specifically developed for this purpose. The second part will review domain-specific and sub-domain-specific measures of perfectionism that are recommended for use and were specifically developed to measure perfectionism in sport.[1]

General Measures

The Importance of Contextualization

Since individuals who are invested in sport, dance, or exercise show higher levels of perfectionism in these domains than other areas of life (e.g. Dunn et al., 2005), if the intention is to measure perfectionism in sport, dance, and exercise, general measures of perfectionism need to be contextualized to make sure they capture individual differences in perfectionism in sport, dance, and exercise, not general perfectionism.

To do so, research in personality and individual differences differentiates between tagging, instructional contextualization, and fully contextualized measures (e.g. Holtrop et al., 2014). Tagging refers to telling participants that the items of a measure should be responded to with reference to a specific domain by adding a "tag" in front of the item section (e.g. "In competitive rowing, …"; Hill et al., 2014). Instructional contextualization refers to adapting the instructions so to tell participants what domain the items should be responded to (e.g. "Below are a number of statements regarding attitudes toward sport and sport performance. Please read each statement and decide to what degree this statement characterizes *your attitudes toward competitive rowing*"; Hill et al., 2014).

This, however, is often not sufficient for providing a reliable and valid assessment of domain-specific perfectionism, so general measures of perfectionism need to be fully contextualized. The reason is that these measures contain items that refer to life in general (e.g. "My parents rarely expected me to excel in all aspects of my life"; Hewitt & Flett, 1991) or to areas of life, activities, and people outside sport, dance, and exercise (e.g. "If I fail at work/school, I am a failure as a person"; Frost et al., 1990). Such items need to be adapted (i.e. revised or rewritten), for example, by replacing "work/school" with "my sport" (e.g. Hill et al., 2014). Only when general measures of perfectionism are contextualized, can researchers be sure that they capture perfectionism in sport, dance, and exercise and not general perfectionism in athletes, dancers, and exercisers.

This is different if researchers intend to examine the correlates and consequences of general perfectionism in athletes – for example, does general perfectionism predict general life satisfaction in athletes? In that case, researchers are advised to make clear to participants that the items do not refer to their sport, but to life in general (cf. Gaudreau & Verner-Filion, 2012). Most of the time, though, researchers should seek to use tagging or instructional contextualization when using general measures.

Frost Multidimensional Perfectionism Scale (F-MPS)

Description

The F-MPS (Frost et al., 1990) differentiates six dimensions of perfectionism: personal standards, concern over mistakes, doubts about actions, parental expectations, parental criticism, and organization. Personal standards reflect perfectionists' exceedingly high standards of performance. Concern over mistakes reflects perfectionists' fear about making mistakes and the negative consequences that mistakes have for their self-evaluation, whereas doubts about actions reflect a tendency towards indecisiveness related to an uncertainty about doing the right thing. In contrast, parental expectations and parental criticism reflect perfectionists' perceptions that their parents expected them to be perfect and were critical if they failed to meet these expectations. Finally, organization reflects tendencies to be organized and value order and neatness. To capture these aspects, Frost et al. (1990) developed the F-MPS. The F-MPS is composed of thirty-five items forming six subscales: Personal Standards (seven items; e.g. "I have extremely high goals"), Concern over Mistakes (nine items; "If I fail at work/school, I am a failure as a person"), Doubts about Actions (four items; "I usually have doubts about the simple everyday things that I do"), Parental Expectations (five items; "My parents wanted me to be the best at everything"), Parental Criticism (four items; "As a child, I was punished for doing things less than perfect"), and Organization (six items; "Organization is very important to me").

Short Form

Cox, Enns, and Clara (2002) published a twenty-two-item short form of the F-MPS, with five subscales: Personal Standards (five items), Concern over Mistakes (five items), Doubts about Actions (three items), Parental Pressure (five items from the Parental Expectations and Parental Criticism subscales), and Organization (four items). The short form has shown good factorial validity, but scores from the Doubts about Actions subscale have shown Cronbach's alphas (α) < .70 (Cox et al., 2002). Because α = .70 is generally considered the lower threshold for acceptable reliability (e.g. Nunnally & Bernstein, 1994), the reliability of the short form's Doubts about Actions scores may be regarded as questionable.[2] All subscales showed correlations with their original counterparts of r >.86 suggesting a strong alignment between the short and long versions.

Reliability and Validity

The F-MPS has shown reliability and validity in numerous studies outside sport, dance, and exercise (see Flett & Hewitt, 2015, for a comprehensive review). In this regard, Personal Standards scores have shown to be a key indicator of perfectionistic strivings and Concern over Mistakes scores a key indicator of perfectionistic concerns (Stoeber & Otto, 2006).

The use of the F-MPS in sport and dance, however, is limited and mainly restricted to the time before the sport adaptation of the F-MPS was published (discussed shortly). Moreover, most of these studies used the F-MPS without contextualizing it (e.g. Gould, Udry, Tuffey, & Loehr, 1996). The same is true for research examining the F-MPS in exercise (Taranis & Meyer, 2010). Consequently, it is unclear to what degree the studies captured perfectionism in sport and exercise (rather than general perfectionism in athletes and exercisers).

A few studies, however, continue to use contextualized versions of the F-MPS subscales and show satisfactory reliabilities. Mouratidis and Michou (2011), for example, contextualized Personal Standards and Concerns over Mistakes to examine perfectionism in sport, motivation, and coping in junior athletes; and Nordin-Bates et al. (2017) contextualized Personal Standards, Concerns over Mistakes, and Doubts about Actions to examine perfectionism in dance, motivation, and burnout in ballet dancers.

Translations

Given that the F-MPS was one of the first multidimensional measures of perfectionism, it is not surprising that there are several available translations. This includes Chinese (Cheng et al., 1999), Korean (Lee & Park, 2011), Polish (Piotrowski & Bojanowska, 2021), Portuguese (Amaral et al., 2013), Romanian (Magurean et al., 2016), and Spanish versions (Gelabert et al., 2011). On the whole, the F-MPS has stood up well to translation with most versions maintaining at least evidence for the reliability and validity of its major subscales. The Portuguese and Spanish translations have also been used in sport (e.g. González-Hernández et al., 2021).

Critique

There are a number of critical points researchers should be aware of when using the F-MPS. First, the factorial validity of the F-MPS is unclear. Factor analyses of the F-MPS items usually find between three and five, rather than six factors, combining Concern over Mistakes and Doubts about Actions items to one factor, or Parental Expectations and Parental Criticism items, or both (e.g. Cox et al., 2002). Second, two items of the Personal Standards subscale ("If I do not set the highest standards for myself, I am likely to end up a second-rate person"; "It is important to me that I be thoroughly competent in everything I do") seem to capture contingent self-worth rather than personal standards (DiBartolo et al., 2004). Hence researchers interested in capturing "pure" personal standards may consider using the reduced five-item version suggested by DiBartolo et al. (2004). Third, because three Concern over Mistakes items make reference to other people (e.g. "People will probably think less of me if I make a mistake"), the scale confounds personal and social aspects of perfectionistic concerns (cf. Hewitt & Flett, 1991). Finally, most of the Parental Expectations and Parental Criticism items are in the past tense. Consequently, the scales capture how participants remember their parents (and how their parents raised them) rather than how participants perceive their parents today. This has two implications. First, it is unclear how accurate these retrospective reports are (cf. Halverson, 1988). Second, as discussed, it is unclear if the scales capture aspects of perfectionism or if they should better be conceptualized as antecedents of perfectionism, that is, aspects that lead to the development of perfectionism (e.g. Damian, Stoeber, Negru, & Băban, 2013).

It is also important to note that the items of the Organization subscale are not included when computing total perfectionism scores (Frost et al., 1990). The reason is that Frost et al. considered order and organization a characteristic closely associated with perfectionism, but not a defining component of perfectionism. This view is supported by factor analyses showing that order and organization form a factor separate from perfectionistic strivings and perfectionistic concerns (Kim et al., 2015). This also means that organization should not be regarded as an indicator of perfectionistic strivings or be included in composite measures of perfectionistic strivings (Stoeber & Otto, 2006).

Recommendation

Since there are two reliable and valid domain-specific measures of perfectionism in sport available that follow Frost et al.'s (1990) model of perfectionism – the S-MPS (Dunn et al., 2002) and the S-MPS-2 (Gotwals & Dunn, 2009) – the continued use of the F-MPS to measure perfectionism in sport and dance is difficult to justify, even if the measure is fully contextualized. Hence researchers interested in measuring the aspects of perfectionism in sport and dance following the model of Frost et al. (1990) should refrain from using the F-MPS and instead use the S-MPS or S-MPS-2 contextualizing the items to specific domains (e.g. dance) if necessary. Researchers interested in measuring perfectionism in exercise, however, may find it difficult to use the S-MPS or S-MPS-2 because of the items' reference to competition and training and may instead prefer to use contextualized versions of the F-MPS.

Hewitt–Flett Multidimensional Perfectionism Scale (HF-MPS)

Description

The HF-MPS (Hewitt & Flett, 1991) is based on a multidimensional model of perfectionism differentiating three forms of perfectionism: self-oriented, other-oriented, and socially prescribed. Self-oriented perfectionism reflects internally motivated beliefs that striving for perfection and being perfect are important. Self-oriented perfectionists have exceedingly high personal standards, strive for perfection, expect to be perfect, and are highly self-critical if they fail to meet these expectations. In contrast, other-oriented perfectionism reflects internally motivated beliefs that it is important for others to strive for perfection and be perfect. Other-oriented perfectionists expect others to be perfect, and are highly critical of others who fail to meet these expectations. Finally, socially prescribed perfectionism reflects externally motivated beliefs that striving for perfection and being perfect are important to others. Socially prescribed perfectionists believe that others expect them to be perfect, and that others will be highly critical of them if they fail to meet their expectations (Hewitt & Flett, 2004). The HF-MPS is a forty-five-item measure with three subscales: Self-Oriented Perfectionism (fifteen items; e.g. "I demand nothing less than perfection of myself"), Other-Oriented Perfectionism (fifteen items; "If I ask someone to do something, I expect it to be done flawlessly"), and Socially Prescribed Perfectionism (fifteen items; "People expect nothing less than perfection from me").

Short Form

Cox et al. (2002) published a fifteen-item short form of the HF-MPS (with each subscale comprising five items) that has shown excellent factorial validity, but may be problematic when used to measure other-oriented perfectionism. The reasons are two-fold. First, Other-Oriented Perfectionism scores showed $\alpha < .70$ questioning the reliability of the scores. Second, all Other-Oriented Perfectionism items are reverse-scored whereas none of the Self-Oriented Perfectionism and Socially Prescribed Perfectionism items are. Because reverse-scored items of the HF-MPS can form a separate method factor (De Cuyper et al., 2015), the short form of Cox et al. (2002) confounds content and method. Whereas self-oriented and socially prescribed perfectionism are measured with positively scored items (the more participants agree with the item content, the higher their perfectionism), other-oriented perfectionism is measured with reverse-scored items (the less participants agree with the item content, the higher their perfectionism). This is not a problem when only Self-Oriented Perfectionism and Socially Prescribed Perfectionism are used (e.g. Jowett et al., 2013), but presents difficulties of interpretation when using Other-Oriented Perfectionism because disagreeing with statements that it is OK for others to be imperfect may not be the same as agreeing with statements that others should be perfect (Hill et al., 2014). The Self-Oriented and Socially Prescribed subscales from the short measure show strong correlations of $r > .94$ with their original counterparts, and can therefore be recommended in situations where it is less feasible to use all items from the original version. The short and long version of Other-Oriented Perfectionism have a notably lower correlation of $r = .73$ which again raises questions about this particular subscale.

Children and Adolescent Version

Researchers should note that there is also a twenty-two-item version of the HF-MPS specifically created for use with children and adolescents called the

Child–Adolescent Perfectionism Scale (CAPS; Flett et al., 2016) which captures self-oriented perfectionism (twelve items) and socially prescribed perfectionism (ten items). In order to measure other-oriented perfectionism in this population, the CAPS will need to be supplemented by the recently developed Other-Oriented Perfectionism Subscale-Junior Form (Hewitt et al., 2022). Use of the CAPS precedes the more recent publication of assessment of its psychometric properties as it was available for use in an unpublished form (Flett et al., 2000). Subscales have demonstrated acceptable reliabilities of $\alpha > .81$ in samples aged 8 years and older (Hewitt et al., 2022).

Reliability and Validity

The HF-MPS has shown reliability and validity in numerous studies outside sport, dance, and exercise (see Flett & Hewitt, 2015, for a review). Furthermore, Self-Oriented Perfectionism scores have been shown to be a key indicator of perfectionistic strivings and Socially Prescribed Perfectionism scores a key indicator of perfectionistic concerns (Stoeber & Otto, 2006). The HF-MPS and its short form have been used frequently in sport, both in their original form and contextualised version. For example, Curran and Hill (2018) explored general perfectionism and responses to performance failure in a sample of athletes whereas Grugan et al. (2020) examined contextualized perfectionism and antisocial behaviour in athletes. Studies have also used the HF-MPS in exercise domains. Deck et al. (2021), for example, examined perfectionism and exercise dependence. The CAPS has begun to be used more frequently, too, and has been used in sport (e.g. Donachie et al., 2019) and dance (e.g. Molnar et al., 2021). These studies are generally supportive of the use of the HF-MPS, particularly the shorter versions of the instrument.

Translations

Similar to the F-MPS, there are several translations available of the HF-MPS for those interested in employing the scales in a non-English language. This includes Dutch (De Cuyper et al., 2015), Italian (Rice et al., 2020), Indonesian (Safitri & Preston, 2020), and Turkish versions (Yasar, 2015). Again, the majority of alternative iterations of the original HF-MPS have translated well and have shown reliability and validity evidence for its multidimensional structure. I am not aware, however, of any instances where these versions have been used in sport, dance, or exercise.

Critique

There are, however, a number of open questions regarding the HF-MPS. First, the position of socially prescribed perfectionism in relation to the two-factor model of perfectionism is not 100% clear (cf. Sironic & Reeve, 2015). Whereas

SPP has been shown to be a reliable and valid indicator of perfectionistic concerns across numerous studies, there are researchers who consider socially prescribed perfectionism – that is, the perception that others are expecting one to be perfect – to be associated with perfectionism, but not an integral part of perfectionism (Shafran, Cooper, & Fairburn, 2002). Moreover, one item ("My parents rarely expected me to excel in all aspects of my life", reverse-scored) has a similar content as the items of the F-MPS Parental Expectations subscale capturing developmental antecedents of perfectionism rather than perfectionism itself (cf. Damian et al., 2013). Second, the factorial validity of the full-length scale has been questioned. Using confirmatory factor analysis (CFA) to test the three-factor structure of the scale, Cox et al. (2002) found most fit indices indicating an unsatisfactory fit, which lead them to develop the fifteen-item short form described above. The reason for Cox et al.'s finding of unsatisfactory fit may be that the HF-MPS contains a significant number of reverse-scored items (e.g. "I never aim for perfection in my work"). In support of this idea, in one study these items formed a separate factor (De Cuyper et al., 2015). When this "method factor" was included in the CFA, the model fit improved significantly. Finally, some researchers have suggested that there are factors within the subscales of self-oriented and socially prescribed perfectionism that show different predictive validities (e.g. Trumpeter et al., 2006). In particular, Campbell and Di Paula's (2002) suggestion to differentiate perfectionistic striving and importance of being perfect (when regarding self-oriented perfectionism) and conditional acceptance and others' high standards (when regarding socially prescribed perfectionism) has been empirically supported (Stoeber & Childs, 2010), but so far this has not been taken up in research on perfectionism in sport, dance, and exercise with the exception of one study in which perfectionistic striving and importance of being perfect were differentiated (Hill et al., 2010).

Recommendation

Researchers interested in measuring the aspects of perfectionism in sport, exercise, and dance following Hewitt and Flett's (1991) multidimensional model of perfectionism have a number of choices depending on their aims. If the goal is to measure general perfectionism, then researchers should use the HF-MPS, if the goal is to capture the proxies of perfectionistic strivings and perfectionistic concerns in sport – self-oriented and socially prescribed perfectionism – then researchers should use and contextualize the respective five-item subscales of Cox et al.'s (2002) HF-MPS short form, but if the goal is to capture sub-domain aspects of perfectionism, the PPS-S (discussed shortly) is more appropriate. There is mixed evidence that Other-Oriented Perfectionism should be included in the two-factor model of perfectionism and was excluded by Cox et al. (2002). With its distinct focus on demands on others, it is not a clear proxy of either perfectionistic strivings nor perfectionistic concerns so is best excluded.

Domain-Specific Measures

Sport–Multidimensional Perfectionism Scale (S-MPS) and S-MPS-2

Description

The S-MPS (Dunn et al., 2002) was the first published sport-specific measure of perfectionism and is based on Frost et al.'s (1990) multidimensional model. The S-MPS is composed of thirty-four items forming four subscales: Personal Standards (seven items; e.g. "I have extremely high goals for myself in my sport"), Concern over Mistakes (eight items; "If I fail in competition, I feel like a failure as a person"), Perceived Parental Pressure (nine items; "I feel like I am criticized by my parents for doing things less than perfectly in competition"), and Perceived Coach Pressure (six items; "Only outstanding performance during competition is good enough for my coach").

Whereas the S-MPS is based on the F-MPS, there are some important differences to note. First, the S-MPS follows Stoeber (1998) in combining parental expectations and parental criticism to one dimension labelled perceived parental pressure (see also Cox et al., 2002). Second, the S-MPS adds another dimension that is of key importance to athletes: perceived coach pressure (see also the MIPS described below). Moreover, except for one Perceived Parental Pressure item, all items of the two pressure scales in the F-MPS are in the past tense, not present tense as is the case in the S-MPS. Third, the S-MPS omits Doubts about Actions and Organization which were, however, added in a later revision of the S-MPS, the S-MPS-2 (Gotwals & Dunn, 2009).

In the S-MPS-2, Doubts about Actions (six items; e.g. "I usually feel unsure about the adequacy of my pre-competition practices") reflects on doubts about the adequacy of pre-competition training, whereas Organization (six items; "I follow pre-planned steps to prepare myself for competition")[3] reflects on having an organized pre-competition training regime and – for the same reasons as F-MPS Organization detailed previously – should not be used as an indicator of perfectionistic strivings.

Reliability and Validity

The S-MPS is the most widely used domain-specific measure of multidimensional perfectionism in sport and has demonstrated reliability and validity in numerous studies (e.g. Dunn et al., 2006). The S-MPS-2 is less frequently used – most researchers continue to use the S-MPS or use the S-MPS-2 ignoring Doubts about Actions and Organization (e.g. Crocker et al., 2014) – but has demonstrated reliability and validity as well (e.g. Gotwals et al., 2010). As with the F-MPS, Personal Standards and Concern over Mistakes scores have been shown to be key indicators of perfectionistic strivings and perfectionistic concerns (e.g. Stoeber et al., 2009). To my knowledge, the S-MPS has not yet been used to measure perfectionism in dance or exercise.

Translations

Like the F-MPS, on which the S-MPS is based, there are now several trans-lated versions available. This includes Brazilian (Nascimento Junior et al., 2015), Czech (Květon et al., 2022), Mexican Spanish (Pineda-Espejel et al., 2017), and Turkish versions (Ercan & Kabakçi, 2020). All are translations of the S-MPS-2 rather than the original version so include the two additional subscales. It would appear that for the most part the scale translates well into these other languages with evidence to support their validities and reliabilities.

Critique

There are a few minor issues to note. First, one Personal Standards item ("If I do not set the highest standards for myself in my sport, I am likely to end up a second-rate player") seems to capture contingent self-worth rather than perso-nal standards (see DiBartolo et al., 2004, and the F-MPS critique above). The absence of the mention of perfection from these items has also recently been raised as a possible concern (see Chapter 13). Second, whereas both S-MPS and S-MPS-2 have shown good factorial validity (e.g. Gotwals et al., 2010), some items have shown low loadings (loadings < .30) on their target factor or cross-loadings (loadings of > .30 on a different factor than the target factor). Third, the scales measuring perceived parental pressure and perceived coach pressure comprise a different number of items and items with different content. Hence, scores are not directly comparable and therefore one cannot test, for example, if athletes perceive more pressure to be perfect coming from their coach or their parents (see e.g. Madigan, 2016). Finally, there are some inconsistencies across and within the S-MPS subscales regarding training and competition. Whereas all Concern over Mistakes items mention competition, only five of the Per-ceived Parental Pressure items, four of the Perceived Coach Pressure items, and none of the Personal Standards items do. Conversely, one Personal Standards item mentions training whereas no other S-MPS item does. In contrast, all S-MPS-2 Doubts about Actions and Organization items concern training.

Recommendation

Notwithstanding these issues, both the S-MPS and the S-MPS-2 are reasonable domain-specific measures of perfectionism in sport. Consequently, researchers interested in measuring the aspects of perfectionism in sport and dance follow-ing Frost et al.'s (1990) model of perfectionism should use the S-MPS or S-MPS-2 to measure perfectionism in sport and use contextualized versions where needed (e.g. dance). Note however that some items need to be adapted for different sports (e.g. items mentioning "players" need to be revised for sports that do not have players such as track or figure skating; Dunn et al., 2011). The Personal Standards and Concerns over Mistakes subscales are the most appropriate to represent perfectionistic strivings and concerns. The S-MPS and S-MPS-2 cannot be recommended for measuring perfectionism in exercise as its items are not applicable or easily adapted for use in that domain.

Multidimensional Inventory of Perfectionism in Sports (MIPS)

Description

The MIPS is based on a combination of different models of multidimensional perfectionism: Frost et al.'s (1990), Hewitt & Flett's (1991), and the two-factor model (Stoeber & Otto, 2006). The MIPS was developed in German (Stoeber, Otto, & Stoll, 2004) and later translated to English (Stoeber, Otto, & Stoll, 2006). The original MIPS comprised 72 items forming nine subscales, each with eight items: Perfectionistic Aspirations during Training (e.g. "During training, I strive to be as perfect as possible"), Perfectionistic Aspirations during Competitions ("During competitions, I strive to be as perfect as possible"), Negative Reactions to Nonperfect Performance during Training (e.g. "During training, I feel extremely stressed if everything does not go perfectly"), Negative Reactions to Nonperfect Performance during Competitions ("During competitions, I feel extremely stressed if everything does not go perfectly"), Perceived Pressure from Parents ("My parents expect my performance to be perfect"), Perceived Pressure from Coach ("My coach expects my performance to be perfect"), Perceived Pressure from Teammates ("My teammates expect my performance to be perfect"), Perfectionistic Pressure on Teammates ("I expect perfect performance of my teammates"), and Negative Reactions to Nonperfect Performance of Teammates ("I feel extremely stressed if everything does not go perfectly for my teammates") with the latter two subscales reflecting other-oriented perfectionism directed at teammates.

In the journal publications following the construction of the MIPS, the first four scales were renamed Striving for Perfection during Training/Competition and Negative Reactions to Imperfection during Training/Competition (Stoeber et al., 2007; Stoeber et al., 2008). Moreover, the scales were reduced to five items to improve factorial validity (Stoeber et al., 2007). The parent and coach subscales were also renamed Parental Pressure to be Perfect and Coach Pressure to be Perfect (cf. Madigan, 2016).

Reliability and Validity

The five-item scales capturing striving for perfection and negative reaction to imperfection have shown reliability and validity in numerous studies (e.g. Mallinson-Howard et al., 2021). Moreover, in structural equation models, Striving for Perfection and Negative Reactions to Mistakes scores have been shown to be reliable indicators of perfectionistic strivings and perfectionistic concerns (e.g. Madigan et al., 2018). The Parental Pressure and Coach Pressure subscales have also shown reliability and validity in more recent studies (e.g. Madigan, 2016). The MIPS has been used on one occasion to examine perfectionism and creativity in dancers (Nordin-Bates et al., 2020), but has yet to be used in exercisers.

Translations

In addition to the original German version of the MIPS, these are also Italian (De Maria et al., 2021) and Spanish versions (Atienza et al., 2020). The Spanish version focuses only on the Striving for Perfection and Negative Reactions to Imperfection subscales, but provides evidence for their reliability and validity. The Italian version on the other hand includes all subscales from the original German version of the MIPS and was broadly supportive of the original factor structure in sport.

Critique

Even though the Negative Reactions to Imperfection scale has been shown to be a reliable and valid indicator of perfectionistic concerns (e.g. Gotwals et al., 2012), the scale captures negative reactions to imperfection rather than perfectionistic concerns per se, that is, anxiety and worry about imperfection (e.g. concern over making mistakes) or about the consequences of imperfection (e.g. negative evaluation from others). Furthermore, the MIPS scales capturing perfectionistic pressure on teammates and negative reactions to nonperfect performance of teammates have never been properly tried and tested. Consequently, it is unclear what to make of these scales. This is different for the scales capturing perceived pressure to be perfect, where researchers are beginning to use them more frequently with athlete samples (e.g. Madigan et al., 2019).

Recommendation

Even though there are conceptual questions of whether Negative Reactions to Imperfection captures perfectionistic concerns (if we take "concerns" literally), both Striving for Perfectionism and Negative Reactions to Imperfection have been shown to be reliable and valid indicators of perfectionistic strivings and perfectionistic concerns in numerous studies and can be recommended. Moreover, it is recommended that researchers consider using the MIPS scales capturing perceived pressure from teammates even though there is so far only limited information on their reliability and validity (cf. Madigan et al., 2016). This is because teammates are likely a significant influence on athletes' experiences in sport, and while there are measures of parental pressure and coach pressure, there is currently no other measure of teammate pressure.

Sub-Domain-Specific Measures

Performance Perfectionism Scale for Sport (PPS-S)

The most recent addition to the field has been the PPS-S (Hill et al., 2016). The PPS-S is based on Hewitt and Flett's conceptualization of perfectionism and comprises twelve items forming three sub-scales: Self-Oriented Performance Perfectionism (four items; "I put pressure on myself to perform perfectly"), Socially Prescribed Performance Perfectionism (four items; "People criticize me if I do not perform perfectly"), and Other-Oriented Performance Perfectionism (four items; "I criticize people if they do not perform perfectly"). The items are focused on the sub-domain of sport performance, rather than life or sport generally.

Reliability and Validity

Hill et al. (2016) provided reliability and validity evidence for all sub-scales of the PPS-S. This was across five samples of junior athletes (two for exploratory analyses, and three for confirmatory analyses). There is also evidence for reliability in adult athlete samples (e.g. Olsson et al., 2022). The scale has yet to be used in a dance domain.

Translations

There are also a few recent translations of the PPS-S. This includes a Brazilian version (Angelo et al., 2019), Polish version (Waleriańczyk et al., 2022), and a Turkish version (Esentas et al., 2020). A note of caution, however, is warranted in relation to the Turkish translation. Their analyses provided support for a unidimensional model. As the PPS-S purports to measure a multidimensional construct, at this time, the Turkish version cannot be recommended. The other translations appear to be adequate in terms of their reliability and validity.

Critique

There are a couple of points of critique to note. There is some evidence that one Socially Prescribed Performance Perfectionism item ("People always expect my performances to be perfect") cross-loads onto Self-Oriented Performance Perfectionism. This was found in two of three samples when adopting exploratory structural equation modelling (Hill et al., 2016). In addition, because the PPS-S is a relatively new addition to the perfectionism literature, it has yet to be used (and evaluated) in large numbers of samples and studies beyond its initial validation.

Recommendation

Those individuals wishing to capture perfectionism in the sub-domain of performance (i.e. sport or dance performance) are recommended to use the PPS-S. In addition, those wishing to adopt the popular Hewitt and Flett approach to conceptualizing perfectionism may prefer to use the PPS-S rather than contextualizing the HF-MPS. With regard to capturing perfectionistic strivings and perfectionistic concerns, I recommend using the self-oriented and socially prescribed sub-scales of the PPS-S. Researchers have recently begun to do so in sport (e.g. Watson et al.,

2021). While the scale has yet to be used in dance settings, it is recommended to those interested in capturing dance performance perfectionism as its items seem readily applicable. However, the scale cannot currently be recommended for use in exercise settings where the concept of performance and item phraseology in the scale may not easily apply.

Overall Recommendations

Based on the above discussions, I have some further broad recommendations regarding measuring perfectionism in sport, dance, and exercise. As noted in Table 2.1, there are now various proxies of perfectionistic strivings and perfectionistic concerns and these are available across various different measures. This includes three measures specifically developed for the sport domain. As such, so as to capture the two higher dimensions of perfectionism across the range of relevant aspects of sport, it is recommended to use multiple sport-specific measures simultaneously (see Watson et al., 2021, for an example of how to do this). Adopting this approach has the benefit of capturing the breadth of perfectionistic strivings and perfectionistic concerns while counteracting some of the potential inadequacies and nuances found in individual subscales.

I note here, however, that the subscales have different numbers of items and different response scales. Consequently, as highlighted in the first edition of this chapter, researchers should either use the scales as indicators in structural equation modelling (e.g. Stoeber et al., 2009) or − if this is not feasible − researchers should first standardize all scores to make sure the scores are on the same scale ($M = 0$, $SD = 1$) before they are combined. This will ensure that all subscales combined get the same weight and avoid the situation where scales that have more items or use response scales with more categories (e.g. a one-to-seven scale compared to a one-to-five scale) will get a disproportionate weight in the aggregate score (e.g. Madigan et al., 2015).

The idea to use multiple measures may not be universally agreed upon. Notably, Dunn et al. (2016) argued that using multiple subscales from one measure − the S-MPS-2 − is sufficient to capture perfectionistic strivings and perfectionistic concerns. I respectfully disagree with this proposal. This is for two main reasons. First, conceptually, some particular aspects measured by the S-MPS-2, namely, parent and coach pressure, are best considered antecedents of perfectionism rather than defining features (see Madigan et al., 2019, in sport; Curran & Hill, 2022, more generally). Second, empirically, in factor analyses, the inclusion of the recommended proxy measures into a higher-order model suggests they better represent the higher order dimensions. This is perhaps best illustrated in Dunn et al.'s own study where the addition of Multidimensional Inventory of Perfectionism in Sport (MIPS) subscales to the model results in reductions in factor loadings of other S-MPS-2 subscales, and the recommended proxies emerge as the strongest loading dimensions. Finally, it is worth noting that Dunn and colleagues have subsequently chosen to adopt a multiple measures approach (e.g. Lizmore et al., 2019).

Table 2.1 Recommended measures to capture perfectionistic strivings and perfectionistic concerns in sport, dance, and exercise.

Measures	Reference	Best/Recommended subscales of …		Suboptimal subscales of …		Inappropriate subscales
		Perfectionistic strivings	Perfectionistic concerns	Perfectionistic strivings	Perfectionistic concerns	
General measures[a]						
F-MPS	Frost et al. (1990)	Personal Standards	Concern over Mistakes	–	Doubts about Action	Parental Expectations Parental Criticism Organization
HF-MPS	Hewitt & Flett (1991, 2004)	Self-Oriented Perfectionism	Socially Prescribed Perfectionism	–	–	Other-Oriented Perfectionism
Domain-specific measures						
S-MPS, S-MPS-2	Dunn et al. (2002); Gotwals et al. (2009)	Personal Standards	Concern over Mistakes	–	Doubts about Action	Perceived Parental Pressure Perceived Coach Pressure Organization
MIPS	Stoeber et al. (2004); Stoeber et al. (2006)	Striving for Perfection	Negative Reactions to Imperfection	–	–	Parental Pressure Coach Pressure
Sub-domain-specific measures						
PPS-S	Hill et al. (2016)	Self-Oriented Performance Perfectionism	Socially Prescribed Performance Perfectionism	–	–	Other-Oriented Performance Perfectionism

Note: Measures are listed in the order as discussed in this chapter. F-MPS = Frost Multidimensional Perfectionism Scale; HF-MPS = Hewitt–Flett Multidimensional Perfectionism Scale; S-MPS = Sport Multidimensional Perfectionism Scale; PPS–S = Performance Perfectionism Scale-Sport; MIPS = Multidimensional Inventory of Perfectionism in Sport.

[a] Note that general measures need to be contextualized or have their items adapted (or both) to measure perfectionistic strivings and perfectionistic concerns in sport, exercise, and dance.

The recommendation that multiple instruments are used to capture the two factors of perfectionism necessitates best proxies are identified and used from domain-specific measures. In addition, it also requires exclusion of other proxies that are either sub-optimal or inappropriate (see again Table 2.1).

In terms of sub-optimal proxies, there is one subscale – Doubts about Action – that could be used but only in instances where it is not possible to use other, better proxies (e.g. availability of translations). The main reason for this recommendation is based on evidence from the original F-MPS that it is difficult to differentiate Doubts about Action from Concerns over Mistakes. In fact, in many instances, both form a single factor (Stoeber, 1998). Given that Concerns over Mistakes better represents the idea of perfectionistic concerns and overly critical evaluations that underpin perfectionistic concerns, in this instance, Doubts about Action should be considered second-best. In addition, this subscale could be considered to be too narrow to capture perfectionistic concerns in sport (at the domain level) – reflecting only doubts about the adequacy of pre-competition training – and therefore not in line with the rest of the S-MPS subscales.

Finally, in terms of inadequate proxies, for the aforementioned reasons, parental and coach aspects (antecedents of perfectionism), organization (peripheral to perfectionism), and other-oriented perfectionism (distinctive in its focus on demands of others) cannot be recommended for use to represent perfectionistic strivings and perfectionistic concerns. Doing so weakens the construct validity of perfectionistic strivings and perfectionistic concerns. In addition, it provides sub-optimal measurement that may contribute to increased measurement error and confusion regarding the correlates and consequences of perfectionism in sport, dance, and exercise.

Concluding Comments

Measurement is the foundation on which the study of perfectionism is built. It is hoped that the recommendations that I have offered in this chapter provide more solid ground from which to further advance our understanding of perfectionism in sport, dance, and exercise. I have reviewed current instruments and made recommendations for their use. I have also identified the subscales that should be used to capture the broad higher-order dimensions of perfectionistic strivings and perfectionistic concerns. In doing so, I have advocated for the use of multiple measures of perfectionism and identified suboptimal subscales and subscales that are best avoided. Adhering to these recommendations will improve measurement of perfectionism and our understanding of its effects in sport, dance, and exercise.

Acknowledgement

The author would like to thank and acknowledge the contributions of Joachim Stoeber, first author of the first edition of this chapter, on which a large proportion of the present ideas and text are based.

Notes

1 In this review, to aid clarity, the names of scales and subscales are capitalized (e.g. Personal Standards, Concern over Mistakes) whereas the psychological concepts the scales and subscales capture are in lowercase letters (e.g. personal standards, concern over mistakes).

2 Note that here and in the rest of the chapter when discussing the scores' reliability, I refer to Cronbach's alpha (α, internal consistency) which is the most commonly used statistic to assess reliability, but there are other statistics (e.g. test–retest correlation). Moreover, there are textbooks that regard Cronbach's alphas between.60 and.70 as acceptable (e.g. George & Mallery, 2003).

3 Beware of the formatting error in Gotwals and Dunn's (2009) table 2.1. Item 31 captures doubts about actions, not organization.

References

Amaral, A. P. M., Soares, M. J., Pereira, A. T., Bos, S. C., Marques, M., Valente, J., … & Macedo, A. (2013). Frost multidimensional perfectionism scale: The Portuguese version. *Archives of Clinical Psychiatry (São Paulo)*, 40, 144–149. https://doi.org/10.1590/S0101-60832013000400004.

Angelo, D. L., Neves, A. N., Correa, M., Sermarine, M., Zanetti, M. C., & Brandão, M. R. F. (2019). Propiedades Psicométricas de la Escala de Perfeccionismo en el Deporte (PPS-S) para el contexto brasileño. *Cuadernos de Psicología del Deporte*, 19(2), 1–11.

Appleton, P. R., & Hill, A. P. (2012). Perfectionism and athlete burnout in junior elite athletes: The mediating role of motivation regulations. *Journal of Clinical Sport Psychology*, 6, 129–145. https://doi.org/10.1123/jcsp.6.2.129.

Atienza, F., Appleton, P., Hall, H. K., Castillo, I., & Balaguer, I. (2020). Validation of the Spanish version of multidimensional inventory of perfectionism in young footballers. *Cuadernos de Psicología del Deporte*, 20(1), 118–129.

Campbell, J. D., & Di Paula, A. (2002). Perfectionistic self-beliefs: Their relation to personality and goal pursuit. In G. L. Flett & P. L. Hewitt (eds), *Perfectionism* (pp. 181–198). Washington, DC: APA. https://doi.org/10.1037/10458-007.

Cheng, S. K., Chong, G. H., & Wong, C. W. (1999). Chinese frost multidimensional perfectionism scale: A validation and prediction of self-esteem and psychological distress. *Journal of Clinical Psychology*, 55(9), 1051–1061. https://doi.org/10.1002/(SICI)1097-4679(199909)55:9<1051:AID-JCLP3>3.0.CO;2-1.

Correia, M., Rosado, A., & Serpa, S. (2017). Psychometric properties of the Portuguese version of the Frost Multidimensional Perfectionism Scale. *International Journal of Psychological Research*, 10, 8–17. https://10.21500/20112084.2109.

Cox, B. J., Enns, M. W., & Clara, I. P. (2002). The multidimensional structure of perfectionism in clinically distressed and college student samples. *Psychological Assessment*, 14, 365–373. https://doi.org/10.1037/1040-3590.14.3.365.

Crocker, P. R. E., Gaudreau, P., Mosewich, A. D., & Kljajic, K. (2014). Perfectionism and the stress process in intercollegiate athletes: Examining the 2 × 2 model of perfectionism in sport competition. *International Journal of Sport Psychology*, 45, 325–348.

Cumming, J., & Duda, J. L. (2012). Profiles of perfectionism, body-related concerns, and indicators of psychological health in vocational dance students: An investigation of the 2 × 2 model of perfectionism. *Psychology of Sport and Exercise*, 13, 729–738. https://doi.org/10.1016/j.psychsport.2012.05.004.

Curran, T., & Hill, A. P. (2018). A test of perfectionistic vulnerability following competitive failure among college athletes. *Journal of Sport and Exercise Psychology*, 40, 269–279. https://doi.org/10.1123/jsep.2018-0059.

Curran, T., & Hill, A. P. (2022). Young people's perceptions of their parents' expectations and criticism are increasing over time: Implications for perfectionism. *Psychological Bulletin*, 148, 107–128. https://doi.org/10.1037/bul0000347.

Damian, L. E., Stoeber, J., Negru, O., & Băban, A. (2013). On the development of perfectionism in adolescence: Perceived parental expectations predict longitudinal increases in socially prescribed perfectionism. *Personality and Individual Differences*, 55, 688–693. https://doi.org/10.1016/j.paid.2013.05.021.

Deck, S., Roberts, R., & Hall, C. (2021). The 2× 2 model of perfectionism and exercise dependence. *Personality and Individual Differences*, 180, 111001. https://doi.org/10.1016/j.paid.2021.111001.

De Cuyper, K., Claes, L., Hermans, D., Pieters, G., & Smits, D. (2015). Psychometric properties of the Multidimensional Perfectionism Scale of Hewitt in a Dutch-speaking sample: Associations with the Big Five personality traits. *Journal of Personality Assessment*, 97(2), 182–190. https://doi.org/10.1080/00223891.2014.963591.

De Maria, A., Mallia, L., Lombardo, C., Vacca, M., & Zelli, A. (2021). The Personal and Interpersonal Components of Perfectionism: The Italian Validation of "Multidimensional Inventory of Perfectionism in Sport". *International Journal of Environmental Research and Public Health*, 18(5), 2657. https://doi.org/10.3390/ijerph18052657.

DiBartolo, P. M., Frost, R. O., Chang, P., LaSota, M., & Grills, A. E. (2004). Shedding light on the relationship between personal standards and psychopathology: The case for contingent self-worth. *Journal of Rational-Emotive & Cognitive-Behavior Therapy*, 22, 241–254. https://doi.org/10.1023/B:JORE.0000047310.94044.ac.

Donachie, T. C., Hill, A. P., & Madigan, D. J. (2019). Perfectionism and precompetition emotions in youth footballers: A three-wave longitudinal test of the mediating role of perfectionistic cognitions. *Journal of Sport and Exercise Psychology*, 41(5), 309–319. https://doi.org/10.1123/jsep.2018-0317.

Dunn, J. G. H., Causgrove Dunn, J., & Syrotuik, D. G. (2002). Relationship between multidimensional perfectionism and goal orientations in sport. *Journal of Sport & Exercise Psychology*, 24, 376–395. https://10.1123/jsep.24.4.376.

Dunn, J. G. H., Causgrove Dunn, J., Gotwals, J. K., Vallance, J. K. H., Craft, J. M., & Syrotuik, D. G. (2006). Establishing construct validity evidence for the Sport Multidimensional Perfectionism Scale. *Psychology of Sport and Exercise*, 7, 57–79. https://doi.org/10.1016/j.psychsport.2005.04.003.

Dunn, J. G. H., Craft, J. M., Causgrove Dunn, J., & Gotwals, J. K. (2011). Comparing a domain-specific and global measure of perfectionism in competitive female figure skaters. *Journal of Sport Behavior*, 34, 25–46.

Dunn, J. G. H., Gotwals, J. K., & Causgrove Dunn, J. (2005). An examination of the domain specificity of perfectionism among intercollegiate student-athletes. *Personality and Individual Differences*, 38, 1439–1448. https://doi.org/10.1016/j.paid.2004.09.009.

Dunn, J. G., Gotwals, J. K., Dunn, J. C., Selzler, A. M., Lizmore, M. R., Vaartstra, M., … & Gamache, V. E. (2016). A multi-sample investigation of the higher-order latent dimensionality of the Sport-Multidimensional Perfectionism Scale-2. *Psychology of Sport and Exercise*, 27, 150–156. https://doi.org/10.1016/j.psychsport.2016.08.006.

Ercan, Ö., & Kabakçi, A. C. (2020). The Adaptation and Validation of Sport Multidimensional Perfectionism Scale-2 for Turkish Athletes. *Uluslararası Kültürel ve Sosyal Araştırmalar Dergisi (UKSAD)*, 6(1), 392–401.

Esentaş, M., Güzel, P., & Tez, Ö. Y. (2020). Sporda Mükemmel Performans Ölçeği'nin (PPS-S) Çocuk ve Yetişkin Sporcular için Geçerlik ve Güvenirliğinin İncelenmesi: Kısa Form. *Ulusal Spor Bilimleri Dergisi*, 4(1), 18–34.

Filaire, E., Rouveix, M., Pannafieux, C., & Ferrand, C. (2007). Eating attitudes, perfectionism and body-esteem of elite male judoists and cyclists. *Journal of Sports Science and Medicine*, 6, 50–57.

Flett, G. L., & Hewitt, P. L. (2006). Positive versus negative perfectionism in psychopathology: A comment on Slade and Owens's dual process model. *Behavior Modification*, 30, 472–495. https://doi.org/10.1177/0145445506288026.

Flett, G. L., & Hewitt, P. L. (2015). Measures of perfectionism. In G. J. Boyle, D. H. Saklofske, & G. Matthews (eds), *Measures of personality and social psychological constructs* (pp. 595–618). Academic Press.

Flett, G. L., Hewitt, P. L., Blankstein, K. R., & Gray, L. (1998). Psychological distress and the frequency of perfectionistic thinking. *Journal of Personality and Social Psychology*, 75, 1363–1381. https://doi.org/10.1037/0022-3514.75.5.1363.

Flett, G. L., Hewitt, P. L., Boucher, D. J., Davidson, L. A., & Munro, Y. (2000). The Child–Adolescent Perfectionism Scale: Development, validation, and association with adjustment. Unpublished manuscript, Department of Psychology, University of British Columbia, Canada.

Flett, G. L., *et al.* (2016). The Child–Adolescent Perfectionism Scale: Development, psychometric properties, and associations with stress, distress, and psychiatric symptoms. *Journal of Psychoeducational Assessment*, 34(7), 634–652.

Frost, R. O., & Henderson, K. J. (1991). Perfectionism and reactions to athletic competition. *Journal of Sport & Exercise Psychology*, 13, 323–335. https://doi.org/10.1123/jsep.13.4.323.

Frost, R. O., Heimberg, R. G., Holt, C. S., Mattia, J. I., & Neubauer, A. L. (1993). A comparison of two measures of perfectionism. *Personality and Individual Differences*, 14, 119–126. https://doi.org/10.1016/0191-8869(93)90181–90182.

Frost, R. O., Marten, P., Lahart, C., & Rosenblate, R. (1990). The dimensions of perfectionism. *Cognitive Therapy and Research*, 14, 449–468. https://doi.org/10.1007/BF01172967.

Gaudreau, P., & Antl, S. (2008). Athletes' broad dimensions of dispositional perfectionism: Examining changes in life satisfaction and the mediating role of sport-related motivation and coping. *Journal of Sport & Exercise Psychology*, 30, 356–382.

Gaudreau, P., & Verner-Filion, J. (2012). Dispositional perfectionism and well-being: A test of the 2 × 2 model of perfectionism in the sport domain. *Sport, Exercise, and Performance Psychology*, 1, 29–43. https://doi.org/10.1037/a0025747.

Gelabert, E., García-Esteve, L., Martín-Santos, R., Gutiérrez, F., Torres, A., & Subirà, S. (2011). Psychometric properties of the Spanish version of the Frost Multidimensional Perfectionism Scale in women. *Psicothema*, 133–139.

George, D., & Mallery, P. (2003). *SPSS for Windows step by step: A simple guide and reference* (4th ed.). Allyn & Bacon.

González-Hernández, J., Baños, R., Morquecho-Sánchez, R., Pineda-Espejel, H. A., & Chamorro, J. L. (2021). Perfectionism patterns, dark personality, and exercise addiction trend in high-intensity sports. *International Journal of Mental Health and Addiction*, 1–13. https://doi.org/10.1007/s11469-021-00595-y.

Gotwals, J. K., & Dunn, J. G. H. (2009). A multi-method multi-analytic approach to establish internal construct validity evidence: The Sport Multidimensional

Perfectionism Scale 2. *Measurement in Physical Education and Exercise Science*, 13, 71–92. https://doi.org/10.1080/10913670902812663.

Gotwals, J. K., Dunn, J. G. H., Causgrove Dunn, J., & Gamache, V. (2010). Establishing validity evidence for the Sport Multidimensional Perfectionism Scale-2 in intercollegiate sport. *Psychology of Sport and Exercise*, 11, 423–432. https://doi.org/10.1016/j.psychsport.2010.04.013.

Gotwals, J. K., Stoeber, J., Dunn, J. G. H., & Stoll, O. (2012). Are perfectionistic strivings in sport adaptive? A systematic review of confirmatory, contradictory, and mixed evidence. *Canadian Psychology*, 53, 263–279. https://doi.org/10.1037/a0030288.

Gould, D., Udry, E., Tuffey, S., & Loehr, J. (1996). Burnout in competitive junior tennis players: I. A quantitative psychological assessment. *Sport Psychologist*, 10, 322–340. https://doi.org/10.1123/tsp.10.4.322.

Grugan, M. C., Jowett, G. E., Mallinson-Howard, S. H., & Hall, H. K. (2020). The relationships between perfectionism, angry reactions, and antisocial behavior in team sport. *Sport, Exercise, and Performance Psychology*, 9, 543. https://doi.org/10.1037/spy0000198.

Hall, H. K., Hill, A. P., Appleton, P. R., & Kozub, S. A. (2009). The mediating influence of unconditional self-acceptance and labile self-esteem on the relationship between multidimensional perfectionism and exercise dependence. *Psychology of Sport and Exercise*, 10, 35–44. https://doi.org/10.1016/j.psychsport.2008.05.003.

Halverson, C. F., Jr. (1988). Remembering your parents: Reflections on the retrospective method. *Journal of Personality*, 56, 435–443. https://doi.org/10.1111/j.1467-6494.1988.tb00895.x.

Hewitt, P. L., & Flett, G. L. (1990). Perfectionism and depression: A multidimensional analysis. *Journal of Social Behavior and Personality*, 5, 423–438.

Hewitt, P. L., & Flett, G. L. (1991). Perfectionism in the self and social contexts: Conceptualization, assessment, and association with psychopathology. *Journal of Personality and Social Psychology*, 60, 456–470. https://doi.org/10.1037/0022-3514.60.3.456.

Hewitt, P. L., & Flett, G. L. (2004). *Multidimensional Perfectionism Scale (MPS): Technical manual*. Multi-Health Systems.

Hewitt, P. L., Flett, G. L., & Mikail, S. F. (2017). *Perfectionism: A relational approach to conceptualization, assessment, and treatment*. The Guilford Press.

Hewitt, P. L., Flett, G. L., Sherry, S. B., Habke, M., Parkin, M., Lam, R., et al. (2003). The interpersonal expression of perfection: Perfectionistic self-presentation and psychological distress. *Journal of Personality and Social Psychology*, 84, 1303–1325. https://doi.org/10.1037/0022-3514.84.6.1303.

Hewitt, P. L., Smith, M. M., Flett, G. L., Ko, A., Kerns, C., Birch, S., & Peracha, H. (2022). Other-Oriented Perfectionism in Children and Adolescents: Development and Validation of the Other-Oriented Perfectionism Subscale-Junior Form (OOPjr). *Journal of psychoeducational assessment*, 40(3), 327–345. https://doi.org/10.1177/07342829211062009.

Hill, A. P., & Appleton, P. R. (2011). The predictive ability of the frequency of perfectionistic cognitions, self-oriented perfectionism, and socially prescribed perfectionism in relation to symptoms of burnout in youth rugby players. *Journal of Sports Sciences*, 29, 695–703. https://doi.org/10.1080/02640414.2010.551216.

Hill, A. P., Appleton, P. R., & Mallinson, S. H. (2016). Development and initial validation of the Performance Perfectionism Scale for Sport (PPS-S). *Journal of Psychoeducational Assessment*, 34, 653–669. https://doi.org/10.1177/0734282916651354.

Hill, A. P., Hall, H. K., & Appleton, P. R. (2010). A comparative examination of the correlates of self-oriented perfectionism and conscientious achievement striving in male cricket academy players. *Psychology of Sport and Exercise*, 11, 162–168. https://doi.org/10.1016/j.psychsport.2009.11.001.

Hill, A. P., Hall, H. K., Appleton, P. R., & Kozub, S. A. (2008). Perfectionism and burnout in junior elite soccer players: The mediating influence of unconditional self-acceptance. *Psychology of Sport and Exercise*, 9, 630–644. https://doi.org/10.1016/j.psychsport.2007.09.004.

Hill, A. P., Mallinson-Howard, S. H., & Jowett, G. E. (2018). Multidimensional perfectionism in sport: A meta-analytical review. *Sport, Exercise, and Performance Psychology*, 7(3), 235. https://doi.org/10.1037/spy0000125.

Hill, A. P., Robson, S. J., & Stamp, G. M. (2015). The predictive ability of perfectionistic traits and self-presentational styles in relation to exercise dependence. *Personality and Individual Differences*, 86, 176–183. https://doi.org/10.1016/j.paid.2015.06.015.

Hill, A. P., Stoeber, J., Brown, A., & Appleton, P. R. (2014). Team perfectionism and team performance: A prospective study. *Journal of Sport & Exercise Psychology*, 36, 303–315.

Holtrop, D., Born, M. P., de Vries, A., & de Vries, R. E. (2014). A matter of context: A comparison of two types of contextualized personality measures. *Personality and Individual Differences*, 68, 234–240. https://doi.org/10.1123/jsep.2013-0206.

Jowett, G. E., Hill, A. P., Hall, H. K., & Curran, T. (2013). Perfectionism and junior athlete burnout: The mediating role of autonomous and controlled motivation. *Sport, Exercise, and Performance Psychology*, 2, 48–61. https://doi.org/10.1037/a0029770.

Kim, L. E., Chen, L., MacCann, C., Karlov, L., & Kleitman, S. (2015). Evidence for three factors of perfectionism: Perfectionistic strivings, order, and perfectionistic concerns. *Personality and Individual Differences*, 84, 16–22. https://doi.org/10.1016/j.paid.2015.01.033.

Květon, P., Jelínek, M., & Burešová, I. (2022). Psychometric Properties of the Sport Multidimensional Perfectionism Scale-2 in Czech Adolescent Athletes: An Exploratory Approach. *SAGE Open*, 12(3), 21582440221109581. https://doi.org/10.1177/21582440221109581.

Lee, D. G., & Park, H. J. (2011). Cross-cultural validity of the frost multidimensional perfectionism scale in Korea. *The Counseling Psychologist*, 39(2), 320–345. https://doi.org/10.1177/0011000010365910.

Lizmore, M. R., Dunn, J. G., Dunn, J. C., & Hill, A. P. (2019). Perfectionism and performance following failure in a competitive golf-putting task. *Psychology of Sport and Exercise*, 45, 101582. https://doi.org/10.1016/j.psychsport.2019.101582.

Longbottom, J.-L., Grove, J. R., & Dimmock, J. A. (2010). An examination of perfectionism traits and physical activity motivation. *Psychology of Sport and Exercise*, 11, 574–581. https://doi.org/10.1016/j.psychsport.2010.06.007.

Longbottom, J.-L., Grove, J. R., & Dimmock, J. A. (2012). Trait perfectionism, self-determination, and self-presentation processes in relation to exercise behavior. *Psychology of Sport and Exercise*, 13, 224–235. https://doi.org/10.1016/j.psychsport.2011.11.003.

Madigan, D. J. (2016). Confirmatory factor analysis of the Multidimensional Inventory of Perfectionism in Sport. *Psychology of Sport and Exercise*, 26, 48–51. https://doi.org/10.1016/j.psychsport.2016.06.003.

Madigan, D. J., Curran, T., Stoeber, J., Hill, A. P., Smith, M. M., & Passfield, L. (2019). Development of perfectionism in junior athletes: A three-sample study of coach and parental pressure. *Journal of Sport and Exercise Psychology*, 41(3), 167–175. https://doi.org/10.1123/jsep.2018-0287.

Madigan, D. J., Stoeber, J., Culley, T., Passfield, L., & Hill, A. P. (2018). Perfectionism and training performance: The mediating role of other-approach goals. *European Journal of Sport Science*, 18, 1271–1279. https://doi.org/10.1080/17461391.2018.1508503.

Madigan, D. J., Stoeber, J., & Passfield, L. (2016). Perfectionism and attitudes towards doping in junior athletes. *Journal of sports sciences*, 34(8), 700–706. https://doi.org/10.1080/02640414.2015.1068441.

Madigan, D. J., Stoeber, J., & Passfield, L. (2015). Perfectionism and burnout in junior athletes: A three-month longitudinal study. *Journal of Sport and Exercise Psychology*, 37(3), 305–315. https://doi.org/10.1123/jsep.2014-0266.

Magurean, S., Sălăgean, N., & Tulbure, B. T. (2016). Factor structure and psychometric properties of two short versions of Frost Multidimensional Perfectionism Scale in Romania. *Romanian Journal of Experimental Applied Psychology*, 7.

Mallinson-Howard, S. H., Madigan, D. J., & Jowett, G. E. (2021). A three-sample study of perfectionism and field test performance in athletes. *European Journal of Sport Science*, 21, 1045–1053. https://doi.org/10.1080/17461391.2020.1811777.

McArdle, S., & Duda, J. L. (2008). Exploring the etiology of perfectionism and perceptions of self-worth in young athletes. *Social Development*, 17, 980–997. https://doi.org/10.1111/j.1467-9507.2007.00456.x.

Molnar, D. S., Blackburn, M., Zinga, D., Spadafora, N , Methot-Jones, T., & Connolly, M. (2021). Trait perfectionism and dance goals among young female dancers: An application of the 2× 2 model of perfectionism. *Journal of Sport and Exercise Psychology*, 43(3), 234–247. https://doi.org/10.1123/jsep.2020-0118

Mouratidis, A., & Michou, A. (2011). Perfectionism, self-determined motivation, and coping among adolescent athletes. *Psychology of Sport and Exercise*, 12, 355–367. https://doi.org/10.1016/j.psychsport.2011.03.006.

Nascimento Junior, J. R. A. D., Vissoci, J. R. N., Lavallee, D., & Vieira, L. F. (2015). Adaptation and validation of the Sport Multidimensional Perfectionism Scale-2 (SMPS-2) for the Brazilian sport context. *Motriz: Revista de Educação Física*, 21, 125–136. https://doi.org/10.1590/S1980-65742015000200003.

Nordin-Bates, S. M. (2020). Striving for Perfection or for Creativity? A Dancer's Dilemma. *Journal of dance education*, 20, 23–34. https://doi.org/10.1080/15290824.2018.1546050.

Nordin-Bates, S. M., Raedeke, T. D., & Madigan, D. J. (2017). Perfectionism, burnout, and motivation in dance: A replication and test of the 2× 2 model of perfectionism. *Journal of Dance Medicine & Science*, 21, 115–122. https://doi.org/10.12678/1089-313X.21.3.115.

Nunnally, J. C., & Bernstein, I. H. (1994). *Psychometric theory* (3rd ed.). McGraw-Hill.

Olsson, L. F., Madigan, D. J., Hill, A. P., & Grugan, M. C. (2022). Do athlete and coach performance perfectionism predict athlete burnout? *European Journal of Sport Science*, 22(7), 1073–1084. https://doi.org/10.1080/17461391.2021.1916080.

Pineda-Espejel, A., Arrayales, E., Morquecho-Sánchez, R., & Trejo, M. (2017). Validation of the Sport Multidimensional Perfectionism Scale-2 for the Mexican sport context. *International Journal of Human Movement and Sports Sciences*, 5(2), 27–32.

Piotrowski, K., & Bojanowska, A. (2021). Factor structure and psychometric properties of a Polish adaptation of the Frost Multidimensional Perfectionism Scale. *Current Psychology*, 40(6), 2754–2763. https://doi.org/10.1007/s12144-019-00198-w.

Rice, S. P., Loscalzo, Y., Giannini, M., & Rice, K. G. (2020). Perfectionism in Italy and the USA: Measurement invariance and implications for cross-cultural assessment.

European Journal of Psychological Assessment, 36(1), 207. https://doi.org/10.1027/1015-5759/a000476.

Safitri, S., & Preston, M. (2020). The development of Indonesian Multidimensional Perfectionism Scale for senior high school students.

Shafran, R., Cooper, Z., & Fairburn, C. G. (2002). Clinical perfectionism: A cognitive-behavioural analysis. *Behaviour Research and Therapy*, 40, 773–791. https://doi.org/10.1016/S0005-7967(01)00059–00056.

Sironic, A., & Reeve, R. A. (2015). A combined analysis of the Frost Multidimensional Perfectionism Scale (FMPS), Child and Adolescent Perfectionism Scale (CAPS), and Almost Perfect Scale – Revised (APS-R): Different perfectionist profiles in adolescent high school students. *Psychological Assessment*, 27, 1471. https://doi.org/10.1037/pas0000137.

Stoeber, J. (1998). The Frost Multidimensional Perfectionism Scale revisited: More perfect with four (instead of six) dimensions. *Personality and Individual Differences*, 24, 481–491. https://doi.org/10.1016/S0191-8869(97)00207–00209.

Stoeber, J. (2011). The dual nature of perfectionism in sports: Relationships with emotion, motivation, and performance. *International Review of Sport and Exercise Psychology*, 4, 128–145. https://doi.org/10.1080/1750984X.2011.604789.

Stoeber, J. (2014a). How other-oriented perfectionism differs from self-oriented and socially prescribed perfectionism. *Journal of Psychopathology and Behavioral Assessment*, 36, 329–338. https://doi.org/10.1007/s10862-013-9397-7.

Stoeber, J. (2014b). Perfectionism in sport and dance: A double-edged sword. *International Journal of Sport Psychology*, 45, 385–394.

Stoeber, J., & Childs, J. H. (2010). The assessment of self-oriented and socially prescribed perfectionism: Subscales make a difference. *Journal of Personality Assessment*, 92, 577–585. https://doi.org/10.1080/00223891.2010.513306.

Stoeber, J., & Eismann, U. (2007). Perfectionism in young musicians: Relations with motivation, effort, achievement, and distress. *Personality and Individual Differences*, 43, 2182–2192. https://doi.org/10.1016/j.paid.2007.06.036.

Stoeber, J., & Madigan, D. J. (2016). Measuring perfectionism in sport, dance, and exercise: Review, critique, recommendations. In A. P. Hill (ed.), *The psychology of perfectionism in sport, dance and exercise*, 47–72. Routledge.

Stoeber, J., & Otto, K. (2006). Positive conceptions of perfectionism: Approaches, evidence, challenges. *Personality and Social Psychology Review*, 10, 295–319. https://doi.org/10.1207/s15327957pspr1004_2.

Stoeber, J., & Rambow, A. (2007). Perfectionism in adolescent school students: Relations with motivation, achievement, and well-being. *Personality and Individual Differences*, 42, 1379–1389. https://doi.org/10.1016/j.paid.2006.10.015.

Stoeber, J., & Rennert, D. (2008). Perfectionism in school teachers: Relations with stress appraisals, coping styles, and burnout. *Anxiety, Stress, & Coping*, 21, 37–53. https://doi.org/10.1080/10615800701742461.

Stoeber, J., & Stoeber, F. S. (2009). Domains of perfectionism: Prevalence and relationships with perfectionism, gender, age, and satisfaction with life. *Personality and Individual Differences*, 46, 530–535. https://doi.org/10.1016/j.paid.2008.12.006.

Stoeber, J., Harvey, L. N., Almeida, I., & Lyons, E. (2013). Multidimensional sexual perfectionism. *Archives of Sexual Behavior*, 42, 1593–1604. https://doi.org/10.1007/s10508-013-0135-8.

Stoeber, J., Hoyle, A., & Last, F. (2013). The Consequences of Perfectionism Scale: Factorial structure and relationships with perfectionism, performance perfectionism, affect, and depressive symptoms. *Measurement and Evaluation in Counseling and Development*, 46, 178–191. https://doi.org/10.1177/074817561348198.

Stoeber, J., Kobori, O., & Tanno, Y. (2010). The Multidimensional Perfectionism Cognitions Inventory–English (MPCI-E): Reliability, validity, and relationships with positive and negative affect. *Journal of Personality Assessment*, 92, 16–25. https://doi.org/10.1080/00223890903379159.

Stoeber, J., Otto, K., & Stoll, O. (2004). Mehrdimensionales Inventar zu Perfektionismus im Sport (MIPS) [Multidimensional Inventory of Perfectionism in Sport (MIPS)]. In J. Stoeber, K. Otto, E. Pescheck, & O. Stoll (eds), *Skalendokumentation "Perfektionismus im Sport" (Hallesche Berichte zur Pädagogischen Psychologie Nr. 7)* (pp. 4–13). Department of Educational Psychology, Martin Luther University of Halle.

Stoeber, J., Otto, K., & Stoll, O. (2006). MIPS: Multidimensional Inventory of Perfectionism in Sport. Retrieved from https://kar.kent.ac.uk/41560/.

Stoeber, J., Otto, K., Pescheck, E., Becker, C., & Stoll, O. (2007). Perfectionism and competitive anxiety in athletes: Differentiating striving for perfection and negative reactions to imperfection. *Personality and Individual Differences*, 42, 959–969. https://doi.org/10.1016/j.paid.2006.09.006.

Stoeber, J., Stoll, O., Pescheck, E., & Otto, K. (2008). Perfectionism and achievement goals in athletes: Relations with approach and avoidance orientations in mastery and performance goals. *Psychology of Sport and Exercise*, 9, 102–121. https://doi.org/10.1016/j.psychsport.2007.02.002.

Stoeber, J., Stoll, O., Salmi, O., & Tiikkaja, J. (2009). Perfectionism and achievement goals in young Finnish ice-hockey players aspiring to make the Under-16 national team. *Journal of Sports Sciences*, 27, 85–94. https://doi.org/10.1080/02640410802448749.

Stoeber, J., Uphill, M. A., & Hotham, S. (2009). Predicting race performance in triathlon: The role of perfectionism, achievement goals, and personal goal setting. *Journal of Sport & Exercise Psychology*, 31, 211–245. https://doi.org/10.1123/jsep.31.2.211.

Taranis, L., & Meyer, C. (2010). Perfectionism and compulsive exercise among female exercisers: High personal standards or self-criticism? *Personality and Individual Differences*, 49, 3–7. https://doi.org/10.1016/j.paid.2010.02.024.

Trumpeter, N., Watson, P. J., & O'Leary, B. J. (2006). Factors within multidimensional perfectionism scales: Complexity of relationships with self-esteem, narcissism, self-control, and self-criticism. *Personality and Individual Differences*, 41, 849–860. https://doi.org/10.1016/j.paid.2006.03.014.

Waleriańczyk, W., Hill, A. P., & Stolarski, M. (2022). A re-examination of the 2 × 2 model of perfectionism, burnout, and engagement in sports. *Psychology of Sport and Exercise*, 61, 102190. https://doi.org/10.1016/j.psychsport.2022.102190.

Watson, D. R., Hill, A. P., & Madigan, D. J. (2021). Perfectionism and Attitudes Toward Sport Psychology Support and Mental Health Support in Athletes. *Journal of Clinical Sport Psychology*, 1, 1–16. https://doi.org/10.1123/jcsp.2020-0052.

Yang, H., Stoeber, J., & Wang, Y. (2015). Moral perfectionism and moral values, virtues, and judgments: A preliminary investigation. *Personality and Individual Differences*, 75, 229–233. https://doi.org/10.1016/j.paid.2014.11.040.

Yasar, B. A. R. U. T. (2015). Confirmatory factor analysis of the Hewitt-multidimensional perfectionism scale. *Educational Research and Reviews*, 10(22), 2854–2859.

Zarghmi, M., Ghamary, A., Shabani, S. E., & Varzaneh, A. G. (2010). Perfectionism and achievement goals in adult male elite athletes who compete at the national level and above. *Journal of Human Kinetics*, 26, 147–155.

3 Revisiting the Development of Perfectionism in Sport, Dance, and Exercise

Paul R. Appleton and Thomas Curran

The aim of this chapter is to revisit Flett et al.'s model of perfectionism develop-ment as it applies to sport, dance, and exercise. In doing so, we discuss the four pathways that are used to explain how perfectionism can develop - via social learning, the presence of parental expectations, the absence of parental warmth, and due to anxious rearing. In each case, we include the latest research from gen-eral psychology, and from sport, exercise, and dance domains. Readers will find that we have made some progress with regard to understanding why and how perfectionism develops. We also update our previous discussions of this topic by introducing Hewitt et al.'s concept of asynchrony. This new concept cuts across all developmental pathways and identifies insecure interpersonal attachment as the root cause of perfectionism. We close the chapter by expanding our previous dis-cussion of coach/instructor pathways via the climates they create and describing the process by which perfectionism is internalized.

Development of Perfectionism in Sport, Dance, and Exercise

The importance of perfectionism in sport, dance, and exercise has consistently been demonstrated in empirical studies. Through this research we have learned a great deal about the likely consequences of perfectionism and, to some degree, the psychological mechanisms that may explain these effects. However, we continue to know far less about the development of perfectionism. As suggested by Flett et al. (2002), this is an important area of enquiry because examining the factors that contribute to the development of perfectionism offers additional means of under-standing the characteristic and how to prevent it. In sport and dance, research lags behind work examining the development of perfectionism in other contexts. This is surprising given the perfectionistic environments created in these domains and how important coaches, teachers, and instructors can be in shaping the experiences and identities of young athletes and dancers.

The lack of research is also surprising because although perfectionism has around 30–40% genetic variance associated with its development (e.g. Tozzi et al., 2004), what's left over after that genetic variance is subtracted out leaves much for the environment to explain (Curran, 2023). Thanks to recent research we have begun to gain a clearer understanding of who is important in

DOI: 10.4324/9781003288015-4

shaping perfectionism, how this happens and what key features of the environment are important. These advances extend to sport and dance, and are supportive of studying coaches and instructors, in particular, their expectations, and the different climates they create. This updated chapter overviews recent conceptual and empirical advances and highlights where we have most to gain in developing our understanding further.

A multi-pathway Model of Perfectionism Development

To date, research on the origins of perfectionism has been mostly guided by Flett et al.'s (2002) conceptual model of perfectionism development (see Figure 3.1). This model is a forerunner of Hewitt et al.'s (2017) Comprehensive Model of Perfectionistic Behaviour (CMPB), discussed in more detail in Chapter 8, and addresses the developmental origins of three distinct trait dimensions of perfectionism; self-oriented (demanding perfection of oneself), other-oriented perfectionism (demanding perfection of others), and socially prescribed perfectionism (believing that others demand perfection). Flett et al.'s (2002) model was a significant and seminal contribution to research and continues to provide the only model that makes detailed reference to how different dimensions of perfectionism develop. As such, in the same way that it guides general perfectionism research, it is the most appropriate point of reference for examining the development of perfectionism sport, dance, and exercise.

Self-oriented perfectionism has an intrapersonal focus and is characterized by intemperate striving to attain perfection and the tendency to respond to imperfection with negative self-appraisal (Hewitt & Flett, 1991). Even a single failure can be debilitating to an individual scoring high in self-oriented perfectionism because it confirms fears that the successful accomplishment of self-set high standards may not be possible, despite maximal effort (Hall, 2006). This is particularly problematic because the perceived achievement of perfection is a necessary condition for the individual to feel worthy (Flett & Hewitt, 2005). As such, although this perfectionism dimension may contribute to positive achievement outcomes, it is conceptualized as a vulnerability factor for motivational and psychological difficulties (Flett & Hewitt, 2006).

Socially prescribed perfectionism involves the beliefs that others impose unrealistic standards on the self, that one's performance is evaluated stringently by others, and that others withhold approval until perfect standards are obtained (Hewitt & Flett, 1991). As socially prescribed perfectionism entails motivation towards standards determined by others, and one's performance is critically evaluated by these same individuals, perceptions of control over performance outcomes becomes largely external (Periasamy & Ashby, 2002). As a result of this limited control, the individual can mistakenly believe that their efforts have been futile when the result of the achievement striving is perceived as discrepant from externally set standards (Hall, 2006). The resulting implications are a range of motivationally dysfunctional behaviours such as helplessness, poor coping, procrastination, and hopelessness (Hewitt & Flett, 1991). Unlike

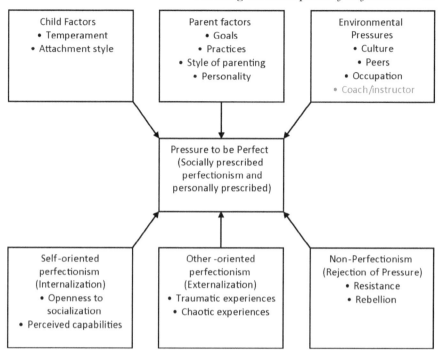

Figure 3.1 Model of the development of perfectionism.
Adapted from "Perfectionism in children and their parents: A developmental analysis",
by G. L. Flett, P. L. Hewitt, J. M. Oliver, and S. Macdonald's (2002), In G. L. Flett &
P. L. Hewitt (eds), *Perfectionism: Theory, Research, and Treatment* (pp. 89–132). Washington,
DC: American Psychological Association. Copyright 2002 by American Psychological
Association.

self-oriented perfectionism, socially prescribed perfectionism therefore appears
to hold no benefits and is uniformly debilitating.

Other-oriented perfectionism has a distinctly interpersonal focus. It is the
tendency to impose unrealistic standards on others and to evaluate others
stringently (Hewitt & Flett, 1991). This form of perfectionism is associated with
other-focused conditional acceptance (Lundh, 2004). Therefore, acceptance
and approval of significant others are also limited to the rare occasions when
they attain unrealistically high standards. As a result, although other-oriented
perfectionism may represent high self-confidence and assertiveness, it also has
hostile and aggressive overtones (Habke & Flynn, 2002).

When originally describing the trait dimensions of their approach, Hewitt
and Flett's (1991) proposed that the development of self-oriented, socially
prescribed and other-oriented perfectionism occurs within a relational context,
and is determined by the quality of interpersonal attachment the child's developing world (Greenspon, 2008). Such attachment is reflected in Flett et al.'s
(2002) conceptual model of perfectionism development. Although studies

outside of sport, dance, and exercise settings have identified a genetic component to perfectionism (e.g. Wade et al., 2008), Flett et al.'s model is a social psychological approach that emphasizes the role of social agents and formative environments in perfectionism development. In particular, parent-child interactions are considered especially influential to a child's proclivity towards perfectionism. The various environments and influences are captured in Flett et al.'s original model via four pathways, with each pathway emphasizing the different influences parents can have. These pathways offer a means of understanding research into the aetiology of perfectionism in sport, dance, and exercise. The next section introduces each pathway and provides an up-to-date account of research in general psychology and in these domains, in particular.

Pathway One: Social Learning Model

Flett et al.'s (2002) social learning model captures the child's tendency to imitate the perfectionism that is displayed by their parents. Flett et al. proposed that a child's tendency to imitate is underpinned by an idealized notion of their seemingly "perfect" parent. It is also hypothesized in this model that gifted children will be especially inclined to imitate their parent's perfectionism because, for this population of children, the achievement of perfection is deemed possible. This suggestion may be relevant to young elite athletes and dancers, for example, who may not only consider perfection a realistic goal, but for whom perfection can be an expected standard.

Empirical tests of the social learning model have taken place in general psychology. Notably, this includes a large recent meta-analytical study by Smith et al. (2022). This study used 46 studies, including 13,364 participants, to test the social learning model (and social expectations model). The findings provided evidence of a positive relationship between parent self-oriented perfectionism and child self-oriented perfectionism, and parent socially prescribed perfectionism and child socially prescribed perfectionism. In addition, there was minimal cross-over effects (e.g. parent self-oriented perfectionism predicting child socially prescribed perfectionism). The size of the relationships was, however, small and accounted for only 4% and 3% variance, respectively. As such, it may be that other influences or pathways are more important than direct social learning or imitation of perfectionism.

This meta-analysis also provided insight into two alternative social learning hypotheses for the development of perfectionism. The first is a primary caregiver hypothesis that children acquire perfectionism by imitating their mothers' perfectionism because mothers typically retain child-rearing responsibilities (and thus children have greater exposure to mother's perfectionism) (Frost et al., 1991). The second is a same-sex hypothesis that children model perfectionism displayed by their same-sex parent (Frost et al., 1991), and reject the perfectionism of their opposite sex-parent (Vieth & Trull, 1999). Previous research findings have provided a mix of support for both hypotheses and often include complex patterns of findings (e.g. Frost et al., 1991, Soenens et al., 2005a, 2005b). Smith et al.'s (2022) meta-analysis was similarly inconclusive in that, while the relationship between father's self-oriented perfectionism and children's self-oriented perfectionism was stronger for sons than daughters (supporting the same-sex hypothesis), the same was not found for mothers and daughters (not supporting the same-sex hypothesis)

With regard to research in sport, the first test of the social learning model in athletes was provided by Appleton et al.'s (2010). Appleton and colleagues recruited mothers and fathers and their athletic children. Separate regression analyses were conducted for mother–child and father–child dyads. Findings revealed athletes' perceptions of their fathers' or mothers' self-oriented perfectionism was the sole positive predictor of athletes' self-oriented perfectionism. In addition, athletes' perceptions of their fathers' or mothers' other-oriented perfectionism emerged as the strongest positive predictor of athletes' self-reported other-oriented perfectionism. Finally, athletes' perceptions of their fathers' or mothers' socially prescribed perfectionism emerged as the strongest positive predictor of athletes' socially prescribed perfectionism. Moderation analyses showed that the association between parents' and athletes' perfectionism were not limited to same-sex parent–child dyads. Therefore, Appleton et al.'s findings provide initial support for social learning model of perfectionism development in sport, but did not offer support for the same-sex hypothesis.

In explaining the findings of Appleton et al.'s (2010) study, and findings of Smith et al. (2022), it may be that rather than same-sex modelling, a child's modelling tendencies are guided by a desire to acquire characteristics most appropriate to their own developmental goals (Maccoby, 1998). This may tend to be the father for sons, generally. However, it does not preclude the significance of the mother. For elite junior athletes, whose sporting progression may depend on the production of perfect performances, they may actively seek out, and subsequently model, their parent (or parents) who demonstrate perfectionistic tendencies regardless of the caregiver's gender. In this regard, just as both mothers and fathers may be relevant to the overall development of athletic children (e.g. Wuerth et al., 2004), they may also be relevant to the development of their children's perfectionism in sport.

More recently researchers have sought to disentangle the roles of actual parents' perfectionism and perceived parents' perfectionism in the development of athlete perfectionism. To do so, Olsson et al. (2020) examined the social learning model in junior athletes and their parent who was most involved with their child's sport participation. Building on Appleton et al.'s (2010) study and guided by Bandura (1977) symbolic coding theory (that actual behaviour is the initial basis from which later impressions are formed), Olsson and colleagues proposed that actual *and* perceived parental perfectionism are likely to be important in the development of perfectionism in junior athletes. As a statistical model, this was tested with the relationship between parents' self-reported perfectionism and athletes' self-reported perfectionism being mediated by athletes' perceptions of their parents' perfectionism. Their findings were supportive of this model. As such, it appears that accounts of the social learning pathway should also include parents' actual perfectionism as well as athletes' perceptions.

Extending the Social Learning Model: Parenting Styles and Practices

The social learning model provides a starting point from which to investigate perfectionism development in sport, dance, and exercise. However, it is also important to take heed of Darling and Steinberg's (1993) recommendations that models of parenting should account for the processes through which parents influence children. For example, perfectionism may in fact be "transmitted" from parent to their children indirectly through specific parenting styles and practices, as well as directly modelled. In support of this possibility, research in the general perfectionism literature has confirmed an association between mothers' and fathers' perfectionism and various parental practices such as overcontrolling (e.g. Affrunti & Woodruff-Borden, 2015), over-protective (e.g. Enns et al., 2002), and guilt- and shame-inducing parenting (e.g. Curran et al., 2020). Moreover, other research has statistically modelled how such parenting practices explain the intergenerational transmission of perfectionism from parent to child.

One especially important explanatory process appears to be parents' use of psychological control. Psychological control is an insidious form of parenting that inhibits a child's psychological development (Barber, 1996). Research supports the link between parents' perfectionism and psychological control (e.g. Smith et al., 2017; Soenens et al., 2005b) and between psychological control and children's perfectionism (e.g. Filippello et al., 2017; Gong et al., 2016; Smith et al., 2017). In addition, as provided by Soenens et al. (2005a), there is direct evidence that psychological control mediates the relationship between maternal and paternal perfectionism and children's perfectionism (in this case daughters). In explaining these findings, they argued that perfectionistic parents may ultimately be less attuned to their child's behaviour and development needs, and may inadvertently use psychological control as a consequence.

In sport and exercise, a number of studies have examined the inter-relationships between parents' and their children's perfectionism and parental psychological control. For example, in a group of young adults who were regular exercisers, Costa et al. (2016) found that mother's and father's psychological control (as perceived by the exercisers) were positively correlated with exercisers' self-reported perfectionism (concerns over mistakes and doubts about action). This was the case for both male and female exercisers regardless of whether the mother or father was the source of psychological control. However, this study did not assess psychological control as a mediating mechanism. Rather, perfectionism was itself considered a mechanism through which psychological control exerted an effect on eating disorder symptoms and exercise dependence symptoms.

In a study in sport, Appleton et al. (2009) examined the mediating role of psychological control in the relationships between parents' and elite junior athletes' self-oriented and socially prescribed perfectionism. In addition, Appleton et al. (2009) also examined the mechanisms that explain the association between parents' perfectionism and their psychological control in the form of the mediating role of (a lack of) empathy. Mediation between parents' perfectionism and psychological control was expected because perfectionistic parents are suggested to be preoccupied with their own psychological development and attainment of perfection, experience difficulties in developing secure relationships with their offspring, and are unable to identify the needs of their child. As a result, when parent–child interactions occur, the caregiver lacks the necessary sensitivity and empathetic concern towards their child, and thus he/she engages in an intrusive and autonomy-inhibiting child rearing style characteristic of psychological control (Soenens et al., 2005a).

Using structural equation modelling, Appleton et al. (2009) found that empathy partially mediated the relationship between parents' socially prescribed perfectionism and psychological control. In turn, the relationship between parents' socially prescribed perfectionism and athletes' socially prescribed perfectionism was partially mediated by empathy and psychological control. The relationship between parents' and athletes' self-oriented perfectionism was significant but not mediated by either empathy or psychological control. Thus, the initial evidence provided by Appleton et al. (2009) suggests that similar parenting styles and practices found to operate outside of sport (i.e. psychological control and a lack of empathy) may also explain intergenerational transmission of socially prescribed perfectionism from parents to their athletic children.

Pathway Two: Social Expectations Model

The major premise guiding the social expectations model is that children who develop perfectionism do so within an environment of extreme parental expectations and conditional parental acceptance (Flett et al., 2002). That is, parents exert considerable pressure on their children to obtain exceptionally high standards and approval is only forthcoming when these standards are met.

Evidence from the general perfectionism literature has supported the social expectations model. This evidence was recently summarized in a large meta-analytical study of perfectionism and parental pressure. Drawing on the findings of 21 studies, including 7060 participants, Curran and Hill (2022) found that all three trait dimensions of perfectionism – self-oriented, other-oriented, and socially prescribed – were positively correlated with perceptions of parental expectations and parental criticism. The relationships were strongest for socially prescribed perfectionism, as might be expected given that this dimension encompasses perceptions of external pressure. Perhaps more intriguingly, the relationships were generally also stronger for parental expectations than parental criticism. Curran and Hill argued that, in regard to directing behaviour, excessive expectations may be experienced as more overtly perfectionistic and explicitly instructive by children than criticism. Regardless, with effects notably stronger than for direct social learning (Smith et al., 2022), their findings provide strong support for the social expectations model.

Other evidence for the social expectations pathway by research that has examined perfectionism and parental conditional regard. Curran et al. (2017; Curran, 2018) have provided evidence that perceptions of parental conditional regard are common to different dimensions of perfectionism in sport. These include perfectionistic strivings, perfectionistic concerns, self-critical perfectionism, and narcissistic perfectionism. In a recent study of child-parent dyads, too, Curran et al. (2020) found that the relationships between parent self-oriented perfectionism and both child self-oriented perfectionism and child socially prescribed perfectionism were mediated by parental conditional regard (as reported by the child). As such, parental conditional regard should be considered central to the development of perfectionism.

In other sport samples, support for the social expectations models can be inferred from the finding that parental expectations are typically positively correlated with core dimensions of athletes' perfectionism. Most studies that have used the Sport-Multidimensional Perfectionism Scale (S-MPS, S-MPS-2; Dunn et al., 2006; Gotwals et al., 2009), that includes a measure of parental pressure (a combination of perceptions of parental expectation and criticism) along with other dimensions of perfectionism, find this relationship. In their study with soccer and figure skaters, for example, Dunn et al. (2005) found that a perceived parental pressure dimension of perfectionism was positively related to athletes' self-reported self-oriented, socially prescribed, and other-oriented perfectionism.

One particularly noteworthy study in terms of the social expectations model has been provided by McArdle and Duda (2004). With a sample of young athletes, and using cluster analysis, McArdle and Duda's (2004) identified four groups that differed in terms of perfectionism and other motivation-related factors. Among the four groups identified, the two reporting higher parental expectations and criticism also reported higher concerns over mistakes. However, there were no differences in terms of personal standards between the four groups. In this sense, parental pressure appears to be particularly important in terms of the development of more problematic dimensions of perfectionism.

The study by Appleton et al. (2010) described earlier also provides support for the social expectations model in sport. Appleton et al. argued that other-oriented perfectionism captures the defining parenting behaviours central to the social expectations model, including holding unreasonable high standards for others and withholding approval until those standards are attained (Hewitt & Flett, 1991). If parents demonstrate other-oriented perfectionistic tendencies within the home and that is directed to their offspring, the sense of conditional self-worth that would ensue in children could be reflected in high socially prescribed perfectionism scores (Flett et al., 2002). In support of this idea, Appleton et al. found that, in addition to parents' socially prescribed perfectionism (as indicative of social learning), parents' other-oriented perfectionism was a positive (albeit weaker) predictor of athletes' socially prescribed perfectionism. This finding supports a social expectations explanation for the development of socially prescribed perfectionism in sport and alludes to the possibility of multiple interwoven pathways (i.e. both modelling and responding to social expectations) in the development of perfectionism in junior athletes.

Pathway Three: Social Reaction Model

In addition to high expectations and conditional approval, children who develop perfectionism are thought to do so through exposure to a harsh family environment (Flett et al., 2002). A harsh family environment can take many forms; from physical abuse through to psychological maltreatment, including the withdrawal of love and exposure to shame, or a chaotic family environment that involves a sense of unpredictability (Flett et al., 2002). This is labelled the social reaction model by Flett et al. (2002).

In proposing their different pathways, Flett et al. (2002) noted the substantial overlap between the social expectations model and the social reaction model. This overlap exists because both models examine parental behaviors and attitudes that are subsequently directed towards their child. However, the models were viewed separately by Flett and colleagues because each approach addresses a particular dimension of parenting. Specifically, parental demands are captured in the social expectations model, and range from exceedingly high expectations and overcontrolling tendencies to a lack of interest in the child's development. In contrast, parental warmth are captured in the social reaction model, and ranges from extreme harshness and criticalness to extreme warmth and unconditional approval.

Parental expectations and warmth were conceived as orthogonal dimensions by Flett et al. (2002), and thus different combinations may exist. Some parents have high expectations, and are warm and accepting of their child, regardless of performance outcome. These parents respond to mistakes with encouragement and value the attainment of realistic standards. It is hypothesized children exposed to this desirable form of parenting will respond with an adaptive pattern of achievement striving. This is because the child's self-worth is unconditionally accepted regardless of whether parental standards are attained. Moreover, the child does not fear failure because the parent is generally accepting of achievement outcomes and adopts a developmental stance towards performance errors.

Another subset of parents, in contrast, not only expect impossibly high standards but are austere, critical, and lack warmth and acceptance when evaluating their child. This combination of parenting dimensions (i.e. high parental expectations, low parenting warmth) is labelled affectionless control within the parental literature (see Parker et al., 1979). In the confines of the family home, children are increasingly vulnerable to the development of perfectionism when their parents are affectionless controlling because the attainment of parental approval, or the avoidance of parental disproval, becomes central to the child's self-worth. In turn, only by attaining unrealistic performance standards can the child reaffirm their self-worth (Flett et al., 2002).

Research in the general perfectionism has established an indirect link between affectionless controlling parents and children's perfectionism. This has been provided by research that has examined authoritarian and authoritative styles of parenting (Baumrind, 1971, 1991). Authoritarian parents are highly controlling, highly demanding, and relatively non-responsive towards their children, and thus are characterized as affectionless and controlling. Authoritative parents are also highly demanding but, in contrast to authoritarian parents, are much less controlling and more responsive and supportive of their children's development. Flett et al. (1995) reported positive correlations between socially prescribed perfectionism and parents' authoritarianism, and Speirs Neumeister (2004) and Kawamura et al. (2002) found similar links for the same, as well as other, perfectionism dimensions (socially prescribed perfectionism, concern over mistakes, and doubts about actions) in samples of undergraduate students.

In sport, Sapieja et al. (2011) examined the relationship between authoritativeness parenting and children's perfectionism in a sample of young male soccer players. A cluster analysis revealed three perfectionism groups, which were labelled as "healthy perfectionism", "unhealthy perfectionism", and "non-perfectionism". A subsequent analysis revealed the groups differed on parents' authoritativeness scores. Healthy perfectionists and non-perfectionists had higher perceptions of both mother and father authoritativeness than unhealthy perfectionists. However, healthy perfectionists and non-perfectionists did not differ in their perceptions of either mother or farther authoritativeness. The findings from Sapieja et al.'s study provides initial, albeit indirect, evidence for the role of affectionless controlling parenting in the development of athletes' perfectionism.

The social reaction model was also recently tested in sport by Fleming et al. (2022). In a sample of adolescent soccer players, they examined whether parent-child warmth – defined as the tendency for the relationship to be imbued by support, affection, and sensitive interactions (Dorsch et al., 2016) – mediated the relationship between perceptions of maternal and parental pressure and athletes' perfectionistic striving and concerns. Structural equation modelling revealed no direct or indirect effects for maternal pressure. However, paternal pressure had both direct and indirect effects on athletes' perfectionistic striving and perfectionistic concerns. Paternal pressure was directly related to higher perfectionistic strivings and higher perfectionistic concerns. However, indirectly, paternal pressure was related to lower perfectionistic strivings and concerns. This latter, unexpected, finding was due to a *positive* correlation between paternal warmth and dimensions of perfectionism in the model. It is not clear at the moment whether this finding reflects a direct challenge to one aspect of the social reaction model, offers new insight (i.e. perfectionism developing even when or because parental warmth is high), or is an artifact of the analyses and statistical model (e.g. due to statistical suppression).

Pathway Four: Anxious Rearing Model

The fourth pathway identified by Flett et al. (2002) considered the role of anxious parents, who are preoccupied with mistakes and the negative consequences of mistakes, in the development of perfectionism. An anxious rearing parenting style may be reflected in overprotection, where the mother and/or father constantly reminds their offspring about being on the "lookout" for possible errors that may pose a threat to the child, because mistakes will be evaluated unfavourably by significant others.

This particular pathway has received growing attention in the general perfectionism literature. Flett et al. (2002) reported on an unpublished study (Flett, Sherry, & Hewitt, 2001) in which anxious parental rearing was positively associated with socially prescribed, but not self- and other-oriented perfectionism in undergraduate students. More recently, anxious rearing parenting has emerged as a positive predictor a children's perfectionism (Affrunti & Woodruff-Borden, 2017) and university students' perfectionism (Segrin et al., 2019). Notably, in a short-term longitudinal study by Domocus and Damian (2018), it was also demonstrated that anxious rearing parenting predicted increases in adolescents' socially prescribed perfectionism over three months.

In sport, there is indirect evidence that supports the role of anxious parental rearing in the development of athletes' perfectionism in the form of research examining the relationship between the parent-initiated motivational climate and athletes' perfectionism. The motivational climate is a central construct within Achievement Goal Theory (Nicholls, 1989), which proposes parents can create a task-involving (where parents encourage their child to derive enjoyment and personal satisfaction from skill acquisition) or ego-involving climates (where parents create a worry-conducive environment and/or reserve approval for success that is achieved without effort) (White, 1996). A parent-initiated ego-involving climate, and specifically a preoccupation with ensuring their child is aware of, and subsequently avoids making, mistakes (i.e. a worry conducive environment), has conceptual overlap with the description of anxious rearing parenting provided by Flett et al. (2002).

Appleton et al. (2011) proposed that athletes enveloped by a parent-initiated ego-involving climate will report higher perfectionism scores because he/she is taught the negative implications of mistakes and learns that performance errors means parental disapproval is forthcoming. Appleton et al. (2011) tested the hypothesized relationship between the parent-initiated motivational climate and athletes' perfectionistic cognitions in a sample of elite junior athletes from individual and team sports. Perfectionistic cognitions are automatic thoughts characterized by images involving a desire to be perfect (Flett et al., 1998). Regression analyses revealed that the father-initiated worry-conducive climate positively predicted male athletes' perfectionistic cognitions, and a mother-initiated worry-conducive climate positively predicted female athletes' perfectionistic cognitions, thus providing indirect support for the role of anxious parenting in the prediction of athletes' perfectionism.

The relationship between a parent-initiated motivational climate and athletes' perfectionism was also examined by Gustafsson et al. (2016) in a sample of junior athletes. Using latent profile analysis, Gustafsson et al. identified four groups within the sample that differed in their perfectionism and parental climate scores. These included three groups with high, moderate, and low levels of perfectionism in a largely task-involving climate and a fourth group that was high in perfectionism in a mixed task- and ego-involving climate. The fourth group included the highest level of a worry-conducive and its existence provides at least some support for the notion that the presence of this element may result in perfectionism. In addition, of the three aspects of the parent-initiated climate, in this study it was a worry-conducive climate that was most strongly related to dimensions of perfectionism.

Recent Advances in Development Theory

Hewitt et al. (2017) have recently advanced their thinking on the development of perfectionism. In their new book, they integrate the pathways described in Flett et al. (2002) and explain the development of perfectionism in terms of parent-child "asynchrony". From this perspective, perfectionism emerges in response to parental socialization that only intermittently fulfils attachment needs of self-esteem and belonging. Germane to asynchrony is the (non)availability and (non)responsiveness of parents to such attachment needs. Parental behaviours understood to promote asynchrony cut across the discussed pathways to include pressurizing, punitive, anxious and controlling socialization, which involves a combination of high expectations and harsh criticism (Flett et al., 2002). Perfectionism ultimately develops because being perfect promises to satisfy unmet needs ("if I am perfect, then there'll be nothing to criticize or reject").

Studies outside of sport support the major tenets of Hewitt et al.'s (2017) concept of asynchrony. The work of Chen and colleagues, for example, shows that facets of perfectionism including socially prescribed perfection were positively correlated with insecure parental attachment in adolescents and college students (Chen et al., 2015; Chen et al., 2012). More recently, Ko et al. (2019) similarly found that attachment anxiety mediated the relationship between adverse parenting (i.e. lack of autonomy support, warmth, and involvement) and socially prescribed perfectionism in college students. To our knowledge, no studies have tested links between insecure and anxious forms of attachment and perfectionism in sport. However, Hewitt et al.'s (2017) model shows promise in adjacent research. Insecure attachment styles, for example, are positively correlated with image-related pathology such as eating disorders in athlete populations (e.g. Shanmugam et al., 2012). Likewise, in sport, parental attachment is an important predictor of social functioning and self-esteem (e.g. Kang et al., 2015).

In subsuming and extending Flett et al.'s (2002) pathways, Hewitt et al. (2017) provide a more comprehensive model of perfectionism development. This model essentially views perfectionism as a product of prolonged attachment anxiety, which is implanted from an early age and by particular parental styles and practices (i.e. anxious, harsh, controlling, and conditionally regarding parenting). The concept of asynchrony is an important theoretical advance because it provides a way of understanding how a variety different styles and behaviours, from previously formalized pathways and beyond, might affect universal needs (for belonging and self-esteem). Moreover, the concept is generalisable and readily applied to a range of different domains, including sport, dance, and exercise.

Extending the Conceptual Model of Perfectionism Development for Sport, Dance, and Exercise

Within their conceptual models, Hewitt and Flett recognized the influence of wider societal factors and social actors in perfectionism development. Within the context of sport-related literature it has been consistently emphasized that one additional social actor that is central to the development of athletes' perfectionism is the coach (Anshel & Eom, 2003; Dunn et al., 2006). Here, we propose an extension to Flett et al.'s model in the form of an additional pathway to the development of perfectionism that is specific in sport, dance, and exercise via coaches and instructors.

The first source of evidence for the inclusion of the coach/instructor is provided by research using sport- (or dance-) specific measures of perfectionism that include coach (or instructor) "pressures" (reflecting expectations and criticism) (e.g. Gotwals & Dunn, 2009; Sport-Multidimensional Perfectionism Scale-2). As discussed earlier in context of the social expectations model, empirical research in sport (e.g. Sapieja et al., 2011) adopting one or more of these sport-specific measures of perfectionism has reported a positive relationship between athletes' self-reported perfectionism (e.g. high personal standards, concern over mistakes) and perceptions of parent and coach pressures, while similar findings have also emerged with classical ballet and contemporary dancers (Nordin-Bates et al., 2011). Interestingly, research has now also demonstrated that when parental- and coach-related pressures are examined simultaneously, it is the latter (and not the former) that emerges as a significant predictor of changes in athletes' perfectionistic striving and concerns over time (3 and 6 months) (Madigan et al., 2019).

The second source of evidence for the coach/instructor-based pathway of perfectionism development is available via the motivational climate literature. The coach-created motivational climate has received considerable attention from sport psychologists (see Duda et al., 2017, for a summary), and in the dance psychology literature (e.g. Quested & Duda, 2010). As with the parental motivational climate, the coach climate from an AGT perspective is considered to be task- or ego-involving. An ego-involving climate reflects the coach's concern for his/her athletes' attaining success without effort and outperforming opponents. In contrast, a task-involving climate encourages enjoyment throughout the learning process, enables athletes to cooperate and work together, and is thought to facilitate positive cognition, affect, and behaviour (Duda et al., 2017). Consistent with the theorizing presented earlier in this chapter regarding the parental motivational climate, it is expected that a coach/instructor–created ego-involving climate will foster perfectionistic tendencies within athletes and dancers.

Evidence for the proposed relationship between the coach-created motivational climate and athletes' perfectionism is provided by Lemyre et al. (2008). In their study they examined the relationship between social cognitive motivational variables, including athletes' perfectionism and perceptions of the coach-created motivational climate, and burnout in 141 current Olympic and junior elite winter athletes. They found that a task-involving coach climate was negatively correlated with athletes' concern over mistakes and doubts about actions. In contrast, an ego-involving climate was positively associated with athletes' high personal standards, concern over mistakes and doubts about actions.

Appleton et al.'s (2011) study with elite junior athletes provides further evidence for the association between the coach-created motivational climate and athletes' perfectionism. As a secondary purpose to their study, Appleton et al. examined whether the coach-created motivational climate predicted athletes' perfectionistic cognitions after controlling for the effects of the parent-initiated climate. Hierarchical regression analyses revealed that, after controlling for the effects of the parent-initiated climate, an ego-involving coaching climate emerged as a positive predictor of athletes' perfectionistic cognitions. For female athletes, in particular, task- and ego-involving coaching climates were significant predictors of perfectionistic cognitions after controlling for the parental climate.

The relationship between the instructor-created climate and dancers' self-reported perfectionism has also been examined. Carr and Wyon (2003) conducted a study with 181 dance students, and regression analyses revealed that task- and ego-involving climate dimensions predicted dancers' tendency to experience concern over making mistakes, high personal standards, and doubts about their actions. Further inspection of the regression analyses revealed that features of a task-involving climate negatively predicted concern over mistakes and positively predicted personal standards, and facets of an ego climate positively predicted concern over mistakes and doubts about actions.

In a second study in dance, Nordin-Bates et al. (2014) used a cross-lagged design to examine the relationship between the instructor-created climate and dancers' perfectionism over time. Young dancers completed measures of the instructor-created climate, striving for excellence and concerns over mistakes on two occasions, six months apart. Nordin-Bates et al. (2014) found that perceptions of a task-involving climate at time one was associated with increased perfectionistic striving over time. Furthermore, perfectionistic concerns at time one were associated with increased perceptions of an ego climate and decreased perceptions of a task climate over time. These findings suggest an interesting relationship between perfectionism and the motivational climate that at least in part includes the potential for a task-involving climate to contribute to the development of perfectionistic strivings in dance.

In addition to AGT, researchers have recently begun to employ self-determination theory as a framework for investigating additional aspects of the coach-created motivational climate and its role in the development of perfectionism. In sport, research that has adopted SDT when investigating perfectionism has focused on autonomy-supportive and controlling behaviours of coaches. In an autonomy-supportive coach-created motivational climate, athletes' preferences are recognized and their perspectives are considered, their feelings are acknowledged, they are provided with meaningful choices, their input into decision making (when and where possible) is welcomed, and a rationale is provided when they are asked to do something (Mageau & Vallerand, 2003). This kind of climate is hypothesized to be negatively correlated with perfectionism. Conversely, controlling coaching behaviours pressurize, coerce, and intimidate sports participants (Bartholomew et al., 2010). This kind of climate and is expected to be positively correlated with perfectionism.

A small number of recent studies have adopted this approach. For example, Jowett et al. (2020) found a negative relationship between perceptions of dance instructors' autonomy-support and adolescent dancers' perfectionistic concerns. These initial studies suggest future research on the origins of perfectionism in athletes and dancers may benefit from examining SDT and AGT facets of the coach- (and parent) created motivational climate.

In broadening the examination of climates, there will also be value in examining the concept of perfectionistic climate (Hill & Grugan, 2020). As outlined in Chapter 8 of this book, the perfectionistic climate comprises features of the social environment that promote the value of perfect performances and the view imperfect performances are unacceptable. As part of their theorizing, Hill and Grugan proposed that perfectionistic climates will likely hold implications for the development of perfectionism. Specifically, in defining the perfectionistic climate, Hill and Grugan drew from three of the four pathways identified by Flett et al. (2002) regarding the influence of parents' behaviours, practices, and relational styles: social expectations, social reactions and anxious rearing. In addition, the perfectionistic climate as defined by Hill and Grugan has conceptual similarities with ego-involving and controlling climates. A perfectionistic climate is one where the social actor has unrealistic expectations, is critical of mistakes, demonstrates coercive and controlling behaviour, and uses the withdrawal and manipulation of recognition in response to the level of performance (imperfect vs. perfect) of others. Intuitively, perfectionistic climates will be involved in the development of perfectionism in sport and dance.

The aforementioned studies provide support for Flett et al.'s (2002) suggestion that parent-child interactions *and* environmental pressures are both important to perfectionism development. Thus, an understanding of the multiple pathways to perfectionism in athletes and dancers will undoubtedly be strengthened via a consideration of the role of coaches and instructors. In light of this suggestion, Flett et al.'s original model (see Figure 3.1) has been extended and adapted to sport and dance to include the influence of coach- and instructor-related factors (highlighted in grey).

Completing the Conceptual Model of Perfectionism Development

The model presented in Figure 3.1 depicts Flett et al.'s (2002) model in full. The model makes clear that the specific perfectionism dimension/s acquired by the individual will be determined by the pathways that are in operation. However, Flett and colleagues also argued that the extent to which perfectionism develops, and the type of perfectionism acquired, also depends on factors outlined in the lower half of their model. According to the lower half of the model, whether perfectionism develops depends upon the individual internalizing socially imposed standards into a coherent self-view. Because children, in particular, vary in the degree to which they are open to socialization and subsequent internalization of values (Flett et al., 2002), young athletes, dancers, or exercisers may or may not develop perfectionism in response to parental and environment pressures. Children who are more open to parental and societal influence are vulnerable to the acquisition of perfectionism. Other children may choose to reject external pressures for a number of reasons; children may want to avoid modelling their mother and/or father, for example, because they have come to despise their parent's perfectionism. A further reason for the rejection of external pressure is because the child views perfection as an unrealistic goal. Flett et al. expanded upon this second reason, and suggested children will most likely strive for perfection in domains where feelings of competence are experienced and the achievement of high-performance standards is deemed possible. Thus, when a personal history of success and achievement has been attained (e.g. gifted performers), the performer may subsequently believe that perfection is a realistic goal for future performance.

Once the child is exposed to external pressures to be perfect, and has subsequently accepted the pressures into their self-view (see centre box of Figure 3.1), a number of important factors determine the type of perfectionism on display. According to the conceptual model of perfectionism development, the internalization of external pressures leads to the development of socially prescribed perfectionism. This is consistent with the social expectations and reaction models, which outline the role of parental demands, conditional acceptance, and fear over mistakes as sources of socially prescribed perfectionism. When external pressures to be perfect are translated into expectations on the self, self-oriented perfectionism will emerge. However, the translation of external pressures into one's self-concept is far from simple. Flett et al. (2002) proposed a complex set of factors that determine whether external pressures to be perfect subsequently develop into self-oriented perfectionism, including the degree to which the child is open to socialization, whether the child decides to model self-oriented perfectionism, whether important environments (e.g. family, sport/dance/exercise) emphasize the achievement of perfection, whether the child has the skills and abilities to achieve perfection, and whether the child has a personality characterized by extreme persistence and fearfulness.

External pressures to be perfect may also be externalized in the form of expectations on others, which is subsequently reflected in other-oriented perfectionism. A number of factors also determine the extent to which external pressures to be perfect are directed towards others, including exposure to an environment that is extremely evaluative in nature, in which the child acquires a similar need to evaluate; maintaining a self-view that perfection is possible and therefore others should also perform to a similar standard; the need for social support within a chaotic environments; and a reaction to a history or perception of being mistreated or disappointed by others (Flett et al., 2002).

Concluding Comments

Research examining the development of perfectionism has made recent conceptual and empirical advances. This work continues to be grounded in Flett et al.'s (2002) model and its refinement. The notion of multiple interwoven parental pathways provides a framework that can readily be applied to sport and dance by researchers and practitioners. It also provides the basis for understanding the role of significant others, such as the coach. Some of the key findings in this regard is evidence of the especial importance of social expectations and how these can be rooted in multiple social agents. Emerging evidence to support coaching/instructor specific pathways point to the need to further examine motivational climates.

Despite the many advances made, more research is sorely needed. Indeed, the development of perfectionism remains an understudied aspect of the trait, both inside and outside sport. Recent evidence suggests that perfectionism is on the rise in adolescents and young adults, with the implication being that more and more young people will arrive on the sports field with underlying vulnerabilities (Curran & Hill, 2019). Better understanding the origins of perfectionism, and the various mechanisms that link parent and coaching practices to perfectionism, will be essential for effective prevention and intervention in sport and dance, environments that may commonly be experienced as perfectionistic.

References

Affrunti, N. W., & Woodruff-Borden, J. (2015). Negative affect and child internalizing symptoms: The mediating role of perfectionism. *Child Psychiatry & Human Development*, 47(3), 358–368. https://doi.org/10.1007/s10578-015-0571-x.

Affrunti, N. W., & Woodruff-Borden, J. (2017). Emotional control mediates the association between dimensions of perfectionism and worry in children. *Child Psychiatry & Human Development*, 48(1), 73–81. https://doi.org/10.1007/s10578-016-0654-3.

Anshel, M. H., & Eom, H.-J. (2003). Exploring the dimensions of perfectionism in sport. *International Journal of Sport Psychology*, 34(3), 255–271.

Appleton, P. R., Hall, H. K., & Hill, A. P. (2009). *Examining the mediating role of psychological control and empathy in the intergenerational transmission of athlete's perfectionism.* 12th ISSP Conference, Marrakesh, Morocco, June.

Appleton, P. R., Hall, H. K., & Hill, A. P. (2010). Family patterns of perfectionism: An examination of elite junior athletes and their parents. *Psychology of Sport and Exercise*, 11(5), 363–371. https://doi.org/10.1016/j.psychsport.2010.04.005.

Appleton, P. R., Hall, H. K., & Hill, A. P. (2011). Examining the influence of the parent-initiated and coach-created motivational climates upon athletes' perfectionistic cognitions. *Journal of Sports Sciences*, 29(7), 661–671. https://doi.org/10.1080/02640414.2010.551541.

Bandura, A. (1977). *Social learning theory*. Prentice-Hall.

Barber, B. K. (1996). Parental psychological control: Revisiting a neglected construct. *Child Development*, 67(6), 3296–3319. https://doi.org/10.1111/j.1467-8624.1996.tb01915.x.

Bartholomew, K. J., Ntoumanis, N., & Thøgersen-Ntoumani, C. (2010). The controlling interpersonal style in a coaching context: Development and initial validation of a psychometric scale. *Journal of Sport and Exercise Psychology*, 32(2), 193–216. https://doi.org/10.1123/jsep.32.2.193.

Baumrind, D. (1971). Current patterns of parental authority. *Developmental Psychology*, 4(1, Pt.2), 1–103. https://doi.org/10.1037/h0030372.

Baumrind, D. (1991). Parenting styles and adolescent development. In J. Brooks-Gunn & R. Lerner (eds), *The encyclopedia of adolescence*. Garland.

Carr, S., & Wyon, M. (2003). The impact of motivational climate on dance students' achievement goals, trait anxiety, and perfectionism. *Journal of Dance Medicine and Science*, 7(4), 105–114.

Chen, C., Hewitt, P. L., & Flett, G. L. (2015). Preoccupied attachment, need to belong, shame, and interpersonal perfectionism: An investigation of the perfectionism social disconnection model. *Personality and Individual Differences*, 76, 177–182. https://doi.org/10.1016/j.paid.2014.12.001.

Chen, C., Hewitt, P. L., Flett, G. L., Cassels, T. G., Birch, S., & Blasberg, J. S. (2012). Insecure attachment, perfectionistic self-presentation, and social disconnection in adolescents. *Personality and Individual Differences*, 52(8), 936–941. https://doi.org/10.1016/j.paid.2012.02.009.

Costa, S., Coppolino, P., & Oliva, P. (2016). Exercise dependence and maladaptive perfectionism: The mediating role of basic psychological needs. *International Journal of Mental Health and Addiction*, 14, 241–256.

Curran, T. (2018). Parental conditional regard and the development of perfectionism in adolescent athletes: The mediating role of competence contingent self-worth. *Sport, Exercise, and Performance Psychology*, 7(3), 284–296. https://doi.org/10.1037/spy0000126.

Curran, T. (2023). *The perfection trap: The power of good enough in a world that always wants more*. Penguin.

Curran, T., & Hill, A. P. (2019). Perfectionism is increasing over time: A meta-analysis of birth cohort differences from 1989 to 2016. *Psychological Bulletin*, 145(4), 410–429. https://doi.org/10.1037/bul0000138.

Curran, T., & Hill, A. P. (2022). Young people's perceptions of their parents' expectations and criticism are increasing over time: Implications for perfectionism. *Psychological Bulletin*. https://doi.org/10.1037/bul0000347.

Curran, T., Hill, A. P., & Williams, L. J. (2017). The relationships between parental conditional regard and adolescents' self-critical and narcissistic perfectionism. *Personality and Individual Differences*, 109, 17–22. https://doi.org/10.1016/j.paid.2016.12.035.

Curran, T., Hill, A. P., Madigan, D. J., & Stornæs, A. V. (2020). A test of social learning and parent socialization perspectives on the development of perfectionism. *Personality and Individual Differences*, 160, 109925. https://doi.org/10.1016/j.paid.2020.109925.

Darling, N., & Steinberg, L. (1993). Parenting style as context: An integrative model. *Psychological Bulletin*, 113(3), 487–496. https://doi.org/10.1037/0033-2909.113.3.487.

Domocus, I. M., & Damian, L. E. (2018). The role of parents and teachers in changing adolescents' perfectionism: A short-term longitudinal study. *Personality and Individual Differences*, 131, 244–248. https://doi.org/10.1016/j.paid.2018.05.012.

Dorsch, T. E., Smith, A. L., & Dotterer, A. M. (2016). Individual, relationship, and context factors associated with parent support and pressure in organized youth sport. *Psychology of Sport and Exercise*, 23, 132–141. https://doi.org/10.1016/j.psychsport.2015.12.003.

Duda, J. L., Appleton, P. R., Stebblings, J., & Balaguer, I. (2017). Towards more empowering and less disempowering environments in youth sport: Theory to evidenced-based practice. In C. J. Knight, C. G. Harwood, & D. Gould (eds), *Sport Psychology for Young Athletes* (pp. 81–93). Routledge.

Dunn, J. G. H., Dunn, J. C., Gotwals, J. K., Vallance, J. K. H., Craft, J. M., & Syrotuik, D. G. (2006). Establishing construct validity evidence for the Sport Multidimensional Perfectionism Scale. *Psychology of Sport and Exercise*, 7(1), 57–79. https://doi.org/10.1016/j.psychsport.2005.04.003.

Dunn, J. G. H., Gotwals, J. K., & Dunn, J. C. (2005). An examination of the domain specificity of perfectionism among intercollegiate student-athletes. *Personality and Individual Differences*, 38(6), 1439–1448. https://doi.org/10.1016/j.paid.2004.09.009.

Enns, M. W., Cox, B. J., & Clara, I. (2002). Adaptive and maladaptive perfectionism: Developmental origins and association with depression proneness. *Personality and Individual Differences*, 33(6), 921–935. https://doi.org/10.1016/s0191-8869(01)00202-00201.

Filippello, P., Larcan, R., Sorrenti, L., Buzzai, C., Orecchio, S., & Costa, S. (2017). The mediating role of maladaptive perfectionism in the association between psychological control and learned helplessness. *Improving Schools*, 20(2), 113–126. https://doi.org/10.1177/1365480216688554.

Fleming, D. J. M., Dorsch, T. E., & Dayley, J. C. (2022). The mediating effect of parental warmth on the association of parent pressure and athlete perfectionism in adolescent soccer. *International Journal of Sport and Exercise Psychology*, 1–17. https://doi.org/10.1080/1612197x.2022.2058584.

Flett, G. L., & Hewitt, P. L. (2005). The perils of perfectionism in sports and exercise. *Current Directions in Psychological Science*, 14(1), 14–18. https://doi.org/10.1111/j.0963-7214.2005.00326.x.

Flett, G. L., & Hewitt, P. L. (2006). Positive versus negative perfectionism in psychopathology. *Behavior Modification*, 30(4), 472–495. https://doi.org/10.1177/0145445506288026.

Flett, G. L., Hewitt, P. L., & Singer, A. (1995). Perfectionism and parental authority styles. *Individual Psychology: Journal of Adlerian Theory, Research & Practice*, 51, 50–60.

Flett, G. L., Hewitt, P. L., Blankstein, K. R., & Gray, L. (1998). Psychological distress and the frequency of perfectionistic thinking. *Journal of Personality and Social Psychology*, 75(5), 1363–1381. https://doi.org/10.1037/0022-3514.75.5.1363.

Flett, G. L., Hewitt, P. L., Oliver, J. M., & Macdonald, S. (2002). Perfectionism in children and their parents: A developmental analysis. In G. L. Flett & P. L. Hewitt (eds), *Perfectionism: Theory, research, and treatment* (pp. 89–132). American Psychological Association.

Flett, G. L., Sherry, S. B., & Hewitt, P. L., (2001). Perfectionism, parental punitiveness, and anxious parent rearing. Unpublished manuscript, Faculty of Health, York University, Canada.

Frost, R. O., Lahart, C. M., & Rosenblate, R. (1991). The development of perfectionism: A study of daughters and their parents. *Cognitive Therapy and Research*, 15(6), 469–489. https://doi.org/10.1007/bf01175730.

Gong, X., Paulson, S. E., & Wang, C. (2016). Exploring family origins of perfectionism: The impact of interparental conflict and parenting behaviors. *Personality and Individual Differences*, 100, 43–48. https://doi.org/10.1016/j.paid.2016.02.010.

Gotwals, J. K., & Dunn, J. G. H. (2009). A multi-method multi-analytic approach to establishing internal construct validity evidence: The Sport Multidimensional Perfectionism Scale 2. *Measurement in Physical Education and Exercise Science*, 13(2), 71–92. https://doi.org/10.1080/10913670902812663.

Greenspon, T. S. (2008). Making sense of error: A view of the origins and treatment of perfectionism. *American Journal of Psychotherapy*, 62(3), 263–282. https://doi.org/10.1176/appi.psychotherapy.2008.62.3.263.

Gustafsson, H., Hill, A. P., Stenling, A., & Wagnsson, S. (2016). Profiles of perfectionism, parental climate, and burnout among competitive junior athletes. *Scandinavian Journal of Medicine & Science in Sports*, 26(10), 1256–1264. https://doi.org/10.1111/sms.12553.

Habke, A. M., & Flynn, C. A. (2002). Interpersonal aspects of trait perfectionism. In G. L. Flett & P. L. Hewitt (eds), *Perfectionism: Theory, research, and treatment* (pp. 151–180). American Psychological Association.

Hall, H. K. (2006). Perfectionism: A hallmark quality of world class performers, or a psychological impediment to athletic development? In D. Hackfort & G. Tenenbaum (eds), *Perspectives in sport and exercise psychology: Essential processes for attaining peak performance* (pp. 178–211). Meyer & Meyer.

Hewitt, P. L., & Flett, G. L. (1991). Perfectionism in the self and social contexts: Conceptualization, assessment, and association with psychopathology. *Journal of Personality and Social Psychology*, 60(3), 456–470. https://doi.org/10.1037/0022-3514.60.3.456.

Hewitt, P. L., Flett, G. L., & Mikail, S. F. (2017). *Perfectionism: A relational approach to conceptualization, assessment, and treatment*. The Guilford Press.

Hill, A., & Grugan, M. (2020). Introducing Perfectionistic Climate. *Perspectives on Early Childhood Psychology and Education*, 4(2), 263–276.

Jowett, G. E., Hill, A. P., Curran, T., Hall, H. K., & Clements, L. (2020). Perfectionism, burnout, and engagement in dance: The moderating role of autonomy support. *Sport, Exercise, and Performance Psychology*. https://doi.org/10.1037/spy0000232.

Kang, S., Jeon, H., Kwon, S., & Park, S. (2015). Parental attachment as a mediator between parental social support and self-esteem as perceived by Korean sports middle and high school athletes. *Perceptual and Motor Skills*, 120(1), 288–303. https://doi.org/10.2466/10.pms.120v11x6.

Kawamura, K. Y., Frost, R. O., & Harmatz, M. G. (2002). The relationship of perceived parenting styles to perfectionism. *Personality and Individual Differences*, 32(2), 317–327. https://doi.org/10.1016/s0191-8869(01)00026–00025.

Ko, A., Hewitt, P. L., Cox, D., Flett, G. L., & Chen, C. (2019). Adverse parenting and perfectionism: A test of the mediating effects of attachment anxiety, attachment avoidance, and perceived defectiveness. *Personality and Individual Differences*, 150, 109474. https://doi.org/10.1016/j.paid.2019.06.017.

Lemyre, P.-N., Hall, H. K., & Roberts, G. C. (2008). A social cognitive approach to burnout in elite athletes. *Scandinavian Journal of Medicine & Science in Sports*, 18(2), 221–234. https://doi.org/10.1111/j.1600-0838.2007.00671.x.

Lundh, L.-G. (2004). Perfectionism and acceptance. *Journal of Rational-Emotive & Cognitive-Behavior Therapy*, 22(4), 251–265. https://doi.org/10.1023/b:jore.0000047311.12864.27.

Maccoby, E. E. (1998). *The two sexes*. Belknap Press.

Madigan, D. J., Curran, T., Stoeber, J., Hill, A. P., Smith, M. M., & Passfield, L. (2019). Development of perfectionism in junior athletes: A three-sample study of coach and parental pressure. *Journal of Sport and Exercise Psychology*, 41(3), 167–175. https://doi.org/10.1123/jsep.2018-0287.

Mageau, G. A., & Vallerand, R. J. (2003). The coach–athlete relationship: A motivational model. *Journal of Sports Sciences*, 21(11), 883–904. https://doi.org/10.1080/0264041031000140374.

McArdle, S., & Duda, J. L. (2004). Exploring Social? Contextual Correlates of Perfectionism in Adolescents: A Multivariate Perspective. *Cognitive Therapy and Research*, 28(6), 765–788. https://doi.org/10.1007/s10608-004-0665-4.

Neumeister, K. L. S. (2004). Factors influencing the development of perfectionism in gifted college students. *Gifted Child Quarterly*, 48(4), 259–274. https://doi.org/10.1177/001698620404800402.

Nicholls, J. G. (1989). *The competitive ethos and democratic education*. Harvard University Press.

Nordin-Bates, S. M., Cumming, J., Aways, D., & Sharp, L. (2011). Imagining yourself dancing to perfection? Correlates of perfectionism among ballet and contemporary dancers. *Journal of Clinical Sport Psychology*, 5(1), 58–76. https://doi.org/10.1123/jcsp.5.1.58.

Nordin-Bates, S. M., Hill, A. P., Cumming, J., Aujla, I. J., & Redding, E. (2014). A longitudinal examination of the relationship between perfectionism and motivational climate in dance. *Journal of Sport and Exercise Psychology*, 36(4), 382–391. https://doi.org/10.1123/jsep.2013-0245.

Olsson, L. F., Hill, A. P., Madigan, D. J., & Woodley, G. (2020). Development of perfectionism in junior athletes: Examination of actual and perceived parental perfectionism. *Journal of Sports Sciences*, 38(6), 669–675. https://doi.org/10.1080/02640414.2020.1723387.

Parker, G., Tupling, H., & Brown, L. B. (1979). A parental bonding instrument. *British Journal of Medical Psychology*, 51, 1–10.

Periasamy, S., & Ashby, J. S. (2002). Multidimensional perfectionism and locus of control. *Journal of College Student Psychotherapy*, 17(2), 75–86. https://doi.org/10.1300/j035v17n02_06.

Quested, E., & Duda, J. L. (2010). Exploring the social-environmental determinants of well- and ill-being in dancers: A test of basic needs theory. *Journal of Sport and Exercise Psychology*, 32(1), 39–60. https://doi.org/10.1123/jsep.32.1.39.

Sapieja, K. M., Dunn, J. G. H., & Holt, N. L. (2011). Perfectionism and perceptions of parenting styles in male youth soccer. *Journal of Sport and Exercise Psychology*, 33(1), 20–39. https://doi.org/10.1123/jsep.33.1.20.

Segrin, C., Kauer, T. B., & Burke, T. J. (2019). Indirect effects of family cohesion on emerging adult perfectionism through anxious rearing and social expectations. *Journal of Child and Family Studies*, 28(8), 2280–2285. https://doi.org/10.1007/s10826-019-01444-2.

Shanmugam, V., Jowett, S., & Meyer, C. (2012). Eating psychopathology amongst athletes: Links to current attachment styles. *Eating Behaviors*, 13(1), 5–12. https://doi.org/10.1016/j.eatbeh.2011.09.004.

Smith, M. M., Hewitt, P. L., Sherry, S. B., Flett, G. L., & Ray, C. (2022). Parenting behaviors and trait perfectionism: A meta-analytic test of the social expectations and social learning models. *Journal of Research in Personality*, 96, 104180. https://doi.org/10.1016/j.jrp.2021.104180.

Smith, M. M., Sherry, S. B., Gautreau, C. M., Mushquash, A. R., Saklofske, D. H., & Snow, S. L. (2017). The intergenerational transmission of perfectionism: Fathers' other-oriented perfectionism and daughters' perceived psychological control uniquely predict daughters' self-critical and personal standards perfectionism. *Personality and Individual Differences*, 119, 242–248. https://doi.org/10.1016/j.paid.2017.07.030.

Soenens, B., Elliot, A. J., Goossens, L., Vansteenkiste, M., Luyten, P., & Duriez, B. (2005a). The intergenerational transmission of perfectionism: Parents' psychological control as an intervening variable. *Journal of Family Psychology*, 19(3), 358–366. https://doi.org/10.1037/0893-3200.19.3.358.

Soenens, B., Vansteenkiste, M., Luyten, P., Duriez, B., & Goossens, L. (2005b). Maladaptive perfectionistic self-representations: The mediational link between psychological control and adjustment. *Personality and Individual Differences*, 38(2), 487–498. https://doi.org/10.1016/j.paid.2004.05.008.

Tozzi, F., Aggen, S. H., Neale, B. M., Anderson, C. B., Mazzeo, S. E., Neale, M. C., & Bulik, C. M. (2004). The structure of perfectionism: A twin study. *Behavior Genetics*, 34(5), 483–494. https://doi.org/10.1023/b:bege.0000038486.47219.76.

Vieth, A. Z., & Trull, T. J. (1999). Family patterns of perfectionism: An examination of college students and their parents. *Journal of Personality Assessment*, 72(1), 49–67. https://doi.org/10.1207/s15327752jpa7201_3.

Wade, T. D., Tiggemann, M., Bulik, C. M., Fairburn, C. G., Wray, N. R., & Martin, N. G. (2008). Shared temperament risk factors for anorexia nervosa: A twin study. *Psychosomatic Medicine*, 70(2), 239–244. https://doi.org/10.1097/psy.0b013e31815c40f1.

White, S. A. (1996). Goal orientation and perceptions of the motivational climate initiated by parents. *Pediatric Exercise Science*, 8(2), 122–129. https://doi.org/10.1123/pes.8.2.122.

Wuerth, S., Lee, M. J., & Alfermann, D. (2004). Parental involvement and athletes' career in youth sport. *Psychology of Sport and Exercise*, 5(1), 21–33. https://doi.org/10.1016/s1469-0292(02)00047-x.

Part II
Established Approaches and Models

4 An Update and Extension of the Independent Effects Approach to Perfectionism in Sport, Dance, and Exercise

Gareth E. Jowett, Sarah H. Mallinson-Howard, Andrew P. Hill and Daniel J. Madigan

Most research on perfectionism in sport, dance, and exercise continues to examine the effects of dimensions of perfectionism separately. In this chapter, we describe this independent-effects approach and revisit our previous review of research that has adopted it in sport, dance, and exercise. In doing so, we provide an updated account of the thoughts, emotions, and behaviours related to multidimensional perfectionism. In a further extension of our previous work, we also include a focus on the total unique effect of perfectionism. This is a new approach to examining the effects of multidimensional perfectionism and can be used to help determine whether, overall, perfectionism is adaptive, maladaptive, or neutral. Our updated review shows that research in this area continues to grow, most notably in sport. In addition, consistent with our previous review perfectionistic concerns and perfectionistic strivings continue to be associated with contrasting patterns of effects. In illustrating the use of total unique effects, we show for the first time that, overall, perfectionism is likely to be maladaptive in these domains, largely due to the relative influence of perfectionistic concerns.

Perfectionistic Strivings and Concerns in Sport, Dance, and Exercise

Perfectionism in Sport, Dance, and Exercise

As described in previous chapters in this book, there are several different multi-dimensional models of perfectionism that have been adopted in research in sport, dance, and exercise. Here, we follow the hierarchical model described in Chapter 1. Specifically, we consider the dimensions of perfectionism drawn from separate models to be indicative of two higher-order dimensions. Perfectionistic strivings capture "aspects of perfectionism associated with self-oriented striving for perfection and the setting of very high personal performance standards" (Gotwals et al., 2012, p. 264). Perfectionistic concerns capture "aspects associated with concerns over making mistakes, fear of negative social evaluation, feelings of discrepancy between one's expectations and performance, and negative reactions to imperfection" (Gotwals et al., 2012, p. 264). When considering how these two broad

DOI: 10.4324/9781003288015-6

dimensions of perfectionism might manifest in sport, dance, and exercise, it might be apparent that they have the potential to have opposing effects. One might visualize this as a tug of war, with perfectionistic strivings pulling hard in one direction and perfectionistic concerns pulling hard in the other.

The competing forces of perfectionistic strivings and concerns are often evident in the personal accounts of perfectionistic athletes. One recent illustrative example is provided from tennis, in the case of Emma Raducanu. At the 2021 US Open, Raducanu, a self-identified perfectionist, became the first qualifier to win a coveted grand slam since the open era began in 1968. Both perfectionistic strivings and perfectionistic concerns appear to have been instrumental in her development and in shaping her experiences. When recounting her formative years, Raducanu (2022) has expressed the importance of her drive for exacting and perfectionistic standards for her success. However, she also cited the strain of an inability to accept even minor mistakes, how it could be "really self-destructive", and recognized the need to try to let go of her unrealistic pursuit of perfection.

Capturing the Independent Effects of Perfectionistic Strivings and Concerns

One of the most common approaches to examining perfectionistic behaviours in sport, dance, and exercise, is to focus on the effects of perfectionistic strivings and perfectionistic concerns separately. This approach is based firmly on the notion that perfectionism is multidimensional and that the two main dimensions ought to be differentiated. The differentiation between the two dimensions is important because perfectionistic strivings and perfectionistic concerns have long been shown to have a contrasting pattern of relationships with various criterion variables (Stoeber & Otto, 2006). Consequently, research that considers the two dimensions separately helps address this issue and, in turn, provides insight into the opposing effects of dimensions of perfectionism (Stoeber, 2012). This approach contrasts to other approaches described later in this book that attempt to examine different combinations or interactive effects of perfectionistic strivings and perfectionistic concerns (see Chapters 5 and 6 for discussion of the tripartite model and 2 × 2 model of perfectionism, respectively).

The first approach to examining the effects of perfectionistic strivings and perfectionistic concerns separately is to do so in a manner that ensures each dimension is conceptually "intact" and statistically unaltered. That is, any relationship between the two dimensions is not statistically controlled or taken into account. Here, we are referring to an approach that examines the linear relationship between perfectionistic strivings or perfectionistic concerns and some other criterion variable. This approach can be observed in research examining perfectionism in sport, dance, and exercise (and research more widely) when using bivariate correlations (e.g. Madigan et al., 2016a) or error-free correlations among latent factors in structural equation modelling (e.g. Curran, 2018).

A second approach to examining the effects of perfectionistic strivings and perfectionistic concerns separately focuses on their unique effects. This entails examination of the effects of perfectionistic strivings and perfectionistic concerns after statistically controlling for their relationship. This is achieved via statistical partialling. Statistical partialling involves holding the effects of one variable constant while examining the effects of another (Lynam, Hoyle, & Newman, 2006). Partialling can take place among predictor variables only (creating semi-partial correlations) or among predictor variables and the criterion variable (creating partial correlations). In the case of the former, new residualized predictor variables are created and the criterion variable is unchanged. In the case of the latter, new residualized predictor variables and a new residualized criterion variable are created. Partialling can be observed in research examining perfectionism in sport, dance, and exercise (and research more widely) when using multiple regression (regression coefficients; e.g. Květon et al., 2021) and structural equation modelling (path coefficients; e.g. Wang et al., 2020).

The new dimensions of perfectionism that are created following partialling have previously been referred to as "pure" perfectionistic strivings and "pure" perfectionistic concerns (Hill, 2014; Hill & Curran, 2016; Stoeber, 2014). These terms were used to portray the notion that perfectionistic strivings and perfectionistic concerns are not "contaminated" by the other (Stoeber & Otto, 2006). We now consider the terms "residual perfectionistic strivings" and "residual perfectionistic concerns" to be a more accurate and less misleading labels. This is because the "pure" label suggests that following partialling the two dimensions are unrelated to each other when, in fact, it is the residualized variable and the unresidualized opposite that are unrelated (e.g. residual perfectionistic strivings and perfectionistic concerns) (Hill et al., 2018). The term "pure" is also used in the 2 × 2 model of perfectionism when labelling subtypes of perfectionism (see Chapter 6) so confusion can be avoided in that regard, too.

Partialling is illustrated in Figure 4.1 which depicts the unpartialled, partialled, and semi-partialled relationship between perfectionistic strivings and perfectionistic concerns with a criterion variable. The conceptual ramifications of the creation of residual perfectionistic strivings and residual perfectionistic concerns are discussed later. For now, the reader can simply note that

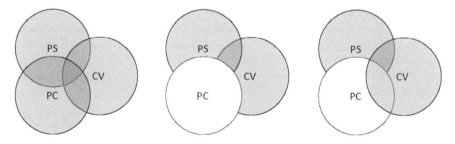

Figure 4.1 A depiction of unpartialled (left), partialled (middle), and semi-partialled (right) relationship of perfectionistic strivings on a criterion variable controlling for perfectionistic concerns.

perfectionistic strivings and perfectionistic concerns are altered following statistical partialling and, therefore, warrant new labels.

Partialling perfectionistic strivings and perfectionistic concerns is warranted for several reasons. Firstly, perfectionistic strivings and perfectionistic concerns typically display a positive and moderate relationship with each other. Consequently, if one is interested in whether a particular relationship is due to the unique features of perfectionistic strivings or the unique features of perfectionistic concerns, partialling is necessary. Secondly, perfectionistic strivings and perfectionistic concerns often display opposing relationships with the same criterion variable (e.g. depressive symptoms; Smith et al., 2018). Therefore, examining their unique effects provides a clearer reflection of these divergent relationships. Thirdly, there is evidence that perfectionistic strivings and perfectionistic concerns supress each other and this is especially pronounced for perfectionistic strivings. That is, before partialling, perfectionistic strivings can often appear ambiguous in terms of its correlates but is more clearly adaptive after partialling. Due to these issues, there is value in partialling perfectionistic strivings and perfectionistic concerns and to studying residual perfectionistic strivings and residual perfectionistic concerns (see Hill, 2014, for consideration of some of the pitfalls).

A Review of Research Examining Perfectionistic Strivings and Concerns

A large amount of research has examined perfectionistic strivings and perfectionistic concerns separately. Outside of sport, dance, and exercise, Stoeber and Otto (2006) conducted the first substantial review of perfectionism research and adopted this approach. In terms of perfectionistic strivings and concerns, the first aim of their review was to examine whether the two could be differentiated based on their associations with positive and negative characteristics. The second aim was to investigate whether perfectionistic strivings might be considered positive due to its association with positive characteristics. Studies were considered for inclusion if perfectionistic strivings and perfectionistic concerns had been measured using established multidimensional instruments. This resulted in the inclusion of thirty-five studies published between 1993 and 2005. The samples in these studies were drawn from undergraduate students, outpatients, and academically gifted children. Of these studies, fifteen examined the correlates of perfectionistic strivings and concerns (the other studies used group-based approaches). To address the second aim, the fifteen studies were graded in terms of the support provided for the notion that perfectionistic strivings are positive or adaptive (viz. positive evidence, negative evidence, mixed evidence, and inconclusive/null findings).

Across the fifteen studies there was a clear distinction between perfectionistic strivings and perfectionistic concerns. The pattern of findings for perfectionistic concerns was straightforward in that they were positively related to negative characteristics (e.g. neuroticism, depression, and avoidant coping) and either unrelated or inversely related to positive characteristics (e.g. self-esteem, positive affect, and social support). However, for perfectionistic strivings, the pattern of findings was more equivocal. That is, in six of the fifteen studies, perfectionistic strivings were found to be positively related to positive characteristics only (e.g. conscientiousness, positive affect, and satisfaction with life). These studies provided positive evidence. In four studies, perfectionistic strivings were related to negative characteristics only (e.g. self-blame, depression, and anxiety). These studies were taken as negative evidence. A further four studies indicated that perfectionistic strivings were related to both positive and negative characteristics (e.g. conscientiousness and neuroticism). These studies were taken as mixed evidence. There was one inconclusive, null finding, where perfectionistic strivings were found to be unrelated to a positive characteristic (self-esteem).

While this initial categorization of findings provided useful insight into perfectionistic strivings and perfectionistic concerns, Stoeber and Otto (2006) noted and then addressed a key limitation. Specifically, they identified that findings from the fifteen correlational studies seemed to relate to how strongly perfectionistic strivings and perfectionistic concerns were correlated, with high correlations ($.45 \leq rs \leq .70$) tending to result in negative evidence or mixed evidence. In accord, the studies were re-examined using partial correlations. The purpose was to identify any change in findings for perfectionistic strivings when the overlap with perfectionistic concerns was controlled for (i.e. when examining residual perfectionistic strivings). Based on partial correlations, ten of the fifteen studies (versus six of fifteen previously) could now be categorized as positive evidence. Of the remaining five studies, no studies were categorized as negative evidence, three provided mixed evidence, and two had inconclusive/ null findings. Therefore, controlling for the relationship between perfectionistic strivings and concerns helped to clarify the distinction between the two dimensions, as well as the associations of perfectionistic strivings, in the form of residual perfectionistic strivings.

Building on this work and others (e.g. Stoeber, 2011), Gotwals et al. (2012) conducted the first systematic review of perfectionistic strivings and perfectionistic concerns in sport. The particular focus of the review was on the nature of perfectionistic strivings and its associations with adaptive and maladaptive characteristics, processes, and outcomes. Studies were included if bivariate correlations between indicators of perfectionistic strivings and perfectionistic concerns were reported and at least one characteristic examined could be clearly identified as adaptive (e.g. positive affect, task orientation, and self-esteem) or maladaptive (e.g. negative affect, ego orientation, and symptoms of athlete burnout). This resulted in the inclusion of twenty-six research articles, reporting thirty-one studies, published between 1998 and 2010. Across the thirty-one studies, ninety-two bivariate and partial correlations with adaptive characteristics and one hundred nine bivariate and partial correlations with maladaptive characteristics were examined. These correlations were categorized in terms of support for the degree to which perfectionistic strivings, with perfectionistic concerns unpartialled and partialled, were associated with adaptive versus maladaptive characteristics (viz. supportive evidence, contrary evidence, mixed evidence, and non-significant findings).

The findings of the review demonstrated a mixed profile for perfectionistic strivings when unpartialled from perfectionistic concerns. In terms of emotions, perfectionistic strivings were positively related to positive emotional experiences, including positive affect, self-confidence, and self-esteem (e.g. Kaye et al., 2008; McArdle & Duda, 2008; Stoeber et al., 2007). They were also positively related to negative emotional experiences, including negative affect, anger, cognitive anxiety, and self-esteem instability (e.g. Dunn et al., 2006; Hall et al., 2009; Kaye et al., 2008). In terms of motivation, perfectionistic strivings were positively related to hope of success, mastery-approach goals, and a task orientation, but also fear of failure, mastery-avoidance goals, performance-avoidance goals, and an ego orientation (e.g. Appleton et al., 2009; Stoeber & Becker, 2008; Stoeber, Stoll, Salmi, & Tiikkaja, 2009). In addition, they were positively related to intrinsic motivation, identified regulation, introjected regulation, and external regulation (McArdle & Duda, 2004). Finally, in terms of performance, perfectionistic strivings were positively related with performance in training and performance in competition (Stoeber, Uphill, & Hotham, 2009; Stoll et al., 2008).

The profile of residual perfectionistic strivings mirrored the profile of perfectionistic strivings in relation to performance. However, a more adaptive profile was evident for residual perfectionistic strivings in relation to emotions and motivation. When residual perfectionistic strivings were examined, the relationships with positive emotions became stronger (e.g. Kaye et al., 2008; McArdle & Duda, 2008; Stoeber et al., 2007); the relationships with negative affect, anger, and self-esteem instability became non-significant (e.g. Dunn et al., 2006; Hall et al., 2009; Kaye et al., 2008); and residual perfectionistic strivings displayed an inverse relationship with cognitive and somatic anxiety (e.g. Stoeber et al., 2007). Regarding motivation, the relationships between residual perfectionistic strivings and adaptive motivation were comparable or stronger (e.g. Appleton et al., 2009; McArdle & Duda, 2004; Stoeber et al., 2008). Specifically, the relationship with fear of failure became inverse (e.g. Stoeber & Becker, 2008); the positive relationships with ego orientation and external regulation were smaller (e.g. Dunn et al., 2002; McArdle & Duda, 2004); and the relationships with mastery-avoidance goals, performance-avoidance goals, and introjected regulation became non-significant (e.g. McArdle & Duda, 2004; Stoeber, Stoll et al., 2009).

The growing body of studies available by the mid-2010s enabled the first meta-analysis of multidimensional perfectionism in sport by Hill et al. (2018). The aim of this meta-analytical review was to update and extend previous reviews by calculating effect sizes across studies for the unpartialled and partialled relationships that perfectionistic strivings and perfectionistic concerns shared with motivation, emotion/well-being, and performance. Hill et al. (2018) included criterion variables providing there were at least three studies to calculate effects and, unlike previous reviews where only clearly adaptive or maladaptive criterion variables were examined, also included criterion variables that were neither clearly adaptive nor maladaptive (e.g. performance approach goals). They were also able to use the meta-analytical approach to assess potential moderators of the effects of perfectionism (gender, age, sport type and the instrument/subscale used to measure perfectionism). The meta-analysis comprised 52 studies and 361 effect sizes.

Consistent with Gotwals et al. (2012), unpartialled perfectionistic strivings displayed a mixed profile of motivation, emotion/well-being and performance. Specifically, Hill et al. (2018) found that perfectionistic strivings shared negligible (task-involving coach climate) to medium (intrinsic motivation, mastery approach) positive relationships with adaptive motivation, small positive relationships with mastery avoidance and fear of failure, small to medium relationships with identified and introjected regulation, and a medium to large positive relationship with performance approach goals. Further, perfectionistic strivings shared small positive relationships with self-esteem and self-confidence but also trait anxiety, cognitive anxiety and worry, small-to-medium positive relationships with positive affect and enjoyment, and a medium positive relationship with self-criticism. Perfectionistic strivings was unrelated to negative affect, rumination, depressive symptoms and satisfaction. It shared a small-to-medium positive relationship with athletic performance. In line with previous reviews, the profile of residual perfectionistic strivings was more adaptive in terms of motivation and emotion. For example, residual perfectionistic strivings was unrelated to fear of failure and shared a small negative relationship with cognitive anxiety. The relationship with athletic performance remained positive and small-to-medium.

Unpartialled perfectionistic concerns displayed a largely maladaptive profile of motivation and emotion/wellbeing. Specifically, perfectionistic concerns was unrelated to intrinsic motivation, mastery approach goals, shared a small-to-medium positive relationship with ego orientation, medium positive relationships with performance approach goals, performance avoidance goals, mastery avoidance goals and amotivation, a medium-to-large positive relationship with ego-involving coach climate, introjected regulation, external regulation, and fear of failure, and a small negative relationship with task-involving coach climate. Perfectionistic concerns also shared a small-to-medium positive relationship with negative affect, medium positive relationships with trait anxiety, cognitive anxiety, self-criticism, rumination, and depressive symptoms, small-to-medium negative relationships with self-confidence and satisfaction, a medium-to-large negative relationship with self-esteem, and was unrelated to positive affect, enjoyment and athletic performance. As expected, for some variables residual perfectionistic concerns displayed more maladaptive associations (e.g. a large positive relationship with cognitive anxiety, small negative relationship with intrinsic motivation). However, there were a small number of other instances where residual perfectionistic concerns displayed a relatively less maladaptive profile (e.g. negligible relationship with ego orientation).

Some initial evidence of moderation by gender, age, sport type, and instrument were also found. However, these findings should be interpreted tentatively given they are based on a relatively small number of studies (Hill et al., 2018). For gender, the relationships found for predominantly female samples appeared to be typically more maladaptive than for predominantly male samples (e.g. perfectionistic strivings and negative affect). For age, the differences in the relationships for predominantly adult and adolescent samples were mixed with some relationships more adaptive for adolescents (e.g. perfectionistic strivings and perceived athletic ability) and others more maladaptive for adolescents (e.g. perfectionistic strivings and negative affect). For sport type, some relationships also differed in direction as well as magnitude and significance depending on team versus individual sport (e.g. the relationship between perfectionistic concerns and self-confidence was small, negative and significant for team sports but small, positive and non-significant for individual sports). Finally, for instrument, there was evidence that relationships differed depending on the specific subscales used to measure perfectionistic strivings and perfectionistic concerns. For example, the positive relationship between residual perfectionistic concerns and cognitive anxiety was small and significant when the concern over mistakes subscale was used but large and significant when negative reactions to imperfection was used.

Taken together, we now have an extensive body of knowledge documenting and reviewing the independent effects of perfectionistic strivings and perfectionistic concerns in sport. This work has highlighted perfectionistic concerns to be maladaptive with regard to emotion/wellbeing and motivation. By contrast, perfectionistic strivings are more complex and ambiguous, sharing a mixed pattern of relationships with the same criterion variables but seemingly more advantageous than perfectionistic concerns when it comes to performance. Also, it is clear from the reviews to date that partialling matters. That is, when the variance between perfectionistic strivings and perfectionistic concerns and the relevant outcome is controlled, the magnitude and in some cases the direction of the relationships can change. Of particular note, while residual perfectionistic concerns are largely similar to perfectionistic concerns, residual perfectionistic strivings often appear much more adaptive than perfectionistic strivings.

An Updated Review of the Independent Effects of Perfectionism

For this current chapter, we have revisited and updated our original review of research that was presented in the first edition of this book. It is valuable to do so, first because since the first edition chapter, interest in perfectionism in sport, dance, and exercise appears to have grown considerably. We are now seeing studies examining perfectionism in these domains in academic journals and at scientific conferences much more frequently. Second, while the first meta-analytical review has also appeared since our last review, it focused only on sport, rather than dance and exercise. It has also been five years since the end of the search date in the Hill et al. (2018) meta-analyses. Therefore, for the benefit of researchers and practitioners, we are seeking to re-establish the state of knowledge and what is now known about the separate effects of perfectionism in these domains. Third, in repeating our review, we have been able to check and correct any previous errors when reporting the features of the studies, correlations and partial corrections.

In conducting the new review, we followed the same methodological approach to our original review. The review is based on an electronic search of PsycINFO, PsycARTICLES, and SPORTDiscus using the terms *perfection** (for perfectionism, perfectionist) AND *sport* OR *dance* OR *exercise* for peer-reviewed journal articles published in English. The review spanned from January 1990 to July 2022, and the search took place on 23 June 2022. The search produced $k = 804$ studies. After removing duplicates, and reviewing titles and abstracts for relevance this was reduced to $k = 296$. As in our previous search we excluded qualitative studies, unidimensional measures of perfectionism, or studies reporting only total scores, studies that used instruments with questionable validity, and those that did not include bivariate correlations. The final total was 156 studies. The results of the are shown in Table 4.1.

An obvious initial observation regarding the results of the review is the considerable increase in the number of studies since our first review. The number of studies included in the new review has doubled over a much shorter period (1990 to 2016 versus 2016 to 2022). Most research that has taken place since the first review has done so in a sport domain. Some of this research revisits existing relationships (e.g. burnout) and other research includes previously unexamined variables (e.g. attitudes towards doping). There is also a notable increase in focus on the athlete's social context and performance in newer studies. Of note, too, is that studies in dance and exercise have increased but to a lesser extent. New research in dance and exercise largely includes studies that have examined similar variables found in sport research such as burnout, goals and motives for participation, and psychological needs (e.g. Jowett et al., 2021; Molnar et al., 2021; Nordin-Bates et al., 2020). However, a distinctive focus on exercise dependence and eating pathology is a feature of emerging research in the exercise domain (e.g. Deck et al., 2021).

In regards to the findings of this new research, our updated review supports previous work by again highlighting divergence between perfectionistic strivings (complex/ambiguous) and perfectionistic concerns (maladaptive). With reference to some of the new criterion variables, perfectionistic strivings, when unpartialled, shared a medium positive relationship with failure/evaluation worry, a small positive relationship with optimism in athletes (Dunn et al., 2020), small-to-medium positive relationships with dimensions of engagement in dancers (Jowett et al., 2021), and large positive relationships with the dark triad personality traits in exercisers (González-Hernández et al., 2021). As expected, residual perfectionistic strivings generally displayed a generally more adaptive profile (e.g. a non-significant relationship with failure/evaluation worry, and a medium positive relationship with optimism). By contrast, perfectionistic concerns, when unpartialled, shared a large positive relationship

Table 4.1 A systematic review of research examining multidimensional perfectionism in sport, dance, and exercise

Study	Sample	Domain	Perfectionistic				Criterion variable	PS	PC	PS	PC
			Instru.	Strivings	Concerns	rPS PC		r	r	pr	pr
Anshel & Seipel (2007)	186 undergraduate students/exercisers	Exercise	F-MPS-b	PST	CM	.15	Social physique anxiety	-.08	.15	-.10	**.16**
Appleton & Hill (2012)	231 junior athletes (12% females)	Sport	CAPS	SOP	SPP	**.23**	Intrinsic motivation	**.35**	.05	**.35**	-.03
							Identified regulation	.07	**.14**	.04	**.13**
							Introjected regulation	**.22**	**.30**	**.16**	**.26**
							External regulation	**.24**	**.24**	**.20**	**.20**
							Amotivation	**-.12**	**.25**	**-.19**	**.29**
							BO: Reduced accomplishment	**-.24**	**.21**	**-.30**	**.28**
							BO: Exhaustion	-.03	**.32**	-.11	**.34**
							BO: Devaluation	**-.29**	**.18**	**-.32**	**.26**
Appleton et al. (2009)	201 male junior and senior athletes	Sport	HF-MPS	SOP	SPP	**.24**	Task orientation	**.24**	-.09	**.27**	**-.16**
							Ego orientation	**.32**	.10	**.31**	.02
							BO: Reduced accomplishment	**-.19**	**.27**	**-.27**	**.33**
							BO: Exhaustion	-.07	**.27**	-.14	**.30**
							BO: Devaluation	**-.17**	**.29**	**-.26**	**.35**
							Satisfaction with goal progress	-.06	**-.20**	-.01	**-.19**

					SOP	SPP	—			
Appleton et al. (2010)	324 male junior athletes	Sport	HF-MPS	Coach satisfaction with goal progress	.03	**-.22**	.09	-.23		
				Mother's SOP (MSOP)	.10	.09	—	—		
				Mother's SPP (MSPP)	.01	**.22**	—	—		
				Mother's OOP (MOOP)	.05	**.19**	—	—		
				Athlete's perception of MSOP	**.50**	**.18**	—	—		
				Athlete's perception of MSPP	**.23**	**.54**	—	—		
				Athlete's perception of MOOP	**.25**	**.28**	—	—		
				Father's SOP (FSOP)	**.28**	**.17**	—	—		
				Father's SPP (FSPP)	.03	**.16**	—	—		
				Father's OOP (FOOP)	**.20**	**.22**	—	—		
				Athlete's perception of FSOP	**.57**	**.19**	—	—		
				Athlete's perception of FSPP	**.29**	**.50**	—	—		
				Athlete's perception of FOOP	**.41**	**.34**	—	—		
	237 female junior athletes	Sport	HF-MPS	Mother's SOP (MSOP)	**.20**	.07	—	—		
				Mother's SPP (MSPP)	.09	**.30**	—	—		
				Mother's OOP (MOOP)	.14	.13	—	—		
				Athlete's perception of MSOP	**.42**	**.22**	—	—		
				Athlete's perception of MSPP	**.27**	**.43**	—	—		

Study	Sample	Domain	Perfectionism measure	Subscale	Outcome measure	α	Variable				
Arcelus et al. (2015)	281 junior female dancers	Dance	F-MPS	PST	CM	.67	Athlete's perception of MOOP	.30	.33	—	—
							Father's SOP (FSOP)	-.01	.14	—	—
							Father's SPP (FSPP)	.07	.10	—	—
							Father's OOP (FOOP)	-.01	.20	—	—
							Athlete's perception of FSOP	.39	.20	—	—
							Athlete's perception of FSPP	.13	.38	—	—
							Athlete's perception of FOOP	.15	.38	—	—
							Dieting	.46	.58	.12	.41
							Bulimia	.33	.44	.05	.31
							Oral control	.56	.22	.57	-.25
							Body dissatisfaction	.43	.64	.00	.53
							Depressive symptoms	.45	.61	.07	.47
							Cognitive anxiety	.31	.46	.00	.36
Aruguete et al. (2012)	258 female psychology undergraduates	Exercise	F-MPS	—	CM	—	Trait anger	—	.21	—	—
							Suppressed anger	—	.35	—	—
							Drive for thinness	—	.29	—	—
							Exercise commitment	—	.35	—	—
							Self-loathing	—	.62	—	—
Atienza et al. (2020)	429 junior footballers (12% females)	Sport	MIPS	SP	NRI	.62	Anxiety	.24	.47	-.07	.42

Study	Sample	Context	Instrument				Outcome				
Bae et al. (2017)	198 adult Olympians (48% females)	Sport	HF-MPS-b	SOP			Contingent self-worth	**.40**	**.55**	**.09**	**.42**
					SPP	.57	Anxiety	**.23**	**.20**	**.14**	.09
			AE-MPS	PST			Contingent self-worth	**.34**	**.54**	.05	**.45**
					CM	**.45**	Attitudes towards doping	-.01	**.18**	-.10	**.21**
Barcza-Renner et al. (2016)	487 adult university swimmers (72% females)	Sport	HF-MPS-b	SOP			Task-involving climate	-.04	.11	-.10	**.14**
					SPP	.36	Ego-involving climate	**.16**	**.45**	-.05	**.43**
							Autonomous motivation	**.21**	**-.24**	**.33**	**-.35**
							Controlled motivation	**.18**	**.64**	-.07	**.63**
							Amotivation	.01	**.46**	**-.19**	**.49**
							Coaches' controlling use of rewards	**.18**	**.28**	**.09**	**.23**
							Coaches' conditional regard	**.12**	**.41**	-.03	**.40**
							Coaches' intimidation	.07	**.36**	-.07	**.36**
							Coaches' excessive personal control	**.20**	**.38**	.07	**.34**
							Total burnout	.02	**.39**	**-.14**	**.41**
Blažev et al. (2020)	345 adult and adolescent male bodybuilders	Sport	APS-R	HS			Dissatisfaction with appearance	**-.11**	**.23**	**-.15**	**.25**
					D	.16	Worry about appearance	-.01	**.44**	**-.09**	**.45**
							Attitudes towards disordered eating	**.21**	.07	**.20**	.04
							Intensity of exercise	.10	**.33**	.05	**.32**

Branman et al. (2009)	204 female university athletes	Exercise	F-MPS	PST	CM	.41

Measure				
Perfectionistic self-promotion	.24	.27	.21	.24
Non-display of imperfection	.04	.45	-.04	.45
Non-disclosure of imperfection	.07	.35	.02	.34
Bulimia	.14	.42	-.04	.40
Body-part satisfaction	.03	-.38	.22	-.43
Life orientation	.09	-.31	.25	-.38
Global self-esteem	.08	-.45	.32	-.53
Exercise for health and fitness	.21	-.14	.30	-.25
Exercise for appearance	.21	.27	.11	.21
Exercise for socializing/mood	.25	.16	.20	.07
BMI	-.12	-.01	-.13	.04

Carr & Wyon (2003)	181 dance students (87% females)	Dance	F-MPS	PST	CM	.54

Measure				
Task-involving climate	-.03	-.22	.11	-.24
Effort and learning climate	.18	-.02	.23	-.14
Co-operative learning climate	-.11	-.18	-.02	-.14
Import role climate	-.22	-.37	-.03	-.31
Ego-involving climate	.37	.41	.19	.27
Inter-student rivalry climate	.36	.34	.22	.19
Unequal recognition climate	.36	.38	.20	.24
Punishment of mistakes climate	.30	.41	.10	.31

Study	Sample	Domain	Measure	r	Variable				
Carter & Weissbrod (2011)	Female university athletes (n unspecified; n = 137 in total)	Sport	HF-MPS SOP SPP	**.66**	Task orientation	.13	-.01	**.16**	-.10
					Ego orientation	**.41**	**.45**	**.22**	**.30**
					Total trait anxiety	.10	**.34**	-.11	**.34**
					Somatic anxiety	.03	**.17**	-.07	**.18**
					Worry	**.19**	**.43**	-.06	**.40**
					Concentration disruption	.04	**.26**	-.12	**.28**
					Enjoyment of competition	.08	-.03	.13	-.11
	Male university athletes (n unspecified; n = 137 in total)	Sport	HF-MPS SOP SPP	**.47**	Positive self-perception when winning	**.25**	**.31**	.06	.20
					Negative self-perception when losing	**.41**	**.62**	.00	.51
					Trait anxiety	.18	**.38**	-.09	.35
					Depressive symptoms	**.44**	**.58**	.06	.43
					Somatic anxiety	-.02	**.25**	-.24	.35
					Worry	.10	**.33**	-.15	.35
					Concentration disruption	.02	**.41**	-.30	.53
					Enjoyment of competition	**.37**	-.15	.49	-.34
					Positive self-perception when winning	.25	.17	.19	.06
					Negative self-perception when losing	.22	**.59**	-.05	.54

Study	Sample	Domain	Measure			Outcome				
Chen et al (2008)	320 inter-collegiate athletes (60% females)	Sport	AE-MPS	PST	CM	.18	Trait anxiety	.08	.35	-.09	.35
							Depressive symptoms	.37	.33	.23	.16
							Somatic anxiety	.18	.19	.10	.12
							Worry	.29	.40	.11	.29
							Concentration disruption	-.19	.14	-.29	.26
							Total burnout	-.28	.20	-.33	.27
Chen et al (2009)†	188 high school athletes (46% females)	Sport	MIPS	SP	NRI	.60	BO: Reduced accomplishment (time 1)	-.43	-.12	-.45	.19
							BO: Exhaustion (time 1)	-.39	-.15	-.38	.11
							BO: Devaluation (time 1)	-.13	.06	-.21	.17
							BO: Reduced accomplishment (time 2)	-.22	-.04	-.25	.12
							BO: Exhaustion (time 2)	-.29	-.14	-.26	.04
							BO: Devaluation (time 2)	-.23	-.02	-.27	.15
Cheng & Hardy (2016)	485 university dance students (87% females)	Dance	CPI	PST	CM	–	Regulatory anxiety	.51	–	–	–
Chou et al. (2019)	266 adult dancers (92% females)	Dance	F-MPS	PST	CM	.67	Self-esteem[a]	.48	.51	.22	.29
							Creative thinking[a]	.38	.25	.30	-.01
Correia et al. (2017)	206 adolescent athletes (gender not reported)	Sport	F-MPS	PST	CM	–	Worry	.32	.33	–	–

Study	Sample	Domain			Variable	F-MPS	PC+		
Costa et al. (2015)	169 adult exercisers (50% females)	Exercise	F-MPS —	PC+ —	Concentration disruption	.04	**.21**	—	—
					Fear of failure[a]	**.34**	**.55**	—	—
					Autonomy thwarting	**.30**	—	—	—
					Competence thwarting	**.42**	—	—	—
					Relatedness thwarting	**.47**	—	—	—
					Autonomy satisfaction	**-.17**	—	—	—
					Competence satisfaction	-.14	—	—	—
					Relatedness satisfaction	-.15	—	—	—
					Need thwarting	**.47**	—	—	—
					Need satisfaction	**-.17**	—	—	—
					ED: Withdrawal	**.28**	—	—	—
					ED: Continuance	**.20**	—	—	—
					ED: Tolerance	**.18**	—	—	—
					ED: Lack of control	**.27**	—	—	—
					ED: Reduction in other activities	**.28**	—	—	—
					ED: Time	.06	—	—	—
					ED: Intention effects	**.16**	—	—	—
					ED: Total	**.29**	—	—	—
Costa et al. (2016)	178 male adult exercisers	Exercise	F-MPS —	PC+ —	Psychological control mother	—	**.46**	—	—
					Psychological control farther	—	**.37**	—	—
					Eating disorder symptoms	—	**.36**	—	—
					Exercise dependence	—	**.34**	—	—

Study	Sample	Domain	Measure				Variable	r1	r2	r3	r4
	170 female adult exercisers	Exercise	F-MPS	–	PC+	–	Psychological control mother	.59	–	–	–
							Psychological control farther	.41	–	–	–
							Eating disorder symptoms	.43	–	–	–
							Exercise dependence	.42	–	–	–
Crocker et al. (2014)†	274 university athletes (46% females)	Sport	S-MPS-2	PST	CM	.20	Problem coping	-.01	.03	.03	-.02
							Emotion coping	-.03	.05	.06	-.04
							Avoidance coping	.20	-.09	-.14	.22
							Control appraisal	-.20	.32	.38	-.28
							Challenge appraisal	-.15	.19	.23	-.20
							Threat appraisal	.20	.05	.01	.19
							Goal progress	-.14	.34	.38	-.23
							Positive affect	-.03	.42	.43	-.13
							Negative affect	.30	.00	-.06	.31
Cumming & Duda (2012; Quested et al., 2014)	194 dance students (87% females)	Dance	F-MPS	PST	CM	.33	Social physique anxiety	.35	-.10	-.24	.41
							Positive affect	-.08	.45	.51	-.27
							Negative affect	.54	-.05	-.29	.59
							Physical symptoms	.31	-.02	-.14	.34
							BO: Exhaustion	.20	-.06	-.14	.23
							Intrinsic motivation	.02	.47	.49	-.16
							Fear of failure	.56	-.01	-.25	.60
							Self-esteem	-.42	.25	.45	-.55

Study	Sample	Domain	Scale	SOP	SPP	r
Curran et al. (2014)	266 junior athletes (50% females)	Sport	HF-MPS-b	SOP	SPP	**.25**
Curran & Hill (2018)†	60 university athletes (12% females)	Sport	HF-MPS	SOP	SPP	**.48**
Curran (2018)	153 adolescent athletes (39% females)	Sport	S-MPS-2 MPS	PS+	PC+	**.71**
Deck et al. (2021)	376 university students (65% females)	Exercise	HF-MPS	SOP	SPP	–
Deck et al. (2021)	195 university students (66% females)	Exercise	HF-MPS	SOP	SPP	**.39**
De Muynck et al (2021)†	59 adolescent tennis players (31% females)	Sport	F-MPS	–	PC+	–
Donachie et al. (2018)	206 academy footballers (62% females)	Sport	CAPS	SOP	SPP	**.05**

Variable				
Body dissatisfaction	-.05	**.28**	**-.16**	**.31**
Harmonious passion	**.45**	.01	**.46**	**-.12**
Obsessive passion	**.26**	**.32**	**.20**	**.27**
Pride	**.30**	-.07	**.38**	**-.26**
Shame	-.02	**.26**	-.17	**.31**
Guilt	-.07	.11	-.14	.16
Parental conditional regard	**.29**	**.59**	**-.23**	**.57**
Competence contingent self-worth	**.64**	**.75**	**.23**	**.55**
Exercise dependence	**.26**	**.17**	–	–
Social Physique anxiety	.11	**.17**	.05	**.14**
Total exercise	-.06	.02	-.07	.05
Negative affect	**.13**	**.21**	.05	**.17**
Positive affect	**.01**	**.23**	-.09	**.25**
Competence need satisfaction	–	**-.27**	–	–
Training frequency	–	-.18	–	–
Perfectionistic cognitions	**.34**	**.38**	**.35**	**.39**

Study	Sample					Variable				
Donachie et al. (2019)†	352 academy footballers (gender not reported)	Sport	CAPS	SOP		Anxiety	**.15**	.04	**.15**	.03
						Dejection	.02	**.16**	.01	**.16**
						Excitement	**.22**	-.02	**.22**	-.03
						Anger	.04	**.21**	.03	**.21**
						Happiness	.12	-.01	.12	-.02
				SPP	.32	Perfectionistic cognitions	**.49**	**.51**	**.40**	**.43**
						Anxiety	**.20**	**.30**	**.12**	**.25**
						Dejection	.04	**.24**	-.04	**.24**
						Excitement	**.19**	-.01	**.20**	-.08
						Anger	.03	**.27**	-.06	**.27**
						Happiness	.07	-.02	.08	-.04
						Cognitive anxiety	**.32**	**.51**	**.19**	**.45**
						Somatic anxiety	**.16**	**.30**	.07	**.27**
						Feel anger	**.28**	**.15**	**.25**	.07
						Verbal anger	**.28**	**.24**	**.22**	**.17**
						Physical Anger	**.17**	**.29**	.09	.25
Dunn et al. (2021)	251 university athletes (41% females)	Sport	S-MPS-2	PST	CM .31	Consistency of interests	.09	**-.15**	.15	**-.19**
						Perseverance of effort	**.33**	**-.19**	**.42**	**-.33**
				SP	NRI .47	Consistency of interests	.11	**-.15**	**.21**	**-.23**
						Perseverance of effort	**.24**	**-.14**	**.35**	**-.30**

Study	Sample	Type	Measure				Variable				
Dunn et al. (2011)	119 female junior figure skaters	Sport	S-MPS	PST	CM	.55	Appearance orientation	.50	.49	.32	.30
							Appearance evaluation	-.02	-.34	.21	-.39
							Overweight preoccupation	.42	.49	.21	.34
							Self-classified weight	.13	.33	-.07	.31
							Body satisfaction	-.04	-.36	.20	-.41
							Body image ideal	.14	.43	-.13	.43
			HF-MPS	SOP	SPP	.44	Appearance orientation	.42	.33	.32	.18
							Appearance evaluation	-.12	-.30	.01	-.28
							Overweight preoccupation	.39	.41	.26	.29
							Self-classified weight	.31	.26	.23	.14
							Body satisfaction	-.21	-.35	-.07	-.29
							Body image ideal	.32	.35	.20	.25
Dunn et al. (2002)	174 male adolescent Canadian footballers	Sport	S-MPS	PST	CM	.40	Task orientation	.20	-.16	.29	-.27
							Ego orientation	.23	.23	.15	.15
Dunn et al. (2006)	138 male adolescent Canadian footballers	Sport	S-MPS	PST	COM	.54	Feel angry after mistakes	.38	.35	.24	.19
							Anger at something after mistakes	.16	.18	.08	.11
							Express anger verbally after mistakes	.16	.21	.06	.15
							Trait anger: Angry temperament	.16	.23	.04	.17
							Trait anger: Angry reaction	.36	.45	.16	.33

Study	Sample	Domain	Measure	Sub. 1	Sub. 2	r	Variable				
Dunn et al. (2020)	144 male high school and senior Canadian football players	Sport	S-MPS-2	PST	COM	.51	Failure/evaluation worry	.38	.61	.10	.52
							Uncertainty worry	.14	.40	-.08	.39
							Injury worry	.03	.08	-.01	.08
							Optimism	.20	-.20	.36	-.36
Elison & Partridge (2012)	285 university athletes (46% females)	Sport	PI	SE	CM	—	Attack self	.22	.53	—	—
							Withdrawal	.04	.45	—	—
							Attack other	-.13	.37	—	—
							Avoidance	-.10	.14	—	—
Eusanio et al. (2014)	24 university students from dance classes (79% females)	Dance	HF-MPS	SOP	SPP	.60	Self-concept	-.17	-.49	.18	-.49
							Shame	.31	.59	-.07	.53
Fawver et al. (2020)	169 adolescent alpine skiers (52% females)	Sport	S-MPS-2	PST	CM	.20	Grit	.15	-.17	.19	-.21
							MT: Total	.14	-.13	.17	-.16
							MT: Confidence	.18	-.05	.19	-.09
							MT: Constancy	.24	-.13	.27	-.19
							MT: Control	-.10	-.15	-.07	-.13
Fazlagić & Belić (2017)	50 adult athletes (24% females)	Sport	F-MPS	PST	CM	—	Flow	.06	-.15	.09	-.17
Ferrand et al. (2007)	33 female junior swimmers	Sport	HF-MPS	SOP	SPP	.03	Body-esteem/satisfaction: Appearance	-.04	-.42	-.03	-.42

Study	Sample	Domain	Measure				Variable				
Fleming et al. (2022)	149 adolescent footballers (28% females)	Sport	MIPS	SP	NRI	.33	Body-esteem/satisfaction: Attribution	-.43	-.26	-.44	-.27
							Body-esteem/satisfaction: Weight	-.06	.17	-.07	.17
							Dietary restraint	**.49**	.06	**.49**	.05
							Maternal pressure	-.11	.12	**-.16**	**.17**
Freire et al. (2020)	177 school sport participants (41% females)	Sport	S-MPS-2	PST	CM	.08	Paternal pressure	.16	**.44**	.02	**.42**
							Maternal warmth	.22	.16	**.18**	.09
							Paternal warmth	.13	-.09	**.17**	**-.14**
							Somatic anxiety	**-.30**	**.28**	**-.34**	**.32**
Freire, Fiorese et al. (2022)	413 school sport participants (45% females)	Sport	S-MPS-2	PST	CM	.14	Worry	**-.20**	**.28**	**-.23**	**.30**
							Concentration disruption	**-.26**	**.37**	**-.31**	**.41**
							Task cohesion	**.18**	**-.15**	**.21**	**-.18**
Freire, Santos et al. (2022)	413 high school athletes (45% females)	Sport	S-MPS-2	PS/O	CM	.14	Social cohesion	**.15**	-.01	**.15**	-.03
							Task conflict	.08	**.24**	.05	**.23**
							Social conflict	.06	**.24**	.03	**.23**
							Ego orientation	**.18**	**.23**	**.15**	**.21**
Frost & Henderson (1991)	40 female university athletes	Sport	F-MPS	PST	CM	—	Task orientation	**.38**	.06	**.38**	.01
							Competitive anxiety	.31	**.47**	—	—
							Trait confidence	-.03	**-.61**	—	—

Success orientation	**.68**	**.35**	—	—
Failure orientation	**.37**	**.70**	—	—
Social concerns after mistakes	.21	**.68**	—	—
Disappointment after mistakes	.30	**.64**	—	—
Effort after mistakes	.30	.23	—	—
Focus after mistakes	.17	**.55**	—	—
Self-talk after mistakes	.13	**.31**	—	—
Pressure after mistakes	.30	**.55**	—	—
Dwell after mistakes	.27	**.66**	—	—
Move on after mistakes	-.18	**.34**	—	—
Affect after mistakes	.12	-.26	—	—
Images after mistakes	.07	**.61**	—	—
Coaches' ratings: Ability	-.01	-.23	—	—
Coaches ratings: Playing time	-.06	-.11	—	—
Coaches' ratings: Reactions to mistakes	-.21	**-.38**	—	—
Before competition: Fear of mistakes	.24	**.48**	—	—
Before competition: Images of mistakes	.07	**.48**	—	—
Before competition: Self-confidence	-.12	**-.48**	—	—
Before competition: Dreams of perfection	**.43**	.18	—	—
Before competition: Feeling in control	.14	-.21	—	—

Study	Sample	Domain	Measures	r	Variable				
Gaudreau & Antl (2008)†	186 adult and adolescent athletes (43% females)	Sport	HF-MPS F-MPS; PS+; PC+	.58	Before competition: Thoughts of competition	**.36**	.21	—	—
					Before competition: Difficulty concentrating	**.47**	**.49**	—	—
					Before competition: Audience worries	**.31**	**.61**	—	—
					Life satisfaction (time 1)	.08	**-.37**	**.39**	**-.51**
					Life satisfaction (time 2)	-.05	**-.42**	**.26**	**-.48**
					Self-determined motivation	**.43**	.12	**.45**	**-.18**
					Appearance evaluation	-.12	**-.30**	.01	**-.28**
					Overweight preoccupation	**.39**	**.41**	**.26**	**.29**
					Self-classified weight	**.31**	**.26**	**.23**	.14
					Body satisfaction	-.21	**-.35**	-.07	**-.29**
					Body image ideal	**.32**	**.35**	**.20**	**.25**
Dunn et al. (2002)	174 male adolescent Canadian footballers	Sport	S-MPS; PST; CM	.40	Task orientation	**.20**	-.16	**.29**	**-.27**
					Ego orientation	**.23**	**.23**	**.15**	**.15**
Dunn et al. (2006)	138 male adolescent Canadian footballers	Sport	S-MPS; PST; COM	.54	Feel angry after mistakes	**.38**	**.35**	**.24**	**.19**
					Anger at something after mistakes	.16	**.18**	.08	.11
					Express anger verbally after mistakes	.16	**.21**	.06	.15
					Trait anger: Angry temperament	.16	**.23**	.04	**.17**

Study	Sample	Domain	Measure				Outcome				
Dunn et al. (2020)	144 male high school and senior Canadian football players	Sport	S-MPS-2	PST	COM	.51	Trait anger: Angry reaction	.36	.45	.16	.33
							Failure/evaluation worry	.38	.61	.10	.52
Elison & Partridge (2012)	285 university athletes (46% females)	Sport	PI	SE	CM	–	Uncertainty worry	.14	.40	-.08	.39
							Injury worry	.03	.08	-.01	.08
							Optimism	.20	-.20	.36	-.36
							Attack self	.22	.53	–	–
							Withdrawal	.04	.45	–	–
							Attack other	-.13	.37	–	–
							Avoidance	-.10	.14	–	–
Eusanio et al. (2014)	24 university students from dance classes (79% females)	Dance	HF-MPS	SOP	SPP	.60	Self-concept	-.17	-.49	.18	-.49
Fawver et al. (2020)	169 adolescent alpine skiers (52% females)	Sport	S-MPS-2	PST	CM	.20	Shame	.31	.59	-.07	.53
							Grit	.15	-.17	.19	-.21
Fazlagić & Belić (2017)	50 adult athletes (24% females)	Sport	F-MPS	PST	CM	–	MT: Total	.14	-.13	.17	-.16
							MT: Confidence	.18	-.05	.19	-.09
							MT: Constancy	.24	-.13	.27	-.19
							MT: Control	-.10	-.15	-.07	-.13
							Flow	.06	-.15	.09	-.17

Study	Sample	Domain	Measure				Construct				
Ferrand et al. (2007)	33 female junior swimmers	Sport	HF-MPS	SOP	SPP	.03	Body-esteem/satisfaction: Appearance	-.04	**-.42**	-.03	**-.42**
							Body-esteem/satisfaction: Attribution	**-.43**	-.26	**-.44**	-.27
							Body-esteem/satisfaction: Weight	-.06	.17	-.07	.17
							Dietary restraint	**.49**	.06	**.49**	.05
Fleming et al. (2022)	149 adolescent footballers (28% females)	Sport	MIPS	SP	NRI	**.33**	Maternal pressure	-.11	.12	**-.16**	**.17**
							Paternal pressure	.16	**.44**	.02	**.42**
							Maternal warmth	.22	.16	**.18**	.09
							Paternal warmth	.13	-.09	**.17**	**-.14**
Freire et al. (2020)	177 school sport participants (41% females)	Sport	S-MPS-2	PST	CM	.08	Somatic anxiety	**-.30**	**.28**	**-.34**	**.32**
							Worry	**-.20**	**.28**	**-.23**	**.30**
							Concentration disruption	**-.26**	**.37**	**-.31**	**.41**
Freire, Fiorese et al. (2022)	413 school sport participants (45% females)	Sport	S-MPS-2	PST	CM	**.14**	Task cohesion	**.18**	**-.15**	**.21**	**-.18**
							Social cohesion	**.15**	-.01	**.15**	-.03
							Task conflict	.08	**.24**	.05	**.23**
							Social conflict	.06	**.24**	.03	**.23**
Friere, Santos et al. (2022)	413 high school athletes (45% females)	Sport	S-MPS-2	PS/O	CM	**.14**	Ego orientation	**.18**	**.23**	**.15**	**.21**
							Task orientation	**.38**	.06	**.38**	.01
Frost & Henderson (1991)	40 female university athletes	Sport	F-MPS	PST	CM	—	Competitive anxiety	.31	**.47**	—	—

Trait confidence	-.03	-.61	—	—
Success orientation	.68	.35	—	—
Failure orientation	.37	.70	—	—
Social concerns after mistakes	.21	.68	—	—
Disappointment after mistakes	.30	.64	—	—
Effort after mistakes	.30	.23	—	—
Focus after mistakes	.17	.55	—	—
Self-talk after mistakes	.13	.31	—	—
Pressure after mistakes	.30	.55	—	—
Dwell after mistakes	.27	.66	—	—
Move on after mistakes	-.18	.34	—	—
Affect after mistakes	.12	-.26	—	—
Images after mistakes	.07	.61	—	—
Coaches' ratings: Ability	-.01	-.23	—	—
Coaches ratings: Playing time	-.06	-.11	—	—
Coaches' ratings: Reactions to mistakes	-.21	-.38	—	—
Before competition: Fear of mistakes	.24	.48	—	—
Before competition: Images of mistakes	.07	.48	—	—
Before competition: Self-confidence	-.12	-.48	—	—
Before competition: Dreams of perfection	.43	.18	—	—

Study	Domain	Instrument	Dimensions	r	Outcome measure	(1)	(2)	(3)	(4)
Gaudreau & Antl (2008)†	Sport	HF-MPS F-MPS	PS+ / PC+	.58	Before competition: Feeling in control	.14	−.21	—	—
					Before competition: Thoughts of competition	**.36**	.21	—	—
					Before competition: Difficulty concentrating	**.47**	**.49**	—	—
					Before competition: Audience worries	**.31**	**.61**	—	—
					Life satisfaction (time 1)	.08	**−.37**	**.39**	**−.51**
					Life satisfaction (time 2)	−.05	**−.42**	**.26**	**−.48**
					Self-determined motivation	**.43**	.12	**.45**	**−.18**
					Non-self-determined motivation	**.37**	**.49**	.12	**.36**
					Task-oriented coping	**.30**	.17	**.25**	−.01
					Distraction-oriented coping	.16	**.48**	**−.17**	**.48**
					Disengagement-oriented coping	.13	**.43**	**−.16**	**.44**
					Goal attainment	.10	−.02	.14	−.10
Gaudreau & Verner-Filion (2012)	Sport	HF-MPS-b	SOP / SPP	.37	Positive affect	.10	−.04	.12	−.08
					Subjective vitality	.06	**−.19**	.14	**−.23**
					Life satisfaction	.05	**−.24**	.15	**−.28**
Gaudreau et al. (2019)	Sport	HF-MPS	SOP / SPP	.51	First class performance	.11	.18	.02	.14
					Second class performance	.09	.04	.08	−.01

Study	Sample	Domain	Instrument				Outcome measure				
González-Hernández, Díaz et al. (2019)	487 adult and adolescent athletes (44% females)	Sport	F-MPS	—	CM	—	Third class performance	**.24**	.07	**.24**	-.06
							Fourth class performance	.16	-.03	**.20**	-.13
							Fifth class performance	.18	-.03	**.23**	-.14
							Sixth class performance	.04	-.16	.14	-.21
							General impulsiveness	—	**.47**	—	—
González-Hernández, Gómez-López et al. (2019)	127 adolescents (35% females)	Sport	F-MPS	PST	CM	**.46**	Stress	.11	**.40**	-.09	**.40**
González-Hernández et al. (2021)	224 adult crossfitters (gender not reported)	Sport	F-MPS	PST	CM	**.71**	Sport practice (days)	**.31**	.00	**.31**	.00
							Narcissism	**.57**	**.59**	**.27**	**.32**
							Machiavellianism	**.49**	**.39**	**.33**	.07
							Psychopathy	**.51**	**.61**	**.14**	**.41**
							Exercise dependence	**.68**	**.71**	**.35**	**.44**
	201 adult runners (gender not reported)	Sport	F-MPS	PST	CM	**.41**	Narcissism	**.68**	**.70**	**.60**	**.63**
							Machiavellianism	**.72**	**.59**	**.65**	**.47**
							Psychopathy	**.64**	**.50**	**.55**	**.34**
							Exercise dependence	**.73**	**.74**	**.70**	**.71**
Gotwals et al. (2003)	87 university athletes (11% females)	Sport	F-MPS	PST	CM	**.50**	Global self-esteem	.09	-**.43**	**.39**	-**.55**

Study	Sample	Domain	Measure			r	Outcome variable				
Gotwals (2011)	117 university athletes (41% females)	Sport	S-MPS-2	PST	CM	**.45**	Perceived athletic competence	-.00	**-.34**	**.21**	**-.39**
							Satisfaction with performance	-.14	**-.59**	**.22**	**-.61**
							BO: Reduced sense of accomplishment	.04	**-.23**	.17	**-.28**
							BO: Exhaustion	.02	-.05	.05	-.07
							BO: Devaluation	**-.18**	**-.30**	-.05	**-.25**
Gotwals & Dunn (2009)	251 inter-collegiate athletes (46% females)	Sport	S-MPS-2	PST	CM	—	Global self-esteem	.04	**-.45**	—	—
Grainger et al. (2016)	522 university athletes (20% females)	Sport	S-MPS-2	PST	CM	**.46**	Stress	**.18**	**.46**	-.04	**.43**
							Burnout	.04	**.38**	**-.16**	**.41**
Grugan et al. (2019)	257 adult and adolescent athletes (15% females)	Sport	HF-MPS	SOP	SPP	**.51**	Angry reactions to teammates	.08	**.21**	-.03	**.20**
							Antisocial teammate behaviour	.07	**.15**	-.01	**.13**
							Antisocial opponent behaviour	.04	**.15**	-.04	**.15**
Gucciardi et al (2012)	423 adult and junior athletes (58% females)	Sport	S-MPS	PST	CM	**.30**	External regulation	**.14**	**.28**	.06	**.25**
							Intrinsic motivation	**.37**	-.05	**.40**	**-.18**
							Mastery avoidance goal	**.20**	**.41**	.09	**.37**
							Performance avoidance goal	**.15**	**.37**	.04	**.34**
							Mastery approach goal	**.35**	**-.08**	**.39**	**-.21**

Study	Sample						.35	.42	.26	.35
Gustafsson et al. (2016)	237 adolescent athletes (48% females)	Sport	F-MPS-b	PST	CM	.68				
						Performance approach goal	.35	.42	.26	.35
						Fear of failure	.24	.63	.07	.60
						Learning/enjoyment climate	.10	-.14	.27	-.29
						Worry conducive climate	.27	.46	-.07	.39
						Success without effort climate	.12	.18	.00	.14
						BO: Reduced accomplishment	.49	.48	.25	.23
						BO: Exhaustion	.31	.49	-.04	.40
						BO: Devaluation	.62	.45	.48	.05
Hall et al. (1998)	119 high school runners (62% females)	Sport	F-MPS	PST	CM	.62				
						Perceived ability	.33	.12	.33	-.11
						Ego orientation	.34	.38	.14	.23
						Task orientation	.24	-.02	.32	-.22
						State cognitive anxiety (1 week)	.11	.23	-.04	.21
						State somatic anxiety (1 week)	-.11	.03	-.16	.13
						State confidence (1 week)	.35	.15	.33	-.09
						State cognitive anxiety (2 days)	.16	.39	-.11	.38
						State somatic anxiety (2 days)	-.16	.06	-.25	.21
						State confidence (2 days)	.41	.16	.40	-.13
						State cognitive anxiety (1 day)	.13	.32	-.09	.31
						State somatic anxiety (1 day)	-.14	.13	-.28	.28

	PST	CM	SOP	SPP
State confidence (1 day)	.36	.10	**.38**	-.17
State cognitive anxiety (30 mins)	.19	**.23**	.06	.15
State somatic anxiety (30 mins)	-.06	.06	-.12	.12
State confidence (30 mins)	**.20**	.04	**.22**	-.11
Ego orientation (30 mins)	.16	**.21**	.04	.14
Task orientation (30 mins)	**.26**	-.05	**.37**	**-.28**
Perceived ability	**.45**	**.44**	**.26**	**.23**
Ego orientation	**.43**	**.44**	**.23**	**.25**
Task orientation	**.30**	.09	**.31**	-.12
Obligatory exercise	**.45**	**.45**	**.25**	**.25**
Unconditional self-acceptance	**-.30**	**-.48**	**-.11**	**-.41**
Labile self-esteem	.16	**.33**	.02	**.29**
Total exercise dependence	**.25**	**.30**	**.14**	**.22**
ED: Interference	**.15**	**.22**	.06	**.17**
ED: Positive reward	**.18**	**.13**	**.14**	.06
ED: Withdrawal symptoms	**.29**	**.17**	**.24**	.05
ED: Weight control	**.14**	**.14**	.09	.09
ED: Insight into problem	.08	**.24**	-.03	**.23**
ED: Social reasons	.04	**.26**	-.09	**.27**
ED: Health reasons	.05	-.09	.10	**-.12**

Hall et al. (2007) — 246 adult club runners (32% females) — Exercise — F-MPS — PST — CM — **.61**

Hall et al. (2009) — 307 adult club runners (36% females) — Exercise — HF-MPS — SOP — SPP — **.44**

Study	Sample	Domain	Scale 1	Scale 2	Model	Variable				
						ED: stereotyped behaviours	.01	.03	.00	.03
Haraldsen et al. (2019)	171 junior athletes and performing artists (51% females)	Sport	F-MPS	—	CM	Controlling conditions	—	.43	—	—
						Need frustration: competence	—	.59	—	—
						Need frustration: autonomy	—	.49	—	—
						Need frustration: relatedness	—	.50	—	—
						Introjected motivation	—	.48	—	—
						External motivation	—	.37	—	—
						Performance anxiety	—	.33	—	—
Haraldsen et al. (2020)†	259 junior athletes and performing artists (47% females)	Sport	F-MPS-b	PST	CM	Need frustration: competence (time 1)	.06	.48	-.16	.50
					.39	Need frustration: competence (time 2)	.02	.54	-.25	.58
						Need frustration: competence (time 3)	.19	.55	-.03	.53
						Need frustration autonomy (time 1)	.11	.41	-.06	.40
						Need frustration: autonomy (time 2)	.14	.43	-.03	.41
						Need frustration: autonomy (time 3)	.14	.38	-.01	.36
						Need frustration: relatedness (time 1)	.07	.40	-.10	.41
						Need frustration: relatedness (time 2)	.13	.43	-.05	.42

Study	Sample	Domain	Measure			
Hardwick et al. (2022)	173 adult athletes (28% females)	Sport	S-MPS MIPS	PS+	PC+	.70
Hill (2013)	171 male junior soccer players	Sport	HF-MPS-b S-MPS-2	PS+	CM+	.27
Hill (2014)	291 adult athletes (34% females)	Sport	F-MPS	PST	CM	.32

Variable				
Need frustration: relatedness (time 3)	.14	.40	-.02	.38
Anxiety/worry (time 3)	.05	.42	-.14	.44
Self-rated performance level (time 3)	.21	-.03	.24	-.12
Task orientation	.19	.06	.21	-.10
Ego orientation	.41	.42	.18	.20
Attitudes towards doping	.08	.17	-.06	.16
Total burnout	-.23	.29	-.33	.38
BO: Reduced accomplishment	-.33	.22	-.41	.34
BO: Exhaustion	-.22	.27	-.32	.35
BO: Devaluation	-.03	.23	-.10	.25
Performance approach goal	.51	.37	.44	.25
Performance avoidance goal	-.15	.60	-.45	.69
Mastery approach goal	.44	-.02	.47	-.19
Mastery avoidance goal	.15	.58	-.05	.57
Intrinsic motivation (to know)	.57	.14	.56	-.05
Intrinsic motivation (to accomplish)	.54	-.02	.58	-.24
Intrinsic motivation (for stimulation)	.50	.03	.52	-.16
Identified motivation	.19	.00	.20	-.07

Variable				
Introjected motivation	.35	.63	.20	.58
Extrinsic motivation	.49	.68	.39	.63
Amotivation	-.04	.62	-.32	.67
Fear of failure	.23	.75	-.02	.73
Contingent self-worth	.31	.42	.20	.36
Overgeneralisation of failure	.17	.60	-.03	.58
Mental perseveration	.30	.63	.13	.59
Self-criticism	.39	.51	.28	.44
Labile self-esteem	.12	.43	-.02	.42
Rumination	.12	.35	.01	.33
BO: Reduced accomplishment	-.12	.32	-.17	.34
BO: Exhaustion	-.15	.30	-.20	.32
BO: Devaluation	-.45	.14	-.47	.22
Cognitive appraisal	.17	.03	.18	-.06
Expressive suppression	.26	.31	.14	.22
Anger control-in	.11	-.09	.17	-.16
Anger control-out	.10	-.13	.18	-.20

Study	Sample	Domain	Measure			
Hill & Appleton (2011)	202 male junior and adult rugby players	Sport	HF-MPS	SOP	SPP	.12
Hill & Davis (2014)	238 adult coaches (26% females)	Sport	HF-MPS-b FMPS-b	PS+	CM+	.47

Study	Sample	Domain	Measure	SOP	SPP	Outcome				
Hill et al. (2008)	151 male junior soccer players	Sport	HF-MPS	SOP	SPP −.16	Unconditional self-acceptance	−.42	−.25	−.38	−.17
						BO: Reduced accomplishment	.44	−.36	.46	−.39
						BO: Exhaustion	.39	−.20	.41	−.25
						BO: Devaluation	.37	−.39	.40	−.42
Hill, Hall, Appleton, & Murray (2010)	150 junior and adult canoe polo and kayak slalom athletes (43% females)	Sport	HF-MPS	SOP	SPP .26	Satisfaction with goal progress	−.19	.31	−.23	.33
						Coach satisfaction with goal progress	−.26	.31	−.30	.34
						Validation seeking	.49	.09	.52	.21
						Growth seeking	−.25	.37	−.15	.31
						Reduced accomplishment	.38	−.20	.34	−.09
						Exhaustion	.26	−.03	.26	.04
						Devaluation	.27	−.21	.22	−.14
Hill, Hall, & Appleton (2010)	255 male junior cricketers	Sport	HF-MPS	SOP	SPP —	Fear of failure	—	—	—	.18
						Self-criticism	—	—	—	.38
Hill et al. (2015)	248 adult exercisers (41% females)	Exercise	HF-MPS-b	SOP	SPP .38	Perfectionistic self-promotion	.48	.31	.57	.45
						Non-display of imperfection	.41	.14	.47	.29
						Non-disclosure of imperfection	.37	.18	.45	.32
						ED: Withdrawal	.12	.24	.22	.30
						ED: Continuance	.11	.17	.19	.23

Study	Sample	Domain	Measure	Subscale	Outcome (α)				
Hill et al. (2020)	297 adolescent swimmers (54% females)	Sport	MIPS	SP	NRI .86	ED: Tolerance	**.30**	**.18**	**.25**
						ED: Lack of control	**.29**	**.20**	**.24**
						ED: Reduction	**.24**	**.21**	**.18**
						ED: Time	**.26**	.10	**.24**
						ED: Intention effects	**.29**	**.22**	**.23**
						Confidence	**-.15**	**-.19**	.03
						Dedication	-.11	**-.14**	.02
						Vigour	**.15**	**-.21**	**.66**
						Enthusiasm	**-.23**	**-.30**	.06
			HF-MPS	SOP	SPP .44	Confidence	**.37**	.04	**.39**
						Dedication	**.39**	.05	**.41**
						Vigour	**.20**	.05	**.20**
						Enthusiasm	.10	.04	.09
	211 adult athletes (34% females)	Sport	MIPS	SP	NRI .57	Confidence	**.32**	.03	**.37**
						Dedication	**.35**	**.18**	**.31**
						Vigour	**.26**	.07	**.27**
						Enthusiasm	**.28**	.09	**.28**
			S-MPS-2	PST	CM .43	Confidence	**.45**	.02	**.49**
				CM		Dedication	**.58**	.11	**.59**
						Vigour	**.40**	.02	**.43**
						Enthusiasm	**.38**	.08	**.38**

(continued)
.07
.10
.13
.00
.12
-.12
-.09
-.67
-.21
-.15
-.15
-.04
.00
-.20
-.03
-.10
-.09
-.22
-.19
-.18
-.10

Ho et al. (2015)	212 deaf junior and adult athletes (26% females)	Sport	HF-MPS	SOP	SPP	**.37**	BO: Reduced accomplishment	**-.19**	-.03	**-.19**	.04
							BO: Exhaustion	.03	**.17**	-.04	**.17**
							BO: Devaluation	-.12	**.15**	**-.19**	**.21**
							Negative affect	**.14**	.13	.10	.09
							Physical symptoms of ill-health	.02	.11	-.02	.11
	205 junior and adult athletes (38% females)						BO: Reduced accomplishment	**-.38**	.15	**-.45**	**.29**
							BO: Exhaustion	**-.19**	.12	**-.24**	**.19**
							BO: Devaluation	**-.40**	.12	**-.46**	**.27**
							Negative affect	**-.16**	**.21**	**-.24**	**.27**
							Physical symptoms of ill-health	**-.23**	.10	**-.27**	**.18**
Houltberg et al. (2018)	99 adult athletes (gender not reported)	Sport	S-MPS-2	PST	CM	**.39**	Belief in good life after sports	-.17	-.14	-.13	-.08
							Global self-esteem	-.06	**-.59**	**.23**	**-.62**
							Meaning of Life (purpose)	-.02	**-.33**	.13	**-.35**
							Contingent self-worth (competition)	**.30**	**.65**	.07	**.61**
							Fear of failure	**.27**	**.68**	.01	**.65**
							Anxiety	.18	**.43**	.01	**.40**
							Depressive symptoms	.07	**.44**	-.12	**.45**
							Shame	**.25**	**.59**	.03	**.55**
							Life satisfaction	-.03	**-.27**	.08	**-.28**

Study	Sample	Domain	Measure	Dim 1	Dim 2	r	Variable				
Jowett et al. (2021)	244 adolescent dancers (17% females)	Dance	HF-MPS-b S-MPS-2	PS+	PC+	.39	Autonomy support	.16	-.19	.26	-.28
							BO: Reduced accomplishment	-.18	.34	-.36	.45
							BO: Exhaustion	.01	.29	-.12	.31
							BO: Devaluation	-.34	.15	-.44	.33
							Confidence	.23	-.16	.32	-.28
							Dedication	.48	-.11	.57	-.37
							Vigour	.25	-.13	.33	-.26
							Enthusiasm	.30	-.18	.41	-.34
Jowett et al. (2018)	224 adult runners (36% females)	Sport	HF-MPS-b	SOP	SPP	.40	Problem-focused coping	.06	-.17	.14	-.21
							Emotion-focused coping	.18	.13	.14	.06
							Avoidance coping	.14	.26	.04	.22
Jowett et al. (2016)	222 adolescent athletes (56% females)	Sport	HF-MPS-b S-MPS-2	PS+	PC+	.22	Need satisfaction	.44	-.07	.47	-.19
Kaye et al. (2008)	372 college students/exercisers (40% females)	Exercise	HF-MPS	SOP	SPP	.37	Need thwarting	-.16	.42	-.29	.47
							Total engagement	.41	-.07	.44	-.18
							BO: Total	-.26	.36	-.37	.44
							FOF: Shame and embarrassment	.22	.41	.08	.36

	Exercise	F-MPS	PST	CM
FOF: Self esteem	.15	.34	.03	.31
FOF: Uncertain future	.09	.37	-.05	.36
FOF: Losing interest	.15	.46	-.02	.44
FOF: Upsetting others	.14	.47	-.04	.45
Behavioural inhibition	-.19	-.13	-.15	-.07
Behavioural activation	-.10	.14	-.17	.19
Neuroticism	.11	.44	-.06	.43
Extraversion	.08	-.18	.16	-.23
Negative affectivity	.20	.38	.07	.34
Positive affectivity	.21	-.11	.27	-.21
Mastery approach goal	.36	-.06	.41	-.22
Mastery avoidance goal	.08	.16	.02	.14
Performance approach goal	.38	.14	.36	.00
Performance avoidance goal	.14	.22	.06	.18
FOF: Shame and embarrassment	.15	.56	-.05	.55
FOF: Self esteem	.05	.46	-.13	.47
FOF: Uncertain future	-.00	.38	-.15	.40
FOF: Losing interest	.19	.54	.01	.51
FOF: Upsetting others	.10	.35	-.02	.34
Behavioural inhibition	-.12	-.19	-.06	-.16
Behavioural activation	.08	.10	.05	.08
Neuroticism	.25	.40	.13	.35
Extraversion	.06	-.19	.13	-.22

CM .34

Construct	Study	Sample									
Negative affectivity								.21	.43	.08	.39
Positive affectivity								.02	-.14	.07	-.16
Mastery approach goal								-.01	-.00	-.01	.00
Mastery avoidance goal								.21	.23	.14	.17
Performance approach goal								.12	.25	.04	.22
Performance avoidance goal								.11	.27	.02	.25
Total Stress	Krasnow et al. (1999)	19 female junior modern dancers	Dance	F-MPS	—	CM	—	—	.53	—	—
Negative stress								—	.47	—	—
Injury								—	—	—	—
Total Stress		30 female junior artistic gymnasts	Dance	F-MPS	—	CM	—	—	.86	—	—
Negative stress								—	.86	—	—
Injury								—	.68	—	—
Total Stress		16 female junior ballet dancers	Dance	F-MPS	—	CM	—	—	—	—	—
Negative stress								—	.50	—	—
Injury								—	—	—	—
Task-involving climate	Kristiansen et al. (2012)	24 junior and adult swimmers (38% females)	Sport	F-MPS	PST	CM	.50	-.01	-.04	.01	-.04
Ego-involving climate								.36	.59	.09	.51
Different types of recovery								.26	-.09	.35	-.26
Balance of training and recovery								.26	.12	.23	-.01
Knowledge about recovery								.10	.01	.11	-.05
BO: Exhaustion								-.18	-.11	-.15	-.02

Study	Sample	Domain	Instrument			r	Outcome				
Klund & Sæther (2017)	115 male junior football players	Sport	S-MPS	PST	CM	.45	BO: Reduced accomplishment	-.17	.17	-.30	.30
							BO: Devaluation	-.37	.15	-.52	.42
							Self-assessed skills	.24	-.05	.29	-.18
							Coach-assessed skills	.28	-.14	.39	-.31
							Number of organised training sessions	.23	.05	.23	-.06
							Hours of organised training sessions	.26	.01	.29	-.12
							Number of independent training sessions	.02	.03	.01	.02
							Hours of organised training sessions	-.02	-.05	.00	-.05
Kvalon et al. (2021)	251 adolescent athletes (50% females)	Sport	S-MPS-2	PS+	PC+	.14	Total athlete burnout	-.39	.29	-.45	.38
							BO: Reduced accomplishment	-.35	.25	-.40	.32
							BO: Exhaustion	-.06	.22	-.09	.23
							BO: Devaluation	-.43	.17	-.47	.26
							Training distress	-.04	.40	-.11	.41
							Perceived performance	.19	-.20	.22	-.23
Kwon & Cho (2020)	302 university athletes (21% females)	Sport	HF-MPS-b	SOP	SPP	.31	Cognitive anxiety	-.06	.24	-.15	.27
Laborde et al. (2015)	332 university students (37% females)	Sport	F-MPS	PST	CM	.47	BO: Exhaustion	.27	.08	.26	.00
							Subjective vitality	-.07	.19	-.14	.22
							Movement self-consciousness	.13	.21	.04	.17

	Sport	F-MPS	PST	CM
Conscious motor processing	**.14**	.11	.10	.05
Movement-specific reinvestment total	**.17**	**.19**	.09	**.13**
Decision reinvestment	**.28**	**.25**	**.19**	**.14**
Decision rumination	**.15**	**.44**	-.07	**.42**
Decision-specific reinvestment total	**.25**	**.43**	.06	**.37**
Private self-consciousness	**.18**	**.14**	**.13**	.06
Public self-consciousness	.08	**.20**	-.02	**.18**
Self-anxiety	-.06	.06	-.10	.10
Response style: Rumination	.05	**.28**	-.10	**.29**
Response style: Distraction	**.15**	**-.15**	**.25**	-.25
Ego orientation	**.31**	**.33**	.15	**.19**
Task orientation	-.15	**-.20**	-.04	-.14
Ego-involving climate	**.19**	**.43**	-.09	**.40**
Task-involving climate	.08	**-.24**	**.29**	-.36
Perceived ability	**.23**	-.05	**.33**	**-.24**
BO: Exhaustion	**-.22**	.06	**-.32**	**.25**
BO: Reduced accomplishment	**-.19**	**.21**	**-.40**	**.41**
BO: Devaluation	-.15	.00	**-.19**	.11
Total burnout	**-.22**	.12	**-.37**	**.32**
Goal attainment	-.07	**-.20**	.06	**-.20**
Performance satisfaction	-.07	**-.21**	.07	**-.21**

Lemyre et al. (2008) — 141 junior and adult athletes (43% females)

CM .60

Study	Sample	Domain	Measure	PS	PC	r	Variable				
Lizmore et al. (2016)	343 adult curlers (42% females)	Sport	S-MPS-2	PST	CM	**.35**	RM: Anger / low criticality	**.15**	**.46**	-.01	**.44**
							RM: Self-confidence / low criticality	**.12**	**-.26**	**.23**	**-.32**
							RM: Anger / high criticality	**.14**	**.48**	-.03	**.46**
							RM: Self-confidence / high criticality	.10	**-.28**	**.22**	**-.34**
Lizmore et al. (2017)	239 university athletes (43% females)	Sport	S-MPS-2 MIPS	PS+	PC+	**.34**	Self-compassion	-.08	**-.63**	**.18**	**-.64**
							Optimism	**.17**	**-.39**	**.35**	**-.48**
							Pessimism	-.09	**.47**	**-.30**	**.53**
							Rumination	**.24**	**.58**	.06	**.55**
Lizmore et al. (2019)	99 university athletes (53% females)	Sport	S-MPS-2 MIPS	PS+	PC+	**.41**	Putting performance	**-.30**	-.11	**-.28**	.01
							Putting performance (after failure)	**-.29**	-.12	**-.27**	.00
Longbottom et al. (2010)	215 sport science undergraduates (50% females)	Exercise	F-MPS-b	PST	CM	**.46**	Adaptive cognitions	**.22**	.01	**.24**	-.11
							Adaptive behaviours	**.14**	.12	.10	.06
							Impeding cognitions	.02	**.33**	**-.16**	**.36**
							Maladaptive behaviours	-.12	**.23**	**-.26**	**.32**
			HF-MPS-b	SOP	SPP	**.53**	Adaptive cognitions	**.20**	.01	**.23**	-.12
							Adaptive behaviours	**.24**	.11	**.22**	-.02
							Impeding cognitions	**.14**	**.32**	-.04	**.29**
							Maladaptive behaviours	**.53**	**.27**	**.47**	-.02

The table is rotated 90°. Reconstructed in normal reading orientation below. Each outcome row carries four reported correlation values; the perfectionism subscales and their inter-correlation (shown beside each measure) are: FMPS-b → PST, CM (.40); HF-MPS → SOP, SPP (.43); F-MPS → PST, CM (.29).

Study / sample	Domain	Measure	Outcome	(1)	(2)	(3)	(4)
Longbottom et al. (2012) — 257 sport science undergraduates (66% females)	Exercise	FMPS-b — PST, CM (.40)	Amotivation	-.13	**.20**	**-.23**	**.28**
			External regulation	-.01	**.40**	**-.20**	**.44**
			Introjected regulation	**.18**	**.38**	.03	**.34**
			Identified regulation	**.21**	.01	**.22**	-.08
			Intrinsic motivation	**.18**	-.09	**.24**	**-.18**
			Relative autonomy index	**.15**	**-.28**	**.30**	**-.38**
			Impression motivation	**.28**	**.22**	**.21**	**.12**
			Impression construction	**.19**	**.37**	.05	**.33**
			Total exercise behaviour	**.16**	-.03	**-.19**	-.10
	Exercise	HF-MPS — SOP, SPP (.43)	Amotivation	.02	**.27**	-.11	**.29**
			External regulation	.11	**.46**	-.11	**.46**
			Introjected regulation	**.21**	**.18**	**.15**	.10
			Identified regulation	.11	-.11	**.18**	**-.18**
			Intrinsic motivation	.12	**.20**	.04	**.17**
			Relative autonomy index	.01	**-.38**	**.21**	**-.43**
			Impression motivation	**.31**	**.22**	**.24**	.10
			Impression construction	**.21**	**.35**	.07	**.29**
			Total exercise behaviour	.06	-.10	.11	**-.14**
Luszczynska et al. (2015)† — 845 adolescents (59% females)	Exercise	F-MPS — PST, CM (.29)	Fruit and vegetable intake (time 1)	**.21**	.05	**.20**	-.01
			Snack intake (time 1)	**-.14**	-.02	**-.14**	.02
			Moderate/vigorous activity (time 1)	.11	.02	**.11**	-.01

Study	Sample	Domain	Instrument			Variable				
Machida et al. (2012)	206 university athletes (67% females)	Sport	S-MPS-2	PS+	PC+ = -.25	Fruit and vegetable intake (time 2)	.15	.01	.15	-.04
						Snack intake (time 2)	-.17	-.05	-.16	.00
						Moderate/vigorous activity (time 2)	.08	-.04	.10	-.07
						Controllable sources of confidence	.34	.07	.37	.17
						Uncontrollable sources of confidence	.21	.26	.29	.33
						Task orientation	.14	-.01	.14	.03
						Ego orientation	-.21	.15	-.18	.10
						Task-involving climate	-.02	-.11	-.05	-.12
						Ego-involving climate	.10	.49	.26	.53
Madigan et al. (2015)†	103 adolescent athletes (20% females)	Sport	S-MPS MIPS	PS+	PC+ = .54	BO: Total (time 1)	-.31	.08	-.42	.31
						BO: Total (time 2)	-.40	.14	-.57	.46
Madigan et al. (2016a)	130 male adolescent athletes	Sport	S-MPS MIPS	PS+	PC+ = .60	Positive attitudes towards doping	-.08	.10	-.18	.19
Madigan et al. (2016b)†	129 adult athletes (49% females)	Sport	S-MPS MIPS	PS+	PC+ = .78	BO: Reduced accomplishment (time 1)	-.33	-.08	-.43	.30
						BO: Exhaustion (time 1)	-.13	.08	-.31	.29
						BO: Devaluation (time 1)	-.32	-.07	-.43	.30
						BO: Total (time 1)	-.29	-.02	-.44	.34
						BO: Reduced accomplishment (time 2)	.29	-.02	.49	-.41

Study	Sample	Domain	Instrument	PS+	PC+	Variable				
Madigan et al. (2016c; 2017a)†	141 adolescent athletes (11% females)	Sport	S-MPS MIPS	PS+	PC+	BO: Exhaustion (time 2)	**-.21**	-.02	**-.31**	**.24**
						BO: Devaluation (time 2)	**.29**	-.02	**.49**	**-.41**
						BO: Total (time 2)	**-.31**	-.05	**-.43**	**.32**
					.54	Training distress (time 1)	-.07	**.24**	**-.24**	**.33**
						Training distress (time 2)	.09	**.33**	-.11	**.34**
						Autonomous motivation (time 1)	**.35**	.01	**.41**	**-.23**
						Controlled motivation (time 1)	**.17**	**.39**	-.05	**.36**
						Amotivation (time 1)	-.06	.14	**-.16**	**.21**
						Athlete burnout (time 1)	-.04	**.31**	**-.26**	**.39**
						Autonomous motivation (time 2)	**.45**	**.17**	**.43**	-.10
						Controlled motivation (time 2)	**.34**	**.56**	.05	**.48**
						Amotivation (time 2)	-.15	.02	**-.19**	.12
						Athlete burnout (time 2)	-.14	**.40**	**-.46**	**.57**
						Autonomous motivation (time 3)	**.22**	-.15	**.36**	**-.33**
						Controlled motivation (time 3)	.10	**.25**	-.04	**.23**
						Amotivation (time 3)	-.09	.06	-.15	.13
						Athlete burnout (time 3)	-.05	**.32**	**-.28**	**.41**
Madigan et al. (2017b)	136 junior athletes (21% females)	Sport	S-MPS MIPS	PS+	PC+ **.53**	Task-approach	**.26**	-.02	**.32**	**-.19**
						Task-avoidance	-.11	**.18**	**-.25**	**.28**

Study	Sample	Domain	Scale	Dim 1	Dim 2	r	Variable				
Madigan et al. (2017c)	261 adolescent and adult athletes (26% females)	Sport	MIPS	SP	NRI	**.62**	Self-approach	**.21**	-.07	.29	**-.22**
							Self-avoidance	-.11	**.21**	**-.27**	**.32**
							Other-approach	**.27**	**.20**	**.20**	.07
							Other-avoidance	.03	**.30**	-.16	**.34**
							Training for avoidance of negative affect	**.20**	**.31**	.01	**.24**
Madigan, Hill et al. (2018)	171 junior athletes (27% females)	Sport	S-MPS MIPS	PS+	PC+	**.71**	Training for weight control	**.14**	**.28**	-.04	**.25**
							Training for mood control	**.20**	**.14**	**.15**	.02
							Problem-focused coping	**.33**	.11	**.36**	**-.19**
Madigan, Stoeber et al. (2018)	90 adult and adolescent (19% females)	Sport	S-MPS MIPS	PS+	PC+	**.63**	Avoidant coping	-.05	**.17**	**-.25**	**.29**
							Training distress	.01	**.28**	**-.28**	**.39**
							Task-approach	**.43**	.19	**.41**	-.12
Madigan, Stoeber, Forsdyke et al. (2018)	80 junior athletes (19% females)	Sport	S-MPS MIPS	PS+	PC+	**.59**	Task-avoidance	**.27**	.19	.20	.03
							Self-approach	**.28**	.13	**.26**	-.06
							Self-avoidance	**.28**	**.24**	.17	.09
							Other-approach	**.47**	**.36**	**.34**	.09
							Other-avoidance	**.38**	**.43**	.16	**.27**
							Performance	**.29**	.10	**.29**	-.11
							Injury	.16	**.29**	-.01	**.25**

Madigan et al. (2020)	181 adult and adolescent athletes (31% females)	Sport	S-MPS MIPS	PS+	PC+	.59	Attitudes towards doping	-.07	**.16**	**-.21**	**.25**
Mallinson & Hill (2011)	205 junior athletes (57% females)	Sport	S-MPS-2	PST	CM	.66	Autonomy thwarting	**.30**	**.40**	.05	**.28**
							Competence thwarting	**.16**	**.33**	-.08	**.30**
							Relatedness thwarting	**.18**	**.31**	-.03	**.26**
			HF-MPS	SOP	SPP	.46	Autonomy thwarting	**.18**	**.31**	.04	**.26**
							Competence thwarting	.12	**.23**	.02	**.20**
							Relatedness thwarting	.05	**.28**	-.09	**.29**
Mallinson et al. (2014)	241 junior athletes (59% females)	Sport	S-MPS-2	PST	PC+	.58	Enjoyment	**.20**	-.10	**.32**	**-.27**
							Physical self-worth	.01	**-.24**	**.19**	**-.30**
							Friendship: Self-esteem enhancement	**.17**	**-.18**	**.34**	**-.35**
							Friendship: Loyalty	.08	-.10	**.17**	**-.18**
							Friendship: Things in common	**.18**	.03	**.20**	-.09
							Friendship: Companionship	**.16**	-.05	**.23**	**-.18**
							Friendship: Conflict resolution	**.14**	-.10	**.24**	**-.22**
							Friendship: Conflict	.11	**.31**	-.09	**.30**
Mallinson-Howard et al. (2019)	222 youth athletes (71% females)	Sport	S-MPS-2	PST	CM	.69	Negative affect	**.33**	**.52**	-.05	**.43**

						Positive affect	.08	-.24	.35	-.41
						Concentration disruption	-.04	.20	-.25	.31
						Worry	.20	.24	.05	.14
						Somatic anxiety	.16	.23	.00	.17
						Antisocial behaviour–teammates	.36	.35	.17	.15
						Antisocial behaviour–opponents	.44	.43	.22	.19
						Prosocial behaviour–teammates	.05	-.07	.14	-.14
						Prosocial behaviour–opponents	.07	-.06	.15	-.15
						Intentions to dropout	-.08	.10	-.21	.22
Mallinson-Howard et al. (2021)	129 university athletes (44% females)	Sport	MIPS	SP	NRI	.33	Performance (jump test)	.21	-.14	.27	-.23
						Performance (sprint test)	-.24	.16	-.31	.26
	136 university athletes (41% females)	Sport	MIPS	SP	NRI	.47	Performance (agility trial time)	-.24	-.10	-.22	.01
	116 junior athletes (17% females)	Sport	MIPS	SP	NRI	.48	Performance (Yo-Yo test)	.26	.11	.24	-.02
Martin et al (2021)	149 adult athletes (30% females)	Sport	F-MPS-b	PST	PC+	.46	Life stress	.12	.18	.04	.14
						Athletic identity	.40	.27	.32	.11
						Coach–athlete relationship	.20	-.03	.24	-.14
Martinent & Ferrand (2007)	166 adult athletes (47% females)	Sport	S-MPS	PST	CM	—	Somatic anxiety intensity	.27	.33	—	—

Variable				
Cognitive anxiety intensity	.35	.48	—	—
Self-confidence intensity	.20	-.05	—	—
Somatic anxiety frequency	.12	.10	—	—
Cognitive anxiety frequency	.24	.30	—	—
Self-confidence frequency	.13	.14	—	—
Somatic anxiety direction	-.15	-.14	—	—
Cognitive anxiety direction	-.13	-.32	—	—
Self-confidence direction	.19	-.05	—	—
Task orientation	.22	-.07	.27	-.17
Ego orientation	.32	.23	.26	.12
Intrinsic motivation	.35	.06	.35	-.08
Identified regulation	.18	.08	.16	.01
Introjected regulation	.23	.34	.12	.28
External regulation	.30	.36	.19	.28
Amotivation	-.02	.23	-.12	.26
Flexible goal structure	.09	-.15	.16	-.20
Perceived parental task orientation	.10	.19	.03	.17
Perceived parental ego orientation	.24	.00	.26	-.10
Global self-esteem	.31	-.14	.40	-.30
Labile self-esteem	.14	.39	-.01	.37

McArdle & Duda (2004) — 196 junior athletes (61% females) — Sport — F-MPS — PST — CM — .38

McArdle & Duda (2008) — 196 junior athletes (61% females) — Sport — F-MPS — PST — CM — .39

Study	Sample	Domain	Measure				Variable				
Miller & Mesagno (2014)	90 adult exercisers (62% females)	Exercise	HF-MPS	SOP	SPP	.47	Exercise dependence	.32	.35	.19	.24
							Narcissism	.17	.31	.03	.26
Molnar et al. (2021)	425 adolescent female dancers	Dance	CAPS	SOP	SPP	.56	Appearance	.26	.44	.02	.37
							Social goals	.22	.26	.09	.17
							Enjoyment goals	.01	−.13	.10	−.16
							Competence goals	.30	.15	.26	−.02
							Expert goals	.13	.43	−.15	.43
							Health goals	.15	.20	.05	.14
Mouratidis & Michou (2011)	333 junior athletes (32% females)	Sport	F-MPS	PS	CM	.10	Autonomous motivation	.49	.01	.49	−.04
							Controlled motivation	.19	.37	.17	.36
							Coping with adversity	.33	−.20	.36	−.25
							Peaking under pressure	.42	.01	.42	−.04
							Goal setting/mental preparation	.56	.02	.56	−.04
							Concentration	.37	−.13	.39	−.18
							Confidence	.43	−.27	.48	−.35
Nascimento Junior et al. (2017)	301 male adult futsal players	Sport	S–MPS–2	PST	CM	.43	Competence satisfaction	.15	.03	.15	−.04
							Relatedness satisfaction	.06	−.02	.08	−.05
							Autonomy satisfaction	.14	.01	.15	−.06
							Cohesion: Group–Integration task	.07	.07	.04	.04
							Cohesion: Group–Integration social	.08	.08	.05	.05

Study	Sample	Domain	Instrument	Subscale	Outcome	r	Variable				
Nascimento Junior et al. (2020)	29 male adult futsal medal winners	Sport	S-MPS-2	PS+	CM	.32	Cohesion: Attraction to group task	**.31**	**.31**	.21	.21
							Cohesion: Attraction to group social	.11	**.11**	.07	.07
							Scored goals	**.32**	.06	**.32**	-.05
							Conceded goals	**-.32**	-.06	**-.32**	.05
							Number of wins	.13	-.09	.17	-.14
							Number of defeats	-.13	.09	-.17	.14
							Total score in competition	.13	-.10	.17	-.15
	111 male adult futsal non-medal winners	Sport	S-MPS-2	PS+	CM	.30	Scored goals	.08	.08	.06	.06
							Conceded goals	.13	.04	.12	.00
							Number of wins	-.10	.05	-.12	.08
							Number of defeats	.13	-.03	.15	-.07
							Total score in competition	-.08	.08	-.11	.11
Nordin-Bates (2020)	77 adolescent dance students (77% females)	Dance	MIPS	SP	NRI	.49	Creativity	.17	-.01	.20	-.11
Nordin-Bates, Cumming et al. (2011)	250 adult dancers (66% females)	Dance	PI	SE	CM	.44	Autonomy satisfaction	.12	**-.30**	**.32**	**-.41**
							Competence satisfaction	.16	-.16	**.28**	**-.28**
							Relatedness satisfaction	.23	.02	**.25**	-.11
							Facilitative imagery	**.25**	**-.02**	**.29**	**-.15**
							Debilitative imagery	**.15**	**.47**	-.07	**.46**
							Cognitive anxiety intensity	**.22**	**.48**	.01	**.44**

Study	Sample	Domain					Outcome				
Nordin-Bates et al. (2014)†	271 junior dancers (74% females)	Dance	PI	SE	CM	.43	Cognitive anxiety direction	-.11	**-.18**	-.03	**-.15**
							Somatic anxiety intensity	.11	**.37**	-.06	**.36**
							Somatic anxiety direction	-.05	-.13	.01	-.12
							Self-confidence	-.02	**-.35**	**.16**	**-.38**
							Task-involving climate (time 1)	.04	**-.20**	**.14**	**-.24**
							Ego-involving climate (time 1)	**.21**	**.41**	.04	**.36**
							Task-involving climate (time 2)	-.06	**-.24**	.05	**-.24**
							Ego-involving climate (time 2)	**.26**	**.36**	**.12**	**.28**
Nordin-Bates, Walker et al. (2011)	261 adolescent female dancers	Dance	PI	PS+	PC+	.56	Eating attitudes	**.27**	**.42**	.05	**.34**
							Self-esteem	**-.32**	**-.31**	**-.19**	**-.17**
	85 adolescent male dancers	Dance	PI	PS+	PC+	.50	Eating attitudes	**.24**	**.31**	.10	**.23**
							Self-esteem	-.16	-.20	-.07	-.14
Nordin-Bates et al. (2017)	91 adolescent ballet dancers (43% females)	Dance	F-MPS	PST	CM	.28	BO: Reduced accomplishment	-.18	**.40**	**-.33**	**.48**
							BO: Exhaustion	**.13**	**.38**	.03	**.36**
							BO: Devaluation	-.02	**.31**	-.12	**.33**
							Intrinsic motivation	**-.26**	.24	**-.35**	**.34**
							Identified regulation	**-.33**	.03	**-.35**	.14
							External regulation	-.12	.06	-.14	.10

Study	Sample	Domain	Measure				Variable				
Olivera et al. (2015)‡	63 adolescent professional soccer players (gender not reported)	Sport	F-MPS	PS+	PC+	–	Amotivation	.21	-.32	**.33**	**-.40**
							Intrinsic motivation to know	**.40**	–	–	–
							Intrinsic motivation for accomplishment	**.42**	–	–	–
							Intrinsic motivation for stimulation	**.53**	–	–	–
							External regulation	**.42**	–	–	–
	119 adolescent non-professional soccer players (gender not reported)	Sport	F-MPS	PS+	PC+	–	Intrinsic motivation to know	–	–	–	–
							Intrinsic motivation for accomplishment	–	–	–	–
							Intrinsic motivation for stimulation	–	–	–	–
							External regulation	–	**.41**	–	–
Ommundsen et al. (2005)	1719 junior soccer player (28% females)	Sport	F-MPS	PST	PC+	.53	Task orientation	.14	-.06	.20	**-.16**
							Ego orientation	.30	.22	.22	.08
							Task-involving climate	.05	-.09	.12	**-.14**
							Ego-involving climate	.31	.53	.04	.45
							Friendship quality: Loyalty	.01	-.23	.16	**-.28**
							Friendship quality: Companionship	-.07	-.33	.13	**-.35**

Study	Sample	Domain	Measure				Variable				
Olsson et al. (2020)	150 adolescent athlete–parent dyads (gender not reported)	Sport	MIPS	SP	NRI	**.53**	Friendship quality: Conflict	.04	.17	-.06	**.18**
							Peer acceptance	-.01	**-.18**	**.10**	**-.21**
							Actual parental perfectionistic strivings	**.20**	.09	**.18**	-.02
							Actual parental perfectionistic concerns	**.24**	**.17**	**.18**	.05
							Perceived parental perfectionistic strivings	**.44**	**.34**	**.33**	.14
							Perceived parental perfectionistic concerns	**.29**	**.48**	.05	**.40**
Olsson et al. (2021)	256 adult athletes (50% females)	Sport	MIPS	SP	NRI	**.41**	Stress	.11	**.35**	-.04	**.34**
							Total burnout	-.06	**.20**	**-.16**	**.25**
							BO: Reduced accomplishment	-.05	**.23**	**-.16**	**.27**
							BO: Exhaustion	.04	**.20**	-.05	**.20**
							BO: Devaluation	**-.13**	.02	**-.15**	.08
Pacewicz et al. (2018)	173 university athletes (50% females)	Sport	S-MPS-2	PST	CM	**.39**	Total burnout	**-.19**	**.41**	**-.42**	**.54**
							BO: Reduced accomplishment	-.01	**-.27**	.11	**-.29**
							BO: Exhaustion	**-.18**	**.32**	**-.35**	**.43**
							BO: Devaluation	**-.25**	**.31**	**-.42**	**.46**
							Problem-focused coping	.12	-.07	**.16**	-.13
							Emotion-focused coping	.08	**-.27**	**.21**	**-.33**

Study	Sample	Domain	PI	PS+	PC+	r	Variable				
Padlam & Aujla (2014)	92 adult dancers (75% females)	Dance					Avoidant coping	-.06	**.20**	-.15	**.24**
							Harmonious passion	-.01	-.02	.00	-.02
			PI	PS+	PC+	.65	Obsessive passion	**.32**	**.39**	.10	**.25**
							Attitudes towards disordered eating	.17	**.31**	-.04	**.27**
							Food preoccupation	.07	**.17**	-.05	.16
							Dieting	**.23**	**.38**	-.02	**.31**
							Oral control	.01	.02	.00	.02
							Global self-esteem	-.16	**-.35**	.09	**-.33**
Paulson & Rutledge (2014)	204 female undergraduates	Exercise	APS-R	HS	D	-.11	Attitudes towards disordered eating	-.04	**.30**	-.01	**.30**
							Cardiovascular exercise	**.15**	.00	**.15**	.02
							Strength exercise	.03	.02	.03	.02
	110 male undergraduates	Exercise	APS-R	HS	D	.14	Attitudes towards disordered eating	-.15	.11	-.17	.13
							Cardiovascular exercise	**.26**	.10	**.25**	.07
							Strength exercise	**.43**	-.01	**.44**	-.08
Penniment & Egan (2012)	142 adult female ballet and jazz dancers	Dance	F-MPS	PST	CM	.88	Dietary restraint	**.75**	**.79**	**.19**	**.41**
							Eating concern	**.76**	**.80**	**.20**	**.43**
							Shape concern	**.84**	**.84**	**.39**	**.39**
Puente-Díaz et al. (2013)	204 adolescent tennis players	Sport	F-MPS	PST	CM	.32	Hope	**.19**	-.01	**.20**	-.08
							Enjoyment	.10	**.20**	.04	**.18**
							Performance avoidance	.06	.12	.02	.11

Study	Sample	Sport type	Measure			Variable				
Raedeke et al. (2021)	254 aesthetic performers (80% females)	Sport/ Dance	F-MPS	PST	CM **.65**	Performance approach	**.29**	-.04	**.32**	**-.15**
						Mastery avoidance	-.02	-.03	-.01	-.02
						Mastery approach	**.26**	**.28**	**.19**	**.22**
						Fear of failure	**.16**	**.32**	.06	**.29**
						Self-esteem	**-.19**	**-.50**	**.21**	**-.50**
Friere et al. (2022)	413 high school athletes (gender not reported)	Sport	S-MPS-2	PS/O	CM **.14**	Contingent self-worth	**.49**	**.59**	**.17**	**.41**
						BO: Exhaustion	.12	**.25**	-.06	**.23**
						BO: Reduced accomplishment	**.22**	**.37**	-.03	**.31**
						BO: Devaluation	.00	**.13**	-.11	**.17**
						Life satisfaction	**-.14**	**-.37**	**.14**	**-.37**
						Ego orientation	**.18**	**.23**	**.15**	**.21**
Sapieja et al. (2011)	194 male junior soccer players	Sport	S-MPS-2	PST	CM **.49**	Task orientation	**.38**	.06	**.38**	.01
						Perceived maternal authoritativeness	-.01	**-.37**	**.21**	**-.42**
						Perceived paternal authoritativeness	.07	**-.33**	**.28**	**-.42**
Sagar & Stoeber (2009)	388 university athletes (46% females)	Sport	S-MPS	PST	CM **.56**	Positive affect after success	**.11**	.02	**.12**	-.05
						Negative affect after failure	**.11**	**.30**	-.07	**.29**
						FOF: Shame and embarrassment	**.20**	**.51**	-.12	**.49**
						FOF: Self esteem	**.21**	**.46**	-.06	**.42**

Study	Sample	Domain	Perfectionism measure	FOF measure	Outcome				
					FOF: Losing interest	.23	.45	-.03	**.40**
					FOF: Upsetting others	**.32**	**.50**	.06	**.41**
					FOF: Uncertain future	**.31**	**.42**	**.10**	**.31**
Shanmugam & Davies (2015)	192 adult athletes (44% females)	Sport	F-MPS	PST	Eating psychopathology	**.18**	—	—	—
Shanmugam et al. (2011)	588 adult athletes (59% females)	Sport	F-MPS	PST	Avoidant attachment	**.10**	—	—	—
					Anxious attachment	.05	—	—	—
					Parent support	**.07**	—	—	—
					Parent conflict	**.11**	—	—	—
					Coach support	**.12**	—	—	—
					Coach conflict	**.11**	—	—	—
					Self-criticism	**.29**	—	—	—
					Self-esteem	.04	—	—	—
					Depressive symptoms	**.08**	—	—	—
					Dietary restraint	**.11**	—	—	—
					Eating concern	.04	—	—	—
					Shape concern	**.08**	—	—	—
					Weight concern	.07	—	—	—
Shanmugam et al. (2012)‡	411 junior and adult athletes (61% females)	Sport	F-MPS	PST	Avoidant attachment	.08	—	—	—
					Anxious attachment	.04	—	—	—
					Self-criticism	**.28**	—	—	—

Study	Sample	Domain	Measure	Subscale 1	Subscale 2	r	Outcome	(1)	(2)	(3)	(4)
							Self-esteem	.04	—	—	—
							Depressive symptoms	.08	—	—	—
							Eating psychopathology	.06	—	—	—
Smith et al. (2018)†	162 male adolescent soccer players	Sport	HF-MPS	SOP	SPP	-.03	Depressive symptoms (time 1)	**-.20**	**.27**	**-.20**	**.27**
							BO: Reduced accomplishment (time 1)	**-.25**	**.27**	**-.25**	**.27**
							BO: Exhaustion (time 1)	**-.32**	.24	**-.32**	**.24**
							BO: Devaluation (time 1)	**-.40**	.16	**-.40**	**.16**
							Depressive symptoms (time 2)	**-.23**	**.27**	**-.23**	**.27**
							BO: Reduced accomplishment (time 2)	-.16	.16	**-.16**	**.16**
							BO: Exhaustion (time 2)	**-.20**	**.27**	**-.20**	**.27**
							BO: Devaluation (time 2)	-.18	**.27**	**-.18**	**.27**
Somasundaram & Burgess (2018)	478 female students and athletes	Sport	F-MPS-b	PST	CM	.39	Body dissatisfaction	.09	**.30**	-.03	**.29**
							Eating attitudes	**.14**	**.30**	.03	**.27**
							Hope of success	**.28**	.18	.22	.02
Stoeber & Becker (2008)	74 female soccer players	Sport	MIPS	SP	NRI	.58	Fear of failure	-.07	.16	-.20	**.25**
							Success internal attributions	**.21**	-.07	**.31**	**-.24**
							Success external attributions	.14	**.23**	.01	.18
							Failure internal attributions	-.14	.07	-.22	.19
							Failure external attributions	-.04	**-.20**	.10	-.22
							Self-serving attributions	.05	**-.24**	.24	**-.33**

Study	Sample	Domain	Measure				Variable				
Stoeber et al. (2007)	115 university athletes (54% females)	Sport	MIPS	SP	NRI	.63	Competitive trait cognitive anxiety	**.20**	**.54**	-.21	.54
							Competitive trait somatic anxiety	.11	**.42**	-.22	**.45**
							Competitive trait self-confidence	.15	**-.26**	**.42**	**-.46**
	74 female soccer players	Sport	MIPS	SP	NRI	.58	Competitive trait cognitive anxiety	.20	**.67**	**-.31**	**.69**
							Competitive trait somatic anxiety	.17	**.43**	-.11	**.41**
							Competitive trait self-confidence	-.03	**-.28**	.17	**-.32**
	204 high school athletes (36% females)	Sport	MIPS	SP	NRI	.35	Competitive trait cognitive anxiety	.03	**.57**	**-.22**	**.60**
							Competitive trait somatic anxiety	.04	**.54**	**-.19**	**.56**
							Competitive trait self-confidence	**.18**	**-.39**	**.37**	**-.49**
	142 university athletes (39% females)	Sport	MIPS	SP	NRI	.56	Competitive trait cognitive anxiety	.10	**.46**	**-.21**	**.49**
							Competitive trait somatic anxiety	.07	**.31**	-.13	**.33**
							Competitive trait self-confidence	.02	**-.34**	**.27**	**-.42**
Stoeber et al. (2008)	204 high school athletes (36% females)	Sport	MIPS	SP	NRI	.35	Mastery goal	**.16**	-.09	**.21**	**-.16**
							Performance approach	**.19**	**.25**	.11	.20
							Performance avoidance	.02	**.39**	-.14	**.41**

Study	Sample	Domain	Measure			r	Variable				
		Sport	MIPS	SP	NRI	**.41**	Mastery goal	**.32**	-.04	**.37**	**-.20**
							Performance approach goal	**.28**	**.26**	**.20**	**.17**
							Performance avoidance goal	.13	**.37**	-.03	**.35**
	147 sport science undergraduates (39% females)	Sport	MIPS	SP	NRI	**.56**	Mastery approach goal	**.49**	**.23**	**.45**	-.06
							Mastery avoidance goal	**.21**	**.42**	-.03	**.37**
							Performance approach goal	**.35**	**.35**	**.20**	**.20**
							Performance avoidance goal	.10	**.22**	-.03	**.20**
		Sport	MIPS	SP	NRI	**.53**	Mastery approach goal	**.50**	**.29**	**.43**	.03
							Mastery avoidance goal	.06	**.27**	-.10	**.28**
							Performance approach goal	**.34**	**.37**	**.18**	**.24**
							Performance avoidance goal	.12	.15	.05	.10
Stoeber, Stoll et al. (2009)	138 male junior ice hockey players	Sport	MIPS	SP	NRI	**.49**	Mastery approach goal	**.49**	**.21**	**.45**	-.04
							Performance avoidance goal	**.47**	**.44**	**.32**	**.27**
							Mastery avoidance goal	**.30**	**.48**	.08	**.40**
							Performance avoidance goal	**.23**	**.37**	.06	**.30**
			S-MPS	PST	CM	**.41**	Mastery approach goal	**.40**	**.27**	**.33**	.13
							Performance avoidance goal	**.53**	**.48**	**.42**	**.34**
							Mastery avoidance goal	**.32**	**.52**	.14	**.45**
							Performance avoidance goal	**.26**	**.30**	.16	**.22**
Stoeber, Uphill, et al. (2009)	112 adult triathletes (22% females)	Sport	S-MPS	PST	CM	**.59**	Season best performance: Swimming	**.39**	.16	**.37**	-.09

321 adult triathletes (17% females)	Sport	S-MPS	PST	CM
Season best performance: Cycling	.23	.17	.16	.04
Season best performance: Running	.22	.23	.11	.13
Performance approach goal	.53	.49	.34	.26
Performance avoidance goal	.12	.47	-.22	.50
Mastery approach goal	.38	.13	.38	-.13
Mastery avoidance goal	.24	.46	-.04	.41
Race performance	.43	.18	.41	-.10
Season best performance: Swimming	.26	.00	.34	-.22
Season best performance: Cycling	.18	.04	.20	-.10
Season best performance: Running	.25	.08	.26	-.11
Personal best performance: Swimming	.21	-.01	.28	-.19
Personal best performance: Cycling	.20	.08	.19	-.06
Personal best performance: Running	.20	.09	.19	-.05
Performance approach goal	.61	.52	.42	.21
Performance avoidance goal	.17	.30	-.03	.25
Mastery approach goal	.47	.30	.38	.00
Mastery avoidance goal	.35	.51	.04	.40
Performance goal: Total time	.20	.04	.23	-.12
Performance goal: Expectancy	.13	-.09	.25	-.23

CM: .64

Study	Sample	Domain	Scale	Type	Stat	Variable				
Stornæs et al. (2019)	832 students and students from elite sports schools (53% females)	Sport	F-MPS	PST	CM .58	Outcome goal: Rank	.43	.18	.42	-.14
						Outcome goal: Expectancy	-.11	-.24	.06	-.22
						Race performance	.28	.05	.32	-.18
						Anxiety	.25	.50	-.06	.45
Stoll et al. (2008)	122 sport science undergraduates (53% females)	Sport	MIPS	SP	NRI .30	Depressive symptoms	.20	.48	-.11	.46
						Weight concern	.12	.35	-.11	.35
						Resilience	.08	-.25	.29	-.37
						Self-worth	-.14	.43	-.53	.63
						Average increment in points per series	.00	-.15	.05	-.16
						Points in basketball task (series 1)	.21	.02	.21	-.05
						Points in basketball task (series 2)	.21	.06	.20	.00
						Points in basketball task (series 3)	.13	-.04	.15	-.08
						Points in basketball task (series 4)	.24	-.04	.26	-.12
						Total points in basketball task	.25	.11	.23	.04
Taranis & Meyer (2010)	97 female adult exercisers	Exercise	F-MPS	PST	— —	CE: Avoidance and rule driven behaviour	.27	—	—	—
						CE: Weight control exercise	.05	—	—	—
						CE: Mood improvement	.07	—	—	—

Study	Sample	Domain	Measure			r
Tashman et al. (2010)	177 adult coaches (36% females)	Sport	PI	SE	CM	.46
Thienot et al. (2014)	343 adult and junior athletes (48% females)	Sport	HF-MPS-b F-MPS-b	PS+	PC+	.33
Vaarstra et al. (2018)	216 adolescent soccer players (75% females)	Sport	S-MPS-2	PST	CM	.35
Vallance et al. (2006)	227 male junior ice hockey players	Sport	S-MPS	PST	CM	.28

Variable				
CE: Lack of exercise enjoyment	.11	—	—	—
CE: Exercise rigidity	.17	—	—	—
BO: Exhaustion	.28	.45	.09	.38
BO: Depersonalisation	.24	.48	.02	.43
BO: Personal accomplishment	.03	-.29	.19	-.34
Perceived stress	.15	.17	.08	.12
Mindfulness: Awareness	.33	-.03	.36	-.16
Mindfulness: Non-judgemental	-.21	-.33	-.11	-.28
Mindfulness: Refocusing	.11	-.24	.21	-.29
Worry	.12	.46	-.04	.45
Concentration disruption	-.01	.46	-.19	.49
Dispositional flow	.17	-.19	.25	-.26
Mindful attention and awareness	-.05	-.51	.15	-.52
Rumination	-.01	.07	-.04	.08
Perceived social loafing of teammates	.23	.06	.22	-.02
Social loafing acceptability	-.15	.03	-.17	.09
Trait anger: Angry reaction	.21	.35	.12	.31

Study	Sample	Setting	Measure	Subscale		Outcome variable				
Van Dyke et al. (2021)	224 female university gymnasts	Sport	S-MPS-2	PST	CM .47	Trait anger: Angry temperament	.08	.22	.02	.21
						Present moment attention	.28	-.14	.40	-.32
						Awareness	.16	-.15	.26	-.26
						Acceptance	.01	-.42	.26	-.48
Vink & Raudsepp (2018)	172 adolescent athletes (45% females)	Sport	S-MPS-2 MIPS	PS+	—	Autonomous motivation (time 1)	.49	—	—	—
						Autonomous motivation (time 2)	.42	—	—	—
						Sport-specific practice/activities (time 1)	.31	—	—	—
						Sport-specific practice/activities (times 2)	.28	—	—	—
Vink & Raudsepp (2020)†	188 adolescent athletes (60% females)	Sport	S-MPS-2	PST	PC+ .51	Quantity of sport specific practice (time 1)	.39	-.09	.51	-.36
						Quantity of sport specific practice (time 2)	.34	-.05	.43	-.28
						Quantity of sport specific practice (time 3)	.31	.06	.33	-.12
						Quality of sport specific practice (times 1)	.40	.04	.44	-.21
						Quality of sport specific practice (times 2)	.35	-.07	.45	-.31
						Quality of sport specific practice (times 3)	.33	-.04	.41	-.26
Walerianczyk & Stolarski (2021)	332 adult runners (43% females)	Sport	PSQ	PS	PC .19	Race performance	.42	.20	.40	.13
						Personal best performance	.29	.05	.29	-.01

Study	Sample	Domain	Measure			Outcome	(1)	(2)	(3)	(4)
Waleriańczyk, Stolarski & Matthews (2022)	188 adult runners (46% females)	Sport	PSQ	PS	PC .11	Anticipate performance	**.43**	.12	**.42**	.04
						Intellect	.15	**-.30**	**.22**	**-.34**
						Extraversion	.09	**-.20**	**.13**	**-.22**
						Agreeableness	-.09	**-.39**	-.02	**-.38**
						Emotional stability	-.18	**-.49**	-.10	**-.47**
						Conscientiousness	**.25**	-.08	**.27**	-.13
						Energetic arousal	**.23**	**-.22**	**.26**	**-.25**
						Tense arousal	-.10	**.33**	-.15	**.34**
						Hedonic tone	.02	**-.30**	.06	**-.30**
						Personal best performance	**.24**	**.17**	**.23**	**.15**
						Anticipated performance	**.32**	.14	**.31**	.11
						Race performance	**.32**	.12	.31	.09
						Anticipated/actual performance	-.05	-.04	-.05	-.03
Waleriańczyk, Hill, & Matthews (2022)	401 adult athletes (50% females)	Sport	S-MPS-2	PST	CM **.51**	Absorption	**.33**	**.12**	**.31**	-.06
						Dedication	**.34**	-.08	**.44**	**-.31**
						Vigor	**.40**	.01	**.46**	**-.25**
						BO: Reduced accomplishment	**-.14**	**.23**	**-.31**	**.35**
						BO: Exhaustion	.06	**.34**	**-.14**	**.36**
						BO: Devaluation	-.02	**.21**	**-.15**	**.26**
		Sport	PPS-S	SOP	SPP .56	Absorption	**.33**	.08	**.35**	**-.13**

Wang et al. (2020)	243 adult athletes (47% females)	Sport	S-MPS-2	PS+	PC+	.11			
			Dedication				**.22**	-.03	**.29**	**-.19**
			Vigor				**.25**	.04	**.27**	**-.12**
			BO: Reduced accomplishment				-.01	**.16**	**-.12**	**.20**
			BO: Exhaustion				**.13**	**.33**	-.07	**.31**
			BO: Devaluation				.05	**.24**	**-.10**	**.26**
			Autonomous motivation				**.52**	**-.12**	**.54**	**-.21**
			Controlled motivation				-.10	**.64**	**-.22**	**.66**
			Attitudes toward doping				**-.54**	**.51**	**-.70**	**.68**

Note.; Intru. = Instrument, CAPS = Child and Adolescent Perfectionism Scale (Flett et al., 2001), HF-MPS = Multidimensional Perfectionism Scale (Hewitt & Flett, 1991), HF-MPS-b = Brief version of Multidimensional Perfectionism Scales (Cox, Enns, & Clara, 2002 or Burgess, Frost, & DiBartolo, 2016), APS-R = Almost Perfect Scale-Revised (Slaney et al., 2001), F-MPS = Multidimensional Perfectionism Scale (Frost et al., 1990); FMPS-b = Brief version of Multi-dimensional Perfectionism Scale (Cox et al., 2002); S-MPS Sport Multidimensional Perfectionism Scale for Sport (Anshel & Eom, 2003); S-MPS-2 Sport Multidimensional Perfectionism Scale 2 (Gotwals et al., 2010); AE-MPS = Multiple Perfectionism Scale for Sport (Anshel & Eom, 2003); MIPS = Multidimensional Inventory of Perfectionism in Sport (Stoeber, Otto, & Stoll, 2006); PI = Perfectionism Inventory (R. W. Hill et al., 2004); CPI = Chinese Perfectionism Inventory (Cheng & Hardy, 2016); PSQ = Perfectionism in Sport Questionnaire (Waleriańczyk & Stolarski, 2016); SOP = self-oriented perfectionism, HS = High standards, SP = Striving for perfection, PST = Personal standards, SE = Striving for excellence; PS+ = A composite of multiple subscales indicative of perfectionistic strivings; SPP = Socially prescribed perfectionism, D = Discrepancy, CM = Concern over mistakes, DA = Doubts about action, NRI = Negative reactions to imperfection; PS/O = subscale that includes both personal standards and organisation; PS = single subscale of perfectionistic strivings from PSQ; PC = single subscale of perfectionistic concerns from PSQ; PS+ = a composite of multiple subscales indicative of perfectionistic strivings; PC+ = a composite of multiple subscales indicative of perfectionistic concerns; CP = A combination of subscales from labelled Conscientious Perfectionism derived from subscales of Perfectionism Inventory; SP = A combination of subscales from labelled Self-Evaluative Perfectionism derived from subscales of Perfectionism Inventory; BO = Burnout; ED = Exercise dependence, FOF = Fear of failure; CE = Compulsive exercise; MT = Mental toughness; [a] = Sub-facets also available in article; r = bivariate correlation coefficient; pr = partial correlation coefficient. † = correlations presented are for perfectionism scores measured at time one and/or pre-intervention. ‡ = Spearman's rank correlations. Bold = p <.05

with failure/evaluation worry and a small negative relationship with optimism (Dunn et al., 2020), medium-to-large positive relationships with the dark triad (González-Hernández et al., 2021), and small negative relationships with engagement (Jowett et al., 2021). Residual perfectionistic concerns displayed a more maladaptive profile with some variables (e.g. small-to-medium negative relationships with engagement), but also a more adaptive profile with others (e.g. small-to-medium relationships with the dark triad).

New research also suggests similar patterns for perfectionistic strivings and perfectionistic concerns in relation to social interactions with coaches and parents. Unpartialled and residual perfectionistic strivings shared small positive correlations with the coach-athlete relationship (Martin et al., 2021) and parental conditional regard (Curran, 2018). By contrast, unpartialled and residual perfectionistic concerns shared non-significant correlations with the coach-athlete relationship, and large positive relationships with parental conditional regard (Curran, 2018). The picture for interactions with peers is less consistent. In the study by Grugan et al. (2019), perfectionistic strivings (unpartialled and residual) shared non-significant relationships with angry reactions towards teammates as well as antisocial behaviour towards teammates and opponents. By contrast, perfectionistic concerns (unpartialled and residual) shared small positive relationships with these negative peer interactions. Conversely, Mallinson-Howard et al. (2019) found that perfectionistic strivings and perfectionistic concerns, when unpartialled, shared medium positive relationships with antisocial behaviour toward teammates and opponents, and that residual perfectionistic strivings and perfectionistic concerns shared small positive relationships with antisocial behaviour.

More research has begun to emerge examining the relationship between perfectionism and performance. Research findings appear relatively consistent. With regard to perceived performance, perfectionistic strivings was typically positively related to perceived performance and perfectionistic concerns was unrelated (e.g. Haraldsen, et al., 2020), or was negatively related (e.g. Květon et al., 2021), to perceived performance. With regard to actual performance, a similar pattern is evident. Perfectionistic strivings were typically positively related to actual performance whereas perfectionistic concerns was typically negatively related or unrelated to actual performance. This pattern was evident for golf putting (Lizmore et al., 2019), basketball free throws (Madigan et al., 2018), and a range of physical fitness testing (Mallinson-Howard et al., 2021).

In summary, based on the findings of previous reviews and our new review, we see some consensus for the independent effects of perfectionistic concerns and perfectionistic strivings. Perfectionistic concerns are typically problematic as they demonstrate inverse relationships with a range of adaptive characteristics (e.g. positive affect, self-esteem, and social support) and positive relationships with a range of maladaptive characteristics (e.g. negative affect, fear of failure, and avoidant coping) in sport, dance and exercise. When perfectionistic concerns are partialled from perfectionistic strivings, residual perfectionistic concerns do not appear to be discernibly different in terms of their effects. By contrast, perfectionistic strivings are more ambiguous. Specifically, perfectionistic strivings demonstrate positive relationships with both adaptive (e.g. positive affect, task orientation, and self-confidence) and maladaptive characteristics (e.g. negative affect, ego orientation, and self-blame) in sport, dance and exercise. Some of this ambiguity is explained by the positive correlation between perfectionistic strivings and perfectionistic concerns. That is, when perfectionistic strivings are partialled from perfectionistic concerns, residual perfectionistic strivings can demonstrate positive relationships with adaptive characteristics (e.g. hope for success, mastery-approach goals, and social support) and non–significant or inverse relationships with maladaptive characteristics (e.g. anxiety, fear of failure, and negative affect).

The Case for Total Unique Effects and Relative Weights

A shortcoming of previous reviews in this area, including our own, is that they fail to resolve the tug of war between perfectionistic strivings and perfectionistic concerns. On one hand, we have perfectionistic concerns pulling towards more problematic outcomes and, on the other hand, we have perfectionistic strivings pulling towards less problematic outcomes and some desirable outcomes such as better athletic performance. For many researchers and practitioners this is an unhelpful state of affairs when seeking to advise, educate, and inform others about perfectionism. It is also unnecessary because the partialling approaches described in this chapter can be used to determine the overall effects of perfectionism. That is, they can be used to understand whether athletes, dancers, and exercisers are typically better or worse off because of perfectionism depending on the criterion variable being measured. This is achieved by determining the overall effect of perfectionism and weighing the relative contributions of perfectionistic strivings and perfectionistic concerns to that effect.

Creating total perfectionism scores is not new. Indeed, in the first study of perfectionism in sport, Frost and Henderson (1991) proposed that a total perfectionism score could be calculated as the sum of the subscales included on his multidimensional perfectionism instrument. However, simply adding subscales together provides us with little means to account for the different and unique effects of each dimension. Stoeber et al. (2020) recently attempted to address this shortcoming by calculating a *combined effect* of perfectionistic strivings and concerns. To do so, they adapted the regression equations from the 2 × 2 model of perfectionism (see Chapter 6 in this book) so to compare the effects of a non–perfectionism subtype of perfectionism (low in both perfectionistic strivings and perfectionistic concerns) with a mixed perfectionism subtype (high in both perfectionistic strivings and perfectionistic concerns). The combined effect approach provides a useful way for researchers to assess differences in outcomes between two important subtypes and was the first to recognize the usefulness of deriving an overall effect of perfectionism.

With Stoeber et al.'s (2020) combined effects approach as impetus, Hill et al. (2021) proposed the idea of a *total unique effect* (TUE) that could also be used to determine if perfectionism is, overall, adaptive, maladaptive, or neutral. Unlike, the combined effect approach, the total unique effect does not rely on a "pick-a-point" approach (viz. high versus low scores) or comparison of subtypes. Rather, it is based on summing the unique effects of perfectionistic strivings and perfectionistic concerns to derive a total effect. TUE is calculated by summing the two standardized residual regression coefficients (TUE = βPS + βPC). These are partialled effects that are very similar to the semi-partial correlations introduced earlier. By adding the effects together, TUE is interpreted as the change in the criterion variable following a one standard deviation increase in both perfectionistic strivings and perfectionistic concerns.

As should be evident, TUE is determined by the strength and the direction of the effects of perfectionistic strivings and perfectionistic concerns. This means that when perfectionistic strivings and perfectionistic concerns pull equally in opposing directions in relation to a given outcome, the TUE will signal perfectionism as neutral. When the pull of perfectionistic concerns is stronger (or in cases where perfectionistic strivings and perfectionistic concerns pull in the same direction for an undesirable outcome), the TUE will signal perfectionism as, overall, maladaptive. When the pull of perfectionistic strivings is stronger, the TUE will typically signal that perfectionism is, overall, adaptive (again depending on the criterion variable, though of course). We can test the significance of the TUE by calculating its standard error (SE) and 95% confidence intervals. A computational example for how to calculate TUE is provided in Hill et al. (2021). Code for R is also available (Hill, 2022a), as is a more user-friendly web-based application (Hill, 2022b).

Once TUE is calculated, the contribution of residual perfectionistic strivings and residual perfectionistic concerns to the overall effects is determined by calculating their relative weights. By calculating relative weights, we can assess the percentage of variance in the criterion variable explained by residual perfectionistic strivings or residual perfectionistic concerns. The relative weight can be considered an effect size for residual perfectionistic strivings and residual perfectionistic concerns in context of the TUE. As such, the relative weights also tell us which dimension is more important for a particular criterion variable. So far, the use of TUE has been illustrated using research outside of sport, dance, and exercise (Hill et al., 2021). To show what insight can be gained from applying it to research in these domains, we have illustrated the approach for some of the effects observed in Hill et al.'s (2018) meta-analysis. The results are displayed in Table 4.2.

In applying the TUE to the meta-analytical data in sport we can draw conclusions regarding the likely overall effects of perfectionism as an athlete becomes more perfectionistic. Starting with motivation, for task orientation, the non-significant TUE suggests that perfectionism is, overall, neutral. This might be surprising as there is a clear positive effect for perfectionistic strivings but as perfectionistic concerns is pulling in the opposing direction to a similar degree there is no "net gain" for perfectionistic athletes in regards to motivation for this goal orientation. For ego orientation, TUE suggests that, overall,

Table 4.2 Meta-analytical relationships, total unique effects and relative weights

Criterion variables	k	N	$r_{(PS\ PC)}$	$r_{(PS\ Y)}$	$r_{(PC\ Y)}$	β_{PS}	β_{PC}	TUE [95% CI]	RW_{PS} (%)	RW_{PC} (%)	R^2_{MODEL}
Task orientation	8	2877	.36	.15	-.07	.20	-.14	.06 [-.00,.12]	.03 (71.91)	.01 (28.09)	.04
Ego orientation	8	2877	.36	.22	.22	.16	.16	.32 [.27,.38]	.04 (50.00)	.04 (50.00)	.07
Self-confidence	9	1300	.47	.16	-.24	.35	-.41	-.05 [-.15,.04]	.06 (39.55)	.09 (60.45)	.15
Depressive symptoms	5	963	.35	.17	.42	.03	.41	.44 [.34,.53]	.01 (8.33)	.16 (91.67)	.18
Athletic performance	6	684	.45	.23	.06	.25	-.06	.20 [.07,.33]	.05 (94.60)	.00 (5.40)	.06

Note. k = Number of effect sizes. N = Number of participants; DV = Dependent variable. β = Standardized regression coefficient. TUE = Total unique effect (βPS + βPC; units of standard deviations of DV per standard deviation of PS + PC). RW = Relative weight. PS = Perfectionistic strivings. PC = Perfectionistic concerns. Rounding to two decimal places accounts for any differences between βPS + βPC and TUE. If 95% CI (confidence intervals) do not include zero, the TUE is statistically significant ($p < .05$). Harmonic mean of sample size and average PS–PC correlation used to calculate effects.

perfectionism is maladaptive. So, as athletes become more perfectionistic, we can expect to deal with the problematic motivation issues that arise from being more ego- oriented (and not task-oriented). In examining the relative weights, we can see that perfectionistic strivings largely accounts for the prediction of task orientation whereas perfectionistic strivings and perfectionistic concerns are equally important in predicting ego orientation.

To consider athlete wellbeing we can use self-confidence and depression as proxies. Like with task orientation, calculation of TUE suggests that there is no net gain of being perfectionistic for self-confidence with increases in perfectionistic strivings and perfectionistic concerns resulting in, overall, a neutral effect. However, based on TUE we can expect athletes to report higher depressive symptoms so in this regard perfectionism is, overall, maladaptive. Indeed, this was the largest total effect we observed in this set of examples. In reviewing the relative weights, we can see a similar contribution to the prediction of self-confidence for the two dimensions of perfectionism but, by some way, perfectionistic concerns accounts for the prediction of depressive symptoms.

The last criterion variable we consider is athletic performance. In this case we see an overall adaptive effect with increases in perfectionism resulting in better athletic performance. There are complexities to this relationship, of course, and we remain unconvinced of the benefits of perfectionism for athlete performance for most people, most of the time. Nonetheless, we have illustrated here that current evidence suggests perfectionism may aid athlete performance, albeit to a small degree. The relative weights in this regard are important, too, as they show, as you would expect, the prediction of performance is almost entirely due to perfectionistic strivings.

Although these TUEs and relative weights are only a small set of examples and are limited to sport, they provide us with important insight into whether, overall, perfectionism is neutral, maladaptive or adaptive. Driven predominantly by perfectionistic strivings, perfectionism appears to offer some small benefit to athletic performance, but at what cost? An overall association with an ego orientation and neutral effects for task orientation and self-confidence alludes to potential motivational difficulties. Furthermore, due predominantly to the pull of perfectionistic concerns, perfectionism is associated with increased risk of maladjustment in the form of depressive symptoms. This is aligned with the TUEs we have seen outside of sport that show maladaptive effects for anxiety, burnout, depression, eating disorders and suicide ideation (Hill et al., 2021). Based on this evidence, we contend that perfectionism is most likely, overall, maladaptive for athletes, dancers, and exercisers.

Concluding Comments

In this chapter we described an independent effects approach to examining the two main dimensions of perfectionism and a new approach that focuses on deriving their overall effect and relative weights. Based on previous reviews and our updated review, we believe there is now sufficient evidence to derive consensus regarding the likely effects of perfectionistic strivings and perfectionistic concerns in sport, dance, and exercise. Because perfectionistic concerns are consistently associated with maladaptive characteristics, we can expect higher levels to undermine motivation and contribute to personal difficulties. Because perfectionistic strivings display a mixed pattern of adaptive and maladaptive characteristics, they are best considered ambiguous. In addition, when examining residual perfectionistic strivings, they appear more adaptive in relation to well-being, motivation, and performance. Beyond these conclusions, if we wish to determine whether, overall, perfectionism is adaptive, maladaptive, or neutral, we need to add the contributions of perfectionistic strivings and perfectionistic concerns to calculate a total effect. Doing so suggests that, overall, perfectionism may aid performance to a small degree but to a much larger degree is likely to be maladaptive for athletes due to the contribution of perfectionistic concerns. Further research is required to establish whether these total effects and conclusions are also evident in dance and exercise, as well as for a broader range of psychological outcomes.

References

Anshel, M. H., & Seipel, S. J. (2007). Relationship between perfectionism and social physique anxiety among male and female college student exercisers. *Perceptual and Motor Skills*, 104(3), 913–922. https://doi.org/10.2466/pms.104.3.913-922.

Anshel, M. H., & Eom, H.-J. (2003). Exploring the Dimensions of Perfectionism in Sport. *International Journal of Sport Psychology*, 34(3), 255–271.

Appleton, P. R., Hall, H. K., & Hill, A. P. (2009). Relations between multidimensional perfectionism and burnout in junior-elite male athletes. *Psychology of Sport and Exercise*, 10(4), 457–465. https://doi.org/10.1016/j.psychsport.2008.12.006.

Appleton, P. R., Hall, H. K., & Hill, A. P. (2010). Family patterns of perfectionism: An examination of elite junior athletes and their parents. *Psychology of Sport and Exercise*, 11(5), 363–371. https://doi.org/10.1016/j.psychsport.2010.04.005.

Appleton, P. R., & Hill, A. P. (2012). Perfectionism and athlete burnout in junior elite athletes: The mediating role of motivation regulations. *Journal of Clinical Sport Psychology*, 6(2), 129–145. https://doi.org/10.1123/jcsp.6.2.129.

Arcelus, J., Garcia-Dantas, A., Sánchez-Martin, M., & Del Rio, C. (2015). Influence of perfectionism on variables associated to eating disorders in dance students. *Revista de Psicología Del Deporte*, 24(2), 297–303. http://hdl.handle.net/11441/59679.

Aruguete, M. S., Edman, J. L., & Yates, A. (2012). The relationship between anger and other correlates of eating disorders in women. *North American Journal of Psychology*, 14(1), 139–148.

Atienza, F., Appleton, P., Hall, H. K., Castillo Fernández, I., & Balaguer Solá, I. (2020). Validation of the Spanish version of multidimensional inventory of perfectionism in young athletes. *Cuadernos de Psicología Del Deporte*, 20(1), 118–129. https://doi.org/10.6018/cpd.397951.

Bae, M., Yoon, J., Kang, H., & Kim, T. (2017). Influences of perfectionism and motivational climate on attitudes towards doping among Korean national athletes: a cross sectional study. *Substance Abuse Treatment, Prevention, and Policy*, 12(1). https://doi.org/10.1186/s13011-017-0138-x.

Barcza-Renner, K., Eklund, R. C., Morin, A. J. S., & Habeeb, C. M. (2016). Controlling coaching behaviors and athlete burnout: Investigating the mediating roles of perfectionism and motivation. *Journal of Sport and Exercise Psychology*, 38(1), 30–44. https://doi.org/10.1123/jsep.2015-0059.

Blažev, M., Blažev, D., Lauri Korajlija, A., & Blažev, V. (2020). Predictors of social physique anxiety among recreational bodybuilders. *Psihologijske Teme*, 29(3), 507–524. https://doi.org/10.31820/pt.29.3.2.

Brannan, M., Petrie, T. A., Greenleaf, C., Reel, J., & Carter, J. (2009). The relationship between body dissatisfaction and bulimic symptoms in female collegiate athletes. *Journal of Clinical Sport Psychology*, 3(2), 103–126. https://doi.org/10.1123/jcsp.3.2.103.

Burgess, A. M., Frost, R. O., & DiBartolo, P. M. (2016). Development and validation of the frost multidimensional perfectionism scale–brief. *Journal of Psychoeducational Assessment*, 34(7), 620–633. https://doi.org/10.1177/07342829166513

Carr, S., & Wyon, M. (2003). The impact of motivational climate on dance students' achievement goals, trait anxiety, and perfectionism. *Journal of Dance Medicine & Science*, 7(4), 105–114.

Carter, M. M., & Weissbrod, C. S. (2011). Gender differences in the relationship between competitiveness and adjustment among athletically identified college students. *Psychology*, 02(02), 85–90. https://doi.org/10.4236/psych.2011.22014.

Chen, L. H., Kee, Y. H., & Tsai, Y. M (2009). An examination of the dual model of perfectionism and adolescent athlete burnout: A short-term longitudinal research. *Social Indicators Research*, 91, 189–201.

Chen, L. H., & Kee, Y. H. (2008). Gratitude and adolescent athletes' well-being. *Social Indicators Research*, 89(2), 361–373. https://doi.org/10.1007/s11205-008-9237-4.

Chen, L. H., Kee, Y. H., & Tsai, Y.-M. (2008). An examination of the dual model of perfectionism and adolescent athlete burnout: A short-term longitudinal research. *Social Indicators Research*, 91(2), 189–201. https://doi.org/10.1007/s11205-008-9277-9.

Cheng, W.-N. K., & Hardy, L. (2016). Three-dimensional model of performance anxiety: Tests of the adaptive potential of the regulatory dimension of anxiety. *Psychology of Sport and Exercise*, 22, 255–263. https://doi.org/10.1016/j.psychsport.2015.07.006.

Chou, C.-C., Huang, M.-Y., Lin, T.-W., Lu, F. J.-H., Chiu, Y.-H., & Chen, J.-F. (2019). Moderating effect of self-esteem on the relationship between perfectionism and creative thinking among collegiate dancers. *Creativity Research Journal*, 31(2), 188–197. https://doi.org/10.1080/10400419.2019.1606620.

Correia, M., Rosado, A., & Serpa, S. (2017). Psychometric properties of the Portuguese version of the Frost Multidimensional Perfectionism Scale. *International Journal of Psychological Research*, 10(1), 8–17. https://doi.org/https://10.21500/20112084.2109.

Costa, S., Coppolino, P., & Oliva, P. (2015). Exercise dependence and maladaptive perfectionism: The mediating role of basic psychological needs. *International Journal of Mental Health and Addiction*, 14(3), 241–256. https://doi.org/10.1007/s11469-015-9586-6.

Costa, S., Hausenblas, H. A., Oliva, P., Cuzzocrea, F., & Larcan, R. (2016). Maladaptive perfectionism as mediator among psychological control, eating disorders, and exercise dependence symptoms in habitual exerciser. *Journal of Behavioral Addictions*, 5(1), 77–89. https://doi.org/10.1556/2006.5.2016.004.

Cox, B. J., Enns, M. W., & Clara, I. P. (2002). The multidimensional structure of perfectionism in clinically distressed and college student samples. *Psychological assessment*, 14(3), 365. https://doi.org/10.1037/1040-3590.14.3.365

Crocker, P. R., Gaudreau, P., Mosewich, A. D., & Kljajic, K. (2014). Perfectionism and the stress process in intercollegiate athletes: Examining the 2 × 2 model of perfectionism in sport competition. *International Journal of Sport Psychology*, 45(4), 325–348. https://doi.org/doi:10.7352/IJSP 2014.45.325.

Cumming, J., & Duda, J. L. (2012). Profiles of perfectionism, body-related concerns, and indicators of psychological health in vocational dance students: An investigation of the 2 × 2 model of perfectionism. *Psychology of Sport and Exercise*, 13(6), 729–738. https://doi.org/10.1016/j.psychsport.2012.05.004.

Curran, T. (2018). Parental conditional regard and the development of perfectionism in adolescent athletes: The mediating role of competence contingent self-worth. *Sport, Exercise, and Performance Psychology*, 7(3), 284–296. https://doi.org/10.1037/spy0000126.

Curran, T., & Hill, A. P. (2018). A test of perfectionistic vulnerability following competitive failure among college athletes. *Journal of Sport and Exercise Psychology*, 40(5), 269–279. https://doi.org/10.1123/jsep.2018-0059.

Curran, T., Hill, A. P., Jowett, G. E., & Mallinson, S. H. (2014). The relationship between multidimensional perfectionism and passion in junior athletes. *International Journal of Sport Psychology*, 45(4), 369–384. https://doi.org/doi: 10.7352/IJSP 2014.45.369.

De Muynck, G.-J., Vansteenkiste, M., Morbée, S., Vandenkerckhove, B., Vande Broek, G., & Soenens, B. (2021). The interplay between normative feedback and self-critical perfectionism in predicting competitive tennis players' competence, tension, and enjoyment: An experimental study. *Sport, Exercise, and Performance Psychology*, 10(3), 345–358. https://doi.org/10.1037/spy0000234.

Deck, S., Roberts, R., & Hall, C. (2021). The 2 × 2 model of perfectionism and exercise dependence. *Personality and Individual Differences*, 180, 111001. https://doi.org/10.1016/j.paid.2021.111001.

Deck, S., Roberts, R., Hall, C., & Kouali, D. (2021). Perfectionism and social physique anxiety using the 2×2 model. *International Journal of Sport and Exercise Psychology*, 19 (5), 895–905. https://doi.org/10.1080/1612197x.2020.1826998.

Donachie, T. C., Hill, A. P., & Hall, H. K. (2018). The relationship between multidimensional perfectionism and pre-competition emotions of youth footballers. *Psychology of Sport and Exercise*, 37, 33–42. https://doi.org/10.1016/j.psychsport.2018.04.002.

Donachie, T. C., Hill, A. P., & Madigan, D. J. (2019). Perfectionism and precompetition emotions in youth footballers: A three-wave longitudinal test of the mediating role of perfectionistic cognitions. *Journal of Sport and Exercise Psychology*, 41(5), 309–319. https://doi.org/10.1123/jsep.2018-0317.

Dunn, J. G. H., Cormier, D., Kono, S., Causgrove Dunn, J., & Rumbold, J. (2021). Perfectionism and grit in competitive sport. *Journal of Sport Behavior*, 44(2), 199–223.

Dunn, J. G. H., Craft, J. M., Causgrove Dunn, J., & Gotwals, J. K. (2011). Comparing a domain-specific and global measure of perfectionism in competitive female figure skaters. *Journal of Sport Behavior*, 34(1), 25–46.

Dunn, J. G. H., Dunn, J. C., & Syrotuik, D. G. (2002). Relationship between multidimensional perfectionism and goal orientations in sport. *Journal of Sport and Exercise Psychology*, 24(4), 376–395. https://doi.org/10.1123/jsep.24.4.376.

Dunn, J. G. H., Gotwals, J. K., Dunn, J. C., & Lizmore, M. R. (2020). Perfectionism, pre-competitive worry, and optimism in high-performance youth athletes. *International Journal of Sport and Exercise Psychology*, 18(6), 749–763. https://doi.org/10.1080/1612197x.2019.1577900.

Dunn, J. G. H., Gotwals, J. K., Dunn, J. C., & Syrotuik, D. G. (2006). Examining the relationship between perfectionism and trait anger in competitive sport. *International Journal of Sport and Exercise Psychology*, 4(1), 7–24. https://doi.org/10.1080/1612197x.2006.9671781.

Elison, J., & Partridge, J. A. (2012). Relationships between shame-coping, fear of failure, and perfectionism in college athletes. *Journal of Sport Behavior*, 35(1), 19–39.

Eusanio, J., Thomson, P., & Jaque, S. V. (2014). Perfectionism, shame, and self-concept in dancers: A mediation analysis. *Journal of Dance Medicine & Science*, 18(3), 106–114. https://doi.org/10.12678/1089-313x.18.3.106.

Fawver, B., Cowan, R. L., DeCouto, B., Lohse, K. R., Podlog, L., & Williams, A. M. (2020). Psychological characteristics, sport engagement, and performance in alpine skiers. *Psychology of Sport and Exercise*, 47, 101616. https://doi.org/10.1016/j.psychsport.2019.101616.

Fazlagić, A. R., & Belić, M. (2017). The connection of perfectionism and flow with athletes of a different performance level. *Fizička Kultura*, 71(2), 111–117. https://doi.org/doi:10.5937/fizkul1702117F.

Ferrand, C., Magnan, C., Rouveix, M., & Filaire, E. (2007). Disordered eating, perfectionism and body-esteem of elite synchronized swimmers. *European Journal of Sport Science*, 7(4), 223–230. https://doi.org/10.1080/17461390701722168.

Fleming, D. J. M., Dorsch, T. E., & Dayley, J. C. (2022). The mediating effect of parental warmth on the association of parent pressure and athlete perfectionism in adolescent soccer. *International Journal of Sport and Exercise Psychology*, 1–17. https://doi.org/10.1080/1612197x.2022.2058584.

Flett, G. L., Hewitt, P. I., Boucher, D. J., Davidson, L. A., & Munro, Y. (2000). The Child–Adolescent Perfectionism Scale: Development, validation, and association with adjustment. Unpublished manuscript, Department of Psychology, University of British Columbia, Canada.

Freire, G. L. M., Fiorese, L., Moraes, J. F. V. N. d., Codonhato, R., Oliveira, D. V. de, & Nascimento Junior, J. R. de A. d. (2022a). Do perfectionism traits predict team cohesion and group conflict among youth athletes? *Perceptual and Motor Skills*, 129(3), 003151252210870. https://doi.org/10.1177/00315125221087025.

Freire, G. L. M., Santos, M. M. d., Lima-Junior, D. d., Fortes, L. S. d., Oliveira, D. V. d., & Nascimento Junior, J. R. A. d. (2022b). The influence of perfectionistic traits on goal orientations of young athletes. *Cuadernos de Psicología Del Deporte*, 22(1), 116–123.

Freire, G. L. M., Sousa, V. da C., Alves, J. F. N., Moraes, J. F. V. N. de, Oliveira, D. V. de, & Nascimento Junior, J. R. A. do. (2020). Are the traits of perfectionism associated with pre-competitive anxiety in young athletes? *Cuadernos de Psicología Del Deporte*, 20(2), 37–46. https://doi.org/10.6018/cpd.406031.

Frost, R. O., Heimberg, R. G., Holt, C. S., Mattia, J. I., & Neubauer, A. L. (1993). A comparison of two measures of perfectionism. *Personality and Individual Differences*, 14, 119–126. https://doi.org/10.1016/0191-8869(93)90181-90182.

Frost, R. O., & Henderson, K. J. (1991). Perfectionism and reactions to athletic competition. *Journal of Sport and Exercise Psychology*, 13(4), 323–335. https://doi.org/10.1123/jsep.13.4.323.

Garinger, L. M., Chow, G. M., & Luzzeri, M. (2018). The effect of perceived stress and specialization on the relationship between perfectionism and burnout in collegiate athletes. *Anxiety, Stress, & Coping*, 31(6), 714–727.

Gaudreau, P., & Antl, S. (2008). Athletes' broad dimensions of dispositional perfectionism: Examining changes in life satisfaction and the mediating role of sport-related motivation and coping. *Journal of Sport and Exercise Psychology*, 30(3), 356–382. https://doi.org/10.1123/jsep.30.3.356.

Gaudreau, P., Louvet, B., & Kljajic, K. (2019). The performance trajectory of physical education students differs across subtypes of perfectionism: A piecewise growth curve model of the 2 × 2 model of perfectionism. *Sport, Exercise, and Performance Psychology*, 8(2), 223–237. https://doi.org/10.1037/spy0000138.

Gaudreau, P., & Verner-Filion, J. (2012). Dispositional perfectionism and well-being: A test of the 2 × 2 model of perfectionism in the sport domain. *Sport, Exercise, and Performance Psychology*, 1(1), 29–43. https://doi.org/10.1037/a0025747.

González-Hernández, J., Baños, R., Morquecho-Sánchez, R., Pineda-Espejel, H. A., & Chamorro, J. L. (2021). Perfectionism patterns, dark personality, and exercise addiction trend in high-intensity sports. *International Journal of Mental Health and Addiction*. https://doi.org/10.1007/s11469-021-00595-y.

González-Hernández, J., Capilla Díaz, C., & Gómez-López, M. (2019a). Impulsiveness and cognitive patterns. Understanding the perfectionistic responses in Spanish competitive junior athletes. *Frontiers in Psychology*, 10, 1–8. https://doi.org/10.3389/fpsyg.2019.01605.

González-Hernández, J., Gómez-López, M., Pérez-Turpin, J., Muñoz-Villena, A. J., & Andreu-Cabrera, E. (2019b). Perfectly active teenagers. When does physical exercise help psychological well-being in adolescents? *International Journal of Environmental Research and Public Health*, 16(22), 4525. https://doi.org/10.3390/ijerph16224525.

Gotwals, J. K. (2011). Perfectionism and burnout within intercollegiate sport: A person-oriented approach. *The Sport Psychologist*, 25(4), 489–510. https://doi.org/10.1123/tsp.25.4.489.

Gotwals, J. K., & Dunn, J. G. H. (2009). A multi-method multi-analytic approach to establishing internal construct validity evidence: The Sport Multidimensional Perfectionism Scale 2. *Measurement in Physical Education and Exercise Science*, 13(2), 71–92. https://doi.org/10.1080/10913670902812663.

Gotwals, J. K., Dunn, J. G., Dunn, J. C., & Gamache, V. (2010). Establishing validity evidence for the Sport Multidimensional Perfectionism Scale-2 in intercollegiate sport. *Psychology of Sport and Exercise*, 11(6), 423–432. https://doi.org/10.1016/j.psychsport.2010.04.013

Gotwals, J. K., Dunn, J. G. H., & Wayment, H. A. (2003). An examination of perfectionism and self-esteem in intercollegiate athletes. *Journal of Sport Behavior*, 26(1), 17–38.

Gotwals, J. K., Stoeber, J., Dunn, J. G. H., & Stoll, O. (2012). Are perfectionistic strivings in sport adaptive? A systematic review of confirmatory, contradictory, and mixed evidence. *Canadian Psychology/Psychologie Canadienne*, 53(4), 263–279. https://doi.org/10.1037/a0030288.

Grugan, M. C., Jowett, G. E., Mallinson-Howard, S. H., & Hall, H. K. (2019). The relationships between perfectionism, angry reactions, and antisocial behavior in team sport. *Sport, Exercise, and Performance Psychology*, 9(4), 543–557. https://doi.org/10.1037/spy0000198.

Gucciardi, D. F., Mahoney, J., Jalleh, G., Donovan, R. J., & Parkes, J. (2012). Perfectionistic profiles among elite athletes and differences in their motivational orientations. *Journal of Sport and Exercise Psychology*, 34(2), 159–183. https://doi.org/10.1123/jsep.34.2.159.

Gustafsson, H., Hill, A. P., Stenling, A., & Wagnsson, S. (2016). Profiles of perfectionism, parental climate, and burnout among competitive junior athletes. *Scandinavian Journal of Medicine & Science in Sports*, 26(10), 1256–1264. https://doi.org/10.1111/sms.12553.

Hall, H. K., Hill, A. P., Appleton, P. R., & Kozub, S. A. (2009). The mediating influence of unconditional self-acceptance and labile self-esteem on the relationship between multidimensional perfectionism and exercise dependence. *Psychology of Sport and Exercise*, 10(1), 35–44. https://doi.org/10.1016/j.psychsport.2008.05.003.

Hall, H. K., Kerr, A. W., Kozub, S. A., & Finnie, S. B. (2007). Motivational antecedents of obligatory exercise: The influence of achievement goals and multidimensional perfectionism. *Psychology of Sport and Exercise*, 8(3), 297–316. https://doi.org/10.1016/j.psychsport.2006.04.007.

Hall, H. K., Kerr, A. W., & Matthews, J. (1998). Precompetitive anxiety in sport: The contribution of achievement goals and perfectionism. *Journal of Sport and Exercise Psychology*, 20(2), 194–217. https://doi.org/10.1123/jsep.20.2.194.

Haraldsen, H. M., Halvari, H., Solstad, B. E., Abrahamsen, F. E., & Nordin-Bates, S. M. (2019). The role of perfectionism and controlling conditions in Norwegian elite junior performers' motivational processes. *Frontiers in Psychology*, 10. https://doi.org/10.3389/fpsyg.2019.01366.

Haraldsen, H. M., Solstad, B. E., Ivarsson, A., Halvari, H., & Abrahamsen, F. E. (2020). Change in basic need frustration in relation to perfectionism, anxiety, and performance in elite junior performers. *Scandinavian Journal of Medicine & Science in Sports*, 30 (4), 754–765. https://doi.org/10.1111/sms.13614.

Hardwick, B., Madigan, D. J., Hill, A. P., Kumar, S., & Chan, D. K. C. (2022). Perfectionism and attitudes towards doping in athletes: the mediating role of achievement goal orientations. *International Journal of Sport and Exercise Psychology*, 20(3), 743–756. https://doi.org/https://doi.org/10.1080/1612197X.2021.1891124.

Hewitt, P. L., & Flett, G. L. (1991). Perfectionism in the self and social contexts: Conceptualization, assessment, and association with psychopathology. *Journal of Personality and Social Psychology*, 60, 456–470. https://doi.org/10.1037/0022-3514.60.3.456.

Hill, A. P. (2013). Perfectionism and burnout in junior soccer players: A test of the 2 × 2 model of dispositional perfectionism. *Journal of Sport and Exercise Psychology*, 35(1), 18–29. https://doi.org/10.1123/jsep.35.1.18.

Hill, A. P. (2014). Perfectionistic strivings and the perils of partialling. *International Journal of Sport and Exercise Psychology*, 12(4), 302–315. https://doi.org/https://doi.org/10.1080/1612197X.2014.919602.

Hill, A. P. (2022a). Total unique effect (R code). Software; York St. John University. https://doi.org/10.25421/yorksj.19555054.v1.

Hill, A. P. (2022b). Calculate the total unique effect of perfectionism – app to accompany Hill, Madigan, & Olamaie (2021). https://aphill.shinyapps.io/TUEffect/.

Hill, A. P., & Appleton, P. R. (2011). The predictive ability of the frequency of perfectionistic cognitions, self-oriented perfectionism, and socially prescribed perfectionism in relation to symptoms of burnout in youth rugby players. *Journal of Sports Sciences*, 29(7), 695–703. https://doi.org/https://doi.org/10.1080/02640414.2010.551216.

Hill, A. P., & Curran, T. (2016). Multidimensional perfectionism and burnout. *Personality and Social Psychology Review*, 20(3), 269–288. https://doi.org/10.1177/1088868315596286.

Hill, A. P., & Davis, P. A. (2014). Perfectionism and emotion regulation in coaches: A test of the 2 × 2 model of dispositional perfectionism. *Motivation and Emotion*, 38(5), 715–726. https://doi.org/10.1007/s11031-014-9404-7.

Hill, A. P., Hall, H. K., & Appleton, P. R. (2010). Perfectionism and athlete burnout in junior elite athletes: the mediating role of coping tendencies. *Anxiety, Stress & Coping*, 23(4), 415–430. https://doi.org/10.1080/10615800903330966.

Hill, A. P., Hall, H. K., Appleton, P. R., & Kozub, S. A. (2008). Perfectionism and burnout in junior elite soccer players: The mediating influence of unconditional self-acceptance. *Psychology of Sport and Exercise*, 9(5), 630–644. https://doi.org/10.1016/j.psychsport.2007.09.004.

Hill, A. P., Hall, H. K., Appleton, P. R., & Murray, J. M. (2010). Perfectionism and burnout in canoe polo and kayak slalom athletes: The mediating influence of validation and growth-seeking. *The Sport Psychologist*, 24(1), 16–34. https://doi.org/http s://doi.org/10.1123/tsp.24.1.16.

Hill, R. W., Huelsman, T. J., Furr, R. M., Kibler, J., Vicente, B. B., & Kennedy, C. (2004). A new measure of perfectionism: The Perfectionism Inventory. *Journal of Personality Assessment*, 82(1), 80–91.

Hill, A. P., Madigan, D. J., & Jowett, G. E. (2020). Perfectionism and athlete engagement: A multi-sample test of the 2 × 2 model of perfectionism. *Psychology of Sport and Exercise*, 48, 101664. https://doi.org/https://doi.org/10.1016/j.psychsport.2020. 101664.

Hill, A. P., Madigan, D. J., & Olamaie, M. (2021). Combined effects, total unique effects and relative weights of perfectionism. *Personality and Individual Differences*, 183, 111136. https://doi.org/10.1016/j.paid.2021.111136.

Hill, A. P., Mallinson-Howard, S. H., & Jowett, G. E. (2018). Multidimensional perfectionism in sport: A meta-analytical review. *Sport, Exercise, and Performance Psychology*, 7(3), 235–270. https://doi.org/10.1037/spy0000125.

Hill, A. P., Robson, S. J., & Stamp, G. M. (2015). The predictive ability of perfectionistic traits and self-presentational styles in relation to exercise dependence. *Personality and Individual Differences*, 86, 176–183. https://doi.org/10.1016/j.paid.2015.06.015.

Ho, M. S. H., Appleton, P. R., Cumming, J., & Duda, J. L. (2015). Examining the relationship between perfectionism dimensions and burning out symptoms in deaf and hearing athletes. *Journal of Clinical Sport Psychology*, 9(2), 156–172. https://doi. org/https://doi.org/10.1123/jcsp.2014-0035.

Houltberg, B. J., Wang, K. T., Qi, W., & Nelson, C. S. (2018). Self-narrative profiles of elite athletes and comparisons on psychological well-being. *Research Quarterly for Exercise and Sport*, 89(3), 354–360. https://doi.org/10.1080/02701367.2018.1481919.

Jowett, G. E., Hill, A. P., Curran, T., Hall, H. K., & Clements, L. (2021). Perfectionism, burnout, and engagement in dance: The moderating role of autonomy support. *Sport, Exercise, and Performance Psychology*, 10(1), 133–148. https://doi.org/10.1037/sp y0000232.

Jowett, G. E., Hill, A. P., Forsdyke, D., & Gledhill, A. (2018). Perfectionism and coping with injury in marathon runners: A test of the 2×2 model of perfectionism. *Psychology of Sport and Exercise*, 37, 26–32. https://doi.org/https://doi.org/10.1016/j.psychsp ort.2018.04.003.

Jowett, G. E., Hill, A. P., Hall, H. K., & Curran, T. (2016). Perfectionism, burnout and engagement in youth sport: The mediating role of basic psychological needs. *Psychology of Sport and Exercise*, 24, 18–26. https://doi.org/10.1016/j.psychsport.2016.01.001.

Kaye, M. P., Conroy, D. E., & Fifer, A. M. (2008). Individual differences in incompetence avoidance. *Journal of Sport and Exercise Psychology*, 30(1), 110–132. https://doi. org/10.1123/jsep.30.1.110.

Klund, F., & Sæther, S. A. (2017). Relationships between perfectionism, training load and elite junior football players' self-assessed and coach-assessed skills. *The Sport Journal*, 24.

Krasnow, D., Mainwaring, L., & Kerr, G. (1999). Injury, stress, and perfectionism in young dancers and gymnasts. *Journal of Dance Medicine & Science*, 3(2), 51–58.

Kristiansen, E., Abrahamsen, F. E., & Stensrud, T. (2012). Stress-related breathing problems: An issue for elite swimmers. *Journal of Swimming Research*, 19.

Květon, P., Jelínek, M., & Burešová, I. (2021). The role of perfectionism in predicting athlete burnout, training distress, and sports performance: A short-term and long-term longitudinal perspective. *Journal of Sports Sciences*, 39(17), 1969–1979. https://doi.org/10.1080/02640414.2021.1911415.

Kwon, W., & Cho, S. (2020). Associations among perfectionism, anxiety, and psychological well-being/ill-being in college athletes of South Korea. *International Journal of Applied Sports Sciences*, 32(2), 75–83. https://doi.org/https://doi.org/10.24985/ijass.2020.32.2.75.

Laborde, S., Musculus, L., Kalicinski, M., Klämpfl, M. K., Kinrade, N. P., & Lobinger, B. H. (2015). Reinvestment: Examining convergent, discriminant, and criterion validity using psychometric and behavioral measures. *Personality and Individual Differences*, 78, 77–87. https://doi.org/https://doi.org/10.1016/j.paid.2015.01.020.

Lemyre, P. N., Hall, H. K., & Roberts, G. C. (2008). A social cognitive approach to burnout in elite athletes. *Scandinavian Journal of Medicine & Science in Sports*, 18(2), 221–234. https://doi.org/10.1111/j.1600-0838.2007.00671.x.

Lizmore, M. R., Dunn, J. G. H., & Causgrove Dunn, J. (2016). Reactions to mistakes as a function of perfectionism and situation criticality in curling. *International Journal of Sport Psychology*, 47(1), 81–101.

Lizmore, M. R., Dunn, J. G. H., & Causgrove Dunn, J. (2017). Perfectionistic strivings, perfectionistic concerns, and reactions to poor personal performances among intercollegiate athletes. *Psychology of Sport and Exercise*, 33, 75–84. https://doi.org/10.1016/j.psychsport.2017.07.010.

Lizmore, M. R., Dunn, J. G. H., Causgrove Dunn, J., & Hill, A. P. (2019). Perfectionism and performance following failure in a competitive golf-putting task. *Psychology of Sport and Exercise*, 45, 101582. https://doi.org/10.1016/j.psychsport.2019.101582.

Longbottom, J. L., Grove, J. R., & Dimmock, J. A. (2010). An examination of perfectionism traits and physical activity motivation. *Psychology of Sport and Exercise*, 11(6), 574–581. https://doi.org/10.1016/j.psychsport.2010.06.007.

Longbottom, J. L., Grove, J. R., & Dimmock, J. A. (2012). Trait perfectionism, self-determination, and self-presentation processes in relation to exercise behavior. *Psychology of Sport and Exercise*, 13(2), 224–235. https://doi.org/10.1016/j.psychsport.2011.11.003.

Luszczynska, A., Zarychta, K., Horodyska, K., Liszewska, N., Gancarczyk, A., & Czekierda, K. (2015). Original article functional perfectionism and healthy behaviors: The longitudinal relationships between the dimensions of perfectionism, nutrition behavior, and physical activity moderated by gender. *Current Issues in Personality Psychology*, 3(2), 84–93. https://doi.org/10.5114/cipp.2015.52085.

Lynam, D. R., Hoyle, R. H., & Newman, J. P. (2006). The perils of partialling. *Assessment*, 13(3), 328–341. https://doi.org/10.1177/1073191106290562.

Machida, M., Marie Ward, R., & Vealey, R. S. (2012). Predictors of sources of self-confidence in collegiate athletes. *International Journal of Sport and Exercise Psychology*, 10(3), 172–185. https://doi.org/10.1080/1612197x.2012.672013.

Madigan, D. J., Hill, A. P., Antiss, P. A., Mallinson-Howard, S. H., & Kumar, S. (2018). Perfectionism and training distress in junior athletes: The mediating role of coping tendencies. *European Journal of Sport Science*, 18(5), 713–721. https://doi.org/https://doi.org/10.1080/17461391.2018.1457082.

Madigan, D. J., Mallinson-Howard, S. H., Grugan, M. C., & Hill, A. P. (2020). Perfectionism and attitudes towards doping in athletes: A continuously cumulating meta-analysis and test of the 2 × 2 model. *European Journal of Sport Science*, 20(9), 1245–1254. https://doi.org/https://doi.org/10.1080/17461391.2019.1698660.

Madigan, D. J., Stoeber, J., Culley, T., Passfield, L., & Hill, A. P. (2018). Perfectionism and training performance: The mediating role of other-approach goals. *European Journal of Sport Science*, 18(9), 1271–1279. https://doi.org/10.1080/17461391.2018. 1508503.

Madigan, D. J., Stoeber, J., Forsdyke, D., Dayson, M., & Passfield, L. (2017). Perfectionism predicts injury in junior athletes: Preliminary evidence from a prospective study. *Journal of Sports Sciences*, 36(5), 545–550. https://doi.org/10.1080/02640414. 2017.1322709.

Madigan, D. J., Stoeber, J., & Passfield, L. (2015). Perfectionism and burnout in junior athletes: A three-month longitudinal study. *Journal of Sport and Exercise Psychology*, 37 (3), 305–315. https://doi.org/10.1123/jsep.2014-0266.

Madigan, D. J., Stoeber, J., & Passfield, L. (2016a). Perfectionism and attitudes towards doping in junior athletes. *Journal of Sports Sciences*, 34(8), 700–706. https://doi.org/10. 1080/02640414.2015.1068441.

Madigan, D. J., Stoeber, J., & Passfield, L. (2016b). Perfectionism and changes in athlete burnout over three months: Interactive effects of personal standards and evaluative concerns perfectionism. *Psychology of Sport and Exercise*, 26, 32–39. https://doi.org/10. 1016/j.psychsport.2016.05.010.

Madigan, D. J., Stoeber, J., & Passfield, L. (2016c). Motivation mediates the perfectionism–burnout relationship: A three-wave longitudinal study with junior athletes. *Journal of Sport and Exercise Psychology*, 38(4), 341–354. https://doi.org/10.1123/ jsep.2015-0238.

Madigan, D. J., Stoeber, J., & Passfield, L. (2017a). Perfectionism and training distress in junior athletes: a longitudinal investigation. *Journal of Sports Sciences*, 35(5), 470–475. https://doi.org/10.1080/02640414.2016.1172726.

Madigan, D. J., Stoeber, J., & Passfield, L. (2017b). Perfectionism and achievement goals revisited: The 3 × 2 achievement goal framework. *Psychology of Sport and Exercise*, 28, 120–124. https://doi.org/10.1016/j.psychsport.2016.10.008.

Madigan, D. J., Stoeber, J., & Passfield, L. (2017c). Athletes' perfectionism and reasons for training: Perfectionistic concerns predict training for weight control. *Personality and Individual Differences*, 115, 133–136. https://doi.org/10.1016/j.paid.2016.03.034.

Mallinson, S. H., & Hill, A. P. (2011). The relationship between multidimensional perfectionism and psychological need thwarting in junior sports participants. *Psychology of Sport and Exercise*, 12(6), 676–684. https://doi.org/10.1016/j.psychsport.2011.05.009.

Mallinson, S. H., Hill, A. P., Hall, H. K., & Gotwals, J. K. (2014). The 2 × 2 model of perfectionism and school- and community-based sport participation. *Psychology in the Schools*, 51(9), 972–985. https://doi.org/https://doi.org/10.1002/pits.21796.

Mallinson-Howard, S. H., Hill, A. P., & Hall, H. K. (2019). The 2 × 2 model of perfectionism and negative experiences in youth sport. *Psychology of Sport and Exercise*, 45, 101581. https://doi.org/https://doi.org/10.1016/j.psychsport.2019.101581.

Mallinson-Howard, S. H., Madigan, D. J., & Jowett, G. E. (2021). A three-sample study of perfectionism and field test performance in athletes. *European Journal of Sport Science*, 21(7), 1045–1053. https://doi.org/10.1080/17461391.2020.1811777.

Martin, S., Johnson, U., McCall, A., & Ivarsson, A. (2021). Psychological risk profile for overuse injuries in sport: An exploratory study. *Journal of Sports Sciences*, 39(17), 1–10. https://doi.org/10.1080/02640414.2021.1907904.

Martinent, G., & Ferrand, C. (2007). A cluster analysis of precompetitive anxiety: Relationship with perfectionism and trait anxiety. *Personality and Individual Differences*, 43(7), 1676–1686. https://doi.org/https://doi.org/10.1016/j.paid.2007.05.005.

McArdle, S., & Duda, J. L. (2004). Exploring social contextual correlates of perfectionism in adolescents: A multivariate perspective. *Cognitive Therapy and Research*, 28(6), 765–788. https://doi.org/10.1007/s10608-004-0665-4.

McArdle, S., & Duda, J. L. (2008). Exploring the etiology of perfectionism and perceptions of self-worth in young athletes. *Social Development*, 17(4), 980–997. https://doi.org/10.1111/j.1467-9507.2007.00456.x.

Miller, K. J., & Mesagno, C. (2014). Personality traits and exercise dependence: Exploring the role of narcissism and perfectionism. *International Journal of Sport and Exercise Psychology*, 12(4), 368–381. https://doi.org/10.1080/1612197x.2014.932821.

Molnar, D. S., Blackburn, M., Zinga, D., Spadafora, N., Methot-Jones, T., & Connolly, M. (2021). Trait perfectionism and dance goals among young female dancers: An application of the 2 × 2 model of perfectionism. *Journal of Sport & Exercise Psychology*, 43(3), 234–247. https://doi.org/10.1123/jsep.2020-0118.

Mouratidis, A., & Michou, A. (2011). Perfectionism, self-determined motivation, and coping among adolescent athletes. *Psychology of Sport and Exercise*, 12(4), 355–367. https://doi.org/10.1016/j.psychsport.2011.03.006.

Nascimento Junior, J. R. A. do, Freire, G. L. M., da Silva, A. A., Costa, N. L. G., de Sousa Fortes, L., & de Oliveira, D. V. (2020). The predicting role of perfectionism on team cohesion among Brazilian futsal athletes. *Motriz: Revista de Educação Física*, 26(1). https://doi.org/10.1590/s1980-6574202000010201.

Nascimento Junior, J. R. A., Vissoci, J. R. N., Lavallee, D., Codonhato, R., Nascimento, J. V. D., & Vieira, L. F. (2017). The mediating role of basic needs satisfaction on the relationship of perfectionism traits and team cohesion among elite futsal athletes. *International Journal of Sport Psychology*, 48, 591–609. https://doi.org/10.7352/IJSP 2017.48.591.

Nordin-Bates, S. M. (2020). Striving for perfection or for creativity? *Journal of Dance Education*, 20(1), 23–34. https://doi.org/10.1080/15290824.2018.1546050.

Nordin-Bates, S. M., Cumming, J., Aways, D., & Sharp, L. (2011). Imagining yourself dancing to perfection? Correlates of perfectionism among ballet and contemporary dancers. *Journal of Clinical Sport Psychology*, 5(1), 58–76. https://doi.org/10.1123/jcsp.5.1.58.

Nordin-Bates, S. M., Hill, A. P., Cumming, J., Aujla, I. J., & Redding, E. (2014). A longitudinal examination of the relationship between perfectionism and motivational climate in dance. *Journal of Sport and Exercise Psychology*, 36(4), 382–391. https://doi.org/10.1123/jsep.2013-0245.

Nordin-Bates, S. M., Raedeke, T. D., & Madigan, D. J. (2017). Perfectionism, burnout, and motivation in dance: A replication and test of the 2×2 model of perfectionism. *Journal of Dance Medicine & Science*, 21(3), 115–122. https://doi.org/10.12678/1089-313x.21.3.115.

Nordin-Bates, S. M., Walker, I. J., & Redding, E. (2011). Correlates of disordered eating attitudes among male and female young talented dancers: Findings from the UK centres for advanced training. *Eating Disorders*, 19(3), 211–233. https://doi.org/10.1080/10640266.2011.564976.

Oliveira, L. P. de, Vissoci, J. R. N., Nascimento Junior, J. R. A. do, Ferreira, L., Vieira, L. F., Silva, P. N. da, Cheuczuk, F., & Vieira, J. L. L. (2015). The impact of perfectionism traits on motivation in high-performance soccer athletes. *Revista Brasileira de Cineantropometria E Desempenho Humano*, 17(5), 601–611. https://doi.org/10.5007/1980-0037.2015v17n5p601.

Olsson, L. F., Hill, A. P., Madigan, D. J., & Woodley, G. (2020). Development of perfectionism in junior athletes: Examination of actual and perceived parental perfectionism. *Journal of Sports Sciences*, 38(6), 669–675. https://doi.org/10.1080/02640414.2020.1723387.

Olsson, L. F., Madigan, D. J., Hill, A. P., & Grugan, M. C. (2021). Do athlete and coach performance perfectionism predict athlete burnout? *European Journal of Sport Science*, 22(7), 1–33. https://doi.org/10.1080/17461391.2021.1916080.

Ommundsen, Y., Roberts, G. C., Lemyre, P.-N., & Miller, B. W. (2005). Peer relationships in adolescent competitive soccer: Associations to perceived motivational climate, achievement goals and perfectionism. *Journal of Sports Sciences*, 23(9), 977–989. https://doi.org/10.1080/02640410500127975.

Pacewicz, C. E., Gotwals, J. K., & Blanton, J. E. (2018). Perfectionism, coping, and burnout among intercollegiate varsity athletes: A person-oriented investigation of group differences and mediation. *Psychology of Sport and Exercise*, 35, 207–217. https://doi.org/10.1016/j.psychsport.2017.12.008.

Padham, M., & Aujla, I. (2014). The relationship between passion and the psychological well-being of professional dancers. *Journal of Dance Medicine & Science*, 18(1), 37–44. https://doi.org/10.12678/1089-313x.18.1.37.

Paulson, L. R., & Rutledge, P. C. (2014). Effects of perfectionism and exercise on disordered eating in college students. *Eating Behaviors*, 15(1), 116–119. https://doi.org/https://doi.org/10.1016/j.eatbeh.2013.11.005.

Penniment, K. J., & Egan, S. J. (2012). Perfectionism and learning experiences in dance class as risk factors for eating disorders in dancers. *European Eating Disorders Review*, 20(1), 13–22. https://doi.org/10.1002/erv.1089.

Puente-Díaz, R. (2013). Achievement goals and emotions. *The Journal of Psychology*, 147(3), 245–259. https://doi.org/https://doi.org/10.1080/00223980.2012.683893.

Quested, E. J., Cumming, J., & Duda, J. L. (2014). Profiles of perfectionism, motivation, and self-evaluations among dancers: An extended analysis of Cumming and Duda (2012). *International Journal of Sport Psychology*, 45(4), 349–368. https://doi.org/10.7352/IJSP2014.45.349.

Raducanu, E. (2022). Emma Raducanu: Letting go of perfection. Retrieved from www.nike.com/gb/a/emma-raducanu-letting-go-of-perfection.

Raedeke, T. D., Blom, V., & Kenttä, G. (2021). Perfectionism and self-perception profile comparisons on burnout and life satisfaction in aesthetic performers. *Journal of Clinical Sport Psychology*, 15(4), 1–22. https://doi.org/10.1123/jcsp.2019-0007.

Sagar, S. S., & Stoeber, J. (2009). Perfectionism, fear of failure, and affective responses to success and failure: The central role of fear of experiencing shame and embarrassment. *Journal of Sport and Exercise Psychology*, 31(5), 602–627. https://doi.org/10.1123/jsep.31.5.602.

Sapieja, K. M., Dunn, J. G. H., & Holt, N. L. (2011). Perfectionism and perceptions of parenting styles in male youth soccer. *Journal of Sport and Exercise Psychology*, 33(1), 20–39. https://doi.org/10.1123/jsep.33.1.20.

Shanmugam, V., & Davies, B. (2015). Clinical perfectionism and eating psychopathology in athletes: The role of gender. *Personality and Individual Differences*, 74, 99–105. https://doi.org/https://doi.org/10.1016/j.paid.2014.09.047.

Shanmugam, V., Jowett, S., & Meyer, C. (2011). Application of the transdiagnostic cognitive-behavioral model of eating disorders to the athletic population. *Journal of Clinical Sport Psychology*, 5(2), 166–191. https://doi.org/10.1123/jcsp.5.2.166.

Shanmugam, V., Jowett, S., & Meyer, C. (2012). Eating psychopathology amongst athletes: Links to current attachment styles. *Eating Behaviors*, 13(1), 5–12. https://doi.org/https://doi.org/10.1016/j.eatbeh.2011.09.004.

Smith, E. P., Hill, A. P., & Hall, H. K. (2018). Perfectionism, burnout, and depression in youth soccer players: A longitudinal study. *Journal of Clinical Sport Psychology*, 12(2), 179–200. https://doi.org/10.1123/jcsp.2017-0015.

Somasundaram, P., & Burgess, A. M. (2018). The role of Division III sports participation in the relationship between perfectionism and disordered eating symptomology. *Journal of Clinical Sport Psychology*, 12(1), 57–74. https://doi.org/https://doi.org/10.1123/jcsp.2017-0013.

Stoeber, J. (2012). Perfectionism and performance. In S. M. Murphy (ed.), *Oxford handbook of sport and performance psychology* (pp. 294–306). Oxford University Press.

Stoeber, J. (2014). Perfectionism in sport and dance: A double-edged sword. *International Journal of Sport Psychology*, 45(4), 385–394.

Stoeber, J., & Becker, C. (2008). Perfectionism, achievement motives, and attribution of success and failure in female soccer players. *International Journal of Psychology*, 43(6), 980–987. https://doi.org/10.1080/00207590701403850.

Stoeber, J., Madigan, D. J., & Gonidis, L. (2020). Perfectionism is adaptive and maladaptive, but what's the combined effect? *Personality and Individual Differences*, 161, 109846. https://doi.org/10.1016/j.paid.2020.109846.

Stoeber, J., & Otto, K. (2006). Positive conceptions of perfectionism: Approaches, evidence, challenges. *Personality and Social Psychology Review*, 10(4), 295–319. https://doi.org/10.1207/s15327957pspr1004_2.

Stoeber, J., Otto, K., Pescheck, E., Becker, C., & Stoll, O. (2007). Perfectionism and competitive anxiety in athletes: Differentiating striving for perfection and negative reactions to imperfection. *Personality and Individual Differences*, 42(6), 959–969. https://doi.org/10.1016/j.paid.2006.09.006.

Stoeber, J., Stoll, O., Pescheck, E., & Otto, K. (2008). Perfectionism and achievement goals in athletes: Relations with approach and avoidance orientations in mastery and performance goals. *Psychology of Sport and Exercise*, 9(2), 102–121. https://doi.org/10.1016/j.psychsport.2007.02.002.

Stoeber, J., Stoll, O., Salmi, O., & Tiikkaja, J. (2009). Perfectionism and achievement goals in young Finnish ice-hockey players aspiring to make the under-16 national team. *Journal of Sports Sciences*, 27(1), 85–94. https://doi.org/10.1080/02640410802448749.

Stoeber, J., Uphill, M. A., & Hotham, S. (2009). Predicting race performance in triathlon: The role of perfectionism, achievement goals, and personal goal setting. *Journal of Sport and Exercise Psychology*, 31(2), 211–245. https://doi.org/10.1123/jsep.31.2.211.

Stoll, O., Lau, A., & Stoeber, J. (2008). Perfectionism and performance in a new basketball training task: Does striving for perfection enhance or undermine performance? *Psychology of Sport and Exercise*, 9(5), 620–629. https://doi.org/10.1016/j.psychsport.2007.10.001.

Stornæs, A. V., Rosenvinge, J. H., Sundgot-Borgen, J., Pettersen, G., & Friborg, O. (2019). Profiles of perfectionism among adolescents attending specialized elite-and ordinary lower secondary schools: a Norwegian cross-sectional comparative study. *Frontiers in Psychology*, 10, 1–12. https://doi.org/https://doi.org/10.3389/fpsyg.2019.02039.

Taranis, L., & Meyer, C. (2010). Perfectionism and compulsive exercise among female exercisers: High personal standards or self-criticism? *Personality and Individual Differences*, 49(1), 3–7. https://doi.org/https://doi.org/10.1016/j.paid.2010.02.024.

Tashman, L. S., Tenenbaum, G., & Eklund, R. (2010). The effect of perceived stress on the relationship between perfectionism and burnout in coaches. *Anxiety, Stress & Coping*, 23(2), 195–212. https://doi.org/10.1080/10615800802629922.

Thienot, E., Jackson, B., Dimmock, J., Grove, J. R., Bernier, M., & Fournier, J. F. (2014). Development and preliminary validation of the mindfulness inventory for sport. *Psychology of Sport and Exercise*, 15(1), 72–80. https://doi.org/10.1016/j.psychsport.2013.10.003.

Vaartstra, M., Dunn, J. G. H., & Causgrove Dunn, J. (2018). Perfectionism and perceptions of social loafing in competitive youth soccer. *Journal of Sport Behavior*, 41(4), 475–501.

Vallance, J. K. H., Dunn, J. G. H., & Causgrove Dunn, J. L. (2006). Perfectionism, anger, and situation criticality in competitive youth ice hockey. *Journal of Sport and Exercise Psychology*, 28(3), 383–406. https://doi.org/10.1123/jsep.28.3.383.

Van Dyke, E. D., Metzger, A., & Zizzi, S. J. (2021). Being mindful of perfectionism and performance among collegiate gymnasts: A person-centered approach. *Journal of Clinical Sport Psychology*, 15(2), 143–161. https://doi.org/https://doi.org/10.1123/jcsp.2019-0100.

Vink, K., & Raudsepp, L. (2018). Perfectionistic strivings, motivation and engagement in among sport-specific activities adolescent team athletes. *Perceptual and Motor Skills*, 125(3), 003151251876583. https://doi.org/10.1177/0031512518765833.

Vink, K., & Raudsepp, L. (2020). Longitudinal associations between perfectionistic strivings, perfectionistic concerns, and sport-specific practice in adolescent volleyball players. *Perceptual and Motor Skills*, 127(3), 609–625. https://doi.org/https://doi.org/10.1177/0031512520908699.

Waleriańczyk, W., Hill, A. P., & Stolarski, M. (2022). A re-examination of the 2 × 2 model of perfectionism, burnout, and engagement in sports. *Psychology of Sport and Exercise*, 61, 102190. https://doi.org/10.1016/j.psychsport.2022.102190.

Waleriańczyk, W., & Stolarski, M. (2016). Kwestionariusz perfekcjonizmu w sporcie-konstrukcja i walidacja narzędzia psychometrycznego. *Psychologia-Etologia-Genetyka*, 34, 55–68.

Waleriańczyk, W., & Stolarski, M. (2021). Personality and sport performance: The role of perfectionism, Big Five traits, and anticipated performance in predicting the results of distance running competitions. *Personality and Individual Differences*, 169, 109993. https://doi.org/https://doi.org/10.1016/j.paid.2020.109993.

Waleriańczyk, W., Stolarski, M., & Matthews, G. (2021). Perfectionism moderates the effects of goal-realization on post-competition mood in amateur runners. *Journal of Sports Science and Medicine*, 21(1), 1–12. https://doi.org/10.52082/jssm.2022.1.

Wang, K., Xu, L., Zhang, J., Wang, D., & Sun, K. (2020). Relationship between perfectionism and attitudes toward doping in young athletes: the mediating role of autonomous and controlled motivation. *Substance Abuse Treatment, Prevention, and Policy*, 15(1). https://doi.org/10.1186/s13011-020-00259-5.

5 Re-envisioning the Tripartite Model of Perfectionism in Sport and Dance

An Updated Review and Response to Critiques

John K. Gotwals and Michael R. Lizmore

The tripartite model of perfectionism was the first model to identify forms of perfectionism that had distinct dimensional profiles and were associated with different performance, health, and well-being outcomes. Evidence for the model stems largely from research based in academic contexts and was controversial from the outset. The first edition of this chapter used research from sport and dance to evaluate the model and address some of the controversy. Since then, two additional reviews of that same body of research have been published. Both concluded that the sport and dance literature provided limited support for the tripartite model and questioned the model's foundational assumptions. In light of this context, this chapter re-evaluates and re-envisions the tripartite model within sport and dance. This extensive update incorporates recent research not included in any previous review, responds to critiques of the model, and suggests a new perspective on the assumptions of the model. Doing so allowed us to make nuanced conclusions about aspects of the tripartite model that are supported versus challenged by research in sport and dance, and to clarify how the model converges with and diverges from other perfectionism conceptualizations. There are three sections to the chapter. The first presents the foundations and history of the tripartite model. The second evaluates the degree to which research findings from sport and dance support the model. The third responds to recent critiques that have been levied against the model and offers a new perspective that supports its continued use.

Foundations and History of the Tripartite Model

The tripartite model is presented in Figure 5.1. The model is founded on two principles. The first is that perfectionism consists of two overarching continuous dimensions: perfectionistic strivings and perfectionistic concerns (Stoeber & Otto, 2006). As described in previous chapters, perfectionistic strivings represent "aspects of perfectionism associated with self-oriented striving for perfection and the setting of very high personal performance standards" (Gotwals et al., 2012, p. 264). Perfectionistic concerns represent "aspects associated with concerns over making mistakes, fear of negative social evaluation, feelings of

DOI: 10.4324/9781003288015-7

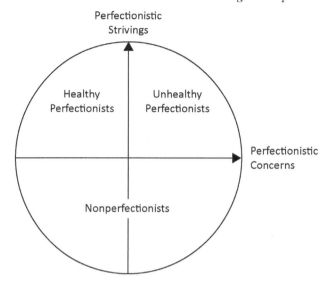

Figure 5.1 The tripartite model of perfectionism. Three orientations (healthy perfec-
        tionism, unhealthy perfectionism, and non-perfectionism) are defined by
        distinct profiles across two overarching dimensions (perfectionistic strivings
        and perfectionistic concerns).

Source: Adapted from "Positive conceptions of perfectionism: Approaches, evidence,
challenges", by J. Stoeber and K. Otto, *Personality and Social Psychology Review*, 10, p. 296.
Copyright 2006 by Lawrence Erlbaum.

discrepancy between one's expectations and performance, and negative reactions
to imperfection" (Gotwals et al., 2012, p. 264).

The second principle of the tripartite model is that when levels across the
two perfectionism dimensions are simultaneously considered, three qualitatively
distinct orientations can be identified: *healthy perfectionism, unhealthy perfectionism,*
and *non-perfectionism* (Parker, 1997; Stoeber & Otto, 2006). Healthy perfectionism is defined by high levels of perfectionistic strivings combined with low
levels of perfectionistic concerns. Unhealthy perfectionism is defined by high levels
of both perfectionistic strivings and perfectionistic concerns. Non-perfectionism is
defined by low levels of perfectionistic strivings and undifferentiated levels of perfectionistic concerns. As indicated by their labels, the three orientations are
proposed to show different patterns of relationships with external constructs.
Healthy perfectionism – in comparison to unhealthy perfectionism and non-
perfectionism – is proposed to be more strongly linked to healthy, positive, and
adaptive characteristics, processes, and outcomes. Unhealthy perfectionism – in
comparison to healthy perfectionism and non-perfectionism – is proposed to
be more strongly linked to unhealthy, negative, and maladaptive characteristics,
processes, and outcomes.

The tripartite model was developed in an inductive manner. The origins of
this process stem from Hamachek's (1978) anecdotal distinction between

normal perfectionists and neurotic perfectionists. Normal perfectionists were proposed to combine a self-oriented drive for high, but realistic, standards of performance with the ability to separate achievement of those standards from evaluations of self-worth. This approach to achievement desensitizes perceptions of socially prescribed performance pressures, alleviates irrational concerns about mistakes, and allows for positive self-worth and satisfaction even when faced with imperfection. As a result, normal perfectionists enter achievement contexts "excited, clear about what needs to be done, and emotionally charged" (ibid., p. 28). In contrast, neurotic perfectionists were proposed to demand unreasonably high performance standards, perceive significant socially prescribed pressures to achieve those standards, and directly tie their ability to do so to evaluations of their self-worth. As a result, neurotic perfectionists tend to be overly sensitive to the perceived expectations and criticisms of significant others, driven by a fear of failure and perceptions of inferiority, chronically dissatisfied with their performances. It is no wonder, then, that neurotic perfectionists enter achievement contexts "feeling anxious, confused, and emotionally drained" (ibid., p. 28). Hamachek's distinction between normal and neurotic perfectionists served as the foundation for the tripartite model's distinction between healthy perfectionists and unhealthy perfectionists.

Inspired by Hamachek's (1978) description of different types of perfectionists (Greenspon et al., 2000), Parker (1997) conducted a study that sparked the line of research and modelled the analytical approach that eventually led to the creation of the tripartite model. Parker used cluster analysis to categorize academically gifted 6th grade students according to their responses to the Multidimensional Perfectionism Scale (F-MPS; Frost et al., 1990). A three-cluster solution was chosen as the best categorization of the participants. Based on their respective profiles across the F-MPS subscales, as well as inter-cluster differences across several positive/negative criterion variables, the clusters were deemed to distinguish between non-perfectionists, healthy perfectionists, and dysfunctional perfectionists. Parker's use of cluster analysis was soon adopted in many studies; especially those by Rice, Ashby, and Slaney (e.g. LoCicero & Ashby, 2000; Rice & Mirzadeh, 2000; Rice & Slaney, 2002). This research team was very prolific, introduced several methodological innovations (including investigating perfectionism through the use of qualitative inquiry and latent profile analysis; e.g. Rice et al., 2003; Rice et al., 2013), and eventually produced much of the research upon which the tripartite model is founded.

Two works proved seminal in codifying the tripartite model. The first was Stoeber and Otto's (2006) review of group-based perfectionism studies from general psychology. The review presented a "common conceptual framework" (p. 296) that is generally accepted as representing the tripartite model (reproduced in Figure 5.1) and concluded that "the great majority" (ibid., p. 312) of findings demonstrated that healthy perfectionists show higher levels of positive characteristics in comparison to unhealthy perfectionists and non-perfectionists. The second was Rice and Ashby's (2007) development of a method of classifying types of perfectionists. Specifically, cut-scores were established across the subscales of the Almost Perfect Scale (Slaney et al., 1996) that could be used to classify people as adaptive perfectionists, maladaptive perfectionists, or non-perfectionists. This approach was especially influential in that it helped to formalize the profiles across perfectionistic strivings and perfectionistic concerns that are associated with each perfectionism orientation.

Dunn and colleagues have been leaders in terms of producing sport-based research that aligns with the tripartite model. The founding principles that guide much of this group's research are that perfectionism is multidimensional, "that an individual's patterns of ratings across all dimensions of perfectionism should be considered" (Dunn et al., 2002, p. 379), and that "examining all perfectionism dimensions simultaneously may shed further light on the correlates of maladaptive and adaptive perfectionism" (Gotwals et al., 2003, p. 20). Dunn and colleagues operationalized this perspective through the use of cluster analysis (e.g. Dunn et al., 2014; Lizmore et al., 2016; Vallance et al., 2006) and canonical correlation (e.g. Gotwals et al., 2003; Gotwals et al., 2010; Dunn et al., 2020). As indicated earlier, and argued again later in the chapter, we feel that these principles should be considered to represent overarching assumptions of the tripartite model.

Evidence from Perfectionism Research in Sport and Dance

This section of the chapter examines the degree to which research from sport and dance supports the tripartite model.[1] Two previous reviews – Hill and Madigan (2017) and Hill et al. (2020) – have been conducted with the same purpose. Both reviews focused solely on research that used cluster analysis. The present review advances these past efforts in two primary ways. First, it re-examines the cluster analytic literature and incorporates recent research that utilized what has been presented as a more sophisticated and appropriate successor to cluster analysis: namely, latent profile analysis (Pastor et al., 2007). Second, the present review incorporates two bodies of literature from sport and dance that we consider applicable to the tripartite model, but that were not included in the previous reviews: namely, research that used canonical correlation analysis and qualitative inquiry. In doing so, we provide an up-to-date and comprehensive review of the tripartite model in sport and dance. The review is broken down into sub-sections by analytical approach. Each sub-section begins by describing the approach and then categorizes studies based on the degree to which the produced findings support the tripartite model.

Studies that Utilized Person-Oriented Approaches to Analysis

In person-oriented approaches the person (as opposed to the variable) is the focus of analysis, is considered holistically, and is distinguished by their profile across multiple meaningful characteristics (Bergman & Andersson, 2010). Cluster analysis is a person-oriented approach that has been connected to the tripartite model since its inception and is the analytical tool used most often when testing the model

(Stoeber & Otto, 2006). The technique uses characteristics pre-selected by the researcher to identify "naturally occurring" groups (or clusters) among a sample (Hair et al., 2010). The general goal is to identify a set of clusters (i.e. a cluster solution) that, in respect to a profile across the pre-selected characteristics, minimizes differences between people within the same cluster and maximizes differences between people in different clusters. Latent profile analysis has emerged more recently as a successor to cluster analysis (Pastor et al., 2007). While both techniques share the same general goal, latent profile analysis differs from cluster analysis in that it is less exploratory, is model based, provides more rigorous criteria that can be used to choose the best cluster solution, and recognizes that cluster membership is a matter of degree (as opposed to all-or-nothing).

Cluster analysis and latent profile analysis are well-suited to the tripartite model because individuals' levels across perfectionistic strivings and perfectionistic concerns can serve as the characteristics upon which they are clustered or grouped. Support for the model is produced if a three-cluster solution emerges as the most optimal solution, if the three clusters demonstrate profiles across perfectionistic strivings and perfectionistic concerns that reflect the expected profiles for healthy perfectionists, unhealthy perfectionists, and non-perfectionists, and if the clusters differ across external criteria in ways that demonstrate their proposed healthy/unhealthy nature. Nine studies have utilized cluster analysis to group athletes or dancers according to their levels of perfectionistic strivings and perfectionistic concerns. Only one study has so far used latent profile analysis to do the same.[2] Table 5.1 identifies and describes these ten studies and indicates the degree to which each supports the tripartite model.

Studies that Support the Tripartite Model

Four of the ten studies produced results that generally support the tripartite model (Dunn et al., 2014; Lizmore et al., 2016; Pacewicz et al., 2018, and Sapieja et al., 2011). Each sampled athletes, clustered those athletes according to their levels across the subscales of the Sport Multidimensional Perfectionism Scale-2 (SMPS-2; Gotwals & Dunn, 2009), and chose a three-cluster solution as providing the best fit. Three of the studies labelled the clusters as *healthy perfectionists, unhealthy perfectionists,* and *non-perfectionists*, whereas Pacewicz et al. (2018) used labels from the 2 × 2 model of perfectionism (i.e. *pure personal standards perfectionists, mixed perfectionists*, and *non-perfectionists*; see Chapter 6). Cluster differences across the SMPS-2 subscales supported use of those labels. For instance, the healthy perfectionists and unhealthy perfectionists generally showed higher levels of subscales representing perfectionistic strivings (e.g. Personal Standards and Organization) than the non-perfectionists, whereas the unhealthy perfectionists consistently showed higher levels of subscales representing perfectionistic concerns (e.g. Concern Over Mistakes and Doubts About Actions) than both the healthy perfectionists and non-perfectionists. Such findings reflect the expected profiles the tripartite model uses to define the three perfectionist orientations (see Figure 5.1).

Table 5.1 Studies that used person–centred analytical approaches to examine perfectionism among athletes or dancers.

Study[a]	Participants	Instrument[b]	Classification Technique	Cluster Labels	Proposed Structure[c]	Cluster Differences[d]		Proposed Differences[e]
Dunn et al. (2014)	137 adult inter-collegiate volleyball players (100% female)	SMPS-2	Cluster analysis	Healthy perfectionists, unhealthy perfectionists, non-perfectionists	Supported	a	HP more likely to cope via more effort and active coping and less likely to cope via disengagement than UP.	a Supported
						b	HP more likely to cope via more planning, effort, and active coping than NP.	b Supported
						c	UP more likely to cope via more wishful thinking and *planning* than NP.	c Mixed
Lizmore et al. (2016)	343 adult curling athletes (42% female)	SMPS-2	Cluster analysis	Healthy perfectionists, unhealthy perfectionists, non-perfectionists	Supported	a	HP more likely to have less anger/dejection and more confidence/optimism following mistakes than UP	a Supported
						b	–	b ∅
						c	UP more likely to have more anger/dejection following mistakes than NP	c Supported

Study[a]	Participants	Instrument[b]	Classification Technique	Cluster Labels	Proposed Structure[c]	Cluster Differences[d]		Proposed Differences[e]	
Pacewicz et al. (2018)	173 adult inter-collegiate athletes (50% female)	SMPS-2	Latent profile analysis	Pure personal standards perfectionists (HP), mixed perfectionists (UP), non-perfectionists	Supported	a	HP lower general burnout, emotional/physical exhaustion, perceived reduced accomplishment, sport devaluation, emotion focused coping, and lower avoidant coping than NP	a	Supported
						b	–	b	Ø
						c	UP higher general burnout, emotional/physical exhaustion, perceived reduced accomplishment, and sport devaluation than NP	c	Supported
Sapieja et al. (2011)	194 youth soccer players (0% female)	SMPS-2	Cluster analysis	Healthy Perfectionists, unhealthy perfectionists, non-perfectionists	Supported	a	HP more likely to perceive higher maternal and paternal authoritativeness than UP	a	Supported
						b	–	b	Ø
						c	UP more likely to perceive lower maternal and paternal authoritativeness than NP	c	Supported

Study[a]	Participants	Instrument[b]	Classification Technique	Cluster Labels	Proposed Structure[c]	Cluster Differences[d]	Proposed Differences[e]
Cumming & Duda (2012)	194 adolescent vocational dance students (87% female)	F-MPS	Cluster analysis	Pure personal standards perfectionism, mixed perfectionism, non-perfectionism, pure evaluative concerns perfectionism	Challenged: #	N/A	N/A
Gotwals (2011)	117 adult inter-collegiate athletes (41% female)	SMPS-2	Cluster analysis	Healthy perfectionists, doubt-oriented unhealthy Perfectionists, parent-oriented unhealthy perfectionists, non-perfectionists	Challenged: #	N/A	N/A
Gucciardi et al. (2012)	423 adult high-performance athletes (58% female)	SMPS	Cluster analysis	Adaptive perfectionists, maladaptive perfectionists, non-perfectionists	Challenged: dimensional	N/A	N/A
Martinent & Ferrand (2006)	166 adult regional athletes (47% female)	SMPS & HF-MPS	Cluster analysis	Adaptive perfectionists, maladaptive perfectionists, non-perfectionists	Challenged: dimensional	N/A	N/A

Study[a]	Participants	Instrument[b]	Classification Technique	Cluster Labels	Proposed Structure[c]	Cluster Differences[d]	Proposed Differences[e]
Nordin-Bates et al. (2011)	250 dancers (66% female)	PI	Cluster analysis	Perfectionistic tendencies, moderate perfectionistic tendencies, no perfectionistic tendencies	Challenged: dimensional	N/A	N/A
Vallance et al. (2006)	229 youth ice hockey players (0% female)	SMPS	Cluster analysis	High perfectionism, moderate perfectionism, low perfectionism	Challenge: dimensional	N/A	N/A

Note. Studies categorized by degree of support for the tripartite model (see specific notes [c] and [b]) and ordered alphabetically within each category. HP = Healthy perfectionists; UP = Unhealthy perfectionists; NP = Non-perfectionists; N/A = not applicable. Table format adapted from Stoeber & Otto (2006). [a] Technique used to categorize participants in parentheses. [b] Instrument used to measure perfectionism. F-MPS = Multidimensional Perfectionism Scale (Frost et al., 1990); HF-MPS = Multidimensional Perfectionism Scale (Hewitt & Flett, 1991); PI = Perfectionism Inventory (Hill et al., 2004); SMPS = Sport Multidimensional Perfectionism Scale (Dunn, Causgrove Dunn, & Syrotuik, 2002); SMPS-2 = Sport Multidimensional Perfectionism Scale-2 (Gotwals & Dunn, 2009). [c] Supported = The study adopted a cluster solution composed of three clusters and the clusters respectively showed profiles across perfectionistic strivings and perfectionistic concerns that reflected the profiles for healthy perfectionists, unhealthy perfectionists, and non-perfectionists, as defined in the tripartite model; Challenge: # = The study adopted a cluster solution of more than three clusters; Challenge: Dimensional = The study adopted a cluster solution that was dimensional (as opposed to categorical) in nature. [d] (a) = Differences between HP and UP clusters on criterion variables; (b) = Differences between HP and NP clusters on criterion variables; (c) = Differences between UP and NP clusters on criterion variables. Only significant differences ($p < .05$) reported. Contradictory findings italicized. [e] Supported = Significant cluster differences on criterion variables in the expected direction; Mixed = Significant cluster differences on criterion variables both in the expected and contradictory direction; ∅ (inconclusive) = No significant cluster differences on criterion variables. (a) = HP versus UP; (b) = HP versus NP; (c) UP versus NP.

Across the four studies' criterion variables, the clusters were also found to largely differ in ways that aligned with the predictions of the tripartite model. In comparison to both the healthy perfectionists and the non-perfectionists, the unhealthy perfectionists were more likely to experience anger/dejection after committing mistakes in competition (Lizmore et al., 2016), more likely to experience burnout (Pacewicz et al., 2018), and less likely to perceive their parents as authoritative (i.e. demanding, yet responsive, supportive, and empowering; Sapieja et al., 2011). When coping with performance slumps, the unhealthy perfectionists were also less likely to use task-focused strategies and more likely to use avoidance strategies in comparison to healthy perfectionists and more likely to engage in wishful thinking than the non-perfectionists (Dunn et al., 2014). Effect sizes associated with the significant cluster differences in these studies reflected small to large effects (see Hill et al., 2020).[3] All these effects were in the expected direction, except for one: unhealthy perfectionists were more likely to use planning to cope with performance slumps than non-perfectionists (Dunn et al., 2014).

In three of these four studies healthy perfectionists were not found to differ significantly from non-perfectionists across any criterion variable. This included anger in reaction to mistakes (Lizmore et al., 2016), burnout (Pacewicz et al., 2018), and perceptions of parental authoritativeness (Sapieja et al., 2011). However, one study did find that healthy perfectionists were more likely to employ planning, increased effort, and active coping when faced with performance slumps than non-perfectionists (Dunn et al., 2014).

Taken collectively, two trends are evident in the cluster differences presented across these four studies. First, unhealthy perfectionists appear to show a greater propensity towards negative outcomes and a lower propensity towards positive outcomes in comparison to healthy perfectionists and non-perfectionists. Second, while healthy perfectionists and non-perfectionists do not appear to differ in their general propensity towards positive or negative outcomes, healthy perfectionists do appear to adopt more proactive and task-focused coping strategies in response to slumps. These trends generally support the tripartite model but do question whether healthy perfectionists always demonstrate healthier characteristics than non-perfectionists.

Studies that Challenge the Tripartite Model

Six of the ten studies presented in Table 5.1 challenge the tripartite model's foundational principles. For example, two cluster analytic studies – one with vocational dance students (i.e. Cumming & Duda, 2012) and one with university athletes (i.e. Gotwals, 2011) – challenge the model's contention that there are three perfectionistic orientations. Both studies considered a three-cluster solution but found that it was not compatible with the tripartite model and ultimately chose a four cluster solution as the best way to categorize their participants.

Cumming and Duda (2012) contended that their four-cluster solution aligned with the 2 × 2 model of perfectionism (see Gaudreau & Thompson,

2010; Chapter 6, this volume) and labelled the clusters accordingly. The *pure personal standards perfectionism* cluster and the *mixed perfectionism* cluster showed profiles across perfectionistic strivings and perfectionistic concerns that reflected the profiles expected for healthy and unhealthy perfectionists (respectively). However, the final two clusters showed profiles that are not readily associated with any orientation represented in the tripartite model: the *non-perfectionism* cluster was defined by low levels across both perfectionistic strivings and perfectionistic concerns, whereas the *pure evaluative concerns perfectionism* cluster was defined by low perfectionistic strivings and moderate-to-high perfectionistic concerns.[4] Moreover, the pure evaluative concerns cluster reported lower levels of psychological and physical health than both the pure personal standards perfectionism cluster and the non-perfectionism cluster, but did not differ in this regard to the mixed perfectionism cluster.[5] These findings suggest that the tripartite model may benefit from distinguishing between non-perfectionists who show low levels across perfectionistic concerns and those that show high levels across perfectionistic concerns.

In Gotwals's (2011) four cluster solution, one cluster reflected healthy perfectionism, a second cluster reflected non-perfectionism, and the final two clusters both reflected unhealthy perfectionism. The two unhealthy perfectionism clusters could be differentiated by their levels of two perfectionistic concerns subdimensions: one showed the highest score of Doubts About Actions and the other showed the highest score of Perceived Parental Pressure. As such, the two clusters were labelled doubt-oriented unhealthy perfectionists and parent-oriented unhealthy perfectionists. The healthy perfectionists generally reported the lowest levels of burnout across all four clusters. These findings suggest that there may be value in revising the tripartite model to consider if different subdimensions of perfectionistic concerns may serve to distinguish between different variants of unhealthy perfectionism.

Another main tenet of the tripartite model that is challenged by findings from several cluster analytic studies is the appropriateness of distinguishing between qualitatively distinct perfectionist orientations (e.g. healthy perfectionism and unhealthy perfectionism). This challenge is based on the distinction between categorical and dimensional approaches to conceptualizing perfectionism. The tripartite model adopts a categorical approach. That is, in distinguishing between healthy perfectionism, unhealthy perfectionism, and non-perfectionism, the model assumes that different types of perfectionism exist and that these types reflect qualitatively (as opposed to quantitatively) different perspectives on achievement (Flett & Hewitt, 2002). In contrast, a dimensional approach assumes that "people differ in degrees of perfectionism, rather than in kinds of perfectionism" (Flett & Hewitt, 2002, p. 18, italics in original). That is, a dimensional approach assumes that different types of perfectionism do not exist; instead, individuals' perfectionistic tendencies differ quantitatively (as opposed to qualitatively) along a continuum.

It is appropriate to adopt a categorical approach (over a dimensional approach) to interpret a cluster solution when discontinuities exist within the solution (Flett & Hewitt, 2002). Discontinuity is present when the rank order of clusters does not follow the same pattern across one or more subdimensions of perfectionism. As an example, consider the cluster solutions in Dunn et al. (2014), Lizmore et al. (2016), Pacewicz et al. (2018), and Sapieja et al. (2011). Across all four solutions, the cluster of unhealthy perfectionists scored higher than the cluster of healthy perfectionists on the SMPS-2 Concern Over Mistakes, Doubts About Actions, and Perceived Parental Pressure subscales. In contrast, the healthy perfectionists scored higher than the unhealthy perfectionists on Organization. Finally, the two clusters' scores on the Personal Standards subscale did not significantly differ. The presence of these discontinuities helps to justify categorical interpretations of the cluster solutions, such as that offered by the tripartite model.

If discontinuity is not present within a cluster solution (in other words, when cluster solutions demonstrate continuity), then it is more appropriate to utilize a dimensional approach (over a categorical approach) to interpret the solution (Flett & Hewitt, 2002). Continuity is present when the rank-order of clusters remains the same regardless of the perfectionism facet in question. Within the body of literature on perfectionism in sport and dance, there are two studies (specifically, Nordin-Bates et al., 2011; and Vallance et al., 2006) in which the researchers recognized the continuous nature of their cluster solution and accordingly adopted a dimensional approach for interpretive purposes. Both adopted a three-cluster solution where, with regard to their levels across subdimensions of perfectionistic strivings and perfectionistic concerns, one cluster always ranked first, a second cluster always ranked second, and a third cluster always ranked third. The labels chosen for each cluster reflect this high degree of continuity (perfectionistic tendencies, moderate perfectionistic tendencies, and no perfectionistic tendencies in Nordin-Bates et al., 2011; high perfectionism, moderate perfectionism, and low perfectionism in Vallance et al., 2006). As Flett and Hewitt (2002) indicate, such cluster solutions suggest that individual differences in perfectionism are "quantitative rather than qualitative in nature" (p. 19) and, as such, challenge the validity of models—including the tripartite model—that adopt a categorical approach to perfectionism.

It has been suggested that sometimes studies adopt a categorical approach to interpret cluster solutions when a dimensional approach may have been more appropriate (Flett & Hewitt, 2002). Two sport-based cluster analytic studies appear to fit this description: Gucciardi et al. (2012) and Martinent and Ferrand (2006). Both identified a three-cluster solution as the best way to categorize their participants, and interpreted the findings in line with the tripartite model. In both studies the clusters were labelled as non-perfectionists, adaptive perfectionists (i.e. healthy perfectionists), and maladaptive perfectionists (i.e. unhealthy perfectionists). Inspection of the cluster solutions in the two studies, though, reveals no evidence of discontinuity and clear evidence of continuity. As such, it would have been more appropriate to interpret both cluster solutions in line with a dimensional, as opposed to categorical, approach. Accordingly, we have categorized both studies as producing findings that challenge the tripartite model.[6]

Summary

This section reviewed the degree to which 10 studies that used person-oriented analytical approaches to examine perfectionism in sport and dance produced findings that support the tripartite model. There appears to be considerable variability in this regard. Four studies generally supported the model by identifying clusters that reflected the model's three orientations and by supporting the model's contention that unhealthy perfectionists should show higher levels of negative outcomes and lower levels of positive outcomes in comparison to both healthy perfectionists and non-perfectionists. Additionally, while healthy perfectionists and non-perfectionists did not differ across many criteria, when they did, those differences supported the notion that healthy perfectionism is the healthier of the two orientations. In contrast, findings from two studies challenged the number of perfectionism orientations proposed in the tripartite model, while four others challenged the appropriateness of distinguishing between qualitatively different perfectionism orientations in the first place. As a result, the conclusion of the present review parallels that of previous reviews (Hill & Madigan, 2017; Hill et al., 2020): that studies that use person-oriented approaches to examine perfectionism among athletes and dancers provide mixed support for the tripartite model.

Studies that Utilized Canonical Correlation Analysis

Canonical correlation is an additional technique that can be used to investigate the tripartite model. The goal of canonical correlation is to identify relationships between one set of predictor variables and another set of criterion variables. Within canonical correlation terminology, those relationships are presented by *canonical functions*. Each function illustrates the relationship between two *canonical variates*: one defined by a pattern of loadings across the predictor set variables and another defined by a pattern of loadings across the criterion set variables. The *canonical correlation coefficient* reflects the strength and direction of the relationship between two variates depicted within a function.

Canonical correlation has the potential to produce results that align with the tripartite model when subdimensions of perfectionistic strivings and perfectionistic concerns are entered as variables in the predictor set and indicators of (un) healthy characteristics, processes, or outcomes are entered as variables in the criterion set. While such analyses will not produce results pertaining to non-perfectionism, they can support the distinction between healthy and unhealthy perfectionism if: (a) two meaningful canonical functions are extracted, (b) the profile of one predictor variate reflects healthy perfectionism and the profile of the other predictor variate reflects unhealthy perfectionism, and (c) each predictor variate relates to a criterion variate in a manner that is consistent with the tripartite model's contentions. While no studies have used canonical correlation analysis to examine perfectionism among dancers, 12 studies have done so among athletes. These studies are presented in Table 5.2.[7]

Table 5.2 Studies that used canonical correlation to examine how perfectionism profiles relate to healthy and unhealthy characteristics, processes, and outcomes in sport.

Study	Participants	Instrument[b]	Criterion variate	Findings
Dunn et al. (2002)	174 high school Canadian football players (0% female)	SMPS	Achievement goal orientation	Support
Dunn et al. (2011)-sport[a]	119 competitive figure skaters (100% female)	SMPS	Body image	Support
Dunn et al. (2020)	144 youth Canadian football players (0% female)	SMPS-2	Worry; optimism	Support
Gotwals et al. (2010)-sport[a]	181 intercollegiate ice hockey players (0% female)	SMPS-2	Competitive trait anxiety	Support
Vaartstra et al. (2018)	216 youth soccer players (75% female)	SMPS-2	Social loafing	Support
Dunn et al. (2011)-global[a]	119 competitive figure skaters (100% female)	HF-MPS	Body image	Partial Support
Dunn et al. (2006)	138 high school Canadian football players (0% female)	SMPS	Trait anger; state anger	Partial Support
Hall et al. (1998)	119 high school runners (62% female)	F-MPS	Achievement goal orientation	Partial Support
Vallance et al. (2006)	229 youth ice hockey players (0% female)	SMPS	Trait anger	Partial Support
Curran et al. (2014)	266 youth athletes (50% female)	HF-MPS	Passion	Challenge
Gotwals et al. (2010)-global[a]	181 intercollegiate ice hockey players (0% female)	F-MPS	Competitive trait anxiety	Challenge
Gotwals et al. (2003)	87 intercollegiate athletes (59% female)	F-MPS	Self-esteem, satisfaction with performance, perceived athletic competence	Challenge

Notes. Perfectionism instrument: F-MPS = Frost Multidimensional Perfectionism Scale (Frost et al., 1990); HF-MPS = Hewitt and Flett Multidimensional Perfectionism Scale (Hewitt & Flett, 1991); PI = Perfectionism Inventory (Hill et al., 2004); SMPS = The original Sport Multidimensional Perfectionism Scale (Dunn, Causgrove Dunn, & Syrotuik, 2002); SMPS-2 = Sport Multidimensional Perfectionism Scale-2 (Gotwals & Dunn, 2009). Criterion variate: Construct represented by the variables included on the criterion variate. Findings: Support = Findings from the study support the tripartite model; Challenge = Findings form the study challenge the tripartite model.
[a] These studies each conducted two canonical correlation analyses: one with the SMPS(2) and one with the HF-MPS or the F-MPS. [b] Instrument used to measure perfectionism.

Study Findings that Fully Support the Tripartite Model

Five of the twelve studies produced findings that fully supported the tripartite model (Dunn et al., 2002; Dunn et al., 2011; Dunn et al., 2020; Gotwals et al., 2010; and Vaartstra et al., 2018). Each study extracted two canonical functions. In one of these canonical functions, the predictor variate always represented healthy perfectionism. Higher levels of predictor variate was found to relate to stronger task goal orientations (Dunn et al., 2002), more positive body image (Dunn et al., 2011), greater concentration (Gotwals et al., 2010), higher optimism and less worry (Dunn et al., 2020), and less acceptance of social loafing (Vaartstra et al., 2018). In the second canonical function, the predictor variate represented unhealthy perfectionism. Higher levels of this predictor variate was found to relate to stronger ego goal orientations (Dunn et al., 2002), poorer body image (Dunn et al., 2011), higher levels of competitive trait anxiety (Gotwals et al., 2010), lower optimism and greater worry (Dunn et al., 2020), and more acceptance of the social loafing (Vaartstra et al., 2018). This pattern of relationships supports the tripartite model's contention that healthy perfectionism is associated with positive outcomes while unhealthy perfectionism is associated with negative outcomes.

Study Findings that Partially Support the Tripartite Model

Four of the twelve studies in Table 5.2 produced partial support for the tripartite model (Dunn et al., 2006; Dunn et al., 2011; Hall et al., 1998; Vallance et al., 2006). Each study extracted a canonical function in which a predictor variate reflecting unhealthy perfectionism was positively related to characteristics generally perceived to be unhealthy in sport. These characteristics included tendencies to experience anger in reaction to mistakes and negative social evaluation (Dunn et al., 2006; Vallance et al., 2006), to have a negative body image (Dunn et al., 2011), and to be predominantly ego oriented (Hall et al., 1998). However, none of these four studies produced a canonical function with a predictor variate that reflected healthy perfectionism. As such, findings from these studies support the tripartite model's contentions regarding unhealthy perfectionism, but not healthy perfectionism.

Studies that Challenge the Tripartite Model

Three of the twelve studies in Table 5.2 produced findings that challenge the tripartite model (Curran et al., 2014; Gotwals et al., 2003; Gotwals et al., 2010). Across these studies, the predictor variate in every extracted canonical function was defined by subdimensions of perfectionistic strivings or perfectionistic concerns, but not both. Curran et al. (2014) extracted two canonical functions: one containing a predictor variate defined by *self-oriented perfectionism* (a subdimension of perfectionistic strivings) and the other containing a predictor variate defined by *socially prescribed perfectionism* (a subdimension of perfectionistic strivings). Each of Gotwals and colleagues' studies extracted a single canonical function in which the predictor variate was defined only by subdimensions of perfectionistic concerns (Gotwals et al., 2003; Gotwals et al., 2010). In each case, the predictor variate cannot be deemed to reflect healthy perfectionism or unhealthy perfectionism because, in the tripartite model, both orientations are defined by unique profiles across both perfectionistic strivings and perfectionistic concerns. Instead, such findings are better interpreted through an independent effects approach where the dimensions of perfectionism are considered independently as opposed to simultaneously.

Summary

This section examined the degree to which 12 sport-based studies that used canonical correlation produced findings that supported the tripartite model. Five studies produced full support by producing canonical functions that related healthy perfectionism to positive outcomes and unhealthy perfectionism to negative outcomes. Four studies partially supported the model by providing evidence of unhealthy perfectionism, but not of healthy perfectionism. Finally, three studies challenged the model by not producing evidence of any orientation defined in the tripartite model. This body of literature demonstrates mixed support for the tripartite model, provides greater support for the existence of unhealthy perfectionism than healthy perfectionism, and generally parallels the pattern of findings exhibited by studies that adopted person-oriented approaches to analysis.

Studies that Utilized Qualitative Approaches to Analysis

Perhaps the most straightforward way to evaluate the tripartite model is to identify healthy and unhealthy perfectionist athletes and dancers and then to ask them about their perspectives and experiences. Five studies – four based in sport (Gotwals & Spencer-Cavaliere, 2014; Gotwals & Tamminen, 2022; Mallinson-Howard et al., 2018; Sellars et al., 2016) and one based in dance (Nordin-Bates & Kuylser, 2020) – have done this through a two-stage mixed methods approach. In the first stage, a sample of participants completed a perfectionism questionnaire. Individual participants were then identified whose profile of scores on the questionnaire's subscales were prototypical of the dimensional profile that defines healthy perfectionism or unhealthy perfectionism. In other words, the researchers identified athletes or dancers who, based on their subscale score profile, appeared to qualify as healthy perfectionists or unhealthy perfectionists.[8] In the second stage, tools of qualitative inquiry – semi-structured interviews, focus groups, and audio-diaries – were then used to explore these participants' perspectives on achievement, success and failure, and perfectionism. Table 5.3 presents a summary of these five studies.

Table 5.3 Studies that used qualitative inquiry to explore healthy and unhealthy perfectionism in sport and dance.

Study	1st stage sample	Instrument[b]	2nd stage sample	Qualitative methods
Gotwals & Spencer-Cavaliere (2014)	117 adult intercollegiate athletes (41% female)	SMPS-2	11 unhealthy perfectionists & 7 healthy perfectionists	Semi-structured one-on-one interviews
Gotwals & Tamminen (2022)	122 adult intercollegiate athletes (48% female)	SMPS-2	7 unhealthy perfectionists & 3 healthy perfectionists	Semi-structured one-on-one interviews and audio diaries
Mallinson-Howard et al. (2018)	192 adolescent school- or community-based athletes (100% female)	SMPS-2	5 unhealthy perfectionists & 5 healthy perfectionists	Focus groups followed by semi-structured one-on-one interviews
Nordin-Bates & Kuylser (2020)	77 adolescent high performance dance students (77% female)	Dance-MIPS	3 unhealthy perfectionists & 1 healthy perfectionist	Semi-structured one-on-one interviews
Sellars et al. (2016)	67 adult high performance athletes[a]	SMPS-2	10 unhealthy perfectionists	Semi-structured one-on-one interviews

Note. Perfectionism instrument: SMPS-2 = Sport Multidimensional Perfectionism Scale-2 (Gotwals & Dunn, 2009); MIPS = Multidimensional Inventory of Perfectionism in Sport (Stoeber et al., 2007). [a]Sellars et al. (2016) did not report gender in their first-stage sample. [b]Instrument used to measure perfectionism.

Findings that Support the Tripartite Model

Comparison of the themes identified by the five studies in Table 5.3 reveals several trends that support the tripartite model. One was that the healthy perfectionists and unhealthy perfectionists tended to report attitudes, beliefs, and perspectives that reflected the profiles used in the tripartite model to define both orientations. For example, both the healthy perfectionists and the unhealthy perfectionists relentlessly pursued high standards of performance that maximized and exhausted their abilities. This pursuit was self-regulated, fuelled by a desire for continual progress and improvement, and supported through a penchant for preparation, planning, and organization. This suggests that both the healthy and unhealthy perfectionists showed high levels of perfectionistic strivings. The healthy perfectionists were also found to not be overly concerned about mistakes, to generally have positive perceptions of coaches, teammates, and parents, and to not be preoccupied with demonstrating their athletic legitimacy. In contrast, the unhealthy perfectionists were highly sensitive to significant others' expectations, evaluations, and criticisms, driven by desires to not let these people down, and concerned about publicly demonstrating their worth as athletes. They were also highly self-critical when they committed mistakes, did not perform their best, and/or were outperformed by peers. This suggests that the healthy perfectionists also showed low levels of perfectionistic concerns, whereas the unhealthy perfectionists showed high levels of perfectionistic concerns.

A second trend evident across the five qualitative studies is that the healthy and unhealthy perfectionists diverged across a host of other characteristics in ways that aligned with the tripartite model. For example, the healthy perfectionists showed an unwavering appreciation of, and commitment to, hard work, generally adopted a mastery-approach achievement goal orientation, and rationally, effectively, and constructively responded to setbacks. In contrast, the unhealthy perfectionists endorsed a fragile, irrational, and rigid belief in hard work, were generally performance-avoidance oriented, and had difficulty responding to, disengaging from, and coping effectively with setbacks. These divergences support the tripartite model's contention that healthy perfectionism is a more positive type of perfectionism in comparison to unhealthy perfectionism.

Findings that Challenge the Tripartite Model

The five studies in Table 5.3 also produced findings that challenge the tripartite model. For example, in the tripartite model high levels of perfectionistic strivings are a defining feature of all types of perfectionism. Accordingly, the healthy and/or unhealthy perfectionists in each study were selected on grounds that they showed this feature (based on self-report perfectionism measures). High levels of perfectionistic strivings imply "that the person is aiming and striving to be perfect" (Gaudreau, 2019, p. 199). However, no study reported that their perfectionistic athletes or dancers identified *perfection* as the goal of their achievement efforts. Instead, the perfectionists were found to judge success by their ability to perpetually improve and continually progress, give maximum effort, perform to the best of their abilities, and win (Gotwals & Spencer-Cavaliere, 2014; Gotwals & Tamminen, 2022; Mallinson-Howard et al., 2018). It is unclear whether these features should be incorporated into the tripartite model as indicators of perfectionistic strivings or whether these features do not adequately represent the "exceedingly stringent (if not unreasonable) and exacting" (Gaudreau, 2019, p. 199) standards that define perfectionism.

While the tripartite model contends that healthy perfectionists and unhealthy perfectionists have different propensities towards positive and negative experiences, it does not describe factors that might enhance, inhibit, or even reverse these propensities. The reviewed qualitative investigations of perfectionism illuminated several potential factors. For example, Nordin-Bates and Kuylser (2020) found that unhealthy perfectionist dancers' concern over mistakes varied depending on their perceived degree of support from others. Mallinson-Howard et al. (2018) reported that healthy and unhealthy perfectionist athletes' potential to have positive experiences in sport depended on whether they perceived themselves to have superior comparative ability. Gotwals and

Tamminen (2022) chronicled the case of a healthy perfectionist athlete whose reactions to failure transitioned over time to being more in-line with those of unhealthy perfectionists after experiencing a high degree of personal success and being exposed to a more accomplished peer's work ethic. Incorporating such factors into the tripartite model would enhance the model's utility and contribution to the study of perfectionism (see Hill et al., 2020).

Summary

This section reviewed five studies (see Table 5.3) that used qualitative inquiry to explore healthy and unhealthy perfectionist athletes' and dancers' perspectives on a variety of topics including achievement, success and failure, and perfectionism itself. Across the studies the athletes and dancers expressed sentiments that aligned with the profiles that define healthy and unhealthy perfectionism and that reflected the orientations' proposed propensities towards positive and negative outcomes. While such findings support the tripartite model, the studies also produced novel findings that, if incorporated into the model, could enhance its utility to researchers and practitioners. Taken collectively, these findings demonstrate the ongoing value of utilizing qualitative inquiry to investigate the tripartite model within sport and dance contexts.

Summary of Findings across Analytical Approaches

This section of the chapter examined the degree to which the tripartite model is supported by studies on perfectionism in dance and sport that used one of three distinct analytical approaches: person-centred analytical approaches, canonical correlation analysis, and qualitative inquiry. Within each body of literature, a similar pattern emerged. Some studies fully supported the model by producing representations of both healthy and unhealthy perfectionism and showing that the two orientations differ in their association to positive and negative outcomes. In contrast, other studies did not show that healthy perfectionism was more healthy than non-perfectionism, did not produce evidence of both healthy and unhealthy perfectionism, directly challenged the notion of qualitatively distinct perfectionistic orientations altogether, or identified meaningful factors that are not addressed by the model. This pattern of variable support parallels the results produced in two previous reviews of the tripartite model (Hill & Madigan, 2017; Hill et al., 2020) and shows, importantly, that the findings extend to analytical approaches beyond solely cluster analysis.

Responses to Critiques of the Tripartite Model

Having provided a comprehensive review of research that has tested the tripartite model, we now address some critiques that have been directed toward the model. In their respective reviews, Hill and Madigan (2017) and Hill et al. (2020) highlighted and critiqued several contentious aspects of the tripartite model. In combination with the mixed empirical support, the authors contended that these critiques signal the demise of the tripartite model. In this section we respond to these critiques and re-evaluate this conclusion.

(Un)healthy Perfectionism Labels

One critique directed at the tripartite model is that by using the terms healthy and unhealthy to label perfectionism orientations the model is presupposing that those orientations are unconditionally associated with healthy and unhealthy outcomes (Gaudreau, 2016; Hill, 2021). This critique is based on the recognition that "no dimension or subtype of perfectionism is likely to be maladaptive (or adaptive) for everyone, under all circumstances" (Hill et al., 2020, p. 152). As indicated earlier, qualitative investigations of healthy and unhealthy perfectionistic athletes and dancers have provided evidence in support of this contention. As such, we feel that this is a valid critique and suggest that the labels used in the tripartite model to capture perfectionistic orientations should be revised to be valence-free and descriptive of their respective profiles across the two perfectionism dimensions. In recognition of large and expanding amount of research on the 2 × 2 model, and to avoid adding new terms to a field that already has an expansive and confusing lexicon, we would be in favour of adopting *personal standards perfectionism* and *evaluative concerns perfectionism* as labels for the two perfectionism dimensions and changing the labels of *healthy perfectionism* and *unhealthy perfectionism* to *pure personal standards perfectionism* and *mixed perfectionism*, respectively.[9]

Dimensional vs. Categorical Perfectionism

A second critique of the tripartite model concerns what is often considered to be a basic assumption of the tripartite model: namely, that perfectionism has a categorical structure and that "different *types* of perfectionists exist" (Hill et al., 2020, p. 127, italics in original; see also Hill & Madigan, 2017). Unpacked, this assumption infers that every person can be wholly categorized as endorsing one qualitatively distinct type of perfectionism. Given the dimensional solutions produced by some of the cluster analytic studies presently reviewed (e.g. Gucciardi et al., 2012; Nordin-Bates et al., 2011; Vallance et al., 2006), and in consideration of taxometric research suggesting that perfectionism exists in varying degrees (Broman-Fulks et al., 2008), this critique is difficult to argue against.

To determine how best to move forward we feel that it is important to highlight the predominant use of cluster analysis in the empirical development of the tripartite model. The stated purpose of Parker's (1997) seminal article was "to conduct a cluster analysis of the perfectionism scores of academically talented children to determine if there are different types of perfectionism" (p. 548). Rice, Slaney, and Ashby's collaborations repeatedly used cluster analysis to distinguish between groups of adaptive perfectionists, maladaptive perfectionists, or non-perfectionists (e.g. LoCicero & Ashby, 2000; Rice & Mirzadeh, 2000; Rice &

Slaney, 2002). Cluster analysis also featured prominently in the two works that codified the tripartite model. Stoeber and Otto's (2006) review was based on 20 group-based studies, 13 of which relied on cluster analysis to establish the groups (the other 7 studies used some form of dichotomization; e.g. mean- or median-splits). An initial cluster analysis also served as the starting point in Rice and Ashby's (2007) method of classifying perfectionists (see p. 76).

Given that cluster analysis assigns people to one – and only one – cluster (Pastor et al., 2007), it is understandable that a foundational assumption of the tripartite model would be that people can be categorized as one – and only one – type of perfectionist. Overreliance on a single method, though, can make any line of research susceptible to criticism based on the limitations of that method. In the case of the tripartite model, it is that the aim of categorical classification via of cluster analysis contrasts with evidence that perfectionism is an entity that varies by degree. In light of this, we feel that the foundational assumptions of the tripartite model should be re-envisioned.

Instead of basing the model on a method-based assumption of perfectionism typologies, we suggest shifting focus to assumptions that are more integral to perfectionism and more aligned with the construct's foundational structure. As foreshadowed earlier in the chapter, we propose a set of three assumptions. First, that perfectionism is composed of two overarching dimensions that are distributed *quantitatively* (as opposed to *categorically*) along a continuum. Second, that three different prototypical *forms* (as opposed to *types*) of perfectionism can be distinguished by distinct profiles of levels across the two continuous dimensions. Third, that different degrees of endorsement of these forms of perfectionism tend to be differentially associated with positive/ negative outcomes.

Cluster analysis partially aligns with the proposed set of assumptions in that the method can be used to group people into clusters based on their profile of scores across the two perfectionism dimensions and the clusters can subsequently be tested for differences on positive/negative criterion variables. However, the categorical and typological nature of these clusters does not reflect the assumption that people can endorse forms of perfectionism to different degrees. There are other methods, though, that do not show this limitation. Percentiles across the perfectionism dimensions have been used, for example, to identify participants who strongly endorse a certain form of perfectionism and who, as a result, are suitable candidates for subsequent interviews (e.g. Gotwals & Tamminen, 2022; Nordin-Bates & Kuylser, 2020). In addition, latent profile analysis "allows membership of a person to each cluster to a certain degree, allowing for fractional cluster membership as captured in the posterior probabilities" (Pastor et al., 2007, p. 20). As a result, in comparison to the original perfectionism typology assumption, the proposed set of assumptions are more amenable to examination through a diversity of methods and more resilient to criticism based on the limitations of any single method.

The proposed set of assumptions also align well with several contentions in the 2 × 2 model of perfectionism (Gaudreau & Thompson, 2010). This includes contentions that the two perfectionism dimensions "differ across individuals in terms of 'degree' (i.e. quantity) rather than in terms of 'kind' (i.e. types)" (Gaudreau, 2016, p. 175) that subtypes represent "different ways of being a perfectionist", (ibid., p. 175) and that endorsement of a perfectionism subtype "is probabilistic rather than deterministic" (ibid., p. 195). As a result, we feel that the proposed set of assumptions better position the tripartite model as a forebearer of the 2 × 2 model. This enhanced alignment also allows for examination of key differences between the two models. We address one of these key differences next.

Pure Evaluative Concerns Perfectionism

A third critique of the tripartite model is that it does not recognize pure evaluative concerns perfectionism (Hill & Madigan, 2017). In the 2 × 2 model of perfectionism, pure evaluative concerns perfectionism is defined by low levels of perfectionistic strivings in combination with high levels of perfectionistic concerns. In comparison to other perfectionism subtypes, the 2 × 2 model hypothesizes that pure evaluative concerns should show the strongest association with negative outcomes. Research findings in sport, dance, and exercise that test the 2 × 2 model tend to support this hypothesis (Hill et al., 2020). Accordingly, we agree that the absence of this group is worthy of investigation.

It is interesting that pure evaluative concerns perfectionism was generally not represented in the studies reviewed in this chapter. To be specific, we reviewed 22 studies that examined perfectionism through cluster analysis, latent profile analysis, or canonical correlation. Only 1 of those studies (Cumming & Duda, 2012) produced findings that included a representation (e.g. a cluster, a class, or a variate) of pure evaluative concerns perfectionism. There are several potential explanations for this. One is that perhaps researchers did not know to look for pure evaluative concerns perfectionism. The 2 × 2 model was originally presented by Gaudreau and Thompson (2010). Many of the cluster analytic studies we reviewed were published around that time or earlier (7 out of 9 studies were published in or before 2012). Given that relevance to theory is a characteristic to consider when selecting cluster solutions (Hair et al., 2010), perhaps at the time researchers were not aware enough of the 2 × 2 model to recognize the theoretical meaningfulness of clusters defined by low perfectionistic strivings and high perfectionistic concerns.

A second explanation could be that most of the studies reviewed in this chapter were contextualized within high performance sport or dance. As argued by Pacewicz et al. (2018), these contexts encourage and reward perfectionistic strivings and are rife with socially imposed pressures, expectations, and criticism. People who endorse pure evaluative concerns perfectionism, with their weak self-oriented drives for exceptional performance and strong sensitivities to socially prescribed pressures, may not fare well in such contexts and may thus be underrepresented. Analytical approaches highlighted in this review could be used to examine this speculation. For example, cluster analysis and latent profile analysis could be used across competition levels (e.g. intramural sport vs. club sport vs. varsity sport in North American colleges and universities) to identify differences in prevalence and degree of endorsement of pure evaluative concerns perfectionism. Qualitative methods could also be used to explore the experiences of pure evaluative concerns perfectionists as they progress through different levels of sport and dance. Such examinations would advance understanding this key difference between the tripartite model and the 2 × 2 model.

Summary

On basis of these criticisms of the tripartite model, in combination with the mixed evidence from sport- and dance-based cluster analytic research, Hill and Madigan (2017) concluded that the tripartite model and the 2 × 2 model are "contradictory" and that and that the rise of the latter "signals the end of the tripartite model" (p. 74). In contrast, in this section we offer a re-envisioned version of the tripartite model – one that shares considerable conceptual overlap with the 2 × 2 model. We have also recognized key differences between the two models and identified research directions that could potentially advance understanding of those differences. As such, we feel that the new version of the tripartite model that we have presented is analogous to the 2 × 2 model, that signalling the end of the tripartite model was perhaps premature, and that additional research using analytical tools covered in this chapter would likely benefit both models.

Concluding Comments

The purpose of this chapter was to use literature from sport and dance to evaluate the tripartite model. A review of three bodies of literature that used distinct analytical approaches identified a pattern of mixed support. On one hand, findings consistently showed that healthy perfectionism was more strongly linked to positive characteristics, processes, and outcomes than unhealthy perfectionism. On the other hand, the orientations specified in the model were often not reproduced, it is unclear if it is always better to be a healthy perfectionist than a non-perfectionist, and the model does not account for important moderating factors. We took this as an opportunity to respond to critiques of the model and to re-envision the foundational assumptions of the model. When seen from the suggested perspective, we feel that the tripartite model is better aligned with the multidimensional structure of perfectionism, more resilient to criticism, and better positioned as a predecessor to the 2 × 2 model. In line with the inductive manner in which the model was developed, analytically diverse research efforts are now needed to advance understanding of when and under what circumstances the principles of the tripartite model will be supported. It is hoped that this chapter inspires those kinds of research efforts within sport, dance, and exercise.

Notes

1 The chapter does not incorporate research from exercise because, to the best of our knowledge, no exercise-based studies on perfectionism have adopted analytical approaches that are amenable to the tripartite model.
2 Several studies that used cluster analysis or latent profile analysis to examine perfectionism among athletes or dancers were excluded from this review. This included studies that incorporated additional achievement motivation constructs as classification criteria (e.g. Gustaffson et al., 2016; Lemyre et al., 2008) and studies that conducted their analyses in a confirmatory, as opposed to exploratory, manner (e.g. Nordin-Bates et al., 2017).
3 Hill et al. (2020) presents effect sizes for all of these studies except for Pacewicz et al. (2018), who found that "mixed perfectionists" (i.e. unhealthy perfectionists) had significantly higher general burnout (d = 1.02), emotional and physical exhaustion (d = 0.72), perceptions of reduced accomplishment (d = 0.91), and sport devaluation (d = 1.22) compared to "pure personal standards perfectionists" (i.e. healthy perfectionists).
4 There is also some concern over the degree to which Cumming and Duda's (2012) cluster solution reflects the 2 × 2 model (see Stoeber, 2014).
5 These cluster differences were reported in two articles using the same samples: Cumming and Duda (2012) and Quested, Cumming, and Duda (2014).
6 In Hill et al.'s (2020) review, the cluster solutions produced by Gucciardi et al. (2012) and Martinent and Ferrand (2006) were treated as representative of the tripartite model. We do not feel that this is appropriate given the dimensional nature of the solutions. This is noteworthy because Hill et al. documented six instances in which differences between clusters of 'healthy perfectionists' and 'non-perfectionists' were not in the expected direction. These instances were judged as contradictory to the tripartite model. However, all six instances came from Gucciardi et al.'s and Martinent and Ferrand's studies. While we agree that these two studies challenge the tripartite model, we feel that it is not because differences between the clusters do not evidence the proposed healthy nature of healthy perfectionism. Instead, the studies challenge the model because their cluster solutions were dimensional and, as a result, did not represent healthy perfectionism in the first place.
7 Dunn et al. (2011) and Gotwals et al. (2010) each conducted two separate canonical correlation analyses: one involving assessments of global perfectionism and one involving assessments of sport perfectionism. In this review, each analysis is considered to represent a separate 'study.' Some other sport-based studies that also used canonical correlation were not included (e.g. Lemyre et al., 2008; Ommundsen et al., 2005) because they incorporated additional achievement motivation constructs within the predictor variates (see also Footnote 2).
8 None of these studies identified athletes whose subscale score profile reflected non-perfectionism as defined in the tripartite model. Additionally, two of the studies – Mallinson-Howard et al. (2018) and Nordin-Bates and Kuylser (2020) – identified examples of all four subtypes in the 2 × 2 model of perfectionism. For these studies the present review summarizes findings pertaining only to the examples of "pure personal standards perfectionism" and "mixed perfectionism". This is because the dimensional profile that defines these two subtypes matches those of healthy and unhealthy perfectionists (respectively).
9 Despite this, we continue to use the tripartite model's original labels through the remainder of the chapter in an effort to maintain consistency with earlier sections and reflect current usage.

References

Bergman, L. R., & Andersson, H. (2010). The person and the variable in developmental psychology. *Journal of Psychology*, 218(3), 155–165. https://doi.org/10.1027/0044-3409/a 000025.

Broman-Fulks, J. J., Hill, R. W., & Green, B. A. (2008). Is perfectionism categorical or dimensional? A taxometric analysis. *Journal of Personality Assessment*, 90(5), 481–490. https://doi.org/10.1080/00223890802248802.

Cumming, J., & Duda, J. L. (2012). Profiles of perfectionism, body-related concerns, and indicators of psychological health in vocational dance students: An investigation of the 2 × 2 model of perfectionism. *Psychology of Sport and Exercise*, 13(6), 729–738. https://doi.org/10.1016/j.psychsport.2012.05.004.

Curran, T., Hill, A. P., Jowett, G. E., & Mallinson, S. H. (2014). The relationship between multidimensional perfectionism and passion in junior athletes. *International Journal of Sport Psychology*, 45(4), 369–384. https://doi.org/10.7352/IJSP 2014.45.369.

Dunn, J. G. H., Causgrove Dunn, J., Gamache, V., & Holt, N. L. (2014). A person-oriented examination of perfectionism and slump-related coping in female inter-collegiate volleyball players. *International Journal of Sport Psychology*, 45(4), 298–324. https://doi.org/10.7352/IJSP 2014.45.298.

Dunn, J. G. H., Causgrove Dunn, J. L., & Syrotuik, D. G. (2002). Relationship between multidimensional perfectionism and goal orientations in sport. *Journal of Sport & Exercise Psychology*, 24(4), 376–395.

Dunn, J. G. H., Craft, J. M., Causgrove Dunn, J., & Gotwals, J. K. (2011). Comparing a domain-specific and global measure of perfectionism in competitive female figure skaters. *Journal of Sport Behavior*, 34(1), 25–46.

Dunn, J.G.H., Gotwals, J. K., Causgrove Dunn, J., & Lizmore, M. R. (2020). Perfectionism, pre-competitive worry, and optimism in high-performance youth athletes. *International Journal of Sport and Exercise Psychology*, 18(6), 749–763.

Dunn, J. G. H., Gotwals, J. K., Causgrove Dunn, J., & Syrotuik, D. G. (2006). Examining the relationship between perfectionism and trait anger in competitive sport. *International Journal of Sport and Exercise Psychology*, 4(1), 7–24. https://doi.org/10.1080/1612197X.2006.9671781.

Flett, G. L., & Hewitt, P. L. (2002). Perfectionism and maladjustment: An overview of theoretical, definitional, and treatment issues. In G. L. Flett & P. L. Hewitt (eds), *Perfectionism: Theory, research and practice* (pp. 33–62). American Psychological Association.

Frost, R. O., Marten, P., Lahart, C., & Rosenblate, R. (1990). The dimensions of perfectionism. *Cognitive Therapy and Research*, 14(5), 449–468. https://doi.org/10.1007/BF01172967.

Gaudreau, P. (2016). The 2 × 2 model of perfectionism in sport, dance, and exercise. In A. P. Hill (ed.), *The psychology of perfectionism in sport, dance and exercise* (pp. 174–200). Routledge.

Gaudreau, P. (2019). On the distinction between personal standards perfectionism and excellencism: A theory elaboration and research agenda. *Perspectives on Psychological Science*, 14(2), 197–215. https://doi.org/10.1177/1745691618797940.

Gaudreau, P., & Thompson, A. (2010). Testing a 2 × 2 model of dispositional perfectionism. *Personality and Individual Differences*, 48(5), 532–537. https://doi.org/10.1016/j.paid.2009.11.031.

Gotwals, J. K. (2011). Perfectionism and burnout within intercollegiate sport: A person-oriented approach. *The Sport Psychologist*, 25(4), 489–510.

Gotwals, J. K., & Dunn, J. G. H. (2009). A multi-method multi-analytic approach to establishing internal construct validity evidence: The Sport Multidimensional Perfectionism Scale 2. *Measurement in Physical Education & Exercise Science*, 13(2), 71–92. https://doi.org/10.1080/10913670902812663.

Gotwals, J. K., Dunn, J. G. H., Causgrove Dunn, J., & Gamache, V. (2010). Establishing validity evidence for the Sport Multidimensional Perfectionism Scale-2 in intercollegiate sport. *Psychology of Sport and Exercise*, 11(6), 423–432. https://doi.org/10.1016/j.psychsport.2010.04.013.

Gotwals, J. K., Dunn, J. G. H., & Wayment, H. A. (2003). An examination of perfectionism and self-esteem in intercollegiate athletes. *Journal of Sport Behavior*, 26(1), 17–37.

Gotwals, J. K., & Spencer-Cavaliere, N. (2014). Intercollegiate perfectionistic athletes' perspectives on achievement: Contributions to the understanding and assessment of perfectionism in sport. *International Journal of Sport Psychology*, 45(4), 271–297. https://doi.org/10.7352/IJSP 2014.

Gotwals, J. K., Stoeber, J., Dunn, J. G. H., & Stoll, O. (2012). Are perfectionistic strivings in sport adaptive? A systematic review of confirmatory, contradictory, and mixed evidence. *Canadian Psychology*, 53(4), 263–279. https://doi.org/10.1037/a0030288.

Gotwals, J. K., & Tamminen, K. A. (2022). Intercollegiate perfectionistic athletes' perspectives on success and failure in sport. *Journal of Applied Sport Psychology*, 34(1), 25–46. https://doi.org/10.1080/10413200.2020.1740826.

Greenspon, T. S., Parker, W. D., & Shuler, P. A. (2000). The author's dialogue. *Journal of Secondary Gifted Education*, 11(4), 209–214.

Gucciardi, D. F., Mahoney, J., Jalleh, G., Donovan, R. J., & Parkes, J. (2012). Perfectionistic profiles among elite athletes and differences in their motivational orientations. *Journal of Sport & Exercise Psychology*, 34(2), 159–183.

Gustafsson, H., Hill, A. P., Stenling, A., Wagnsson, S. (2016). Profiles of perfectionism, parental climate, and burnout among competitive junior athletes. *Scandinavian Journal of Medicine & Science in Sports*, 26(10), 1256–1264.

Hair, J. F., Anderson, R. E., Tatham, R. L., & Black, W. C. (1998). *Multivariate data analysis* (5th ed.). Prentice Hall.

Hair, J. F., Black, W. C., Babin, B. J., & Anderson, R. E. (2010). *Multivariate data analysis* (7th ed.). Pearson Education.

Hall, H. K., Kerr, A. W., & Matthews, J. (1998). Precompetitive anxiety in sport: The contribution of achievement goals and perfectionism. *Journal of Sport & Exercise Psychology*, 20(2), 194–217.

Hamachek, D. E. (1978). Psychodynamics of normal and neurotic perfectionism. *Psychology*, 15(1), 27–33.

Hewitt, P. L., & Flett, G. L. (1991). Perfectionism in the self and social contexts: Conceptualization, assessment, and association with psycho-pathology. *Journal of Personality and Social Psychology*, 60(3), 456–470. https://doi.org/10.1037/0022–3514.60.3.456.

Hill, A. P. (2021). Perfectionism myths. In I. Taylor & C. Englert (eds), *Handbook of Self-Regulation and Motivation* (pp. 76–86). Taylor & Francis.

Hill, A. P. & Madigan, D. (2017). A short review of perfectionism in sport, dance, and exercise: Out with the old, in with the 2 × 2. *Current Opinion in Psychology*, 16, 72–77.

Hill, A. P., Mallinson-Howard, S., Madigan, D. J., & Jowett, G. E. (2020). Perfectionism in sport, dance, and exercise: An extended review and re-analysis. In G. Tenenbaum & R. C. Eklund (Eds.), *Handbook of Sport Psychology* (4th ed., pp. 121–157). Wiley.

Hill, R.W., Huelsman, T.J., Furr, R.M., Kibler, J., Vicente, B.B., & Kennedy, C. (2004). A new measure of perfectionism: The Perfectionism Inventory. *Journal of Personality Assessment*, 82(1), 80–91. https://doi.org/10.1207/s15327752jpa8201_13.

Lemyre, P. N., Hall, H. K., & Roberts, G. C. (2008). A social cognitive approach to burnout in elite athletes. *Scandinavian Journal of Medicine & Science in Sports*, 18(2), 221–234. https://doi.org/10.1111/j.1600–0838.2007.00671.x.

Lizmore, M. R., Dunn, J. G. H., & Causgrove Dunn, J. (2016). Reactions to mistakes as a function of perfectionism and situation criticality in curling. *International Journal of Sport Psychology*, 47(1), 81–101.

LoCicero, K., & Ashby, J. S. (2000). Multidimensional perfectionism and self-reported self-efficacy in college students. *Journal of College Student Psychotherapy*, 15(2), 47–56. https://doi.org/10.1300/J035v15n02_06.

Mallinson-Howard, S. H., Knight, C. J., Hill, A. P., & Hall, H. K. (2018). The 2 × 2 model of perfectionism and youth sport participation: A mixed-methods approach. *Psychology of Sport & Exercise*, 36, 162–173. https://doi.org/10.1016/j.psychsport.2018.02.011.

Martinent, G., & Ferrand, C. (2006). A cluster analysis of perfectionism among competitive athletes. *Psychological Reports*, 99(3), 723–738. https://doi.org/10.2466/PR0.99.7.723–738.

Nordin-Bates, S. M., Cumming, J., Aways, D., & Sharp, L. (2011). Imagining yourself dancing to perfection? Correlates of perfectionism among ballet and contemporary dancers. *Journal of Clinical Sport Psychology*, 5(1), 58–76.

Nordin-Bates, S. M., Raedeke, T. D., & Madigan, D. J. (2017). Perfectionism, burnout, and motivation in dance: A replication and test of the 2 × 2 model of perfectionism. *Journal of Dance Medicine & Science*, 21(3), 115–122. https://doi.org/10.12678/1089–1313X.21.3.115.

Nordin-Bates, S. M., & Kuylser, S. (2020). High striving, high costs? A qualitative examination of perfectionism in high-level dance. *Journal of Dance Education*, 21(4), 212–223. https://doi.org/10.1080/15290824.2019.1709194.

Ommundsen, Y., Roberts, G. C., Lemyre, P. N., & Miller, B. W. (2005). Peer relationships in adolescent competitive soccer: Associations to perceived motivational climate, achievement goals and perfectionism. *Journal of Sports Sciences*, 23(9), 977–989. https://doi.org/10.1080/02640410500127975.

Pacewicz, C. E., Gotwals, J. K., & Blanton, J. E. (2018). Perfectionism, coping, and burnout among intercollegiate varsity athletes: A person-oriented investigation of group differences and mediation. *Psychology of Sport and Exercise*, 35, 207–217. https://doi.org/10.1016/j.psychsport.2017.12.008.

Parker, W. D. (1997). An empirical typology of perfectionism in academically talented children. *American Educational Research Journal*, 34(3), 545–562. https://doi.org/10.3102/00028312034003545.

Pastor, D. A., Barron, K. E., Miller, B. J., & Davis, S. L. (2007). A latent profile analysis of college students' achievement goal orientation. *Contemporary Educational Psychology*, 32(1), 8–47. https://doi.org/10.1016/j.cedpsych.2006.10.003.

Quested, E., Cumming, J., & Duda, J. L. (2014). Profiles of perfectionism, motivation, and self-evaluations among dancers: An extended analysis of Cumming and Duda (2012). *International Journal of Sport Psychology*, 45(4), 349–368. https://doi.org/10.7352/IJSP 2014.45.349.

Rice, K. G., & Ashby, J. S. (2007). An efficient method for classifying perfectionists. *Journal of Counseling Psychology*, 54(1), 72–85. https://doi.org/10.1037/0022-0167.54.1.72

Rice, K. G., Bair, C. J., Castor, J. R., Cohen B. N., & Hood, C. A. (2003). Meanings of perfectionism: A quantitative and qualitative analysis. *Journal of Cognitive*

Psychotherapy: An International Quarterly, 17(1), 39–58. https://doi.org/10.1891/jcop.17.1.39.58266.

Rice, K. G., Lopez, F., G., & Richardson, C. M. E. (2013). Perfectionism and performance among STEM students. *Journal of Vocational Behavior*, 82(2), 124–134. https://doi.org/10.1016/j.jvb.2012.12.002.

Rice, K. G., & Mirzadeh, S. A. (2000). Perfectionism, attachment, and adjustment. *Journal of Counseling Psychology*, 47, 238–250. https://doi.org/10.1037/0022–0167.47.2.238.

Rice, K. G., & Slaney, R. B. (2002). Clusters of perfectionists: Two studies of emotional adjustment and academic achievement. *Measurement and Evaluation in Counseling and Development*, 35(1), 35–48. https://doi.org/10.1080/07481756.2002.12069046.

Sapieja, K. M., Dunn, J. G. H., & Holt, N. L. (2011). Perfectionism and perceptions of parenting styles in male youth soccer. *Journal of Sport & Exercise Psychology*, 33(1), 20–39.

Sellars, P. A., Evans, L., & Thomas, O. (2016). The effects of perfectionism in elite sport: Experiences of unhealthy perfectionists. *The Sport Psychologist*, 30(3), 219–230. https://doi.org/10.1123/tsp.2014–0072.

Slaney, R. B., Mobley, M., Trippi, J., Ashby, J., & Johnson, D. G. (1996). The Almost Perfect Scale–Revised. Unpublished manuscript, Pennsylvania State University, University Park Campus.

Stoeber, J. (2014). *Perfectionism in sport and dance: A double-edged sword. International Journal of Sport Psychology*, 45(4), 385–394. https://doi.org/10.7352/IJSP 2014.45.385.

Stoeber, J., & Otto, K. (2006). Positive conceptions of perfectionism: Approaches, evidence, challenges. *Personality and Social Psychology Review*, 10(4), 295–319. https://doi.org/10.1207/s15327957pspr1004_2.

Stoeber, J., Otto, K., Pescheck, E., Becker, C., & Stoll, O. (2007). Perfectionism and competitive anxiety in athletes: Differentiating striving for perfection and negative reactions to imperfection. *Personality and Individual Differences*, 42, 959–969. https://doi.org/10.1016/j.paid.2006.09.006.

Vaartstra, M., Dunn, J. G. H., & Causgrove Dunn, J. (2018). Perfectionism and perceptions of social loafing in competitive youth soccer. *Journal of Sport Behaviour*, 41(4), 475–500.

Vallance, J. K. H., Dunn, J. G. H., & Causgrove Dunn, J. (2006). Perfectionism, anger, and situation criticality in competitive youth ice hockey. *Journal of Sport & Exercise Psychology*, 28(3), 383–406.

6 The 2 × 2 Model of Perfectionism in Sport, Dance, and Exercise

An Updated and Critical Review

Patrick Gaudreau

More than a decade ago, the 2 × 2 model of perfectionism was proposed to revisit and reformulate the effects studied in the multidimensional perfectionism literature. The model has received a fair amount of empirical attention and the 2 × 2 literature has been summarized in several reviews. In this chapter, I will start with a brief overview of the four subtypes of perfectionism and four hypotheses of this model. Then, I will present an updated review of studies that specifically investigated the 2 × 2 model with athletes, dancers, and exercisers. Attention will also be paid to a recent review that reinterpreted the whole perfectionism literature in sport, dance, and exercise in light of the 2 × 2 model. Finally, critical issues will be discussed to further enrich our understanding of the 2 × 2 model.

The 2 × 2 Model of Perfectionism

Key Definitions, Assumptions, and Hypotheses

Perfectionism is operationalized as a personality system composed of two broad dimensions applicable to all individuals: Personal Standards Perfectionism (PSP) and Evaluative Concerns Perfectionism (ECP). The 2 × 2 model proposes that crossing these two broad dimensions reveals four distinct within-person configurations of PSP and ECP (hereafter referred as *subtypes of perfectionism*). Although everyone probably has a unique way of being a perfectionist, the 2 × 2 model tries to parsimoniously summarize key individual differences situated at the intersections of low and high levels of PSP and ECP in a quadripartite framework that differentiates four *prototypical ways of being a perfectionist* (see Figure 6.1).

The first subtype, *non-perfectionism* is positioned as a control condition in the 2 × 2 model. As its name implies, it represents people with low scores on both PSP and ECP. If we agree that perfectionism is unhealthy, then we inherently assume that non-perfectionism should be the most optional subtype in the 2 × 2 model. If there is one way of being a perfectionist that could potentially yield positive outcomes, it would be the second subtype, *pure PSP*, which portrays individuals with a combined high score on PSP and low score on ECP. The

DOI: 10.4324/9781003288015-8

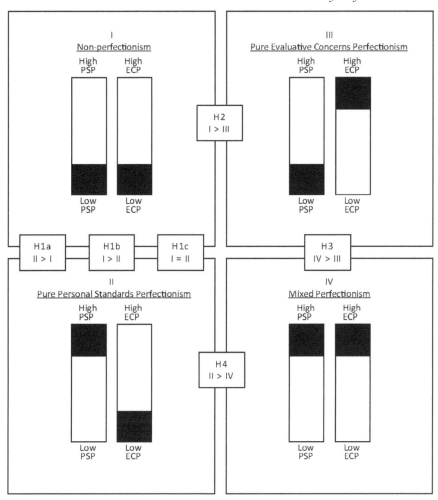

Figure 6.1 Four subtypes of perfectionism and four hypotheses of the 2 × 2 model of perfectionism. > denotes better psychological adjustment. = denotes equivalent psychological adjustment

third subtype, *mixed perfectionism*, describes the prototypical case of people with combined high levels of both PSP and ECP. Finally, the 2 × 2 model differentiates this subtype from a fourth within-person combination – *pure ECP* – that depicts individuals with a high level of ECP combined with a low level of PSP.

The 2 × 2 model of perfectionism is advantageous because it proposes testable and refutable hypotheses. The model was developed after nearly 20 years of research, at a time at which a priori and falsifiable hypotheses were needed to move our research from an exploratory to a theory-driven paradigm. After a decade of research, the 2 × 2 model remains a flexible open-ended system composed of four hypotheses (see Figure 6.1). It has proven useful to encourage further theorizing, both inside (Gaudreau, 2019) and outside the perfectionism literature (Schellenberg et al., 2018). As expected, the model guided research, facilitated the interpretation of findings, and provided a framework to compare findings across studies.

Ten years ago, many researchers and practitioners highlighted the need to investigate the possible healthiness of perfectionism because several empirical studies showed positive associations between PSP and desirable outcomes such as positive affectivity, subjective well-being, and task performance (Gotwals et al., 2012; Stoeber, 2011). Since then, meta-analytical reviews provided evidence for a positive association between PSP and a mixture of desirable and undesirable outcomes (e.g. Hill & Curran, 2015; Hill et al., 2018; Limburg et al., 2017). The subtype of pure PSP still remains at the forefront of fruitful discussions regarding the healthiness and unhealthiness of perfectionism (Hill, 2014; Stoeber & Gaudreau, 2017) and the three alternative versions of Hypothesis 1 are still relevant to examine whether pure PSP is associated with better (*Hypothesis 1a*), worse (*Hypothesis 1b*), or equivalent (*Hypothesis 1c*) outcomes compared to a subtype of non-perfectionism.

As shown in previous chapters of this book, the unhealthiness of ECP has been commonly accepted in the perfectionism literature. Even when the 2 × 2 model was developed, ample evidence had already accumulated to indicate that ECP relates to a myriad of undesirable outcomes in sport, dance, and other life domains. Therefore, *Hypothesis 2* was meant to foreshadow that a subtype of pure ECP should be associated to worse outcomes compared to a subtype of non-perfectionism. Another important question addressed in the 2 × 2 model is whether pure ECP is actually the worst subtype of perfectionism. Before the 2 × 2 model, the tripartite model had already proposed that high levels of both PSP and ECP should be worse than other subtypes of perfectionism (e.g. Rice & Ashby, 2007). The last two hypotheses of the 2 × 2 model stood in contrast to this assertion. A within-person combination with high levels of PSP and ECP is defined as mixed perfectionism rather than as inherently maladaptive perfectionism. In mixed perfectionism, the person tends to perceive that others are exerting pressure to be perfect, to evaluate accordingly, and to doubt one's capacity to reach exceedingly high outcomes that are socially prescribed. Yet, the person also has a self-directed tendency to set, embrace, and pursue exacting standards that are deemed important, valuable, and consequential for one's self-worth. The combinatory presence of high levels of ECP and PSP denotes a partial internalization in which the perceived external contingencies are cohabiting in relative harmony with personal standards, values, and priorities. This form of person-environment congruence is likely to buffer some of the negative effects of ECP associated with the socially pressuring and evaluative characteristics of perfectionism. Considering the aforementioned rationale, the 2 × 2 model hypothesized that mixed perfectionism should be associated to relatively better outcomes compared to pure ECP (*Hypothesis 3*) but to worse outcomes compared to pure PSP (*Hypothesis 4*). In that sense, the 2 × 2 model proposes that pure ECP is potentially the most debilitative subtype of perfectionism.

Conceptual, Analytical, and Interpretational Considerations

In a typical study on the 2 × 2 model of perfectionism, participants complete questionnaires designed to measure core dimensions of perfectionism (i.e. PSP and ECP) and/or their underlying characteristics. A majority of studies relied on Frost et al. (1990; F-MPS) and Hewitt and Flett (1991; HF-MPS) Multi-dimensional Perfectionism Scale or scales inspired by these frameworks (e.g. Dunn et al., 2006). Researchers have relied on different measures because the 2 × 2 model is not prescriptive regarding which ones should preferably be used in empirical studies. At a first glance, the variety of measurement decisions made by researchers could be seen as an obstacle to compare findings across studies. However, this variety is an opportunity to evaluate the extent to which different conceptual frameworks generate comparable findings. As such, some studies have found important differences depending on which questionnaires were used to test the model (Hill, Madigan, & Jowett, 2020; Waleriańczyk, Hill, & Stolarski, 2022).

Studies on the 2 × 2 model have operationalized perfectionism at different levels of analysis. The F-MPS and HF-MPS ask individuals to refer to their lives in general. This global level of generality has proven useful to predict global life outcomes (e.g. life satisfaction, depression) as well as outcomes that are specific to a life domain (e.g. academic achievement). Sport scientists have also adopted a domain-specific approach in which the participants rate their perfectionism in reference to their experience in sport (e.g. Mallinson-Howard et al., 2019) or dance (e.g. Jowett et al., 2021). Domain-specific ratings can capture some of the idiosyncrasies of being a perfectionist in sport or dance without necessarily being a perfectionist across all other areas of one's lives. Overall, both approaches remain acceptable given that researchers have yet to consensually determine if perfectionism is better operationalized at the dispositional or the domain-specific level.

Subtypes of perfectionism are not known and directly observable subgroups in the population. Scores of PSP and ECP (or scores from their specific facets) are analysed with multivariable statistical analyses to evaluate and compare the consequences associated with the subtypes of perfectionism proposed in the 2 × 2 model. These statistical analyses have fallen into two broad families of multivariate statistics: A group-centred approach (e.g. cluster analyses, latent class modelling) and a variable-centred approach (e.g. multiple regression, structural equation modelling). Multiple regression, with and without interaction terms, is a straight-forward approach to test the model. A methodological tutorial is available to help the interpretation of results from multiple regressions in light of the hypotheses of the 2 × 2 model (Gaudreau, 2012). These guidelines can also be used to interpret the findings obtained with more advanced analytical approaches that corrects for measurement errors (i.e. structural equation modelling) and non-independence of the data (i.e. multilevel modelling). The variable-centred approach offers flexibility to incorporate categorical (Franche et al., 2012) and continuous (Crocker et al., 2014) variables that can moderate the associations between subtypes of perfectionism and outcomes. Of foremost importance, multiple regressions and their extensions are treating perfectionism dimensions as continuous distributions. Suboptimal or unwarranted partitioning of the total sample into subgroups is therefore avoided. "Breaking up" can be difficult (Streiner, 2002). Arbitrary divisions performed with "eye balling" or median split are known to create spurious effects hardly replicable across samples (Bissonnette et al., 1990) and should not be used in the 2 × 2 model.

Technically appropriate cluster analyses and latent class modelling have been performed in the 2 × 2 literature (e.g. Cumming & Duda, 2012; Nordin-Bates et al., 2017; Quested et al., 2014). This approach, however, require larger samples to divide them in smaller subgroups. The number and the definition of the subgroups obtained with these techniques are often misaligned with the operational definitions of the 2 × 2 model (Gaudreau et al., 2018). Better alignment with the theory could be obtained by placing specific constraints on the parameters of the latent class model. Researchers espousing the group-centred tradition should test the 2 × 2 model with confirmatory rather than exploratory latent class modelling (Finch & Bronk, 2011). For all these reasons, the current review focused on studies that relied on the variable-centred approach.

In the following section, the results of studies are reported and interpreted in terms of their effect size rather than statistical significance. Statistical significance was relied on only when effect sizes were not published or calculable. First, null hypothesis significance testing offers a dichotomous portrait of whether evidence exists to support a hypothesis. Second, moderate effects, like the ones typically observed in personality psychology (Richard et al., 2003), are likely to reach statistical significance in larger samples while failing to reach the same threshold with relatively smaller samples. Consequently, null hypothesis significance testing offers an ambiguous metric to evaluate and compare findings across studies. Effect sizes, like the Cohen's d, offer a more nuanced interpretation that helps evaluate the strength of effects in each study and across studies. The Cohen's d estimates of .20, .50, and .80 were interpreted as weak, medium, and strong effects, respectively (Johnson & Boynton, 2008).

Research in Sport, Dance, and Exercise

For more than a decade, the 2 × 2 model has offered refutable hypotheses to guide research. Many researchers have cited, discussed, and even praised the model as a significant contribution to the literature. However, far less empirical effort has been invested to directly test the model. Given the growing acceptance of the model (e.g. Hill & Madigan, 2017; Stoeber, 2014), Hill, Mallinson-Howard, Madigan, & Jowett (2020) reanalysed and reinterpreted the independent effects of PSP and ECP using the 2 × 2 model as an integrative framework. Their results are summarized before focusing on studies that carried specific tests of the 2 × 2 model.

Reanalysing the Independent Effects of PSP and ECP with the 2 × 2 Model of Perfectionism

Hill, Mallinson-Howard, Madigan, & Jowett (2020) reanalysed the extant literature conducted in sport, dance, and exercise using the 2 × 2 model as a framework to reinterpret and integrate the findings. Sixty-three studies totalling 1772 effect sizes were included in their review. Robust support (94% of the time) was found for *Hypotheses 2 and 4* across different types of affective, motivational, and performance outcomes. This finding indicates that pure ECP and mixed perfectionism are quite systematically associated with a bad outcome (i.e. low adjustment or high maladjustment) compared non-perfectionism and pure PSP, respectively. Results for *Hypotheses 1 and 3* showed more variability, which could suggest potential impact of moderating influences. Support was found 70% of the time, meaning that pure PSP (compared to non-perfectionism) and mixed perfectionism (compared to pure ECP) were mostly associated with a good outcome (i.e. high adjustment or low maladjustment) while being less frequently (30% of the time) associated with a bad outcome (i.e. low adjustment or high maladjustment). Overall, results of the studies using the independent effects approach closely matched the four hypotheses even if they were not formally conducted to test the 2 × 2 model of perfectionism.

Direct Tests of the 2 × 2 Model of Perfectionism

Research that directly studied the 2 × 2 model was mostly conducted with athletes using a sport-specific operationalization of perfectionism. Summarizing this growing literature is a complex task because researchers have measured different types of outcomes. In this review, studies are regrouped depending on whether they mostly focused on indicators of positive/negative sport experiences, burnout and engagement, coping and emotion regulation, doping in sport, and performance. When available the effect sizes of these studies are summarized based on the four hypotheses of the model (see Table 6.1).

Positive/Negative Sport Experiences

Gaudreau and Verner-Filion (2012) presented the first test of the 2 × 2 model of perfectionism in sport. A sample of 208 athletes (aged between 14 and 28 years) rated their general perfectionism and their affective (i.e. positive affect), eudemonic (i.e. vitality), and cognitive (i.e. life-satisfaction) subjective well-being.

Results for *Hypothesis 1* indicated that pure PSP was not associated with significantly better overall subjective well-being than non-perfectionism. The absolute average Cohen's *d* effect size was 0.14, thus indicating a very small

Table 6.1 Review of the studies examining the hypotheses of the 2 × 2 model of perfectionism and effect sizes (Cohen's *d*) in sport, dance, and exercise.

Authors and Outcomes	H1 Pure PSP vs. Non	H2 Non vs. Pure ECP	H3 Mixed vs. Pure ECP	H4 Pure PSP vs. mixed	Scales	Level of Generality	Sample
Gaudreau & Verner-Filion (2012)					HF-MPS (SOP, SPP)	DISPO	208 athletes
Life satisfaction	d = 0.21	d = 0.85	d = 0.63	d = 0.43			
Subjective vitality	d = 0.12	d = 0.90	d = 0.82	d = 0.20			
Positive affect	d = 0.08	d = 0.63	d = 0.83	d = −0.13*			
Hill (2013)					HF-MPS (SOP, SPP) and Sport-MPS-2 (PS, COM, DAA, PP)	CON	167 junior male soccer players
Total burnout	d = −0.67	d = −0.76	d = −0.67	d = −0.76			
Reduced sense of accomplishment	d = −0.85	d = −0.67	d = −0.85	d = −0.67			
Physical/emotional exhaustion	d = −0.22	d = −0.59	d = −0.22	d = −0.59			
Sport devaluation	d = −0.31	d = −0.97	d = −0.94	d = −0.34			
Mallinson et al. (2014)					Sport MPS2 (PS, COM, DAA)	CON	219 young sport participants
Sport enjoyment	d = 0.79	d = 0.65	d = 0.79	d = 0.65			
Physical self-worth	d = 0.38	d = 0.69	d = 0.38	d = 0.69			
Self-esteem enhancement and supportiveness	d = 0.83	d = 0.84	d = 0.83	d = 0.84			
Loyalty and intimacy	d = 0.41	d = 0.43	d = 0.41	d = 0.43			
Things in common	d = 0.33	d = 0.67	d = 0.87	d = 0.13			
Companionship and pleasant play	d = 0.56	d = 0.43	d = 0.56	d = 0.43			
Conflict resolution	d = 0.28	d = 0.86	d = 0.90	d = 0.23			
Friendship conflict	d = −0.20	d = −0.75	d = −0.20	d = −0.75			

Authors and Outcomes	H1 Pure PSP vs. Non	H2 Non vs. Pure ECP	H3 Mixed vs. Pure ECP	H4 Pure PSP vs. mixed	Scales	Level of Generality	Sample
Hill & Davis (2014)					HF-MPS (SOP, SPP) and F-MPS (PS, COM, DAA, and PP)	DISPO	227 coaches
Internal control of anger	$d = 0.32$	$d = 0.24$	$d = 0.32$	$d = 0.24$			
External control of anger	$d = 0.35$	$d = 0.32$	$d = 0.35$	$d = 0.32$			
Cognitive reappraisal	$d = 0.35$	$d = 0.23$	$d = 0.35$	$d = 0.23$			
Suppression	$d = 0.05*$	$d = -0.25$	$d = 0.53*$	$d = -0.72$			
Crocker et al. (2014)					Sport-MPS-2 (PS, COM)	CON	179 university athletes
Positive affect	$d = 0.71$	$d = 0.24$	$d = 0.71$	$d = 0.24$			
Control appraisal	$d = 0.61$	$d = 0.54$	$d = 0.61$	$d = 0.54$			
Challenge appraisal	$d = 0.38$	$d = 0.39$	$d = 0.38$	$d = 0.39$			
Goal progress	$d = 0.60$	$d = 0.41$	$d = 0.60$	$d = 0.41$			
Negative affect	$d = -0.12$	$d = -0.62$	$d = -0.12$	$d = -0.62$			
Threat appraisals	$d = 0.01*$	$d = -0.40$	$d = 0.01*$	$d = -0.40$			
Problem-focused coping	$d = 0.07$	$d = 0.03$	$d = 0.07$	$d = 0.03$			
Avoidance-focused coping	$d = -0.22$	$d = -0.43$	$d = -0.22$	$d = -0.43$			
Internal control of anger	$d = 0.32$	$d = 0.24$	$d = 0.32$	$d = 0.24$			
External control of anger	$d = 0.35$	$d = 0.32$	$d = 0.35$	$d = 0.32$			
Cognitive reappraisal	$d = 0.35$	$d = 0.23$	$d = 0.35$	$d = 0.23$			
Suppression	$d = 0.05*$	$d = -0.25$	$d = 0.53*$	$d = -0.72$			

Authors and Outcomes	H1 Pure PSP vs. Non	H2 Non vs. Pure ECP	H3 Mixed vs. Pure ECP	H4 Pure PSP vs. mixed	Scales	Level of Generality	Sample
Madigan et al. (2016)					Sport MPS (PS, COM) MIPS (PeS, NRI).	CON	111 varsity and local club athletes
Change total burnout	$d = -0.48$	$d = -0.61$	$d = -0.75$	$d = -0.30$			
Change reduced sense of achievement	$d = -0.72$	$d = -0.64$	$d = -0.72$	$d = -0.64$			
Change exhaustion	$d = -0.21$	$d = -0.53$	$d = -0.61$	$d = -0.04$			
Change sport devaluation	$d = -0.49$	$d = -0.32$	$d = -0.49$	$d = -0.32$			
Mallinson-Howard et al. (2019)					Sport MPS2 (PS, COM)	CON	222 young sport participants
Negative affect	$d = -0.26$	$d = -0.86$	$d = 0.16*$	$d = 0.-1.28$			
Positive affect	$d = 0.86$	$d = 0.1.10$	$d = 0.88$	$d = 0.1.09$			
Concentration disruption	$d = -0.32$	$d = 0.-1.25$	$d = 0.-1.06$	$d = -0.51$			
Cognitive anxiety (worry)	$d = 0.10*$	$d = -0.45$	$d = 0.10*$	$d = -0.45$			
Somatic anxiety	$d = 0.21*$	$d = -0.83$	$d = -0.39$	$d = -0.23$			
Antisocial behaviours teammates	$d = 0.04*$	$d = 0.18*$	$d = 0.1.01*$	$d = -0.79$			
Antisocial behaviours opponents	$d = 0.28*$	$d = -0.07$	$d = 0.93*$	$d = -0.72$			
Intentions to dropout	$d = -0.50$	$d = -0.53$	$d = -0.50$	$d = -0.53$			
Madigan et al. (2020)					Sport MPS (PS, COM) MIPS (PeS, NRI)	CON	181 athletes
Attitude toward doping	$d = -0.31$	$d = 0.-1.01$	$d = -0.99$	$d = -0.33$			
Gaudreau et al. (2019)					HF-MPS (SOP, SPP)	GEN	97 physical education students
Change in performance	n/a	n/a	n/a	n/a			

Authors and Outcomes	H1 Pure PSP vs. Non	H2 Non vs. Pure ECP	H3 Mixed vs. Pure ECP	H4 Pure PSP vs. mixed	Scales	Level of Generality	Sample
Hill, Madigan, & Jowett (2020)					Many; Different in each sample	CON	297 and 222 adolescents; 211 adults. All athletes
Confidence	n/a	n/a	n/a	n/a			
Dedication	n/a	n/a	n/a	n/a			
Vigour	n/a	n/a	n/a	n/a			
Enthusiasm	n/a	n/a	n/a	n/a			
Waleriańczyk and Stolarski (2021)					PSQ (PS, COM, DAA, RUM).		332 runners 10km;115 runners half marathon
Performance	n/a	n/a	n/a	n/a			
Waleriańczyk and Stolarski (2022)					Sport-MPS-2 (PS, COM) PPS–S (SOP, DAA)	CON	173 athletes
Change total burnout	n/a	n/a	n/a	n/a			
Change reduced sense of achievement	n/a	n/a	n/a	n/a			
Change exhaustion	n/a	n/a	n/a	n/a			
Change sport devaluation	n/a	n/a	n/a	n/a			
Waleriańczyk, Hill, & Stolarski (2022)					Many	CON	377 athletes
Vigour, dedication, absorption	n/a	n/a	n/a	n/a			
Three indicators of burnout	n/a	n/a	n/a	n/a			

Note. A Cohen's *d* effect size marked with * indicates that the effect was in opposite direction than expected. n/a = not enough information to calculate the effect size. SOP = self-oriented perfectionism. SPP = socially prescribed perfectionism. PS = personal standards. PP = parental pressure. PeS = perfectionistic standards. NRI = negative reactions to imperfection. RUM = mistake rumination. DISPO = global level of analysis, CON = contextual level of analysis. COM = concerns over mistakes. DAA = doubts about actions.

advantage of pure PSP over non-perfectionism. This advantage, which was more marked for life-satisfaction ($d = 0.21$) than positive affect ($d = 0.08$) and vitality ($d = 0.12$), nonetheless remained small. Overall, weak support was provided for *Hypothesis 1* and the idea that pure PSP relates to healthy outcomes compared to non-perfectionism.

The 2 × 2 model is unique in proposing that pure ECP and non-perfectionism should be treated as two distinct subtypes of perfectionism (*Hypothesis 2*). It also diverges from the tripartite model because it proposes that mixed perfectionism is associated with better (rather than worse) outcomes than pure ECP (*Hypothesis 3*). On the one hand, results indicated that non-perfectionism was significantly associated with higher scores on each indicator of subjective well-being than pure ECP (*Hypothesis 2*); effects were medium ($d = .63$) to strong ($d = 0.90$). On the other hand, similar effects and support were found for *Hypothesis 3*. Overall, these findings provided strong support for these two original hypotheses of the 2 × 2 model.

Mixed support was obtained for *Hypothesis 4*. Pure PSP was associated with significantly higher life-satisfaction than a subtype of mixed perfectionism ($d = 0.43$). However, the findings for positive affect and vitality did not reach statistical significance. It could be said that the difference between pure PSP and mixed perfectionism was limited to the cognitive indicator of subjective well-being, but there was nonetheless a small advantage of pure PSP compared to mixed perfectionism in relation to vitality ($d = 0.20$).

Mallinson et al. (2014) recruited 219 adolescents from various school- and community-based sports. Enjoyment of sport, positive views of one's physical skills, and positive friendship experiences are important to promote active living and positive development during and beyond adolescence. Participants rated their sport-related perfectionism and their sport enjoyment, physical self-worth, and six characteristics of friendship experience in sport.

Results for sport enjoyment, physical self-worth, and three characteristics of friendship experience in sport (i.e. enhancement and supportiveness of self-esteem, loyalty and intimacy, and companionship and pleasant play) supported the four hypotheses of the 2 × 2 model. Pure PSP was associated with higher scores on each of these outcomes than non-perfectionism (*Hypothesis 1*) and mixed perfectionism (*Hypothesis 4*). Pure ECP was associated with lower scores on each of these outcomes compared to non-perfectionism (*Hypothesis 2*) and mixed perfectionism (*Hypothesis 3*). Effects varied from medium ($d = 0.41$) to strong ($d = 0.84$).

Two characteristics of friendship experience were useful to illustrate the advantages of reinterpreting non-significant findings with their effect sizes. The findings for *Hypothesis 1* and *Hypothesis 4* did not reach statistical significance but showed a small to moderate advantage of pure PSP compared to non-perfectionism on sharing things in common ($d = 0.33$) and conflict resolution ($d = 0.28$) as well as a small advantage of pure PSP over mixed perfectionism on these two characteristics of friendship in sport ($d = 0.13$; $d = 0.23$). Finally, *Hypothesis 2 and 3* were supported with medium to strong advantage for non-perfectionism and mixed perfectionism compared to pure ECP on sharing things in common ($d = .67$; $d = .87$) and conflict resolution ($d = .85$; $d = .90$).

Mallinson-Howard et al. (2019) turned their attention to negative experiences in youth sport. They recruited 222 adolescents from various school- and community-based sports who rated their sport-related perfectionism, both their positive and negative affect as well as their anxiety, antisocial behaviours, and intention to dropout from sport.

Eighteen of the 32 effects reached statistical significance (in the expected direction) with more consistent support for *Hypothesis 2* (6 out of 8) and *Hypothesis 4* (7 out of 8) and largely unsupportive evidence for *Hypothesis 1* (2 out of 8) and *Hypothesis 3* (3 out of 8). Results outlined the antagonistic nature of pure PSP. On the one hand, young sport participants with pure PSP displayed higher positive affect ($d = .86$) and lower intention to dropout ($d = -.50$). On the other hand, their worry ($d = .10$), somatic anxiety ($d = .21$), and antisocial behaviours toward their opponents ($d = .28$) were higher than a subtype of non-perfectionism. Many differences did not reach significance, but these findings nonetheless indicate that a subtype of pure PSP may not always be adaptive. Nevertheless, pure PSP appears preferable to a subtype of mixed perfectionism (*Hypothesis 4*), with a weak effect for somatic anxiety ($d = -.23$), medium effects for concentration disruption, worry, and intention to dropout ($d = -.45$ to $-.53$), and strong effects for antisocial behaviours, positive affect, and negative affect ($d = -.72$ to -1.28). Overall, these results illustrate that pure PSP (compared to non-perfectionism and other subtypes of perfectionism) may provide some motivational advantages (e.g. being enthusiastic and positively aroused; having the intention to persevere) without necessarily dampening the negative emotions and behaviours experienced by youth sport participants.

Burnout and Engagement

Hill (2013) was the first to revisit the associations between perfectionism and burnout through the lens of the 2 × 2 model. A sample of 167 male adolescent soccer players from academies of professional clubs in England rated their sport-related perfectionism and burnout.

Good support was found for the four hypotheses of the 2 × 2 model for total athletic burnout and reduced sense of accomplishment, with a medium effect size (ds from -0.67 to -0.76). In contrast, only two hypotheses were supported when looking at exhaustion and sport devaluation. The difference between non-perfectionism and pure PSP (*Hypothesis 1*) was smaller for exhaustion ($d = -0.22$) and sport devaluation ($d = -0.31$). The difference between mixed perfectionism and pure ECP was also smaller for exhaustion (*Hypothesis 3; d = -0.22*), just like the difference between pure PSP and mixed perfectionism was smaller for sport devaluation (*Hypothesis 4; d = -0.34*). Although appealing, a total burnout score may obscure important differences in how symptoms of burnout are experienced by athletes across subtypes of perfectionism.

Hill, Madigan, and Jowett (2020) followed by examining athletes' engagement. Engagement can be positioned as the opposite of burnout, but it also offers a unique window into the experience of persistent motivation toward one's sport. In sport, engagement can be operationalized using indicators of vigour, dedication, enthusiasm, and confidence. Three samples of adolescent ($N = 297$ and 222) and adult athletes ($N = 211$) completed various measures of sport-related perfectionism and a measure of sport engagement.

Distinct ways of measuring perfectionism generated different results. *Hypotheses 1 and 3* were supported in samples 1 and 2 across all four indicators of engagement, but only when PSP/ECP were operationalized as self-oriented/socially prescribed perfectionism or as personal standards/concerns over mistakes. In sample 1, very limited support was found when PSP/ECP were operationalized as perfectionistic standards/negative reactions to imperfection; only 4 of the 16 effects supported the hypotheses. In contrast, 10 of the 16 effects supported the hypotheses when reusing this operationalization in sample 3. Overall, the ways of measuring perfectionism, the specific characteristics of the samples (e.g. adolescents versus adults), or a complex *sample by measurement interaction* appear to substantially alter the results. This finding raises serious conceptual and methodological concerns not only for the 2 × 2 model but also for the entire literature on perfectionism in sport, dance, exercise, and beyond.

Support for *Hypothesis 2 and 4* was even less systematic across the four indicators of engagement. More support was found for confidence and dedication (15 of the 24 effects supported the hypotheses) compared to vigour and enthusiasm (7 of the 24 effects supported the hypotheses). Overall, these findings could suggest that positive self-beliefs and motivation are more likely to differ across subtypes of perfectionism compared to the feelings of energy/liveness and excitement.

Waleriańczyk, Hill, and Stolarski (2022) moved this literature forward by including and contrasting engagement and burnout in a sample of 377 athletes from various sports. Across all three indicators of engagement (i.e. vigour, dedication, absorption), *Hypotheses 1, 2, and 3* were supported regardless of whether PSP/ECP were operationalized as self-oriented/socially prescribed perfectionism or as personal standards/concerns over mistakes. Less support was found for *Hypothesis 4* (2 of the 6 effects supported the hypothesis), which indicates that pure PSP and mixed perfectionism are associated with more comparable level of engagement.

Pure PSP was associated with lower burnout (compared to non-perfectionism; *Hypothesis 1*) only when it was operationalized as personal standards/concerns over mistakes. The same conclusion applied to the difference between mixed perfectionism and pure ECP (*Hypothesis 3*). In contrast, support for *Hypotheses 2 and 4* was found regardless of how perfectionism was operationalized. Overall, these results suggest that the four hypotheses of the 2 × 2 model are distinctly affected when small variations are introduced in the operationalization of PSP and ECP.

Madigan et al. (2016) further advanced this literature by conducting a first longitudinal test. A sample of 129 young adults from varsity and local clubs participated in a three-month longitudinal study that focused sport-specific perfectionism and residual changes in athlete burnout. The four hypotheses of the model were supported for changes in total athletic burnout and reduced sense of accomplishment, with medium to strong effects (*d*s from −0.30 to −0.75). Of note, pure ECP was the only subtype showing increased burnout over the three-month period. Change in sport devaluation closely mirrored the four hypotheses of the 2 × 2 model, with medium effects (*d*s from −0.32 to −0.49). The change in exhaustion associated with pure PSP did not significantly differ from non-perfectionism (*d* = −0.21; *Hypothesis 1*) and mixed perfectionism (*d* = −0.04; *Hypothesis 4*). Findings from this study mostly replicated the results of Hill (2013) − this time using a longitudinal design.

Waleriańczyk and Stolarski (2022) pursued this line of research in a five-month longitudinal study of 173 athletes from various sports that focused sport-specific perfectionism and residual changes in both engagement and burnout. Changes in total athletic burnout and reduced change in accomplishment again supported the hypotheses of the 2 × 2 model. This time, the change in exhaustion also matched the hypotheses of the model. However, the four hypotheses of the model were not supported for the change in sport devaluation. Effects sizes could not be calculated. Statistical significance should be prudently interpreted because 49% of the original sample of 377 did not participate in the five-month follow-up.

Change in total engagement, absorption, and vigour provided support for *Hypothesis 2 and 4*. Engagement was significantly higher for pure PSP (compared to mixed perfectionism; *Hypothesis 2*) and non-perfectionism (compared to pure ECP; *Hypothesis 4*). Elevated levels of engagement for non-perfectionists could potentially explain why they not significantly differed from athletes with pure PSP (*Hypothesis 1*). Changes in dedication supported the four hypotheses of the 2 × 2 model, which again suggests the motivational ingredients that undergird sport engagement are more likely to differ across subtypes of perfectionism compared to the elements of positive energy and attention respectively entailed vigour and absorption.

Coping and Emotion Regulation

Hill and Davis (2014) recruited 238 coaches from various sports. The capacity to optimally manage one's emotions − particularly anger − appears pivotal to ensure that coaches can thrive and flourish over the long haul while maximizing their capacity to create a secure and nurturing training climate for their protégés. Coaches rated their general perfectionism. They also evaluated their current tendency to use cognitive reappraisal and suppression as well as their capacity to control outward and inward expression of anger in general in their lives.

Results concerning the tendency to control expression of anger provided support for the four hypotheses of the 2 × 2 model of perfectionism with small (*d* = 0.24) to medium (*d* = 0.35) effect sizes.

Cognitive reappraisals and expression suppression are typically associated with adaptive and maladaptive emotional outcomes, respectively. Pure PSP was associated with significantly stronger cognitive reappraisals than non-perfectionism (*Hypothesis 1; d* = 0.35). Pure PSP was not more nor less likely to suppress their emotions (*d* = 0.05). As expected, pure PSP was associated with significantly lower suppression (*d* = −0.72) and with non-significant higher cognitive reappraisals (*d* = 0.23) than mixed perfectionism (*Hypothesis 4*).

Mixed perfectionism in relation to pure ECP (*Hypothesis 3*) yielded both expected and unexpected effects. As expected, mixed perfectionism was associated with significantly higher cognitive appraisals than pure ECP (*d* = 0.35). Contrary to expectations, mixed perfectionism was associated with significantly higher expressive suppression than pure ECP (*d* = 0.53). Suppression, which is generally associated with negative outcomes in the general population, might enable coaches to maintain composure and dampen their emotions while managing the ongoing demands of a sport competition. Therefore, the finding that mixed perfectionism is associated to higher suppression of emotions might reflect the need of coaches to develop a broad and diversified repertoire of emotion regulation strategies.

Crocker et al. (2014) conducted the first longitudinal study that relied on the 2 × 2 model of perfectionism in sport. They recruited 274 varsity athletes from various sports. At Time 1, they rated their sport-related perfectionism. At Time 2, four weeks later, a sample of 179 athletes evaluated their cognitive appraisals, coping strategies, affective states, and goal progress during their recent sport competitions.

Results yielded more consistent support for *Hypothesis 2* and *Hypothesis 4* across the eight outcome variables, with an absolute average Cohen's *d* effect size of 0.38. Results yielded mixed support for *Hypothesis 1* and *Hypothesis 3*. Across eight outcomes, the absolute average Cohen's *d* effect size was 0.34, thus indicating a small to medium advantage of pure PSP over non-perfectionism (*Hypothesis 1*) and mixed perfectionism over pure ECP (*Hypothesis 3*). These advantages were moderate to strong for outcomes that are generally associated with positive adjustment such as positive affect (*d* = 0.71), perceived control (*d* = 0.61), appraisal of challenge (*d* = 0.38), and goal progress (*d* = 0.60), but they were weak for outcomes such as negative affect (*d* = −0.12) and appraisal of threat (*d* = 0.01). Coping strategies were not markedly different across non-perfectionism and pure PSP and across mixed perfectionism and pure ECP. Pure PSP (versus non-perfectionism) and mixed perfectionism (versus pure ECP) were associated with similar problem-focused coping (*d* = 0.07) and slightly lower avoidance-focused coping (*d* = −0.22). Overall, we can conclude that support (or lack of thereof) for *Hypothesis 1* and *Hypothesis 3* was largely dependent on the type of outcomes under investigation.

Doping in Sport

Madigan et al. (2020) studied the associations between perfectionism and attitudes toward doping through the lens of the 2 × 2 model. A sample of 181 competitive athletes rated their sport-related perfectionism and their attitudes about performance enhancement drug. Differences between the subtypes were consistent with the four hypotheses of the model (with medium to strong effect sizes), but only two hypotheses reached statistical significance. The differences of pure PSP with non-perfectionism ($d = -0.31$; *Hypothesis 1*) and mixed perfectionism ($d = -0.33$; *Hypothesis 4*) were smaller than the differences of pure ECP with non-perfectionism ($d = -1.01$; *Hypothesis 2*) and mixed perfectionism ($d = -0.99$; *Hypothesis 3*). Overall, athletes with pure ECP showed the highest tolerance toward doping.

Performance

Crocker et al. (2014) found support for the longitudinal association between subtypes of perfectionism and progress made by athletes on their athletic goals in a subsequent competition in the study described earlier. All four hypotheses of the model were supported.

Gaudreau et al. (2019) followed 97 high school students as they were learning a new skill across six physical education classes. During the first class, students performed simple acrobatic gymnastic figures before being introduced to more complex figures in the second class. Objective performance (rated by the teacher) decreased from the first to the third classes as students learned their novel and complex movements. The grades of students with pure PSP did not significantly decrease whereas the grades of non-perfectionism, pure ECP, and mixed perfectionism respectively decreased by 6%, 12%, and 6%. Pure PSP was associated with the best performance trajectory compared to both non-perfectionism (*Hypothesis 1*) and mixed perfectionism (*Hypothesis 4*). Pure ECP was associated with the poorest performance trajectory compared to both non-perfectionism (*Hypothesis 2*) and mixed perfectionism (*Hypothesis 3*). Performance improved across the last three classes, but the rate of improvement did not significantly differ across subtypes of perfectionism. Overall, subtypes of perfectionism can differentially influence learning outcomes when students are introduced and try to acquire novel and increasingly complex motor movements.

Waleriańczyk & Stolarski (2021) estimated the association between sport-specific perfectionism measured before a competition and the objective performance of 332 runners in a 10-kilometre race (Study 1) and 115 runners in a half-marathon (Study 2). PSP (but not ECP) was a significant positive predictor of performance. Once reinterpreted through the lens of the 2 × 2 model, this result indicates that only *Hypotheses 1 and 3* were supported. Pure PSP performed significantly better than non-perfectionism while mixed perfectionism performed significantly better than pure ECP. Results replicated across the 10-kilometre and half-marathon races.

A similar effect was found to predict anticipated performance (i.e. a rating of one's expected time for the upcoming race). The main effects of PSP disappeared after entering anticipated performance in the regression model and complex interactions (i.e. PSP × anticipated performance in both studies; PSP × ECP in Study 1) turned significant. Three possible interpretations are equally defendable. First, anticipated performance potentially acted as a mediator of the differences between pure PSP and non-perfectionism and between mixed perfectionism and pure ECP. Second, the positive beta weight of the PSP × anticipated performance effect suggests that support for *Hypotheses 1 and 3* potentially increased for runners who anticipated a better race time. As such, it could be said that holding positive performance expectancies boosted the advantage of pure PSP compared to non-perfectionism. Third, anticipated performance radically changed (i.e. potential suppression; Stoeber & Gaudreau, 2017) the associations between perfectionism and performance. For two runners with equal anticipated performance (Study 1), pure PSP was still associated with better performance than non-perfectionism (*Hypothesis 1*). However, pure ECP was now associated with better performance than non-perfectionism and mixed perfectionism, thus contradicting *Hypotheses 2 and 3*. With interpretation difficulties in mind, more research is warranted to investigate the role of anticipated performance in the associations between perfectionism and performance.

Potential Moderators in the 2 × 2 Model

Performance in sport (e.g. goal progress, winning/losing) is not only an important outcome; it is also a potential achievement stressor capable of altering the psychological experience of perfectionists. Consistent with a *stress-diathesis framework* (e.g. Flett et al., 1995) failure to attain meaningful athletic goals could attenuate the potentially desirable effects of pure PSP (compared to non-perfectionism; *Hypothesis 1*). Athletes spend a significant amount of their lives in the sport environment. For them to optimally learn, perform, and thrive, they need to train and compete in environments that are supportive rather than unsupportive or adversarial.

Gaudreau et al. (2018) introduced the *differential susceptibility hypothesis* to formulate the potential impact of achievement and environmental stressors in the 2 × 2 model of perfectionism. Advantages associated with pure PSP are potentially accentuated when people partake in non-distressful situations (e.g. after attaining an important goal) or supportive environments (e.g. receiving autonomy support). However, these advantages can vanish in stressful situations (e.g. not attaining an important goal in one competition) or unsupportive environments (e.g. laissez-faire leadership style). They could even be replaced by negative outcomes in distressful situations (e.g. not attaining an important goal across multiple competitions) or adverse environments (e.g. abusive, toxic, overly autocratic). In surveying the literature, four studies are particularly relevant in regards to the *differential susceptibility hypothesis*.

In the study of Crocker et al. (2014), support was found for this moderating effect but only for 2 of the 8 outcomes (i.e. control appraisals, positive affect). Athletes with pure PSP (compared to non-perfectionism) who reported *high level of goal progress* displayed more perceived control and positive affect. How-ever, the advantage associated with pure PSP vanished for athletes who repor-ted *low level of goal progress*. These findings are consistent with the differential susceptibility hypothesis introduced by Gaudreau et al. (2018).

Waleriańczyk, Stolarski, & Matthews (2022) offered indirect evidence for the impact of sport performance in the associations between perfectionism and affective states. A sample of 154 runners was followed before and a few days after a 10-kilometre street run. Runners who exceeded their expected perfor-mance (e.g. goal attainment) experienced lower tense arousal a few days after the race – a typical effect expected by self-regulation theories (e.g. Carver & Scheier, 1998). However, this effect differed across subtypes of perfectionism. Runners with pure PSP (compared to non-perfectionism) who reported *higher level of goal attainment* experienced lower tense arousal. However, the advantage associated with pure PSP vanished for runners who failed to attain their expected running time (i.e. *low level of goal progress*).

Jowett et al. (2021) offered convincing support for the differential susceptibility hypothesis in a study of burnout and engagement among 244 adolescent dancers. Dancers with pure PSP (compared to non-perfectionism) who reported that their teacher provided them with a *high level of autonomy support* displayed higher engagement and lower burnout. However, the advantage associated with pure PSP vanished for dancers who reported *low level of teacher's autonomy support*. Low autonomy support could be seen as an unsupportive rather than an adversarial environment. More research is needed to evaluate what would happen to the burnout and engagement of performers with pure PSP if their teachers and coa-ches create abusive, toxic, and psychologically unsafe (e.g. need thwarting envir-onment). Whether these moderating effects generalize to parenting environments is another question in need to investigation.

Gaudreau et al. (2018) discussed the implications of the *differential susceptibility hypothesis* specifically for the difference between pure PSP and non-perfectionism (*Hypothesis 1*). However, the same principles could generalize to other hypotheses of the 2 × 2 model. For example, Curran and Hill (2018) focused on Hypothesis 3 in their examination of the self-conscious emotions of perfectionists when exposed to successive failures. A sample of 60 students participated in four 4-minute trials of a cycling sprinting task in which the goal was to outperform other cyclists. After each trial, all participants received false failure feedback; they were told that they ranked last among their group of three or four cyclists. Such a condition of suc-cessive failures can be distressful for everybody, and the results showed that shame and guilt increased across the four successive experiences of failure. Increases in guilt and shame were significantly stronger for mixed perfectionism compared to pure ECP. This finding, which contradicted *Hypothesis 3* of the 2 × 2 model, was obtained in a distressful situation of successive and repeated failures. Finishing last across multiple competitions is rare and upsetting and appears to create the needed condition to overturn the positive advantages of mixed perfectionism (compared to pure ECP) into significant emotional disadvantages. In this extreme and potentially distressful achievement situation, none of the four hypotheses of the 2 × 2 model was supported. Increases in guilt and shame were also comparable across pure PSP and non-perfectionism (*Hypothesis 1*). This study did not directly compare athletes across success and failure scenarios, but these findings are nonetheless consistent with a differential susceptibility hypothesis.

Taking Stock and Moving Forward

The results of studies in sport and dance have offered partial support for the hypotheses of the 2 × 2 model. As such, a few caveats need to be discussed to help moving this literature forward.

First, the 2 × 2 model requires a good understanding of multivariate statistics. Over the years, most researchers have maintained a preference for a dualistic approach in which the main effects (e.g. beta weights) of PSP and ECP are interpreted independently of each other. This has resulted in a literature in which PSP and ECP are interpreted as if they were characteristics of two different individuals rather than characteristics that co-exist to a certain degree within everyone. The 2 × 2 model has been increasingly discussed and cited, but direct and complete tests remain far less frequent. Parameter estimates (the intercept and unstandardized beta weights) from a multiple regression can easily be used to calculate predicted values and effect sizes for each of the four subtypes of perfectionism. This step requires some technical knowledge and skills, which have been obstacles in the implementation and scaling-up of this theoretical model. Several published studies did not calculate the predicted values and effect sizes, thus making it difficult to grasp and non-ambiguously interpret their findings. Other studies not reviewed in this chapter apparently made mistakes that called into question our capacity to trustworthily interpret their findings. Technically demanding models – even if parsimonious in their conceptual logic – run the risk of being undervalued, misunderstood, and simply put away on the sidings. This caveat has limited our capacity to build a large corpus of knowledge to identify the boundary conditions of some of the effects observed in the 2 × 2 model.

Second, scales designed to measure PSP appear to be lacking construct validity. More precisely, results of factor analytical research revealed that several items from these scales are measuring high standards rather than perfectionistic standards (Blasberg et al., 2016). Pursuing high standards can be a healthy approach toward goal pursuit and self-regulation (e.g. Gaudreau, 2019; Gaudreau et al., 2022). In contrast, perfectionistic standards are often unrealistic, unattainable, and unreasonably taxing for one's self-regulatory resources. The measurement of high standards in scales designed to measure perfectionism may have inadvertently boosted and overestimated the potentially adaptive outcomes associated with PSP. Not all scales have the same percentage of items tapping into high standards. Therefore, the potential overestimation of the pure PSP effects likely depends on the precise scale(s) used in each study. Even if support was found for *Hypothesis 1* in several studies, it remains unclear if pure PSP is *really* associated with desirable outcomes compared to a subtype of non-perfectionism (Gaudreau, 2019).

Third, the 2 × 2 model assumed that a subtype of non-perfectionism could be used as a control condition to estimate the effects associated with pure PSP. Although defendable, this assumption is questionable because individuals in the subtype of non-perfectionism might be pursuing lower standards than non-perfectionistic standards. Pursuing low standards potentially lacks some of the motivational ingredients seen in individuals pursuing excellence. Those individuals – characterized as *excellence strivers* in the Model of Excellencism and Perfectionism (e.g. Gaudreau, 2019; Gaudreau et al., 2022) – offer a much better control condition upon which to estimate the effects of perfectionistic standards. Comparing pure PSP to a subtype of low standards was not intended in the 2 × 2 model, and potentially boosted and overestimated some of the adaptive outcomes associated with a subtype of pure PSP.

Given all the above, one could easily wonder if time has come to retire the 2 × 2 model of perfectionism. The independent effects approach still undisputedly remains the dominant paradigm in sport, dance, and exercise. However, as eloquently demonstrated by Hill, Mallinson-Howard, Madigan, & Jowett (2020), this line of research can easily be reanalysed and reinterpreted through the lens of the 2 × 2 model. Noteworthy insights are offered when crossing the dimensions of PSP and ECP *within each person* rather than isolating their respective effects as if they were the effects of *two separate persons*. However, research from both the 2 × 2 model and the independent effects approaches has failed to neatly separate the pursuit of perfection from the pursuit of high personal standards. This limitation applies to the entire perfectionism literature and is not bounded to the 2 × 2 model. Better measurement, like the ones developed in the Model of Excellencism and Perfectionism (Gaudreau et al., 2022), have already started to move the perfectionism literature in the right direction (e.g. Cheek & Goebel, 2020; Goulet-Pelletier et al., 2022; Grieve et al., 2021).

Years of labour will be needed for these advances to widely penetrate and influence research and practice. However, this is urgently required for three main reasons. First, we cannot afford to lure performers, coaches, teachers, and parents into thinking that perfectionism is a desirable personality dimension. Ample evidence now suggests that perfectionism is a transdiagnostic risk factor for psychopathologies (e.g. Limburg et al., 2017). Second, recent research suggests that excellencism rather than perfectionistic standards is associated with desirable achievement outcomes (Gaudreau et al., 2021; Gaudreau et al., 2022; Goulet-Pelletier et al., 2022). More of this research is warranted to help convince the sport community to abandon the pursuit perfection because the pursuit of excellence can be more than good enough. Third, perfectionistic standards and concerns are often experienced together as indicated by their moderately high intercorrelation. Promoting perfectionistic standards without increasing perfectionistic concerns is likely undoable. Cross-sectional and short-term longitudinal studies are insightful, but they often fail to account for the many ways through which the long-term development and the daily enactment of perfectionistic standards and concerns can co-occur. As noted across many definitions, perfectionism is a "personality disposition characterized by striving for flawlessness and setting exceedingly high standards of performance accompanied by overly critical evaluations of one's behavior" (Stoeber, 2018, p. 3). If we accept that perfectionistic concerns are frequently experienced by those who possess high perfectionistic standards, we then accept that perfectionistic standards are directly and indirectly involved in making perfectionism a risk factor for psychopathologies for many perfectionists at least once during their lives (Gaudreau, 2021). Prudence is therefore warranted when interpreting the good outcomes (i.e. high adjustment and low maladjustment) associated to a subtype of pure PSP.

Concluding Comments

So far, the 2 × 2 model of perfectionism has been used as an alternative way of studying perfectionism. However, as shown by Hill, Mallinson-Howard, Madigan, & Jowett (2020), the model offers a framework to revisit, reanalyse, and reinterpret the extant literature on the independent effects of PSP and ECP. Time has come to start seeing and using the 2 × 2 model of perfectionism as a hub to integrate the literature rather than as a separate, orphan or niche model of perfectionism.

Contexts in which high levels of achievement is valued and reinforced – such as sport, dance, and higher education – might create the needed conditions to attract perfectionists and increase their propensity toward the pursuit of perfection. Parental pressure and perfectionism are on the rise among newer generations (Curran & Hill, 2019; Curran & Hill, 2022) and teachers, coaches, and parents should try to mitigate the risks associated with perfectionism rather than promote it in a despairing way of boosting performance. Evidence currently exists to suggest that some of the advantages of pure PSP vanish when the going gets tough or when athletes experience stress from performance difficulties and unsupportive environments. Results also differ across dependent variables, which indicate that pure PSP is not a panacea. Future work is needed to explore mental health outcomes (e.g. anxiety, depression, eating disorders) of athletes and dancers to comprehensively assess many dangers associated with perfectionism.

Research on the 2 × 2 model acted as a springboard for the elaboration of the Model of Excellencism and Perfectionism (e.g. Gaudreau, 2019; Gaudreau, 2021). After drawing a clear distinction between excellencism and perfectionism, little evidence will remain for the position that perfectionistic standards (i.e. including a subtype of pure PSP)[1] are associated with healthy outcomes. The pursuit of perfection is psychologically taxing and likely to yield diminishing returns compared to the pursuit of excellence. Even when they equally attain their athletic goals, perfection strivers (compared to excellence strivers) may end up paying a higher psychological price for the same amount of goal success (Gaudreau et al., 2021). In that sense, perfectionism is both inefficient and unsustainable. Perfectionistic standards are inextricably associated with perfectionistic concerns; they accompany the pursuit of perfection. The perfectionistic concerns, doubts, fears, automatic thoughts, self-presentation schemes, and social pressure derive from the pursuit of perfection. They characterize the ongoing and recurrent phenomenological experience of the perfection strivers as they strive toward perfection. As such, these expressions of perfectionism play an essential role in explaining the many ways through which perfectionistic standards participate in the multifarious difficulties experienced by perfection strivers (Gaudreau, 2021). Overall, the Model of Excellencism and Perfectionism provides the theoretical roadmap to revisit and clarify perfectionistic standards and their associations with affective, motivational, social, performance, health, and psychopathological outcomes.

Acknowledgements

Preparation of this chapter was facilitated by a research grant from Social Sciences and Humanities Research Council of Canada (435-2015-0649) and a teaching release from the Faculty of Social Science awarded to Patrick Gaudreau.

Note

1 Perfectionistic concerns are highly prevalent in perfection strivers; much more compared to excellence strivers (Cohen's *d* from 0.69 to 1.25; Gaudreau et al., 2022). Therefore, pure PSP (i.e. high personal standards with low evaluative concerns) may have inadvertently measured a subtype of excellencism (i.e. high personal standards and low perfectionistic standards) rather than a subtype of perfectionism.

References

Bernerth, J. B., & Aguinis, H. (2016). A critical review and best-practice recommendations for control variable usage. *Personnel Psychology*, 69, 229–283. https://doi.org/10.1111/peps.12103.

Bissonnette, V., Ickes, W., Bernstein, I. H., & Knowles, E. (1990). Personality moderating variables: A warning about statistical artifact and a comparison of analytic techniques. *Journal of Personality*, 58, 567–587. https://doi.org/10.1111/j.1467-6494.1990.tb00243.x.

Blasberg, J. S., Hewitt, P. L., Flett, G. L., Sherry, S. B., & Chen, C. (2016). The importance of item wording: The distinction between measuring high standards versus measuring perfectionism and why it matters. *Journal of Psychoeducational Assessment*, 34, 702–717. https://doi.org/10.1177/0734282916653701.

Carver, C. S., & Scheier, M. F. (1998). *On the self-regulation of behavior*. Cambridge University Press.

Cheek, N. N., & Goebel, J. (2020). What does it mean to maximize? "Decision difficulty," indecisiveness, and the jingle-jangle fallacies in the measurement of maximizing. *Judgment and Decision Making*, 15(1), 7–24.

Crocker, P. R. E., Gaudreau, P., Mosewich, A. D., & Kljajic, K. (2014). Perfectionism and the stress process in intercollegiate athletes: Examining the 2 × 2 model of perfectionism in sport competition. *International Journal of Sport Psychology*, 45, 325–348. https://doi.org/10.7352/IJSP2014.45.325.

Cumming, J., & Duda, J. L. (2012). Profiles of perfectionism, body-related concerns, and indicators of psychological health in vocational dance students: An investigation of the 2 × 2 model of perfectionism. *Psychology of Sport and Exercise*, 13, 729–738. https://doi.org/10.1016/j.psychsport.2012.05.004.

Curran, T., & Hill, A. P. (2018). A test of perfectionistic vulnerability following competitive failure among college athletes. *Journal of Sport and Exercise Psychology*, 40, 269–279. https://doi.org/10.1123/jsep.2018-0059.

Curran, T., & Hill, A. P. (2019). Perfectionism is increasing over time: A meta-analysis of birth cohort differences from 1989 to 2016. *Psychological Bulletin*, 145, 410–429. https://doi.org/10.1037/bul0000138.

Curran, T., & Hill, A. P. (2022). Young people's perceptions of their parents' expectations and criticism are increasing over time: Implications for perfectionism. *Psychological Bulletin*, 148, 107–128. https://doi.org/10.1037/bul0000347.

Dunn, J. G., Dunn, J. C., Gotwals, J. K., Vallance, J. K., Craft, J. M., & Syrotuik, D. G. (2006). Establishing construct validity evidence for the Sport Multidimensional Perfectionism Scale. *Psychology of Sport and Exercise*, 7, 57–79. https://doi.org/10.1016/j.psychsport.2005.04.003.

Finch, W. H., & Bronk, K. C. (2011). Conducting confirmatory latent class analysis using Mplus. *Structural Equation Modeling: A Multidisciplinary Journal*, 18(1), 132–151. https://doi.org/10.1080/10705511.2011.532732.

Flett, G. L., Hewitt, P. L., Blankstein, K. R., & Mosher, S. W. (1995). Perfectionism, life events, and depressive symptoms: A test of a diathesis-stress model. *Current Psychology* 14, 112–137. https://doi.org/10.1007/BF02686885.

Franche, V., Gaudreau, P., & Miranda, D. (2012). The 2 × 2 model of perfectionism: A comparison across Asian Canadians and European Canadians. *Journal of Counseling Psychology*, 59, 567–574. https://doi.org/10.1037/a0028992.

Frost, R. O., Marten, P., Lahart, C., & Rosenblate, R. (1990). The dimensions of perfectionism. *Cognitive Therapy and Research*, 14, 449–468. https://doi.org/10.1007/BF01172967.

Gaudreau, P. (2012). A methodological note on the interactive and main effects of dualistic personality dimensions: An example using the 2 × 2 model of perfectionism. *Personality and Individual Differences*, 52, 26–31. https://doi.org/10.1016/j.paid.2011.08.022.

Gaudreau, P. (2019). On the distinction between personal standards perfectionism and excellencism: A theory elaboration and research agenda. *Perspectives on Psychological Science*, 14, 195–215. https://doi.org/10.1177/1745691618797940.

Gaudreau, P. (2021). Separating the core definitional feature and the signature expressions of dispositional perfectionism: Implications for theory, research, and practice. *Personality and Individual Differences*, 181, 110975. https://doi.org/10.1016/j.paid.2021.110975.

Gaudreau, P., Boileau, L., & Schellenberg, B. J. I. (2021). Peur de l'échec à l'école et dans les sports: Apport du modèle de l'excellencisme et du perfectionnisme [Fear of failure in sport and school: Contribution of the model of excellencism and perfectionism]. *Revue Québécoise de Psychologie*, 42(3), 173–194.

Gaudreau, P., Franche, V., Kljajic, K., & Martinelli, G. (2018). The 2 × 2 model of perfectionism: Assumptions, trends, and potential developments. In J. Stoeber (ed.), *The psychology of perfectionism: Theory, research, applications* (pp. 44–67). Routledge.

Gaudreau, P., Louvet, B., & Kljajic, K. (2019). The performance trajectory of physical education students differs across subtypes of perfectionism: A piecewise growth curve model of the 2 × 2 model of perfectionism. *Sport, Exercise, and Performance Psychology*, 8, 223–237. https://doi.org/10.1037/spy0000138

Gaudreau, P., Schellenberg, B. J. I., Gareau, A., Kljajic, K., & Manoni-Millar, S. (2022). Because excellencism is more than good enough: On the need to distinguish the pursuit of excellence from the pursuit of perfection. *Journal of Personality and Social Psychology*, 122, 1117–1145. https://doi.org/10.1037/pspp0000411.

Gaudreau, P., & Thompson, A. (2010). Testing a 2 × 2 model of dispositional perfectionism. *Personality and Individual Differences*, 48, 532–537. https://doi.org/10.1016/j.paid.2009.11.031.

Gaudreau, P., & Verner-Filion, J. (2012). Dispositional perfectionism and well-being: A test of the 2 × 2 model of perfectionism in the sport domain. *Sport, Exercise, and Performance Psychology*, 1, 29–43. https://doi.org/10.1037/a0025747.

Gotwals, J. K., Stoeber, J., Dunn, J., & Stoll, O. (2012). Are perfectionistic strivings in sport adaptive? A systematic review of confirmatory, contradictory, and mixed evidence. *Canadian Psychology*, 53, 263–279. https://doi.org/10.1037/a0030288.

Goulet-Pelletier, J.-C., Gaudreau, P., & Cousineau, D. (2022). Is perfectionism a killer of creative thinking? A test of the model of excellencism and perfectionism. *British Journal of Psychology*, 113, 176–207. https://doi.org/10.1111/bjop.12530.

Grieve, P., Egan, S. J., Andersson, G., Carlbring, P., Shafran, R., & Wade, T. D. (2021). The impact of internet-based cognitive behaviour therapy for perfectionism on different measures of perfectionism: a randomised controlled trial. *Cognitive Behaviour Therapy*, 1–13. https://doi.org/10.1080/16506073.2021.1928276.

Hewitt, P. L., & Flett, G. L. (1991). Perfectionism in the self and social contexts: Conceptualization, assessment, and association with psychopathology. *Journal of Personality and Social Psychology*, 60, 456–470. https://doi.org/10.1037/0022-3514.60.3.456.

Hill, A. P. (2013). Perfectionism and burnout in junior soccer players: A test of the 2 × 2 model of dispositional perfectionism. *Journal of Sport & Exercise Psychology*, 35, 18–29. https://doi.org/10.1123/jsep.35.1.18.

Hill, A. P. (2014). Perfectionistic strivings and the perils of partialling. *International Journal of Sport and Exercise Psychology*, 12(4), 302–315. https://doi.org/10.1080/1612197X.2014.919602.

Hill, A. P., & Curran, T. (2015). Multidimensional perfectionism and burnout: A meta-analysis. *Personality and Social Psychology Review*, 20, 269–288. https://doi.org/10.1177/1088868315596286.

Hill, A. P., & Davis, P. A. (2014). Perfectionism and emotion regulation in coaches: A test of the 2× 2 model of dispositional perfectionism. *Motivation and Emotion*, 38, 715–726. https://doi.org/10.1007/s11031-014-9404-7

Hill, A. P., & Madigan, D. J. (2017). A short review of perfectionism in sport, dance and exercise: Out with the old, in with the 2 × 2. *Current Opinion in Psychology*, 16, 72–77. https://doi.org/10.1016/j.copsyc.2017.04.021.

Hill, A. P., Madigan, D. J., & Jowett, G. E. (2020). Perfectionism and athlete engagement: A multi-sample test of the 2 × 2 model of perfectionism. *Psychology of Sport and Exercise*, 48, 101664. https://doi.org/10.1016/j.psychsport.2020.101664.

Hill, A. P., Mallinson-Howard, S. H., & Jowett, G. E. (2018). Multidimensional perfectionism in sport: A meta-analytical review. *Sport, Exercise, and Performance Psychology*, 7(3), 235–270. https://doi.org/10.1037/spy0000125.

Hill, A. P., Mallinson-Howard, S. H., Madigan, D. J., & Jowett, G. E. (2020). Perfectionism in sport, dance, and exercise: An extended review and reanalysis. In G.

Tennenbaum & R. C. Eklund (eds), *Handbook of sport psychology* (4th ed., pp. 121–157). Wiley.

Johnson, B. T., & Boynton, M. H. (2008). Cumulating evidence about the social animal: Meta-analysis in social-personality psychology. *Social and Personality Psychology Compass*, 2, 817–841. https://doi.org/10.1111/j.1751-9004.2007.00048.x.

Jowett, G. E., Hill, A. P., Curran, T., Hall, H. K., & Clements, L. (2021). Perfectionism, burnout, and engagement in dance: The moderating role of autonomy support. *Sport, Exercise, and Performance Psychology*, 10. https://doi.org/10.1037/spy0000232.

Limburg, K., Watson, H. J., Hagger, M. S., & Egan, S. J. (2017). The relationship between perfectionism and psychopathology: A meta-analysis. *Journal of Clinical Psychology*, 73, 1301–1326. https://doi.org/10.1002/jclp.22435.

Madigan, D. J., Mallinson-Howard, S. H., Grugan, M. C., & Hill, A. P. (2020). Perfectionism and attitudes towards doping in athletes: A continuously cumulating meta-analysis and test of the 2 × 2 model. *European Journal of Sport Science*, 20(9), 1245–1254. https://doi.org/10.1080/17461391.2019.1698660.

Madigan, D. J., Stoeber, J., & Passfield, L. (2016). Perfectionism and changes in athlete burnout over three months: Interactive effects of personal standards and evaluative concerns perfectionism. *Psychology of Sport and Exercise*, 26, 32–39. https://doi.org/10.1016/j.psychsport.2016.05.010.

Mallinson-Howard, S. H., Hill, A. P., & Hall, H. K. (2019). The 2 × 2 model of perfectionism and negative experiences in youth sport. *Psychology of Sport and Exercise*, 45, 101581. https://doi.org/https://doi.org/10.1016/j.psychsport.2019.101581.

Mallinson, S. H., Hill, A. P., Hall, H. K., & Gotwals, J. K. (2014). The 2 × 2 model of perfectionism and school- and community-based sport participation. *Psychology in the Schools*, 51, 972–985. https://doi.org/10.1002/pits.21796.

Nordin-Bates, S. M., Raedeke, T. D., & Madigan, D. J. (2017). Perfectionism, burnout, and motivation in dance: A replication and test of the 2 × 2 model of perfectionism. *Journal of Dance Medicine & Science*, 21(3), 115–122. https://doi.org/10.12678/1089-313X.21.3.115.

Quested, E., Cumming, J., & Duda, J. L. (2014). Profiles of perfectionism, motivation, and self-evaluations among dancers: An extended analysis of Cumming and Duda (2012). *International Journal of Sport Psychology*, 45, 349–368. https://doi.org/10.7352/IJSP 2014.45.349.

Rice, K. G., & Ashby, J. S. (2007). An efficient method for classifying perfectionists. *Journal of Counseling Psychology* 54, 72–85. https://doi.org/10.1037/0022-0167.54.1.72.

Richard, F. D., BondJr., C. F., & Stokes-Zoota, J. J. (2003). One hundred years of social psychology quantitatively described. *Review of General Psychology*, 7, 331–363. https://doi.org/10.1037/1089-2680.7.4.331.

Schellenberg, B. J., Verner-Filion, J., Gaudreau, P., Bailis, D. S., Lafrenière, M. A. K., & Vallerand, R. J. (2018). Testing the dualistic model of passion using a novel quadripartite approach: A look at physical and psychological well-being. *Journal of Personality*, 87, 163–180. https://doi.org/10.1111/jopy.12378.

Stoeber, J. (2011). The dual nature of perfectionism in sports: Relationships with emotion, motivation, and performance. *International Review of Sport and Exercise Psychology*, 4, 128–145. https://doi.org/10.1080/1750984x.2011.604789.

Stoeber, J. (2014). Perfectionism in sport and dance: A double-edged sword. *International Journal of Sport Psychology*, 45(4), 385–394.

Stoeber, J. (2018). The psychology of perfectionism: An introduction. In J. Stoeber (ed.), *The psychology of perfectionism: Theory, research, and applications* (pp. 3–16). Routledge.

Stoeber, J., & Gaudreau, P. (2017). The advantages of partialling perfectionistic strivings and perfectionistic concerns: Critical issues and recommendations. *Personality and Individual Differences*, 104, 379–386. https://doi.org/10.1016/j.paid.2016.08.039.

Streiner, D. L. (2002). Breaking up is too hard to do: The heartbreak of dichotomizing continuous data. *The Canadian Journal of Psychiatry*, 47, 262–266. https://doi.org/10.1177/070674370204700307.

Waleriańczyk, W., Hill, A. P., & Stolarski, M. (2022). A re-examination of the 2 × 2 model of perfectionism, burnout, and engagement in sports. *Psychology of Sport and Exercise*, 61, 102190. https://doi.org/https://doi.org/10.1016/j.psychsport.2022.102190.

Waleriańczyk, W., & Stolarski, M. (2021). Personality and sport performance: The role of perfectionism, Big Five traits, and anticipated performance in predicting the results of distance running competitions. *Personality and Individual Differences*, 169, 109993. https://doi.org/https://doi.org/10.1016/j.paid.2020.109993.

Waleriańczyk, W., & Stolarski, M. (2022). Perfectionism, athlete burnout, and engagement: A five-month longitudinal test of the 2 × 2 model of perfectionism. *Personality and Individual Differences*, 195, 111698. https://doi.org/https://doi.org/10.1016/j.paid.2022.111698.

Waleriańczyk, W., Stolarski, M., & Matthews, G. (2022). Perfectionism moderates the effects of goal-realization on post-competition mood in amateur runners. *Journal of Sports Science & Medicine*, 21, 1–12. https://doi.org/https://doi.org/10.52082/jssm.2022.1.

Part III

New Approaches and Concepts

7 Perfectionistic Tipping Points and How to Find Them

Andrew P. Hill

While there are a number of disagreements regarding perfectionism, most agree that in order to gain a fuller understanding of its effects we will need to study different combinations of its dimensions and the way in which its dimensions interact. As seen in the chapters in this book on the Tripartite model and the 2 × 2 model of perfectionism, there is growing evidence that different profiles of perfectionism are associated with different outcomes in sport, dance, and exercise, and that quite often the effects of one dimension of perfectionism – perfectionistic strivings – can depend on the degree to which the other dimension of perfectionism – perfectionistic concerns – is present. With this in mind, the aim of the current chapter is to describe a new conceptual and analytical approach to examining the interaction between the two main perfectionism dimensions. The focus of the approach is on the identification of perfectionistic tipping points. That is, the precise level of perfectionistic concerns at which the effects of perfectionistic strivings are altered and become helpful or harmful. The chapter also aims to provide a practical illustration of how to identify perfectionistic tipping points. Readers will be able to follow the instructions provided to identify perfectionistic tipping points in their own work and contribute to efforts to better understand the effects of perfectionism.

Multidimensional Perfectionism

Can athletes, dancers and exercisers ever be too motivated or strive too hard? There probably is a point at which we could agree that the behaviours necessary to be successful in these domains – hard work, dedication, discipline – become excessive and unhealthy. Arguably, this is when these behaviours become counterproductive and have a detrimental impact on the individual, their health and performance, or on other people. Train too much, for example, and you may injure yourself. Similarly, invest too much of your identity in these domains and you will be vulnerable to mental health issues when things don't pan out the way you hoped. If this is the case, it would be useful to know at what point the pursuit of important goals tip from being helpful to harmful. This idea and the notion that there maybe points at which seemingly desirable behaviours become problematic underlies the content of this chapter

DOI: 10.4324/9781003288015-10

and recent efforts to understand the effects of perfectionism and perfectionistic striving, in particular.

The effects of perfectionism in sport, dance, and exercise continue to be a contested issue. Researchers have previously argued that pursuing perfection may be reflective of a healthy pursuit of excellence (e.g. Stoeber, 2011). Others have suggested that it is inevitably problematic (e.g. Hall, 2006). Moving away from these perspectives, more lately the focus has turned towards the challenging task of identifying *when* and for *who* perfectionism may be helpful, harmful or neutral in sport, dance, and exercise. To do so has required new theoretical and conceptual approaches, the use of more complex designs in our research, and novel ways of analysing and reanalysing new and old data. In these regards, this chapter will provide readers with an understanding of a novel concept – *perfectionistic tipping points* – and is intended to be instructional of the practical steps required to conduct the statistical analyses used to identify them.

Before we get to perfectionistic tipping points, though, it is useful if we first briefly highlight aspects of perfectionism research that have provided impetus for this approach. Perfectionism is multidimensional – it includes a range of different dimensions. The dimensions depend on the particular model (and measure) of perfectionism you use. In sport psychology we tend to use three main models. The first model includes a focus on whether perfectionistic standards and evaluation are directed to the self ("My performances need to be perfect"), to other people ("My teammates performances need to be perfect") or are perceived to be directed from others ("Others expect my performances to be perfect") (Hill et al., 2016). The second model separates out personal standards ("I hate being less than the best at things in my sport.") from an array of other qualities such as being overly concerned by mistakes ("If I fail in competition, I feel like a failure as a person.") and doubts about the quality of one's actions ("I rarely feel that my training fully prepares me for competition.") (Gotwals et al., 2010). The third model, like the second one, includes a striving for perfection dimension ("I strive to be as perfect as possible.") but has only one other feature which is a strong aversion to mistakes in the form of negative reactions to imperfection ("I get completely furious if I make mistakes.") (Stoeber et al., 2007). Each of these models requires us to consider the separate, combined, and interactive effects of different dimensions of perfectionism.

Researchers also often combine multiple measures to create two composite scores – one for perfectionistic strivings (PS) and one for perfectionistic concerns (PC). There are a number of studies that suggest this approach makes sense as most measures of perfectionism appear to include dimensions that are indicators of either one of these two broad dimensions. This approach also maps on nicely to one of the early definitions of perfectionism as being a combination of excessively "high standards of performance which are accompanied by tendencies for overly critical evaluations of one's own behavior" (Frost et al., 1990, p. 450). PS primarily capture the personal standards and striving elements of perfectionism in the definition whereas PC primarily capture the critical evaluative concerns, negative reactions, and perceived pressures of perfectionism. Here, too, researchers must consider the interplay between PS and PC when seeking to understand the effects of perfectionism.

As a multidimensional and complex personality characteristic, it has not been easy to get a clear picture or agreement on the likely effects of perfectionism. In our meta-analytical work in sport, for example, we have found that, on one hand, PC is consistently related to motivation and wellbeing problems for athletes (see Hill et al., 2018). This includes, for example, a higher ego orientation, higher fear of failure and higher depressive symptoms (with little or no relationship with athletic performance). On the other hand, PS is much more ambiguous and is often related to both positive and negative outcomes for athletes. This includes indicators of better and worse quality motivation (e.g. ego and task orientation) and wellbeing (e.g. self-confidence and anxiety). There is also evidence that PS may contribute to better athletic performance. With the opposing effects of PS and PC in mind, whether perfectionism is likely to be "good, bad, or both" (Bieling et al., 2004, p. 1373) for athletes, dancers, and exercisers remains a difficult question to answer.

A clearer picture has begun to emerge thanks to research that has examined combinations or profiles of perfectionism and how PS and PC interact with each other. Much of the progress is owed to researchers who have tested the Tripartite model of perfectionism and the 2 × 2 model of perfectionism (see Chapters 5 and 6). These two models encourage researchers to compare the outcomes associated with different combinations of high and low PS and PC. The 2 × 2 model of perfectionism, in particular, has provided especial impetus to shift attention to the interaction between PS and PC, and includes a set of a priori hypotheses and statistical methods to guide research in this area. Though not without limitations, research testing this model has typically provided support for its use and has strongly suggested that it is the presence of high or low PC that is the critical factor in determining the effects of the different combinations of PS and PC (see Hill & Madigan, 2017).

With these issues as a backdrop, and in keeping with a focus on the interaction between PS and PC, the concept of *perfectionistic tipping points* has recently been proposed (Hill, 2021). Perfectionistic tipping points are the precise level of perfectionistic concerns at which the effects of perfectionistic strivings are altered. They are proposed to be conceptual, statistical, and practical points of interest. Notably, they are intended to help identify for *whom* perfectionism may be problematic in sport based on levels of PS and PC, but PC in particular. In addition, a focus on perfectionistic tipping points is also proposed as a means of progressing our understanding of PS by clarifying when we can expect PS to be helpful, harmful, or neutral for athletes – an unresolved and enduring issue. A final note is that while the usefulness of perfectionistic tipping points was first illustrated in context of the 2 × 2 model of perfectionism, they can be examined independent of the 2 × 2 model providing that the interaction between PS and PC remains the focus of the research question.

Identification of perfectionistic tipping points requires a statistical test of the interaction between PS and PC in predicting a given dependent variable (e.g. athlete burnout). This interaction signals whether the size and/or direction of the relationship between PS and the dependent variable depends (or is "conditional") on the level of PC. If the interaction is statistically significant ($p <$ .05), the J-N technique is then used to probe and plot the interaction (Johnson & Neyman, 1936). The J-N technique has been around for a long time but is not widely used in sport psychology. Instead, the most common technique for probing interactions is the pick-a-point approach which tests the conditional effect of the predictor variable (e.g. PS) on the dependent variable (e.g. burnout) at a small number of arbitrary values of the moderator (e.g. PC), normally one standard deviation above and below the mean of the moderator. Unlike the pick-a-point approach, however, the J-N technique tests the relationship between the predictor variable and the dependent variable at all recorded values of the moderator. This is a key strength of the technique that allows perfectionistic tipping points to be identified and is a notable departure to the approach used in the 2 × 2 model of perfectionism.

In his excellent book on moderation and mediation, Hayes (2013) provides a summary of the three possible outcomes of the J-N technique. The outcomes focus on "regions of significance" that signal when the conditional effect of the predictor variable (x) on the dependent variable (y) is statistically significant.

- The first outcome is the identification of a single value of the moderator (M) that marks the *start* of a region of significance. In this case, the conditional effect of x on y becomes statistically significant when M is equal to or more than a certain value ($M \geq$ J-N$_{M1}$) or equal to or less than a certain value ($M \leq$ J-N$_{M1}$).
- The second outcome is the identification of two values of M that mark the *start and end* of a region of significance. In this case, the conditional effect of x on y is statistically significant when M is within the range of the two values ($M \geq$ J-N$_{M1}$ and $M \leq$ J-N$_{M2}$) or outside the range of these two values ($M \leq$ J-N$_{M1}$ and $M \geq$ J-N$_{M2}$).
- The third outcome is that there are no values of M that signal the start or end of a region of significance. In this case, the conditional effect of x on y is either statistically significant across the entire range of M or none of it.

These three possible outcomes of the J-N technique, may be somewhat abstract and confusing at this point so some examples may be helpful. The concept of perfectionistic tipping points is relatively new so there is not a great deal of research to draw upon. However, while there are only a few studies, those that do exist are illustrative. Evidence comes from attempts to re-examine previous statistically significant interactions between PS and PC in sport to identify perfectionistic tipping points (Hill, 2021) and precursory work using the J-N technique in perfectionism research (e.g. Lizmore et al., 2019; Curran & Hill, 2018). Collectively, so far, this work suggests that perfectionistic tipping points may exist for athlete burnout, athlete engagement, coach emotion regulation, and athlete performance and emotions following competitive failure. The use of the J-N technique and findings for athlete burnout, athlete engagement, coach emotion regulation, and athlete performance following failure are used as examples of the three outcomes described by Hayes (2013) next.

Evidence for a perfectionistic tipping point for athlete burnout comes from a study that examined perfectionism and burnout in junior soccer players (Hill, 2013). Athlete burnout has three main symptoms – physical and emotional exhaustion, reduced sense of athletic accomplishment and sports devaluation. The initial study found a statistically significant interaction between PS and PC when predicting sports devaluation. When the interaction was re-examined using the J-N technique it was found that at the point at which soccer players reported PC greater than or equal to 2.54 (on a scale of 1 to 7) PS became significantly related to lower sports devaluation. Although this finding might be counterintuitive at first glance (presuming you expect perfectionism to be related to higher burnout), it makes at least some sense that higher PC may intensify commitment to sport due to the additional importance its presence would attach to performance.

Evidence for a similar type of perfectionistic tipping point comes from a study that examined perfectionism and emotion regulation in sports coaches (Hill & Davis, 2014). When attempting to control or regulate emotions you can seek to either inhibit and hide emotion, called expressive suppression, or try to alter perceptions of the situation, called reappraisal. While neither is good or bad for you in all circumstances, when used habitually, research suggests that expressive suppression is problematic as it requires ongoing management of unresolved emotions (Gross & John, 2003). The initial study found a statistically significant interaction between PS and PC when predicting the use of this emotion regulation strategy. When the interaction was re-examined using the J-N technique it was found that at the point at which coaches reported PC greater than or equal to 2.83 (on a scale of 1 to 7) PS became significantly related to higher expressive suppression. In this case, it suggests that higher levels of PC may inhibit effective emotion regulation for coaches.

These two studies illustrate how levels of PC "tip" the conditional effect of PS on different outcomes into being statistically significant at one single point – potentially making PS more or less problematic for athletes and coaches. They are examples of the first outcome of the J-N technique described by Hayes (2013). However, perfectionistic tipping points can also be more complex. This is illustrated by a study examining perfectionism and athlete performance following competitive failure (Lizmore et al., 2019). Which is also the first study in which we used the term "tipping point" to describe what we were observing. In this study student-athletes were told that they were being outperformed by an opponent on a golf putting task. After receiving this feedback, initially PS was significantly related to better performance. However, as PC increased and was greater than or equal to 2.80 (on a response scale of 1 to 5) the relationship between PS and performance became non-significant. Eventually, when PC was greater than or equal to 4.53, PS became significantly related to worse performance. This is an example of the second outcome of the J-N technique described by Hayes (2013). It is also indicative of how higher PC may eventually subvert any initial benefits of PS for athletes.

A final recent study provides an example of the third outcome of the J-N technique described by Hayes (2013). In this study, the interaction between different measures of PS and PC was examined in context of predicting burnout symptoms and what some have argued to be the opposite – athlete engagement – among adult athletes from various sports (Waleriańczyk et al., 2022). A statistically significant interaction was found between PS and PC when predicting all dimensions of engagement (vigour, dedication, and absorption). Using the J-N technique to probe the interactions, it was also found that the conditional effect of PS on vigour and dedication was statistically significant ($p < .05$) at all reported values of PC when using one measure of perfectionism and the conditional effect of PS on absorption was statistically significant ($p < .05$) at all report values of PC when using another measure of perfectionism. In these four cases PS was associated with higher engagement regardless of the level of PC exhibited by the athletes.

Illustrative Research Example

What follows next is a demonstration of how to identify perfectionistic tipping points. The demonstration uses data from Hill (2021) which sought to identify perfectionistic tipping points in previous research that had found evidence of statistically significant interactions between PS and PC. To start, the study by Hill (2021) is briefly described with a focus on the design, methods, and findings. The subsequent sections then focus on three main steps: (1) how to conduct and interpret moderated regression, (2) how to interpret the results of the J-N technique and identify perfectionistic tipping points, and (3) how to plot the results of the J-N technique. The three steps are illustrated using SPSS (version 26) and Hayes's (2013) PROCESS macro (version 3.4). You will need access to this software if you would like to follow along and complete your own analyses.

Hill (2021) presented a reanalysis of data from Hill and Davis (2014). As described earlier, the original study examined the relationship between perfectionism and emotion regulation in coaches. Two-hundred and thirty-eight coaches from various team and individual sports took part in the study. They completed short measures of perfectionism which were then combined to create measures of PS and PC (Cox et al. 2002). PS and PC were labelled Personal Standards Perfectionism and Evaluative Concerns Perfectionism in the study which are the labels used in the 2 × 2 model of perfectionism. Coaches also completed the Emotion Regulation Questionnaire (Gross & John, 2003) and the control of anger subscales of the State-Trait Anger Expression Inventory-2 (STAXI-2; Spielberger, 1999). The design was cross-sectional, so the survey was completed once. A statistically significant interaction between PS and PC was found for expressive suppression but not the other variables. This interaction was later re-examined by Hill (2021) using the J-N technique.

Step One – Moderated Regression Analyses

Step one is the completion of a moderated regression. Before doing so, a quick note on preliminary analyses is in order. It is always worthwhile to conduct initial checks on any data before the primary analysis. This can include checking for missing data, missing data imputation, screening for univariate outliers and multivariate outliers, and assessing the reliabilities of the measures used. Most statistics textbooks provide guidelines on how to do each of these things. One text that I have found especially helpful is Tabachnick and Fidell (2007) which I tend to follow for preliminary analyses. Preliminary analyses are not discussed in detail in this chapter so you are encouraged to read about the topic elsewhere.

I usually remove participants with missing data that exceed 5%, as suggested by Tabachnick and Fidell (2007), and use a simple technique of replacing missing values with the mean of the reported items for that subscale and participant (ipsative mean substitution; Graham et al., 2003). This is typically one or two questions for a very small number of people. I also screen for univariate and multivariate outliers to help minimize issues with non-normal distribution of the data and ensure that findings are less likely to be due to a small number of extreme scores and individuals. Finally, I assess the reliability of instruments. This can be done in a number of ways, although slowly being replaced by better approaches, most commonly this involves assessing internal reliability (e.g. Cronbach's alpha). Each of these things were done in Hill and Davis (2014) and resulted in a final sample of 227 coaches.

Preliminary analyses also include checking the assumptions of the primary analyses. Hayes (2013) discusses the assumptions of moderated regression in his book which include (1) the relationships between the predictors and the dependent variable are linear (linearity), (2) differences between estimates of the dependent variable and the actual dependent variable are normally distributed (normally distributed residuals), (3) differences between estimates of dependent variable and the actual dependent variable are equally variable (homoscedasticity of residuals), and (4) differences between estimates of the dependent variable and the actual dependent variable for one person is not related to differences in another person (independence of residuals). These assumptions are typically checked or it is assumed that they are not violated to a degree that it is problematic. On this issue, Hayes (2013, p. 52) advises that, while not downplaying their importance, we "should not lose too much sleep" over violating these assumptions providing we are mindful of the properties of our data.

Once you are satisfied with the preliminary analyses, the moderated regression is straightforward. The instructions to conduct the analyses using SPSS and the PROCESS macro are presented in Figure 7.1 and the output is presented in Figure 7.2 and Figure 7.3. Note that the PROCESS macro must be downloaded and installed before it can be used in SPSS (see Hayes, 2022).

The first set of key features of the output in Figure 7.1 to take note of are multiple "R" (the correlation between the estimated dependent variable scores,

In SPSS, select...

> "Analyze" Tab
> "Regression"
> "PROCESS vX.X by Andrew F. Hayes"

In the PROCESS menu,

> Insert the dependent variables (e.g., expressive suppression) into the "Y variable:" box,
> Insert PS into the "X variable:" box,
> Insert PC into the "moderator variable W:" box,
> Ensure that "Model number:" is "1",

Then, click "Options"

> Change "Probe interactions...if p < .10" to "...if p <.05",
> Select "Johnson-Neyman output",
> Select "-SD, Mean, +1SD" for "Conditioning values"

Click "Continue" and then "OK".

Figure 7.1 Instructions for moderated regression using SPSS and the PROCESS macro

using a combination of the predictor variables and their interaction scores as predictors, and the actual dependent variables scores), "R-sq" (the squared multiple correlation or amount of variance explained in the actual dependent variable scores by the predictors and their interaction scores, ranging from 0% to 100%), corresponding F-statistic for the model, its degrees of freedom, and whether the model is statistically significant (or better than no predictors at all). These all provide an indication of model fit. That is, how closely the predicted values of expressive suppression from our model correspond with the actual scores. The better the fit, the more variance explained, and the more useful the model. In this case, PS, PC, and their interaction explained 13.6% of variance in expressive suppression, and the model was statistically significant ($p < .001$).

Next, we consider the individual predictors. First note though that the "constant" tells us the value of the score of the estimated expressive suppression score when all the predictors are zero (i.e. where the regression line intersects zero on the y-axis, the intercept). Whether this is meaningful or useful depends on scaling of the predictor variables and whether zero is actually a possible response (i.e. whether people score zero on your response format). Quite often it isn't useful or meaningful. For the purpose of the illustration here it is not important.

In regression analyses, the focus is normally on the regression weights or, as labelled in SPSS, unstandardized B-values ("coeff" in the PROCESS output). These indicate the change in the dependent variable for every one unit increase in the predictor variable in the original units (e.g. a 1 to 7 response format). So, here, for every one unit increase in PS, expressive suppression decreases by .401

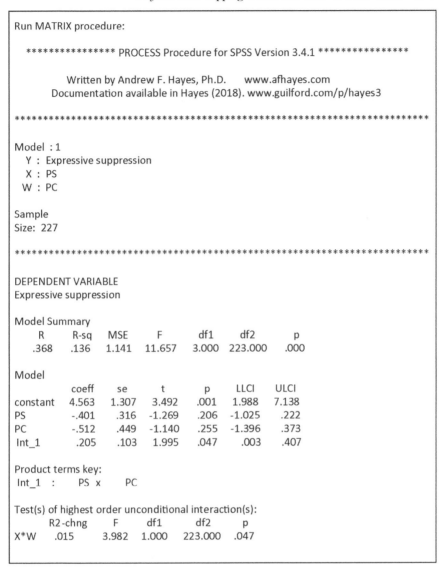

Run MATRIX procedure:

*************** PROCESS Procedure for SPSS Version 3.4.1 ***************

Written by Andrew F. Hayes, Ph.D.   www.afhayes.com
Documentation available in Hayes (2018). www.guilford.com/p/hayes3

****

Model : 1
  Y : Expressive suppression
  X : PS
  W : PC

Sample
Size: 227

****

DEPENDENT VARIABLE
Expressive suppression

Model Summary
    R   R-sq   MSE   F   df1   df2   p
  .368   .136   1.141   11.657 3.000   223.000   .000

Model
           coeff   se   t   p   LLCI   ULCI
constant   4.563   1.307 3.492   .001   1.988   7.138
PS   -.401   .316   -1.269 .206   -1.025   .222
PC   -.512   .449   -1.140 .255   -1.396   .373
Int_1   .205   .103   1.995   .047   .003   .407

Product terms key:
  Int_1 :   PS x   PC

Test(s) of highest order unconditional interaction(s):
        R2-chng   F   df1   df2   p
X*W   .015   3.982 1.000   223.000   .047

Figure 7.2 PROCESS output for moderated regression analyses

(because the unstandardized *B*-value is −0.401) and, likewise, for every one unit increase in PC, expressive suppression decreases by .512 (because the unstandardized *B*-value is −0.512). When multiple predictors are included in the model, the estimates are provided after statistically controlling for (or "partialling") the relationship between the predictors.

In moderated regression analyses, the individual or main effects of the predictors need to be ignored as an interaction term is included in the model. The interpretation of the interaction unstandardized B-value for the interaction terms is more complex. The inclusion of the term tests a hypothesis that the effect of a predictor on a dependent variable is conditional on the level of the other predictor (the moderator variable). The size of the unstandardized B-value for the interaction term tells us the amount of change in the dependent variable when there is a one unit increase in the predictor at different levels of the moderator. Here, then, it indicates that for every one unit increase in PC, the impact of PS on expressive suppression increases by .205 on our response format.

Whether the unstandardized B-values, including for the interaction term, are statistically significant is reported in two ways. The first way is via a *t*-test that assesses whether the difference between the unstandardized B-value (remember, "coeff") and zero exceeds sampling error ("s.e."). Sampling error is an estimate of the difference we would expect anyway as a consequence of selecting a sample of coaches from the entire population of coaches. The probability of the resulting t-score indicates whether the unstandardized B-value is statistically significant. For our interaction term, it can be seen that the size of the unstandardized B-value for the interaction term is significantly different from zero as the *p*-value is less than .05 (e.g. 0 minus .205 [coeff] / 1.03 [s.e.] = $t = 1.995$, $p = .047$).

The second way the statistical significance of the unstandardized B-values is displayed is via reporting confidence intervals. If the confidence intervals include zero, the unstandardized B-value is not statistically significant (note that 95% confidence intervals signal statistical significance at $p < .05$ and 99% confidence intervals at $p < .01$). The range of the confidence intervals are also useful because they provide the other likely values of the unstandardized B-value. Here, as our confidence interval excludes zero, we know that our interaction is statistically significant. Also, we are 95% confident that the unstandardized B-value for our interaction term is between .003 and .407. However, note, if we used a more stringent criteria, and wanted to be 99% confident, the interaction would not be considered statistically significant.

The change in the model associated with the inclusion of the interaction term is also displayed ("R^2-chng"). This is important as it tells us whether the model that includes the interaction term (PS × PC) is better than a model that includes only PS and PC. A model with only two predictors, rather than three, that explains a similar mount of variance in the dependent variable would be more parsimonious and therefore more desirable. However, here, the results signal that the interaction accounts for 1.5% of the model (or 1.5% of a total of 13.6%) and that this is a significant improvement in comparison to a model that includes only PS and PC ($p = .047$). While only a small amount of variance, this is typical of interaction effects.

The results of this moderated regression analyses are reported in Hill (2021, p. 9) as follows:

> The interaction model for expressive suppression was statistically significant, F (3, 223) = 11.66, $p < .001$. The two dimensions of perfectionism and their

interaction term explained 13.56% of variance in expressive suppression (ΔR2 interaction term =.02). PS was not a significant predictor (B = −0.40 [95% CI = −1.03 to 0.22], t = −1.27, p = .206) and neither was PC (B = −0.51 [95% CI = −1.40 to −0.37], t =−1.24, p =.255). The interaction term was statistically significant (B = 0.20 [95% CI = 0.003–0.41], t = 2.00, p = .047).

You can therefore see the correspondence between the PROCESS output and what and how things are reported.

Step Two – Interpret the Results of the J-N Technique

The PROCESS output also includes the information required to probe the interaction. The first part of the output is the pick-a-point approach that tests the conditional effect of PS on the dependent variable at three specific levels of PC: (1) at one standard deviation below the mean of PC (2.196), (2) at the mean of PC (2.652), and (3) at one standard deviation above the mean of PC (3.708). As mentioned earlier, these are only a small number of possible values of PC and are arbitrary indicators of "high" and "low" scores of PC so offer limited insight in comparison to the J-N technique that follows next in the output. Notably, by testing conditional effects only at a small number of values of PC, statistically significant effects that take place outside of those the values tested are missed.

The part of the output for the J-N technique displays the conditional effect of PS on expressive suppression ("Effect") across all reported PC scores in the sample from the lowest recorded PC score (1.300) to the highest (4.683), along with 95% confidence intervals for the conditional effect ("LLCI" and "ULCI"). It also tests whether the conditional effect at every level of PC is statistically significant in the same way described earlier. Herein lies the usefulness of the J-N technique for identifying perfectionistic tipping points. It allows you to identify the precise level of PC that corresponds with changes in the effect of PS on the dependent variable. In this example, when values of PC exceed 2.826 (rounded to 2.83), the effect of PS on expressive suppression becomes statistically significant. This marks the start of a region of significance. Prior to this level of PC, the effect of PS on expressive suppression was not statistically significant. The J-N technique also provides the percentage of the sample that report a PC score above 2.826 (53.744%) and the percentage that report below 2.826 (46.256%). In terms of the three possible outcomes discussed earlier, the finding is indicative of the first outcome – the identification of a single value of a moderator that marks the start of a region of significance.

Step Three – Plotting the Results of the J-N Technique

Having identified the perfectionistic tipping point, it is useful to depict the inter-action graphically and display the results of the J-N technique. This can be done using any software with a graphing function. Lin (2020) provides a review of software that can be used to plot the results of the J-N technique. In Figure 7.4, I

Focal predict: PS (X)
Mod var: PC (W)

Conditional effects of the focal predictor at values of the moderator(s):

PC	Effect	se	t	p	LLCI	ULCI
2.196	.048	.119	.408	.684	-.185	.282
2.952	.203	.089	2.284	.023	.028	.378
3.708	.358	.118	3.045	.003	.126	.590

Moderator value(s) defining Johnson-Neyman significance region(s):

Value	% below	% above
2.826	46.256	53.744

Conditional effect of focal predictor at values of the moderator:

PC	Effect	se	t	p	LLCI	ULCI
1.300	-.135	.192	-.704	.482	-.514	.243
1.469	-.101	.177	-.568	.570	-.449	.248
1.638	-.066	.162	-.407	.685	-.385	.254
1.807	-.031	.148	-.211	.833	-.323	.260
1.977	.003	.134	.025	.980	-.262	.268
2.146	.038	.122	.312	.756	-.202	.278
2.315	.073	.111	.656	.513	-.146	.291
2.484	.107	.101	1.058	.291	-.093	.307
2.653	.142	.094	1.505	.134	-.044	.328
2.822	.177	.090	1.961	.051	-.001	.354
2.826	.177	.090	1.971	.050	.000	.355
2.992	.211	.089	2.373	.018	.036	.387
3.161	.246	.091	2.692	.008	.066	.426
3.330	.281	.097	2.899	.004	.090	.471
3.499	.315	.105	3.007	.003	.109	.522
3.668	.350	.115	3.044	.003	.123	.576
3.837	.384	.127	3.036	.003	.135	.634
4.007	.419	.140	3.004	.003	.144	.694
4.176	.454	.153	2.960	.003	.152	.756
4.345	.488	.168	2.911	.004	.158	.819
4.514	.523	.183	2.863	.005	.163	.883
4.683	.558	.198	2.816	.005	.167	.948

************* ANALYSIS NOTES AND ERRORS **************

Level of confidence for all confidence intervals in output:
  95.0000

W values in conditional tables are the 16th, 50th, and 84th percentiles.

------ END MATRIX -----

Figure 7.3 PROCESS output for J-N technique

In SPSS, enter the data from J-N technique into four columns with 22 rows for PC, Effect, LLCI, and ULCI.

```
1.300   -.135   -.514   .243
1.469   -.101   -.449   .248
1.638   -.066   -.385   .254
```

Etc.

In "Variable View,"

Label the four variables "PC," "Effect," "LLCI," and "ULCI" in the "Name" column.

Select…

    "Graphs" Tab
    "Legacy Dialogs"
    "Scatter/Dot…"
    "Overlay Scatter"
    "Define"

In Overlay Scatterplot menu,

    In the "Pairs" box,
    Insert "EFFECT" as "Y variable" and "PC" as "X variable",
    Insert "LLCI" as "Y variable" and "PC" as "X variable",
    Insert "ULCI" as "Y variable" and "PC" as "X variable",

Click "OK".

Figure 7.4 Instructions to graph results of J-N technique in SPSS

have provided the instructions to produce a graph in SPSS. Once the graph is produced, you will need to edit the graph and add labels to each axis so it is clear what is being displayed. If you want to formally present it somewhere, the more editing work required. If you follow the instructions, the x-axis is the response format for PC and the y-axis is the conditional effect of PS on expressive suppression. The estimate of the conditional effect of PS on expressive suppression is plotted on the graph along with 95% confidence intervals. An edited version of the SPSS graph produced here is displayed in Hill (2021, p. 8, fig. 7.1). Having now followed all three steps, you have reproduced the findings of Hill (2021), replicated in Figure 7.5.

Future Directions and Questions

I close the chapter with some brief consideration of future directions for research. The idea of perfectionistic tipping points is new in sport, dance, and exercise (and other domains). Therefore, there is considerable scope for novel

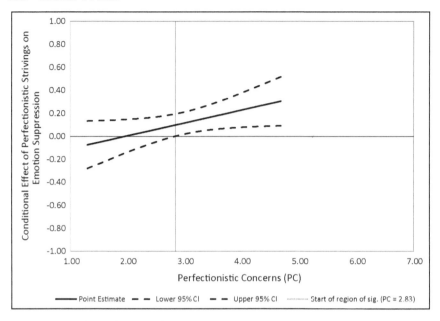

Figure 7.5 Conditional effect of PS on Emotion Suppression as PC increases
Adapted from Hill, A. P. (2021). Perfectionistic tipping points: Re-probing interactive effects of perfectionism. *Sport, Exercise, and Performance Psychology*, 10(2), 177–190. Copyright 2021 by American Psychological Association.

research in this area and there is much we don't know. As illustrated in the examples provided in the current study, revisiting previous research and applying this approach can be valuable. Most studies that have found evidence of interactions between PS and PC would benefit from being revisited in the same way. Recent studies that spring to mind is those that have been conducted in domains other than sport and include a focus on interesting variables such as social physique anxiety in exercisers (Deck et al., 2021) and enjoyment goals in young dancers (Molnar et al., 2021). This type of research is a good example of how beneficial secondary analyses can be and how it can bring about new insights. The frequency of this types of analyses generally is also likely to increase as more data is made publicly available.

Examining the replicability of existing findings is also needed using either existing or new data. Such research will be fundamental to determining the usefulness of the concept of perfectionistic tipping points. In doing so, researchers will need to be especially mindful of ensuring adequate statistical power. This is because unlike the 2 × 2 model of perfectionism that can be tested in the absence of a statistically significant interaction, this is not the case for perfectionistic tipping points. Interaction effects are typically small and account for less than 5% of variance in the dependent variable. Although not the only consideration, power analyses suggest that in order to detect effects of 3% to 5% variance, samples between 152 to 252 are required (see Hill, 2021).

In some cases, larger samples will be necessary if smaller effect sizes are considered meaningful.

Other directions for future research include seeking to identify perfectionistic tipping points in new data for dependent variables not yet examined when testing for interactions. For those interested in doing so, I would recommend reviewing the content of Chapter 4 and Chapter 6 of this book because together they provide a comprehensive account of research that has employed independent and interactive approaches. In my view, a focus on some for the features of perfectionistic strivings that might be identified as signalling its desirability would be revealing, like optimism and perseverance of effort (Dunn et al., 2019), for example. I am curious to know if these relationships are affected by the level of perfectionistic concerns athletes also exhibit and what percentage of our samples enjoy (or don't enjoy) the benefits of a more optimistic outlook and determination. These questions could be answered by seeking to identify any perfectionistic tipping points for these variables.

One final suggestion is more general and it is to extend the use of J-N technique to identify other tipping points in sport, dance, and exercise psychology. Some areas in which this would be applicable include the study of passion (obsessive and harmonious), dichotomous achievement goals (ego and task orientation), and narcissism (self-inflated and dominant). The idea of "passion tipping points," for example, might help better understand the interplay between obsessive passion and harmonious passion which are similar to PS and PC in that they often have opposing effects (see Curran et al., 2015). Given its comparative benefits, it would also be good to see the J-N technique used more routinely and replace the use of pick-a-point approach when probing significant interactions in research. The J-N technique can be conducted easily mainly due to the excellent PROCESS macro provided by Hayes (2022) and is a valuable addition to the statistical tools at our disposal.

Concluding Comments

This chapter has described perfectionistic tipping points as a new way of conceptualizing and analysing the interaction between dimensions of perfectionism so to better understand their effects. In particular, how the relationship between PS and various dependent variables may depend on the level of PC that is exhibited. Research examining perfectionistic tipping points so far has found support for their existence for a range of common outcomes (e.g. burnout, engagement, and emotion regulation). More research is needed to replicate these findings and identify new perfectionistic tipping points. This might be undertaken by re-examining data from previous studies where statistically significant interactions have been found or by collecting new data. Although there are many merits of this approach, perhaps most of all, its strength lies in its potential to help our ongoing efforts to identify for whom perfectionism is helpful, harmful, or neutral.

References

Bieling, P. J., Israeli, A. L., & Antony, M. M. (2004). Is perfectionism good, bad, or both? Examining models of the perfectionism construct. *Personality and individual differences*, 36(6), 1373–1385.

Cox, B. J., Enns, M. W., & Clara, I. P. (2002). The multidimensional structure of perfectionism in clinically distressed and college student samples. *Psychological Assessment*, 14(3), 365–373. https://doi.org/10.1037/1040-3590.14.3.365.

Curran, T., & Hill, A. P. (2018). A test of perfectionistic vulnerability following competitive failure among college athletes. *Journal of Sport and Exercise Psychology*, 40(5), 269–279. https://doi.org/10.1123/jsep.2018-0059.

Curran, T., Hill, A. P., Appleton, P. R., Vallerand, R. J., & Standage, M. (2015). The psychology of passion: A meta-analytical review of a decade of research on intrapersonal outcomes. *Motivation and Emotion*, 39(5), 631–655. https://doi.org/10.1007/s11031-015-9503-0.

Deck, S., Roberts, R., Hall, C., & Kouali, D. (2021). Perfectionism and social physique anxiety using the 2 × 2 model. *International Journal of Sport and Exercise Psychology*, 19 (5), 895–905. https://doi.org/10.1080/1612197x.2020.1826998.

Dunn, J. G. H., Gotwals, J. K., Dunn, J. C., & Lizmore, M. R. (2019). Perfectionism, pre-competitive worry, and optimism in high-performance youth athletes. *International Journal of Sport and Exercise Psychology*, 18(6), 749–763. https://doi.org/10.1080/1612197x.2019.1577900.

Frost, R. O., Marten, P., Lahart, C., & Rosenblate, R. (1990). The dimensions of perfectionism. *Cognitive Therapy and Research*, 14(5), 449–468. https://doi.org/10.1007/bf01172967.

Gaudreau, P. (2016). The 2 × 2 Model of Perfectionism in sport, dance, and exercise. In A. P. Hill (ed.), *The psychology of perfectionism in sport, dance and exercise* (pp. 174–200). Routledge.

Gotwals, J. K. (2016). The Tripartite Model of perfectionism: Evidence from research in sport and dance. In A. P. Hill (ed.), *The psychology of perfectionism in sport, dance and exercise* (pp. 166–189). Routledge.

Gotwals, J. K., Dunn, J. G. H., Causgrove Dunn, J., & Gamache, V. (2010). Establishing validity evidence for the Sport Multidimensional Perfectionism Scale-2 in intercollegiate sport. *Psychology of Sport and Exercise*, 11(6), 423–432. https://doi.org/10.1016/j.psychsport.2010.04.013.

Graham, J. W., Cumsille, P. E., & Elek-Fisk, E. F. (2003). Methods for handling missing data. In J. A. Schinka & W. F. Velicer (eds), *Research methods in psychology* (pp. 87–112). Wiley.

Gross, J. J., & John, O. P. (2003). Individual differences in two emotion regulation processes: Implications for affect, relationships, and well-being. *Journal of Personality and Social Psychology*, 85(2), 348–362. https://doi.org/10.1037/0022-3514.85.2.348.

Hall, H. K. (2006). Perfectionism: A hallmark quality of world class performers, or a psychological impediment to athletic development. In D. Hackfort & G. Tenenbaum (eds), *Perspectives in sport and exercise psychology* (pp. 178–211). Meyer & Meyer Publishers.

Hayes, A. F. (2013). *Mediation, moderation and conditional process analysis: A regression-based approach*. The Guilford Press.

Hayes A. (2022). The PROCESS macro for SPSS, SAS, and R. Retrieved from www.processmacro.org/index.html.

Hill, A. P. (2013). Perfectionism and burnout in junior soccer players: A test of the 2×2 model of dispositional perfectionism. *Journal of Sport and Exercise Psychology*, 35(1), 18–29. https://doi.org/10.1123/jsep.35.1.18.

Hill, A. P. (2021). Perfectionistic tipping points: Re-probing interactive effects of perfectionism. *Sport, Exercise, and Performance Psychology*, 10(2), 177–190. https://doi.org/10.1037/spy0000226.

Hill, A. P., Appleton, P. R., & Mallinson, S. H. (2016). Development and initial validation of the Performance Perfectionism Scale for Sport (PPS-S). *Journal of Psychoeducational Assessment*, 34(7), 653–669. https://doi.org/10.1177/0734282916651354.

Hill, A. P., & Davis, P. A. (2014). Perfectionism and emotion regulation in coaches: A test of the 2×2 model of dispositional perfectionism. *Motivation and Emotion*, 38(5), 715–726. https://doi.org/10.1007/s11031-014-9404-7.

Hill, A. P., & Madigan, D. J. (2017). A short review of perfectionism in sport, dance and exercise: Out with the old, in with the 2 × 2. *Current Opinion in Psychology*, 16, 72–77. https://doi.org/10.1016/j.copsyc.2017.04.021.

Hill, A. P., Madigan, D. J., & Jowett, G. E. (2020). Perfectionism and athlete engagement: A multi-sample test of the 2×2 model of perfectionism. *Psychology of Sport and Exercise*, 48, 101664. https://doi.org/10.1016/j.psychsport.2020.101664.

Hill, A. P., Mallinson-Howard, S. H., & Jowett, G. E. (2018). Multidimensional perfectionism in sport: A meta-analytical review. *Sport, Exercise, and Performance Psychology*, 7(3), 235–270. https://doi.org/10.1037/spy0000125.

Johnson, P. O., & Neyman, J. (1936). Tests of certain linear hypotheses and their application to some educational problems. *Statistical Research Memoirs*, 1, 57–93.

Lin, H. (2020). Probing two-way moderation effects: A review of software to easily plot Johnson-Neyman figures. *Structural Equation Modeling: A Multidisciplinary Journal*, 27 (3), 494–502.

Lizmore, M. R., Dunn, J. G. H., Causgrove Dunn, J., & Hill, A. P. (2019). Perfectionism and performance following failure in a competitive golf-putting task. *Psychology of Sport and Exercise*, 45, 101582. https://doi.org/10.1016/j.psychsport.2019.101582.

Molnar, D. S., Blackburn, M., Zinga, D., Spadafora, N., Methot-Jones, T., & Connolly, M. (2021). Trait perfectionism and dance goals among young female dancers: An application of the 2 × 2 model of perfectionism. *Journal of Sport & Exercise Psychology*, 43(3), 1–14. https://doi.org/10.1123/jsep.2020-0118.

Nicholls, J. G. (1989). *The competitive ethos and democratic education*. Harvard University Press.

Spielberger, C. D. (1999). *STAXI-2: State-Trait Anger Expression Inventory-2: Professional manual*. Psychological Assessment Resources.

Stoeber, J. (2011). The dual nature of perfectionism in sports: Relationships with emotion, motivation, and performance. *International Review of Sport and Exercise Psychology*, 4(2), 128–145. https://doi.org/10.1080/1750984x.2011.604789.

Stoeber, J., Otto, K., Pescheck, E., Becker, C., & Stoll, O. (2007). Perfectionism and competitive anxiety in athletes: Differentiating striving for perfection and negative reactions to imperfection. *Personality and Individual Differences*, 42(6), 959–969. https://doi.org/10.1016/j.paid.2006.09.006.

Tabachnick, B. G., & Fidell, L. S. (2007). *Using multivariate statistics*. Pearson Education.

Waleriańczyk, W., Hill, A. P., & Stolarski, M. (2022). A re-examination of the 2 × 2 model of perfectionism, burnout, and engagement in sports. *Psychology of Sport and Exercise*, 61, 102190. https://doi.org/10.1016/j.psychsport.2022.102190.

8 Perfectionism Cognitions in Sport, Dance, and Exercise

Tracy Donachie, Andrew P. Hill and Marianne E. Etherson

The chapters of this book have so far focused on trait perfectionism – which has been the main focus of perfectionism research in sport, dance, and exercise. However, perfectionism manifests at multiple levels and includes cognitive elements that are essential when seeking to understand its full effects. With this in mind, this chapter focuses on perfectionism cognitions and how this type of ruminative over-thinking offers further insight into the inner experiences of athletes, dancers, and exercisers. Only a handful of studies have examined perfectionism cognitions in these domains so far. However, these studies show the importance of perfectionism cognitions and mirror more extensive work outside of sport. The chapter starts with a brief overview of the Comprehensive Model of Perfectionistic Behaviour and Perfectionism Cognitions Theory. We then review and discuss existing research examining perfectionism cognitions in sport, dance, and exercise. We conclude the chapter by identifying future directions for research and key research questions that should be prioritized.

Comprehensive Model of Perfectionistic Behaviour

Research examining perfectionism in sport, dance, and exercise domains has mainly focused on trait (or dispositional) perfectionism. However, trait perfectionism sits at only one level of a larger model used to study perfectionism. As presented by Hewitt et al. (2017), the Comprehensive Model of Perfectionistic Behaviour (CMPB) is an encompassing approach that views perfectionism as a "multifaceted and multilevel personality style" (p. 3). In the CMPB, perfectionism functions at trait, interpersonal (or other-relational), and intrapersonal (or self-relational) levels, and there are components at each level which themselves include multidimensional traits, multifaceted self-presentational styles, and automatic thoughts (or perfectionism cognitions). In deriving the model, Hewitt et al. (2017) emphasize the importance of including, and differentiating between, these levels and what people "have" with regard to perfectionism (their traits and the content of their traits) and what people "do" in terms of its expression (how they hide imperfection from others or experience perfectionistic thoughts).

As described by Hewitt et al. (2017), at the trait level, the focus is on the motivation and requirement to be perfect. Traits include intrapersonal and

DOI: 10.4324/9781003288015-11

interpersonal dimensions that reflect different targets of the requirement to be perfect. The requirement can be for the self to be perfect (self-oriented perfectionism), for others to be perfect (other-oriented perfectionism), or to meet other people's requirements to be perfect (socially prescribed perfectionism). These dimensions of trait perfectionism are separate entities, but covary and interact, allowing people to be higher in one, two or all traits, and creating "complex blends" of trait perfectionism that determine its effects (Hewitt et al., 2017).

At the interpersonal (or other-relational) level, the focus is on the expression of perfectionism to others via perfectionistic self-presentational styles. Perfectionistic self-presentation is composed of three facets: perfectionistic self-promotion (displaying perfection to others), non-display of imperfection (concealing and avoiding behavioural demonstrations of imperfection), and nondisclosure of imperfection (avoiding verbal admissions of imperfection) (Hewitt et al., 2003). Perfectionistic self-promotion is the presentation of the perfect self so to impress others and gain admiration (Hewitt et al., 2017). By contrast, the other two facets of perfectionistic self-presentation are passive and concealing styles and involve preventing any signs of imperfection being known to others (Hewitt et al., 2003).

At the intrapersonal (or self-relational) level, the focus is on the inner expression of perfectionism. In particular, the manner in which an individual's need to be perfect manifests in perfectionistic thoughts and images (Flett et al., 1998). These thoughts and images include automatic negative self-statements and rumination, and a paucity of positive self-statements (Flett et al., 1998). Perfectionism cognitions are more state-like in comparison to trait perfectionism and perfectionistic self-presentational styles as they are more directly linked to daily events and immediate concerns (Flett et al., 2018). However, they can become chronically activated and serve as a subconscious cognitive filter for people's everyday experience (Hewitt et al., 2017). They also provide an additional source of internal pressure to be perfect (Flett et al., 2018).

In formalizing the CMPB, Hewitt and Flett have brought together lines of research that span over thirty years – it is perhaps the most complete account of perfectionism available. The CMPB highlights the various ways perfectionism can exist and, through the way in which components within and between levels interact, shows the large heterogeneity we can expect with regard to manifestations of perfectionism and the variability in its effects. Research in sport, dance, and exercise is heavily skewed towards trait perfectionism with few studies of the other two levels. As such, currently we have only part of a view of the overall picture of perfectionism. However, this is changing and an increasing number of studies are including multiple components in these domains. In the current chapter, we focus on the intrapersonal level and perfectionism cognitions as this has been the focus of most of the research that has included more than just trait perfectionism. In addition, the interpersonal level is also key to understanding the inner turmoil of perfectionism, regardless of whether outwardly any desirable behaviours are being exhibited in sport, dance, and exercise.

Perfectionism Cognitions Theory

Perfectionism Cognitions Theory (PCT; Flett et al., 2015, 2018) is a sub-theory of the CMPB that seeks to explain the cognitive elements and mechanisms related to perfectionism. Building on historical cognitive approaches to perfectionism, PCT is derived from the work of Hewitt and Genest (1990) and Flett et al. (1998). This work focused on the cognitive processing of self-relevant information and the role of different self-schemas (or beliefs about ourselves and our characteristics). Notably, this included the role of the "ideal self" in the inner expression of perfectionism and the thoughts that can arise that are focused on the need to be perfect. In this work, the salience of the ideal-self was proposed to make those higher in trait perfectionism prone to the experience of negative, automatic thoughts centred on perfectionistic themes such as personal shortcomings and failures. Flett et al. (1998) labelled these thoughts perfectionism cognitions.

In revisiting their work, Flett et al. (2015, 2018) expanded the approach based on the cognitive taxonomy proposed by Ingram and colleagues (Ingram, 1990; Ingram & Kendall, 1986; Ingram et al., 1998) and their four-level framework: (a) structural level, (b) propositional level, (c) operational level, and (d) cognitive products level. The structural level contains self-schemas, long-term memories, and deep neural networks. At this level, perfectionism is evident in the content of both actual self- and ideal self-schemas and the interconnectedness of perceived negative attributes and personal deficits. Perfectionism is also evident at this level via its influence on important long-term memories of success and failures that have merged to create generalized views of the self as being imperfect.

The propositional level contains beliefs and attitudes stored in various cognitive structures. According to Flett et al. (2018), for perfectionism, the cognitive content of these beliefs and attitudes are dysfunctional and reflect contingencies of self-worth and irrational perfectionistic beliefs. They also highlight the prominence of two conflicts and sources of tension associated with perfectionism at this level. The first conflict is between "emotional perfectionism" – a dysfunctional belief about the importance of maintaining perfect emotional control – and the routine experience of intense negative emotions. The second conflict is the "approach-avoidance conflict" which pertains to the experience of the need to balance the perceived rewards of perfection against the consequences of striving but failing to be perfect.

The operational level contains ongoing cognitive operations and functions. Perfectionism is proposed to be influential at this level by creating attentional biases and reactivity towards perceived threats and evaluative cues, and any other perfectionism-relevant cues. This includes information from social and performance contexts, particularly those that pertain to possible rejection or failure. Perfectionism is also evident at this level in how this kind of preoccupation and sensitivity impedes other cognitive processes, creates cognitive interference, and limits working cognitive capacity. These latter effects are proposed to be especially evident under conditions of negative mood, emotional distress, and stress or pressure.

The final product level contains cognitive outputs – thoughts, images, and self-statements. At this level, the products of perfectionism include ruminative thoughts and other forms of overthinking such as worry (Flett et al., 2018). It is at this level that perfectionism cognitions sit. Perfectionism cognitions are frequent, uncontrollable, and negative thoughts centred on perfectionistic themes. Flett et al. (2018) draw on theories of ruminative cognitions to conceptualize perfectionism cognitions as a form of perseverative thought that accompanies failed goal pursuit. Cognitive interference is also evident at this level in the form of mind-wandering, with onus placed on the difficulty associated with suppressing perfectionism cognitions due to the reasons for their occurrence lying deep within the lower levels of the model and the importance of the goals and objectives associated with perfectionism (being perfect or appearing to be perfect).

Measuring Perfectionism Cognitions

To measure perfectionism cognitions, Flett and colleagues developed the Perfectionism Cognitions Inventory (HF-PCI; Flett et al., 1998). The measure is a unidimensional scale with 25-items that are used to calculate a total score. The instructions ask responders to indicate how frequently, if at all, they have experienced particular thoughts in the last week. The thoughts are those such as "Why can't I be perfect?" and "I should be perfect". The response format is from "Not at all" [0] to "All the time" [4]. There has been a number of studies that have examined the psychometric properties of the HF-PCI including in its original development and validation (Flett et al., 1998), and subsequent work focused on particular populations such as adult psychiatric patients (Flett et al., 2007), students (Rudolph et al., 2007), and adolescents (Flett et al., 2012a). The findings of these studies tend to be similar and are supportive of the use of the HF-PCI.

By way of example, in the initial validation of the HF-PCI Flett et al. (1998) used 11 samples of university students and one sample of adult psychiatric patients in five studies. The HF-PCI was assessed in regard to factor structure (using exploratory factor analysis), test-retest reliability (r), and internal consistency (using Cronbach's alpha). Evidence was found to support the unidimensional structure in that all items appeared to load meaningfully on one factor (study 1). Test–retest reliability over a three-month period was also reasonably high in both a student sample ($r = .67$; study 2) and adult psychiatric patient sample ($r = .85$; study 4). The scale was considered internally consistent in all samples in which it was assessed ($\alpha \geq .90$).

In the initial validation, Flett et al. (1998) also examined the predictive ability of the HF-PCI in six samples of university students and one sample of adult psychiatric patients. They found that more frequent perfectionism cognitions were related to higher performance difficulties, negative affect, and general distress. In addition, perfectionism cognitions predicted unique variance in psychological distress (anxiety and depressive symptoms) after controlling for trait perfectionism dimensions, trait neuroticism, and general measures of negative automatic thoughts. In other words, perfectionism cognitions were found to be an important predictor of maladjustment regardless of whether trait perfectionism was being exhibited or general tendencies to experience similar types of negative thoughts.

Multidimensional versus Unidimensional Measurement

The conceptualization and measurement of perfectionism cognitions have not been without controversy. Notably, there has been disagreement among researchers with regard to whether perfectionism cognitions are best treated as unidimensional or multidimensional. Disagreement followed the publication of a Multidimensional Perfectionism Cognitions Inventory (MPCI) first published by Kobori (Kobori, 2006; Kobori & Tanno, 2004, 2005) in Japanese and then subsequently published in English (MPCI-E) by Stoeber et al. (2010). The MPCI-E is a 15-item scale that uses the same instructions and time frame as the HF-PCI, and a similar response format ("Not at all" [1] to "Always" [4]). However, it includes multiple dimensions that distinguish between positive and negative perfectionism cognitions. The dimensions are *personal standards cognitions* (e.g. "It's important to set high standards for myself"), *pursuit of perfection cognitions* (e.g. "I must be perfect at any cost") and *concern over mistakes cognitions* (e.g. "I'll blame myself if I make a mistake"). Personal standards cognitions are considered positive and concern over mistakes cognitions are considered negative with pursuit of perfection cognitions somewhere in-between (Stoeber et al., 2014).

The validation of the MPCI-E included rigorous tests of its validity and reliability. In a sample of university students, Stoeber et al. (2010) found evidence for the three-factor structure (using confirmatory factor analysis) and satisfactory internal consistency for all subscales (using Cronbach's alpha). In addition, supporting the distinction between dimensions of perfectionism cognitions, personal standards cognitions displayed a significant, positive, and small relationship with positive affect, whereas concerns over mistakes cognitions displayed a significant, negative, and small relationship with positive affect. In addition, both concerns over mistakes cognitions and pursuit of perfection cognitions displayed significant, positive, and small-moderate relationship with negative affect. MPCI-E subscales also predicted positive and negative affect beyond trait perfectionism (self-oriented and socially prescribed perfectionism).

In a subsequent study, Stoeber et al. (2014) sought to compare multidimensional versus unidimensional assessment of perfectionism cognitions. In critiquing the unidimensional approach of Flett et al (1998), they reasoned that (1) as trait perfectionism is multidimensional, so should perfectionism cognitions, (2) inspection of the items of the HF-PCI suggest close alignment between items on the scale and those on other measures indicative of the two broad dimensions of perfectionism (perfectionistic strivings and perfectionistic concerns), and (3) re-examination of the statistical analyses in Flett et al. (1998) suggests that the HF-PCI has two or three underlying dimensions. Stoeber et al.'s (2014) study included assessing the factor structure of the HF-PCI, deriving a multidimensional version of the HF-PCI (which we will call the HF-MPCI), and comparing unidimensional and multidimensional versions of the instruments when predicting positive and negative affect and depressive symptoms. After finding greater predictive ability when using the multidimensional version, they argued that multidimensional assessment of perfectionism cognitions is more advantageous than unidimensional assessment.

This study led to a rejoinder by Flett and Hewitt (2014a) who reiterated their position that, in their model, perfectionism cognitions are conceptualized as unidimensional and should be measured as such. Key to their position was how they viewed perfectionism cognitions as part of their CMPB as an intrapersonal level component focused on the self, and the underlying mechanisms they considered key to explaining *why* and *when* they arise. Notably, their perspective is in keeping with general theories of rumination and how this type of thinking is typically considered to be negative, unintentional and unwanted, and the result of failed goal pursuit (e.g. Klinger, 1996; Nolen-Hoeksema, 1996; Pyszczynski & Greenberg, 1987). Flett and Hewitt (2014a) also questioned the interpretability of the three factors of the HF-MPCI, the appropriateness of the factor labels, and the distinctiveness of the factors. In all, Flett and Hewitt (2014a) argued that any multidimensional approach to perfectionism cognitions was an alternative to their own.

To help resolve this issue, Hill and Donachie (2020) adopted the view that theory should take precedence over the findings regarding the factor structure of the HF-PCI and sought to create a more robust unidimensional version of the instrument. In doing so, the HF-PCI and the version derived by Stoeber et al. (2014) (HF-MPCI) were also compared. Across two adolescent athlete samples, and using more robust tests of factor structure than used in both previous studies (confirmatory and exploratory-confirmatory factor analysis), it was confirmed that the HF-PCI was most likely multidimensional, but support for the HF-MPCI version was also mixed. A new short version of the HF-PCI (the PCI-10) was developed that was superior in comparison to both the HF-PCI and HF-MPCI. The new version was also highly correlated with the original ($r = .94$ in both samples) providing some reassurance of comparability for studies using the two versions.

Given these circumstances, what should researchers in sport, dance and exercise do in regards to conceptualizing and measuring perfectionism cognitions? It is our view that when adopting Hewitt and Flett's approach, perfectionism cognitions are best conceptualized and measured as unidimensional. In addition, although Stoeber et al. (2014) illustrated that there may be merit in using a multidimensional approach, doing so currently lacks the theoretical basis of Hewitt and Flett's approach. As such, it is more difficult to hypothesize why and when positive versus negative perfectionism cognitions would arise. For the same reason, at the moment, we are unconvinced of the utility of this approach and its ability to inform applied practice in sport, dance, and exercise. Until this changes, we therefore recommend that those in sport, dance, and exercise domains adopt a unidimensional approach to perfectionism cognitions and use the PCI-10 when doing so.

Research Examining Perfectionism Cognitions

There is a considerable amount of research that has examined perfectionism cognitions outside of sport, dance, and exercise. This research attests to the negative effects of the experience of more frequent perfectionism cognitions. Some of the most common findings pertain to the relationship with emotional experiences, including stress (e.g. Flett et al., 2016), anxiety (e.g. Flett et al., 2002), and depressive symptoms (e.g. Flett et al., 2012a). These findings are in keeping with research that has also illustrated that perfectionism cognitions are related to deficits in emotion regulation (Rudolph et al., 2007), coping (Kobori et al., 2011), and cognitive self-management (e.g. Flett et al., 2007). In addition, on the more extreme and clinical end, the experience of frequent perfectionism cognitions is related to a host of anxiety-related disorders, including generalized anxiety disorder, obsessive compulsive disorder, and social anxiety disorder (e.g. Tyler et al., 2021).

As we noted earlier, perfectionism cognitions have been found to predict some of these outcomes, including anxiety and depressive symptoms, after controlling for trait perfectionism (e.g. Flett et al., 1998, 2007, 2012b). The implication being that the experience of perfectionism cognitions is important regardless of more stable perfectionistic qualities. Building on this idea, more recent research has found support for the notion that the experience of more frequent perfectionism cognitions is an explanation for *why* trait perfectionism is associated with a range of difficulties. So far, research testing a mediation model has included negative affect (e.g. Kobori et al., 2005), eating disturbances (e.g. Downey et al., 2014), and anxiety and depression (e.g. Macedo et al., 2017). Some of the most impressive work testing this model has demonstrated these effects over time (e.g. Besser et al., 2020).

To our knowledge, six studies have included perfectionism cognitions in sport, dance, and exercise, and all of the studies have been conducted in sport. The focus of these studies mirror those outside of sport in that they have included an emphasis on emotional experiences, tested predictive ability above traits, and more recently sought to model perfectionism cognitions as a mediating factor between traits and various outcomes. To account for the current state of knowledge in sport, we have described each of these studies in detail below and provided a shorthand account of their features and findings in Table 8.1. Of the six studies, two focus on pre-competition emotions, three focus on athlete burnout, and one focuses on motivational climate.

Table 8.1 A summary of research examining perfectionism cognitions in sport, exercise, and dance.

Study	Sample	Domain	Measure	Criterion variable	T1	T2	T3
Appleton et al. (2011)	73 female adolescent athletes	Sport	PCI	Coach-created mastery climate	.25	–	–
				Coach-created performance climate	**.34**	–	–
				Mother-initiated learning-enjoyment climate	−.11	–	–
				Father-initiated learning-enjoyment climate	.05	–	–
				Mother-initiated success-without-effort climate	**.22**	–	–
				Father-initiated success-without-effort climate	.17	–	–
				Mother-initiated worry-conducive environment	**.45**	–	–
				Father-initiated worry-conducive environment	**.23**	–	–
	117 male adolescent athletes	Sport	PCI	Coach-created mastery climate	.05	–	–
				Coach-created performance climate	**.31**	–	–
				Mother-initiated learning-enjoyment climate	−.04	–	–
				Father-initiated learning-enjoyment climate	−.03	–	–
				Mother-initiated success-without-effort climate	−.12	–	–
				Father-initiated success-without-effort climate	**−.21**	–	–
				Mother-initiated worry-conducive environment	.01	–	–
				Father-initiated worry-conducive environment	**.19**	–	–
Hill & Appleton (2011)	202 male adult rugby players	Sport	PCI	BO: Reduced accomplishment	**.27**	–	–
				BO: Exhaustion	**.21**	–	–
				BO: Devaluation	.03	–	–
Donachie et al. (2018)	206 adolescent soccer players (62% females)	Sport	PCI-10	Anxiety	**.32**	–	–
				Anger	**.29**		
				Dejection	**.24**	–	–
				Happiness	.12	–	–
				Excitement	.13	–	–

Study	Sample	Domain	Measure	Criterion variable	r		
					T1	*T2*	*T3*
Donachie et al. (2019)	352 adolescent soccer players (33% females)	Sport	PCI-10	Anxiety	**.30**	**.44**	**.41**
				Anger	**.27**	**.39**	**.39**
				Dejection	**.24**	**.39**	**.35**
				Happiness	.10	**.13**	**.22**
				Excitement	−.01	**.13**	**.33**
				Cognitive anxiety	**.46**	**.49**	**.53**
				Somatic anxiety	**.37**	**.39**	**.41**
				Feeling anger	**.25**	**.29**	**.24**
				Verbal anger	**.31**	**.30**	**.24**
				Physical anger	**.32**	**.33**	**.33**
Hassmén et al. (2020)	272 adult sports coaches (15% females)	Sport	PCI	BO: Exhaustion	**.41**	–	–
				Working hours	**.14**	–	–
Crowell & Madigan (2021)	170 university athletes (44% females)	Sport	PCI	BO: Exhaustion	.14	.14	–
				BO: Reduced accomplishment	.07	.11	–
				BO: Devaluation	−.04	.01	–
			PCI-10	BO: Exhaustion	**.18**	.14	–
				BO: Reduced accomplishment	**.15**	**.18**	–
				BO: Devaluation	.05	.08	–
			PSC	BO: Exhaustion	.04	−.03	–
				BO: Reduced accomplishment	−.09	−.12	–
				BO: Devaluation	**−.17**	−.14	–
			PCC	BO: Exhaustion	**.23**	**.29**	–
				BO: Reduced accomplishment	**.22**	**.36**	–
				BO: Devaluation	.12	**.24**	–
			PD	BO: Exhaustion	.05	.05	–
				BO: Reduced accomplishment	.03	−.05	–
				BO: Devaluation	−.12	**−.16**	–

Notes: PCI = Perfectionism Cognitions Inventory (Flett et al., 1998); PCI-10 = Perfectionism cognitions Inventory-10 (Hill & Donachie, 2020); PSC = Perfectionistic Strivings Cognitions (Stoeber et al., 2014) PCC = Perfectionistic Concerns Cognitions (Stoeber et al., 2014); PD = Perfectionistic Demands Cognitions (Stoeber et al., 2014). All correlations for longitudinal studies are within timepoints.

Motivational Climates and Perfectionism Cognitions

We start with the study examining perfectionism cognitions and motivational climate in sport (Appleton et al. 2011). This is one of the few studies in any domain to examine if the experience of perfectionism cognitions is related to perceptions of the social environment. The study adopted Achievement Goal Theory (AGT; Nicholls, 1989) to test the relationship between perfectionism cognitions and perceptions of different motivational climates created by parents and coaches in youth sport. Within AGT, coaches create a mastery climate (emphasizing effort and personal development) and a performance climate (emphasizing the importance of normative ability and comparative superiority). Similarly, parents are considered to initiate a learning-enjoyment climate (emphasis on enjoyment derived from skill acquisition), worry-conducive climate (emphasis on negative consequences of mistakes), and success-without-effort climate (reserving approval for occasions of success with minimal effort) (White, 1996). Athletes report the subjective experience of these climates by commenting on the behaviours, expectations, and values of their coach and parents.

Perceptions of the motivational climate have an important influence on how athletes feel about themselves and their sport (Duda & Balaguer, 2007). Based on the last review of research in this area (Harwood et al., 2015), we know for instance that a mastery climate is typically positively related to valuing effort, intrinsic motivation, self-esteem, and prosocial moral attitudes. By contrast, a performance climate is typically positively related to valuing ability, extrinsic motivation, negative affect, and antisocial moral attitudes. These relationships are mirrored when it comes to parents. In terms of outcomes, a learning-enjoyment climate is akin to a mastery climate, and worry-conducive and a success-without-effort climates are akin to a performance climate (e.g. Gustafsson et al., 2016; Kolayiş et al., 2017; Wagnsson et al., 2016).

Appleton et al. (2011) examined whether perceived parent and coach-created motivational climates predicted perfectionism cognitions in a sample of youth athletes. In doing so, they also sought to test alternative hypotheses on the development of perfectionism whereby perfectionism in children is more strongly related to the primary caregiver (mother) or same-sex parent (mother–daughters and father–sons). For female athletes, mother-worry-conducive climate predicted more frequent perfectionism cognitions, as did father-learning-enjoyment climate. For male athletes, father-worry-conducive climate predicted more frequent perfectionism cognitions and father-success-without-effort climate predicted less frequent perfectionism cognitions, as did mother-worry-conducive climate. After controlling for these effects, coach performance climate predicted more frequent perfectionism cognitions for both male and female athletes, and coach mastery climate predicted more frequent perfectionism cognitions for female athletes.

In a second analysis they examined whether athlete gender and age moderated the relationships between parent and coach motivational climates and perfectionism cognitions. Age did not moderate any of the relationships. However, it was found that gender moderated the relationship of one of the climate measures – mother-worry-conducive climate – with perfectionism cognitions. The moderation showed that, for female athletes, as perceptions of mother-worry-conducive climate increased, the frequency of perfectionism cognitions increased. However, for male athletes, as perceptions of the mother-worry-conducive climate increased, the frequency of perfectionism cognitions decreased.

The findings of this study are complex and include some unexpected findings (e.g. a father-learning-enjoyment climate predicting higher perfectionism cognitions in female athletes). However, the findings are noteworthy with regard to a coach performance climate predicting more frequent perfectionism cognitions in junior athletes. This is the first indication that coaches are important in the experience of perfectionism cognitions. In addition, findings are also noteworthy with regard to an interesting same-sex effect for parents whereby a worry-conducive climate predicts more frequent perfectionism cognitions when there is a gender match (mothers–daughters and father–sons). More research is needed to follow-up this study to better understand its findings, but for now it provides a clear indication that the social environment created in sport may be important for the experience of perfectionism cognitions.

Perfectionism Cognitions and Burnout

One of the most examined relationships involving perfectionism in sport is trait perfectionism and burnout (see Curran & Hill, 2018). Likewise, most studies in sport that include perfectionism cognitions also include a focus on burnout. Athlete burnout is a syndrome that includes three symptoms: reduced sense of accomplishment, physical and emotional exhaustion, and sport devaluation (Raedeke & Smith, 2001). There are different models of burnout but the most popular and well-supported model views burnout as the result of chronic stress (Smith, 1986). Trait perfectionism is implicated in the development of burnout because of its role in the stress process – making appraisals of threat and the experience of stress more likely. In a similar manner, perfectionism cognitions may also be important because of the internal sense of pressure they can generate and their potential to magnify and maintain stressful experiences (Flett et al., 2018).

The first study to examine perfectionism cognitions and athlete burnout was conducted by Hill and Appleton (2011). They examined whether perfectionism cognitions were related to burnout symptoms in male youth and adult rugby union players and whether perfectionism cognitions predicted burnout symptoms after controlling for trait perfectionism. The trait dimensions they controlled for were self-oriented perfectionism and socially prescribed perfectionism. Results showed that perfectionism cognitions had a significant, positive, and small-to-medium relationship with two burnout symptoms – reduced sense of athletic accomplishment and emotional and physical exhaustion. In addition, perfectionism cognitions also predicted variance in all three symptoms of athlete burnout after controlling for the two trait dimensions of perfectionism.

The findings suggest that perfectionism cognitions are likely to increase the risk of burnout for athletes. It may be that perfectionism cognitions maintain and exacerbate stress experiences leaving them physically and emotionally exhausted. Alternatively, ruminating about imperfect performances may undermine their motivation and lead athletes to feel dissatisfied with their accomplishments in sport. Regardless, as found outside of sport, the study provides evidence that perfectionism cognitions are a unique feature of perfectionism and need to be considered alongside whether athletes are typically more or less perfectionistic (i.e. trait perfectionism). As such, perfectionism cognitions may warrant additional attention when examining the perfectionism-athlete burnout relationship, when considering who is most at risk to burnout, and when devising interventions aimed at reducing burnout.

A second study by Crowell and Madigan (2021) has examined the relationship between perfectionism cognitions and burnout in sport over time. Crowell and Madigan (2021) built on Hill and Appleton's (2011) study by using a two-wave, three-month longitudinal design with measures taken at the start and end of season. In this study the sample were university athletes from various sports. The study is noteworthy, too, because it also examined all versions of the HF-PCI (HF-PCI, PCI-10, and HF-MPCI). Scores on the PCI-10 and HF-MPCI were related to burnout symptoms at Time 1 and Time 2. However, only concern over mistakes cognitions (labelled perfectionistic concerns cognitions in their study) from the HF-MPCI predicted changes in athlete burnout over time. Specifically, concern over mistakes cognitions predicted increases in reduced accomplishment and sport devaluation over the course of the season.

With controversy regarding the use of the HF-MPCI in mind, we believe some caution is required when extrapolating from this study. However, as the only test of the perfectionism cognitions and burnout relationship over time to date, it clearly has evidential value and is potentially informative. In this regard, it suggests that the relationship between perfectionism cognitions and athlete burnout symptoms may be something that is evident over time. If this is the case, there is a considerable amount we still do not know about this finding such as why the relationship exists for some symptoms of burnout (and possibly some cognitions) but not others. More longitudinal research of this kind is sorely needed to address these issues and further our understanding of the role of perfectionism cognitions in the development of athlete burnout.

One final study has examined the relationship between perfectionism cognitions and burnout (Hassmén et al., 2020). In this study, the focus was not on athlete burnout but on coach burnout. This built on the two aforementioned studies as well as a small number of studies that have examined trait perfectionism and burnout in coaches (e.g. Vealey et al., 2020). There are similarities and differences between the circumstances athletes and coaches find themselves. For example, both share irregular working hours, long seasons with limited breaks, and can be focus of harsh criticism from others (e.g. Bentzen et al., 2016). However, coaches have the additional burden of stress associated with being responsible for overall team performance and the emotional investment in both the sport and their athletes (e.g. Lee & Cho, 2021). It may be, then, that coaches are even more prone to burnout than athletes.

Noting the differences and the additional stressors for coaches, Hassmén et al. (2020) examined the relationship between perfectionism cognitions and one symptom of burnout (exhaustion) in a sample of professional soccer coaches. They also examined the predictive ability of a range of demographic and work factors, as well as a perfectionistic self-presentational style. Perfectionism cognitions were found to have a significant, positive, and moderate relationship with exhaustion. The relationship remained after demographic and work factors were taken into account (gender, age, civil status, and level of coaching, work hours). It also remained when considered alongside the three facets of a perfectionistic self-presentational style (one of which also predicted higher exhaustion – non-display of imperfection).

The study by Hassmén et al. (2020) illustrates that coaches may, like athletes, also be susceptible to burnout when they experience more frequent perfectionism cognitions. We believe it is noteworthy that this relationship was evident beyond perfectionistic self-presentational styles, too. Typically, research has focused on traits when examining incremental predictive ability. It appears that *thinking* you should be perfect places coaches at risk to burnout even if they are also trying to *appear* perfect. It would be interesting to see if perfectionism cognitions still emerged as a unique predictor alongside both trait perfectionism and perfectionistic self-presentation styles. There are few studies that include all three, generally. One examining burnout in sport would be especially useful given we now know that components at all levels of the CMPB are related to higher burnout symptoms.

Perfectionism Cognitions and Emotions in Sport

Two studies in sport have examined the relationship between perfectionism cognitions and pre-competition emotions (Donachie et al., 2018; Donachie et al., 2019). Pre-competition emotions are complex and their influence depends on a number of factors (Jekauc et al., 2021). However, athletes experiencing positive pre-competition emotions (e.g. excitement) are typically considered to be braced for competition and energized. By contrast, athletes experiencing negative pre-competition emotions (e.g. anger) are typically considered more prone to being distracted and having displaced energy (e.g. Vast et al., 2010). Over time, too, pre-competitive emotions are a key aspect of the overall sport experience. With these issues in mind, a better understanding of why some athletes report more negative and less positive pre-competition emotions, and vice versa, provides an opportunity to better support athletes with their wellbeing and their performance.

In the first study, Donachie et al. (2018) examined the relationship between trait perfectionism, perfectionism cognitions, and pre-competition emotions in youth soccer players. Youth soccer players completed a questionnaire once approximately a day before their next match. Perfectionism cognitions displayed significant, positive, and small-to-moderate relationships with pre-competition anxiety, dejection, and anger. After controlling for trait perfectionism, perfectionism cognitions predicted unique variance in all of these pre-competition emotions. In the same way that perfectionism cognitions predicted burnout symptoms in an incremental fashion, then, they also did the same for the negative pre-competition emotions soccer players were reporting.

In a follow-up study, Donachie et al. (2019) examined whether perfectionism cognitions act as a mediator between trait perfectionism and pre-competition emotions. Youth footballers completed questionnaires three times, three-weeks apart, and approximately three days before their next match. The mediation was modelled at both between-person (changes relative to other athlete's scores) and within-person level (changes relative to an individual's own scores). At the between-person level, perfectionism cognitions mediated the relationships between trait perfectionism (self-oriented and socially prescribed perfectionism) and all pre-competition emotions, as well as multidimensional anxiety and anger. At the within-person level, again, perfectionism cognitions mediated the relationship between trait perfectionism and general pre-competition anxiety and anger, as well as multidimensional anxiety and anger. That is, it was found that as self-oriented and socially prescribed perfectionism increase over time so do perfectionism cognitions and, subsequently, so do pre-competition anxiety and anger.

This study provides one of the strongest indications yet that the experience of perfectionism cognitions explain why perfectionistic athletes will be prone to more negative emotional experiences. In this regard, the findings are very much consistent with research outside of sport. Pre-competition anxiety and anger, in particular, appear to be a key aspect of their emotional experiences and may pose particular difficulties with regard to emotion regulation. Of note, too, the experience of more negative pre-competition emotions is related to perfectionism cognitions regardless of whether an athlete typically expects perfection of themselves or believes others expects it of them. Hence, whether the result of trait perfectionism or the social environment, as perfectionism cognitions become more frequent athletes will likely experience more emotional difficulties.

Managing Perfectionism Cognitions in Sport

As evidenced in previous sections, perfectionism cognitions predict both burn-out and negative emotions beyond trait perfectionism. In addition, perfectionism cognitions appear to be the mechanism by which trait perfectionism is related to undesirable emotional experiences. Therefore, it is important to find ways to protect athletes (and coaches) from the harmful consequences of perfectionism cognitions. Despite the evidence that perfectionism can be problematic in sport, studies testing the effectiveness of interventions for perfectionism are scarce. As trait perfectionism is relatively stable and may not be as amenable to change, it may even be that a focus on perfectionism cognitions, which is more state-like, may be a better focus for this work and is more likely to be successful.

Outside of sport, at least two intervention studies have found evidence that perfectionism cognitions can be reduced. The first study examined a 12-week web-based cognitive behavioural therapy (CBT) intervention with university students (Radhu et al., 2012). While they found that perfectionism cognitions (and concerns over mistakes) significantly reduced from pre- to post-intervention, no significant difference between the intervention group and control post-intervention was found. The second study also examined a web-based CBT intervention in students albeit slightly shorter (10 weeks) and compared it to both a general stress intervention and a control group in university students (Arpin-Cribbie et al., 2012). They found that perfectionism cognitions significantly reduced from pre- to post- for both intervention groups. In addition, the CBT group reported significantly lower perfectionism cognitions compared to the general stress intervention group and the control group post-intervention, when pre-intervention scores were controlled. As such, while limited and somewhat mixed, there is at least some emerging evidence that perfectionism cognitions can be reduced via intervention.

There are two studies that have tested interventions aimed at reducing perfectionism cognitions in the three domains this book is focused on. The first is by Karin and Nordin-Bates (2020) in dance and the second in by Donachie and Hill (2020) in sport. In the first study, Karin and Nordin-Bates's (2020) used a pre-test–post-test design to examine the influence of a five-day intervention on 13 adolescent vocational ballet students. The intervention was pedagogical (rather than therapeutic or psychoeducational) with an emphasis on the use of implicit- learning and sensori-kinetic imagery as a means of improving creativity and reducing perfectionism cognitions. They found support for the intervention with statistically significant reductions in perfectionism cognitions pre- to post-intervention. Limitations of the design aside, these are intriguing findings and suggest that educational and indirect interventions may be useful in reducing perfectionism cognitions in dance and other domains.

In the second study, Donachie and Hill (2020) examined the effectiveness of a CBT-based self-help book ("When Perfect Isn't Good Enough"; Antony & Swinson, 2009) for reducing trait perfectionism and perfectionism cognitions among athletes. This approach, and book, had successfully been used in previous intervention research focused on trait perfectionism outside of sport (Pleva & Wade, 2007; Steele & Wade, 2008). One hundred and fifteen soccer players were randomly allocated to the self-help intervention group or a control group. The intervention group had access to the book for 8-weeks and were encouraged to read its 16 chapters and complete as many of its 53 exercises as possible. In support of the intervention, there were statistically significant, moderate-to-large, differences found between the two groups post-intervention in perfectionism cognitions which were also evident three months later.

The results from the two studies provide early indication that the experience of perfectionism cognitions is amenable to intervention in dance and sport. The use of implicit-learning and sensori-kinetic imagery is particularly novel. It may be that a focus on multisensory images and absorption in the task leaves less "cognitive room" for negative thoughts. By contrast, CBT-based practices may provide the opportunity to abate perfectionism cognitions by challenging and changing some of the preceding beliefs and behaviours. However, given that the origins of perfectionism cognitions lie at a deep structural level, fundamental change is likely to be more involved and difficult, and possibly require other types of intervention (see Hewitt et al., 2017). While we wait for more research, we recommend practitioners consider the content of studies reviewed here in their own applied work and use them as the basis for interventions aimed at reducing perfectionism cognitions.

Other Future Directions for Research

We close the chapter by briefly considering avenues for future research. Perhaps the most obvious avenue for future research is the general need to increase the number of studies of perfectionism cognitions in sport, dance, and exercise. Our view is that the importance of perfectionism cognitions is currently underappreciated in these domains. Perfectionism cognitions are likely to be extremely influential with regard to the experiences of athletes, dancers, and exercisers, and revealing in regards to the consequences of being perfectionistic. Perfectionism cognitions are a unique aspect of perfectionism that can help distinguish the characteristic from other personal qualities and is an important explanatory factor for the effects of trait perfectionism. This includes, in our view, being part of a key indirect pathway that links ambiguous dimensions of perfectionism – perfectionistic strivings – to negative outcomes such as burnout and emotional difficulties. As such, we believe research examining perfectionistic cognitions as an explanatory factor and mediator for outcomes associated with perfectionism to be an important avenue for future research.

One related future avenue pertains to broadening the focus of research to include other outcomes. So far research has focused mainly on pre-competition emotions and burnout. We would encourage researchers in sport, dance, and exercise to consider examining more clinically oriented outcomes (e.g. depressive symptoms and eating disorder symptomology). As noted by others, this would mirror research outside of sport and address concerns that we are in danger of painting too positive a picture of perfectionism in these domains (e.g. Flett & Hewitt, 2014b). We would also encourage researchers to examine how the experience of perfectionism cognitions undermines the presence of positive outcomes, such as enjoyment, confidence, and satisfaction. These types of outcomes have the potential to show how perfectionism cognitions not only increase the likelihood of problems, but also deny athletes, dancers, and exercisers experiences that are considered central to the value of participation in these domains.

A final future avenue pertains to the types of designs that are used to test these relationships. There have been many calls for more longitudinal research in the perfectionism area (e.g. Hill & Curran, 2016; Stoeber, 2018; Crowell &

Madigan, 2021). These calls are applicable to perfectionism cognitions, too, and maybe especially important when considering their more state-like features and the situational and momentary changes that can only be captured over time. As such, some of the longitudinal designs and methods we have seen in trait perfectionism research would be useful for perfectionism cognitions like the use of daily diaries (e.g. MacKinnon et al., 2019). Other designs and methods used in sport, dance, and exercise capable of capturing more momentary changes such as the think aloud method would also be useful in this regard (see Eccles & Arsal, 2017). Such designs are necessary if we are to capture the experience of perfectionism cognitions in ecologically valid ways.

Many of the same merits apply to the use of more experimental designs. Again, while in short supply, some of the more revealing studies in the perfectionism area include attempts to observe the consequences of failure and negative feedback in competitive scenarios (e.g. De Muynck et al., 2021; Curran & Hill, 2018; Lizmore et al., 2019). To date, perfectionism cognitions have not featured in this research but, arguably, may be more relevant and revealing in regards to immediate responses to these types of manipulations. It would be interesting to see how responsive perfectionism cognitions are in these scenarios and their impact on state thoughts, feelings and behaviour such as performance. As such, we also call for more routine inclusion of perfectionism cognitions in these types of studies.

Concluding Comments

This chapter focused on perfectionism cognitions and their role in revealing the inner experiences of athletes, dancers, and exercisers. The chapter begun by outlining the Comprehensive Model of Perfectionistic Behaviour and Perfectionism Cognitions Theory (Flett et al., 2018) which illustrated the deep-rooted nature of perfectionism cognitions and how they differ from other components of perfectionism. We then reviewed and discussed the research examining perfectionism cognitions in sport, dance, and exercise. These studies are indicative of the importance of perfectionism cognitions, particularly in regards to the emotional experiences of athletes and coaches, and suggest perfectionism cognitions are amenable to interventions aimed at reducing them. We concluded the chapter by identifying future directions for research and called for a greater focus on perfectionism cognitions and different outcomes, the use of more sophisticated research designs and methods, and the inclusion of perfectionism cognitions in research that examines responses to negative feedback and competitive failure.

References

Antony, M. M., & Swinson, R. P. (2009). *When perfect isn't good enough: Strategies for coping with perfectionism.* New Harbinger Publications.

Appleton, P. R. & Curran, T. (2016). The origins of perfectionism in sport, dance, and exercise: An introduction to the conceptual model of perfectionism development. In

A. P. Hill (ed.), *The psychology of perfectionism in sport, dance, and exercise* (pp. 57–82). Routledge.

Appleton, P. R., Hall, H. K., & Hill, A. P. (2011). Examining the influence of the parent-initiated and coach-created motivational climate upon athletes' perfectionism cognitions. *Journal of Sports Sciences*, 29(7), 661–671.

Arpin-Cribbie, C., Irvine, J., & Ritvo, P. (2012). Web-based cognitive-behavioral therapy for perfectionism: a randomized controlled trial. *Psychotherapy Research*, 22(2), 194–207. https://doi.org/10.1080/10503307.2011.637242.

Atkins, M. R., Johnson, D. M., Force, E. C., & Petrie, T. A. (2015). Peers, parents, and coaches, oh my! The relation of the motivational climate to boys' intention to continue in sport. *Psychology of Sport and Exercise*, 16, 170–180. https://doi.org/10.1016/j.psychsport.2014.10.008.

Belli, G. (2009). Nonexperimental quantitative research. In S. D. Lapan & M. T. Quartaroli (eds), *Research essentials: An introduction to designs and practices* (pp. 59–77). Jossey-Bass.

Bentzen, M., Lemyre, P. N., & Kenttä, G. (2016). Development of exhaustion for high-performance coaches in association with workload and motivation: A person-centered approach. *Psychology of Sport and Exercise*, 22, 10–19. https://doi.org/10.1016/j.psychsport.2015.06.004

Besser, A., Flett, G. L., Sherry, S. B., & Hewitt, P. L. (2020). Are perfectionistic thoughts an antecedent or a consequence of depressive symptoms? A cross-lagged analysis of the Perfectionism Cognitions Inventory. *Journal of Psychoeducational Assessment*, 38(1), 99–111. https://doi.org/10.1177/0734282919877764.

Burns, D. D. (1980). *Feeling good: The new mood therapy*. The New American Library.

Campo, M., Champely, S., Lane, A.M., Rosnet, E., Ferrand, C., & Louvet, B. (2016). Emotions and performance in rugby. *Journal of Sport and Health Science*, 294, 1–6. https://doi.org/10.1016/j.jshs.2016.05.007.

Casale, S., Fioravanti, G., Rugai, L., Flett, G.L., & Hewitt, P.L. (2020) What lies beyond the superordinate trait perfectionism factors? The Perfectionistic Self-Presentation and Perfectionism Cognitions Inventory versus the Big Three Perfectionism Scale in predicting depression and social anxiety. *Journal of Personality Assessment*, 102(3), 370–379. https://doi.org/10.1080/00223891.2019.1573429.

Crowell, D. & Madigan, D.M. (2021). Perfectionistic concerns cognitions predict burnout in college athletes: a three-month longitudinal study. *International Journal of Sport and Exercise Psychology*, 20(2), 532–550. https://doi.org/10.1080/1612197X.2020.1869802.

Curran, T., & Hill, A. P. (2018). A test of perfectionistic vulnerability following competitive failure among college athletes. *Journal of Sport and Exercise Psychology*, 40(5), 269–279. https://doi.org/10.1123/jsep.2018-0059.

Curran, T., Hill, A. P., Hall, H. K., & Jowett, G. E. (2015). Relationships between the coach-created motivational climate and athlete engagement in youth sport. *Journal of Sport and Exercise Psychology*, 37(2), 193–198. https://doi.org/10.1123/jsep.2014-0203.

De Muynck, G. J., Vansteenkiste, M., Morbée, S., Vandenkerckhove, B., Vande Broek, G., & Soenens, B. (2021). The interplay between normative feedback and self-critical perfectionism in predicting competitive tennis players' competence, tension, and enjoyment: An experimental study. *Sport, Exercise, and Performance Psychology*. https://doi.org/10/1037/spy0000234.

Donachie, T. C., & Hill, A. P. (2020). Helping soccer players help themselves: Effectiveness of a psychoeducational book in reducing perfectionism. *Journal of Applied Sport Psychology*, 1–21. https://doi.org/10.1080/10413200.2020.1819472.

Donachie, T. C., Hill, A. P., & Hall, H. K. (2018). The relationship between multidimensional perfectionism and pre-competition emotions of youth footballers. *Psychology of Sport and Exercise*, 37, 33–42. https://doi.org/10.1016/j.psychsport.2018.04.002.

Donachie, T. C., Hill, A. P., & Madigan, D. J. (2019). Perfectionism and pre-competition emotions in youth footballers: A three-wave longitudinal test of the mediating role of perfectionism cognitions. *Journal of Sport and Exercise Psychology*, 41(5), 309–319. https://doi.org/10.1123/jsep.2018-0317.

Donahue, E. G., Forest, J., Vallerand, R. J., Lemyre, P. N., Crevier-Braud, L., & Bergeron, É. (2012). Passion for work and emotional exhaustion: The mediating role of rumination and recovery. *Applied Psychology: Health and Well-Being*, 4(3), 341–368. https://doi.org/10.1111/j.1758-0854.2012.01078.x.

Downey, C. A., Reinking, K. R., Gibson, J. M., Cloud, J. A., & Chang, E. C. (2014). Perfectionistic cognitions and eating disturbance: Distinct mediational models for males and females. *Eating Behaviors*, 15(3), 419–426. https://doi.org/10.1016/j.eatbeh.2014.04.020.

Duda, J. L., & Balaguer, I. (2007). Coach-created motivational climate. In S. Jowette & D. Lavallee (eds), *Social psychology in sport* (pp. 117–130). Human Kinetics. https://doi.org/10.5040/9781492595878.ch-009

Eccles, D. W., & Arsal, G. (2017). The think aloud method: what is it and how do I use it? *Qualitative Research in Sport, Exercise and Health*, 9(4), 514–531.

Ferrari, J. R. (1995). Perfectionism cognitions with nonclinical and clinical samples. *Journal of Social Behaviour and Personality*, 10(1), 143–156.

Flett, G. L., & Hewitt, P. L. (2014a). The multidimensional assessment of perfectionistic automatic thoughts: A commentary on "Examining mutual suppression effects in the assessment of perfectionism cognitions: Evidence supporting multidimensional assessment". *Assessment*, 21(6), 661–665. https://doi.org/10.1177/1073191114553015.

Flett, G. L., & Hewitt, P. L. (2014b). The perils of perfectionism in sports" revisited: Toward a broader understanding of the pressure to be perfect and its impact on athletes and dancers. *International Journal of Sport Psychology*, 45(4), 395–407.

Flett, G. L., Hewitt, P. L., Blankstein, K. R., & Gray, L. (1998). Psychological distress and the frequency of perfectionistic thinking. *Journal of Personality and Social Psychology*, 75(5), 1363–1381. https://doi.org/10.1037/0022-3514.75.5.1363.

Flett, G. L., Hewitt, P. L., Demerjian, A., Sturman, E. D., Sherry, S. B., & Cheng, W. (2012a). Perfectionistic automatic thoughts and psychological distress in adolescents: An analysis of the Perfectionism Cognitions Inventory. *Journal of Rational-Emotive & Cognitive-Behavior Therapy*, 30(2), 91–104. https://doi.org/10.1007/s10942-011-0131-7.

Flett, G. L., Hewitt, P. L., Nepon, T., & Besser, A. (2018). Perfectionism cognitions theory: The cognitive side of perfectionism. In J. Stoeber (ed.), *The psychology of perfectionism: Theory, research and applications* (pp.89–110). Routledge.

Flett, G. L., Hewitt, P. L., Whelan, T., & Martin, T. R. (2007). The perfectionism cognitions inventory: Psychometric properties and associations with distress and deficits in cognitive self-management. *Journal of Rational-Emotive and Cognitive Therapy*, 25(4), 255–277. https://doi.org/10.1007/s10942-007-0055-4.

Flett, G. L., Madorsky, D., Hewitt, P. L., & Heisel, M. J. (2002). Perfectionism cognitions, rumination, and psychological distress. *Journal of Rational-Emotive and Cognitive-Behavior Therapy*, 20(1), 33–47. https://doi.org/10.1023/A:1015128904007.

Flett, G. L., Molnar, D. S., Nepon, T., & Hewitt, P. L. (2012b). A mediational model of perfectionistic automatic thoughts and psychosomatic symptoms: The roles of negative affect and daily hassles. *Personality and Individual Differences*, 52(5), 565–570. https://doi.org/10.1016/j.paid.2011.09.010.

Flett, G. L., Nepon, T., & Hewitt, P.L. (2016). Perfectionism, worry and rumination in health and mental health: A review and a conceptual framework for a cognitive theory of perfectionism. In. F. S. Sirois & D. S. Molnar (eds), *Perfectionism, health and well-being* (pp.121–155). Springer International.

Garinger, L. M., Chow, G. M., & Luzzeri, M. (2018). The effect of perceived stress and specialization on the relationship between perfectionism and burnout in collegiate athletes. *Anxiety, Stress, & Coping*, 31(6), 714–727. https://doi.org/10.1080/10615806.2018.1521514.

Gustafsson, H., Hill, A. P., Stenling, A., & Wagnsson, S. (2016). Profiles of perfectionism, parental climate, and burnout among competitive junior athletes. *Scandinavian Journal of Medicine & Science in Sports*, 26(10), 1256–1264. https://doi.org/10.1111/sms.12553.

Gustafsson, H., DeFreese, J. D., & Madigan, D. J. (2017). Athlete burnout: Review and recommendations. *Current Opinion in Psychology*, 16, 109–113. https://doi.org/10.1016/j.copsyc.2017.05.002.

Harwood, C. G., Keegan, R. J., Smith, J. M., & Raine, A. S. (2015). A systematic review of the intrapersonal correlates of motivational climate perceptions in sport and physical activity. *Psychology of Sport and Exercise*, 18, 9–25. https://doi.org/10.10.16/j.psychsport.2014.11.005.

Hassmén, P., Lundkvist, E., Flett, G. L., Hewitt, P. L., & Gustafsson, H. (2020). Coach burnout in relation to perfectionism cognitions and self-presentation. *International Journal of Environmental Research and Public Health*, 17(23), 8812–8821. https://doi.org/10.3390/ijerph17238812.

Hewitt, P. L., & Flett, G. L. (1991). Perfectionism in the self and social contexts: Conceptualization, assessment, and association with psychopathology. *Journal of Personality and Social Psychology*, 60(3), 456–470. https://doi.org/10.1037/0022-3514.60.3.456.

Hewitt, P. L., Flett, G. L., & Mikail, S. F. (2017). *Perfectionism: A relational approach to conceptualization, assessment, and treatment*. Guilford Publications.

Hewitt, P. L., & Genest, M. (1990). The ideal self: Schematic processing of perfectionistic content in dysphoric university students. *Journal of Personality and Social Psychology*, 59(4), 802–808. https://doi.org/10.1037/0022-3514.59.4.802

Hewitt, P. L., *et al.* (2003). The interpersonal expression of perfection: perfectionistic self-presentation and psychological distress. *Journal of Personality and Social Psychology*, 84(6), 1303.

Hill, A. P., & Appleton, P. R. (2011). The predictive ability of the frequency of perfectionism cognitions, self-oriented perfectionism, and socially prescribed perfectionism in relation to symptoms of burnout in youth rugby players. *Journal of Sports Sciences*, 29(7), 695–703. https://doi.org/10.1080/02640414.2010.551216.

Hill, A. P., & Curran, T. (2016). Multidimensional perfectionism and burnout: A meta-analysis. *Personality and Social Psychology Review*, 20(3), 269–288. https://doi.org/10.1177/1088868315596286.

Hill, A. P., & Donachie, T. C. (2020). Not all perfectionism cognitions are multi-dimensional: Evidence for the Perfectionism Cognitions Inventory–10. *Journal of Psychoeducational Assessment*, 38(1), 15–25. https://doi.org/10.1177/0734282919881075.

Hill, A. P., Hall, H. K., Duda, J. L., & Appleton, P. R. (2011). The cognitive, affective and behavioural responses of self-oriented perfectionists following successive failure on a muscular endurance task. *International Journal of Sport and Exercise Psychology*, 9(2), 189–207. https://doi.org/10.1080/1612197x.2011.567108.

Hill, A. P., Madigan, D. J., Smith, M. M., Mallison-Howard, S. H., & Donachie, T. C. (2020). Perfectionism. In D. Hackfort, & R. J. Schinke (eds), *The Routledge international encyclopaedia of sport and exercise psychology: Theoretical and methodological concepts* (pp. 405–412). (Key Issues in Sport and Exercise Psychology). Routledge.

Hill, A. P., Mallinson-Howard, S. H., & Jowett, G. E. (2018). Multidimensional perfectionism in sport: A meta-analytical review. *Sport, Exercise, and Performance Psychology*, 7(3), 235–270. https://doi.org/10.1037/spy0000125.

Ingram, R. E. (1990). Self-focused attention in clinical disorders: Review and a conceptual model. *Psychological Bulletin*, 107(2), 156–176. https://doi.org/10.1037/0033-2909.107.2.156.

Ingram, R. E., & Kendall, P. C. (1986). Cognitive clinical psychology: Implications of an information processing perspective. In R. E. Ingram (ed.), *Information processing approaches to clinical psychology* (pp. 3–21). Academic Press.

Ingram, R. E., Miranda, J., & Segal, Z. V. (1998). *Cognitive vulnerability to depression*. Guilford Press.

Isoard-Gautheur, S., Guillet-Descas, E., & Gustafsson, H. (2016). Athlete burnout and the risk of dropout among young elite handball players. *Sport Psychologist*, 30(2). https://doi.org/10.1123/tsp.2014-0140.

Jekauc, D., Fritsch, J., & Latinjak, A. T. (2021). Toward a theory of emotions in competitive sports. *Frontiers in Psychology*, 12. https://doi.org/10.3389/fpsyg.2021.790423.

Karin, J., & Nordin-Bates, S. M. (2020). Enhancing creativity and managing perfectionism in dancers through implicit learning and sensori-kinetic imagery. *Journal of Dance Education*, 20(1), 1–11. https://doi.org/10.1080/15290824.2018.1532572.

Klinger, E. (1996). *The contents of thoughts: Interference as the downside of adaptive normal mechanisms in thought flow*. In I. G. Sarason, G. R. Pierce, and B. R. Sarason (eds), *Cognitive interference*. Routledge.

Kobori, O. (2006). A cognitive model of perfectionism: The relationship of perfectionism personality to psychological adaptation and maladaptation (Unpublished doctoral dissertation). Department of Cognitive and Behavioral Science, University of Tokyo, Japan.

Kobori, O., & Tanno, Y. (2004). Development of multidimensional perfectionism cognition inventory. *Japanese Journal of Personality*, 13(1), 34–43.

Kobori, O., & Tanno, Y. (2005). Self-oriented perfectionism and its relationship to positive and negative affect: The mediation of positive and negative perfectionism cognitions. *Cognitive Therapy and Research*, 29(5), 555–567. https://doi.org/10.1007/s10608-005-2835-4.

Kobori, O., Yoshie, M., Kudo, K., & Ohtsuki, T. (2011). Traits and cognitions of perfectionism and their relation with coping style, effort, achievement, and performance anxiety in Japanese musicians. *Journal of Anxiety Disorders*, 25, 674–679. https://doi.org/10.1016/j.janxdis.2011.03.001.

Kolayiş, H., Sarı, İ & Çelik, N. (2017). Parent-initiated motivational climate and self-determined motivation in youth sport: how should parents behave to keep their child in sport? *Kinesiology*, 49(2), 217–224.

Lee, Y. H., & Cho, H. (2021). The roles of different types of passion in emotional exhaustion and turnover intention among athletic coaches. *International Journal of Sports Science & Coaching*, 16(3): 465–476.

Lemelin, E., Verner-Filion, J., Carpentier, J., Carbonneau, N., & Mageau, G. A. (2022). Autonomy support in sport contexts: The role of parents and coaches in the promotion of athlete well-being and performance. *Sport, Exercise, and Performance Psychology*. https://doi.org/10.1037/spy0000287.

Lizmore, M. R., Dunn, J. G., Dunn, J. C., & Hill, A. P. (2019). Perfectionism and performance following failure in a competitive golf-putting task. *Psychology of Sport and Exercise*, 45, 101582. https://doi.org//10.1016/j.psychsport.2019.101582.

Macedo, A., Marques, C., Quaresma, V., Soares, M. J., Amaral, A. P., Araújo, A. I., & Pereira, A. T. (2017). Are perfectionism cognitions and cognitive emotion regulation strategies mediators between perfectionism and psychological distress? *Personality and Individual Differences*, 119(1), 46–51. https://doi.org/10.1016/j.paid.2017.06.032.

MacKinnon, S. P., Ray, C. M., Firth, S. M., & O'Connor, R. M. (2019). Perfectionism, negative motives for drinking, and alcohol-related problems: A 21-day diary study. *Journal of Research in Personality*, 78, 177–188. https://doi.org/10.1016/j.jrp.2018.12.003.

Madigan, D. J., Gustafsson, H., Smith, A., Raedeke, T. D., & Hill, A. P. (2019). The BASES expert statement on burnout in sport. *The Sport and Exercise Scientist*, 61, 6–7.

Madigan, D. J., Stoeber, J., & Passfield, L. (2015). Perfectionism and burnout in junior athletes: A three-month longitudinal study. *Journal of Sport and Exercise Psychology*, 37(3), 305–315. https://doi.org/10.1123/jsep.2014-0266.

Madigan, D. J., Stoeber, J., & Passfield, L. (2016). Motivation mediates the perfectionism-burnout relationship: A three-wave longitudinal study with junior athletes. *Journal of Sport and Exercise Psychology*, 38(4), 341–354. https://doi.org/10.1123/jsep.2015-0238.

Mandel, T., Dunkley, D. M., Lewkowski, M., Zuroff, D. C., Lupien, S. J., Juster, R.-P., Ng Ying Kin, N. M. K., Foley, J. E., Myhr, G., & Westreich, R. (2018). Self-critical perfectionism and depression maintenance over one year: The moderating roles of daily stress–sadness reactivity and the cortisol awakening response. *Journal of Counseling Psychology*, 65(3), 334–345. https://doi.org/10.1037/cou0000284.

Martinent, G., & Ferrand, C. (2009). A naturalistic study of the directional interpretation process of discrete emotions during high-stakes table tennis matches. *Journal of Sport and Exercise Psychology*, 31(3), 318–336. https://doi.org/10.1123/jsep.31.3.318.

Moen, F., Hrozanova, M., Stiles, T. C., & Stenseng, F. (2019). Burnout and perceived performance among junior athletes: Associations with affective and cognitive components of stress. *Sports*, 7(7), 171. https://doi.org/10.3390/sports7070171.

Molnar, D. S., Moore, J., O'Leary, D. D., MacNeil, A. J., & Wade, T. J. (2021). Perfectionism cognitions, Interleukin-6, and C-Reactive protein: A test of the perfectionism diathesis stress model. *Brain, Behavior, & Immunity-Health*, 13, 100211. https://doi.org/10.1016/j.bbih.2021.100211.

Mosewich, A. D., Crocker, P. R., Kowalski, K. C., & DeLongis, A. (2013). Applying self-compassion in sport: An intervention with women athletes. *Journal of Sport and Exercise Psychology*, 35(5), 514–524.

Nicholls, J. G. (1989). *The competitive ethos and democratic education*. Harvard University Press.

Nolen-Hoeksema, S. (1996). Chewing the Cud and Other. *Ruminative Thoughts*, 9, 135.

Nolen-Hoeksema, S. (1991). Responses to depression and their effects on the duration of depressive episodes. *Journal of Abnormal Psychology*, 100(4), 569–582.

Nolen-Hoeksema, S., Wisco, B. E., & Lyubomirsky, S. (2008). Rethinking rumination. *Perspectives on Psychological Science*, 3(5), 400–424. https://doi.org/10.1111/j.1745-6924.2008.00088.x.

Nordin-Bates, S. M., Cumming, J., Sharp, L., &. Aways, D. (2011). Imagining Yourself Dancing to Perfection? Correlates of Perfectionism in Ballet and Contemporary Dance. *Journal of Clinical Sport Psychology*, 5, 58–76. https://doi.org/10.1123/jcsp.5.1.58.

Oliver, J. M., Hart, B. A., Ross, M. J., & Katz, B. M. (2001). Healthy perfectionism and positive expectations about counseling. *North American Journal of Psychology*, 3(2), 229–242.

O'Rourke, D. J., Smith, R. E., Smoll, F. L., & Cumming, S. P. (2014). Relations of parent-and coach-initiated motivational climates to young athletes' self-esteem, performance anxiety, and autonomous motivation: who is more influential? *Journal of Applied Sport Psychology*, 26(4), 395–408. https://doi.org/10.1080/10413200.2014. 907838.

Patterson, H., Firebaugh, C. M., Zolnikov, T. R., Wardlow, R., Morgan, S. M., & Gordon, B. (2021). A systematic review on the psychological effects of perfectionism and accompanying treatment. *Psychology*, 12(1), 1–24. https://doi.org/10.4236/psych. 2021.121001.

Pleva, J., & Wade, T.D. (2007). Guided self-help versus pure self-help for perfectionism: A randomised control trial. *Behaviour Research and Therapy*. 45(5), 849–861. https://doi.org/10.1016/j.brat.2006.08.009.

Pyszczynski, T., & Greenberg, J. (1987). Self-regulatory perseveration and the depressive self-focusing style: a self-awareness theory of reactive depression. *Psychological Bulletin*, 102(1), 122–138. https://doi.org/10.1037/0033-2909.102.1.122.

Radhu, N., Daskalakis, Z. J., Arpin-Cribbie, C. A., Irvine, J., & Ritvo, P. (2012). Evaluating a web-based cognitive-behavioral therapy for maladaptive perfectionism in university students. *Journal of American College Health*, 60(5), 357–366. https://doi.org/10.1080/07448481.2011.630703.

Raedeke, T. D., & Smith, A. L. (2001). Development and preliminary validation of an athlete burnout measure. *Journal of Sport and Exercise Psychology*, 23(4), 281–306.

Rudolph, S. G., Flett, G. L., & Hewitt, P. L. (2007). Perfectionism and deficits in cognitive emotion regulation. *Journal of Rational-Emotive & Cognitive-Behavior Therapy*, 25(4), 343–357. https://doi.org/10.1007/s10942-007-0056-3.

Sagar, S.S., & Stoeber, J. (2009). Perfectionism, fear of failure, and affective responses to success and failure: The central role of fear of experiencing shame and embarrassment. *Journal of Sport & Exercise Psychology*, 31(5). 602–627. https://doi.org/10.1123/jsep.31. 5.602.

Smith, R. E. (1986). Toward a cognitive-affective model of athletic burnout. *Journal of Sport and Exercise Psychology*, 8(1), 36–50. https://doi.org/10.1123/jsp.8.1.36.

Steele, A. L., & Wade, T. D. (2008). A randomised trial investigating guided self-help to reduce perfectionism and its impact on bulimia nervosa: A pilot study. *Behaviour Research and Therapy*, 46(12), 1316–1323. https://doi.org/10.1016/j.brat.2008.09.006.

Stoeber, J. (2018). The psychology of perfectionism: Critical issues, open questions, and future directions. In J. Stoeber (ed.), *The psychology of perfectionism: Theory, research, applications* (pp. 333–352). Routledge.

Stoeber, J., Kobori, O., & Brown, A. (2014). Examining mutual suppression effects in the assessment of perfectionism cognitions: Evidence supporting multidimensional assessment. *Assessment*, 21(6), 647–660. https://doi.org/10.1177/1073191114534884.

Stoeber, J., Kobori, O., & Tanno, Y. (2010). The multidimensional perfectionism cognitions inventory–English (MPCI-E): Reliability, validity, and relationships with positive and negative affect. *Journal of Personality Assessment*, 92(1), 16–25. https://doi.org/10.1080/00223890903379159.

Sysko, R., & Walsh, B. T. (2008). A critical evaluation of the efficacy of self-help interventions for the treatment of bulimia nervosa and binge-eating disorder. *International Journal of Eating Disorders*, 41(2), 97–112. https://doi.org/10.1002/eat.20475.

Tyler, J., Mu, W., McCann, J., Belli, G., & Asnaani, A. (2021) The unique contribution of perfectionistic cognitions to anxiety disorder symptoms in a treatment-seeking sample, *Cognitive Behaviour Therapy*, 50(2) 121–137. http://doi.org/10.1080/16506073.2020.1798497.

Vast, R. L., Young, R. L., & Thomas, P. R. (2010). Emotions in sport: Perceived effects on attention, concentration, and performance. *Australian Psychologist*, 45(2), 132–140. https://doi.org/10.1080/00050060903261538.

Vealey, R. S., Martin, E., Coppola, A., Ward, R. M., & Chamberlin, J. (2020). The slippery slope: Can motivation and perfectionism lead to burnout in coaches?. *International Sport Coaching Journal*, 7(1), 1–10. https://doi.org/10.1123/iscj.2018-0043.

Wagnsson, S., Stenling, A., Gustafsson, H., & Augustsson, C. (2016). Swedish youth football players' attitudes towards moral decision in sport as predicted by the parent-initiated motivational climate. *Psychology of Sport and Exercise*, 25, 110–114. https://doi.org/10.1016/j.psychsport.2016.05.003.

White, S. A. (1996). Goal orientation and perceptions of the motivational climate initiated by parents. *Pediatric Exercise Science*, 8, 122–129. https://doi.org/10.1123/pes.8.2.122.

Xie, Y., Kong, Y., Yang, J., & Chen, F. (2019). Perfectionism, worry, rumination, and distress: A meta-analysis of the evidence for the perfectionism cognition theory. *Personality and Individual Differences*, 139, 301–312. https://doi.org/10.1016/j.paid.2018.11.028.

9   Studying Perfectionistic Climates

Michael C. Grugan, Laura C. Fenwick and Luke F. Olsson

In studying perfectionism in sport, dance, and other performance environments, researchers have typically conceptualized perceptions of external pressure to be perfect as a reflection of a performer's perfectionistic personality. However, we believe that when some performers report the experience of external pressure, their experiences are not solely generated internally. Rather, for many performers, they are reporting experiences that are to a much greater degree rooted in the behaviour of others. The major theme forwarded in this chapter is that some performers – regardless of how perfectionistic they are themselves – will have the misfortune of encountering specific others and environments that are highly perfectionistic. We are referring particularly to coaches, teachers and instructors, and clubs, teams, and classes, and how these leaders can imbue these environments with perfectionistic messages and cues. To elaborate on this theme, in the current chapter, we introduce, define, and discuss a new construct that captures the degree to which an environment is perfectionistic – perfectionistic climate.

Introducing and Conceptualizing Perfectionistic Climate

To introduce the notion that experiences of pressure to be perfect can be externally rooted in the behaviour of others – rather than generated internally by the perfectionistic personality of performers – Hill and Grugan (2019) proposed the construct of perfectionistic climate. They defined perfectionistic climate as the *informational cues and goal structures that align with the view that performances must be perfect and less than perfect performances are unacceptable*. In the first part of the definition, the terms *informational cues* and *goal structures* refer to leader behaviours, practices, and relational styles that shape how performers experience their environment. The second part of the definition helps to delineate a perfectionistic climate from other types of climate experience. That is, the key feature of a perfectionistic climate is that it is shaped by leader interactions and practices that emphasize to performers that nothing less than perfect performance will be tolerated.

There are two major rationales underpinning the introduction of perfectionistic climate. The first rationale, which is emphasized in the opening to this chapter, is that the perfectionistic pressure experienced by many performers exists independent from their perfectionistic personality. Instead, for some

DOI: 10.4324/9781003288015-12

performers, experiences of perfectionistic pressure are rooted in the behaviours of others, and this is demonstrably so. The second rationale is that current approaches to studying climates in sport, dance, and other performance environments (e.g. Achievement Goal Theory, AGT; Nicholls, 1984; Self-Determination Theory, SDT; Ryan and Deci, 2017) do not adequately account for the full range of practices that shape how performers experience their environment (Morgan, 2017). In particular, existing approaches do not account for how environments can be imbued with unrealistic and perfectionistic messages.

The definition of perfectionistic climate lends language from AGT and seminal work on motivational climate and, as such, is intended to sit alongside other motivational climate constructs (Ames, 1981; Ames & Ames, 1984; Ames, 1992). In line with classical climate-based research, perfectionistic climate is a construct that captures the characteristics of a social environment created by leaders (e.g. coaches, teachers, or instructors). In addition, there is the same focus on the goal structures and informational cues (i.e. behaviours, practices, and relational styles) that shape how performers experience the environment. This includes the demands and expectations, evaluative criterion, and values that are set and governed by leaders. In this sense, as with other climate-based constructs, perfectionistic climate captures a performers perceptions of the external environment shaped by the actions and behaviours of others. The key factor that distinguishes perfectionistic climate from existing climate constructs, though, is that it focusses on a unique set of behaviours that give rise to perceptions that only perfect performance is acceptable.

The behaviours, practices, and relational styles that populate the content of the perfectionistic climate construct are drawn from theory on perfectionism development. As such, the models of perfectionism development outlined by Flett, Hewitt, and colleagues (Flett et al., 2002; Hewitt et al., 2017) are also a key touchstone for the perfectionistic climate construct. These models, which are outlined by Appleton and Curran (Chapter 3), explain the various ways leaders shape environments and instil in children and adolescents the need to be perfect. The theme emphasized across these models is that perfectionism develops in environments where leaders are seen as being extremely demanding and difficult to please, highly critical and intolerant of mistakes, and extremely worried about the potential for anything other than perfect performance. On this basis, perfectionistic climate includes five specific components that capture these perfectionistic behaviours.

The first component of perfectionistic climate is *expectations*. In context of perfectionistic climate, the expectations component is the perception that leaders hold and demand unrealistically high performance expectations of others. This component is primarily grounded in the *social expectations model* or pathway of perfectionism development. In line with this model, the focus is on the extent to which young people believe a leader sets and demands unrealistically high goals. In defining this component, emphasis was placed on the distinction between high standards and unrealistically high standards. As Flett and Hewitt (2006) have emphasized, there is a difference between someone who thinks, "My parents demand absolute perfection, and nothing else will do", *versus* someone who thinks "My parents have high expectations of me" (p. 476). In this regard, *unrealistically high performance expectations* (as opposed to *high* or *very high performance expectations*) are a notable part of the definition.

The second component of perfectionistic climate is *criticism*. In context of perfectionistic climate, the criticism component is the perception that leaders engage in harsh criticism whenever the performance of others is not perfect. This component is primarily grounded in the *social reaction model* or pathway of perfectionism development. In line with this model, the focus is on the extent to which young people believe a leader is being overly critical. In defining this component, it was important to distinguish between perfectionistic criticism and criticism that might be considered reasonable or constructive. The defining characteristics of perfectionistic criticism are that it is harsh, unreasonable, and follows almost all mistakes, no matter how small or inconsequential. This includes being criticized despite best effort, personal improvement, or task difficulty.

The third component of perfectionistic climate is *control*. In context of perfectionistic climate, the control component is the perception that leaders employ externally controlling strategies that place pressure on others to perform perfectly. In line with the externally controlling socialization strategies emphasized in SDT, the focus in this component is on tangible, external, and overt contingencies that put pressure on young people (Soenens & Vansteenkiste, 2010). These are structural in the sense that they are features of the environment created by the coach and what a coach explicitly does to motivate perfect performances. This includes use of punishment and sanctions or an overemphasis on rewards. In terms of models of perfectionism development, the control component is primarily grounded in the *social reaction model* or pathway. This is because, like criticism, controlling practices shape a highly intimidating and challenging environments in which young people feel extreme pressure to be perfect.

The fourth component of perfectionistic climate is *conditional regard*. In context of perfectionistic climate, the conditional regard component is the perception that leaders employ internally controlling strategies that place pressure on others to perform perfectly. In line with the internally controlling socialization strategies emphasized in SDT, the focus in this component is on communications that express disappointment, disregard for personal feelings and opinions, and love withdrawal. Unlike with the strategies for control, the behaviours for conditional regard appeal primarily to forces and regulations that reside within performers (Soenens & Vansteenkiste, 2010). This component is primarily grounded in the *social expectations model* or pathway of perfectionism development. This is because this model focusses on the extent to which young people believe a leader is extremely difficult to please, reluctant to provide approval, and quick to disapprove of anything less than perfection. The behaviours emphasized in this model activate an internal compulsion to engage in perfectionistic behaviour with the aim of pleasing others.

The fifth component of perfectionistic climate is *anxiousness*. In context of perfectionistic climate, anxiousness is the perception that leaders are extremely worried and vigilant about mistakes and the consequences of others not performing perfectly. This component is primarily grounded in the *anxious rearing model* or pathway of perfectionism development. In line with this model, the focus is on the extent to which young people believe a leader is concerned over mistakes and wants mistakes to be avoided. In line with the other components of perfectionistic climate, anxiousness captures an excessive level of worry, rather than any due concern. That is, young people believe that leaders worry about all mistakes, go to extreme lengths to limit the potential for mistakes, and express a level of concern that is experienced as disproportionate to any actual consequences of being imperfect.

Applying Perfectionistic Climate to Sport

The model of perfectionistic climate outlined above can be applied to various performance environments and the leaders that operate in those environments (e.g. coach-created perfectionistic climate in sport or teacher-created perfectionistic climate in dance). Our research on perfectionistic climate has so far been in youth sport and has focused on the development of the first scale to measure the construct (Grugan et al., 2021a). The first stage of this process involved identifying and addressing key considerations pertaining to the applicability, conceptualization, and measurement of perfectionistic climate in youth sport. In this regard, we and other colleagues outlined several guiding proposals that helped to provide a sound foundation for the development of the Perfectionistic Climate Questionnaire-Sport (PCQ-S).

The first proposal we made was that while there are various leaders who may be influential in shaping perfectionistic climates in youth sport, the coach is especially important. This is because coaches are directly responsible for designing and delivering training activities, setting expectations and evaluative standards, and managing the overall performance environment (Alvarez et al., 2012). The influence that coaches have over athletes starts to become particularly prominent in middle-to-late childhood (Kipp, 2018). This means that even from a young age coaches play a key role in shaping the overall sporting experiences of athletes (Horn, 2008). We know now that when coaches provide appropriate reinforcement and encouragement, athletes are likely to experience positive outcomes (e.g. increased enjoyment, team unity, and stronger motives to continue participation). By contrast, when coaches provide poor social support and engage in controlling behaviours, athletes are likely to experience negative outcomes (e.g. diminished motivation, stronger motives to dropout, and athlete burnout; Duda et al., 2014).

The coach is also an important figure who can shape the extent to which youth athletes experience pressure to be perfect. Based on qualitative research in youth sport, media accounts provided by athletes, and governing body consensus statements, there is growing evidence that many youth athletes experience inappropriate and unrealistic demands and expectations from coaches (e.g. Bergeron et al., 2015; Ingle, 2021; Lavallee & Robinson, 2007). This includes accounts of coaches using physical punishment and humiliation in response to performance mistakes, putting pressure on athletes to meet increasingly high levels of performance, and responding angrily to performance errors. In terms of quantitative research, there is also evidence that coach pressure to be perfect (i.e. unrealistic coach expectations in combination with overly harsh criticism) shares positive correlations with dimensions of athlete perfectionism (Gotwals, 2011; Madigan et al., 2019; Sagar & Stoeber, 2009). This body of evidence provides further support for the importance of considering coaches as important leaders responsible for shaping perfectionistic climates in sport.

The second proposal we made was that there is a need to revise how we have typically conceptualized and measured coach pressure to be perfect. There are at least two problematic issues that apply to perfectionism measures that incorporate coach pressure dimensions. The first issue is that current perfectionism measures may be confounding etiological factors with core characteristics of trait perfectionism. This issue is highlighted by other researchers who argue that measures of pressure to be perfect from a specific significant other (such as a coach or parent) represent developmental features of perfectionism rather than core characteristics of perfectionism (e.g. Damian et al., 2013; Sirois & Molnar, 2016; Rice et al., 2005). To avoid any potential confusion regarding what features should constitute core definitional components of perfectionism (*versus* more peripheral components of perfectionism), the model of perfectionistic climate re-locates dimensions of coach pressure in a model capturing experiences of pressure in the environment of performers.

The second issue is that dimensions of coach pressure in existing perfectionism measures fail to distinguish between *coach expectations* and *coach criticism*. While measures typically include separate items for each component (e.g. "My coach *sets very high standards* for me in competition" *versus* "I feel like my coach *criticizes me* for doing things less than perfectly in competition"), these items are collapsed to form broader measures of coach pressure. This approach is understandable and based on factor analytical evidence (e.g. Dunn, Dunn, Gotwals, Vallance, Craft, & Syrotuik, 2006). However, expectations and criticism are separate components in models of perfectionism development. Specifically, in line with Flett et al.'s (2002) developmental framework, leaders can have different levels of expectations and propensity for harsh criticism. In addition, different combinations of expectations and criticism exist and contribute to differences in perfectionism development. In support of this argument, McArdle and Duda (2008) found evidence for distinguishing between *parental expectations* and *parental criticism* when examining perfectionism development in youth athletes. In line with this evidence, it is important that perfectionistic climate has both components represented separately.

The third, and final, proposal we made was that other behaviours contribute to experiences of perfectionistic coach pressure in sport. As such, focusing only on expectations and criticism would mean perfectionistic climate underrepresented the other various ways it manifests. In SDT-based research, for example, Barcza-Renner et al. (2016) found that controlling coach behaviours (including controlling use of rewards and negative conditional regard) were positively correlated with perfectionism in youth athletes. Likewise, Curran and colleagues found parental conditional regard to be positively corelated with perfectionism in athletes (Curran et al., 2017; Curran, 2018). In AGT-based research, too, there are examples that suggest a wider range of coach behaviours need to be considered. Gustafsson et al. (2016), for instance, found that perceptions of worry-conducive behaviour from parents (i.e. actions signalling an extreme focus on mistakes and the importance of avoiding errors) were positively correlated with perfectionism in youth athletes. In these regards, we consider control, conditional regard, and anxiousness to all be important and unique components of perfectionistic climate in sport.

Initial Validity and Reliability Evidence for the PCQ-S

The conceptual model of perfectionistic climate and key guiding proposals outlined above were used to guide the development of the PCQ-S. The scale development project included multiple stages and data from four samples of youth athletes. The result of the rigorous procedure was a five-factor 20-item scale with evidence supporting multiple aspects of validity and reliability (e.g. factor structure, factor stability, scale reliability, construct validity, and measurement invariance). In terms of factor structure, a five-factor model was supported based on exploratory factor analysis (EFA), confirmatory factor analysis (CFA) and exploratory structural equation modelling (ESEM) techniques. The finding across multiple independent samples provided evidence for well-defined and discernible factors measuring expectations, criticism, control, conditional regard, and anxiousness. This evidence demonstrates that the five-factor PCQ-S adequately represents the generalized model of perfectionistic climate.

In addition to testing the first-order structure identified in the models above, we also examined the potential for a second-order PCQ-S structure using an ESEM-within-CFA modelling technique (Morin et al., 2020). In line with the results above, this model provided support for five well-defined PCQ-S factors. The key distinction in this model is that evidence was provided for the five PCQ-S factors providing meaningful second-order factor loadings onto a hierarchical perfectionistic climate factor. This evidence suggests that researchers can either study the PCQ-S components as individual factors or statistically model them in a manner to study the overall construct. This level of modelling flexibility is advantageous as it provides scope to examine the relative influence of each PCQ-S factor in relation to a specified outcome or examine the broader influence of an overall perfectionistic climate factor. This latter modelling strategy will help to reduce model complexity when examining perfectionistic climate using a structural equation modelling (SEM) framework.

To provide further evidence of construct validity for the PCQ-S, we then estimated a nomological network of relations between test scores on the PCQ-S and established coach climate measures. This network was initially assessed using a more traditional EFA approach. The results of this analysis provided support for the distinction between the PCQ-S dimensions and measures of coach-created climate guided by AGT (task- and ego-involving coach dimensions) and SDT (autonomy supportive and controlling coach dimensions). The three-factor structure identified in the EFA provided support for the integration of AGT- and SDT-based dimensions into higher-order empowering (task-involving and autonomy supportive dimensions) and disempowering (ego-involving and controlling dimensions) coach climate factors (Duda, 2013). Importantly, the PCQ-S dimensions were found to uniquely load on a perfectionistic coach climate factor that was separate from these other factors. This finding is important as it is consistent with our view that the PCQ-S measures a climate experience that is not currently accounted for by other measures of motivational climate.

The network of relations between coach climate variables was also examined using *network analysis* (Epskamp & Fried, 2018). This approach provided a visualization of the complex covariation between the measures under investigation. In the estimated network diagram, *nodes* (circles) represented different coach climate dimensions and *edges* (lines connecting nodes together) represented associations between variables. In terms of dimensionality, exploratory graph analysis (Golino et al., 2020) provided confirmation that the coach climate data was best represented by three factors. In line with the EFA results, the nodes in each factor were representative of perfectionistic, empowering, and disempowering coach climate features. Thus, while AGT and SDT coach climate measures can be integrated to capture empowering and disempowering climate experiences, again, the PCQ-S captures a unique and independent climate experience.

Based on these findings, it is possible to further surmise how a perfectionistic climate differs from other climates. Our view is that perfectionistic coach behaviours (e.g. unrealistic demands, harsh criticism, and anxiousness over mistakes) will lead to a climate experience that is more extreme than an environment shaped by disempowering coach behaviours. For example, a perfectionistic climate emphasizes a level of expectation that is more excessive than in an ego-involving climate. In a perfectionistic climate, it would not be sufficient to simply win and outperform others, even with minimal effort. The performance must be without any flaws, exceed personal expectations and the expectations of others, and be unquestionable. In this kind of climate, success over weaker opponents may even come to be viewed as an indictment on the athletic or personal qualities of the individual (e.g. "good athletes compete only against the best"). In this way, satisfaction and enjoyment are not inevitable consequences of outperforming others in a perfectionistic climate as they are in an ego-involving climate.

The distinction between perfectionistic coach behaviour and disempowering coach behaviour is also evident when focussing on components of coach control. The components of control emphasized in perfectionistic climate (control and conditional regard) capture more extreme and specific motivational strategies than SDT-based components of control. That is, controlling practices that pressure performers to feel, think, and behave in line with a specific requirement for perfection. This differs from the more general controlling practices emphasized in SDT-based climate models. This is evident in Bartholomew et al.'s (2010) model of controlling coach behaviour, for example, which emphasizes controlling practices that encourage athletes to "do well", "train harder", and "stay focussed". These outcomes are much broader and less demanding than the perfectionistic controlling practices that pressure athletes to "stop mistakes in performances" and "make performances perfect" (Grugan et al., 2021a).

The final psychometric examination we provided was a test of measurement invariance. In line with previous scale validation studies, the aim was to evaluate whether the PCQ-S functions equivalently across different age and gender groups (e.g. Checa et al., 2021; Crocker et al., 2018; Gucciardi et al., 2011). This type of assessment is important as many studies in sport psychology are focussed on comparing groups of athletes (e.g. perfectionism scores in younger *versus* older athletes; Dunn et al., 2022). An important assumption in such research is that the underlying factor structure is the same for the specified groups and their responses are not confounded by other characteristics (Marsh et al., 2014; Schellenberg et al., 2014). In line with this assumption, important initial evidence was presented for the equivalence of the PCQ-S regardless of age (younger *versus* older youth athletes) and gender (males *versus* female athletes). As a result, researchers and practitioners can be confident that the PCQ-S will provide valid scores when comparing these groups or using samples which include different ages and a mix of genders.

Expanding the Nomological Network of Perfectionistic Climate

As the PCQ-S has only recently been published, research using it is extremely limited. Most of the work of our research group is in progress with some preliminary findings presented at scientific conferences (e.g. Grugan et al., 2021b). Therefore, we consider the most immediate priority for research in this area is to expand understanding of the nomological network of perfectionistic climate in sport. By reviewing relevant theoretical frameworks and empirical research, it is possible to identify potential outcomes of the perfectionistic climate construct. Once potential outcomes have been identified, researchers can use the PCQ-S and examine whether empirical relationships match the theoretical relationships. This process of expanding and testing the nomological network of perfectionistic climate in sport will help to build our understanding of the perfectionistic climate phenomenon and provide important validity information for the PCQ-S.

In terms of an existing empirical evidence base, the most relevant source of information that researchers can draw upon when identifying potential outcomes of perfectionistic climate at present is research examining perceptions of coach pressure to be perfect. While coach pressure to be perfect and perfectionistic climate are not the same – one is operationalized at a personal level (e.g. "The coach criticizes *me* if *my performances* are not perfect") and the other at a climate level (e.g. "The coach criticizes performances that are not perfect") – the constructs are similar. Therefore, reviewing existing correlates of coach pressure provides a starting point for researchers designing studies on perfectionistic climate in sport and other performance environments. To aid researchers in this regard, we have reported the results of a systematic review of research that has used the subscales of coach pressure from the Sport Multidimensional Perfectionism Scale ("*Perceived coach pressure*"; Dunn et al., 2002; Dunn, Dunn, Gotwals, Vallance, Craft, & Syrotuik, 2006; Gotwals & Dunn, 2009) and Multidimensional Inventory for Perfectionism in Sports ("*Perceived pressure from coach*"; Stoeber et al., 2006) in Table 9.1.[1]

Table 9.1 A systematic review of research examining coach pressure to be perfect.

Study	Sample(s)	Domain	Instr.	Criterion variable	r
De Maria et al. (2021)	644 junior, adolescent, and adult athletes (43% females)	Sport	MIPS	Cognitive anxiety	**.12**
				Somatic anxiety	.07
				Self-confidence	.07
Dunn, Gotwals, Dunn, & Syrotuik (2006)	138 adolescent athletes (26% females)	Sport	S-MPS-2	Reactions to mistakes: Feeling angry	**.31**
				Reactions to mistakes: Feeling like expressing anger at someone/ something	**.19**
				Reactions to mistakes: Feeling like expressing anger verbally	**.33**
				Trait anger: Angry temperament	**.26**
				Trait anger: Angry reaction	**.40**
Dunn et al. (2011)	119 female junior athletes	Sport	S-MPS-2	Body image: Appearance orientation	**.27**
				Body image: Appearance evaluation	**−.33**
				Body image: Overweight preoccupation	**.29**
				Body image: Self-classified weight	**.22**
				Body image: Body areas satisfaction	**−.28**
				Body image: Body image ideal	**.30**
Dunn et al. (2020)	144 male junior athletes	Sport	S-MPS-2	Worry about failure / Negative social evaluation	**.40**
				Worry about the unknown	**.33**
				Worry about injury	**.18**
				Optimism	**−.17**
Dunn et al. (2021)	251 student athletes (41% females)	Sport	S-MPS-2	Grit: Consistency of interests	**−.13**
				Grit: Perseverance of effort	.03
Fawver et al. (2020)	169 junior athletes (52% females)	Sport	S-MPS-2	Grit	**−.17**
				Mental toughness: Total	**−.13**
				Mental toughness: Confidence	−.05
				Mental toughness: Constancy	**−.13**
				Mental toughness: Control	**−.15**
Gotwals (2011)	117 student athletes (41% females)	Sport	S-MPS-2	Athlete burnout: Exhaustion	**.42**
				Athlete burnout: Reduced accomplishment	**.31**
				Athlete burnout: Devaluation	**.24**
Gotwals & Dunn (2009)	251 student athletes (46% females)	Sport	S-MPS-2	Global self-esteem	**−.14**

Study	Sample(s)	Domain	Instr.	Criterion variable	r
Gucciardi et al. (2012)	423 junior, adolescent, and adult athletes (58% females)	Sport	S-MPS	External regulation	**.12**
				Intrinsic motivation	−.07
				Mastery avoidance goals	**.24**
				Performance avoidance goals	**.25**
				Mastery approach goals	−.02
				Performance approach goals	**.27**
				Fear of failure	**.39**
Ismaili et al. (2013)	55 male athletes	Sport	S-MPS-2	Positive attitudes toward doping	**.33**
Klund & Sæther (2017)	115 male junior athletes	Sport	S-MPS	Player self-assessed skills	.04
				Coach assessed player skills	−.08
				Training volume: Number of organized training sessions	.02
				Training volume: Hours of organized training	−.02
				Training volume: Number of independent training sessions	−.11
				Training volume: Hours of independent training	−.09
Madigan et al. (2016)	130 male junior athletes	Sport	MIPS	Positive attitudes toward doping	.10
Madigan et al. (2017)	261 junior, adolescent, and adult athletes (26% females)	Sport	MIPS	Reasons for training: Avoidance of negative affect	**.13**
				Reasons for training: Weight control	.08
				Reasons for training: Mood improvement	.01
Mallinson & Hill (2011)	205 junior athletes (57% females)	Sport	S-MPS-2	Autonomy thwarting	**.41**
				Competence thwarting	**.31**
				Relatedness thwarting	**.28**
Martinent et al. (2010)	642 junior, adolescent, and adult athletes (47% females)	Sport	S-MPS-2	Somatic anxiety: Intensity	.12
				Cognitive anxiety: Intensity	.15
				Self-confidence: Intensity	**.25**
				Somatic anxiety: Frequency	.10
				Cognitive anxiety: Frequency	**.18**
				Self-confidence: Frequency	**.17**
				Somatic anxiety: Direction	−.11
				Cognitive anxiety: Direction	−.14
				Self-confidence: Direction	**.18**

Study	Sample(s)	Domain	Instr.	Criterion variable	r
Pacewicz et al. (2018)	173 student athletes (50% females)	Sport	S-MPS-2	Athlete burnout: Total	**.31**
				Athlete burnout: Exhaustion	**.26**
				Athlete burnout: Reduced accomplishment	**.23**
				Athlete burnout: Devaluation	**.26**
				Problem-focussed coping	−.01
				Emotion-focussed coping	−.11
				Avoidant coping	**.23**
Pineda-Espejel et al. (2021)	377 junior athletes (57% females)	Sport	MIPS	Task-involving coach climate	−.13
				Ego-involving coach climate	**.53**
				Coach autonomy support	.13
Sagar & Stoeber (2009)	388 student athletes (46% females)	Sport	MIPS	Fear of experiencing shame and embarrassment	**.29**
				Fear of devaluing one's self-estimate	**.12**
				Fear of important others losing interest	**.25**
				Fear of upsetting important others	**.40**
				Fear of having an uncertain future	**.20**
				Positive affect after success	**.12**
				Negative affect after failure	**.21**
Sapieja et al. (2011)	194 junior athletes (0% females)	Sport	S-MPS-2	Mother authoritativeness	**−.34**
				Father authoritativeness	**−.22**
Sindik et al. (2011)	74 male adult athletes	Sport	S-MPS	Hardiness: Commitment	−.07
				Hardiness: Control	.07
				Hardiness: Challenge	−.07
				Personality: Extraversion	−.14
				Personality: Agreeableness	−.07
				Personality: Conscientiousness	−.09
				Personality: Emotional stability	−.05
				Personality: Intellect	−.19
				Group cohesion: Individual attractions to the group-social	−.19
				Group cohesion: Individual attractions to the group-task	**−.27**
				Group cohesion: Group integration-social	**−.26**
				Group cohesion: Group integration-task	**−.32**
Šíp & Burešová (2020)	180 junior athletes	Sport	S-MPS	Perceived training load	**.18**

Study	Sample(s)	Domain	Instr.	Criterion variable	r
Skwiot et al. (2020)	207 junior, adolescent, and adult athletes (36% females)	Sport / Dance	S-MPS-2	Athlete burnout: Exhaustion	**.25**
				Athlete burnout: Reduced accomplishment	.09
				Athlete burnout: Devaluation	**.24**
Vaartstra et al. (2018)	216 junior athletes (75% females)	Sport	S-MPS-2	Perceived social loafing	.04
				Social loafing acceptability	.04
Vallance et al. (2006)	229 junior athletes (0% females)	Sport	S-MPS-2	Trait anger: Angry temperament	**.22**
				Trait anger: Angry reaction	**.29**

Notes: MIPS = Multidimensional Inventory of Perfectionism in Sport (Stoeber et al., 2006); S-MPS = Sport Multidimensional Perfectionism Scale (Dunn et al., 2002); S-MPS-2; Sport-Multidimensional Perfectionism Scale 2 (Dunn et al., 2006a; Gotwals & Dunn, 2009). Bold typeface denotes a significant correlation. All study designs were non-experimental and cross-sectional.

The systematic literature search identified 24 independent studies involving 5,702 participants and a range of criterion variables. In reviewing the 98 correlation coefficients retrieved, we identified four broad themes. The first theme was a link between coach pressure to be perfect and apprehensiveness. This theme was evident in that coach pressure to be perfect was positively correlated with cognitive anxiety, competitive worry, and fear of failure (De Maria et al., 2021; Dunn et al., 2020; Gucciardi et al., 2012; Sagar & Stoeber, 2009), as well as negatively correlated with optimism (Dunn et al., 2020). Based on these findings, we would anticipate that perfectionistic climates in sport to invoke a similar sense of fear over competition and various performance-related concerns (e.g. fear of negative social evaluation, making mistakes, and choking under pressure). More perfectionistic climates may also result in lower risk taking, willingness to make decisions, and adaptability to uncontrollable situations.

The second theme identified in the systematic review was a link between coach pressure to be perfect and negative responses to failure. This theme was evident in that coach pressure to be perfect was positively correlated with angry reactions to poor performance and negative affect after failure (Dunn, Gotwals, Dunn, & Syrotuik, 2006; Sagar & Stoeber, 2009). In context of the theme identified above, it may be that concerns over the perceived consequences of failure trigger strong reactions to underperformance. As for why this is the case, it may be that the stakes are perceived to be particularly high when coaches create highly demanding and perfectionistic climates. In line with this evidence, we can expect more perfectionistic climates to be positively correlated with strong feelings of disappointment and dejection following competitive failure. We may even find strong positive feelings when things go well, or at least marked relief when failure is avoided.

The third theme identified in the systematic review was a link between coach pressure to be perfect and athlete resiliency. This theme was firstly evident in that coach pressure to be perfect was negatively correlated with mental toughness and grit (Dunn et al., 2021; Fawver et al., 2020). These are interesting findings and a clear signal of how counterproductive perfectionistic pressure is likely to be in sport. Athletes who perceive higher levels of coach pressure to be perfect seemingly find it difficult to maintain focus on important goals in sport and persist in the face of adversity. Relevant to this theme were also studies that found coach pressure to be perfect was negatively correlated with global self-esteem (Gotwals & Dunn, 2009) and positively correlated with avoidant coping (Pacewicz et al., 2018). With this evidence in mind, we would anticipate that rather than instilling characteristics conducive to dealing with adversity in an effective manner, highly perfectionistic climates in sport will give rise to poor coping and less ability to deal with stress.

The fourth and final theme identified in the systematic review was a link between coach pressure to be perfect and athlete burnout – an experiential state we would expect when athletes face external demands they cannot cope with. This theme was evident in that coach pressure to be perfect was positively correlated with total athlete burnout and the individual burnout symptoms (Gotwals, 2011; Pacewicz et al., 2018; Skwiot et al., 2020). We can expect the greater stress and ineffective coping found in other studies to partly explain this relationship. Additionally, the relationship between coach pressure to be perfect and psychological need thwarting also provides a further explanation (Mallinson & Hill, 2011). So, too, does the positive correlations between coach pressure to be perfect and markers of less adaptive motivation (e.g. avoidance motivation and external regulation; Gucciardi et al., 2012). Mirroring these findings, we would expect more perfectionistic climates to be correlated with greater athlete burnout and other risk factors and markers of motivation "going awry" (Gould, 1996).

To guide ongoing research using the PCQ-S and develop an understanding of perfectionistic climate, researchers can use the evidence in our systematic review of coach pressure to be perfect. The retrieved data provides an important source of information that researchers can draw upon to identify outcomes and develop research questions applicable to the initial study of perfectionistic climate in sport. In reviewing the data, we identified themes of apprehensiveness, negative responses to failure, athlete resiliency, and athlete burnout. These themes are an excellent starting point and signal some of the likely effects of highly perfectionistic coach climates in sport. In considering this research, and the theoretical foundations of the construct, we would envisage that few young or aspiring performers would enjoy the experience of being in a highly perfectionistic climate and that such climates will be ill-equipped to support and nurture performers or their talents.

Advancing Research on Perfectionistic Climate

In addition to expanding the nomological network of perfectionistic climate, there are several other areas of research that would advance the study of perfectionistic climate. We close the chapter by discussing three of them.

Studying Perfectionistic Climate in Dance

One important area for future research is to extend the study of perfectionistic climate to other domains. We believe dance would be a particularly fruitful in this regard. The reason that dance provides an important next step for the study of perfectionistic climate is that, like sport, dance is an environment in which performers often experience a sense of perfectionistic pressure from others. That is, it is common for dancers to view their teachers, artistic directors, and choreographers as sources of extreme demands and unrealistic expectations (Mainwaring & Aujla, 2017). This view is perhaps unsurprising given that many dance schools and companies live by the principle of *"practice makes perfect"* and employ staff whose responsibility is to perfect the technical skills of their students (Ng et al., 2022). Indeed, in a qualitative study of ballet dancers, McEwen and Young (2011) found that dancers repeatedly referred to the presence of hierarchical power structures that underpinned an ultra-competitive atmosphere and drive to achieve perfection.

When applying perfectionistic climate to dance, it will be important for researchers to consider the distinctive ways perfectionistic climate may manifest in this domain. One important consideration in this regard is that a strong dance performance is contingent upon several factors (e.g. body aesthetics, musical timing, and athleticism; Chirban & Rowan, 2017). The key point to emphasize is that, in addition to pressure to learn and execute perfect technical routines, many dancers also experience pressure to achieve and maintain the perfect dancer's body (Quin et al., 2015). Again, drawing on qualitative research, there are accounts of elite dancers who identify teachers as key sources of *pressure for thinness* (Francisco et al., 2012). This pressure came from teachers making negative and critical comments about eating, weight, and food related issues. In this regard, perfectionistic climates in dance will need to capture the particular ways in which teachers put pressure on dancers to have the perfect body, be the perfect dancer, and always give perfect performances (Mainwaring & Aujla, 2017).

In line with this thinking, perfectionistic climates in dance may give rise to outcomes that are common to perfectionistic climates in other domains, such as apprehension, negative responses to failure, and burnout. However, we might also expect that perfectionistic climates in dance will exert a unique influence on issues pertaining to appearance and body ideals. One study of female figure skaters conducted by Dunn et al. (2011) alludes to this possibility. This is evident in that Dunn and colleagues found that coach pressure to be perfect was positively correlated with negative body-image attitudes. In a similar way we would expect highly perfectionistic climates in dance to also predict eating disorder symptomology in dancers (e.g. excessive exercise, body image disturbance, and binge eating behaviours). Eating disorder symptoms are consistently correlated with trait perfectionism and the focus of the work normally emphasizes personal vulnerability. Studying perfectionistic climates locates such vulnerabilities elsewhere and will better highlight the roots of these difficulties.

Perfectionistic Climate as Group-Level Construct

When studying perfectionistic climates in sport and dance in the future, researchers will need to consider the structure of data they collect. When performers are nested within groups that share the same leader (e.g. coach, teacher, or instructor), it will be important for researchers to adopt an approach that accounts for group membership (or nesting). This is especially important given that many researchers argue that climate-based constructs are inherently group-level constructs. This argument is clearly articulated by Papaioannou et al. (2004) who emphasize that climate data are based on responses about the overall group climate created by a single leader for all group members. This means that performers can (and should where possible) be nested into higher-level units (e.g. dancers who share the same teacher). The reason that this nesting is important is because performers who share the same leader are more like each other (in terms of their climate experience) than they are to performers who belong to different groups with different leaders (Papaioannou et al., 2004). This shared experience means that data collected from individuals nested within groups violates the assumption of independence required for basic single-level statistical approaches.

In keeping with the discussion above, researchers with perfectionistic climate data should consider adopting an approach that allows them to model perfectionistic climate as both an individual characteristic and a group-level characteristic (Lüdtke et al., 2008). This can be achieved by using a multilevel modelling approach in which perfectionistic climate is modelled as both an individual experience (i.e. performer-level perfectionistic climate perceptions) and a group experience (i.e. group-level perfectionistic climate perceptions). In doing so, any observed relationship (e.g. perfectionistic climate predicting burnout) can be decomposed into within-group and between-group effects. This is important as there could be differences in how the construct operates at these two levels (Lüdtke et al., 2008). This possibility is evident in a recent study examining a task-involving coach climate in relation to reports of coach-induced effort, coach effectiveness, and satisfaction with coach (Álvarez et al., 2019). In this study, differences in the pattern and magnitude of relationships between these constructs were evident between the group-level and performer-level analyses.

A further reason why a multilevel approach is beneficial is because it will help answer new and important questions about the perfectionistic climate construct. For example, it will be possible to examine whether effects vary from one group to another and identify group characteristics that may account for such variation (e.g. sport type, level of competition, or gender of athletes). In addition to this aim, adopting a multilevel modelling framework would provide a further (and robust) examination of construct validity. That is, it would be possible to examine the degree of similarity in perfectionistic climate data from members in the same group. The idea here is that a high level of agreement about the perfectionistic climate would be expected. This is because, in theory, the external objective reality being assessed is the same (or at least very similar) for all athletes who have the same coach (Morin et al., 2014). If there is high agreement about perfectionistic climate among performers part of the same group, then support for the construct validity of the scores would be provided.

Observed and Perceived Assessments of Perfectionistic Climate

The final important area of future research is the need to develop and validate an observational tool for assessing perfectionistic climate in sport and other performance environments. As perfectionistic climate is conceptualized as the experience of external pressure from the social environment, the behaviours that produce this perception should be amenable to more objective observation. In addition, it should be possible to systematically record and analyse perfectionistic leader interactions (e.g. behaviours signalling extreme expectations or harsh criticism) and correlate them with various performer outcomes. Other observational tools grounded in AGT, SDT, and Duda's (2013) hierarchical model of the coach-created climate are also available (Boyce et al., 2009; Smith et al., 2015; Webster et al., 2013). As such, these tools could be used to validate any new instrument and confirm existing findings on how components of a perfectionistic climate relate to other climate measures.

The development of an observational perfectionistic climate tool would allow researchers to evaluate the *actual behaviour of leaders* rather than *performer perceptions of how leaders behave* (Langdon et al., 2017). There are two major reasons why this approach to data collection would be useful. The first reason is that it would provide data against which the validity of test scores generated using self-report measures of perfectionistic climate could be assessed. That is, it would be possible to examine the degree of similarity in observational perfectionistic climate data (e.g. perfectionistic coach behaviour coded during a specified training session) *versus* self-report perfectionistic climate data (e.g. athlete perceptions of the coach-created perfectionistic climate reported after a specified training session). Once again, as with the group-level approach to assessing construct validity outlined above, a high level of agreement in the data obtained using each method would support the validity of the self-report measure. In research in education, this method of comparing observed *versus* perceived assessments of climate-based constructs has provided evidence to support the validity of self-report climate data from students (e.g. Haerens et al., 2013).

The second reason that an observational approach to data collection would be useful is for developing and evaluating future climate-based interventions aimed at reducing perfectionism. This approach to intervention could be designed to help leaders create less perfectionistic climates for their performers. To evaluate the effectiveness of such an intervention, it will be important for researchers to use both observational and self-report tools. This combination of data collection strategies will help researchers to identify whether an intervention has been effective in relation to both the observable behaviour of leaders and the self-reported experiences of performers. The data provided by self-report measures is important as it evidences intervention-enabled change at a perceptual level. This evidence of change is important given that climate-based perceptions have "functional significance" in terms of how performers feel, think, and behave (Ryan & Grolnick, 1986). The benefit of the observable data is that it allows researchers to evaluate "real" changes in perfectionistic leader behaviour, and as such will be of additional value when assessing intervention-enabled change (Haerens et al., 2013).

Concluding Comments

In this chapter we argued that experiences of external pressure to be perfect are not always explained by a performer's perfectionistic personality. Rather, for many, the pressure for perfection is grounded in the behaviour of others and the features of the social environments they encounter. To formalize this way of conceptualizing pressure to be perfect, we defined perfectionistic climate, summarized a generalized perfectionistic climate model, and described how this model has been operationalized in sport. We then conducted a systematic review of existing research that has examined coach pressure to be perfect and argued that this research suggests that perfectionistic climate will most likely be correlated with markers of apprehensiveness, negative reactions to failure, performer resiliency, and burnout. In addition to testing these relationships, we encouraged researchers to advance the study of perfectionistic climate by studying it in other domains, particularly dance, adopting nested and multi-level approaches, and developing observational tools for assessing perfectionistic climate.

Note

1 The review is based on two electronic searches (Search #1 and Search #2) using PsychINFO, PsychARTICLES, SPORTDiscus and Google Scholar databases. The search terms were "perceived coach pressure" OR "PCP" AND "Sport Multidimensional Perfectionism Scale" (Search #1) and "perceived pressure from coach" OR "coach pressure" AND "multidimensional perfectionism inventory for sports" OR "MIPS" (Search #2). The period of each search spanned publications between December 2002–June 2022 (Search #1) and June 2006–June 2022 (Search #2). No other restrictions were placed on the searches. The searches produced $k = 144$ studies (Search #1) and $k = 56$ studies (Search #2). An abstract and full-text review of the $k = 200$ retrieved articles was then conducted to screen for relevance. This process resulted in the identification of $k = 24$ peer-reviewed journal articles which: (a) provided an empirical examination of coach pressure to be perfect (using the Sport-MPS, Sport-MPS-2, or MIPS); (b) included at least one criterion variable (other than measures of trait perfectionism); (c) reported a correlation coefficient for the relationship between coach pressure to be perfect and the criterion variable(s) examined; and (d) were published in English.

References

Alvarez, M. S., Balaguer, I., Castillo, I., & Duda, J. L. (2012). The coach-created motivational climate, young athletes' well-being and intentions to continue participation. *Journal of Clinical Sport Psychology*, 6(2), 166–179. https://doi.org/10.1123/jcsp.6.2.166.

Álvarez, O., Castillo, I., Molina-García, V., & Tomás, I. (2019). Transformational leadership, task-involving climate, and their implications in male junior soccer players: a multilevel approach. *International Journal of Environmental Research and Public Health*, 16 (19), 3649. https://doi.org/10.3390/ijerph16193649.

Ames, C. (1981). Competitive versus cooperative reward structures: The influence of individual and group performance factors on achievement attributions and affect. *American Educational Research Journal*, 18(3), 273–287. https://doi.org/10.3102/00028312018003273.

Ames, C. (1992). Classrooms: Goals, structures, and student motivation. *Journal of Educational Psychology*, 84(3), 261–271. https://doi.org/10.1037/0022-0663.84.3.261.

Ames, C., & Ames, R. (1984). Systems of student and teacher motivation: Toward a qualitative definition. *Journal of Educational Psychology*, 76(4), 535–556. https://doi.org/10.1037/0022-0663.76.4.535.

Barcza-Renner, K., Eklund, R. C., Morin, A. J. S., & Habeeb, C. M. (2016). Controlling coaching behaviors and athlete burnout: Investigating the mediating roles of perfectionism and motivation. *Journal of Sport and Exercise Psychology*, 38(1), 30–44. https://doi.org/10.1123/jsep.2015-0059.

Bartholomew, K. J., Ntoumanis, N., & Thøgersen-Ntoumani, C. (2010). The controlling interpersonal style in a coaching context: Development and initial validation of a psychometric scale. *Journal of Sport and Exercise Psychology*, 32(2), 193–216. https://doi.org/10.1123/jsep.32.2.193.

Bergeron, M. F., Mountjoy, M., Armstrong, N., Chia, M., Côté, J., Emery, C. A., Faigenbaum, A., Hall, Jr., G., Kriemler, S., Léglise, M., Malina, R. M., Pensgaard, A. M., Sanchez, A., Soligard, T., Sundgot-Borgen, J., van Mechelen, W., Weissensteiner, J. R., & Engebretsen, L. (2015). International Olympic Committee consensus statement on youth athletic development. *British Journal of Sports Medicine*, 49(13), 843–851. https://doi.org/10.1136/bjsports-2015-094962.

Boyce, B. A., Gano-Overway, L. A., & Campbell, A. L. (2009). Perceived motivational climate's influence on goal orientations, perceived competence, and practice strategies across the athletic season. *Journal of Applied Sport Psychology*, 21(4), 381–394. https://doi.org/10.1080/10413200903204887.

Checa, I., Bohórquez, M. R., Arnau, V. M., & Tomás, J. M. (2021). Factor structure and measurement invariance across gender, age and sport psychology experience of the SPA-R in Spanish athletes. *Current Psychology*, 1–9. https://doi.org/10.1007/s12144-021-01447-7.

Chirban, S. A., & Rowan, M. R. (2017). Performance psychology in ballet and modern dance. In R. J. Schinke, & D. Hackfort (eds), *Psychology in professional sports and the performing arts: Challenges and strategies* (pp. 259–274). Routledge.

Crocker, P. R., Pedrosa, I., Mosewich, A. D., & Sabiston, C. M. (2018). Examining gender invariance of the Sport-Multidimensional Perfectionism Scale-2 in intercollegiate athletes. *Psychology of Sport and Exercise*, 34(1), 57–60. https://doi.org/10.1016/j.psychsport.2017.09.005.

Curran, T. (2018). Parental conditional regard and the development of perfectionism in adolescent athletes: The mediating role of competence contingent self-worth. *Sport, Exercise, and Performance Psychology*, 7(3), 284–296. https://doi.org/10.1037/spy0000126.

Curran, T., Hill, A. P., & Williams, L. J. (2017). The relationships between parental conditional regard and adolescents' self-critical and narcissistic perfectionism. *Personality and Individual Differences*, 109(1), 17–22. https://doi.org/10.1016/j.paid.2016.12.035.

Damian, L. E., Stoeber, J., Negru, O., & Băban, A. (2013). On the development of perfectionism in adolescence: Perceived parental expectations predict longitudinal increases in socially prescribed perfectionism. *Personality and Individual Differences*, 55 (6), 688–693. https://doi.org/10.1016/j.paid.2013.05.021.

De Maria, A., Mallia, L., Lombardo, C., Vacca, M., & Zelli, A. (2021). The personal and interpersonal components of perfectionism: The Italian validation of "Multidimensional Inventory of Perfectionism in Sport". *International Journal of Environmental Research and Public Health*, 18(5), 2657. https://doi.org/10.3390/ijerph18052657.

Duda, J. L. (2013). The conceptual and empirical foundations of Empowering Coaching™: Setting the stage for the PAPA project. *International Journal of Sport and Exercise Psychology*, 11(4), 311–318. https://doi.org/10.1080/1612197x.2013. 839414.

Duda, J. L., Papaioannou, A. G., Appleton, P. R., Quested, E., & Krommidas, C. (2014). Creating adaptive motivational climates in sport and physical education. In A. G. Papaioannou & D. Hackfort (eds), *Routledge companion to sport and exercise psychology: Global perspectives and fundamental concepts* (pp. 544–558). Routledge.

Dunn, J. G., Cormier, D. L., Kono, S., Causgrove Dunn, J., & Rumbold, J. (2021). Perfectionism and grit in competitive sport. *Journal of Sport Behavior*, 44(2), 199–223. https://journalofsportbehavior.org/index.php/JSB/article/view/67.

Dunn, J. G., Craft, J. M., Dunn, J. C., & Gotwals, J. K. (2011). Comparing a domain-specific and global measure of perfectionism in competitive female figure skaters. *Journal of Sport Behavior*, 34(1), 25–46.

Dunn, J. G., Dunn, J. C., & Syrotuik, D. G. (2002). Relationship between multidimensional perfectionism and goal orientations in sport. *Journal of Sport and Exercise Psychology*, 24(4), 376–395. https://doi.org/10.1123/jsep.24.4.376.

Dunn, J. G., Dunn, J. C., Gotwals, J. K., Vallance, J. K., Craft, J. M., & Syrotuik, D. G. (2006). Establishing construct validity evidence for the Sport Multidimensional Perfectionism Scale. *Psychology of Sport and Exercise*, 7(1), 57–79. https://doi.org/10. 1016/j.psychsport.2005.04.003.

Dunn, J. G., Gotwals, J. K., Dunn, J. C., & Lizmore, M. R. (2020). Perfectionism, pre-competitive worry, and optimism in high-performance youth athletes. *International Journal of Sport and Exercise Psychology*, 18(6), 749–763. https://doi.org/10.1080/ 1612197x.2019.1577900.

Dunn, J. G., Gotwals, J. K., Dunn, J. C., & Lizmore, M. R. (2022). Perceived parental pressure and perceived coach pressure in adolescent and adult sport. *Psychology of Sport and Exercise*, 59(1), 102100. https://doi.org/10.1016/j.psychsport.2021.102100.

Dunn, J. G., Gotwals, J. K., Dunn, J. C., & Syrotuik, D. G. (2006). Examining the relationship between perfectionism and trait anger in competitive sport. *International Journal of Sport and Exercise Psychology*, 4(1), 7–24. https://doi.org/10.1080/1612197x. 2006.9671781.

Epskamp, S., & Fried, E. I. (2018). A tutorial on regularized partial correlation networks. *Psychological Methods*, 23(4), 617–634. https://doi.org/10.1037/met0000167.

Fawver, B., Cowan, R. L., DeCouto, B. S., Lohse, K. R., Podlog, L., & Williams, A. M. (2020). Psychological characteristics, sport engagement, and performance in alpine skiers. *Psychology of Sport and Exercise*, 47(1), 101616. https://doi.org/10.1016/j. psychsport.2019.101616.

Flett, G. L., & Hewitt, P. L. (2006). Positive versus negative perfectionism in psychopathology: A comment on Slade and Owens's dual process model. *Behavior Modification*, 30(4), 472–495. https://doi.org/10.1177/0145445506288026.

Flett, G. L., Hewitt, P. L., Oliver, J. M., & Macdonald, S. (2002). Perfectionism in children and their parents: A developmental analysis. In G. L. Flett & P. L. Hewitt (eds), *Perfectionism: Theory, research, and treatment* (pp. 89–132). American Psychological Association. https://doi.org/10.1037/10458-004.

Francisco, R., Alarcão, M., & Narciso, I. (2012). Aesthetic sports as high-risk contexts for eating disorders: Young elite dancers and gymnasts perspectives. *The Spanish Journal of Psychology*, 15(1), 265–274. https://doi.org/10.5209/rev_sjop.2012.v15.n1.37333.

Golino, H. F., Shi, D., Christensen, A. P., Garrido, L. E., Nieto, M. D., Sadana, R., Thiyagarajan, J. A., & Martinez-Molina, A. (2020). Investigating the performance of exploratory graph analysis and traditional techniques to identify the number of latent factors: A simulation and tutorial. *Psychological Methods*, 25(3), 292–320. https://doi.org/10.1037/met0000255.

Gotwals, J. K. (2011). Perfectionism and burnout within intercollegiate sport: A person-oriented approach. *The Sport Psychologist*, 25(4), 489–510. https://doi.org/10.1123/tsp.25.4.489.

Gotwals, J. K., & Dunn, J. G. (2009). A multi-method multi-analytic approach to establishing internal construct validity evidence: The Sport Multidimensional Perfectionism Scale 2. *Measurement in Physical Education and Exercise Science*, 13(2), 71–92. https://doi.org/10.1080/10913670902812663.

Gould, D. (1996). Personal motivation gone awry: Burnout in competitive athletes. *Quest*, 48(3), 275–289. https://doi.org/10.1080/00336297.1996.10484197.

Grugan, M. C., Hill, A. P., Mallinson-Howard, S. H., Donachie, T. C., Olsson, L. F., Madigan, D. J., & Vaughan, R. S. (2021a). Development and initial validation of the Perfectionistic Climate Questionnaire-Sport (PCQ-S). *Psychology of Sport and Exercise*, 56(1), 101997. https://doi.org/10.1016/j.psychsport.2021.101997.

Grugan, M. C., Hill, A. P., Mallinson-Howard, S. H., Donachie, T. C., Olsson, L. F., Madigan, D. J., & Vaughan, R. S. (2021b). *"The coach says you will be released if you don't start bucking your idea up": Introducing perfectionistic climate*. Paper presented at Psychological Insights into Coaching Practice, Newcastle University, 23 June.

Gucciardi, D. F., Jackson, B., Coulter, T. J., & Mallett, C. J. (2011). The Connor-Davidson Resilience Scale (CD-RISC): Dimensionality and age-related measurement invariance with Australian cricketers. *Psychology of Sport and Exercise*, 12(4), 423–433. https://doi.org/10.1016/j.psychsport.2011.02.005.

Gucciardi, D. F., Mahoney, J., Jalleh, G., Donovan, R. J., & Parkes, J. (2012). Perfectionistic profiles among elite athletes and differences in their motivational orientations. *Journal of Sport and Exercise Psychology*, 34(2), 159–183. https://doi.org/10.1123/jsep.34.2.159.

Gustafsson, H., Hill, A. P., Stenling, A., & Wagnsson, S. (2016). Profiles of perfectionism, parental climate, and burnout among competitive junior athletes. *Scandinavian Journal of Medicine and Science in Sports*, 26(10), 1256–1264. https://doi.org/10.1111/sms.12553.

Haerens, L., Aelterman, N., Van den Berghe, L., De Meyer, J., Soenens, B., & Vansteenkiste, M. (2013). Observing physical education teachers' need-supportive interactions in classroom settings. *Journal of Sport and Exercise Psychology*, 35(1), 3–17. https://doi.org/10.1123/jsep.35.1.3.

Hewitt, P. L., Flett, G. L., & Mikail, S. F. (2017). *Perfectionism: A relational approach to conceptualization, assessment, and treatment*. The Guilford Press.

Hill, A. P., & Grugan, M. C. (2019). Introducing perfectionistic climate. *Perspectives on Early Childhood Psychology and Education*, 4(2), 263–276. Retrieved from https://press.pace.edu/perspectives-on-early-childhood-psychology-and-education.

Horn, T. S. (2008). Coaching effectiveness in the sport domain. In T. S. Horn (ed.), *Advances in sport psychology* (3rd ed., pp. 239–268). Human Kinetics.

Ingle, S. (2021). British gymnastics faces group-claim lawsuit from 17 alleging abuse. *The Guardian*, 26 February. Retrieved from www.theguardian.com/sport/2021/feb/26/brit ish-gymnastics-faces-class-action-lawsuit-from-17-alleging-abuse-jennifer-pinches.

Ismaili, S. S., Yousefi, B., & Sobhani, Y. (2013). The role of some psychological factors in the doping attitudes of elite wrestlers. *International Journal of Wrestling Science*, 3(1), 35–47. https://doi.org/10.1080/21615667.2013.10878968.

Kipp, L. E. (2018). Developmental considerations for working with young athletes. In C. J. Knight, C. G. Harwood, & D. Gould (eds), *Sport psychology for young athletes* (pp. 32–42). Routledge. https://doi.org/10.4324/9781315545202-4.

Klund, F., & Sæther, S. A (2017). Relationships between perfectionism, training load and elite junior football players' self-assessed and coach-assessed skills. *The Sport Journal*, 20(1), 1–8. https://thesportjournal.org/article/tag/perfectionism/.

Langdon, J. L., Schlote, R., Melton, B., & Tessier, D. (2017). Effectiveness of a need supportive teaching training program on the developmental change process of graduate teaching assistants' created motivational climate. *Psychology of Sport and Exercise*, 28(1), 11–23. https://doi.org/10.1016/j.psychsport.2016.09.008.

Lavallee, D., & Robinson, H. K. (2007). In pursuit of an identity: A qualitative exploration of retirement from women's artistic gymnastics. *Psychology of Sport and Exercise*, 8(1), 119–141. https://doi.org/10.1016/j.psychsport.2006.05.003.

Lüdtke, O., Marsh, H. W., Robitzsch, A., Trautwein, U., Asparouhov, T., & Muthén, B. (2008). The multilevel latent covariate model: a new, more reliable approach to group-level effects in contextual studies. *Psychological Methods*, 13(3), 203–229. https://doi.org/10.1037/a0012869.

Madigan, D. J., Curran, T., Stoeber, J., Hill, A. P., Smith, M. M., & Passfield, L. (2019). Development of perfectionism in junior athletes: A three-sample study of coach and parental pressure. *Journal of Sport and Exercise Psychology*, 41(3), 167–175. https://doi.org/10.1123/jsep.2018-0287.

Madigan, D. J., Stoeber, J., & Passfield, L. (2016). Perfectionism and attitudes towards doping in junior athletes. *Journal of Sports Sciences*, 34(8), 700–706. https://doi.org/10.1080/02640414.2015.1068441.

Madigan, D. J., Stoeber, J., & Passfield, L. (2017). Athletes' perfectionism and reasons for training: Perfectionistic concerns predict training for weight control. *Personality and Individual Differences*, 115(1), 133–136. https://doi.org/10.1016/j.paid.2016.03.034.

Mainwaring, L., & Aujla, I. (2017). Psychological wellness. In M. V. Wilmerding, & D. H. Krasnow (eds), *Dancer wellness* (pp. 71–82). Human Kinetics.

Mallinson, S. H., & Hill, A. P. (2011). The relationship between multidimensional perfectionism and psychological need thwarting in junior sports participants. *Psychology of Sport and Exercise*, 12(6), 676–684. https://doi.org/10.1016/j.psychsport.2011.05.009.

Marsh, H. W., Morin, A. J. S., Parker, P. D., & Kaur, G. (2014). Exploratory structural equation modelling: An integration of the best features of exploratory and confirmatory factor analyses. *Annual Review of Clinical Psychology*, 10(1), 85–110. https://doi.org/10.1146/annurev-clinpsy-032813-153700.

Martinent, G., Ferrand, C., Guillet, E., & Gautheur, S. (2010). Validation of the French version of the Competitive State Anxiety Inventory-2 Revised (CSAI-2R) including frequency and direction scales. *Psychology of Sport and Exercise*, 11(1), 51–57. https://doi.org/10.1016/j.psychsport.2009.05.001.

McArdle, S., & Duda, J. L. (2008). Exploring the etiology of perfectionism and perceptions of self-worth in young athletes. *Social Development*, 17(4), 980–997. https://doi.org/10.1111/j.1467-9507.2007.00456.x.

McEwen, K., & Young, K. (2011). Ballet and pain: Reflections on a risk-dance culture. *Qualitative Research in Sport, Exercise and Health*, 3(2), 152–173. https://doi.org/10.1080/2159676x.2011.572181.

Morgan, K. (2017). Reconceptualizing motivational climate in physical education and sport coaching: An interdisciplinary perspective. *Quest*, 69(1), 95–112. https://doi.org/10.1080/00336297.2016.1152984.

Morin, A. J. S., Myers, N. D., & Lee, S. (2020). Modern factor analytic techniques: Bifactor models, exploratory structural equation modelling (ESEM), and bifactor-ESEM. In G. Tenenbaum, & R. C. Eklund (eds), *Handbook of sport psychology* (Vol. 2, 4th ed., pp. 1044–1073). Wiley. https://doi.org/10.1002/9781119568124.ch51.

Morin, A. J., Marsh, H. W., Nagengast, B., & Scalas, L. F. (2014). Doubly latent multilevel analyses of classroom climate: An illustration. *The Journal of Experimental Education*, 82(2), 143–167. https://doi.org/10.1080/00220973.2013.769412.

Ng, R. YK., Wells, R., Lee, L., & Ng, KK. (2022). Beyond Perfection: Technology as an Enabler to Promote Higher Order Skills in Performing Arts Education. In R. C. Li, S. K. S. Cheung, P. H. F. Ng, LP. Wong, & F. L. Wang (eds), *Blended learning: Engaging students in the new normal era* (pp. 325–335). Springer. https://doi.org/10.1007/978-3-031-08939-8_28.

Nicholls, J. G. (1984). Achievement motivation: Conceptions of ability, subjective experience, task choice, and performance. *Psychological Review*, 91(3), 328–346. https://doi.org/10.1037//0033-295x.91.3.328.

Pacewicz, C. E., Gotwals, J. K., & Blanton, J. E. (2018). Perfectionism, coping, and burnout among intercollegiate varsity athletes: A person-oriented investigation of group differences and mediation. *Psychology of Sport and Exercise*, 35(1), 207–217. https://doi.org/10.1016/j.psychsport.2017.12.008.

Papaioannou, A., Marsh, H. W., & Theodorakis, Y. (2004). A multilevel approach to motivational climate in physical education and sport settings: An individual or a group level construct? *Journal of Sport and Exercise Psychology*, 26(1), 90–118. https://doi.org/10.1123/jsep.26.1.90.

Pineda-Espejel, H. A., León, J., Núñez, J. L., Morquecho-Sánchez, R., Trejo, M., & Morales-Sánchez, V. (2021). Motivational context and perfectionism traits in pediatric sports. *Sustainability*, 13(21), 11639. https://doi.org/10.3390/su132111639.

Quin, E., Rafferty, S., & Tomlinson, C. (2015). *Safe dance practice*. Human Kinetics.

Rice, K. G., Lopez, F. G., & Vergara, D. (2005). Parental/social influences on perfectionism and adult attachment orientations. *Journal of Social and Clinical Psychology*, 24(4), 580–605. https://doi.org/10.1521/jscp.2005.24.4.580.

Ryan, R. M., & Deci, E. L. (2017). *Self-determination theory: Basic psychological needs in motivation, development, and wellness*. The Guilford Press.

Ryan, R. M., & Grolnick, W. S. (1986). Origins and pawns in the classroom: Self-report and projective assessments of individual differences in children's perceptions. *Journal of Personality and Social Psychology*, 50(3), 550–558. https://doi.org/10.1037/0022-3514.50.3.550.

Sagar, S. S., & Stoeber, J. (2009). Perfectionism, fear of failure, and affective responses to success and failure: The central role of fear of experiencing shame and embarrassment. *Journal of Sport and Exercise Psychology*, 31(5), 602–627. https://doi.org/10.1123/jsep.31.5.602.

Sapieja, K. M., Dunn, J. G., & Holt, N. L. (2011). Perfectionism and perceptions of parenting styles in male youth soccer. *Journal of Sport and Exercise Psychology*, 33(1), 20–39. https://doi.org/10.1123/jsep.33.1.20.

Schellenberg, B. J., Gunnell, K. E., Mosewich, A. D., & Bailis, D. S. (2014). Measurement invariance of the Passion Scale across three samples: An ESEM approach. *Measurement in Physical Education and Exercise Science*, 18(4), 242–258. https://doi.org/10.1080/1091367X.2014.942453.

Sindik, J., Nazor, D., & Vukosav, J. (2011). Correlation between the conative characteristics at top senior basketball players. *Sport Science*, 4(1), 78–83. Retrieved from www.sposci.com/PDFS/BR0401/SVEE/04%20CL%2013%20JS.pdf.

Šíp, R., & Burešová, I. (2020). Does personality matter when we are approaching the subjective perception of overtraining among adolescents? *Studia Sportiva*, 14(1), 58–66. https://doi.org/10.5817/sts2020-1-7.

Sirois, F. M., & Molnar, D. S. (2016). Conceptualizations of perfectionism, health, and well-being: An introductory overview. In F. M. Sirois, & D. S. Molnar (eds), *Perfectionism, health, and well-being* (pp. 1–21). Springer. https://doi.org/10.1007/978-3-319-18582-8_1.

Skwiot, M., Śliwiński, Z., & Śliwiński, G. E. (2020). Perfectionism and burnout in sport and dance. *Physikalische Medizin, Rehabilitationsmedizin, Kurortmedizin*, 30(3), 135–140. https://doi.org/10.1055/a-1089-8125.

Smith, N., Tessier, D., Tzioumakis, Y., Quested, E., Appleton, P., Sarrazin, P., Papaioannou, A., & Duda, J. L. (2015). Development and validation of the multidimensional motivational climate observation system. *Journal of sport and exercise psychology*, 37(1), 4–22. https://doi.org/10.1123/jsep.2014-0059.

Soenens, B. & Vansteenkiste, M. (2010). A theoretical upgrade of the concept of parental psychological control: proposing new insights on the basis of self-determination theory. *Developmental Review*, 30(1), 74–99. https://doi.org/10.1016/j.dr.2009.11.001.

Stoeber, J., Otto, K., & Stoll, O. (2006). Multidimensional Inventory of Perfectionism in Sport (MIPS): English version. Unpublished manuscript, Division of Human and Social Sciences, School of Psychology, University of Kent. Retrieved from https://kar.kent.ac.uk/41560/.

Vaartstra, M., Dunn, J. G., & Dunn, J. C. (2018). Perfectionism and perceptions of social loafing in competitive youth soccer. *Journal of Sport Behavior*, 41(4), 475–501.

Vallance, J. K., Dunn, J. G., & Dunn, J. L. C. (2006). Perfectionism, anger, and situation criticality in competitive youth ice hockey. *Journal of Sport and Exercise Psychology*, 28(3), 383–406. https://doi.org/10.1123/jsep.28.3.383.

Webster, C. A., Wellborn, B., Hunt, K., LaFleche, M., Cribbs, J., & Lineberger, B. (2013). MPOWER: An observation system for assessing coach autonomy support in high school varsity boys' soccer practices. *International Journal of Sports Science and Coaching*, 8(4), 741–754. https://doi.org/10.1260/1747-9541.8.4.741.

Part IV

Applied Issues and Practitioner Perspectives

10 Working with Perfectionistic Athletes in Sport

An Acceptance and Commitment Therapy Perspective

Dean Watson, Henrik Gustafsson and Carolina Lundqvist

In this chapter we draw on our applied experiences and research to highlight how perfectionistic athletes can be supported using Acceptance and Commitment Therapy (ACT). The first part of the chapter describes ACT and research that has examined its use for perfectionism. In keeping with other chapters in this section of the book, the second part of the chapter presents a case example of a perfectionistic athlete. Our case example is an aspiring young athlete who in making the transition to the senior performance squad has begun to experience emotional and behavioural problems. Our novel contribution to previous work of this kind is our focus on ACT. Few studies have adopted ACT interventions to reduce perfectionism even though we believe it to be a valuable way of doing so. In addition, there are even fewer exemplars of how to implement this type of intervention in sport. As such, our intention is that the chapter serves as a guide for practitioners unfamiliar with ACT and is a useful addition to other illustrative examples of how to work effectively with perfectionistic athletes.

Context for the Chapter

We knew little about perfectionism during our training and early years as qualified practitioners. It is only really through our research, and subsequent first-hand experiences with perfectionistic athletes, that we have been able to recognize the characteristic and the impact it has on the lives of athletes inside and outside of sport. From our experience, perfectionism is central to many of the difficulties athletes face. From youth athletes to older more experienced athletes, the sense of expectation and pressure to be perfect can be ever-present and can exact a heavy toll. It is because of our applied experiences, and the challenges that we have seen these athletes face, that we think it important that this topic is better understood by fellow practitioners. In addition, to work effectively with these athletes we also need tools to do so. With this in mind, practical guides and illustrations are essential, so we have sought to provide these here, too.

Perfectionism is not something athletes, coaches, and parents are familiar with. We have had countless conversations with these groups about perfectionism and

DOI: 10.4324/9781003288015-14

its inadvertent and undesirable consequences, and it is simply not something they typically consider. In fact, athletes, coaches, and parents more often value the pursuit of perfection and actively push themselves or others to pursue it. The idea of obsessing over goals, working tirelessly and relentlessly, and pushing through the pain barrier, are all things we have seen commended in sport. As a result, as sport psychologists we are often left with the fallout – the inevitable performance and wellbeing difficulties that athletes experience as they struggle with this environment, their own irrational expectations, and the demands of others.

The backdrop for this chapter is a growing body of work outside of sport that has examined the effectiveness of different interventions for perfectionism. One of the most notable of which has been published recently and is a meta-analysis of cognitive behaviour therapy-based interventions (e.g. Galloway et al., 2022). Research examining ACT and perfectionism, specifically, is sparse. However, evidence of the efficacy of ACT generally is provided in a recent review of meta-analyses by Gloster et al. (2020) who found that ACT is effective for a range of issues (e.g. anxiety, substance use, and depression). In these regards, we are seeking to provide guidance that is empirically-informed by existing research. Inevitably, we have also drawn on our own experiences and used a number of excellent resources to help inform our approach (e.g. Kemp, 2021; White et al., 2021; Sinclair & Beadman, 2016). In providing our perspective, we acknowledge this work and encourage readers to seek out to inform their own practice.

Cognitive Behavioural Therapy (CBT) and Acceptance and Commitment Therapy (ACT)

Cognitive Behavioural Therapy (CBT) is the name of a broad set of approaches that combine cognitive therapy and behavioural therapy. It is also a term used to identify a specific and discreet type of therapy. To avoid confusion, we use the term "cognitive behavioural approaches" hereafter when referring to the broad category and CBT when referring to the discreet therapy. As described by Hayes (2004) in his excellent overview of how cognitive behavioural approaches have changed over time, cognitive behavioural approaches can be viewed as having arrived in three waves. The first wave focused on learned behaviour and the association between stimuli and problematic behaviour (viz. neo-behaviourism as exemplified by operant conditioning; Skinner, 1953). The second wave of cognitive behavioural approaches had a much greater emphasis on cognitive mediation and cognitive concepts (e.g. irrational thoughts and faulty information processing styles) as a means of understanding psychopathology. This wave is synonymous with Beck's (1976) cognitive therapy and the CBT which we referred to earlier. The third wave of cognitive behavioural approaches has a greater emphasis on social constructivism and the notion of changing the function of thoughts (or consequences) without needing to change their form (or content).

ACT is a third wave cognitive behavioural approach with particular philosophical (Functional Contextualism) and theoretical (Relational Frame Theory) underpinnings. For a detailed discussion of these underpinnings, we recommend readers consult Hayes (2004) and colleagues (e.g. Fletcher & Hayes, 2005; Hayes et al., 2006; Hayes et al., 2013). Here, we highlight that these underpinnings set this therapy apart from those in the first two waves and directs those using the approach to think in terms of subjective, value-led experiences, and contextual and relational (acquired) bases for experiences. In practice, when using ACT we aim to support people to accept their difficult thoughts and feelings, and to break both the link between them and the desire to avoid them (Hayes, 2004).

The ability to accept the experience of problematic thoughts and feelings, remain present in the moment, and still behave aligned with one's values, is referred to as psychological flexibility (Bond et al., 2011.). Increasing psychological flexibility is consider one of the main processes of change in ACT and is developed through six core processes: Being Present, Acceptance, Defusion, Values, Self, and Commitment (Hayes et al., 1999). Being present promotes direct contact with psychological events as they occur in that moment, rather than flicking between the future or the past. Acceptance involves embracing and accepting inner experiences rather than avoiding certain emotions and feelings. Defusion seeks to change the relationship with problematic thoughts. Values are activities that give life meaning and provide direction. Self is being aware of experiences without being attached or invested in them. Commitment is about setting goals in order to take action (Hayes et al., 2006).

To illustrate, a football player may report they find it difficult to be involved in the game and receive passes in defensive areas from teammates out of fear of making a mistake. This situation leads to an emotional response (e.g. anxiety) and the athlete's behavioural response is to avoid the anxiety by hiding during a game and discouraging players from passing to him. The result is temporarily lower anxiety. However, this is followed by feelings of guilt and shame, and self-critical thoughts ("I am not a good player or teammate"). This type of behaviour might also go against his values (e.g. wanting to try one's best), which can create more anxiety, stress, and a lost sense of self. Whereas CBT would focus on eliminating or correcting the negative thoughts and feelings in this situation, ACT would focus on helping him to accept his experiences and understanding that they are not themselves harmful. In ACT, his personal values would also be used as a reference point for his experience and would guide the understanding of why his thoughts and feelings are problematic and help realign his behaviours towards his personal and professional goals.

ACT shares characteristics with other approaches with regard to how it conducted. For example, during ACT interventions there is reliance on homework to completed by clients between sessions. In addition, the success or failure of an ACT intervention will be influenced by how much the individual participates and engages in the homework (see LeBeau et al., 2013). Again, as with other CBT interventions, there is also a strong emphasis on the therapeutic alliance which in ACT is described as "important, powerful, and deliberately equal" (Hayes, 2004, p. 652). Forming a strong therapeutic alliance is likely to lead to greater athlete disclosure (Katz & Hemmings, 2009). However, this is something that both therapists and clients can find difficult (Eubank et al., 2014). The importance of the therapeutic alliance is especially noteworthy here as there are suggestions that perfectionism can interfere with its development (Miller et al., 2017; Hewitt et al., 2020). Therefore, practitioners will need to be aware of the additional challenges they may face in this regard when working with perfectionistic athletes.

ACT and Managing Perfectionism

There is now ample evidence that perfectionism is something that can be reduced and managed. A lot of this evidence comes from community and education settings with individuals displaying higher perfectionism but not (as yet) clinical problems (e.g. Olton-Weber et al., 2020; Shafran et al., 2017; Arana et al., 2017). Intervention research on perfectionism in sport is still quite rare. But, the findings from current studies are promising. Some notable examples in sport include Donachie and Hill (2020) and Mosewich et al. (2013). Donachie and Hill (2020) found support for the effectiveness of a CBT-based self-help book in reducing perfectionism in adult soccer players. Similarly, Mosewich et al. (2013) found support for the effectiveness of a compassionate-based intervention in reducing concern over mistakes in female university athletes. These studies are notable because of their robust randomized-controlled (RCT) designs and positive findings, but also because they both used cognitive behavioural approaches.

There are other studies in sport that provide more preliminary evidence for the use of third wave cognitive behavioural approaches as an intervention for perfectionism. Notably, Kaufman et al. (2009) assessed the effectiveness of a 4-week mindfulness intervention to reduce perfectionism in archers and golfers. Similarly, De Petrillo et al. (2009) assessed the effectiveness of the same 4-week mindfulness intervention in long-distance runners. These studies found decreases in dimensions of perfectionism – perceived parental expectations, perceived parental criticism, and personal standards following the intervention. Unfortunately, neither of the studies used an RCT design and instead used weaker pre-test–post-test designs. However, combined with study discussed below outside of sport, we consider these studies to be at least indicative of the possible usefulness of third-wave interventions like ACT for perfectionism in sport.

To our knowledge, there is one study that has examined the use of ACT outside of sport, and this found ACT to be effective in reducing perfectionism. In the study, Ong et al. (2019, 2020) delivered a ten-week intervention to a community sample with higher scores on an obsessive-compulsive scale (so to screen for what was described as "clinical perfectionism" in this study). The intervention included sessions on acceptance, defusion, values, commitment, and relapse prevention. Using an RCT design, they found that following the intervention the ACT intervention group reported lower perfectionistic concerns (concern over mistakes and doubts about action), as well as reduced psychological inflexibility, and increased self-compassion and quality of life, in comparison to a waitlist control group. Many of these changes were considered clinically significant and reliable immediately after the treatment and one-month follow-up. Tentative evidence of changes in neural activation indicative of more efficient cognitive processing and reduced reactivity to negative stimuli were also reported in additional analyses (Ong et al., 2020).

It is hopefully evident from the description of ACT, and review of studies that have adopted the approach or similar approaches in sport and other domains, that ACT is a promising intervention for perfectionism. The experience of negative thoughts and emotions are common for perfectionistic athletes (see Chapter 4 of this book). Indeed, the experience of negative thoughts centred on themes of perfection are so deeply engrained that they may be difficult to avoid (see Chapter 8 of this book). There is also a stark contrast between the concept of psychological flexibility and the rigid perfectionistic mindset that makes it difficult to envisage that perfectionistic athletes would not benefit from ACT and the techniques it uses. As such, we now present a case example of how ACT can be used to support perfectionistic athletes.

A Case Example of Perfectionism in High-Performance Sport

In order to describe the process of working with perfectionistic athletes using ACT, we have provided a case description of a real athlete the lead author encountered in their work and have described the work together during different phases of ACT. This is based on the Hexaflex model of ACT (Bach & Moran, 2008). So not to reveal the identity of the athlete, minor changes have been made to the case or information omitted. However, overall, it is an accurate reflection of the case and the support that was provided. Quotes are provided from notes and sessions for illustrative effect.

Case Description – Sophie

Sophie's coach initially contacted the lead author to request sport psychology support, as Sophie was finding the transition to senior field hockey "difficult". Sophie is a high-performance field hockey player. She has just turned 18 years old and has been competing mainly with junior squads in national and international competitions. She trains six times a week and attends regular regional and national training camps. This requires a lot of time and travel across the UK. Sophie has recently joined the senior squad at her club and has begun competing in senior competitions. She lives at home with her parents who support her and take her to most training sessions and competitions. Based on her achievements, she is highly talented and among the best young players in the country. Her coaches and peers expect her to eventually gain a place in the senior national squad.

In discussing Sophie with her coaches and parents, Sophie's regional coach said that over the past few weeks her engagement with training has been "shoddy" and that she had appeared disinterested at times. He also explains that she is becoming forgetful (for example, missing items from her kit and turning up late). Sophie's parents later explain that she has been more "upset" and "emotional" than usual. They say that she is very demanding of herself and is trying her best. They don't have an explanation for her behaviour but are concerned that her schedule is too demanding and she feels under pressure. However, they want to support her ambition, which has always been to play field hockey for her country.

Table 10.1 ACT delivery plan and session overview.

Module	ACT	Perfectionism	Aim	Module Components
1	Analysis	N/A	To build background information	1.1 Build rapport 1.2 Outline of the problems 1.3 Expectations of one another
2	Case formulation	N/A	Conceptualization of the issues	2.1 Function of perfectionism 2.2 Sources of psychological inflexibility 2.3 Presenting problems
3	Psychoeducation	N/A	An outline of sport psychology and ACT	3.1 Increase confidence in sport psychology 3.2 Welcome to ACT 3.3 Iron out pre-conceptions
4	Contact with the present moment	Concerns Over Mistakes	Staying focused in competition/training	4.1 What is being present? 4.2 Contacting the present moment 4.3 Using senses (e.g. dropping anchor)
5	Mindfulness	Fear of Failure	To be able to control the body and mind	5.1 What is mindfulness? 5.2 Emptying the mind 5.3 Pink elephant
6	Acceptance	Self-Criticism	To be able to accept mistakes/the self	6.1 How do I accept? 6.2 Struggling vs opening up 6.3 Thoughts – emotions – actions
7	Cognitive defusion	Doubt About Actions	To disconnect thoughts	7.1 Removing doubt (e.g. hands Infront of face) 7.2 Being more compassionate to the self 7.3 Getting hooked
8	Values	Managing Expectations	Leading a values led life	8.1 Values vs goals 8.2 Exploring values 8.3 Overcoming expectations
9	Self	Negative Reactions to Imperfections	Increase awareness of the self	9.1 How do you want to be seen? 9.2 Overcoming imperfections 9.3 Obituary
10	Commitment	Healthy Striving	Setting realistic and healthy goals	10.1 Committing to the plan 10.2 What if planning 10.3 FEAR

Below is a description of ten sessions conducted with Sophie. Each description explains what was done and why. The session outline will be one that will provide perfectionistic athletes with a space to allow their thoughts to pass, for them to remain present, and to live a values-led life. Ultimately, the ACT intervention is designed to create psychological flexibility, which for perfectionistic athletes is a stark contrast from their rigid, dichotomous thinking they routinely experience (see Table 10.1).

Description of the Sessions

Session One – Analysis

In the first meeting the aim is to get more background information about the athlete and collect information about his/her problem(s) and what maintains them, as well as information on his/her strengths. This first meeting provides an important opportunity to begin building rapport with the athlete. It is also used to provide information to the athlete about ACT and the possible schedule of work (Hayes & Strosahl, 2004).

In this first session, Sophie talked about problems that related to feeling stressed during training and being anxious about competitions. Soon, it was evident that these problems were related to perfectionism. Sophie described herself as being a perfectionist in many aspects of life, but mostly in sport. Sophie felt pressure from herself and others to do everything perfectly and felt both fear and anxiety over making mistakes. Sophie described that most of her thoughts and feelings come from her own expectations: "I constantly feel like things need to be done perfectly. If they are not, I can get really upset with myself". Sophie also described that she feels her coach and some of her teammates can be very critical of her. Sophie said, "If I misplace a pass, I tend to go into my shell to protect me from what they might say or think." Sophie is normally incredibly organized, a meticulous planner, and also highly prudent. Sophie explained that if she doesn't perform how she wants to, or things don't go as planned, she gets very critical of herself.

Sophie's perfectionism showed itself in many respects, such as demanding and rigid personal standards, obsessing over her goals, being very self-critical, and trying to hide her flaws from the judgement of others. This way of behaving and thinking is extremely difficult and challenging for Sophie. She finds it difficult to accept criticism from her parents and coaches partly because it adds to the weight of her own criticism but also because it feels like they are not supporting her. This belief often created feelings of anxiety which is not only problematic for her performance but also her wellbeing. The idea of not being perfect, not performing perfectly, or things not going perfectly, are things that Sophie finds difficult to accept.

As mentioned earlier, in order for ACT to be effective, compliance to homework is important (Mausbach et al., 2010). As such, it is vital that the athlete is a part of the development of the home assignments as this improves adherence and the likelihood of successful intervention (Robinson, 2008). Successfully completing homework will provide a more detailed understanding of her perfectionism and the impact it has on her. It will also create a space for her to begin noticing her thoughts and behaviours and increase awareness of herself. Giving an assignment in the first session is also a way to enhance engagement with Sophie as well as build longer-term adherence. The home assignment is evaluated in the first part of the next session, this provides an opportunity for Sophie to discuss any problems she might have experienced or questions she might have. It can also allow for an easier transition into the content of the next session.

Session Two – Case Formulation

In this session the work with the analysis continues and the problem is explored in more detail. The aim is to develop a case formulation or conceptualization of the issues being described where we can better understand the function of Sophie's perfectionism in context (Hayes et al., 2004). At this stage, it is important to understand how the various processes relate to psychological (in) flexibility. This is because it will provide an in-depth account of Sophie's rigid thinking, and the behaviours that do not allow her to be present. It is also important the process remains evidence-based and underpinned by relevant theory. To understand the underlying problems of Sophie's perfectionism, we used a set of questions to guide the conceptualization process, as outlined by Hayes et al. (2004) (see Table 10.2). In addition, we used the Hexaflex model as a framework (Harris, 2009).

Table 10.2 ACT case formulation – core questions.

	Case Formulation		
Sources of Psychological Flexibility	Factors that Contribute to Psychological Inflexibility	Factors that Contribute to Psychological Flexibility	Treatment Implications
Contacting the present moment	Making a mistake in a game and not being able to move past it	Not applicable	Excessive worry and regret
Acceptance	Preference to avoid conversations with parents	Some positive, honest chats with her coach	Always thinks she is right
Defusion	Constant need to evaluate herself	Not applicable	Change is not possible
Self as context	She feels like she is judged by her hockey ability	Not applicable	Fear of unsatisfying relationships with parents and coach
Contact with values	Wants to be a loving daughter and friend	Not applicable	May be seen differently to others
Committed action	Tried making changes to attitudes and thoughts previously	Some positive self-control	Fear of the unknown

Source: Adapted from S. C. Hayes, K. D. Strosahl, J. Luoma, A. A. Smith, & K. G. Wilson (2004). ACT case formulation. In *A practical guide to acceptance and commitment therapy* (pp. 59–73). Springer.

Sophie's home assignment was to identify the areas of her life that she is perfectionistic and revealed that the main area in which she was perfectionistic was in sport, but this was also the case for schoolwork. Sophie liked things done in a particular way. She has previously described herself as a "control freak". It was apparent that Sophie found making *any* mistakes difficult to accept even when made by others, but she mostly kept these feeling to herself. Sophie is incredibly critical towards herself and focussed intensely on mistakes she made (for example, "I misplaced a really easy pass last week, I beat myself up about it for a week"). Sophie believed that she was difficult to be around, especially when she was critical towards herself. She feels that she ultimately doesn't want to make mistakes and has described rigid rules (e.g. "I must be perfect"). These thoughts and feelings are creating psychological inflexibility as they prevent Sophie from contacting the present moment.

Based on the analysis and case formulation session, as well as conversations with her coach and parents, a description of her perfectionism was presented to Sophie (see Table 10.3) and based on those created by Harris (2009). This table includes an integration of the fundamental aspects of the Hexaflex model of perfectionism as well as the personal experiences Sophie described regarding her perfectionism. This model also outlines the specific thoughts and behaviours that create psychological inflexibility. Creating a diagram of the case formulation provides a good opportunity to explore the factors that maintain Sophie's perfectionism and how to proceed to break the cycle of perfectionism

Table 10.3 An Acceptance and Commitment Therapy model of Sophie's perfectionism based on Hexaflex model (Harris, 2009).

	Psychological Inflexibility
Dominance of Past and Future	Unable to focus in training after making a mistake (e.g. misplaced pass followed by dominate thoughts of the mistake)
Lack of Value Clarity	Lack of value clarity and crippled by expectations from themselves (e.g. neglected values of self-compassion and caring)
Unworkable Action	Constant rumination and worry with little persistence (e.g. "I feel like they judge me for every mistake I make so it's easier not to try")
Conceptualized Self	Feel they are not good enough and that they constantly make mistakes (e.g. feel unloved and unwanted within the team)
Cognitive Fusion	Hooked by rigid thoughts leading to concerns about making mistakes (e.g. "I must win every challenge and score every opportunity")
Experiential Avoidance	Unable to accept mistakes and highly self-critical of themselves and others (e.g. avoiding opening up to anyone)

(Egan et al., 2014). However, using the Hexaflex model can sometimes be confusing for the athletes (Twoihig et al., 2021), so it is important to remain clear and concise with them during each phase of the model.

Session Three – Psychoeducation

After the analysis of the problem, the next phase is psychoeducation and introduction to ACT. Knowledge about sport and performance can be helpful here, but not essential. If the therapist or practitioner has knowledge of the sport they may be seen as more credible. But there is also benefit for the therapist or practitioner knowing very little about the sport. This can strengthen the relationship building process as it provides the athlete with plenty of opportunities to talk and be the "expert" (Miller & Rollnick, 2013). For us, the need to build strong relationships with perfectionistic athletes is essential in order to have successful outcomes. To do this, we used core skills from Motivational Interviewing (e.g. open-ended questions; see Miller & Rollnick, 2013). As discussed earlier, perfectionism can undermine the development of the therapeutic alliance. This places even more emphasis on building strong working relationships with perfectionistic athletes.

One important part of the work is to reduce any stigma or pre-conceptions towards sport psychology (Watson et al., 2021). Previous research has found that athletes with higher levels of some dimensions of perfectionism have less confidence in sport psychologists, are "psychologically closed" to discussing personal problems, and attach a sense of stigma to seeking support. Therefore, it is important to provide clear explanations and rationales as to what sport psychology is, how it will help them, and what the benefits are for their perfectionism. It is also important to remember that some athletes with higher levels of perfectionism value the perceived benefits of perfectionism (Hill et al., 2015). A primary focus on self-evaluation processes, rather than lowering standards, is also beneficial in this regard (Egan et al., 2014), particularly for athletes. These points should provide practitioners with a sense of caution around the early part of the consultancy process.

Session Four – Contact with the Present Moment

In this session, we focussed on identifying specific moments where Sophie is unable to be present with her thoughts and actions. Having a focus on the past (i.e. rumination) or future (i.e. worry) is a common problem for athletes with high levels of perfectionism. Sophie described that in training and games she would feel under pressure from herself and her coach to constantly play well and play the "perfect" game. She said if she made a mistake, she always ruminated over it. This inability to be present in her thoughts played an instrumental role in her psychological inflexibility. Being drawn towards mistakes or situations that are yet to happen will contribute to losing focus, more anxiety, and less control. By being present in one's thoughts, athletes can better focus on the cues that are relevant to them in that moment.

The aim of the session was to provide Sophie with (a) an understanding of what being present felt like and (b) a clear process to follow in order to be present. The intention was to help her stay focussed in training and in games. Metaphors can play an important role in the delivery of ACT interventions (Varra et al., 2009). One metaphor that was relevant to Sophie and one that she found relatable was "leaves on a stream". This metaphor describes the need to allow thoughts to pass by without examining each one. Taking that step back and not being drawn into every thought. Just being present and allowing each leaf to pass by. This would help Sophie understand that some of her own thoughts can be left without the need to control them. The homework for the next session was to identify situations where it is common for her to focus on mistakes or generally not to be present in her thoughts. In the session Sophie described several situations where she had lost focus and been "overly concerned of making a mistake". In the homework, we decided to focus on one or two situations where this is the case. Sophie was to use one of the metaphors from the session that would encourage her to be present and take a step back.

Session Five – Mindfulness

In the next session, we introduced mindfulness. Mindfulness can be used as a standalone intervention or within an ACT intervention (Röthlin & Birrer, 2020). Mindfulness has also been used within interventions for perfectionism with some promising results (e.g. De Petrillo et al., 2009; Kaufman et al., 2009; Steele & Wade, 2008). Mindfulness is about trying to draw attention to, and connect to, the wider environment and observe the present experience with an accepting and open attitude (Bishop et al., 2004). Sophie has previously described generally feeling stressed in training and competitions. So, we wanted Sophie to engage in mindfulness to reduce her feelings of stress and overriding fear of failure.

The session included practicing mindfulness. This comprises a range of different exercises including body scanning. Body scanning involves paying attention to parts of the body in order to notice tension and ultimately increase awareness to the self. These are exercises that are helpful in noticing thoughts, to be in the present moment, and avoiding trying to change the experience (see Segal et al., 2013). These aspects are all really important elements within ACT. We also encouraged Sophie to practice mindfulness in moments that she notices herself struggling with perfectionistic thoughts or behaviours. To help her with this, we suggested that Sophie used a diary to log her thoughts and behaviours. This would help us better understand how and when she might use mindfulness.

Session Six – Acceptance

In this session, we focussed on a fundamental part of ACT – acceptance. Acceptance is about accepting thoughts and emotions. It is an active process of engaging with one's emotions, which will allow for greater compassion to oneself (Hayes et al., 2011). It is hoped that accepting one's thoughts and emotions will create a

more mindful and flexible perspective, making a shift from avoidance to engagement. In perfectionism, avoiding inner experiences (e.g. procrastinating to avoid
seeming imperfect) is common (Ong et al., 2019). This avoidance also extends to
perfectionistic thoughts or cognitions (e.g. "I'm not good enough"). ACT
addresses these perfectionistic thoughts without needing to change their content.

Sophie has described how she felt overwhelmed by her thoughts, specifically
after making a mistake in a game. Our aim for this session was to help Sophie
open up and describe her thoughts, and to provide opportunities to take a "step
back" and see the thoughts as just thoughts. When Sophie is overwhelmed by
these thoughts, she notices and analyses each individual thought. These
thoughts, and subsequent emotions, played a critical role in Sophie's level of
self-criticism. Therefore, it was also hoped that this session would help address
this aspect of perfectionism and accept rather attend to her negative thoughts.

After providing perspective on some of her self-critical thoughts, we provided
Sophie with the choice of struggling vs opening-up. Opening-up makes room for
problematic thoughts and feelings, rather than struggling and fighting them. Previously, Sophie has struggled to accept mistakes, to move on from the thoughts
that follow mistakes, and to provide compassion to herself. She had tried to wrestle
with these thoughts and feelings but doing so hadn't resolved them or provided
her with a space to feel content. We suggested opening-up rather than struggling
with these thoughts and feelings. In order to overcome the difficulty in opening-
up, she needed to show courage and willingness. This is also called Creative
Hopelessness. Creative Hopelessness is a fundamental part of acceptance, which
reflects Sophie's resistance and opposition to acceptance, and willingness to
examine the workability of her perfectionism (Hayes et al., 2011).

Session Seven – Cognitive Defusion

Here we focussed on defusing Sophie's problematic thoughts (e.g. "I must do
things perfectly"). Defusing thoughts in ACT is key as it shows Sophie that she
is not her thoughts and that they don't define her. Sophie has historically
struggled with this concept. Defusion attempts to alter the context so that
Sophie isn't punished by her own idiosyncratic thinking. Altering the context
will allow Sophie to be free to think and act in accordance with her values.
Unlike the first and second waves of cognitive behavioural approaches, the aim
in this session isn't to control, suppress, or avoid the thoughts that Sophie is
having. A metaphor that worked well within this session is the Sushi Train.
Sophie is encouraged to see thoughts pass by (as if they were pieces if sushi)
rather than engage and examine each piece of sushi (or each thought).

For homework, we provided Sophie with different exercises to explore some of
her more difficult thoughts and provide an opportunity to take a step back and not
to engage with them as often. For example, to help Sophie understand her struggle
with her own thoughts, she was asked to put her hands up to her eyes. Sophie is
asked what she can see, and how she feels. The answer is that she can't see anything
and that she feels uncomfortable. She's asked to slowly move her hands away from

her face, continually recognizing what she can begin to see. She was asked what she could now notice, what she could feel and see. At the end of the exercise, it's important to help Sophie recognize that her hands (or indeed her thoughts) are still here, but that they are not controlling or absorbing, allowing her greater focus.

Session Eight – Values

In this session, Sophie is encouraged to move towards a values-led life. Values are verbally construed desired life consequences that guide us in the choices that we make (Hayes et al., 1999). Therefore, values give direction and purpose to our behaviour. When Sophie doesn't live in line with her values, she becomes more critical towards herself and feels less confident about her abilities. The discrepancies between her values and her current behaviour, in turn, create and further fuel her perfectionism. Sophie has described how she is very "goal-focussed", and typically sets extremely high and even unrealistic goals for herself. Better understanding values will provide Sophie will help maintain her sense of motivation and energy, because she will know what matters to her.

As part of the session, Sophie was asked "What do you want your life to stand for?" A useful exercise that runs alongside this is the Bulls Eye (Larsen et al., 2019). Sophie writes down her values for work, leisure, health, and relationships. She indicates how strongly she is living by each of these values on a 7-point scale (1 = "living by them inconstantly" and 7 = "living by them fully"). These provide us both with an outlook in regards to whether she is living by her values or not (e.g. "What do you need to do to live by them more fully?"). A second exercise that was useful was the *BUS* acronym (Breath, Unhook, See). Sophie was encouraged to *breath* to help slow down her body and mind and be present. To *unhook* from thoughts, seeing them as just thoughts. And finally, to *see* what matters to her. Sophie was encouraged to use this in training and games at times when she either made a mistake or lost focus.

Session Nine – Self

In the penultimate session, we focussed on the self. Recently, it has been referred to the *noticer* mode of mind (Hayes & Ciarrochi, 2015). This is because it refers to our ability to be aware of, or notice, what is happening to us or around us (White et al., 2021). An aim of focusing on the self is to distinguish between the content of private events and the context in which they occur (Strosahl et al., 2004). Understanding the self (i.e. the perfectionistic self-descriptions Sophie makes about herself) will allow Sophie to adopt different perspectives on her thoughts and feelings, and help overcome the trappings of her perfectionistic thinking. To help Sophie understand this part of the session, we used the following metaphor from Belmont (2019):

> The observer self can be linked to the sky. Your thoughts and feelings being like the weather. No matter how turbulent the hurricanes, blizzards

and rainstorms, blue skies and balmy breezes will replace the turbulent weather if you are patient and have faith that the storm will pass. We don't try to change the weather, we cannot control it – rather, we can observe it and be detached from it, knowing the storm will pass and there will again be sunny days and calm breezes again. Likewise, your thoughts will also pass and by not reacting to the storm, you will develop equanimity and patience.

Sophie has already described how her perfectionism makes it very hard to move on from mistakes. She sets extremely high standards for herself and is overly critical of her own achievements. It is suggested to Sophie, that she can move into a space where she can observe some of these painful thoughts and experiences without getting caught up in them. The control and avoidance that she has previously explored (e.g. missed training sessions) has had little success. An exercise that Sophie found useful was the chessboard metaphor. Here we discuss the pieces to be like her thoughts – some positive, some negative. Her experience has been a "battle" between these pleasant and unpleasant chess pieces (or thoughts). We encourage Sophie to be more like the chessboard and observe the thoughts that she has, without engaging or reacting to them.

Session Ten – Commitment

The aim of the final session in the intervention was to provide Sophie with perspective and an established method of setting goals that don't fuel her perfectionism. As is the case for most perfectionistic athletes, setting unrealistic goals often undermines how they deal with setbacks and failure (Lizmore et al., 2019). So, better goal setting is an imperative part of the intervention process that supports a greater drive for healthy striving and realistic goal setting. Commitment (or committed action) is defined as engaging in a pattern of behaviour, in pursuit of short- and medium-term health related goals, that is consistent with a person's values (Hayes et al., 1999). As previously covered from session eight, Sophie wasn't living by her values. She wasn't living a values-led life and was instead setting goals that encouraged self-criticism and fear.

Sophie has previously discussed how she sometimes "hides away" in training or games if she makes mistakes. Avoidance helps preserve or protect her perceived imperfections. So, what we want is for Sophie to see that even in the presence of obstacles, she can overcome them if she is directed and committed towards her values. In the session we used goal setting that was incorporated some of her values. To help with this, we used the Life Compass exercise (Dahl & Lundgren, 2006). Here, we discussed her values (those that were written from session eight) and developed an appropriate action plan which proposes several questions. Firstly, why is this goal meaningful? Secondly, what are the obstacles that may prevent you achieving this goal? Thirdly, which of these are you willing to make room for? Finally, which skills will you use to combat the uncomfortable thoughts? By ending the session and intervention in this way, it provides an effective way to maintain the impact of the intervention and support her in utilizing the previous sessions.

Case Study Evaluation and Outcomes

There were several important and successful outcomes for Sophie. To understand and determine these outcomes, we employed a number of different evaluative techniques. Firstly, we used social validation to understand the quality of support that was provided to Sophie. Social validation is often used in single case research (Barker et al., 2011), but also as a standalone exercise, which can offer an in-depth analysis of the intervention from the athlete's perspective. Sophie described how she now felt "more in control" of her perfectionistic thoughts. She described being present in practice and used several of the techniques after making mistakes, which previously caused her to be overly self-critical. The second technique we used was performance based. We used a subjective measure of performance to determine improvements. Importantly, Sophie's parents described how they noticed Sophie being more "in the zone" in the car on the way to games. This made them feel less inclined to ask questions or make statements. Given that Sophie's parents often outlined their own expectations in these situations, this was seen as an important outcome.

However, like with most interventions, there were areas it could be improved. Firstly, we did not measure Sophie's psychological flexibility directly. Despite understanding Sophie's thoughts and feelings that contributed to her psychological inflexibility (in the needs analysis and case conceptualization phase), we could have included the Acceptance and Action Questionnaire (AAQ 2; Bond et al., 2011). The AAQ-2 has been validated in several domains, including sport, so we encourage practitioners to consider using it. Secondly, after having several conversations with her coach, he suggested that Sophie still become overwhelmed at times and can still apply pressure on herself to be perfect. Practitioners should be reminded that interventions do not always go to plan (or work perfectly). There are often elements of an intervention that require adjustment, revisiting or abandoning. What is important is the conversation we had with her coach to understand how things were developing and better evaluate the impact of the intervention.

Moving forward, Sophie was encouraged to use self-reflection. One useful technique that we asked Sophie to engage with was to record, reflect, and learn from her performances (e.g. Ravizza, 1990). Sophie was asked to record three things that went well in each game and training session, two things that didn't go so well (so to reduce or cap the amount of self-criticism), and one thing that she intends to improve on. This reflective process will support how she reacts to situations and provide her with a space for growth. Sophie is also encouraged to reach out for support if she finds that things are becoming difficult again. This includes from those providing psychological support, from her parents, coach, friends, and teammates.

Reflections

As it should be with all sport psychology interventions, reflecting is an essential part of the practice and should be conducted by the sport psychologists. Reflective practice offers a useful and appropriate framework for professional training and development (Anderson et al., 2004). Here we used Gibbs's Reflective Cycle (Gibbs, 1988), but there are several alternative models available (e.g. Kolb, 1984; Schon, 1991; Johns, 1995). Regardless of the model used, the main basis of reflecting is for the practitioner to develop their practice and approach, and for the practitioner to increase their self-awareness (Knowles et al., 2014). In sharing professional reflections, it can also be beneficial to others.

A key question we asked ourselves from this process of reflecting was whether we engaged and worked with Sophie's coach enough? Given the coaches role in fuelling perfectionism in this case, it may have been more beneficial for Sophie if we had also worked with the coach, too. Providing coach education workshops may be an additional way of supporting Sophie. Similarly, greater involvement of Sophie's parents may have been useful and provided for a more effective intervention. Like coaches, parents are instrumental in the way athletes view themselves and the expectations they establish. There are often logistical issues that need to be overcome and consideration of ethical issues when inviting parents and coaches to be a part of interventions but, if carefully navigated, their involvement may serve the athlete better.

Something that this particular case study highlighted is the benefit of delivering more remote or online based interventions. When working with Sophie, some of the sessions (e.g. session nine) were delivered online but doing more sessions online may have been beneficial. Delivering support online is beginning to gain more attention as a mode of intervention within sport psychology (Price et al., 2020). There is also evidence that this mode of delivery is equally effective as face-to-face delivery when working with perfectionism (Suh et al., 2019). This is partly explained by the increase in flexibility and access the mode of delivery offers. In our experience, athletes are familiar with using digital technologies as they regularly use them to communicate with friends and family while travelling. So, following initial meetings to build rapport and trust, using new technologies may be more desirable for athletes who are "on the road".

Concluding Comments

In this chapter we described ACT and provided an illustrative example of the approach to working with a perfectionistic athlete. Evidence is beginning to emerge in support of ACT in sport and in our own applied work we have found it useful and effective. Unlike other cognitive behavioural approaches, ACT focusses on accepting rather than changing negative thoughts and feelings. In this regard, we consider ACT to be suited to working with perfectionistic athletes for whom negative cognitive and emotional experienced may be deeply engrained. We hope that this chapter encourages sport psychologists to consider utilizing ACT interventions when working with perfectionistic athletes, that our practical illustrations are useful, and that our own reflections can inform the effective future practice of others.

References

Anderson, A. G., Knowles, Z., & Gilbourne, D. (2004). Reflective practice for sport psychologists: Concepts, models, practical implications, and thoughts on dissemination. *The Sport Psychologist*, 18(2), 188–203. https://doi.org/10.1123/tsp.18.2.188.

Arana, F. G., Miracco, M. C., Galarregui, M. S., & Keegan, E. G. (2017). A brief cognitive behavioural intervention for maladaptive perfectionism in students: A pilot study. *Behavioural and Cognitive Psychotherapy*, 45(5), 537–542. https://doi.org/10.1017/S1352465817000406.

Bach, P. A., & Moran, D. J. (2008). *ACT in practice: Case conceptualization in acceptance and commitment therapy*. New Harbinger Publications.

Barker, J., McCarthy, P., Jones, M., & Moran, A. (2011). *Single-case research methods in sport and exercise psychology*. Routledge. https://doi.org/10.4324/9780203861882.

Beck, A. T. (1976). *Cognitive therapy and the emotional disorders*. International Universities Press.

Belmont, J. (2019). *Embrace your greatness: Fifty ways to build unshakable self-esteem*. New Harbinger Publications.

Bishop, S. R., Lau, M., Shapiro, S., Carlson, L., Anderson, N. D., Carmody, J., … & Devins, G. (2004). Mindfulness: A proposed operational definition. *Clinical Psychology, Science and practice*, 11(3), 230–241. https://doi.org/10.1093/clipsy.bph077.

Bond, F. W., Hayes, S. C., Baer, R. A., Carpenter, K. M., Guenole, N., Orcutt, H. K., … & Zettle, R. D. (2011). Preliminary psychometric properties of the Acceptance and Action Questionnaire–II: A revised measure of psychological inflexibility and experiential avoidance. *Behavior Therapy*, 42(4), 676–688. https://doi.org/10.1016/j.beth.2011.03.007.

Dahl, J., & Lundgren, T. (2006). *Living beyond your pain: Using acceptance and commitment therapy to ease chronic pain*. New Harbinger Publications.

De Petrillo, L. A., Kaufman, K. A., Glass, C. R., & Arnkoff, D. B. (2009). Mindfulness for long-distance runners: An open trial using Mindful Sport Performance Enhancement (MSPE). *Journal of Clinical Sport Psychology*, 25, 357–376. https://doi.org/10.1123/jcsp.3.4.357.

Donachie, T. C., & Hill, A. P. (2020). Helping soccer players help themselves: Effectiveness of a psychoeducational book in reducing perfectionism. *Journal of Applied Sport Psychology*, 34(3), 564–584. https://doi.org/10.1080/10413200.2020.1819472.

Egan, S. J., Noort, E., Chee, A., Kane, R. T., Hoiles, K. J., Shafran, R., & Wade, T. D. (2014). A randomised controlled trial of face to face versus pure online self-help cognitive behavioural treatment for perfectionism. *Behaviour Research and Therapy*, 63, 107–113. https://doi.org/10.1016/j.brat.2014.09.009.

Egan, S. J., Wade, T. D., Shafran, R., & Antony, M. M. (2014). *Cognitive-behavioral treatment of perfectionism*. Guilford Publications.

Eubank, M., Nesti, M., & Cruickshank, A. (2014). Understanding high performance sport environments: impact for the professional training and supervision of sport psychologists. *Sport & Exercise Psychology Review*, 10(2), 30–36.

Fletcher, L., & Hayes, S. C. (2005). Relational frame theory, acceptance and commitment therapy, and a functional analytic definition of mindfulness. *Journal of Rational-Emotive and Cognitive-Behavior Therapy*, 23(4), 315–336. https://doi.org/10.1007/s10942-005-0017-7.

Galloway, R., Watson, H., Greene, D., Shafran, R., & Egan, S. J. (2022). The efficacy of randomised controlled trials of cognitive behaviour therapy for perfectionism: a systematic review and meta-analysis. *Cognitive Behaviour Therapy*, 51(2), 170–184. https://doi.org/10.1080/16506073.2021.1952302.

Gibbs, G. (1988). *Learning by doing. A guide to teaching and learning methods.* Oxford Brooks University.

Gloster, A. T., Walder, N., Levin, M. E., Twohig, M. P., & Karekla, M. (2020). The empirical status of acceptance and commitment therapy: A review of meta-analyses. *Journal of Contextual Behavioral Science*, 18, 181–192. https://doi.org/10.1016/j.jcbs.2020.09.009.

Harris, R. (2009). *ACT made simple: An easy-to-read primer on acceptance and commitment therapy.* New Harbinger Publications.

Hayes, S. C. (2004). Acceptance and commitment therapy, relational frame theory, and the third wave of behavioral and cognitive therapies. *Behavior Therapy*, 35(4), 639–665. https://doi.org/10.1016/S0005-7894(04)80013–80013.

Hayes, L. L., & Ciarrochi, J. V. (2015). *The thriving adolescent: Using acceptance and commitment therapy and positive psychology to help teens manage emotions, achieve goals, and build connection.* New Harbinger Publications.

Hayes, S. C., Levin, M. E., Plumb-Vilardaga, J., Villatte, J. L., & Pistorello, J. (2013). Acceptance and commitment therapy and contextual behavioral science: Examining the progress of a distinctive model of behavioral and cognitive therapy. *Behavior Therapy*, 44(2), 180–198. https://doi.org/10.1016/j.beth.2009.08.002.

Hayes, S. C., Luoma, J. B., Bond, F. W., Masuda, A., & Lillis, J. (2006). Acceptance and commitment therapy: Model, processes and outcomes. *Behaviour research and therapy*, 44(1), 1–25. https://doi.org/10.1016/j.brat.2005.06.006.

Hayes, S. C., & Strosahl, K. D. (2004). *A practical guide to acceptance and commitment therapy.* Springer.

Hayes, S. C., Strosahl, K.D., Luoma, J., Smith, A.A., Wilson, K. G. (2004). ACT case formulation. In S. C. Hayes & K. D. Strosahl (eds), *A practical guide to acceptance and commitment therapy* (pp. 59–73). Springer. https://doi.org/10.1007/978-0-387-23369-7_3.

Hayes, S. C., Strosahl, K., & Wilson, K. G. (1999). *Acceptance and commitment therapy: An experiential approach to behavior change.* Guilford Press.

Hayes, S. C., Strosahl, K. D., & Wilson, K. G. (2011). *Acceptance and commitment therapy: The process and practice of mindful change.* Guilford Press.

Hewitt, P. L., Chen, C., Smith, M. M., Zhang, L., Habke, M., Flett, G. L., & Mikail, S. F. (2020). Patient perfectionism and clinician impression formation during an initial interview. *Psychology and Psychotherapy: Theory, Research and Practice*, 94(1), 45–62. https://doi.org/10.1111/papt.12266.

Hewitt, P. L., & Flett, G. L. (2002). Perfectionism and stress processes in psychopathology. In G. L. Flett & P. L. Hewitt (eds), *Perfectionism: Theory, research, and treatment* (pp. 255–284). American Psychological Association. https://doi.org/10.1037/10458-011.

Hill, A. P., Witcher, C. S., Gotwals, J. K., & Leyland, A. F. (2015). A qualitative study of perfectionism among self-identified perfectionists in sport and the performing arts. *Sport, Exercise, and Performance Psychology*, 4(4), 237–253. https://doi.org/10.1037/spy0000041.

Johns, C. (1995). Framing learning through reflection within Carper's fundamental ways of knowing in nursing. *Journal of Advanced Nursing*, 22(2), 226–234. https://doi.org/10.1046/j.1365-2648.1995.22020226.x.

Katz, J., & Hemmings, B. (2009). *Counselling Skills Handbook for the Sport Psychologist.* Division of Sport & Exercise Psychology of the British Psychological Society.

Kaufman, K. A., Glass, C. R., & Arnkoff, D. B. (2009). Evaluation of Mindful Sport Performance Enhancement (MSPE): A new approach to promote flow in athletes. *Journal of Clinical Sport Psychology*, 3(4), 334–356. https://doi.org/10.1123/jcsp.3.4.334.

Kemp, J. (2021). *The ACT workbook for perfectionism: Build your best (imperfect) life using powerful Acceptance and Commitment Therapy and self-compassion skills*. New Harbinger Publications.

Knowles, Z., Gilbourne, D., Cropley, B., & Dugdill, L. (2014). *Reflective practice in the sport and exercise sciences: Contemporary issues*. Routledge.

Kolb, D. A. (1984). *Experiential learning: experience as the source of learning and development*. Prentice Hall.

Larsen, C. H., Reinebo, G., & Lundgren, T. (2019). Helping athletes clarify their values and become grounded in their sport venture. In K. Henriksen, J. Hansen, & C. H. Larsen (eds), *Mindfulness and acceptance in sport: How to help athletes perform and thrive under pressure* (pp. 35–46). Routledge. https://doi.org/10.4324/9780429435232.

LeBeau, R. T., Davies, C. D., Culver, N. C., & Craske, M. G. (2013). Homework compliance counts in cognitive-behavioral therapy. *Cognitive Behaviour Therapy*, 42(3), 171–179. https://doi.org/10.1080/16506073.2013.763286.

Lizmore, M. R., Dunn, J. G., Dunn, J. C., & Hill, A. P. (2019). Perfectionism and performance following failure in a competitive golf-putting task. *Psychology of Sport and Exercise*, 45, 101582. https://doi.org/10.1016/j.psychsport.2019.101582.

Mausbach, B. T., Moore, R., Roesch, S., Cardenas, V., & Patterson, T. L. (2010). The relationship between homework compliance and therapy outcomes: An updated meta-analysis. *Cognitive Therapy and Research*, 34, 429–438. https://doi.org/10.1007/s10608-010-9297-z.

Miller, R., Hilsenroth, M. J., & Hewitt, P. L. (2017). Perfectionism and therapeutic alliance: A review of the clinical research. *Research in Psychotherapy: Psychopathology, Process, and Outcome*, 20(1), 19–29. https://doi.org/10.4081/ripppo.2017.264.

Miller, W. R., & Rollnick, S. (2013). *Motivational interviewing: Helping people change (applications of Motivational Interviewing)*. The Guilford Press.

Mosewich, A. D., Crocker, P. R. E., Kowalski, K. C., & DeLongis, A. (2013). Applying self-compassion in sport: An intervention with women athletes. *Journal of Sport and Exercise Psychology*, 35(5), 514–524. https://doi.org/10.1123/jsep.35.5.514.

Olton-Weber, S., Hess, R., & Ritchotte, J. A. (2020). Reducing levels of perfectionism in gifted and talented youth through a mindfulness intervention. *Gifted Child Quarterly*, 64(4), 319–330. https://doi.org/10.1177/0016986220953392.

Ong, C. W., Hancock, A. S., Barrett, T. S., Lee, E. B., Wan, N., Gillam, R. B., … & Twohig, M. P. (2020). A preliminary investigation of the effect of acceptance and commitment therapy on neural activation in clinical perfectionism. *Journal of Contextual Behavioral Science*, 18, 152–161. https://doi.org/10.1016/j.jcbs.2020.09.007.

Ong, C. W., Lee, E. B., Krafft, J., Terry, C. L., Barrett, T. S., Levin, M. E., & Twohig, M. P. (2019). A randomized controlled trial of acceptance and commitment therapy for clinical perfectionism. *Journal of Obsessive-Compulsive and Related Disorders*, 22, 100444. https://doi.org/10.1016/j.jocrd.2019.100444.

Price, D., Wagstaff, C. R., & Thelwell, R. C. (2020). Opportunities and considerations of new media and technology in sport psychology service delivery. *Journal of Sport Psychology in Action*, 13(1), 4–15. https://doi.org/10.1080/21520704.2020.1846648.

Ravizza, K. (1990). Sport psych consultation issues in professional baseball. *The Sport Psychologist*, 4(4), 330–340. https://doi.org/10.1123/tsp.4.4.330.

Robinson, P. (2008). Putting it on the street: Homework in cognitive behavioral therapy. In W. T. O'Donahue, & J. E. Fisher (eds), *General principles and empirically supported techniques of cognitive behavior therapy* (pp. 407–413). Wiley.

Röthlin, P., & Birrer, D. (2020). Mental training in group settings: Intervention protocols of a mindfulness and acceptance-based and a psychological skills training program. *Journal of Sport Psychology in Action*, 11(2), 103–114. https://doi.org/10.1080/21520704.2018.1557771.

Schon D. (1991) *The reflective practitioner*. Jossey-Bass. https://doi.org/10.1002/chp.4750090207.

Segal, Z. V., Williams, J. M. G., & Teasdale, J. D. (2013). *Mindfulness-based cognitive therapy for depression*. Guilford Press.

Shafran, R., Wade, T. D., Egan, S. J., Kothari, R., Allcott-Watson, H., Carlbring, P., … & Andersson, G. (2017). Is the devil in the detail? A randomised controlled trial of guided internet-based CBT for perfectionism. *Behaviour Research and Therapy*, 95, 99–106. https://doi.org/10.1016/j.brat.2017.05.014.

Sinclair, M., & Beadman, M. (2016). *The little ACT workbook*. Hachette.

Skinner, B. F. (1953). Some contributions of an experimental analysis of behavior to psychology as a whole. *American Psychologist*, 8(2), 69–78. https://doi.org/10.1037/h0054118.

Strosahl, K. D., Hayes, S. C., Wilson, K. G., & Gifford, E. V. (2004). An ACT primer. In S. C. Hayes, & K. D. Strosahl (eds), *A practical guide to acceptance and commitment therapy* (pp. 31–58). Springer.

Steele, A. L., & Wade, T. D. (2008). A randomised trial investigating guided self-help to reduce perfectionism and its impact on bulimia nervosa: A pilot study. *Behaviour Research and Therapy*, 46(12), 1316–1323. https://doi.org/10.1016/j.brat.2008.09.006.

Suh, H., Sohn, H., Kim, T., & Lee, D. G. (2019). A review and meta-analysis of perfectionism interventions: Comparing face-to-face with online modalities. *Journal of Counseling Psychology*, 66(4), 473–486. https://doi.org/10.1037/cou0000355.

Twohig, M. P., Levin, M. E., & Ong, C. W. (2021). *ACT in steps: A transdiagnostic manual for learning Acceptance and Commitment Therapy*. Oxford University Press.

Varra, A. A., Drossel, C., & Hayes, S. C. (2009). The use of metaphor to establish acceptance and mindfulness. In F. Didonna (eds), *Clinical handbook of mindfulness* (pp. 111–123). Springer.

Watson, D. R., Hill, A. P., & Madigan, D. J. (2021). Perfectionism and attitudes toward sport psychology support and mental health support in athletes. *Journal of Clinical Sport Psychology*, online ahead of print. https://doi.org/10.1123/jcsp.2020-0052.

White, R. G., Bethell, A., Charnock, L., Leckey, S., & Penpraze, V. (2021). *Acceptance and commitment approaches for athletes' wellbeing and performance*. Springer Nature.

11 Applying Self-compassion to Perfectionism in Sport

Leah J. Ferguson, Kent C. Kowalski,
Danielle L. Cormier and Abimbola O. Eke

In this chapter we introduce and apply self-compassion as a resource to effectively manage challenges that can result from perfectionism in sport. The chapter is organized around an opening case study that presents a difficult sport experience, including elements of perfectionistic concerns such as unrealistic performance expectations, need for approval, and responding to failure with self-criticism. We introduce self-compassion as an understanding, kind, and connected way of relating to oneself during times of difficulty, and present a brief overview of relevant self-compassion literature. We consider links between self-compassion and perfectionism in the general psychology literature and sport domain. We then discuss athletes' development of self-compassion and interventions in sport before returning to the case study to consider how self-compassion might be helpful when supporting athletes with common problems associated with perfectionism. Evidence-based self-compassion exercises are included that demonstrate the utility of self-compassion to navigate perfectionistic concerns in sport.

A Case Study of Perfectionism in Sport

Chleo is a varsity ice hockey player in her third year of eligibility. She was pursued by multiple universities when she was in high school due to her exceptional technical skills, performance record, and athletic potential. Chleo ended up selecting a university that has a strong record of regional- and national-level success across a range of sports, including ice hockey. Chleo's coaches, Ash and Blair, repeatedly told Chleo at the start of her varsity sport career that she should expect immediate success. Chleo lived up to these expectations during her first two years as a student-athlete; she often out-performed veteran athletes on the team, and she even clinched a starting position during last year's regional championship. Chleo recalls being excited and optimistic about that performance, describing herself as the underdog who had nothing to lose. She found that mindset conducive to a solid individual performance at the championship (which her team won). Overall, Chleo's first two years of varsity sport included considerable success, and Chleo became used to receiving praise from Ash and Blair for her consistently improving performance.

DOI: 10.4324/9781003288015-15

Due to strike action at Chleo's university, Chleo's team was unable to compete during the first half of the new hockey season. Training and practices were also limited due to ongoing restrictions to campus facilities (including the rink, fitness centre, and the team's locker room). Initially, Chleo channelled her extra time and energy into her academic coursework. As time progressed, Chleo noticed that her strength and endurance had started to deteriorate during her at-home workouts. She became angry with herself for letting her fitness slide and disappointed with how her body was failing her. She began to crave competition for the opportunity to refine and advance her skills, as well as to demonstrate her abilities to others. Following the strike, varsity sports were able to return as normal. Chleo, however, indicated that her return to sport was anything but "normal".

Chleo didn't seem to be performing at her usual level during practices. Ash and Blair initially assumed this was due to a disrupted season (i.e. very little training and practice, no competition), but Chleo's performance still did not return after a few months. Chleo believed that people expected more from her, and she grew more and more concerned about her inability to perform. After all, multiple universities had tried to recruit her, and she felt she owed it to her coaches to not disappoint them. As a veteran and former stand-out athlete on her team, Chleo believed she needed to carry the team to the top of the standings for another regional – or even national – victory. As the season continued, Chleo was given less playing time than usual. She grew increasingly frustrated with her inability to be in season-ready shape. She worried that she was failing to meet expectations and often reprimanded herself for taking time off from training to focus on academic work during the strike.

Chleo convinced herself that extreme discipline and dedication to training and practice was needed and would allow her to perfect her skills and showcase her full potential, translating into more playing time. Throughout her newly enhanced training and practice regimen, she constantly compared her performance to last season's performance, and she scrutinized the ways she was currently underperforming. She was determined to identify and correct every mistake or error. While Ash and Blair admired Chleo's drive and determination, they reminded her that hockey is a team sport, and that the team's standing and season outcomes don't rest solely on her performance. They often observed Chleo reacting strongly (e.g. verbal self-belittlement) to errors she made during practice, and they wondered if her enhanced training regimen was being used as self-punishment when mistakes were made. Chleo was unwilling to settle for anything less than last season's performance, if not better, and felt she would be letting herself, her teammates, and her coaches down if the team didn't win the regional championship.

Self-Compassion

If you were one of Chleo's good friends, family members, or close teammates, you might notice that she is going through a difficult time and have compassion for her. In other words, you might direct feelings of kindness and care towards her, as well as have the desire to help alleviate her difficult experience in some way. You might even have an appreciation for Chleo's circumstances; after all, we can all relate to going through difficult experiences now and again. Though this type of social support may be helpful for Chleo, you might not always be around or available to support her when she is struggling. Fortunately, just as you might have compassion for Chleo in these circumstances, she can also be *self*-compassionate. Self-compassion involves being open to one's own suffering, generating the desire to heal one's suffering with kindness, and seeing one's circumstances as part of the larger human experience (Neff, 2003a). In short, self-compassion is compassion turned inward.

Kristin Neff (2003a) introduced self-compassion to the general psychology literature two decades ago, which sparked an explosion of research on self-compassion as an adaptive self-attitude. Neff's conceptualization of self-compassion consists of three components that mutually interact to create a self-compassionate frame of mind: *mindfulness* (keeping thoughts and feelings in balance rather than exaggerating or avoiding them), *self-kindness* (being kind and accepting – rather than harshly self-critical – during adversity), and *common humanity* (recognizing that one's experiences are not isolating, but rather we are all connected through imperfection).[1] Extending compassion toward the self is particularly useful during times of difficulty and failure (Neff, 2003a). As the sport domain is replete with the potential for difficult experiences, self-compassion is a relevant tool to help athletes navigate various challenges in sport (see Mosewich, 2020; Mosewich, Ferguson, McHugh, & Kowalski, 2019).

Measures of self-compassion denote the extent to which an individual, such as Chleo, who was introduced in the case study above, is more or less self-compassionate. While there are a few different measures of self-compassion (e.g. the Sussex–Oxford Compassion for the Self Scale; Gu et al., 2020), most self-compassion in sport research has used Neff's (2003b) Self-Compassion Scale or a variation of it (see Röthlin et al., 2019). The Self-Compassion Scale includes 26 items and measures each component (i.e. mindfulness, self-kindness, common humanity) and counter component (i.e. overidentification, self-judgment, isolation) of self-compassion. After responding to scale items, individuals can calculate a total mean score (ranging from 1.00 to 5.00) representing their level of self-compassion. Neff specified that scores between 1.00 and 2.49 are indicative of low self-compassion, those between 2.50 and 3.50 are moderate, and scores between 3.51 and 5.00 are representative of high self-compassion. Neff (2022a) has made her scale, as well as scoring procedures and additional information, available on her website.

In a way, having self-compassion is similar to having an unconditional friend or ever-available ally. In Chleo's experiences as a varsity athlete, regardless of what is happening, who is present, or any other contextual features, she always has the opportunity to be self-compassionate. This, however, might be easier said than done. Individuals who have high expectations of themselves and place an emphasis on performance may fear that self-compassion may limit goal attainment (Gilbert, 2009). Through our research and that of our colleagues, we have found that some athletes express concern that self-compassion might generate a lack of motivation and lead to complacency (e.g. Reis et al., 2022). Being fearful of, or resistant to, extending compassion towards oneself is known as *fear of self-compassion* (Gilbert et al., 2011), and it often manifests as psychological distress and high self-criticism in athletes (Ceccarelli et al., 2019; Walton et al., 2020). Thus, in the same way athletes can be concerned about being self-compassionate, some athletes feel they are reliant on self-criticism, expressing that they need to be self-critical to reach their potential in sport (Ferguson et al., 2014; Mosewich et al., 2014). This is despite a robust body of literature boasting the advantages of self-compassion in sport that challenges concerns of adopting a self-compassionate mindset.

Self-Compassion in Sport

Self-compassion is a resource that helps athletes manage difficult emotions and cognitions, manoeuvre through the evaluative aspects of sport, and excel psychologically. Mosewich et al. (2011) found that women[2] athletes with higher levels of self-compassion experienced lower shame proneness, guilt-free shame proneness, objectified body consciousness, body shame, body surveillance, fear of failure, and fear of negative evaluation. Importantly, these associations endured after controlling for self-esteem.[3] Mosewich et al.'s seminal results illustrated the potential of self-compassion as a resource for women athletes and set a robust foundation for a flourishing area of research focused on self-compassion in sport (see Röthlin et al., 2019). Since then, researchers have found self-compassion to be related to a range of desirable cognitions, emotions, and behaviours in athletes more generally (e.g. authentic pride, positive affect, behavioural equanimity; see Mosewich, 2020).

Self-compassion also plays a role in the stress process of athletes. For instance, Sereda et al. (2021) found that varsity women athletes high in self-compassion can adaptively appraise (e.g. logically assess) and effectively cope (e.g. regulate emotions) with various stressors in sport, including difficult interactions with others (e.g. coaches), injury, and conceding points. As a result of having higher control appraisals, lower threat appraisals, and effective coping (e.g. higher task-focused coping), varsity women athletes with higher self-compassion have higher perceived goal progress, more positive affect, and lower negative affect (Mosewich, Sabiston, Kowalski, Gaudreau, & Crocker, 2019). Women and men athletes with higher self-compassion have been found to have more adaptive reactions (i.e. perseverant, positive, and responsible) and lower maladaptive reactions (i.e. passive, ruminative, and self-critical) to emotionally difficult sport situations (Ferguson et al., 2014, 2015; Reis et al., 2019), suggesting that self-compassionate athletes are equipped to manage challenging events with a determined, optimistic, and accountable mindset. Moreover, adult athletes with higher levels of self-compassion have higher parasympathetic nervous system activity in response to stress, suggesting they are better able to regulate their physiological response to stress activity (Ceccarelli et al., 2019). Thus, evidence suggests that self-compassion promotes desirable psychological and physiological responses to stressors in sport.

Beyond stress and coping, researchers, including our team, have also found self-compassion to be relevant to athletes' psychological well-being. Women athletes with higher self-compassion have higher eudaimonic well-being, which reflects optimal psychological functioning and development, including autonomy, environmental mastery, personal growth, positive relations with others, purpose in life, and self-acceptance (Ferguson et al., 2014). Specific to the sport context, members of our team found that self-compassionate women athletes also had higher proxy indicators of eudaimonic well-being in sport, in particular autonomy (i.e. choice, internal perceived locus of causality, and volition), sense of meaning, subjective vitality, and body appreciation (Ferguson et al., 2015). Wasylkiw and Clairo (2016) found that self-compassion predicted more positive attitudes toward help-seeking (i.e. favourable attitudes toward getting professional help for psychological issues) among intercollegiate men athletes, which we feel is critically important given the ongoing need to support athletes' mental health and consider ways of decreasing perceived barriers to help-seeking for mental health (Poucher et al., 2021). Overall, research findings suggest that self-compassion is an important construct when considering athletes' well-being and their propensity to seek help for mental health concerns.

Given that sport participation inherently places an emphasis on athletes' physical selves (e.g. performance and appearance demands/expectations), the body is another focus of challenging sport-related experiences. However, women athletes with higher levels of self-compassion are more appreciative of their bodies, less critical about their bodies, and have fewer negative feelings towards their bodies, thus protecting against negative body-related experiences (Adam, Kowalski, Duckham, Ferguson, & Mosewich, 2021; Pila et al., 2022). The link between self-compassion and body image suggests that taking a compassionate approach to one's body may be useful for overcoming challenges related to the body in sport. Indeed, members of our team described *body self-compassion* as the extension of kindness and non-judgmental attitudes towards the body despite perceived physical imperfections and limitations (Berry et al., 2010). We further positioned body self-compassion as a coping mechanism for adolescent women athletes' body-related challenges in sport, as it allows them to focus on what the body is capable of doing in sport (i.e. a productive body) while strengthening positive emotions toward the body (Eke et al., 2020). An adaptive focus on the body creates a shift away from *how the body looks* to *what the body can do* in sport.

In addition to stress and coping, psychological well-being, and body-related matters, performance is an essential topic when considering athletes' sport experiences, as it is core to athletic development and progress in sport. Self-compassion has been linked with elite women athletes' mental toughness (Wilson et al., 2019) and varsity women and men athletes' perseverance of effort (Mosewich et al., 2021), suggesting that self-compassionate athletes are better equipped to persist and pursue their sport-related goals when facing setbacks in sport. In support of this view, Killham et al. (2018) found that self-compassion was positively related to women athletes' perceived sport performance, while self-criticism was *not* related to perceived sport performance. This is an important result that counters the reliance on self-criticism that some athletes have indicated is necessary to reach their potential in sport. In addition, Doorley et al. (2022) found that higher self-compassion boosted collegiate women and men athletes' perceived sport performance at a key moment: following poor performances. However, few researchers have examined the relationship between self-compassion and objective assessments of performance in sport, with some evidence indicating no direct immediate impact (e.g. Alipour Ataabadi et al., 2022). This suggests that any relationship with performance may be indirect – via buffering against self-criticism, fear of failure, and fear of negative evaluations, and enhancing sport experiences generally.

Self-Compassion and Perfectionism

Athletes report having higher levels of perfectionism in the sport domain compared to other domains (i.e. school; Dunn et al., 2005), and it is common for athletes to describe themselves as perfectionistic or at least have extremely high standards and goals. However, given the many challenges that can be experienced in sport – such as injuries, performance plateaus, poor performance, and failing to meet personal goals – this domain is rife with instances where perfection cannot be achieved. Thus, as sport psychology researchers and practitioners we need to consider factors that might buffer the less desirable effects of perfectionism in sport. Self-compassion offers reprieve to athletes experiencing demands, setbacks, and failures in sport, generally, and may be especially useful for perfectionistic athletes who have a proclivity for unrealistic expectations, fear of failure, and self-criticism. While there is minimal research focused on self-compassion and perfectionism in the sport domain, there is an abundance of research in the general psychology literature that suggests it will be helpful.

Self-Compassion and Perfectionistic Concerns in the General Psychology Literature

It may not come as a surprise that higher levels of perfectionistic concerns (i.e. concerns, fears, doubts, discrepancies, and negative reactions to imperfections; Gotwals et al., 2012) have generally been found to be related to lower levels of self-compassion (e.g. Linnett & Kibowski, 2019). As self-compassion can help an individual gently acknowledge their own suffering, soften negative thoughts and emotions about oneself, and facilitate the understanding that all human beings make mistakes and are imperfect by nature (Neff, 2003a), it seems reasonable that it will be antithetical to the punitive self-judgements associated with perfectionistic concerns (Stoeber, 2012). Indeed, when validating her first measure of self-compassion, Neff (2003b) found that perfectionistic concerns were negatively related to self-compassion, and that this relationship even remained statistically significant when controlling for self-criticism (more on the role of self-criticism later). The negative relationship between perfectionistic concerns and self-compassion has since been replicated in several studies including among adolescents and adults (Ferrari et al., 2018; Turk et al., 2021), as well as various student groups (e.g. undergraduates, nursing students; Hiçdurmaz & Aydin, 2017; Stoeber et al., 2020).

Researchers have also considered more complex connections between self-compassion and perfectionistic concerns. For instance, self-compassion has been examined as an explanatory or mediating mechanism to understand why or how perfectionistic concerns may be linked with various outcomes. Pereira et al. (2022) analysed self-compassion as a mediating variable between perfectionism (in this case self-critical perfectionism, rigid perfectionism, and narcissistic perfectionism) and burnout among medical and dentistry students. They found that perfectionism positively predicted burnout through lower self-compassion, suggesting that self-compassion may help prevent burnout in perfectionistic students. Barnett and Sharp (2016) also examined the mediating role of self-compassion, with their work focused on the link between perfectionistic concerns and body image satisfaction among college females. In a series of two studies, they found support for the mediating role of self-compassion, such that the negative relationship between perfectionism and body image satisfaction was explained by lower self-compassion. The results from these studies support the development of self-compassion-based programs (e.g. interventions) to reduce undesirable outcomes associated with perfectionistic concerns.

Self-compassion has also been considered as a protective factor against the effects of perfectionistic concerns. As an example, Abdollahi et al. (2020) examined the moderating role of self-compassion in the relationship between perfectionism and depression among a sample of inpatients with clinical diagnoses of depression. They found self-compassion moderated the relationship between perfectionistic concerns (labelled evaluative concerns perfectionism in their study) and depression, such that there was a statistically significant relationship between perfectionistic concerns and depression among inpatients with low self-compassion, but the relationship was not statistically significant for those with high self-compassion. In one impressive longitudinal study, Tobin and Dunkley (2021) found that adults with high perfectionistic concerns (labelled self-critical perfectionism in their study) and low self-compassion had greater distress and anxious arousal symptoms two years later, highlighting the importance of fostering self-compassion to reduce anxiety and depressive symptoms in individuals with higher perfectionistic concerns. Self-compassion can therefore be considered as a *buffer* against negative emotions, thoughts, and mental health symptoms that may be heightened due to perfectionistic concerns.

Self-Compassion and Perfectionistic Strivings in the General Psychology Literature

The relationship between perfectionistic strivings (i.e. self-oriented striving for perfection and setting of very high personal standards; Gotwals et al., 2012) and self-compassion appears to be both less investigated and more complex than that between perfectionistic concerns and self-compassion. Neff (2003b) initially hypothesized that self-compassionate individuals would not have lower levels of perfectionistic strivings, and that the two constructs would be unrelated. Indeed, she found that perfectionistic strivings was not statistically significantly related to self-compassion. Others have proposed that perfectionistic strivings should be positively related to self-compassion. Abdollahi and colleagues (2020), for example, posited that people higher in perfectionistic strivings ("personal standard perfectionists") should have a higher degree of flexibility in accepting their mistakes, report positive affect, and have higher levels of mindfulness and self-kindness (two of the components of self-compassion). They found a positive relationship between perfectionistic strivings and self-compassion. This positioning reflects Neff's (2021) most recent conceptualization of self-compassion, where self-compassionate individuals not only provide themselves with tenderness while experiencing setbacks, but with the fierceness needed to take action to improve one's circumstances. At the same time, Neff (2021) explained that "too much" fierceness without tenderness can slide into problematic perfectionism.

Reflecting contradictory findings in the literature, current research on self-compassion and perfectionistic strivings is ambivalent. While self-compassion has been shown to be positively related to perfectionistic strivings in some studies (e.g. among undergraduate students; Wei et al., 2021), there is also evidence of negative relationships in others (e.g. among nursing students; Hiçdurmaz & Aydin, 2017). Moreover, the subcomponents of self-compassion appear to have weaker (or statistically non-significant) relationships with perfectionistic strivings among adults in comparison to their relationships with perfectionistic concerns (Linnett & Kibowski, 2019; Tobin & Dunkley, 2021). We hypothesize that the stronger relationship between self-compassion and perfectionistic concerns might be attributed to self-compassion's initial conceptualization (and operationalization) as a "desire to alleviate one's suffering and to heal oneself with kindness" (Neff, 2003a, p. 87), as this may be inherently connected to the less desirable aspects of perfectionism. Future research focused on fierce self-compassion may find positive relationships between perfectionistic strivings and this more activating form of self-compassion, as both constructs are tied to goal achievement (Neff, 2021; Stoeber, 2012).

Like with perfectionistic concerns, self-compassion has been examined as a mediating mechanism for perfectionistic strivings. For example, Wei et al. (2021) explored the relationships between perfectionistic strivings, self-compassion, and depression (or common characteristics of depression) among undergraduate students. Perfectionistic strivings were found to have both a negative direct and negative indirect relationship with depression. That is, students with higher levels of perfectionistic strivings had lower levels of depression partly because they also reported higher self-compassion. In another study with undergraduate students, Stoeber et al. (2020) found that self-compassion (and compassion for others) fully mediated the positive relationship between perfectionistic strivings and subjective well-being. Therefore, if there is a positive relationship between perfectionistic strivings and self-compassion, this relationship may explain why perfectionistic strivings is sometimes related to aspects of well-being.

Self-Compassion and Perfectionism in Sport

Against this backdrop, a handful of studies have examined self-compassion and perfectionism in sport. We are familiar with three studies, in particular, that examined the relationship between athletes' self-compassion and concern over mistakes (a dimension of perfectionistic concerns). Mosewich et al. (2013) conducted an intervention study with self-critical varsity women athletes, which we discuss in the next section. Next, Reis et al. (2019) examined self-compassion, masculinity, and psychological well-being among men athletes, and found self-compassion to be negatively related to concern over mistakes. More recently, Alipour Ataabadi et al. (2022) examined how male and female team sport athletes respond to biomechanical feedback, and how self-compassion and concern over mistakes are associated with those responses. Again, they found self-compassion to be negatively related to concern over mistakes before engaging in a set of sprint trials. We interpret the results of these studies as evidence that athletes with higher self-compassion will tend to react less negatively to mistakes, are less likely to interpret mistakes as failures, and are less likely to believe they will lose the respect of others following failure.

In support of our thinking, in addition to the above studies, Lizmore et al. (2017) examined if varsity women and men team sport athletes' perfectionism was related to the way they tended to response to poor performances. They expected perfectionistic strivings to be positively related to self-compassion, as being kind to oneself in moments of suffering doesn't include abating one's personal standards, and they expected perfectionistic concerns to be negatively related to self-compassion. In partial support of their expectations, Lizmore et al. found no relationship between perfectionistic strivings and self-compassion but a negative relationship between perfectionistic concerns and self-compassion. However, they did find a positive relationship between perfectionistic strivings and self-compassion after controlling for perfectionistic concerns. This aligns with reviews demonstrating that perfectionistic strivings are more adaptive when perfectionistic concerns are controlled (e.g. Gotwals et al., 2012; Hill et al., 2018). It also suggests that the overlap between perfectionistic strivings and perfectionistic concerns may be important to consider when seeking to understand the relationship between perfectionistic strivings and self-compassion.

Worthy of note in this regard is that both perfectionistic strivings and perfectionistic concerns include self-evaluative components, including self-criticism (Hill, 2014). Self-criticism is an often-overlooked construct in sport psychology research (Walton et al., 2020) and is especially important as an opposing force to self-compassion. Among the research that has been done so far, for example, self-criticism has been found to interfere with goal pursuit (Powers et al., 2011) and has been identified as a robust predictor of perfectionism outside of sport (Dunkley et al., 2006; Gilbert et al., 2006). Other researchers have found positive relationships between self-criticism and perfectionism in athletes, including Alipour Ataabadi et al. (2022), whom we introduced earlier. Hill (2014) also found self-criticism to be positively related to perfectionistic strivings in male and female individual and team sport athletes, as did Hill et al. (2010) among male junior cricket players. In this way, mixed evidence of the relationship between perfectionistic strivings and self-compassion can be expected. In addition, we can understand the basis of some of the difficulties associated with perfectionism to be both the absence of self-compassion and the presence of self-criticism.

We are not suggesting that all self-evaluation is maladaptive and/or harmful. Constructive self-criticism can be useful to make corrections or improvements to help avoid making future performance mistakes. However, another harsher form of self-criticism includes persecution and punishment (Castilho et al., 2017). Chleo's situation, in the opening case of our chapter, highlights a form of self-criticism that goes beyond constructive correction for improvement. As Neff (2021) explains, those who engage in harsh self-criticism tear themselves down when they fail, which can undermine one's ability to achieve in a performance domain. In contrast, self-compassionate individuals do not berate themselves when they fail, but rather are accepting of their mistakes, setbacks, and flaws (Neff, 2021). Indeed, self-compassion is related to *lower* fear of failure and fear of negative evaluation (Mosewich et al., 2011), which is particularly relevant to our focus in this chapter. Researchers have also found that self-compassion can reduce athletes' self-criticism and concern over mistakes (Mosewich et al., 2013). Athletes who are self-compassionate are likely to work hard and challenge themselves because they know that even if they fail, they won't harshly criticize themselves or overly worry about how others are perceiving them (Adam, Eke, & Ferguson, 2021). Rather, they know they will still be there for themselves regardless of degree of success or failure. As such, enhancing athletes' self-compassion will help athletes navigate the challenges that can be associated with perfectionism.

Self-Compassion Development and Interventions in Sport

Researchers have identified both intrapersonal and interpersonal factors as playing critical roles in athletes' self-compassion development. Regarding intrapersonal factors, developing self-compassion is a highly individual process that requires substantial personal processing (Ferguson et al, 2022; Frentz et al., 2019; Ingstrup et al., 2017). Self-awareness is key, whereby self-reflection and an openness to learn from one's experiences fosters a journey towards self-acceptance. Being able to reflect on negative experiences without excessive self-criticism permits more self-awareness and self-compassion. Thus, overcoming self-criticism is necessary for self-compassion development.

Regarding interpersonal factors, athletes' self-compassion development is influenced by a variety of support persons inside and outside of sport, including coaches, parents, peers, siblings, sport psychologists, and teammates (Crozier et al., 2019; Ferguson et al., 2022; Frentz et al., 2019; Ingstrup et al., 2017; Jeon et al., 2016). These individuals may (a) directly or indirectly "teach" self-compassion (e.g. athletes observe these individuals extending compassion towards themselves), (b) be available for athletes to seek assistance with their difficult experiences (rather than isolating themselves); and (c) help put difficult sport experiences into perspective. For example, coaches can help interpret performance errors and encourage focusing on the present or future rather than dwelling on past mistakes or failures. These individuals, however, can also deter athletes' self-compassion development, as might be the case in challenging coach-athlete relationships or when negativity from others impedes the use of self-compassion. To illustrate, a teammate who unrelentingly scrutinizes a mistake during competition or a coach who constantly compares athletes to unrealistic performance standards may deter athletes from being self-compassionate. The individuals that comprise the sport environment there-fore have the opportunity (and power) to generate contexts that nurture (or hinder) self-compassion.

With a growing understanding of how self-compassion might be fostered, researchers have developed interventions to enhance athletes' self-compassion and corresponding desirable outcomes in sport. Mosewich et al. (2013) devel-oped the first sport-specific self-compassion intervention for varsity women athletes who identified as being self-critical. The intervention included a psy-choeducation session and writing components completed over a 7-day period. The psychoeducation session overviewed the basic tenets of stress and coping in sport, introduced self-compassion and relevant research, and explained why self-compassion might be effective for managing sport demands. The psychoe-ducation session also included an example of an applied writing exercise that required identifying and describing a difficult sport experience and responding to prompts designed to promote thinking about the event in a self-compassionate way (we present the specific writing prompts later in this chapter). Participants then received a booklet of modules containing writing exercises to be completed over the next seven days. Modules included reflecting on and processing previous negative sport experiences and responding with common humanity, self-kindness, and mindfulness.

Mosewich et al.'s (2013) intervention, which was the first self-compassion intervention to target perfectionism in sport using a robust randomized control design, was effective. Participants in the intervention group reported higher self-compassion and lower self-criticism, rumination, and excessive concerns over mistakes (a dimension of perfectionistic concerns) than an attention control group one week after the intervention. Moreover, these results were maintained one-month post-intervention. The results are particularly relevant to our previous dis-cussion around self-compassion, perfectionism, and self-criticism, demonstrating that providing athletes with an opportunity to learn, apply, and practice the prin-ciples of self-compassion in sport can help them manage negative events in sport, including challenges linked with perfectionism.

Other studies assessing the effectiveness of compassion-based interventions (though not including perfectionism) provide a compelling case for their use in sport. Voelker et al. (2019), for example, examined Bodies in Motion, which is an intervention based on cognitive dissonance and mindful self-compassion that integrates positive components of social media to improve female athletes' body image. The program, comprising a 35-minute introductory session and four 75-minute sessions, included interactive small group sessions to build supportive relationships among participants. Structured activities included mindful breathing and walking, self-compassion affirmations, self-compassion imagery, and body celebration tasks. Participants were also encouraged to use the program's social media platform to provide support and positive feedback to each other. The program resulted in decreased thin-ideal internalization and increased self-compassion and mindfulness among female collegiate athletes in comparison to a control group.

Researchers have also combined self-compassion with mindfulness-based interventions, which have become a mainstream approach for enhancing athletes' performance and sport experiences. For example, Cote at al. (2019) integrated self-compassion into their mindfulness meditation training for sport (MMTS) 2.0 intervention, which is designed to increase athletes' concentration, adaptability in performance, and tolerance of negative internal states. The MMTS 2.0 consisted of six modules, each lasting one hour (or two 30-minute segments) and including psychoeducation, guided practice, and group discussion. Athletes were also encouraged to listen to daily sport-specific meditations. The modules included self-compassion strategies, such as compassionate thinking to help athletes cope with sport distress by modifying their relationship with negative internal states rather than trying to stop the distress. In exploring the experiences of collegiate tennis players in the intervention, Cote et al. identified that self-compassion helped the athletes manage their sport distress by providing them with the courage to respond to, and not avoid, difficult sport situations.

The number of interventions in sport that integrate self-compassion is accelerating (e.g. Carraça et al., 2018; Röthlin & Leiggener, 2021; Shortway et al., 2018). Given the increasing interest in enhancing athletes' self-compassion, it is important to identify ways to optimally integrate self-compassion in sport. Thoughtful consideration is needed in terms of intervention design (e.g. length), delivery (e.g. in-person, remote, on-demand), and content modality (Mosewich, Ferguson, McHugh, & Kowalski, 2019). Though writing activities have been a primary intervention practice for athletes, there are diverse self-compassion practices to consider, as presented in Table 11.1. Many evidence-based self-compassion practices are informed by Neff's research and available on her website or in Neff and Germer's (2018) workbook.

Consideration of *who* is involved in a self-compassion intervention (e.g. coaches, teammates, parents, peers) is another important factor. Given the role that others can play in athletes' self-compassion development, we believe there is a need to consider interventions for sport support persons. For example, Hägglund et al. (2021) found that an SMS-delivered mindful self-reflection intervention for high performance coaches resulted in behaviours aligned with

Table 11.1 Examples of self-compassion exercises.

Exercise	Brief Description
Affectionate breathing	Training the mind to be focused and calm through breath meditation that incorporates affection
Compassionate listening	Listening in an embodied way (i.e. with your whole body) to maintain an emotional connection
Compassionate movement	Moving compassionately, from the inside out, through anchoring your awareness to your feet, opening your awareness to your whole body, responding compassionately with movement to any places of discomfort, and coming to stillness
Cues	Creating phrases or cue words that remind you to do three things: (1) acknowledge the difficult moment; (2) extend kindness toward yourself; and (3) recognize that everyone struggles at times
Journaling	Keeping a journal to process difficult events through a self-compassion lens to help make mindfulness, self-kindness, and common humanity part of daily life
Self-compassion break	Thinking about a difficult situation and bringing to mind the three components of self-compassion
Sense and savour walk	Taking a 15-minute walk to notice and savour any positive internal experiences using all your senses
Supportive touch	Activating your parasympathetic nervous system by comforting and supporting yourself through supportive touch (e.g. a gentle hand squeeze) to feel calm, cared for, and safe

self-compassion, including learning from mistakes, engaging in perspective taking, developing gratitude, and ruminating less. These are important findings given that coaches' self-compassion appears to be relatively stable over time without intervention (Ackeret et al., 2022). Increasing coaches' self-compassion might position them to support themselves *and* the athletes they work with. Overall, identifying optimal ways to enhance athletes' self-compassion will provide a readily available resource for managing difficult sport experiences.

Applying Self-Compassion to Chleo's Case

When athletes are experiencing setbacks in sport, harsh self-criticism, and unrealistic performance expectations, such as in the opening case of this chapter, self-compassion may be a useful resource. But how might we apply self-compassion to Chleo's case? The complexity of Chleo's experiences highlights the importance and value of using an integrated approach to help athletes effectively manage challenges associated with perfectionism. In other words, although the purpose of this chapter is to demonstrate how self-compassion might be helpful as a strategy to deal with things like high expectations and harsh self-criticism stemming from perfectionism, it seems essential we recognize that no single self-compassion exercise, or even self-compassion exercises alone, likely offers the most effective approach. As such, as we work through the case, we try to show how self-compassion can be *part of* an approach to helping athletes navigate through perfectionism. And, of course, some strategies might work more effectively than others across different athletes, contexts, and time; hence, our goal is not to offer a cookbook solution, but to offer ideas and options within a self-compassion framework that might be considered when working with athletes experiencing challenges associated with perfectionism.

One option that might be available is to work with Chleo in the role of mental performance consultant. Based on the description of the case, we identify three key areas upon which to focus when working with Chleo. First, it is clear that not being able to return to a previous performance level is creating some negative emotions for Chleo, predominantly frustration and anxiety. Second, her harsh self-critical response to not achieving her performance standard, including belittling self-talk, is posing another layer of emotional challenge. Third, Chleo is trying to live up to an exceptionally high standard that she has set for herself and feels others are expecting of her. We support a focus on self-compassion as part of an effective strategy to significantly improve Chleo's sport experience and (hopefully) put her on a path to giving her the best chance possible to achieve her sporting goals.

One strength of taking a self-compassion approach is that doing so doesn't require a lowering of standards. In other words, Chleo can retain her performance goals, even if they seem a bit beyond reach at present. What self-compassion offers is an opportunity to work towards those goals in a way that retains (and likely enhances) her motivation and prioritizes a growth mindset versus a path filled with harsh self-criticism, frustration, anxiety, and fear of failure. An effective starting point might be to engage in a goal setting activity with Chleo. Our intent of the goal setting exercise wouldn't be to steer Chleo away from her "dream" goals, as they are likely core to her sport experience. Rather, our focus would be to help her identify (a) other goals that are also important and meaningful as part of her sporting journey, and (b) specific process goals (and steps to achieve those goals) that work to link her current performance level with her desired one. As such, we are not necessarily looking to change her performance standards, but rather focus on how she experiences those performance standards.

As part of the goal setting exercise, in addition to her current goals of returning to a starting position and winning a championship, Chleo might set goals such as (a) learning to deal with her own and others' expectations in a healthy way, (b) focusing on ways to learn and grow when she faces inevitable setbacks and failures, (c) developing more effective communication strategies with her coaches, (d) working to be more supportive of her teammates' success (i.e. enhance leadership skills), (e) ensuring self-health and self-care, (f) valuing the balance between sport and academics (and the unique opportunity being a varsity athlete offers), and perhaps most importantly, (g) ensuring she enjoys her sporting journey regardless of the path it takes. These are just a few examples, but within each there are a considerable number of strategies that could be used by Chleo to enhance the richness of her sporting experience, such that if she doesn't achieve her ultimate performance goals the attempted striving towards those goals is still perceived as a success.

Once the broader goals have been identified in collaboration with Chleo, the next focus of the goal setting exercise would be to identify more specific, manageable process goals. For example, to help Chleo achieve her performance goals, she might need to work with her coaches, Ash and Blair, to find ways to develop a more "Chleo-specific" strength training, fitness, and nutrition program to help her return to previous strength and endurance levels, because what worked for her before might no longer be sufficient. To achieve her communication goals, Chleo might set weekly meetings with Ash and Blair to discuss her progress and to identify ongoing supports that are needed. To achieve her enjoyment goals, she might start a gratitude journal and begin to identify small successes at practice or training sessions. To help achieve her self-health and self-care goals, she might commit to ensuring adequate sleep and spending time with friends and family (amidst a busy schedule). The intent of the goal setting exercise is to ensure that Chleo has multiple, meaningful goals to strive to achieve and to provide a roadmap to guide her along the way. Self-compassion can be an invaluable resource for an athlete on that journey.

As a first step to introducing Chleo to self-compassion, it would be important to have an "education" phase, as the term self-compassion likely isn't all that familiar to her. Furthermore, the term might be faced with resistance over fears that it could lead to complacency. Given the details of the case and the challenges perfectionism is causing Chleo, we would want to discuss the pitfalls of retaining harsh self-criticism as an approach when facing failure; as Neff describes in her work, although harsh self-criticism might offer some short-term motivation, it ultimately leads to anxiety, fear of failure, and decreased confidence. We would then share an overview of research supporting self-compassion as not only important to mental health, especially when dealing with emotional challenges associated with perfectionism, but that by being self-compassionate, Chleo can keep just as high of standards with an accompanying motivation to persist in the face of adversity. We would also discuss research showing links between self-compassion, self-criticism, and performance, which should help address concerns that being self-compassionate will undermine her performance goals. It would also be important to have these conversations with Chleo's coaches, if possible, because, ideally, both Ash and Blair would gain self-compassion skills for their own toolbox and having them model self-compassion would likely further demonstrate their support of such an approach for Chleo (as demonstrated by Miller and Kelly, 2020, self-compassion can be contagious).

Once there was an initial level of buy-in or interest in the potential value of self-compassion, it would be important to provide Chleo with some applied experiences of self-compassion. In Chleo's case, we would likely start with (a) self-compassionate writing, and/or (b) the Self-Compassion Break. The self-compassionate writing could be based on the three prompts used by Mosewich et al. (2013), representing each component of self-compassion. Specifically, Chleo would be asked to (a) "List ways in which other people experience similar events" (i.e. common humanity), (b) "Write a paragraph expressing understanding, kindness, and concern to yourself … as if you are communicating to a close friend in the same situation" (i.e. self-kindness), and (c) "Describe the event in an objective and unemotional manner" (i.e. mindfulness). We think that this type of writing exercise would be extremely valuable for Chleo to help her begin to reframe her emotionally challenging experiences related to perfectionism in a more self-compassionate way.

Because the self-compassion writing prompts require an individualized response, it's hard to predict what Chleo might include in her responses, and because it is new to her (and challenges her traditional ways of thinking) she might struggle to come up with responses. If so, we could provide examples to help guide her towards thinking more self-compassionately. For example, to help her find a response to the common humanity writing prompt we might ask her if she thought other athletes with very high standards face setbacks in chasing those standards (which we are confident she would say "yes" to). As just one example for Chleo, we could discuss Hayley Wickenheiser, one of the world's top hockey players, who faced missing a world hockey championship due to a foot injury. We could share Hayley's lesson-filled response to her setback, "It's frustrating to miss worlds, but at the same time, I need to do this right and come back strong for next season and that's my goal" (Denette, 2015, para. 5). Helping Chleo recognize that she isn't alone in her experiences should help combat some of the feelings of isolation she might be experiencing.

We typically find the second writing prompt (i.e. self-kindness) particularly helpful for athletes to connect with self-compassion, as the conversations athletes have with themselves are often quite different than what they would say to teammates experiencing similar setbacks. Particularly because some of the harsh criticism and belittling self-talk that Chleo is unleashing upon herself, thinking of how she would support a teammate, and then turning that same compassion inward, should help her (a) develop awareness of how she is currently treating herself, and (b) find an alternative, more self-compassionate way to support herself during an emotionally difficult time. We would want Chleo to acknowledge that what she is experiencing is indeed difficult (e.g. "What you are experiencing must be very hard"), and that she can be there to support herself (e.g. "What can I do to help?"). Especially if combined with positive, supportive statements (e.g. "I know you can get through this"), Chleo might begin to experience some of the personal care and support that self-compassion offers to help her soothe difficult emotions and find the motivation to move forward with productive action.

The third prompt, focused on mindfulness, is designed to allow Chleo a bit more clarity as to what she is experiencing in the present moment, so that she can experience her emotions just as they are, rather than denying those negative emotions (and hence increasing their power). Particularly for someone with a perfectionistic approach to sport, learning skills to live in the moment can be invaluable to help performance in critical moments (e.g. rather than being worried about missing a shot or making a mistake). It would be important for Chleo to acknowledge and describe her frustration, anxiety, and fear of failure about returning to previous performance levels. Some ways to introduce athletes to mindfulness can include (a) focused breathing, (b) sound or body sensation meditations, and (c) mindfulness-based yoga. Learning mindfulness skills can also help shift focus when attention is directed towards perceived expectations of others, in that it can bring an athlete back to a moment-by-moment awareness of the present.

Introducing Chleo to the Self-Compassion Break can also be an effective way for her to experience self-compassion through a guided meditation. A benefit of this exercise is that it takes only 5 minutes to complete and is freely available for download on Neff's website (Neff, 2022a). When doing the Self-Compassion Break, Chleo would be asked to reflect on something that is causing her emotional suffering, perhaps something like her worry about failing to live up to others' expectations or how she is using increased training as self-punishment. She would then think about important details of the situation (e.g. the ways she feels she has been underperforming) and be guided through a series of phrases reflecting the three components of self-compassion. The first phrase is "This is a moment of suffering" or "This is really hard right now", to acknowledge that it is an emotionally difficult experience. The second phrase is "Suffering is a part of life" or "Many people are going through similar situations", to recognize that difficult emotional experiences are part of everyone's journey through life. The third phrase is "May I be kind to myself in this moment" or "I'm here for you. It's going to be okay", during which a soothing touch (e.g. hands over the heart) is encouraged. It concludes with a recognition and acceptance of current body sensations. The Self-Compassion Break might be particularly helpful for Chleo if she struggles with the writing exercise to think of phrases on her own that represent each component of self-compassion.

If Chleo was open to it, we would then develop a broader plan for learning self-compassion, largely facilitated by the variety of self-compassion guided meditations that Kristin Neff has made freely available and encouraging further self-compassionate writing in a journal. Guided meditations that we think might be particularly promising for Chleo appear in Table 11.2. There are

Table 11.2 Examples of guided meditation self-compassion exercises.

Guided Meditation	Brief Description
Compassionate body scan	24-minute meditation emphasizing awareness of and connection to the body in a kind and compassionate way
Loving-kindness meditation	20-minute meditation intended to generate feelings of goodwill and kindness for others and oneself
Self-compassion/loving-kind-ness meditation	20-minute variation of the loving-kindness meditation tailored specifically to cultivate self-compassion
Soften, sooth, allow	15-minute meditation that entails working with difficult emotions in the moment and emphasizing awareness of and connection to the body

Note. These meditations are available as guided audio meditations from Neff (2022b).

other guided meditations available as well, all of which could be considered. With a dedicated self-compassion practice, we are confident that Chleo would learn to approach her sport in a more self-compassionate (and less self-critical) way, thereby reducing the emotional suffering of her sport experience, particularly that associated with her perfectionistic concerns.

Concluding Comments

Athletes can experience a range of difficult experiences in sport. In this chapter we introduced self-compassion, a resource for athletes to help manage difficult sport experiences by extending kind and connected understanding towards the self. We summarized research on self-compassion and perfectionism from general psychology and sport psychology bodies of literature. Based on the literature, it is evident that self-compassion is useful for athletes navigating challenges associated with perfectionism, such as unrealistic expectations from others, personally demanding standards, concern over mistakes, and continual self-belittlement. We discussed how athletes can develop self-compassion and overviewed self-compassion interventions in sport. Working through a case study, we applied evidence-based self-compassion exercises that may be useful when working with athletes who are managing challenges linked with perfectionism.

Notes

1 Neff (2021) continues to advance her conceptualization of self-compassion and has positioned *fierce self-compassion* as a more action-oriented form of self-compassion that allows us to take appropriate action to alleviate suffering (Neff & Germer, 2018). In contrast to the more soothing or tender self-compassion (as described here), fierce self-compassion involves protecting, providing for, and motivating ourselves. Researchers have yet to empirically examine fierce self-compassion, and the discussion of self-compassion in this chapter is focused primarily on the original conceptualization.

2 Throughout this chapter we intentionally apply language that reflects gender identification (e.g. women, men), and where needed honour the language used by original authors (i.e. females, males) when integrating past research.

3 This demonstrates the usefulness of self-compassion beyond self-esteem, which has limitations to the development of a healthy self. Self-esteem is often linked with narcissism and social comparisons, and it is contingent on positive outcomes. Self-compassion, in comparison, does not require social comparisons or the adoption of an unrealistic view of oneself, and it allows individuals to feel positively about themselves without self-judgment and evaluation (Neff, 2003a, 2003b). Thus, self-compassion appears to offer unique advantages beyond that of self-esteem.

References

Abdollahi, A., Allen, K. A., & Taheri, A. (2020). Moderating the role of self-compassion in the relationship between perfectionism and depression. *Journal of Rational-Emotive & Cognitive-Behavior Therapy*, 38(4), 459–471. https://doi.org/10.1007/s10942-020-00346-3.

Ackeret, N., Röthlin, P., Allemand, M., Krieger, T., Berger, T., Znoj, H., Kenttä, G., Birrer, D., & Horvath, S. (2022). Six-month stability of individual differences in sports coaches' burnout, self-compassion and social support. *Psychology of Sport & Exercise*, 61, article 102207. https://doi.org/10.1016/j.psychsport.2022.102207.

Adam, M. E. K., Eke, A. O., & Ferguson, L. J. (2021). "Know that you're not just settling": Exploring women athletes' self-compassion, sport performance perceptions, and well-being around important competitive events. *Journal of Sport and Exercise Psychology*, 43(3), 268–278. https://doi.org/10.1123/jsep.2020-0196.

Adam, M. E. K., Kowalski, K. C., Duckham, R. L., Ferguson, L. J., & Mosewich, A. D. (2021). Self-compassion plays a role in Canadian women athletes' body appreciation and intuitive eating: A mixed methods approach. *International Journal of Sport Psychology*, 52(4), 287–309. https://doi.org/10.7352/IJSP.2021.52.287.

Alipour Ataabadi, Y., Cormier, D. L., Kowalski, K. C., Oates, A. R., Ferguson, L. J., & Lanovaz, J. L. (2022). The associations among self-compassion, self-esteem, self-criticism, and concern over mistakes in response to biomechanical feedback in athletes. *Frontiers in Sports and Active Living*, 4, article 868576. https://doi.org/10.3389/fspor.2022.868576.

Barnett, M. D., & Sharp, K. J. (2016). Maladaptive perfectionism, body image satisfaction, and disordered eating behaviors among U.S. college women: The mediating role of self-compassion. *Personality and Individual Differences*, 99, 225–234. https://doi.org/10.1016/j.paid.2016.05.004.

Berry, K. A., Kowalski, K. C., Ferguson, L. J., & McHugh, T.-L. F. (2010). An empirical phenomenology of young adult women exercisers' body self-compassion. *Qualitative Research in Sport and Exercise*, 2(3), 293–312. https://doi.org/10.1080/19398441.2010.517035.

Carraça, B., Serpa, S., Rosado, A., & Palmi, J. (2018). The Mindfulness-Based Soccer Program (MBSoccerP): Effects on elite athletes. *Cuadernos de Psicología del Deporte*, 18, 62–85.

Castilho, P., Pinto-Gouveia, J., & Duarte, J. (2017). Two forms of self-criticism mediate differently the shame-psychopathological symptoms link. *Psychology and Psychotherapy*, 90(1), 44–54. https://doi.org/10.1111/papt.12094.

Ceccarelli, L. A., Giuliano, R. J., Glazebrook, C. M., & Strachan, S. M. (2019). Self-compassion and psycho-physiological recovery from recalled sport failure. *Frontiers in Psychology*, 10, article 1564. https://doi.org/10.3389/fpsyg.2019.01564.

Cote, T., Baltzell, A., & Diehl, R. (2019). A qualitative exploration of division I tennis players completing the Mindfulness Meditation Training for Sport 2.0 program. *The Sport Psychologist*, 33(3), 203–212. https://doi.org/10.1123/tsp.2017-0155.

Crozier, A. J., Mosewich, A. D., & Ferguson, L. J. (2019). The company we keep: Exploring the relationship between perceived teammate self-compassion and athlete self-compassion. *Psychology of Sport and Exercise*, 40, 152–155. https://doi.org/10.1016/j.psychsport.2018.10.005.

Denette, N. (2015). Hayley Wickenheiser to miss world championship with foot injury. *The Canadian Press*, 15 February. Retrieved from www.theglobeandmail.com/sports/hockey/hayley-wickenheiser-to-miss-world-championship-with-foot-injury/article23028347/.

Doorley, J. D., Kashdan, T. B., Weppner, C. H., & Glass, C. R. (2022). The effects of self-compassion on daily emotion regulation and performance rebound among college athletes: Comparisons with confidence, grit, and hope. *Psychology of Sport and Exercise*, 58, article 102081. https://doi.org/10.1016/j.psychsport.2021.102081.

Dunkley, D. M., Zuroff, D. C., & Blankstein, K. R. (2006). Specific perfectionism components versus self-criticism in predicting maladjustment. *Personality and Individual Differences*, 40(4), 665–676. https://doi.org/10.1016/j.paid.2005.08.008.

Dunn, J. G. H., Gotwals, J. K., & Causgrove Dunn, J. (2005). An examination of the domain specificity of perfectionism among intercollegiate student-athletes. *Personality and Individual Differences*, 38(6), 1439–1448. https://doi.org/10.1016/j.paid.2004.09.009.

Eke, A. O., Adam, M. E. K., Kowalski, K. C., & Ferguson, L. J. (2020). Narratives of adolescent women athletes' body self-compassion, performance and emotional well-being. *Qualitative Research in Sport, Exercise and Health*, 12(2), 175–191. https://doi.org/10.1080/2159676X.2019.1628805.

Ferguson, L. J., Kowalski, K. C., Mack, D. E., & Sabiston, C. M. (2014). Exploring self-compassion and eudaimonic well-being in young women athletes. *Journal of Sport & Exercise Psychology*, 36(2), 203–216. https://doi.org/10.1123/jsep.2013-0096.

Ferguson, L. J., Kowalski, K. C., Mack, D. E., & Sabiston, C. M. (2015). Self-compassion and eudaimonic well-being during emotionally difficult times in sport. *Journal of Happiness Studies*, 16(5), 1263–1280. https://doi.org/10.1007/s10902-014-9558-8.

Ferguson, L. J., Saini, S., & Adam, M. E. K. (2022). Safe space or high stakes environments: Comparing self-compassion in differing sport contexts in Canada. *International Journal of Sport Psychology*, 53(1), 1–24. https://doi.org/10.7352/IJSP.2022.53.001.

Ferrari, M., Yap, K., Scott, N., Einstein, D. A., & Ciarrochi, J. (2018). Self-compassion moderates the perfectionism and depression link in both adolescence and adulthood. *PLOS ONE*, 13(2), article e0192022. https://doi.org/10.1371/journal.pone.0192022.

Frentz, D. M., McHugh, T.-L. F., & Mosewich, A. D. (2019). Athletes' experiences of shifting from self-critical to self-compassionate approaches within high-performance sport. *Journal of Applied Sport Psychology*, 32(6), 565–584. https://doi.org/10.1080/10413200.2019.1608332.

Gilbert, P. (2009). *The compassionate mind: A new approach to life's challenges*. New Harbinger.

Gilbert, P., Durrant, R., & McEwan, K. (2006). Investigating relationships between perfectionism, forms and functions of self-criticism, and sensitivity to put-down. *Personality and Individual Differences*, 41(7), 1299–1308. https://doi.org/10.1016/j.paid.2006.05.004.

Gilbert, P., McEwan, K., Matos, M., & Rivis, A. (2011). Fears of compassion: Development of three self-report measures. *Psychology and Psychotherapy*, 84(3), 239–255. https://doi.org/10.1348/147608310X526511.

Gotwals, J. K., Stoeber, J., Dunn, J. G. H., & Stoll, O. (2012). Are perfectionistic strivings in sport adaptive? A systematic review of confirmatory, contradictory, and mixed evidence. *Canadian Psychology*, 53(4), 263–279. https://doi.org/10.1037/a0030288.

Gu, J., Baer, R., Cavanagh, K., Kuyken, W., & Strauss, C. (2020). Development and psychometric properties of the Sussex-Oxford Compassion Scales (SOCS). *Assessment*, 27(1), 3–20. https://doi.org/10.1177/1073191119860911.

Hägglund, K., Kenttä, G., Thelwell, R. & Wagstaff, C. R. D. (2021). Mindful self-reflection to support sustainable high-performance coaching: A process evaluation of a novel method development in elite sport. *Journal of Applied Sport Psychology*, online ahead of print. https://doi.org/10.1080/10413200.2021.1925782.

Hiçdurmaz, D., & Aydin, A. (2017). The relationship between nursing students' self-compassion and multidimensional perfectionism levels and the factors that influence them. *Journal of Psychiatric Nursing*, 8(2), 86–94. https://doi.org/10.14744/phd.2017. 40469.

Hill, A. P. (2014). Perfectionistic strivings and the perils of partialling. *International Journal of Sport and Exercise Psychology*, 12(4), 302–315.

Hill, A. P., Hall, H. K., & Appleton, P. R. (2010). A comparative examination of the correlates of self-oriented perfectionism and conscientious achievement striving in male cricket academy players. *Psychology of Sport and Exercise*, 11(2), 162–168. https://doi.org/10.1016/j.psychsport.2009.11.001

Hill, A. P., Mallinson-Howard, S. H., & Jowett, G. E. (2018). Multidimensional perfectionism in sport: A meta-analytical review. *Sport, Exercise, and Performance Psychology*, 7(3), 235. https://doi.org/10.1037/spy0000125.

Ingstrup, M. S., Mosewich, A. D., & Holt, N. L. (2017). The development of self-compassion among women varsity athletes. *The Sport Psychologist*, 31(4), 317–331. https://doi.org/10.1123/tsp.2016-0147.

Jeon, H., Lee, K., & Kwon, S. (2016). Investigation of the structural relationships between social support, self-compassion, and subjective well-being in Korean elite student athletes. *Psychological Reports*, 119(1), 39–54. https://doi.org/10.1177/0033294116658226.

Killham, M. E., Mosewich, A. D., Mack, D. E., Gunnell, K. E., & Ferguson, L. J. (2018). Women athletes' self-compassion, self-criticism, and perceived sport performance. *Sport, Exercise, and Performance Psychology*, 7(3), 297–307. http://doi.org/10.1037/spy0000127.

Linnett, R. J., & Kibowski, F. (2019). A multidimensional approach to perfectionism and self-compassion. *Self and Identity*, 19(7), 757–783. https://doi.org/10.1080/15298868.2019.1669695.

Lizmore, M. R., Dunn, J. G. H., & Causgrove Dunn, J. (2017). Perfectionistic strivings, perfectionistic concerns, and reactions to poor personal performances among intercollegiate athletes. *Psychology of Sport and Exercise*, 33, 75–84. https://doi.org/10.1016/j.psychsport.2017.07.010.

Miller, K., & Kelly, A. (2020). Is self-compassion contagious? An examination of whether hearing a display of self-compassion impacts self-compassion in the listener. *Canadian Journal of Behavioural Science*, 52(2), 159–170. https://doi.org/10.1037/cbs0000150.

Mosewich, A. D. (2020). Self-compassion in sport and exercise. In G. Tenenbaum & R. C. Eklund (eds), *Handbook of sport psychology* (4th ed.). Wiley-Blackwell. https://doi.org/10.1002/9781119568124.ch8.

Mosewich, A. D., Crocker, P. R. E., & Kowalski, K. C. (2014). Managing injury and other setbacks in sport: Experiences of (and resources for) high-performance women athletes. *Qualitative Research in Sport, Exercise and Health*, 6(2), 182–204. https://doi.org/10.1080/2159676X.2013.766810.

Mosewich, A. D., Crocker, P. R. E., Kowalski, K. C., & DeLongis, A. (2013). Applying self-compassion in sport: An intervention with women athletes. *Journal of Sport & Exercise Psychology*, 35(5), 514–524. https://doi.org/10.1123/jsep.35.5.514.

Mosewich, A. D., Dunn, J. G. H., Causgrove Dunn, J., & Wright, K. S. (2021). Domain-specific grit, identity, and self-compassion in intercollegiate athletes. *Sport, Exercise, and Performance Psychology*, 10, 257–272. https://doi.org/10.1037/spy0000267.

Mosewich, A. D., Ferguson, L. J., McHugh, T.-L. F., & Kowalski, K. C. (2019). Enhancing capacity: Integrating self-compassion in sport. *Journal of Sport Psychology in Action*, 10(4), 235–243. https://doi.org/10.1080/21520704.2018.1557774.

Mosewich, A. D., Kowalski, K. C., Sabiston, C. M., Sedgwick, W. A., & Tracy, J. L. (2011). Self-compassion: A potential resource for young women athletes. *Journal of Sport & Exercise Psychology*, 33(1), 103–123. https://doi.org/10.1123/jsep.33.1.103.

Mosewich, A. D., Sabiston, C. M., Kowalski, K. C., Gaudreau, P. & Crocker, P. R. E. (2019). Self-compassion in the stress process in women athletes. *The Sport Psychologist*, 33(1), 23–34. https://doi.org/10.1123/tsp.2017-0094.

Neff, K. D. (2003a). Self-compassion: An alternative conceptualization of a healthy attitude toward oneself. *Self and Identity*, 2(2), 85–101. https://doi.org/10.1080/15298860309032.

Neff, K. D. (2003b). The development and validation of a scale to measure self-compassion. *Self and Identity*, 2(3), 223–250. https://doi.org/10.1080/15298860390209035.

Neff, K. D. (2021). *Fierce self-compassion: How women can harness kindness to speak up, claim their power, and thrive.* HarperCollins.

Neff, K. (2022a). Self-compassion. Retrieved from https://self-compassion.org/.

Neff, K. (2022b). Self-compassion exercises. Retrieved from https://self-compassion.org/category/exercises/#exercises.

Neff, K. D., & Germer, C. (2018). *The mindful self-compassion workbook: A proven way to accept yourself, build inner strength, and thrive.* Guilford.

Pereira, A. T., Brito, M. J., Cabaços, C., Carneiro, M., Carvalho, F., Manão, A., Araúja, A., Pereira, D., & Macedo, A. (2022). The protective role of self-compassion in the relationship between perfectionism and burnout in Portuguese medicine and dentistry students. *International Journal of Environmental Research and Public Health*, 19(5), 2740. https://doi.org/10.3390/ijerph19052740.

Pila, E., Gilchrist, J. D., Kowalski, K. C., & Sabiston, C. M. (2022). Self-compassion and body-related self-conscious emotions: Examining within- and between-person variation among adolescent girls in sport. *Psychology of Sport and Exercise*, 58, article 102083. https://doi.org/10.1016/j.psychsport.2021.102083.

Poucher, Z. A., Tamminen, K. A., Kerr, G., & Cairney, J. (2021). A commentary on mental health research in elite sport. *Journal of Applied Sport Psychology*, 33(1), 60–82. https://doi.org/10.1080/10413200.2019.1668496.

Powers, T. A., Koestner, R., Zuroff, D. C., Milyavskaya, M., & Gorin, A. A. (2011). The effects of self-criticism and self-oriented perfectionism on goal pursuit. *Personality and Social Psychology Bulletin*, 37(7), 964–975. https://doi.org/10.1177/0146167211410246.

Reis, N. A., Kowalski, K. C., Mosewich, A. D., & Ferguson, L. J. (2019). Exploring self-compassion and versions of masculinity in men athletes. *Journal of Sport and Exercise Psychology*, 41(6), 368–379. https://doi.org/10.1123/jsep.2019-0061.

Reis, N. A., Kowalski, K. C., Mosewich, A. D., & Ferguson, L. J. (2022). "That's how I am dealing with it – that *is* dealing with it": Exploring men athletes' self-compassion through the lens of masculinity. *Qualitative Research in Sport, Exercise and Health*, 14(2), 245–267. https://doi.org/10.1080/2159676X.2021.1920455.

Röthlin, P., Horvath, S., & Birrer, D. (2019). Go soft or go home? A scoping review of empirical studies on the role of self-compassion in the competitive sport setting. *Current Issues in Sport Science*, 4, article 004. https://doi.org/10.15203/CISS_2019.013.

Röthlin, P., & Leiggener, R. (2021). Self-compassion to decrease performance anxiety in climbers: A randomized control trial. *Current Issues in Sport Science*, 6. https://doi.org/10.36950/2021ciss004.

Sereda, B. J., Holt, N. L., & Mosewich, A. D. (2021). How women varsity athletes high in self-compassion experience unexpected stressors. *Journal of Applied Sport Psychology*, online ahead of print. https://doi.org/10.1080/10413200.2021.1897900.

Shortway, K. M., Wolanin, A., Block-Lerner, J., & Marks, D. (2018). Acceptance and commitment therapy for injured athletes: Development and preliminary feasibility of the return to ACTion protocol. *Journal of Clinical Sport Psychology*, 12(1), 4–26. https://doi.org/10.1123/jcsp.2017-0033.

Stoeber, J. (2012). Perfectionism and performance. In S. M. Murphy (ed.), *The Oxford handbook of sport and performance psychology* (pp. 294–306). Oxford University Press. https://doi.org/10.1093/oxfordhb/9780199731763.013.0015.

Stoeber, J., Lalova, A. V., & Lumley, E. J. (2020). Perfectionism, (self-)compassion, and subjective well-being: A mediation model. *Personality and Individual Differences*, 154, article 109708. https://doi.org/10.1016/j.paid.2019.109708.

Tobin, R., & Dunkley, D. M. (2021). Self-critical perfectionism and lower mindfulness and self-compassion predict anxious and depressive symptoms over two years. *Behaviour Research and Therapy*, 136, article 103780. https://doi.org/10.1016/j.brat.2020.103780.

Turk, F., Kellett, S., & Waller, G. (2021). Determining the potential links of self-compassion with eating pathology and body image among women and men: A cross-sectional mediational study. *Body Image*, 37, 28–37. https://doi.org/10.1016/j.bodyim.2021.01.007.

Voelker, D. K., Petrie, T. A., Huang, Q., & Chandran, A. (2019). Bodies in Motion: An empirical evaluation of a program to support positive body image in female collegiate athletes. *Body Image*, 28, 149–158. https://doi.org/10.1016/j.bodyim.2019.01.008.

Walton, C. C., Baranoff J., Gilbert, P., & Kirby, J. (2020). Self-compassion, social rank, and psychological distress in athletes of varying competitive levels. *Psychology of Sport and Exercise*, 50, article 101733. https://doi.org/10.1016/j.psychsport.2020.101733.

Wasylkiw, L., & Clairo, J. (2016). Help seeking in men: When masculinity and self-compassion collide. *Psychology of Men & Masculinity*, 19(2), 234–242. https://doi.org/10.1037/men0000086.

Wei, S., Li, L., Shi, J., Liang, H., & Yang, X. (2021). Self-compassion mediates the perfectionism and depression link on Chinese undergraduates. *Annals of Palliative Medicine*, 10(2), 1950–1960. https://doi.org/10.21037/apm-20-1582.

Wilson, D., Bennett, E. V., Mosewich, A. D., Faulkner, G. E., & Crocker, P. R. E. (2019). "The zipper effect": Exploring the interrelationship of mental toughness and self-compassion among Canadian elite women athletes. *Psychology of Sport and Exercise*, 40, 61–70. https://doi.org/10.1016/j.psychsport.2018.09.006.

12 Perfectionism in Sport

A Rational Emotive Behaviour Therapy Perspective

Anna Jordana and Martin J. Turner

Just as sport can be perfectionistic it can also be irrational, providing messages to athletes of the incredible importance of success and the catastrophe of failure. The study of perfectionism is inextricably linked to irrational beliefs through the seminal work of Albert Ellis and Rational Emotive Behaviour therapy (REBT). However, the synergies between these two areas of work are typically underappreciated and have yet to be fully explored in sport. The current chapter addresses this issue by considering perfectionism and some of the issues perfectionism athletes face from an REBT perspective. The chapter starts with a brief overview of REBT. We then consider REBT research in sport. Thereafter, we explain perfectionism within the context of REBT and irrational beliefs. The chapter closes with an applied case example of an athlete dealing with a common challenge in sport – the experience of a debilitating injury. Though our case example we showcase the REBT approach and highlight some of the techniques that can be used to support perfectionistic athletes and provide a basis for better mental health and performance.

A Brief Overview of Rational Emotive Behaviour Therapy

The challenging situations athletes face throughout their careers are, to some degree, inherent and unavoidable. Some of the most common challenges include competitive stressors (e.g. performance expectations), organizational issues (e.g. travel), personal issues (e.g. family), and managing numerous transitions (e.g. retirement). Two key questions research has sought to answer are why is it that some athletes are able to cope with these situations better than others? And, how can we help those who struggle to cope? According to Rational Emotive Behavioural Therapy (REBT; Ellis, 1957), in these situations, problems are largely the result of *irrational beliefs*. Therefore, in order to support athletes who are struggling with these challenges, we must work to challenge and weaken any unhelpful beliefs about themselves or the situation. Work that has applied REBT in the sports domain has clearly demonstrated the importance of these types of beliefs in regards to athlete mental health and performance (see Jordana et al., 2020). In keeping with this evidence, in the current chapter we emphasize this approach as a means of understanding the

DOI: 10.4324/9781003288015-16

issues athletes with perfectionistic tendencies face and as a way of directing the practical steps that can be taken to support them.

Beliefs are representations of reality imbued with personal meaning (David et al., 2010). They are deeply held, often tacit, propositions, assumptions, rules, ideas, attitudes, and expectations – ways of seeing the world that have cognitive, emotional, and behavioural concomitants and consequences (Turner, 2022). The beliefs people hold can be about oneself, about others, or about the world in general, they are formed during emotional and psychological experiences, and are influenced by various factors (e.g. cultural background, relationships, and education) (Shermer, 2011). Beliefs are open to cognitive biases and are not necessarily true, but can have the appearance of being true and are experienced as such by the holder. Importantly, within REBT, beliefs are key to understanding mental health and influence emotional and behavioural responses to life adversity (David et al., 2005; Ellis & Dryden, 1997). Some beliefs provide the basis for better mental health and adjustment whereas other beliefs make people vulnerable to mental ill-health and maladjustment.

The conceptual core of REBT is two types of beliefs – irrational beliefs and rational beliefs (Ellis, 1957). Irrational beliefs are rigid, extreme and without logical, empirical, and functional support. For example, "demandingness" is an irrational belief characterized by the inflexible and absolutist perspective of "I must" and "I have to" (e.g. "I must perform well"). Deriving from this belief, three other irrational beliefs can arise: "awfulizing" (e.g. "nothing could be worse"), "frustration intolerance" (e.g. "it is unbearable"), and "conditional acceptance" of oneself, others, or life in general (e.g. "I am only acceptable if I am successful"). By contrast, rational beliefs are flexible, non-extreme and with logical, empirical, and functional support. The alternative rational belief to demandingness is "preferences" which emphasizes wants rather than demands (e.g. "I want to perform well, but I do not have to"). The three equivalent subsequent rational beliefs are "anti-awfulizing" (e.g. "this is bad but not awful"), "frustration tolerance" (e.g. "this is tough, but I can tolerate it"), and "unconditional acceptance" of oneself, others, or life in general (e.g. "Win or lose, I accept myself as a fallible and unique human being"). To adopt an REBT perspective in sport, is to view the emotions and behaviours of athletes as significantly influenced by the beliefs they hold about themselves, others, and the world.

The GABCDE Framework

The theory and practice of REBT is articulated through the GABCDE model (David et al., 2010), which proposes that irrational and rational beliefs (B) are triggered in response to activating situations or events (A) that block the achievement of personal goals (G), and underpin emotions, thoughts, and behaviours (C). As Figure 12.1 shows, in this model irrational beliefs underpin dysfunctional, unhealthy, and maladaptive consequences whereas rational beliefs underpin functional, healthy, and adaptive consequences. The concepts of "functional", "healthy", and "adaptive" are used to characterize the

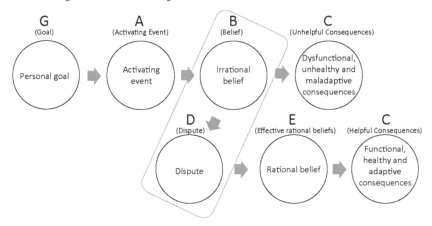

Figure 12.1 Scheme of the GABCDE model for beliefs rationalization.

consequences that facilitate the achievement of personal goals, while the concepts of "dysfunctional", "unhealthy", and "maladaptive" represent those consequences that hinder their achievement. REBT is primarily concerned with encouraging negative consequences to be functional, healthy, and adaptive, rather than only promoting positive consequences (Turner, 2016b).

Goals play an important role in the sports context from an REBT perspective, too, because, depending on the goal, different types of As, Bs and Cs will manifest. However, the central point of typical REBT is to help people challenge and weaken irrational beliefs (D) and to adopt and strengthen other more rational beliefs (E), with the aim of reducing dysfunctional, unhealthy, and maladaptive consequences, and promoting more functional, healthy, and adaptive ones. We have populated Table 12.1 to illustrate how different beliefs (irrational versus rational) might influence the consequences of pursuing the same goal ("To be perfect") and experiencing the same adversity (failure). The key message is that the GABC aspects of the framework can be used to show how two people can think, feel, and behave in different ways, depending on what they say to themselves, in the same situation (MacLaren et al., 2016). From a practical perspective, this approach also offers the possibility of managing challenging situations in sport through addressing beliefs first, before we try to exercise control over external events which may be more difficult (or often impossible) (Turner, 2019).

One important final note is that REBT is underpinned by a humanistic philosophy (Ellis, 1973). As such, it is important to consider the person from a holistic perspective. In sport, this means not only considering the individual as an athlete or focusing solely on their performance. Beyond working on beliefs to promote desirable changes in sport – improved performance, motivation, and emotional experiences – REBT interventions should focus on promoting long-term changes in athletes' irrational beliefs (i.e. identifying, discussing, and replacing them for more rational ones) in order to promote a deep change in

Table 12.1 Completed GABC formulation.

			Consequences (C)		
Goal (G)	*Adversity (A)*	*Beliefs (B)*	*Emotional*	*Cognitive*	*Behavioural*
To be perfect	Failure	*Irrational* "I must be perfect, and it is terrible when I fail to show that I am perfect"	Depressed, anger, panic	Self/other blame, self-flagellation, overthinking, procrastination	Withdrawal, aggression
		Rational "I want to be perfect, but I do not need to be the perfect athlete"	Annoyed, calm, concern	Greater focus, instinctive, helpful self-talk	Coping, assertiveness

irrational schemas that foster more general adaptive and healthy consequences (see Jordana et al., 2020). This underpinning distinguishes REBT from other common therapeutic approaches (e.g. Acceptance and Commitment Therapy) and sets it apart from the techniques sport and exercise psychologists might typically use to support their athletes (e.g. psychological skills training).

REBT and Irrational Beliefs in Sport

One of the reasons why REBT is becoming more popular in sport may be due to the irrational beliefs embedded in sports environments where ideas of "winning at all costs" can be common (Turner, 2014). Social agents in the micro- (e.g. peers, parents, fans, coaches) and macro-environment (e.g. media, key sport stakeholder organizations) of the athlete, can model irrationality through their behaviour and language, and encourage the development and maintenance of irrational beliefs in athletes (King et al. 2022). Some studies evidence the presence of irrational beliefs in coaches, specifically, a fact that allows us to assume the presence of irrational beliefs in other social agents that operate in this setting (Arnold et al., 2019). Irrational beliefs are also readily identifiable in the language used in the narratives used in sport and, although the language may not always appear to directly reflect irrational beliefs, it can play a role in their development (Turner, 2016b). Language used in the sports media, for example, is often very powerful and aimed at magnifying the importance of success and seriousness of failure (Turner, 2019).

The usefulness of REBT is also becoming increasingly recognized in sport due to the growing body of empirical studies that supports the approach.

Irrational beliefs and mental health have been examined in a variety sports and levels of competition, and research supports the tenets of REBT (e.g. Mansell, 2021; Turner et al., 2022; Vîslă et al., 2016). Other research that has taken place has provided validation of psychometric instruments (e.g. Turner & Allen, 2018), professional practice guidelines (e.g. Turner, 2019), and other applied tools (e.g. Turner & Wood, 2021). Consequently, researchers and practitioners now know much more about the adverse effects of irrational beliefs in sport, have an evidence-base to draw on, and practical resources to help guide intervention.

With regard to interventions, in particular, the systematic mapping review provided by Jordana et al. (2020) gives an overview of the literature on REBT interventions with athletes. This extensive review of research (1) classified the type of literature, (b) categorized evidence, (c) identified current trends, and (d) critically appraised the methodological rigour, suitability, and relevance of existing studies. Thirty-nine studies were included in the review and on the basis of these studies it was evident that one-to-one REBT, in particular, is effective for use with athletes, with most evidence indicating that REBT works well in reducing anxiety. However, there is also evidence to support its use for many outcomes across emotional, behavioural, wellbeing, and performance markers, using a variety of modes of working (one to one, group education, group sharing) and doses (from a single session, to eight sessions). Based on research so far, then, REBT can be considered a valuable intervention for use with athletes to promote, restore and maintain mental health, as well as performance.

Two Faces of the Same Coin? Perfectionism and Irrational Beliefs

Perfectionism was defined by Ellis when discussing irrational beliefs as the "the idea that one should be thoroughly competent, adequate, intelligent, and achieving in all possible respects" (Ellis, 1958, p. 41) and "the idea that there is invariable a right, precise, and perfect solution to human problems and that it is catastrophic if this perfect solution is not found" (Ellis, 1962, pp. 86–87). As such, perfectionism and irrational beliefs are inextricably linked. Irrational beliefs and perfectionism are both extreme, rigid, and illogical schemas. Perfectionism is extreme because it represents an ideal (nothing can be better); it is rigid because it is focused only on one outcome (to be perfect); and it is illogical because perfection does not and cannot exist. But if we take seriously the four core irrational beliefs of REBT, it can be noted that "perfectionism" is not explicitly synonymous or analogous to any of the core irrational beliefs. In addition, if we interrogate Ellis's above statement that "one should be thoroughly competent", it is the "should" of the statement that best captures the irrationality, not necessarily the desired, aspired to, and pursued thoroughness of one's competence. On this basis, we argue, from an REBT perspective, that pursuing perfection is not inherently irrational (though perhaps ill-advised in other ways), but it is the *demand* for perfection that is irrational.

In deriving this position, and considering the root of any negative effects of perfectionism from a REBT perspective, we are reminded, too, of the important work of Karen Horney which made her an important progenitor of the humanistic movement, and how her chapter "The tyranny of the should" guided the central theme of rational psychotherapy. Karen Horney (1950) argued that idealized ideas can be severely disturbing as they generated internal dictates – "should" and "musts" – and dysfunctional emotions. Horney (1950) suggested that as we cannot attain idealized goals, or become our idealized self, we enter a vicious cycle of striving and failing. Figure 12.2 illustrates this vicious cycle. The cycle has the potential to explain both the high effort and dedication characteristic of perfectionism but also the futility and emotional toll of pursuing perfection when people believe it should or must be obtained. As such, we argue that it is in the "must" and "should" that perfectionism is irrational and is maladaptive, not in the perfectionist goal or ideal itself.

Within REBT, irrational beliefs can be applied to any idea or goal, including perfectionistic goals (e.g. "I *have* to play perfectly" versus "I *want* to play perfectly"). They can also be used to understand how conditional musts can be invalidated. Conditional musts are not inherently irrational because it often makes sense that "X" (e.g. playing well) needs to happen for "Y" (e.g. winning) to occur. For perfectionism, though, we have an invalid conditional must because "Y" (e.g. being perfect) is not possible no matter how many times you do "X" (e.g. win). As such, Ellis (1994) proposed that having thoughts related to perfectionism results only in anxiety and other emotional problems. So, from an REBT perspective, athletes should be encouraged to challenge and weaken rigid demands for perfection, and to be more flexible and less extreme with regards to their inevitable failure to live up to their ideals (see also Bernard, 2019).

The relationship between perfectionism and irrational beliefs is provided in Figure 12.3 using the GABC model. When faced with perfectionistic goals there is a greater probability of "As" being evaluated as a failure, since the idea of achieving perfection is extreme, rigid, illogical. This fact will trigger the activation of the irrational beliefs and subsequent dysfunctional and unhealthy emotional and behavioural consequences. Critically, perfectionistic athletes are also more likely to perceive discrepancies between expectations and performance on an ongoing basis. This will create an unavoidable incongruence between "G" and "A" which is the basis for longer-term and more severe difficulties (Dickson et al., 2019; Turner, 2022).

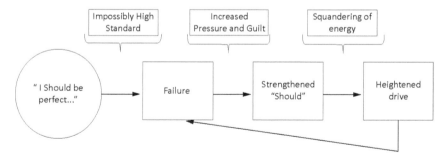

Figure 12.2 An illustration of Horney's vicious cycle.

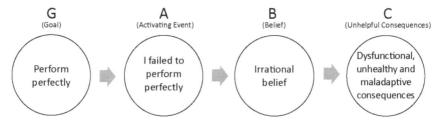

Figure 12.3 GABC scheme for perfectionistic goals.

To illustrate the difference of retaining perfection as a goal versus doings so accompanied by irrational beliefs, we can further consider the role of irrational beliefs in Figure 12.3. The investment in perfectionistic goals already has the potential to bring about negative emotions because with such high expectations, adversity is bound to occur or be perceived, because most (if not all) occurrences will not live up to one's perfectionistic ideals. Thus, the stage is set for negative emotions and consequences. However, when we add irrational beliefs to perfectionistic goals and inevitable adversities, any arising negative emotion is elevated to broader maladaptive and unhealthy negative emotion, turning frustration to anger, concern to anxiety, and sadness to depression. From an REBT perspective, then, the goal of perfection can be problematic, but it is especially dysfunctional if accompanied by or propped up with irrational beliefs.

With regard to empirical research linking perfectionism to irrational beliefs, two studies have examined the relationship between perfectionism and the belief of (un)conditional self-acceptance. That is, the belief of acceptance regardless of the approval, respect or love received from other people (e.g. "I feel I am a valuable person even when other people disapprove of me") (Lundh, 2004). In the first study, Hill et al. (2008) found both socially prescribed perfectionism (perceptions of demands of perfection from others) and self-oriented perfectionism (personal demands of perfection) to be negatively related to unconditional self-acceptance in junior soccer players. Likewise, Hall et al. (2009) found the same in a study of adult middle-distance runners. In support of the approach presented in this chapter, in both these studies, lower levels of this belief partially explained the relationships between the two dimensions of perfectionism and higher levels of both athlete burnout and exercise dependence.

In a more recent study, Michel-Kröhler and Turner (2022) examined the relationship between multiple dimensions of perfectionism (self-critical perfectionism, striving for perfection, and negative reactions to imperfection) and different irrational beliefs (primary irrational beliefs, low frustration tolerance, awfulness, and depreciation) in adult athletes from different sports. They found that on almost all occasions dimensions of perfectionism were positivity related to all irrational beliefs. Interestingly, striving for perfection was not related to depreciation (viz. conditional self-acceptance) in training but was in competition. This suggests potential moderation when stakes are higher, and alludes to additional complexity to the relationship.

In another study, Toth et al. (2022) examined the relationship between perfectionism (high standards and discrepancy), irrational beliefs (demandingness, awfulizing, low frustration tolerance, and depreciation), and competitive anxiety in adult athletes. Again, in this study both dimensions of perfectionism were positively related to all irrational beliefs. The authors also found, using atemporal serial mediation, that athletes who held stronger irrational beliefs and greater perfectionism were more likely to report higher anxiety. Both dimensions of perfectionism were significant mediators for most of the relationships between irrational beliefs and anxiety. In discussing the findings, the authors suggest that REBT with a particular focus upon perfectionism might be a useful approach with athletes.

In reflecting on existing research, it appears that dimensions of perfectionism are related to a range of irrational beliefs and that their interplay may partly explain some of the maladaptive, unhealthy, and dysfunctional consequences of being perfectionistic in sport. But, although irrational beliefs do appear to be related to perfectionism, they are not one in the same. Therefore, irrational beliefs and perfectionism may need to be addressed separately when working with athletes.

Next in this chapter, we detail the applied application of the concepts and ideas we have discussed so far. We do this by offering a hypothetical athlete case and then addressing the case using REBT.

The "Perfect" Case: Using REBT to Help an International Futsal Player

Jason is a 23-year-old male futsal athlete from the United Kingdom who has represented his country in 50 competitive games. In preparation for a World Cup qualifying tournament, Jason suffers a calf strain just before half time in a friendly match. At half time, the team doctor, physio, and head coach decide that it is best for Jason to miss the rest of the game. Following further assessments by the team doctor and physio, it is decided that Jason will not be able to play in the World Cup qualifying games. They estimate that due to the severity of the injury, Jason may require up to 3 months to recover fully. Having worked with Jason for 5 years, the sport psychologist notices that, since the injury, Jason has been distancing himself from the team and it being short with his teammates. He is also being very negative about the World Cup qualifying tournament, and about life in general, and this negativity is being noticed by members of the team. The sport psychologist arranges a one-to-one meeting with Jason to discuss the situation, and to see if they can offer some assistance for the rehabilitation from the injury Jason is undertaking.

It is beyond the scope of the current chapter to provide a full and detailed portrayal of the practice of REBT. Other works can be consulted if the reader is interested in more detail (e.g. Turner, 2022). Instead, what follows is a brief outline of what REBT would likely entail with Jason, taking into consideration his specific situation. Whilst all REBT work is idiosyncratic to the client, there is a general flow or structure that can be used a guide which is in line with

Dryden et al.'s (2010) REBT Competency Scale. We follow this structure. We do not cover the entire process or inevitable flexibility required in the process. Our case is intended to serve as an illustrative example, rather than an exhaustive or definitive account of the approach.

The "Flow" of REBT

There is no single path through REBT, but there is a trajectory that is characterized by the weakening of irrational beliefs and the strengthening of rational beliefs. Turner (2022) proposes that REBT has the broad aim of supporting the athlete in developing and strengthening rational ways of seeing the world in service of long-term wellbeing, biopsychosocial functioning, and goal fulfilment (eudaimonia). In order to achieve this aim, we help the client to understand the function and utility of cognitive mediation and cognitive change, through which their beliefs can be assessed, evaluated, and shaped. Beliefs that do not serve an adaptive purpose are actively rallied against, and beliefs that do serve an adaptive function are instantiated and buttressed. Clients develop their capacity to use the criteria of truth, logic, and function to evaluate and shape their beliefs. The practitioner interacts with the client openly and forthrightly, teaching them skills and ideas that contribute to, rather than detract from, their life. Client learning and development takes place discursively and Socratically for the most part, but also didactically at times, including via the use of homework assignments completed between face-to-face contact. The client is an active collaborator in the work, not a passive participant. The apotheosis of the client's development is the eventual autonomous and independent usage of REBT and the ability to live using rational principles in their engagement with themselves, others, and the world. The practitioner's goal should be to make themselves redundant in the client's life (Dryden et al., 2010).

So where do we start with Jason? We begin by *developing a working alliance* between client and practitioner. Tomes have been written about the working alliance, and the development and maintenance of rapport is a topic worthy of an entire book. But suffice it to say, the development of a strong working alliance is vital (Woody & Adessky, 2002). This is because it is the working alliance that makes core aspects of REBT viable. Indeed, successful REBT is less likely to occur without a good working alliance and a mutual agreement on goals and therapeutic methods (e.g. Castonguay et al., 2010). This strong client-practitioner working alliance is underpinned by a solid bond, openness, clear aims for the work, and the forthright effort expenditure towards those agreed aims (e.g. Dryden, 2009). So with Jason, our first job is to ensure a strong working alliance to set a solid foundation for the work that follows. We will continually strengthen the therapeutic bond with Jason as the work progresses, with rapport building being a feature of every session we have with Jason.

Next, we *establish the aims of the work* by identifying a target problem, and commit to a way forward. We do have some background information about Jason already, but it important not to assume what the target problem is based on brief observations. The goals of REBT are negotiated and agreed upon by client and practitioner together in order to arrive at a viable way forward that the client will actually commit to. One of the ways we can determine the goals of the work is to develop a problem list (Dryden, 2021) and then discuss and determine what we believe to be the most adaptive approaches or responses to these problems. In conversation with Jason, three main problems are identified: (1) he is injured, (2) he has to undergo a difficult rehab process, and (3) he will miss out on the World Cup qualifying games. In REBT terms, we could consider these problems to broadly be adversities or activating events (As), but a fuller assessment needs to take place in order to understand the extent to which these descriptive issues are indeed generative of irrational beliefs at B and unhealthily negative emotions (UNEs) at C. But for now, Jason and the practitioner can discuss these three problems (as defined by Jason) and what might be the most adaptive way/s to engage with these problems. After some discussion, it is agreed that the most adaptive way in which Jason can approach and respond to these issues is to "remain professional, stay connected and be there for the team, and look positively towards the future". In formulating and articulating these ideal self-projections, Jason can see the discrepancy between the maladaptive approaches and responses he is currently enacting, and the approaches and responses that he knows are more adaptive and thus could be striven for.

We can now become more detailed in our assessment of Jason's current approaches and responses to his current situation. Here we are *assessing* C to determine the extent to which Jason's approaches and responses are actually maladaptive for him. We do this carefully because it is important that both Jason and the practitioner have a detailed understanding of the thoughts, feelings, and behaviours Jason is experiencing and enacting in response to his problems (As). It is possible that Jason's responses are appropriate and adaptive, even though they are unpleasant in the short-term. In REBT we do not seek to change negatively valenced responses just because they are unpleasant – rather – we seek to change responses that are detracting from the fulfilment of the client's (eudaimonic) goals. Not all that is negative is subject to change. As we assess C with Jason, it becomes clear that his thoughts, feelings, and behaviours in relation to the problems he faces are maladaptive, as they are not helping him and are actually leading to more suffering.

To expand, Jason is seeing only the negative aspects of situation, and feels hopeless about the future (cognitive Cs), has withdrawn into himself, is pushing people away, bemoans his fate to people around him (behavioural Cs), and is feeling deep sadness accompanied by persistent low mood (emotive C). We could say that Jason is evidencing "unhealthy sadness". Jason wants to get to a place where he is showing "healthy sadness", characterized by seeing negative *and positive* aspects of the situation, and being hopeful for the future (cognitive Cs), expressing his feelings to others, allowing himself to be comforted, seeking and accepting support from those around him (behavioural Cs), and feeling sad but in way they is not so persistent and pervasive (emotive C). He believes that thinking, behaving, and feeling in these new ways would facilitate his ideals of remaining professional, staying connected and being there for the team, and looking positively towards the future.

It is not enough, however, to just know what the adaptive response is, or to want to move to towards this adaptive response – Jason is unable at this moment in time to get to that place and we need to figure out why. So we next undertake an *assessment of A*, which is to say that we try to get some greater depth into the three problems that Jason presented to us earlier (i.e. injured, difficult rehab process, miss out on qualifying games). We can ask Jason which of these problems he believes is leading to his unhealthy sadness. Jason tells us that it is really the prospect of rehab that brings forth his sadness – when he thinks about undergoing rehab, he notices a deepening of his sadness. So, we ask Jason what it is about the prospect of rehab that is so provoking of his sadness. Jason responds with "it is the pain and inconvenience I will go through whilst undertaking rehab" to which we ask what it is about the prospect of pain and inconvenience that is so provoking of his sadness. Jason responds with "the pain and inconvenience are signs that my body is frail – weak". We ask, "what if your body is weak? What would be so sad about that?" to which Jason replies "then I am weak and feeble person who cannot hope to become the athlete I should be". In further dialogue with Jason, he reveals that from all these potential As (prospect of rehab, pain and inconvenience, weak body, not being the athlete he should be) it is having a weak body and not being the athlete he should be that is tightly connected to his sadness. We dig a little deeper and underneath this idea of the athlete he "should" be is a goal to be the perfect athlete. Jason has explicitly set himself the goal of being the perfect athlete in every way, and it seems that having a weak body directly opposes, or incongruent, with that goal.

We *could* challenge the notion that Jason has a weak body and *could* take aim at his perfectionistic goal, of course. But in REBT we would consider this to be low hanging fruit that if picked will only provide short-term benefits for Jason. He might feel better if we try to convince Jason of all the ways in which is body is not weak, but at some point in the future, he will face injury or illness again, and the weak body neuroses will likely return. He might feel better about himself if we convince Jason that the injury does not detract from him being the athlete he should be, but there will be future As that Jason will construe as detracting from his perfectionistic ideal. So in REBT we *assume that the A is true* (Dryden, 2009) and ask "what are you telling yourself about your body being weak that is causing you to feel so sad?" We are assuming A is true because *maybe* Jason's body is weak, *maybe* it isn't. We cannot *prove* or *disprove* this inference and by taking what Jason says at face value, and not focusing on factors that we cannot prove or disprove, we can open the door to deeper cognitions that are more proximal to his unhealthy sadness.

In response to our question "what are you telling yourself about your body being weak that is causing you to feel so sad?", Jason replies "I need to be perfect, and weak people get injured". We ask why he has to be "perfect" to which Jason replies "because I want that for myself". We ask what he means by "weak people get injured" to which Jason replies "me being injured shows that I am a weak and feeble person". Together with Jason, we construct an axiomatic statement that reflects what Jason is saying:

I want to be, and therefore I need to be, the perfect athlete, and being injured shows that I am a weak and feeble human being.

It might not be the "fact" that Jason's body is weak or that his injury detracts from his perfectionistic ideals that is causing such deep sadness all by itself. Rather, it might be the rigid demand to be perfect and the depreciation of the whole self on the basis of being injured, that is most proximal to Jason's unhealthy sadness. In other words, Jason's irrational beliefs concerning his injury and desire to be perfect are causing problems for Jason, beyond the problems manifested by the goal of being perfect and his injury alone. In other words, it is not $G - A = C$, but rather, it is $G - A \times B = C$. In other words, the incongruence between G and A (i.e. the adverse injury thwarts his goal to be perfect) is made more problematic by the demand for G (I need to be perfect) and depreciation of the self on the basis of A (being injured). We work with Jason on this idea to see if it holds water. We can also take this chance to educate Jason about cognitive mediation, and how our cognitions mediate between the situations we face and our emotions (Lazarus, 1999). It is important to help Jason shift from "my injury is making me sad" to "what I am telling myself about my injury is making me sad" because clients are unlikely to attempt to change something that their language implies is not in their control (DiGiuseppe et al., 2014). Jason cannot change the fact that he is injured, but he can work to change his belief about the injury. At this point, it is possible to articulate a *maladaptive (irrational) GABCDE* formulation for Jason (see Table 12.2).

Next, we can Socratically compare this *maladaptive (irrational) GABCDE* formulation to a hypothetical *adaptive (rational) GABCDE* formulation (see Table 12.3) in order to (1) test the idea that Jason's beliefs are indeed problematic, (2) to start to

Table 12.2 A maladaptive (irrational) GABCDE formulation.

Element	Detail
Goals (G)	To be a perfect athlete in every way.
Adversity (concrete)	Short term injury.
Adversity (perception)	I will suffer through inconvenience and pain of rehab.
Adversity (inference)	My body is weak.
Irational beliefs	I want to be, and therefore I need to be, the perfect athlete, and being injured shows that I am a weak and feeble human being.
Consequences (cognitive)	See only negative aspects of situation, hopelessness about future.
Consequences (behavioural)	Withdraw into oneself, push people away, bemoan fate.
Consequences (emotive)	Unhealthy sadness.

Table 12.3 An adaptive (rational) GABCDE formulation.

Element	Detail
Goals (G)	To be a perfect athlete in every way.
Adversity (concrete)	Short term injury.
Adversity (perception)	I will suffer through inconvenience and pain of rehab.
Adversity (inference)	My body is weak.
Rational beliefs	I want to be, but I do not need to be, the perfect athlete, and being injured does not mean that I am weak or feeble, it just shows that I am normal and fallible human being.
Consequences (cognitive)	See negative *and positive* aspects of situation, hope for the future.
Consequences (behavioural)	Express feelings to others, allow self to be comforted, seek support.
Consequences (emotive)	Healthy sadness.

teach Jason the differences between irrational and rational beliefs, and (3) to start to work towards some potential solutions for Jason. To do this, we take Jason's irrational beliefs and create rational alternatives. Then we compare irrational vs. rational beliefs on three criteria of evidence, logic, and function. In REBT this is called disputation (D), which is a collaborative (client-practitioner) argument, or a debate, focussed on challenging the client's ideas, not the client themselves (Turner, 2022). Clients are more likely to abandon their irrational beliefs if considerable tension is caused by a great deal of disconfirming empirical evidence for the belief, new problems exist for which the belief cannot help them, and an alternative, and superior, belief becomes available (DiGiuseppe, 1986). As such, disputation is imbued with a scientific approach to beliefs and belief change such that clients can learn to recognize dis-confirming evidence for their irrational beliefs, to realize that their irrational beliefs do not help them attain their eudaimonic goals, and to generate and strengthen alternative rational beliefs that do help them.

With this comparison between irrational and rational beliefs, we ask the question, which is more true, logical, and functional (helpful for goal attainment)? We also ask which belief Jason would want to strengthen and act upon. Table 12.4 gives a template for how this comparison can be done – Jason is asked to tick the box that applies most – and we add some annotation as to how this decision has been made. As you can see, Jason indicates that his current belief is false, illogical, and unhelpful (dysfunctional), and wants to work to strengthen the alternate belief. This Socratic comparison method, or paired comparison (Neenan & Dryden, 1996) is one way of applying disputation (D), and there are various other methods (see DiGiuseppe et al., 2014; Turner, 2022).

Table 12.4 Socratic comparison for Jason's beliefs.

	Current belief	Alternate belief
	I want to be, and therefore I need to be, the perfect athlete, and being injured shows that I am a weak and feeble human being.	I want to be, but I do not need to be, the perfect athlete, and being injured does not mean that I am weak or feeble, it just shows that I am normal and fallible human being.
Which belief is true and which is false?	*False* Just because I want something, does not mean I need it. It is not the case that my whole self can be defined by one injury.	*True* I do not need the things I want. My injury merely shows that I can be injured, just like everyone else in the world.
Which belief is sensible/ logical and which doesn't make sense or is illogical?	*Makes no sense (illogical)* "I need" does not follow "I want". As a human being, I am too complex to be defined by one event (e.g. injury).	*Logical* "I want" does not beget "I need". Like all humans, I am fallible, and so, I will be injured from time to time.
Which belief is helpful and which is unhelpful?	*Unhelpful* This is making me feel worse about my situation and is taking me away from who I want to be.	*Helpful* This could still lead me to sadness, but a sadness I can cope with and come back stronger from. It also won't lead to me sabotaging my own attainment.
Which of the two beliefs do you want to strengthen and act on?	*Not this one* It is unrealistic and is hindering me.	*This one* It is realistic and could actually help me.

At this point, Jason is able to see the connection between his G, A, Bs, and Cs, has distinguished between irrational and rational beliefs as they pertain to his problems, and has started to commit to developing rational beliefs. Given that we have now arrived at a place where Jason recognizes the role of beliefs in his emotional responding, and has also realized that his current irrational beliefs are not serving him well when compared to potential rational beliefs, we can now move forward to help Jason learn to dispute (D) his irrational beliefs in various other ways, with a view to developing and strengthening rational beliefs (E). While the Socratic comparison method was useful to structure D, we can teach Jason the rules of D so that he can apply them to future beliefs that might undercut his goal attainment. Once Jason demonstrates that he understands D, by applying D to his own beliefs and to other examples that we can use to practice upon, we can move to strengthening

Jason's new rational beliefs (E). To be clear, with Jason, we are working to strengthen the beliefs:

> *I want to be, but I do not need to be, the perfect athlete, and being injured does not mean that I am weak or feeble, it just shows that I am normal and fallible human being.*

Here we help Jason to steelman his new rational beliefs, rehearse them meaningfully, and plan the integration into his life. From Jason, this requires ongoing effort as he strengthens his conviction and commitment to the effective new beliefs over time. This E phase is undertaken in four steps (Turner, 2022); develop, challenge, strengthen, and commit. With Jason, we have already made in roads with "develop" and "challenge", so we can move to helping Jason to "strengthen" and "commit" to the new beliefs. Again, there are many ways we can do this, including rehearsal of rational beliefs (e.g. via cue cards; Turner, 2022), using rational self-talk (Turner et al., 2019), engaging in rational emotive imagery (Maultsby, 1971), developing rational credos (Turner, 2016a), and using debate and role play (DiGiuseppe et al., 2014). Turner (2022) also advocates the use of "if-then" plans (i.e. implementation intentions; Gollwitzer & Sheeran, 2006) to identify both an appropriate goal-directed response and a suitable situation in which to initiate that response (e.g. "IF I feel unhealthily sad about my injury, THEN I will remind myself that although I really want to be perfect, that doesn't mean that I have to be"). We can work with Jason to apply some of these methods, whichever we deem to fit Jason the best based on his likes, dislikes, and needs, before finishing our work.

Finishing the work can happen when client and practitioner are confident that solutions have been reached that help the client to move healthily into the future of their goal pursuits. Through REBT, we have been teaching Jason the rules and tools needed to apply REBT independently, making ourselves as practitioners redundant. This can happen when Jason is able to demonstrate that he has retained his REBT learning and is moving towards emotional insight whereby his is committing to rationality and committing to the work that is required for meaningful change (Ellis, 1963). Is Jason confident with articulating the GABCDE framework for his issues? Can he demonstrate the differences between irrational and rational beliefs? Can he generate his own rational beliefs? Can he apply disputation accurately? We need to answer "yes" to these questions in order to confident that Jason can apply REBT by himself. If we do answer "yes" than the practitioner can recap all that we have done together, a verbal reflection that aids closure at this final juncture. We will end the work with Jason with a statement of confidence that he has the capacity to move forward positively, but that support is here if he needs it. This might sound like:

> I think you have progressed very well in our work and I am sure you will be able to apply what you have learned out in the real world. But if you do feel like you want another check-in down the line, then of course reach out to me and we can have a chat.

But what if the work is not over? It is misconception that once we have aided the client in their irrational-rational transition then we just down tools and part ways. We can of course help the client in myriad other ways that can aid their goal attainment (Turner, 2022). In the case of Jason, what of his goal "I want to be … the perfect athlete"? Even if we remove the demandingness of "needing" to be perfect, is the goal of perfectionism bad in of itself? This is what our work with Jason would focus upon next. When we are shifting this focus to G (i.e. the client's goals) we need to be aware that we are no longer practicing *specific* REBT. Rather, we are now practicing *general* REBT. *Specific* REBT is focussed on belief change primarily, but *general* REBT has a broader focus on change other than deep belief change (Dryden & David, 2008). Thus, in *general* REBT we can work with Jason directly across any element of the GABCDE framework. Once we have helped Jason address his beliefs, we can help Jason to address other aspects of his goal pursuits which may involve reshaping G, physically or inferentially altering A, and or directly modulating C (e.g. via rhythmic breathing; Turner, 2022). Belief change is seen as the optimal and elegant solution because it addresses deeper level schema that can operate across many situations, but direct G, A, and C change is still possible. Thus, with Jason's goal to be "the perfect athlete" we can, if required, proactively help Jason to shape or reshape this goal to ensure that what he orients himself towards in life has some eudaimonic functionality. We are no longer remedially helping Jason with an identified emotional problem, we are paving the way for future functionality by optimizing his goals, thus fundamentally changing the nature of the As he will face as a result.

Thus, given that we know the potential dangers of holding perfectionistic goals especially if this perfectionism is expressed as perfectionistic concerns (including the demands of others, concerns, and doubts), we can work with Jason to first, understand whether his perfectionistic goal is indeed maladaptive, and second, to help him adopt a more adaptive goal that serves a more eudaimonic purpose. This goal might still be perfectionistic, but not necessarily maladaptive. In other words, holding and pursuing an ideal might serve the athlete well, so long as they don't rigidly demand this ideal or depreciate themselves when they don't achieve the ideal. If I hold this perfectionistic goal lightly, it might get me further than if I held no such goal, or if I held this goal tightly (rigidly demanding it). So, this perfectionistic goal could be articulated as a striving towards an ideal, rather than as an impossible self-definition that can be used as a stick to beat himself with. We could also help Jason to adopt a goal that is more eudaimonic that speaks to his broader human self, rather than just his athlete self. We can help Jason to work towards the experience of some positive affect and wellbeing, not just away from poor wellbeing (e.g. Oltean et al., 2019).

For example, here is what Jason's new GA(B)CDE formulation could look like after we address his perfectionistic goals at G and help him to change his inference at A (Table 12.5). Notice that B is in grey in the example offered in Table 12.5 – this is because the inference at A does not trigger B, but Jason can still endorse a rational way of thinking about his goal to be a contented and

Table 12.5 Jason's new GA(B)CDE formulation.

Element	Detail
Goals (G)	To drive towards being a perfect athlete, and to be a contented and fulfilled human being.
Adversity (concrete)	Short term injury.
Adversity (perception)	I will suffer through inconvenience and pain of rehab.
Adversity (inference)	I will suffer in the short term, but I have an opportunity to test myself, and develop as a human being, through rehab and come back stronger.
Rational beliefs	I want to be, but I do not need to be, a contented and fulfilled human being.
Consequences (cognitive)	Be aware of potential downsides but notice opportunities brought about by situation, hope and determination for the future.
Consequences (behavioural)	Exert time and effort diligently in rehab, express feelings to others by sharing rehab journey learnings with others.
Consequences (emotive)	Healthy sadness, optimism, gratitude.

fulfilled human being. In brief, once we have helped Jason address his irrational belief/s, we can then address his perfectionistic goals if they are or could be maladaptive to Jason in some way.

Concluding Comments

In this chapter we described and discussed the relationship between perfectionism and irrational beliefs in the sports context. Our experiences, beyond what happens to us, are determined by the interpretation we make of the facts. Thus, well-being or discomfort is more related to how we interpret what happens to us than to the event itself. Perfectionism and irrational beliefs are both involved in the sense and meaning making of the experiences we have. To dispute irrational beliefs and promote adaptive, realistic and reasonable objectives that protect the athletes' mental health, and to promote and maintain healthy, successful and sustainable athletic career regardless of performance outcomes, the authors propose the use of REBT in work with perfectionistic athletes. Our case study of the application of REBT with an injured athlete will hopefully help illustrate how to do so and how addressing irrationality is the best means of supporting perfectionistic athletes.

References

Arnold, R., Collington, S., Manley, H., Rees, S., Soanes, J., & Williams, M. (2019). "The team behind the team": Exploring the organizational stressor experiences of sport science and management staff in elite sport. *Journal of Applied Sport Psychology*, 31 (1), 7–26. https://doi.org/10.1080/10413200.2017.1407836.

Bernard, M. E. (2019). REBT in the workplace. In *Advances in REBT* (pp. 353–380). Springer.

Bernard, M. E., Ellis, A., & Terjesen, M. (2006). Rational-emotive behavioral approaches to childhood disorders: History, theory, practice and research. In A. Ellis & M. E. Bernard (eds) *Rational emotive behavioral approaches to childhood disorders*. Springer.

Bowman, A. W., & Turner, M. J. (2022). When time is of the essence: The use of rational emotive behavior therapy (REBT) informed single-session therapy (SST) to alleviate social and golf-specific anxiety, and improve wellbeing and performance, in amateur golfers. *Psychology of Sport and Exercise*, 60, 102167. https://doi.org/10.1016/j.psychsport.2022.102167.

Castonguay, L. G., Constantino, M. J., McAleavey, A. A., & Goldfried, M. R. (2010). The therapeutic alliance in cognitive-behavioral therapy. In J. C. Muran & J. P. Barber (eds), *The therapeutic alliance: An evidence-based guide to practice* (pp. 150–171). The Guilford Press.

Chadha, N. J., Turner, M. J., & Slater, M. J. (2019). Investigating irrational beliefs, cognitive appraisals, challenge and threat, and affective states in golfers approaching competitive situations. *Frontiers in Psychology*, 10, 2295. https://doi.org/10.3389/fpsyg.2019.02295.

Collins, D., MacNamara, Á., & McCarthy, N. (2016). Super champions, champions, and almosts: important differences and commonalities on the rocky road. *Frontiers in Psychology*, 6, 2009. https://doi.org/10.3389/fpsyg.2015.02009.

Cunningham, R., & Turner, M. J. (2016). Using Rational Emotive Behavior Therapy (REBT) with Mixed Martial Arts (MMA) Athletes to Reduce Irrational Beliefs and Increase Unconditional Self-Acceptance. *Journal of Rational-Emotive & Cognitive-Behavior Therapy*, 34(4), 289–309. https://doi.org/10.1007/s10942-016-0240-4.

David, D., Lynn, S. J., & Ellis, A. (2010). *Rational and irrational beliefs: Research, theory, and clinical practice*. Oxford University Press.

David, D., Szentagotai, A., Eva, K., & Macavei, B. (2005). A synopsis of rational Emotive Behavior Therapy (REBT); Fundamental and applied research. *Journal of Rational-Emotive & Cognitive-Behavior Therapy*, 23(3), 175–221. https://doi.org/10.1007/s10942-005-0011-0.

Dickson, J. M., Moberly, N. J., & Huntley, C. D. (2019). Rumination selectively mediates the association between actual-ideal (but not actual-ought) self-discrepancy and anxious and depressive symptoms. *Personality and Individual Differences*, 149, 94–99. https://doi.org/10.1016/j.paid.2019.05.047.

DiGiuseppe, R. (1986). The implication of the philosophy of science for rational-emotive theory and therapy. *Psychotherapy: Theory, Research, Practice, Training*, 23(4), 634–639. https://doi.org/10.1037/h0085668.

DiGiuseppe, R. A., Doyle, K. A., Dryden, W., & Backx, W. (2014). *A practitioner's guide to rational emotive behavior therapy* (3rd ed.). Oxford University Press.

Dixon, M., Turner, M. J., & Gillman, J. (2017). Examining the relationships between challenge and threat cognitive appraisals and coaching behaviours in football coaches. *Journal of Sports Sciences*, 35(24), 2446–2452. https://doi.org/10.1080/02640414.2016.1273538.

Donachie, T. C., & Hill, A. P. (2020). Helping soccer players help themselves: Effectiveness of a psychoeducational book in reducing perfectionism. *Journal of Applied Sport Psychology*, 1–21. https://doi.org/10.1080/10413200.2020.1819472.

Dryden, W. (2019). Brief interventions in rational emotive behavior therapy. In M. E. Bernard, & W. Dryden (eds), *Advances in REBT: Theory, practice, research measurement prevention and promotion* (pp. 211–230). Springer.

Dryden, W. (2021). *Reason to change: A rational emotive behaviour therapy workbook* (2nd ed.). Routledge.

Dryden, W. (2009). *Skills in rational emotive behaviour counselling and psychotherapy*. Sage.

Dryden, W., Beal, D., Jones, J., & Trower, P. (2010). The REBT Competency Scale for Clinical and Research Applications. *Journal of Rational-Emotive & Cognitive-Behavior Therapy*, 28(4), 165–216. https://doi.org/10.1007/s10942-010-0111-3.

Dryden, W., & David, D. (2008). Rational emotive behavior therapy: Current status. *Journal of Cognitive Psychotherapy*, 22(3), 195–209. https://doi.org/10.1891/0889-8391.22.3.195.

Dugdale, J. H., Sanders, D., Myers, T., Williams, A. M., & Hunter, A. M. (2021). Progression from youth to professional soccer: A longitudinal study of successful and unsuccessful academy graduates. *Scandinavian Journal of Medicine & Science in Sports*, 31, 73–84. https://doi.org/10.1111/sms.13701.

Ellis, A. (1973). *Humanistic psychotherapy: The rational-emotive approach*. McGraw-Hill.

Ellis, A. (1958). Rational psychotherapy. *The Journal of General Psychology*, 59(1), 35–49.

Ellis, A. (1957). Rational psychotherapy and individual psychology. *Southern Medical Journal*, 7(1), 451–458. https://doi.org/10.1097/00007611-191406000-00006.

Ellis, A. (1962). *Reason and emotion in psychotherapy*. Lyle Stuart.

Ellis, A. (1994). *Reason and emotion in psychotherapy: Revised and updated*. Secaucus.

Ellis, A. (1976). The biological basis of human irrationality. *Journal of Individual Psychology*, 32, 145–168.

Ellis, A. (1963). Toward a more precise definition of "emotional" and "intellectual" insight. *Psychological Reports*, 13(1), 125–126. https://doi.org/10.2466/pr0.1963.13.1.125.

Ellis, A., & Dryden, W. (1997). *The practice of rational-emotive behaviour therapy*. Springer Publishing Company.

Flett, G. L., Besser, A., Davis, R. A., & Hewitt, P. L. (2003). Dimensions of perfectionism, unconditional self-acceptance, and depression. *Journal of Rational-Emotive and Cognitive-Behavior Therapy*, 21(2), 119–138. https://doi.org/10.1023/A:1025051431957.

Flett, G. L., & Hewitt, P. L. (2014). The perils of perfectionism in sports" revisited: Toward a broader understanding of the pressure to be perfect and its impact on athletes and dancers. *International Journal of Sport Psychology*, 45(4), 395–407. https://doi.org/10.7352/IJSP 2014.45.395.

Frost, R. O., Marten, P., Lahart, C., & Rosenblate, R. (1990). The dimensions of perfectionism. *Cognitive Therapy and Research*, 14, 449–468. https://doi.org/10.1007/BF01172967.

Gollwitzer, P. M., & Sheeran, P. (2006). Implementation intentions and goal achievement: A meta-analysis of effects and processes. In M. P. Zanna (ed.), *Advances in experimental social psychology*, 38 (pp. 69–119). Elsevier. https://doi.org/10.1016/S0065-2601(06)38002-38001.

Gorczynski, P., Currie, A., Gibson, K., Gouttebarge, V., Hainline, B., Castaldelli-Maia, J. M., Mountjoy, M., Purcell, R., Reardon, C. L., Rice, S., & Swartz, L. (2020). Developing mental health literacy and cultural competence in elite sport. *Journal of Applied Sport Psychology*, 33(4), 1–15. https://doi.org/10.1080/10413200.2020.1720045.

Grossmann, B., & Lames, M. (2015). From Talent to Professional Football – Youthism in German Football. *International Journal of Sport Science & Coaching*, 10(6), 1103–1113. https://doi.org/10.1260/1747-9541.10.6.1103.

Haase, A. M., Prapavessis, H., & Owens, R. G. (2002). Perfectionism, social physique anxiety and disordered eating: A comparison of male and female elite athletes.

Psychology of sport and Exercise, 3(3), 209–222. https://doi.org/10.1016/S1469-0292 (01)00018-00018.

Hall, H. K., Hill, A. P., & Appleton, P. R. (2012) Perfectionism: A foundation for sporting excellence or an uneasy pathway toward purgatory? In G. C. Roberts & D. C. Treasure (eds), *Advances in motivation in sport and exercise* (3rd, pp. 129–168). Human Kinetics.

Hall, H. K., Hill, A. P., Appleton, P. R., & Kozub, S. A. (2009). The mediating influence of unconditional self-acceptance and labile self-esteem on the relationship between multidimensional perfectionism and exercise dependence. *Psychology of Sport and Exercise*, 10(1), 35–44. https://doi.org/10.1016/j.psychsport.2008.05.003

Henriksen, K., Schinke, R., Moesch, K., McCann, S., Parham, W. D., Larsen, C. H., & Terry, P. (2020). Consensus statement on improving the mental health of high-performance athletes. *International Journal of Sport and Exercise Psychology*, 18(5), 553–560. https://doi.org/10.1080/1612197X.2019.1570473.

Henriksen, K., Storm, L. K., & Larsen, C. H. (2018). Organizational culture and influence on developing athletes. In C. Knight, C. Harwood, & D. Gould (eds), *Sport psychology for young athletes* (pp. 216–228). Routledge.

Hill, A. P. (2013). Perfectionism and burnout in junior soccer players: A test of the 2×2 model of dispositional perfectionism. *Journal of Sport and Exercise Psychology*, 35(1), 18–29. https://doi.org/10.1123/jsep.35.1.18.

Hill, A. P., Hall, H. K., Appleton, P. R., & Kozub, S. A. (2008). Perfectionism and burnout in junior elite soccer players: The mediating influence of unconditional self-acceptance. *Psychology of Sport and Exercise*, 9(5), 630–644. https://doi.org/10.1016/j.psychsport.2007.09.004.

Hill, A. P., Mallinson-Howard, S. H., Madigan, D. J., & Jowett, G. E. (2020). Perfectionism in sport, dance, and exercise: An extended review and reanalysis. In A. P. Hill, S. H. Mallinson-Howard, D. J. Madigan, and G. E. Jowett (eds), *Handbook of sport psychology* (pp. 121–157). Wiley. https://doi.org/10.1002/9781119568124.ch7.

Horney, K. (1950). *Neurosis and human growth*. W. W. Norton.

Jordana, A., Turner, M. J., Ramis, Y., & Torregrossa, M. (2020). A systematic mapping review on the use of Rational Emotive Behavior Therapy (REBT) with athletes. *International Review of Sport and Exercise Psychology*, online ahead of print. https://doi.org/10.1080/1750984X.2020.1836673.

King, A., Barker, J., Turner, M., & Plateau, C. (2022). The socialisation of athlete irrational beliefs. *Journal of Rational-Emotive and Cognitive-Behavior Therapy*, online ahead of print. https://doi.org/10.1007/s10942-022-00460-4.

Kuettel, A., & Larsen, C. H. (2020). Risk and protective factors for mental health in elite athletes: a scoping review. *International Review of Sport and Exercise Psychology*, 13(1), 231–265. https://doi.org/10.1080/1750984X.2019.1689574.

Lazarus, R. S. (1999). *Stress and emotion: A new synthesis*. Springer.

Lundh, L. G. (2004). Perfectionism and acceptance. *Journal of Rational-Emotive & Cognitive-Behavior Therapy*, 22(4), 251.

MacLaren, C., Doyle, K. A., & DiGiuseppe, R. (2016). Rational emotive behavior therapy (REBT): Theory and practice. *Contemporary Theory and Practice in Counseling and Psychotherapy*, 1, 233–263.

Mansell, P. C. (2021). Stress mindset in athletes: Investigating the relationships between beliefs, challenge and threat with psychological wellbeing. *Psychology of Sport and Exercise*, 57, 102020. https://doi.org/10.1016/j.psychsport.2021.102020.

Matweychuk, W., DiGiuseppe, R., & Gulyayeva, O. (2019). A comparison of REBT with other cognitive Behavior therapies. In M. E. Bernard, & W. Dryden (eds), *Advances in REBT* (pp. 47–77). Springer.

MaultsbyJr., M.. (1971). Rational emotive imagery. *Rational Living*, 6(1), 24–27.

Maxwell-Keys, C., Wood, A. G., & Turner, M. J. (2022). Developing decision making in rugby union match officials using rational Emotive Behavior (REBT). *Psychology of Sport and Exercise*, 58(1), 102098. https://doi.org/10.1016/j.psychsport.2021.102098.

Mesagno, C., Tibbert, S. J., Buchanan, E., Harvey, J. T., & Turner, M. J. (2021). Irrational beliefs and choking under pressure: A preliminary investigation. *Journal of Applied Sport Psychology*, 33(6), 569–589. https://doi.org/10.1080/10413200.2020.1737273.

Michel-Kröhler, A., & Turner, M. J. (2022). Link between irrational beliefs and important markers of mental health in a German sample of athletes: Differences between gender, sport-type and performance level. *Frontiers in Psychology*, 3997. https://doi.org/10.3389/fpsyg.2022.918329.

Neenan, M., & Dryden, W. (1996). The intricacies of inference chaining. *Journal of Rational-Emotive and Cognitive-Behavior Therapy*, 14(4), 231–243.

Nordin-Bates, S. M., & Abrahamsen, F. (2016). Perfectionism in dance: A case example and applied considerations. In *The psychology of perfectionism in sport, dance and exercise* (pp. 238–260). Routledge.

Nordin-Bates, S. M., Radeke, T. D., & Madigan, D. J. (2017). Perfectionism, Burnout, and Motivation in Dance: A Replication and Test of the 2 × 2 Model of Perfectionism. *Journal of Dance & Medicine Science*, 21, 115–122.

Oltean, H. R., Hyland, P., Vallières, F., & David, D. O. (2019). Rational beliefs, happiness and optimism: An empirical assessment of REBT's model of psychological health. *International Journal of Psychology*, 54(4), 495–500. https://doi.org/10.1002/ijop.12492.

Pereira-Vargas, M. L. F., Papathomas, A., Williams, T. L., Kinnafick, F. E., & Rhodes, P. (2021). Diverse paradigms and stories: mapping "mental illness" in athletes through meta-study. *International Review of Sport and Exercise Psychology*, online ahead of print. https://doi.org/10.1080/1750984X.2021.2001840.

Pons, J., Ramis, Y., Alcaraz, S., Jordana, A., Borrueco, M., y Torregrossa, M. (2020). Where did all the sport go? negative impact of COVID-19 lockdown on life-spheres and mental health of Spanish young athletes. *Frontiers in Psychology*, 11, 3498. https://doi.org/10.3389/fpsyg.2020.611872.

Ramis, Y., Torregrossa, M., & Latinjak, A. T. (2017). *Perfectionistic strivings and concerns on the emotional experience of young athletes* [Poster]. XIV World Congress of Sport Psychology, International Society of Sport Psychology, Sevilla, Spain, July.

Raue, P. J., & Goldfried, M. R. (1994). Therapeutic alliance in cognitive-behavior therapy. In A. O. Horvath & L. S. Greenberg (eds), *The working alliance: Theory, research and practice* (pp. 131–152). Wiley.

Rumbold, J. L., Fletcher, D., & Daniels, K. (2012). A systematic review of stress management interventions with sport performers. *Sport, Exercise, and Performance Psychology*, 1(3), 173–193. https://doi.org/10.1037/a0026628.

Ruth, W. J. (1992). Irrational thinking in humans: An evolutionary proposal for Ellis" genetic postulate. *Journal of Rational-Emotive and Cognitive-Behavior Therapy*, 10(1), 3–20.

Shermer, M. (2011). The believing brain: Why science is the only way out of the trap of belief-dependent realism. *Scientific American*, 305(1), 85.

Sille, R. A., Turner, M. J., & Eubank, M. R. (2020). "Don't be stupid, Stupid!": Cognitive-behavioral techniques to reduce irrational beliefs and enhance focus in a youth tennis player. *Case Studies in Sport and Exercise Psychology*, 4(1), 40–51. https://doi.org/10.1123/cssep.2019-0018.

Stambulova, N. B., Ryba, T. V., & Henriksen, K. (2021). Career development and transitions of athletes: The international society of sport psychology position stand revisited. *International Journal of Sport and Exercise Psychology*, 19(4), 524–550. https://doi.org/10.1080/1612197X.2020.1737836.

Stoeber, J., & Eismann, U. (2007). Perfectionism in young musicians: Relations with motivation, effort, achievement, and distress. *Personality and Individual Differences*, 43(8), 2182–2192.

Stoeber, J., & Gaudreau, P. (2017). The advantages of partialling perfectionistic strivings and perfectionistic concerns: Critical issues and recommendations. *Personality and Individual Differences*, 104, 379–386. https://doi.org/10.1016/j.paid.2016.08.039.

Stoeber, J., & Otto, K. (2006). Positive conceptions of perfectionism: Approaches, evidence, challenges. *Personality and Social Psychology Review*, 10(4), 295–319. https://doi.org/10.1207/s15327957pspr1004_2.

Terry-Short, L. A., Owens, R. G., Slade, P. D., & Dewey, M. E. (1995). Positive and negative perfectionism. *Personality and Individual Differences*, 18(5), 663–668. http://doi.org/10.1016/0191-8869(94)00192-U.

Tóth, R., Turner, M. J., Kökény, T., & Tóth, L. (2022). "I must be perfect": The role of irrational beliefs and perfectionism on the competitive anxiety of Hungarian athletes. *Frontiers in Psychology*, 13.

Turner, M. J. (2016a). Proposing a rational resilience credo for athletes. *Journal of Sport Psychology in Action*, 7(3), 170–181. https://doi.org/10.1080/21520704.2016.1236051.

Turner, M. J. (2016b). Rational emotive behavior therapy (REBT), irrational and rational beliefs, and the mental health of athletes. *Frontiers in Psychology*, 7(9), 1–16. https://doi.org/10.3389/fpsyg.2016.01423.

Turner, M. J. (2019). REBT in sport. In M. E. Bernard, & W. Dryden (eds), *Advances in REBT* (pp. 307–335). Springer.

Turner, M. J. (2014). Smarter thinking in sport. *The Psychologist*, 27(8), 596–599.

Turner, M. J. (2020). The Olympic Games: The rational pursuit of excellence. *MMU News*, August 6. Retrieved from www.mmu.ac.uk/hpsc/news-and-media/news/story/?id=12703.

Turner, M. J. (2022). *The rational practitioner: The sport and performance psychologist's guide to practicing rational emotive behaviour therapy*. Routledge.

Turner, M. J., & Allen, M. S. (2018). Confirmatory factor analysis of the irrational performance beliefs Inventory (iPBI) in a sample of amateur and semi-professional athletes. *Psychology of Sport and Exercise*, 35(3), 126–130. https://doi.org/10.1016/j.psychsport.2017.11.017.

Turner, M. J., Aspin, G., Didymus, F. F., Mack, R., Olusoga, P., Wood, A. G., & Bennett, R. (2020). One case, four approaches: The application of psychotherapeutic approaches in sport psychology. *The Sport Psychologist*, 34(1), 71–83. https://doi.org/10.1123/tsp.2019-0079.

Turner, M. J., & Barker, J. B. (2014). Using Rational Emotive Behavior Therapy with athletes. *The Sport Psychologist*, 28(1), 75–90. https://doi.org/10.1123/tsp.2013-0012.

Turner, M. J., & Bennett, R. (2018). *Rational emotive behavior therapy in sport and exercise*. Routledge.

Turner, M. J., Miller, A., Youngs, H., Barber, N., Brick, N. E., Chadha, N. J., Chandler, C., Coyle, M., Didymus, F. F.., Evans, A. L., Jones, K., McCann, B.,

Meijen, C., & Rossato, C. J. L. (2022). "I must do this!": A latent profile analysis approach to understanding the role of irrational beliefs and motivation regulation in mental and physical health. *Journal of Sports Sciences*. https://doi.org/10.1080/02640414.2022.2042124.

Turner, M. J., & Wood, A. G. (2021). The Smarter Thinking app. *Sci-Ed*, 11 November. Retrieved from https://thesmarterthinkingproject.com/the-smarter-thinking-app/.

Turner, M. J., Wood, A. G., Barker, J. B., & Chadha, N. (2019). Rational self-talk: A Rational Emotive Behaviour Therapy (REBT) perspective. In A. T. Latinjak, & A. Hatzigeorgiadis (eds). *Self-talk in sport*. Routledge.

Vîslă, A., Flückiger, C., Holtforth, M. G., & David, D. (2016). Irrational beliefs and psychological distress: A meta-analysis. *Psychotherapy and Psychosomatics*, 85, 8–15. https://doi.org/10.1159/000441231.

Watkins, E. R. (2018). *Rumination-focused cognitive-behavioral therapy for depression*. Guilford Press.

Watson, D. R., Hill, A. P., & Madigan, D. J. (2021). Perfectionism and Attitudes Toward Sport Psychology Support and Mental Health Support in Athletes. *Journal of Clinical Sport Psychology*, online ahead of print.

Wood, A. G., Turner, M. J., & Barker, J. B. (2019). Bolstering psychological health using rational emotive behaviour therapy. In G. Breslin, & G. Leavey (eds), *Mental health and well-being interventions in sport: Research, theory and practice* (pp. 45–62). Routledge.

Woody, S. R., & Adessky, R. S. (2002). Therapeutic alliance, group cohesion, and homework compliance during cognitive-behavioral group treatment of social phobia. *Behavior Therapy*, 33, 5–27.

World Health Organization (WHO) (2014) *Data repository: Human resources data by country*. World Health Organization.

Wylleman, P. (2019). An organizational perspective on applied sport psychology in elite sport. *Psychology of Sport and Exercise*, 42(5), 89–99. https://doi.org/10.1016/j.psychsport.2019.01.008.

Part V

Reflections and Future Directions

13 Reflections on 20 Years Studying Multidimensional Perfectionism in Sport

John G. H. Dunn

When Andrew Hill approached me to write this reflection about my 20-year journey studying multidimensional perfectionism in sport, I was both honoured and grateful to receive the invitation. However, I was also a little nervous about undertaking this endeavour given the challenge of living up to the exceptional quality of the concluding chapters that were written for the first edition of this textbook. Despite my trepidation, I was still excited about the prospect of taking a sentimental (and hopefully thought-provoking) trip down memory lane knowing that this chapter will almost certainly be the last piece of academic writing I produce on the topic of perfectionism in sport before I retire. Having kindly hosted me as a visiting scholar for a month at York St John University in 2019, Andrew was aware of my pending retirement and suggested that this chapter might be a fitting way for me to conclude my academic career by discussing issues surrounding perfectionism in sport that have interested me for many years. I also saw this chapter as the perfect opportunity – if you pardon the pun – to highlight the contributions of many researchers and theorists whose work I have long admired, and whose ideas inspired my interest in, and challenged my thinking about, perfectionism in sport.

I start by offering a brief definition of perfectionism to ensure that readers understand how I view the construct. I conceptualize perfectionism in sport as a *domain-specific* multidimensional achievement-motivation disposition on the grounds that levels of perfectionism often differ for individuals across different achievement settings (Stoeber & Stoeber, 2009), with athletes typically reporting higher perfectionistic tendencies in sport than in other achievement contexts (Dunn et al., 2005, 2012). In keeping with the views of Stoeber (2018), given the lack of absolute stability in perfectionism levels across different achievement domains, I also adopt the perspective that it is more appropriate to conceptualize perfectionism as a personality *disposition* than a personality *trait*. I use the term *achievement-motivation* in the definition because perfectionistic tendencies drive (i.e. motivate) many behaviours of individuals who pursue success (i.e. achievement) – or who try to avoid failure – in sport. And finally, I use the term *multidimensional* because this is in keeping with contemporary views of perfectionism in sport where perfectionism is conceptualized as a broad higher-order construct that captures (a) the degree to which athletes strive for flawlessness and the attainment of extremely high standards of personal performance in sport, and (b) the degree to

DOI: 10.4324/9781003288015-18

which athletes are concerned about the consequences of failing to reach these high standards. These higher-order dimensions are typically labelled as *perfectionistic strivings* and *perfectionistic concerns* in the sport perfectionism literature (e.g. Gotwals et al., 2012; Hill et al., 2018; Stoeber & Madigan, 2016) – terms originally coined by Joachim Stoeber and Kathleen Otto in the general psychology literature (Stoeber & Otto, 2006).

Perfectionism Research in Sport: The Early Days

When I was a graduate student (1989–1998) studying for my MA and PhD at the University of Alberta (U of A), my research interests focused largely upon the stress process in sport, and more specifically upon competitive sport anxiety, worry, and perceived threat in athletes. My motivation for studying these aspects of the stress process was twofold. First, I was still competing as a student-athlete on the varsity soccer team at the U of A, and as an athlete who experienced a considerable amount of pre-competition anxiety, I was always looking to better understand my own emotions and to find ways that would enhance my ability to cope more effectively with the pressures of competition (and improve my on-field perfor-mance). Second, I had (and still have) an insatiable desire to understand the psy-chology of human performance in stressful situations, and in particular to answer the question, "*Why do we so often see a wide array of cognitive, emotional, and beha-vioural responses in different people when they are confronted with (what appears to be) the same objective stressor?*" For example, after losing an important competition, why do some athletes get angry, others feel a sense of shame or embarrassment, a few will ruminate on their failure for weeks, and some will even leave their sport entirely, while others remain calm, become more determined to succeed, and quickly turn their attention to the process of trying to learn/grow from their stressful encoun-ter? My desire to understand this (and many related) questions steered me towards the study of personality and emotion in sport, and eventually to the study of perfectionism in athletes.

My interest in athlete perfectionism really began midway through my doc-toral program when I was working on a study that examined characteristics of anxiety-inducing situations in team sports (see Dunn & Nielsen, 1996). This research had nothing to do with perfectionism and there were less than a handful of published studies on perfectionism in sport at the time when I conducted the study. While preparing the manuscript, I came across a series of papers by Tara Scanlan and her colleagues (Scanlan et al., 1989a, 1989b, 1991). These papers outlined a qualitative research project – long before qualitative research had become an established part of the mainstream sport psychology literature – that examined sources of enjoyment and sources of stress in former elite-level figure skaters. The second paper of their project focussed upon sources of enjoyment where Scanlan et al. (1989b) clustered some of the figure skaters' responses into a thematic category labelled *striving for perfection*. The authors presented the following athlete quote to illustrate the conceptual meaning of this theme: "It was just more challenging to try and do the figures perfectly. Working on that, I just really enjoyed that" (p. 69). Scanlan et al. concluded that striving for perfection was an enjoyable part of the mastery process that assisted athletes in their efforts to pursue success at the highest levels of competitive sport.

In contrast to the enjoyment that figure skaters experienced when striving for perfection, Scanlan and colleagues presented findings in the third paper of their project that focussed on sources of stress (Scanlan et al., 1991). Athletes spoke about the stress they experienced when trying to live up to the "performance expectations" (p. 113) set by significant others (i.e. parents, coaches, and teammates). One athlete said, "My parents had high standards for me. And in that sense, I tried to live up to the standards that I think they had set for me. I felt like they really expected me to do perfect" (p. 113). Another athlete talked about stress emanating from the belief that they "could never give enough ... I would try as hard as I could [to meet the standards set by others], but it wouldn't be enough" (p. 113). Readers familiar with the perfectionism literature will recognize that the contents of these athlete quotes reflect central features of *socially prescribed perfectionism* (Hewitt & Flett, 1991) – the interpersonal dimension of perfectionism that captures the degree to which individuals perceive pressure to achieve exactingly high (or perfect) performance standards from other people.

Scanlan et al. (1991) also presented a theme from their sources-of-stress data labelled *perfectionism* – defined by the authors as a source of stress that captured figure skaters' "need to skate flawlessly" and their inability "to accept anything less than an error-free performance" (p. 115). An exemplar quote from an athlete illustrating the meaning of this perfectionism theme read, "I was a perfectionist ... that's probably the hardest thing; I was just a perfectionist all the time ... I would never accept myself not doing it perfectly" (p. 115). On the basis of their findings, Scanlan et al. (1991) concluded that "Skaters feeling the *need* to skate flawlessly experienced stress, but skaters *striving* for perfection experienced enjoyment" (emphases in original: p. 116). I regard Tara Scanlan's work as the first body of research in the sport psychology literature to provide evidence of the potential "dual nature" of perfectionism in sport (see Stoeber, 2011). As such, I have always found it surprising that, despite holding the status of what I believe should be regarded as pioneering work that set the stage for future research examining adaptive versus maladaptive aspects of perfectionism in sport, those who study perfectionism in sport have paid relatively little attention to Scanlan et al.'s (1989b, 1991) work.

Ten years after Scanlan et al.'s (1991) research was published – and one year before I would publish my first research paper on the topic of perfectionism in sport (i.e. Dunn et al., 2002) – I read a chapter by Nate Zinsser et al. (2001) in an applied sport psychology textbook that further stimulated my desire to learn more about perfectionism in athletes. In the context of a discussion about distorted and irrational thinking in sport, Zinsser et al. stated, "There is always value in [athletes] *striving* for perfection, but nothing is gained by [athletes] *demanding* perfection" (emphases in original: p. 302). Seeing what I regarded as a connection between the position of Zinsser et al. and the findings about the dual nature of perfectionism in sport presented by Scanlan et al. (1989b, 1991), I became more intrigued by the idea that the manner in which athletes framed their pursuit of perfection (or framed the meaning of a lack of perfection) might determine the types of cognitive, affective, and behavioural responses athletes experienced during the achievement striving process in sport.

My interest in athlete perfectionism continued to grow as a handful of research papers that examined perfectionism as a multidimensional construct started to appear in the sport psychology literature during the 1990s (e.g. Coen & Ogles, 1993; Frost & Henderson, 1991; Gould et al., 1996). However, it was not until I read two papers that presented very different views about the role of perfectionism in sport that I finally decided to make perfectionism the primary focus of my research. The first paper was written by Dan Gould and his colleagues (2002); their research explored psychological characteristics underlying athletic success among Olympic champions. (It should be noted that ten years before the publication of the study by Gould et al., 2002, Dan Gould had been recognized by 65 of his peers within the academic sport psychology community as one of the leading sport psychologists in North America "who had made the greatest contributions to the advancement of sport psychology during the decade (1980–1990)" [Straub & Hinman, 1992, p. 298]). The second paper was written by Gordon Flett and Paul Hewitt in which the authors presented their views about the role of perfectionism in sport and exercise settings (Flett & Hewitt, 2005). (Readers who are familiar with the perfectionism literature should need no introduction to the immense contributions that Gordon Flett and Paul Hewitt have made to the study of perfectionism over the last 30 years. Their seminal textbook on perfectionism – *Perfectionism: Theory, Research, and Treatment* [Flett & Hewitt, 2002] – has been opened more times than any other book that sits upon the bookshelves in my office).

Gould et al.'s (2002) paper described a mixed-methods study that explored the psychological characteristics of ten US Olympic champions who had won a combined total of 32 Olympic medals (28 gold) during their careers. This sample is truly deserving of the label "elite" – something that I cannot always say about studies in the sport psychology literature that use the term elite to describe their samples. In addition to participating in qualitative interviews, athletes completed a battery of self-report instruments that measured an array of psychological characteristics including (but not limited to) competitive trait anxiety, dispositional optimism, and multidimensional perfectionism. Perfectionism was measured using Frost et al.'s (1990) *Multidimensional Perfectionism Scale* (F-MPS) – an instrument that profoundly influenced the way I would measure athlete perfectionism in my own research for years to come. Following an examination of the pattern of scores across the six subscales contained within the F-MPS – with athletes generally scoring moderately high or high on the *personal standards* and *organization* subscales (sub-dimensions of perfectionistic strivings), but low on the *concern over mistakes, doubts about actions, parental criticism*, and *parental expectations* subscales (sub-dimensions of perfectionistic concerns) – Gould et al. (2002) concluded that this pattern of responses reflected a profile of "adaptive perfectionism" (p. 172) that had been seen in studies outside the sport psychology literature (e.g. Parker, 1997; Rice & Mirzadeh, 2000; Rice & Slaney, 2002) and recommended that "future researchers should explore both the positive and negative aspects of perfectionistic tendencies in athletes and their relationship to athletic success" (p. 198).

Three years after the publication of Gould et al.'s (2002) study, Flett and Hewitt (2005) published their paper titled, *The Perils of Perfectionism in Sports and Exercise*. In the introduction section of their paper, Flett and Hewitt stated, "We adopt the position, consistent with our previous conceptualizations of perfectionism (Hewitt & Flett, 1991) that perfectionism is primarily a negative factor that contributes to maladaptive outcomes among athletes and exercisers" (p. 14). Being a relative newcomer to the field of perfectionism research when Flett and Hewitt published their paper, I was intrigued (and am still intrigued) by the fact that two of the foremost authorities on perfectionism research would maintain a position that perfectionism primarily leads to maladaptive outcomes in sport, yet a leading scholar in the field of applied sport psychology – Dan Gould – would argue that seeking perfection in sport could help athletes attain success at the highest levels of competitive sport. Even as I approach retirement this issue still fascinates me and I believe is still deserving of research attention from the scientific community.

Beyond the intellectual curiosity that these papers stimulated within me as I started to explore perfectionism in sport more deeply, my interest in athlete perfectionism was also fuelled by the degree to which (I thought) I saw perfectionism operating among athletes who competed in elite-level sport. (Readers should know that in addition to conducting research in the field of sport psychology for the last 30 years, I have also had the privilege of working as a mental performance coach with a host of athletes in intercollegiate sport, professional sport, and international sport, including a number of athletes/teams who have stood on top of the podium at World Championships and/or Olympic Games). To illustrate where (I thought) I saw perfectionism operate in elite-level sport beyond what I had read in research papers, I turn to an Entertainment and Sports Programming Network (ESPN) *SportsCentury* documentary that first aired on North American television in August 2004. The documentary focussed upon the early stages of the professional career of future hall-of-fame quarterback, Peyton Manning.

Peyton Manning (now retired) was an elite level quarterback in the National Football League (NFL) who would eventually win Super Bowl titles playing for the Indianapolis Colts (2007) and the Denver Broncos (2016). Interested readers can still find this documentary on YouTube (Quinn, 2014). When the documentary first aired, Manning had just won consecutive NFL Most Valuable Player (MVP) awards in 2003 and 2004, and would eventually go on to win three more League MVP titles before retiring. Part of the documentary focussed on a number of Manning's coaches, teammates, and family members who talked about his obsessive commitment to watching game film and to studying scouting reports as he prepared to face opposing teams. Manning responded to these comments in the documentary saying, "I'm a preparation freak. I've never been embarrassed about that. I feel so accountable and responsible to so many people. I feel guilty if I haven't prepared for the situation."

Tony Dungy – head coach of the Indianapolis Colts – commented in the documentary that Manning "wants to win every game. Not only win the game, but not throw an incomplete pass. Not have anything go wrong in the game. And he can pick apart games that we've scored 50 points in and he still feels bad about certain things." John Ed Bradley – a senior writer for Sports Illustrated magazine – followed Dungy in the documentary saying, "I think he [Manning] expects the world from himself, and he expects the same from his teammates. He's always been a perfectionist." Finally, one of Manning's teammates, Jeff Saturday, said, "He [Manning] wants things to be perfect, and at times when they are not [perfect] he comes down on guys pretty hard. But it's not always reciprocal you know. He doesn't like guys challenging him on occasion."

Watching and listening to the aforementioned extracts from the ESPN documentary strengthened (and continues to maintain) my interest in athlete perfectionism because, on one hand, Manning's quest to be perfect appeared to be associated with a host of potentially unhealthy responses – a finding consistent with Flett and Hewitt's (2005) views about the maladaptive consequences of perfectionism in sport. Specifically, Manning's obsession with preparation was apparently driven by guilt (or the need to avoid guilt), he had an overly critical view of performance (even when great success had been achieved), and he had an intolerance of mistakes or less-than-perfect performances from his teammates (but was not open to receiving critical feedback from others when he failed to reach certain performance expectations). On the other hand, Manning's apparent quest for perfection (and corresponding commitment to preparation) seemed to play a key role in helping him achieve the highest performance standards in one of the most competitive (and high profile) professional sport leagues in the world – an outcome that seemed consistent with Gould et al.'s (2002) views about the potential benefits of athlete perfectionism in elite-level sport. Once again, I could not help but notice the apparent contradictory nature of perfectionism in sport. I determined that the best way to understand the role of perfectionism in sport was to examine the construct through my own research.

Measuring Multidimensional Perfectionism in Sport

A substantial part of my research in perfectionism has been the validation and extensive use of the *Sport Multidimensional Perfectionism Scale-2* (Sport-MPS-2: Gotwals & Dunn, 2009) and its predecessor, the *Sport Multidimensional Perfectionism Scale* (Sport-MPS: Dunn et al., 2002, 2006). When I first became interested in studying perfectionism in athletes, I focussed my attention on two instruments that enabled me to examine dispositional perfectionism as a multidimensional construct – namely, the F-MPS (Frost et al., 1990) and Hewitt and Flett's (1991) measure that is also named the *Multidimensional Perfectionism Scale*

(HF-MPS). Moreover, when I was preparing to conduct my first study of perfectionism in sport, all of the papers I had read in the sport psychology literature that quantitatively assessed multidimensional perfectionism in athletes had used the F-MPS (e.g. Frost & Henderson, 1991; Gould et al., 1996; Hall et al., 1998). Given that I was new to the field of perfectionism and I wanted to heighten the chances of getting my work approved by reviewers (an objective that has influenced many "strategic research decisions" I have made throughout my academic career), I elected to pursue the study of perfectionism in sport using the framework provided by the F-MPS (rather than the HF-MPS). Readers should be aware, however, that I subsequently used variations of the HF-MPS to good effect in a number of studies that examined perfectionism in athletes (e.g. Dunn et al., 2005, 2011, 2012).

The F-MPS was constructed within a theoretical framework that conceptualized perfectionism as a domain-general (or global/generic) personality characteristic. As such, the F-MPS did not provide a specific situational or contextual frame of reference for individuals to consider when responding to items contained within the instrument, though it should be noted that two of the original 35 items contained within the instrument do mention school and/or work contexts. This domain-general conceptualization of perfectionism concerned me because, as mentioned previously, I had examined the construct of competitive anxiety in sport during my graduate studies and there was an extensive body of empirical evidence within the sport psychology literature indicating that anxiety in sport was best conceptualized and measured as a domain-specific construct rather than a domain-general construct (see Martens et al., 1990; Smith et al., 1990). Consequently, I felt that there might be value in pursuing the study of perfectionism in sport using a domain-specific approach; a position that I still advocate today.

The Sport-MPS was initially labelled the Football-MPS because it was used to measure dispositional perfectionism in a sample of high-performance male youth Canadian Football players (see Dunn et al., 2002). To enhance the domain-specificity of the instrument, the words "competition" or "sport" were added to the majority of the items from the F-MPS. Although the F-MPS contained six subscales – *personal standards* (PS), *organization* (ORG), *concern over mistakes* (COM), *doubts about actions* (DAA), *parental expectations* (PE), and *parental criticism* (PC) – factor analysis results indicated that it was appropriate to combine the PE and PC subscales into a single subscale labelled *perceived parental pressure* within the Football-MPS (Dunn et al., 2002). Moreover, the ORG and DAA subscales from the F-MPS were omitted from the Football-MPS due to concerns about the face validity of the items. Specifically, my co-authors (Janice Causgrove Dunn and Dan Syrotuik) and I believed that the athletes in our study might question the relevance of the instrument if they were asked to respond to items that focussed, for example, on being a "neat person" (ORG) or getting "behind in their work" (DAA) after being informed that the "purpose of the questionnaire was to 'identify how players view certain aspects of their competitive experiences in sport'" (Dunn et al., 2002, p. 381).

In addition to dropping the ORG and DAA subscales in the original scale-construction study, we added a number of new items to the Football-MPS that focussed upon the degree to which football players perceived social pressures from *coaches* to live up to very high performance-standards/expectations in sport (Dunn et al., 2002). The newly constructed items mirrored the content and structure of the existing *parental expectations* and *parental criticism* items contained within the F-MPS, with the word "parent" being replaced with the word "coach". Given that Frost et al. (1990) and Hewitt and Flett (1991) had included perceived interpersonal pressures to be perfect in their instruments, and knowing the degree to which coaches can profoundly influence the cognitive, affective, and behavioural experiences of athletes in competitive sport settings, we added these new items to the Football-MPS to measure *perceived coach pressure* (PCP) in sport.

Although some researchers have adopted the position that perceived coach pressure and perceived parental pressure (to reach very high standards of performance in sport) should be regarded as *antecedents* of perfectionistic concerns rather than central dimensions of perfectionistic concerns (e.g. Grugan et al., 2021; Madigan et al., 2019; Stoeber & Otto, 2006), I adhere to the view that perceived coach pressure and perceived parental pressure represent important domain-specific facets of socially prescribed perfectionism in sport (see Dunn et al., 2006, 2011, 2022). Determining whether perceived coach pressure and perceived parental pressure are better regarded as antecedents of perfectionistic concerns or as central sub-dimensions of perfectionistic concerns is a difficult task because, on one hand, it seems likely that pressure from significant others will heighten the degree to which athletes experience elevated levels of perfectionistic concerns in sport (Madigan et al., 2019). However, on the other hand, socially prescribed perfectionism (and corresponding concerns, worries, and fears) is a central sub-dimension of perfectionistic concerns in sport (Stoeber & Madigan, 2016) – where perfectionistic concerns represent "those aspects of perfectionism associated with concerns over making mistakes, fear of negative social evaluation, feelings of discrepancy between one's expectations and performance, and negative reactions to imperfection" (Gotwals et al., 2012, p. 264).

Why do I regard perceived coach pressure (PCP) and perceived parental pressure (PPP) as domain-specific facets of socially prescribed perfectionism, and therefore as *de facto* sub-dimensions of perfectionistic concerns in sport? First, this perspective is consistent with the theoretical framework upon which the PCP and PPP subscales were constructed (see Dunn et al., 2002, 2006; Gotwals & Dunn, 2009; Gotwals et al., 2010). Second, in our instrument-construction work, both PCP and PPP were highly correlated with the socially prescribed perfectionism subscale of the HF-MPS ($rs \geq .60$, $ps < .001$) in a study of competitive figure skaters (Dunn et al., 2011), and moderately correlated with socially prescribed perfectionism ($rs = .42$ and .53 respectively, $ps < .001$) in a study of youth Canadian Football players (Dunn et al., 2006). Third, I see a high degree of conceptual overlap between the content of many PCP and PPP items in the Sport-MPS-2 and the content of items that comprise the socially prescribed perfectionism subscale of the HF-MPS. For example, I see a high degree of conceptual similarity between the PCP item from the Sport-MPS-2, *"I feel like I can never quite live up to my coach's standards"*, and the socially prescribed perfectionism item from the HF-MPS, *"I find it difficult to meet others' expectations of me."* Similarly, I see a high degree of conceptual similarity between the PPP item from the Sport-MPS-2, *"Only outstanding performance during competition is good enough in my family"*, and the socially pre-scribed perfectionism item from the HF-MPS, *"Anything I do that is less than excellent will be seen as poor work by those around me."*

I am also mindful of the results of factor analytic studies using data obtained from domain-general approaches that examined perfectionism in samples from the general population (outside the context of sport). These studies have repeatedly shown that the *parental expectations* and *parental criticism* subscales of the F-MPS and the *socially prescribed perfectionism* subscale of the HF-MPS load on the same higher-order factor – labelled by Frost et al. (1993, p. 124) as "maladaptive evaluative concerns" (also see Slaney et al., 1995; Suddarth & Slaney, 2001). This factor closely resembles the higher-order dimension of perfectionistic concerns in sport. And finally, the PPP and PCP subscales from the Sport-MPS/Sport-MPS-2 have consistently loaded on a *perfectionistic-concerns-in-sport* factor following second-order factor analyses of sport perfectionism data provided by a number of independent samples of athletes (see Dunn et al., 2016). I hope that future research will find a way to determine whether perceived coach pressure and perceived parental pressure are best regarded as domain-specific *antecedents* of perfectionistic concerns in sport or as domain-specific *sub-dimensions* of perfectionistic concerns in sport.

Although the Football-MPS – re-named as the *Sport-MPS* by Dunn et al. (2006) – consistently demonstrated good psychometric properties (in terms of factorial validity and internal reliability), questions remained as to whether the construct of multidimensional perfectionism in sport was underrepresented given that (a) two of the original F-MPS subscales (i.e. organization and doubts about actions) had been omitted from the Sport-MPS (see Vallance et al., 2006), and (b) studies that employed the F-MPS to measure domain-general perfectionism in athletes invariably used one or both of these subscales (e.g. Coen & Ogles, 1993; Gould et al., 2002; Kaye et al., 2008). These circum-stances lead John Gotwals to develop domain-specific versions of the organi-zation and doubts about actions subscales for inclusion in the Sport-MPS-2 (see Gotwals & Dunn, 2009; Gotwals et al., 2010).

I was (and still am) very impressed at the rigorous scale-construction and construct-validation processes that John Gotwals employed when creating the organization and doubts about actions subscales for the Sport-MPS-2. I also believe that the organization and doubts about actions subscales respectively capture important sub-dimensions of perfectionistic strivings and perfectionistic concerns in sport (see Dunn et al., 2016, 2021). However, if I could turn back time, I would have advised against using the labels "organization" and "doubts about actions" in reference to these respective subscales when the Sport-MPS-2 was created. I make this comment because I now believe that the labels have added to the *jingle-jangle problem* that so often surrounds the measurement of constructs in sport psychology research (see Marsh, 1994), whereby instruments/subscales with similar labels are mistakenly assumed to measure the same constructs (the jingle fallacy) and instruments/subscales with different labels are mistakenly assumed to measure different constructs (the jangle fallacy).

If readers look at the subscale labels contained within the Sport-MPS-2 (see Gotwals & Dunn, 2009) and the F-MPS (see Frost et al., 1990), they will see that the labels for the personal standards, concern over mistakes, organization, and doubts about actions subscales are identical for each instrument. Although there is a high degree of parallel structure and conceptual similarity of the items contained within the other subscales, the item content of the *organization* and *doubts about actions* subscales in the Sport-MPS-2 and F-MPS are quite different (see Frost et al., 1990; Gotwals & Dunn, 2009). Moreover, the bivariate correlation (r) between the organization subscales of the Sport-MPS-2 and the F-MPS (reported by Gotwals et al., 2010, using data provided by male intercollegiate ice hockey players) was .29 ($p < .001$), and the bivariate correlation between the doubts about actions subscales of the two instruments was .43 ($p < .001$). Although in a positive direction (and statistically significant), one might expect the relationship to be stronger and greater shared variance between these parallel subscales. I therefore now question the extent these subscales measure the same constructs, and whether it is appropriate to directly compare results from different studies that have used them. If given the chance to have a "research do over", I would be more inclined to use the label "*competitive planning and routines*" in reference to the organization subscale of the Sport-MPS-2 and the label "*preparation uncertainty and dissatisfaction*" in reference to the doubts about actions subscale of Sport-MPS-2.

Upon reflection, I would also consider adding the words "perfect/perfection" or "flawless" to the content of more items within the Sport-MPS-2 to further enhance the content relevance and content representativeness of the instrument as a measure of perfectionism in sport. Only two (of 42) items in the Sport-MPS-2 actually focus on the attainment of perfect/flawless performance (i.e. "*I feel like my coach criticizes me for doing things less than perfectly in competition*" and "*I feel like I am criticized by my parents for doing things less than perfectly in competition*"), although a number of items do infer a lack of perfection/flawlessness without using these specific terms (e.g. "*If I play well but only make one obvious mistake in the entire game, I still feel disappointed with my performance*" and "*Even if I fail slightly in competition, for me, it is as bad as being a complete failure*"). In its current form, I believe that the item content of the Sport-MPS-2 does an excellent job of capturing the degree to which athletes pursue very high standards of performance in sport – a key aspect of perfectionism. However, the instrument could be improved if items also had a greater focus upon the degree to which athletes seek the perfect or flawless achievement of these very high standards – another key aspect of perfectionism. Fortunately, this content-relevance/representativeness issue can be alleviated when researchers use the Sport-MPS-2 in conjunction with other domain-specific measures of perfectionism in sport that do include the word "perfect" or "perfection" to a greater degree in their item content (e.g. the *Multidimensional Inventory of Perfectionism in Sport* [MIPS: Stoeber et al., 2006] or the *Performance Perfectionism Scale for Sport* [PPS-S: Hill et al., 2016]). Using items from these other instruments (that focus on "being perfect") in conjunction with Sport-MPS-2 items ensures that the degree to which athletes pursue very high standards of performance *and* the degree to which athletes seek the flawless attainment of these performance standards is captured during the measurement process. Of course, researchers must carefully balance the number of items they choose to measure perfectionism in sport with the "time burden" that the addition of items/ measures might impose upon the respondents who participate in our studies.

In closing my commentary about future research directions surrounding the measurement of multidimensional perfectionism in sport, I believe that there is still a need for more research that examines the degree to which domain-specific measures of perfectionism in sport (such as the Sport-MPS-2, the MIPS, or the PPS-S) account for unique variance in domain-matched criterion variables in sport beyond the variance that is accounted for by domain-*general* measures of perfectionism (such as the F-MPS or the HF-MPS). I make this comment because (to the best of my knowledge) there are very few published studies in the sport psychology literature that have actually used a combination of domain-specific *and* domain-general measures of perfectionism in the *same* study to predict (or explain) variance in theoretically relevant domain-matched criterion variables. If domain-specific measures of perfectionism are found to provide a greater understanding of the cognitive, affective, and behavioural tendencies of athletes in sport than domain-general measures of perfectionism – which I suspect will often be the case (see Dunn et al., 2011; Gotwals et al., 2010) – such knowledge would be extremely useful for coaches and applied sport psychologists who seek to better understand personality characteristics that underly athlete performance and achievement in sport.

Who (or What) Is a Perfectionist?

During my attempts to better understand the role of multidimensional perfectionism in sport over the last 20 years, I have often faced the question, "*who (or what) is a perfectionist?*" Readers may be surprised (or even disappointed) to hear me say that I still cannot provide a suitable answer to this question. Although we often hear athletes describe themselves as *perfectionists* (as seen previously in the self-description provided by a figure skater in the study by Scanlan et al., 1991) or we see observers refer to athletes as perfectionists (as seen previously in the way that John Ed Bradly described Peyton Manning in the ESPN documentary), I believe that the research community must be held to a higher standard of "scientific proof" if we are going to refer to athletes (or coaches or parents) as *perfectionists*, and I suspect the root of this problem stems from the fact that no single agreed-upon definition of perfectionism currently exists (Stoeber, 2018).

I am confident that the vast majority of perfectionism researchers and theorists believe that striving for flawlessness and the pursuit of very high (as opposed to moderate or low) standards of performance is a core feature of perfectionism. However, I think there is less agreement as to whether the label *perfectionist* should be reserved only for individuals who set standards that are *unattainably* or *unrealistically* high, or whether the label perfectionist can be legitimately applied to athletes who set very high standards of performance that are *attainable* and *realistic* but require immense effort, concentration, practice, and skill to achieve. Furthermore, I believe there is a high degree of consensus among perfectionism researchers and theorists that an *aspect* of perfectionism is reflected in the degree to which individuals experience perfectionistic concerns in achievement settings (i.e. "concerns over making mistakes, fear of negative social evaluation, feelings of discrepancy between one's expectations and performance, and negative reactions to imperfection": Gotwals et al., 2012, p. 264). However, I also believe that there is much less agreement within the research community as to whether an athlete *must* have high perfectionistic concerns (and the harsh self-criticism that this entails) to be labelled as a perfectionist, or whether an athlete can be labelled as a perfectionist if they strive for the flawless attainment of extremely high standards of performance but do not simultaneously hold high perfectionistic concerns.

Howard Hall – one of the pioneers of perfectionism research in sport psychology whose work inspired my interest in this area of inquiry – and his colleagues argued that "the term *perfectionism* refers to individuals who exhibit more than a commitment to high standards" (Hall et al., 2012, p. 134) because "perfectionism is a psychological commitment to exceedingly high standards that is believed to reflect an extreme way of thinking in which the meaning of achievement becomes distorted by irrational beliefs and dysfunctional attitudes" (p. 135). As such, Hall et al. (2012) would almost certainly argue against the label *perfectionist* being ascribed to athletes in the previous paragraph who do not hold high perfectionistic concerns. However, if we adopt Hall et al.'s (2012) position – as many researchers and theorists do – what label should we ascribe to athletes who look to attain flawless performances and very high standards of achievement in every aspect of their competitive sport experiences but do not engage in overly-critical self-evaluations (or hold irrational beliefs) towards sub-standard performance levels in sport?

Given that I do not have a definitive answer to the question, "who (or what) is a perfectionist?", I now adopt the position that it is more appropriate (and certainly more defensible) for researchers and theorists to avoid using the label *perfectionist* entirely, and instead use labels that refer to individuals who possess (or demonstrate) certain *perfectionistic tendencies, perfectionistic characteristics,* or *perfectionistic dispositions*. In doing so, researchers avoid the problem of having to provide validity evidence that adequately answers the question, "who (or what) is a perfectionist?" while also acknowledging (indirectly) that perfectionism is a complex multidimensional disposition that is composed of different cognitive, affective, attitudinal, motivational, and behavioural elements in competitive sport. For a related discussion on this issue readers should refer to Hill et al. (2020a) who also propose that "there is no such thing as a perfectionist" (p. 408), though my views (to be discussed later in the next section of this chapter) differ from Hill et al. when it comes to the appropriateness of differentiating between different *types* or *profiles* of perfectionism in sport.

As a research community, I believe that we run into further validity issues when using the label *perfectionist* or *perfectionists* to describe athletes (or coaches or parents) because, to the best of my knowledge, we have yet to establish or agree upon any specific cut-off or criterion scores on self-report instruments that determine whether an athlete is indeed a perfectionist or not. Notwithstanding the issue I just raised in the previous paragraph, I do not believe that researchers can confidently label athletes as *perfectionists* on the basis of the scores they provide on self-report measures of perfectionism in sport. To illustrate this point, consider the following five items from the *striving for perfection* subscale of the MIPS (Stoeber et al., 2006) that are commonly used to measure a facet of perfectionistic strivings in sport (e.g. Dunn et al., 2016, 2021; Mallinson-Howard et al., 2021; Stoeber et al., 2007): (1) "In sport, I strive to be as perfect as possible", (2) "In sport, I am a perfectionist as far as my targets are concerned", (3) "In sport, it is important for me to be perfect in everything I attempt", (4) "In sport, I want to do everything perfectly", and (5) "In sport, I feel the need to be perfect." Researchers typically ask athletes to rate these items on a 5-point scale (e.g. 1 = *strongly disagree*; 5 = *strongly agree*: Dunn et al., 2016) or a 6-point scale (e.g. 1 = *rarely*; 6 = *always*: Stoeber et al., 2006). In these examples, composite *striving for perfection* subscale scores will range from 5 to 25 (using the 5-point scale) or from 5 to 30 (using the 6-point scale). What score must athletes achieve on this subscale before they can be labelled as *perfectionists*? Is an athlete who scores 20 out of 25 (on the 5-point scale) a perfectionist in sport? What about an athlete who scores 21, 22, 23, or 24 out of 25 (using the 5-point scale)? Or can we only refer to an athlete as a perfectionist if they score 25 out of 25 (on the 5-point scale)?

I am not aware of any established/validated criterion or cut-off scores in the literature around which the label "perfectionist" can be justifiably assigned to athletes based upon their scores from self-report instruments. Similarly, I am also not aware of any established/validated criterion or cut-off scores in the literature around which the label "non-perfectionist" can be justifiably assigned to an athlete. This labelling issue is further complicated by the fact that the preceding example did not consider an athlete's scores on any of the other MIPS subscales that capture different sub-dimensions of perfectionistic concerns (i.e. *Negative Reactions to Imperfection, Parental Pressure to be Perfect, Coach Pressure to be Perfect*). Consequently, I believe it is probably more appropriate (and defensible) for researchers to talk about athletes who vary in the degree to which they hold *perfectionistic tendencies* or *perfectionistic characteristics* (across different subscales of multidimensional measures of perfectionism) than to refer to athletes as *perfectionists* per se. As I look back upon a number of studies I have co-authored (e.g. Dunn et al., 2014; Sapieja et al., 2011; Vallance et al., 2006),

I believe we might have erred using the label *perfectionist* or *perfectionists* to describe athletes within our samples because I am no longer convinced that we had sufficient validity evidence to support our claim that the athletes were indeed perfectionists (or non-perfectionists) in sport.

Patterns or Profiles of Perfectionism in Sport

Although I have just explained why I am no longer comfortable referring to athletes as *perfectionists*, I nevertheless believe that there is considerable value in labelling/describing athletes according to the *patterns* or *profiles* of scores they exhibit on self-report measures of multidimensional perfectionism in sport. Such labels might refer to adaptive, healthy, or functional *patterns/profiles* of perfectionism, or to maladaptive, unhealthy, or dysfunctional *patterns/profiles* of perfectionism. However, in order to use such labels, it is essential that researchers (a) include criterion variables in their studies that are clearly associated with adaptive/healthy/functional or maladaptive/unhealthy/dysfunctional cognitive, affective, and behavioural responses in sport, and (b) demonstrate that the corresponding patterns/profiles of perfectionism are associated with (or exhibit differences across) these criterion variables in theoretically meaningful ways. For example, if a particular pattern or profile of scores on a perfectionism measure (or measures) was associated with high levels of confidence, low levels of anxiety, high levels of grit, low levels of burnout, and high levels of optimism, whereas a different pattern/profile of scores on the same perfectionism measure (or measures) was associated with *comparatively* lower levels of confidence, higher levels of anxiety, lower levels of grit, higher levels of burnout, and lower levels of optimism, it seems reasonable to conclude that the former pattern of scores represents a *more* adaptive/healthy/functional profile of perfectionism than the latter pattern of scores which represents a *more* maladaptive/unhealthy/ dysfunctional profile of perfectionism in sport.

Based upon the content of the preceding paragraph, readers will have likely deduced that I support a view of perfectionism in sport that differentiates between adaptive/healthy/functional and maladaptive/unhealthy/dysfunctional patterns or profiles of perfectionism in sport, and this is evident throughout my work. However, I acknowledge that a number of my colleagues who study perfectionism do not support such adaptive, healthy, or functional conceptualizations (e.g. Flett & Hewitt, 2005; Hall, 2016; Hill et al., 2020a). I suspect the difference of opinions that members of the perfectionism research community have towards this issue comes down to whether or not a researcher maintains the position that athletes *must* have high perfectionistic concerns (*in addition to* high perfectionistic strivings) to be included in any discussion of perfectionism. On the basis of empirical evidence, I believe that an athlete who has a profile or pattern of scores on a multidimensional measure (or measures) of perfectionism that reflects a combination of high perfectionistic strivings with *low* perfectionistic concerns should be regarded as a person who exhibits high perfectionistic *tendencies* in sport – but only in terms of their perfectionistic strivings – and this athlete will likely demonstrate a more adaptive, healthy, or functional set of cognitive/motivational, affective/emotional, and behavioural/performance characteristics in competitive sport settings than an athlete who exhibits high perfectionistic strivings combined with *high* perfectionistic concerns (see Gucciardi et al., 2012; Lizmore et al., 2016; Vaartstra et al., 2018, for examples).

Although many statistical techniques are available to researchers who investigate different patterns, profiles, combinations, or interactions of subscale scores from multidimensional measures of perfectionism in sport (e.g. cluster analysis: Lizmore et al., 2016; latent profile analysis: Pacewicz et al., 2018; canonical correlation analysis: Dunn et al., 2020; or moderated regression analysis: Walerianczyk et al., 2022) the essential feature of these approaches is that they all account for patterns or combinations of scores across different subscales (or dimensions) of perfectionism *simultaneously*. I believe that this is important if we are to fully understand how perfectionism operates in sport because different dimensions of perfectionism that are assessed by multidimensional measures of perfectionism coexist within athletes (to different degrees) and will presumably have a combined or interactive effect upon the cognitive, affective, and behavioural responses of athletes in the real-world situations they encounter when pursuing success in sport. In doing so, researchers need to emphasize that specific profiles, patterns, or combinations of scores on perfectionism measures are *comparatively* more adaptive or *comparatively* more maladaptive within the sample being studied (as opposed to definitively labelling athletes as having profiles of "*adaptive perfectionism*" or "*maladaptive perfectionism*"). In addition, researchers must be open to the possibility that particular profiles or combinations of perfectionism scores in one sample of athletes – and labelled accordingly as being comparatively more or less adaptive/maladaptive than another profile – could be interpreted quite differently in a different sample depending on levels of competition, age and gender (e.g. Dunn et al., 2005, 2022; Rasquinha et al., 2014).

To help interpret different profiles, I also believe that future discussions of perfectionism profiles in sport that describe athletes as having *high, moderate*, or *low* perfectionistic strivings combined with *high, moderate*, or *low* perfectionistic concerns would be enhanced if the scientific community set about establishing norm-referenced standards that reflect typical perfectionism levels in different populations of athletes according to age, competitive level, and gender (or according to other demographic variables that potentially influence perfectionism levels in sport). To the best of my knowledge, subscale norms (e.g. whereby subscales scores correspond to normatively-based percentile ranks within specific populations of athletes) do not currently exist in sport. I believe that establishing such norms would greatly enhance the ability of researchers and practitioners to better understand when it is appropriate (valid) to refer to athletes as possessing *low, moderate*, or *high* perfectionistic tendencies in sport.

Building upon this issue, consider the following (fictitious) example of a 20-year-old female intercollegiate (varsity) volleyball player who completes the Sport-MPS-2. All items within the instrument employ a 5-point response scale

(1 = *not at all like me*; 5 = *very much like me*) whereby higher scores reflect higher perfectionistic tendencies. Given that there are different numbers of items within each of the six Sport-MPS-2 subscales, a composite mean–item score for each subscale is computed by dividing the total subscale score by the number of items within the subscale. Thus, composite subscale scores can range from 1 to 5. The athlete scores 3.4 for *personal standards* (PS), 3.0 for *organization* (ORG), 2.6 for *concern over mistakes* (COM), 1.8 for *perceived parental pressure* (PPP), 2.8 for *perceived coach pressure* (PCP), and 2.4 for *doubts about actions* (DAA). In this example, the two highest scores are reported on the personal standards and organization subscales; these subscales capture sub-dimensions of perfectionistic strivings (Dunn et al., 2016, 2021). In contrast, the scores for concern over mistakes, perceived parental pressure, perceived coach pressure, and doubts about actions are comparatively lower; these subscales capture sub-dimensions of perfectionistic concerns (Dunn et al., 2016, 2021).

It is tempting to conclude that the pattern of scores (i.e. moderate perfectionistic strivings combined with comparatively low perfectionistic concerns) for the athlete described in the previous paragraph resembles an adaptive profile of perfectionism (notwithstanding the fact that scores on theoretically-relevant criterion variables are also required before such an inference can actually be supported). However, if we were to look at descriptive statistics provided by Dunn et al. (2014) in a study of 137 female intercollegiate volleyball players, the pattern of scores across the six Sport-MPS-2 subscales for the athlete has many similarities with a profile/cluster of athletes who were labelled as *non-perfectionists* (based upon the following pattern of mean subscale scores: PS = 3.32, ORG = 2.74, COM = 2.67, PPP = 1.72, PCP = 2.87, DAA = 2.44) in Dunn et al.'s study. The point I am trying to make here, is that without a set of established norms for scores on different measures of perfectionism, it is quite difficult to talk about an athlete having *high, moderate,* or *low* perfectionistic strivings or *high, moderate,* or *low* perfectionistic concerns if we don't actually know what the terms high, moderate, or low represent for perfectionism levels that typically exist in sport. Thus, we must ask the question, how high must an athlete's perfectionistic concerns be before practitioners should become concerned that the level of self-reported perfectionistic concerns may lead to maladaptive responses in sport?

To further complicate matters, as a scientist practitioner who works closely with athletes in applied settings (see Harwood, 2016), I would actually be worried about an athlete in high-performance sport who did not possess *some* level of perfectionistic concerns in sport (see the previous discussion about Peyton Manning) because having little or no concerns about making mistakes, little or no concerns about failing to live up to the performance expectations of coaches, or little or no concerns about failing to achieve very high standards of performance may signal that the athlete simply does not care about how they perform. I have often wondered if there is a point at which we want athletes to have *some* level of perfectionistic concerns in sport given that the evolutionary function of the fear, anxiety, and worry (that frequently accompanies perfectionistic concerns) is to heighten a person's awareness of potential threats that exist in their environment and to plan/initiate responses that (hopefully) lead to successful encounters with the stressors that are faced (Brymer & Schweitzer, 2013; Lazarus, 2000). I also suspect that any level of perfectionistic concerns (and perfectionistic strivings) that potentially benefits athletes in pursuit of athletic success will likely differ for individual athletes with optimal levels varying in the same way that emotions can vary (Hanin, 2000).

Closing Reflections of a Scientist Practitioner

As a scientist practitioner who works with athletes in high-performance sport settings, I have often held the view that the scientific knowledge we derive from our research is only as useful as the degree to which it helps us understand the behaviour (and reactions) of individual athletes in the real-world performance-situations they encounter in sport. Given that the key objective for many athletes/teams in competitive sport is to win the competitive encounter against an opponent (or opponents), it is important that researchers in the field of sport psychology seek to determine whether our scientific knowledge surrounding perfectionism in sport actually helps us understand (or predict) athlete performance/achievement in competitive sport settings. Unfortunately, as I survey the current landscape of sport perfectionism research in the literature, there are relatively few studies that have actually used performance (or achievement) as a criterion variable when assessing the role that perfectionism plays in sport, particularly in contexts where athletes actually compete against opponents (see Lizmore et al., 2019; Stoeber et al., 2009). I hope that researchers will increase their efforts to better understand how perfectionism, perfectionistic tendencies, and/or different profiles of perfectionism are linked to athlete performance and achievement in competitive sport settings where the objective is to outperform the opponent and win the competitive encounter.

I believe that researchers and practitioners should expect to see performance/achievement benefits for athletes who possess high (as opposed to low) perfectionistic strivings in sport, but these performance-enhancement benefits will be most prevalent in athletes who have high perfectionistic strivings accompanied by low perfectionistic concerns. My view on this issue is not new to the sport psychology literature (see Stoeber, 2011, 2012), and evidence of the performance benefits of high (as opposed to low) perfectionistic strivings has also been demonstrated in the context of academic achievement (see Madigan, 2019). In accordance with Stoeber (2011, 2012), I believe that high (as opposed to low) perfectionistic strivings are likely to (a) act as an energizing factor that assists athletes in their efforts to work through the challenging demands of deliberate practice that are integral to success in high-performance sport (Ericsson, 2006), and (b) enhance the motivation of athletes to persevere through the obstacles, adversity, and setbacks that are inevitably encountered during the pursuit of competitive success in sport (Dunn et al., 2021). Of course, the critical caveat here is that high perfectionistic strivings are not accompanied by achievement goals/standards that are *unattainably* high; striving to attain a performance standard that is unattainable will almost certainly lead to frustration, anger, anxiety, disappointment, dejection, and dropout.

Unfortunately, in a practical sense, it is often very difficult to determine when a performance standard or achievement goal is truly unattainable or unrealistic for an athlete or sport team, and this is where coaches (and parents) can play a critical role in determining the mindset that athletes adopt towards the pursuit of high standards (and flawless performance) in sport. On this matter, I am excited to see that researchers are now starting to consider the *perfectionistic climates* that athletes encounter in sport and how perfectionistic climates might shape the behaviours, reactions, performances, and achievement levels of athletes – where perfectionistic climate reflects "the degree to which the social environment [in sport] is experienced as perfectionistic" (Grugan et al., 2021, p. 1) by athletes on the basis of the feedback, performance-expectations, and performance criticism they perceive from coaches (or parents or teammates).

I close my reflection with another example from a sport documentary where I believe I am witnessing high perfectionistic tendencies – in terms of perfectionistic strivings – and a *positive* perfectionistic climate at play in elite-level sport. The Facebook documentary titled "*Tom vs Time*" (Chopra & Sankaran, 2018) provides a behind-the-scenes look into the life of Tom Brady – considered by many to be the greatest NFL quarterback of all time – during the year that immediately followed his fifth Superbowl victory as the quarterback for the New England Patriots. (Brady has since gone on to win two more Superbowl titles as the quarterback for the Patriots in 2019 and the Tampa Bay Buccaneers in 2021, making him the "winningest" quarterback in NFL history). During the second episode (titled "*The Mental Game*") of the 6-part documentary, Tom Brady talks directly to the camera saying, "Knowing what your strengths are and weaknesses are, and trying to build on those things and being open about changing those things, is you know, something that I've really worked hard at, and been coached at. I'm trying to work on my attention to detail with my [throwing] mechanics so that when I cut it loose and I rip it [i.e. the ball/pass] in a meaningful game, does it go *exactly* where I want to go?" Immediately following this dialogue, the next 3 minutes and 15 seconds of the documentary show Brady throwing a football during the off-season under the supervision of throwing coach, Tom House. Twice we hear Tom House using the word "perfect" in reference to Brady's throwing mechanics (e.g. "We are going to try to be perfect") and twice we also hear Brady use the word "perfect" in reference to his throws (e.g. "It's not perfect").

Based upon my scientific knowledge of perfectionism and my applied experiences working with athletes in high-performance sport, I believe that this short extract from the Facebook documentary illustrates Tom Brady's drive for flawless execution and total mastery of his throwing mechanics, and this quest for perfection is indicative of high perfectionistic strivings in sport. I also contend that this apparent drive to be perfect is a key motivational factor underlying Tom Brady's prolonged success as an elite NFL quarterback. Moreover, the film appears to indicate that Tom House creates a "positive" perfectionistic training climate whereby he encourages Tom Brady to *strive* for perfection every time the ball is thrown, but he does not create pressure on Brady by *demanding* or *expecting* that every throw *will/must* be perfect.

I look forward to seeing how the scientific community goes about determining whether different perfectionistic climates that are set by coaches influence the cognitive, affective, and behavioural experiences of athletes in sport, and whether such perfectionistic climates are also linked to the performance/achievement levels of athletes in training and competitive settings. Of course, I am working under the assumption that coaches who continually push their athletes to strive for perfection in sport but who do *not* create unrealistic expectations, who do *not* set unattainable standards, and who do *not* criticize athletes when substandard performance levels occur are actually creating conditions that reflect a "perfectionistic climate". I suspect that Grugan et al. (2021) might not agree with my view that there is such a thing as a *positive/adaptive perfectionistic climate* given that they conceptualize perfectionistic climate as follows:

> the informational cues and goal structures (i.e. components of the environment that emphasise what people are expected to accomplish and how they are to be evaluated) that align with the view that performances must be perfect and less than perfect performances are unacceptable.
>
> (Grugan et al., 2021, p. 1)

I hope readers will critically evaluate the perspectives I have put forward in this chapter, and that future research will confirm or refute the validity of the ideas I have presented. I "sign off" as a member of the perfectionism research community by extending my sincere gratitude to Andrew for allowing me to express my ideas about perfectionism in sport in this chapter. Andrew and I have not always agreed upon the conceptualization of perfectionism in sport, particularly as it relates to whether self-criticism and harsh self-evaluation *must* be present if we are actually talking about athletes who have high perfectionistic tendencies in sport (see Hill et al., 2020b). Nevertheless, despite our differences of opinion, we have built a high level of professional respect for each other's ideas and we both acknowledge that neither of us has (nor should ever have) a monopoly on the "truth" when it comes to understanding the construct of perfectionism in sport (dance and exercise).

References

Brymer, E., & Schweitzer, R. (2013). Extreme sports are good for your health: A phenomenological understanding of fear and anxiety in extreme sport. *Journal of Health Psychology*, 18(4), 477–487. https://doi.org/10.1177/1359105312446770.

Chopra, G., & Sankaran, S. (Executive Producers) (2018). Tom vs time. Chapter II: The mental game. Retrieved from www.facebook.com/vsonwatch/videos/s1e2-the-mental-game/2084671908433217/.

Coen, S. P., & Ogles, B. M. (1993). Psychological characteristics of the obligatory runner: A critical examination of the anorexia analogue hypothesis. *Journal of Sport & Exercise Psychology*, 15(3), 338–354. https://doi.org/10.1123/jsep.15.3.338.

Dunn, J. G. H., Causgrove Dunn, J., Gamache, V., & Holt, N. L. (2014). A person-oriented examination of perfectionism and slump-related coping in female inter-collegiate volleyball players. *International Journal of Sport Psychology*, 45(4), 298–324. doi:10.7352/IJSP2014.45.298.

Dunn, J. G. H., Causgrove Dunn, J., Gotwals, J. K., Vallance, J. K. H., Craft, J. M., & Syrotuik, D. G. (2006). Establishing construct validity evidence for the Sport Multi-dimensional Perfectionism Scale. *Psychology of Sport and Exercise*, 7(1), 57–79. https://doi.org/10.1016/j.psychsport.2005.04.003.

Dunn, J. G. H., Causgrove Dunn, J., & McDonald, K. (2012). Domain-specific per-fectionism in intercollegiate athletes: Relationships with perceived competence and perceived importance in sport and school. *Psychology of Sport and Exercise*, 13(6), 747–755. https://doi.org/10.1016/j.psychsport.2012.05.002.

Dunn, J. G. H., Causgrove Dunn, J., & Syrotuik, D. G. (2002). Relationship between multidimensional perfectionism and goal orientations in sport. *Journal of Sport & Exercise Psychology*, 24(4), 376–395. https://doi.org/10.1123/jsep.24.4.376.

Dunn, J. G. H., Craft, J. M., Causgrove Dunn, J., & Gotwals, J. K. (2011). Comparing a domain-specific and global measure of perfectionism in competitive female figure skaters. *Journal of Sport Behavior*, 34(1) 25–46.

Dunn, J. G. H., Gotwals, J. K., & Causgrove Dunn, J. (2005). An examination of the domain specificity of perfectionism among intercollegiate student-athletes. *Personality and Individual Differences*, 38(6), 1439–1448. https://doi.org/10.1016/j.paid.2004.09.009.

Dunn, J. G. H., Gotwals, J. K., Causgrove Dunn, J., & Lizmore, M. R. (2020). Per-fectionism, pre-competitive worry, and optimism in high-performance youth ath-letes. *International Journal of Sport and Exercise Psychology*, 18(6), 749–763. https://doi.org/10.1080/1612197x.2019.1577900.

Dunn, J. G. H. Gotwals, J. K., Causgrove Dunn, J., & Lizmore, M. R. (2022). Per-ceived parental pressure and perceived coach pressure in adolescent and adult sport. *Psychology of Sport and Exercise*, 59, 102100. https://doi.org/10.1016/j.psychsport.2021.102100.

Dunn, J. G. H., Gotwals, J. K., Causgrove Dunn, J., Selzler, A.-M., Lizmore, M. R., Vaartstra, M., Sapieja, K. M., & Gamache, V. E. (2016). A multi-sample investigation of the higher-order latent dimensionality of the Sport-Multidimensional Perfection-ism Scale-2. *Psychology of Sport and Exercise*, 27, 150–156. https://doi.org/10.1016/j.psychsport.2016.08.006.

Dunn, J. G. H., Kono, S., Cormier, D. L., Causgrove Dunn, J., & Rumbold, J. L. (2021). Perfectionism and grit in competitive sport. *Journal of Sport Behavior*, 44(2), 199–223.

Dunn, J. G. H., & Nielsen, A. B. (1996). A classificatory system of anxiety-inducing situations in four team sports. *Journal of Sport Behavior*, 19(2), 111–131.

Ericsson, K. A. (2006). The influence of experience and deliberate practice in the development of superior expert performance. In K. A. Ericsson, N. Charness, P. J. Feltovich, & R. R. Hoffman (eds), *The Cambridge handbook of expertise and expert performance* (pp. 683–704). Cambridge University Press.

Flett, G. L., & Hewitt, P. L. (2002). *Perfectionism: Theory, research, and treatment.* American Psychological Association.

Flett, G. L., & Hewitt, P. L. (2005). The perils of perfectionism in sports and exercise. *Current Directions in Psychological Science*, 14(1), 14–18. https://doi.org/10.1111/j. 0963-7214.2005.00326.x.

Flett, G. L., & Hewitt, P. L. (2016). Reflections on perfection and the pressure to be perfect in athletes, dancers, and exercisers. In A. P. Hill (ed.), *The psychology of perfectionism in sport, dance and exercise* (pp. 296–319). Routledge.

Frost, R. O., Heimberg, R. G., Holt, C. S., Mattia, J. I., & Neubauer, A. L. (1993). A comparison of two measures of perfectionism. *Personality and Individual Differences*, 14 (1), 119–126. https://doi.org/10.1016/0191-8869(93)90181-90182.

Frost, R. O., & Henderson, K. J. (1991). Perfectionism and reactions to athletic competition. *Journal of Sport & Exercise Psychology*, 13(3), 323–335. https://doi.org/10. 1123/jsep.13.4.323.

Frost, R. O., Marten, P., Lahart, C., & Rosenblate, R. (1990). The dimensions of perfectionism. *Cognitive Therapy and Research*, 14(5), 449–468. https://doi.org/10. 1007/BF01172967.

Gotwals, J. K., & Dunn, J. G. H. (2009). A multi-method multi-analytic approach to establishing internal construct validity evidence: The Sport Multidimensional Perfectionism Scale 2. *Measurement in Physical Education and Exercise Science*, 13(2), 71–92. https://doi.org/10.1080/10913670902812663.

Gotwals, J. K., Dunn, J. G. H., Causgrove Dunn, J., & Gamache, V. (2010). Establishing validity evidence for the Sport Multidimensional Perfectionism Scale-2 in intercollegiate sport. *Psychology of Sport and Exercise*, 11(6), 423–442. https://doi.org/10. 1016/j.psychsport.2010.04.013.

Gotwals, J. K., Stoeber, J., Dunn, J. G. H., & Stoll, O. (2012). Are perfectionistic strivings in sport adaptive? A systematic review of confirmatory, contradictory, and mixed evidence. *Canadian Psychology*, 53(4), 263–279. https://doi.org/10.1037/a0030288.

Gould, D., Dieffenbach, K., & Moffett, A. (2002). Psychological characteristics and their development in Olympic champions. *Journal of Applied Sport Psychology*, 14(3), 172–204. https://doi.org/10.1080/10413200290103482.

Gould, D., Tuffey, S., Udry, E., & Loehr, J. (1996). Burnout in competitive junior tennis players: I. A quantitative psychological assessment. *The Sport Psychologist*, 10(4), 322–340. https://doi.org/10.1123/tsp.10.4.322.

Grugan, M. C., Hill, A. P., Mallinson-Howard, S. H., Donachie, T. C., Olsson, L. F., Madigan, D. J., & Vaughan, R. S. (2021). Development and initial validation of the Perfectionistic Climate Questionnaire-Sport (PCQ-S). *Psychology of Sport and Exercise*, 56, 101997. https://doi.org/10.1016/j.psychsport.2021.101997.

Gucciardi, D. F., Mahoney, J., Jalleh, G., Donovan, R. J., & Parkes, J. (2012). Perfectionistic profiles among elite athletes and differences in their motivational orientations. *Journal of Sport & Exercise Psychology*, 34(2), 159–183. https://doi.org/10.1123/jsep.34.2.159.

Hall, H. K. (2016). Reflections on perfectionism and its influence on motivational processes in sport, dance, and exercise. In A. P. Hill (ed.), *The psychology of perfectionism in sport, dance and exercise* (pp. 275–295). Routledge.

Hall, H. K., Hill, A. P., & Appleton, P. R. (2012). Perfectionism: A foundation for sporting excellence or an uneasy pathway toward purgatory? In G. C. Roberts & D. C. Treasure (eds), *Advances in motivation in sport and exercise* (3rd ed., pp. 129–168). Human Kinetics.

Hall, H. K., Kerr, A. W., & Matthews, J. (1998). Precompetitive anxiety in sport: The contribution of achievement goals and perfectionism. *Journal of Sport & Exercise Psychology*, 20(2), 194–217. https://doi.org/10.1123/jsep.20.2.194.

Hanin, Y. L. (2000). Individual Zones of Optimal Functioning (IZOF) Model: Emotion-performance relationship in sport. In Y. L. Hanin (ed.), *Emotions in sport* (pp. 65–89). Human Kinetics.

Harwood, C. (2016). Doing sport psychology? Critical reflections of a scientist-practitioner. In M. Raab, P. Wylleman, R. Seiler, A.M. Elbe, & A. Hatzigeorgiadis (eds), *Sport and exercise psychology research: From theory to practice* (pp. 229–249). Elsevier. https://doi/10.1016/B978-0-12-803634-1.00011-X.

Hewitt, P. L., & Flett, G. L. (1991). Perfectionism and self and social contexts: Conceptualization, assessment, and association with psychopathology. *Journal of Personality and Social Psychology*, 60(3), 456–470. https://doi.org/10.1037/0022-3514.60.3.456.

Hill, A. P., Appleton, P. R., & Mallinson, S. H. (2016). Development and initial validation of the Performance Perfectionism Scale for Sport (PPS-S). *Journal of Psychoeducational Assessment*, 34(7), 653–669. https://doi.org/10.1177/0734282916651354.

Hill, A. P., Madigan, D. J., Smith, M. M., Mallinson-Howard, S. H., & Donachie, T. C. (2020a). Perfectionism. In D. Hackfort & R. J., Schinke (eds), *The Routledge international encyclopedia of sport and exercise psychology, vol. 1: Theoretical and methodological concepts* (pp. 405–412). Routledge.

Hill, A. P., Mallinson-Howard, S. H., & Jowett, G. E. (2018). Multidimensional perfectionism in sport: A meta-analytic review. *Sport, Exercise, and Performance Psychology*, 7(3), 235–270. https://doi.org/10.1037/spy0000125.

Hill, A. P., Mallinson-Howard, S. H., Madigan, D. J., & Jowett, G. E. (2020b). Perfectionism in sport, dance, and exercise: An extended review and reanalysis. In G. Tenenbaum & R. C. Eklund (eds), *Handbook of sport psychology, volume 1: Social perspectives, cognition, and application* (4th edition, pp. 121–157). Wiley.

Kaye, M. P., Conroy, D. E., & Fifer, A. M. (2008). Individual differences in incompetence avoidance. *Journal of Sport & Exercise Psychology*, 30(1), 110–132. https://doi.org/10.1123/jsep.30.1.110.

Lazarus, R. S. (2000). How emotions influence performance in competitive sports. *The Sport Psychologist*, 14(3), 229–252. https://doi.org/10.1123/tsp.14.3.229.

Lizmore, M. R., Dunn, J. G. H., & Causgrove Dunn, J. (2016). Reactions to mistakes as a function of perfectionism and situation criticality in curling. *International Journal of Sport Psychology*, 47(1), 81–101.

Lizmore, M. R., Dunn, J. G. H., Causgrove Dunn, J., & Hill, A. P. (2019). Perfectionism and performance following failure in a competitive golf-putting task. *Psychology of Sport and Exercise*, 45, 101582. https://doi.org/10.1016/j.psychsport.2019.101582.

Madigan, D. J. (2019). A meta-analysis of perfectionism and academic achievement. *Educational Psychology Review*, 31(4), 967–989. https://doi.org/10.1007/s10648-019-09484-2.

Madigan, D. J., Curran, T., Stoeber, J., Hill, A. P., Smith, M. M., & Passfield, L. (2019). Development of perfectionism in junior athletes: A three-sample study of coach and parental pressure. *Journal of Sport and Exercise Psychology*, 41(3), 167–175. https://doi.org/10.1123/jsep.2018-0287.

Mallinson-Howard, S. H., Madigan, D. J., & Jowett, G. E. (2021). A three-sample study of perfectionism and field test performance in athletes. *European Journal of Sport Science*, 21(7), 1045–1053. https://doi.org/10.1080/17461391.2020.1811777.

Marsh, H. M. (1994). Sport motivation orientations: Beware of jingle-jangle fallacies. *Journal of Sport & Exercise Psychology*, 16(4), 365–380. https://doi.org/10.1123/jsep.16.4.365.

Martens, R., Vealey, R. S., & Burton, D. (1990). *Competitive anxiety in sport*. Human Kinetics.

Pacewicz, C. E., Gotwals, J. K., & Blanton, J. E. (2018). Perfectionism, coping, and burnout among intercollegiate varsity athletes: A person-oriented investigation of group differences and mediation. *Psychology of Sport and Exercise*, 35, 207–217. https://doi.org/10.1016/j.psychsport.2017.12.008.

Parker, W. D. (1997). An empirical typology of perfectionism in academically talented children. *American Educational Research Journal*, 34(3), 545–562. https://doi.org/10.3102/00028312034003545.

Quinn, A. (2014). Discovery Channel Peyton Manning NFL full length football documentary [video]. Retrieved from www.youtube.com/watch?app=desktop&v=K_pnNDa0ytU.

Rasquinha, A., Dunn, J. G. H., & Causgrove Dunn, J. (2014). Relationships between perfectionistic strivings, perfectionistic concerns and competitive sport level. *Psychology of Sport and Exercise*, 15(6), 659–667. https://doi.org/10.1016/j.psychsport.2014.07.008.

Rice, K. G., & Mirzadeh, S. A. (2000). Perfectionism, attachment, and adjustment. *Journal of Counseling Psychology*, 47(2), 238–250. https://doi.org/10.1037/0022-0167.47.2.238.

Rice, K. G., & Slaney, R. B. (2002). Clusters of perfectionists: Two studies of emotional adjustment and academic achievement. *Measurement and Evaluation in Counseling and Development*, 35(1), 35–48. https://doi.org/10.1080/07481756.2002.12069046.

Sapieja, K. M., Dunn, J. G. H., & Holt, N. L. (2011). Perfectionism and perceptions of parenting styles in male youth soccer. *Journal of Sport & Exercise Psychology*, 33(1), 20–39. https://doi.org/10.1123/jsep.33.1.20.

Scanlan, T. K., Ravizza, K., & Stein, G. L. (1989a). An in-depth study of former elite figure skaters: I. Introduction to the project. *Journal of Sport & Exercise Psychology*, 11(1), 54–64. https://doi.org/10.1123/jsep.11.1.54.

Scanlan, T. K., Stein, G. L., & Ravizza, K. (1989b). An in-depth study of former elite figure skaters: II. Sources of enjoyment. *Journal of Sport & Exercise Psychology*, 11(1), 65–83. https://doi.org/10.1123/jsep.11.1.65.

Scanlan, T. K., Stein, G. L., & Ravizza, K. (1991). An in-depth study of former elite figure skaters: III. Sources of stress. *Journal of Sport & Exercise Psychology*, 13(2), 103–120. https://doi.org/10.1123/jsep.13.2.103.

Slaney, R. B., Ashby, J. S., & Trippi, J. (1995). Perfectionism: Its measurement and career relevance. *Journal of Career Assessment*, 3(4), 279–297. https://doi.org/10.1177/106907279500300403.

Smith, R. E., Smoll, F. L., & Schutz, R. W. (1990). Measurement and correlates of sport-specific cognitive and somatic trait anxiety: The Sport Anxiety Scale. *Anxiety Research*, 2(4), 263–280. https://doi.org/10.1080/08917779008248733.

Stoeber, J. (2011). The dual nature of perfectionism in sports: relationships with emotion, motivation, and performance. *International Review of Sport and Exercise Psychology*, 4(2), 128–145. https://doi.org/10.1080/1750984x.2011.604789.

Stoeber, J. (2012). Perfectionism and performance. In S. M. Murphy (ed.), *The Oxford handbook of sport and performance psychology* (pp. 294–306). Oxford University Press.

Stoeber, J. (2018). The psychology of perfectionism: Critical issues, open questions, and future directions. In J. Stoeber (ed.), *The psychology of perfectionism: Theory, research, applications* (pp. 333–352). Routledge.

Stoeber, J., & Madigan, D. J. (2016). Measuring perfectionism in sport, dance, and exercise: Review, critique, recommendations. In A.P. Hill (ed.), *Perfectionism in sport, dance, and exercise* (pp. 32–56). Routledge.

Stoeber, J., & Otto, K. (2006). Positive conceptions of perfectionism: Approaches, evidence, challenges. *Personality and Social Psychology Review*, 10(4), 295–319. https://doi.org/10.1207/s15327957pspr1004_2.

Stoeber, J., Otto, K., Pescheck, E., Becker, C., & Stoll, O. (2007). Perfectionism and competitive anxiety in athletes: Differentiating striving for perfectionism and negative reactions to imperfection. *Personality and Individual Differences*, 42(6), 959–969. https://doi.org/10.1016/j.paid.2006.09.006.

Stoeber, J., Otto, K., & Stoll, O. (2006). MIPS: Multidimensional Inventory of Perfectionism in Sport (English version, November). Retrieved from https://kar.kent.ac.uk/41560/.

Stoeber, J., & Stoeber, F. S. (2009). Domains of perfectionism: Prevalence and relationships with perfectionism, gender, age, and satisfaction with life. *Personality and Individual Differences*, 46(4), 530–535. https://doi.org/10.1016/j.paid.2008.12.006.

Stoeber, J., Uphill, M. A., & Hotham, S. (2009). Predicting race performance in triathlon: The role of perfectionism, achievement goals, and personal goal setting. *Journal of Sport & Exercise Psychology*, 31(2), 211–245. https://doi.org/10.1123/jsep.31.2.211.

Straub, W. F., & Hinman, D. A. (1992). Profiles and professional perspectives of 10 leading sport psychologists. *The Sport Psychologist*, 6(3), 297–312. https://doi.org/10.1123/tsp.6.3.297.

Suddarth, B. H., & Slaney, R. B. (2001). An investigation of the dimensions of perfectionism in college students. *Measurement and Evaluation in Counseling and Development*, 34(3), 157–165. https://doi.org/10.1080/07481756.2002.12069032.

Vaartstra, M., Dunn, J. G. H., & Causgrove Dunn, J. (2018). Perfectionism and perceptions of social loafing in competitive youth soccer. *Journal of Sport Behavior*, 41(4), 475–500.

Vallance, J. K. H., Dunn, J. G. H., & Causgrove Dunn, J. L. (2006). Perfectionism, anger, and situation criticality in competitive youth ice hockey. *Journal of Sport & Exercise Psychology*, 28(3), 383–406. https://doi.org/10.1123/jsep.28.3.383.

Walerianczyk, W., Hill, A. P., & Stolarski, M. (2022). A re-examination of the 2x2 model of perfectionism, burnout, and engagement in sports. *Psychology of Sport and Exercise*, 61, 102190. https://doi.org/10.1016/j.psychsport.2022.102190.

Zinsser, N., Bunker, L., & Williams, J. M. (2001). Cognitive techniques for building confidence and enhancing performance. In J. M. Williams (ed.), *Applied sport psychology: Personal growth to peak performance* (4th ed., pp. 284–311). Mayfield.

14 Questions, Critical Reflections, and Advances with the Model of Excellencism and Perfectionism

A Call to Action

Patrick Gaudreau, Antoine Benoit and Laurence Boileau

We now know a lot about perfectionism. Novel interventions for perfectionists (e.g. online, face-to-face with a therapists) have been created and tested in rigorous randomized controlled trials. Empirical knowledge accumulated at an increasing pace over the last 30 years and has recently been integrated across a series of comprehensive, systematic, and diversified meta-analytical reviews – so much so that the last decade has been accurately portrayed as the era of the meta-analyses. The recent years have also been ones of great promise for conceptual clarifications.

Defining psychological constructs is a difficult and never-ending task. It is the bedrock of sound research, intervention, and professional practice. Without clear and precise definitions, clinicians run the risk of denying services to people who really are perfectionists while devoting their time to those who are not. Given such importance, time has come to take a step back to reconsider some of our assumptions and perhaps even correct some misconceptions. Self-correction may appear as an antithesis of scientific progress. It is indeed a daunting and humbling process. However, it is necessary in order to advance any area of research and practice.

As part of reflecting and self-correcting, some of the things we know and assumed to be true could end up reinforced and reaffirmed. Other things are denied, refined or abandoned. Regardless, the process will help clarify the conceptual domain of perfectionism and its measurement. Some key simple questions may appear obvious, but they often are intellectually challenging. Drafting out clear answers to conceptual and measurement questions is the building block of a sound theoretical elaboration and maturation process. In this chapter, we walk through a series of simple questions that are in desperate need of greater conceptual clarifications in the field of perfectionism.

What is the Core Definitional Feature of Perfectionism?

Clarifying what perfectionism is (and what it is not) is quite a challenge. Providing a straightforward answer to this question is essential. This challenge led us to pay a closer attention to the definitions generally espoused in perfectionism research (Gaudreau, 2021). Striking similarities were found across many contemporary definitions (e.g. Frost et al., 1990; Sirois & Molnar, 2016; Stoeber, 2018a). There appears to be large consensus around the idea that

DOI: 10.4324/9781003288015-19

perfectionistic standards *are accompanied* (among many other things) by evaluative concerns. These concerns become perfectionistic concerns only if they are
experienced by a perfectionist (see also Smith et al., 2021).

To maintain a stronger coherence between the definition and its operationalization, Gaudreau (2021) introduced the distinction between the *core
definitional feature* of perfectionism and the *signature expressions* of perfectionism.
Based on this, perfectionism was redefined as "as a tendency to aim and strive
toward idealized, flawless, and excessively high standards in a relentless manner
(as per Gaudreau, 2019, p. 200) that frequently and recurrently influences many
interrelated cognitive (e.g. cognitions related to perfectionism), socio-cognitive
(e.g. socially prescribed perfectionism, perceived pressure to be perfect), and
socio-behavioural expressions (e.g. other-oriented perfectionism, perfectionism
self-presentation) that contribute to the developmental and maintenance of
perfectionism and their associations with psychological adjustment" (Gaudreau,
2021, p. 6). In other words, perfectionistic concerns are cognitive *expressions of
perfectionism* rather than a core definitional feature of perfectionism per se. And
therefore, the *core definitional feature* of perfectionism is made of the aiming and
striving toward the incredibly high and unreasonable perfectionistic standards.

Our approach is both similar and different from the Comprehensive Model of
Perfectionistic Behavior (CMPB; Hewitt et al., 2017). The CMPB separates the trait
(i.e. self-oriented, socially prescribed, and other-oriented perfectionism) from the
interpersonal (e.g. perfectionistic self-presentation) and intrapersonal (e.g. perfectionistic cognitions) components of perfectionism. Separating dispositional perfectionism from the other components of the conceptual landscape of perfectionism is
consistent with our approach. However, our model places perfectionistic standards as
the definitional core while repositioning socially prescribed and other-oriented perfectionism as socio-cognitive and socio-behavioural expressions of perfectionism.
They are distinctively associated with antecedents, processes, and outcomes (e.g. Hill
et al., 2018) and factor analytical evidence indicates that self-oriented, socially prescribed perfectionism, and other-oriented perfectionism belong to distinct dimensions (e.g. Smith et al., 2016). These conceptual reasons – and many others discussed
by Gaudreau (2021, pp. 4–6) – offer a defendable case for the repositioning of several elements of perfectionism outside the definitional core of the construct. Despite
these differences, the CMPB and our model are not strictly incompatible and they
will certainly feed of each other in the years to come.

Are We Sure That We are Measuring What We Think We Are Measuring?

Over the years, the question mark in the eyes of the students in our undergraduate
courses have forced us to reconsider our overall understanding of the perfectionism
landscape. Students often felt like perfectionism is represented by many tangentially
related constructs. Stoeber (2018b) even questioned whether there were "too many
perfectionisms in perfectionism theory and research" (p. 337). Similarly, many of our
undergraduate and graduate trainees wonder where exactly perfectionism is among

this list of constructs. Their quest for greater conceptual clarity was insightful because it challenged us to rethink our teaching and research program on perfectionism.

Growing empirical support for the unhealthiness of perfectionism created a form of collective conceptual blindfolding. The conceptual elements used to make inferences from empirical data have been uncritically accepted. As a result, perfectionism became more and more defined by its measures. To say that perfectionists frequently experience concerns over mistakes is logically and empirically defendable. However, to say that concerns over mistakes *is perfectionism per se* appears logically flawed. The same argument has been made about self-criticism (Stoeber, 2018b). Using self-criticism as an indicator of perfectionistic concerns conflates perfectionism with a mechanism putatively involved in the development and maintenance of depression (e.g. Cox et al., 2004; Thew et al., 2017). All in all, these conceptual confounds run the risk of overestimating the associations between perfectionism and psychopathologies.

Concerns over mistakes and self-criticism are unquestionably prevalent *signature expressions* involved in perfectionism (Gaudreau, 2021). However, the phenomenological experience of being concerned with mistakes is potentially straddling the conceptual border of anxiety disorders and perfectionism. Evaluative concerns and concerns over mistakes are cardinal features of many cognitive processes (e.g. fear of failure, rumination, fear of negative evaluations, and post-event processing) known to be involved in the development and maintenance of anxiety disorders (e.g. McLaughlin & Nolen-Hoeksema, 2011). Correlations between evaluative concerns and psychological distress can be interpreted as the causal influence of perfectionism itself; this interpretation prevails in the extant perfectionism literature. However, these moderate-to-strong correlations potentially suggest that evaluative concerns (e.g. concerns over mistakes, doubts about actions) potentially fall somewhere between perfectionism and anxiety symptomology. Consequently, it is preferable to consider them as mechanisms involved in symptomatology rather than as key definitional features of perfectionism. If so, evaluative concerns and self-criticism should be seen as *cognitive expressions* of perfectionism rather than inherent constituents of the *core definitional feature of perfectionism* itself.

Where to Draw the Line Between High Personal Standards and Perfectionistic Standards?

Repositioning perfectionistic standards as the core definitional feature raises yet another question – a question frequently asked by students, the public, practitioners, and researchers over the last few years (e.g. Blasberg et al., 2016; Flett et al., 2018; Wade, 2018). How do we determine if a person aims and strives toward excessively high perfectionistic standards?

Conceptual Issues

Gaudreau (2019) recently developed the *Model of Excellencism and Perfectionism* (MEP) to provide a conceptual solution to this important question. The model attempts to fill an important gap by formalizing the distinction between the pursuit of perfection and the pursuit of excellence. The analogy of a journey is useful to illustrate the similarities and differences between excellencism and perfectionism. Many people pursue high personal standards. When they attain these standards, they will feel like their destination has been reached. These people are the ones who pursue excellence without pursuing perfection. They are *excellence strivers*. In contrast, some people pursue high standards but are not fulfilled by the pursuit and attainment of these standards. Even if they were to reach excellence, they would continue to pursue their journey in the hope of attaining their perfectionistic standards. These people are the ones who incidentally pursue excellence in their quest toward perfection. They not only pursue high standards (involved in excellencism) but they resolutely pursue the more extreme, less realistic, more exacting, and less flexible perfectionistic standards. These people are *perfection strivers*. This distinction is illustrated in Figure 14.1.

Words can also be used to distinguish excellence and perfection. Imagine Taylor and Billie – two competitive athletes. Taylor wants to be a competent athlete, obtain very good results, and train in an effortful, dedicated, yet flexible manner. Taylor's aiming and striving are well representative of the pursuit of excellence. Billie wants to be a perfect athlete and needs to obtain extremely good results all the time in the hope of feeling accomplished. This athlete follows an exaggeratedly strict and exacting training regimen that requires flawlessness. Billie's aiming and striving are well representative of the pursuit of perfection. Words that characterize the goal to be very good, competent, accomplished, very productive, skilful, high quality, successful, great, and capable are likely to be espoused by both Taylor and Billie. It can be said that both excellence and perfection strivers are driven, ambitious, and persevering people

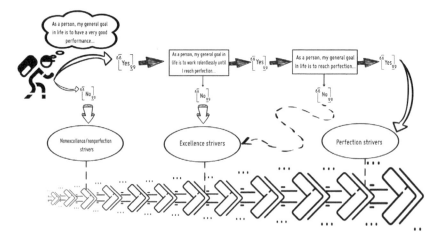

Figure 14.1 Visual definition of nonexcellence/nonperfection, excellence, and perfection strivers in the MEP.

(Besser et al., 2008). However, words that characterize the goal to reach exactness, faultlessness, flawlessness, ideal, error-free, impeccability, and irreproachableness – which go over and above the notion of excellence – will be specifically espoused by Billie. Perfectionism starts where excellencism ends. What happens beyond excellencism is qualitatively different and sets the tone for the phenomenological experiences of being a perfectionist.

Empirical Evidence

Effort has been made to improve the content validity of already existing scales (Blasberg et al., 2016; Lin & Muenks, 2022) and to reinterpret the effects according to whether they assess high personal standards or perfectionistic standards (Osenk et al., 2020). However, many popular measures of perfectionistic standards still contain items tapping into excellencism while scales designed to assess striving toward excellence predominantly measure perfectionism (e.g. Hill et al., 2004).

Gaudreau et al. (2022) developed and validated the Scale of Perfectionism and Excellencism (SCOPE) to differentiate high personal standards (i.e. excellencism) from perfectionistic standards (i.e. perfectionism). Results of exploratory and confirmatory factor analyses showed that excellencism and perfectionism can be separated at the conceptual level. Based on the MEP operational definitions (Gaudreau, 2019, p. 205), scores on the SCOPE can be used to compare non-excellence/nonperfection strivers (i.e. low excellencism and low perfectionism) excellence strivers (i.e. high excellencism and low perfectionism), and perfection strivers (i.e. high excellencism and high perfectionism).

Across five studies with 2,157 university students, various findings also revealed that excellencism and perfectionism can be distinguished at the functional level. Perfection strivers more frequently aim and strive toward the goal of earning a perfect grade (A+) in their courses. Despite their unquestionable ambition, perfection strivers are less likely to earn good academic performance and to improve their level of achievement over time compared to excellence strivers. Another series of studies found similar results to predict performance on divergent thinking tasks used to measure creativity (Goulet-Pelletier et al., 2022). When it comes to academic success and creativity of university students, it appears like aiming and striving for excellence is, in fact, more than good enough.

Gaudreau et al. (2021) conducted the first study on the MEP in the sport domain. A sample of 156 sport participants rated their fear of failure and goal progress in both sport and school as well as their perceived difficulties in balancing their sport and school lives. Perfection strivers and excellence strivers reported similar levels of goal progress in both sport and school. This finding needs to be reinterpreted considering other findings from Gaudreau et al. (2022) who reported that perfection strivers are more likely to attain their socially prescribed goals compared to their personal goals. This tendency to sacrifice the self in quest of social acceptance could explain why perfection strivers experience more fear of failure in both school and sport compared to excellence strivers. This also aligns with findings showing that perfection strivers experience more difficulties in balancing their sport and school lives. Taken together, these results support the idea that perfectionism is not needed and perhaps even harmful for individuals involved in competitive sports.

Another MEP study examined how sport fans reacted when the Houston Astros were found guilty of illegally stealing the signs of their opponents during the 2017 World Series of Baseball (Gaudreau & Schellenberg, 2022a). Results indicated that perfection strivers were more tolerant toward sport-related cheating compared to excellence strivers. When asked to take the perspective of a coach, sport fans were also more likely to espouse a winning-at-all-cost mentality and to show signs of moral disengagement. Overall, it can be said that perfection strivers use cognitive stratagems to justify wrongdoings (e.g. everyone is doing it, therefore it is not cheating) while holding the beliefs that winning (no matter how) is justifiable and more important than fairness and wellness of the sport and their participants.

In summary, these initial findings offer a sample of what can be learned and discovered when we conceptually make a clear distinction between excellencism and perfectionism. The implications for perfectionism research are far reaching. The desirable effects of perfectionistic standards (observed in past studies) were potentially caused by an undifferentiable combination of excellencism and perfectionism. Conflating high standards with perfectionistic standards accidentally boosted the probability of findings supportive evidence for the idea that perfectionism is healthy. If we accept this argument, we accept that researchers need to take a step back to revisit and correct the accumulated evidence in the extant literature. Effects of perfectionistic standards with adjustment and maladjustment have been overestimated and underestimated, respectively. Future research should therefore measure both excellencism and perfectionism using measures – like the SCOPE – that do not conflate the two constructs into a single score. This new corpus of knowledge is urgently required to more precisely re-estimate the effects associated with perfectionistic standards – the core definitional feature of perfectionism.

What is the Role of the Signature Expressions of Perfectionism in the MEP?

The aiming and striving for perfection are the core definitional feature of perfectionism in the MEP. However, the MEP maintains 30 years of research tradition in reaffirming that perfectionism is multidimensional. Signature expressions are not discarded from the perfectionism landscape. They are relocated outside of core definitional feature of perfectionism to give them a central role that better explains the phenomenological experiences and outcomes of perfection strivers.

Perfection strivers (compared to excellence strivers and nonexcellence/nonperfection strivers) are more likely to experience the cognitive expressions (e.g. concerns over mistakes, doubts about actions, automatic perfectionistic thoughts), socio-cognitive (e.g. impression that others require perfection), and socio-behavioural expressions of perfectionism (e.g. expecting others to be perfect). This hypothesis has already been supported in MEP empirical studies (Gaudreau et al., 2022). On the one hand, this idea is consistent with 30 years of research showing a moderate-to-strong correlations between perfectionistic standards and many characteristics of perfectionistic concerns (e.g. Hill et al., 2018). On the other hand, it offers a new integration of the perfectionism landscape. Signature expressions are not just co-occurring with perfectionistic standards; they are the energy that radiates from the nucleus (i.e. the core) of perfectionism. The signature expressions are the fuel that propels the core definitional feature of perfectionism into a transdiagnostic risk factor.

Figure 14.2 illustrates the interplay between perfectionism, its expression, transient episodic states, and downstream developmental influences. In daily lives, perfectionism will frequently activate or enact a series of cognitive (e.g. automatic perfectionistic thoughts, mistake rumination), socio-cognitive (e.g. perceived pressure to be perfect), and socio-behavioural expressions (e.g. imposing one's perfectionism into other, perfectionistic self-presentation) that will increase *transient episodic states* of sadness, stress, anxiety, loneliness, anger, and feelings of personal and social inadequacies. Being concerned about mistakes here and now (or occasionally) will unlikely increase depression six months down the road. However, *frequent re-enactment* of the signature expressions of perfectionism – as already captured through the instructions given by participants in self-report measures – will create the needed conditions for perfectionism to unleash some *downstream developmental influences* on a host of important psychological and life outcomes. How long (e.g. weeks, months, years) exactly does it take for the developmental influences to kick in could depend on a lot of factors. For this reason, these influences are dubbed as *downstream* because they are prospective, ongoing, transactional, cumulative, and developmental rather than automatic, permanent, and

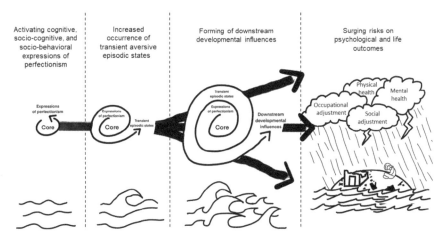

Figure 14.2 Interplay between the core definitional feature and the signature expressions of perfectionism in the MEP.

inherently long-term influences. Overall, these influences happen and build up as we live (Sameroff, 2009); they do not just simply happen at the end of a six-month longitudinal study.

Our model in Figure 14.2 assumes that perfectionism will frequently enact signature expressions of perfectionism. This transactional effect, across frequently reoccurring cycles of enactments and re-enactments, may eventually produce observable developmental outcomes over the long haul. Stopping these naturally occurring cycles – through targeted psychological interventions, changes operated by the people themselves or modifications of social environmental risk factors – can attenuate and perhaps even turn off the transdiagnostic risks associated with perfectionism. However, just like a campfire or a volcano, the effects of perfectionism may often appear to be extinguished. The distribution of episodes experienced in our daily lives usually averages somewhere between small failure to small success; extreme failure and life stress (as well as extreme success and states of elation) occur far less frequently. Therefore, the proverbial pictures taken by researchers generally happen when the fire or the volcano is pretty much sleepy rather than raging. This potentially explains why research often reports relatively weak associations between perfectionistic standards and life outcomes. Even when they appear to be turned off, these perfectionism cycles can be reactivated to refuel the probability that a perfectionist will subsequently experience unhealthy downstream developmental influences. Keeping one's perfectionism under check can be a lifelong challenge for a perfectionist.

A proof of concept was produced by Gaudreau (2021) who re-examined the associations between perfectionistic standards, perfectionistic concerns, and burnout. Correlations from a meta-analysis (Hill & Curran, 2015) and values from a Monte-Carlo simulation were used to test a simple nomological network. Let us provide another example – this time using the correlations for *self-esteem* taken from the meta-analysis of Hill et al. (2018). The correlation matrix to run our analyses is showed in panel A of Figure 14.3. The results of a multiple regression (see panel B) and a meta-analytical path analysis (see panel C) are also displayed in this figure. As expected, perfectionistic standards positively relate to perfectionistic concerns which negatively relate to self-esteem. The positive association between perfectionistic standards and self-esteem (i.e. total effect or the correlation seen in panel A) is smaller compared to the association observed after controlling for perfectionistic concerns (i.e. direct effect) in both analyses (panels B and C).

In the past, this boosted positive association with self-esteem has been interpreted as a suppression effect as well as evidence for the healthiness of perfectionistic standards. Both interpretations are accurate but nonetheless deserve further clarifications. This effect is not the effect of perfectionism for *everyone at the population level*; it is a *partial effect* or the effect of perfectionistic standards when perfectionistic concerns are held constant (Stoeber & Gaudreau, 2017). Holding constant provides an estimate of a *local, residual, or partial effect* of perfectionistic standards for *people who have the same amount of perfectionistic concerns* (Wysocki et al., 2022; see middle panel of their table 2). As illustrated in panel

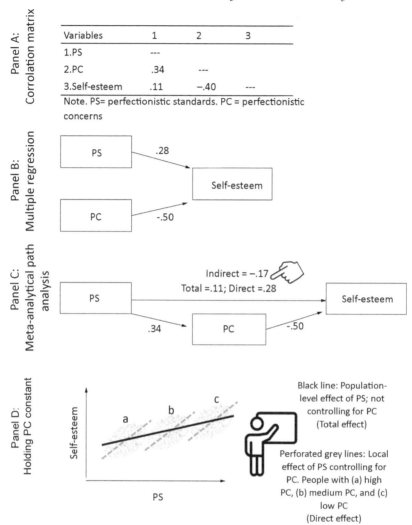

Figure 14.3 Proof of principle for self-esteem.

D of our Figure 14.3, this is similar to Simpson's paradox. In this case, the estimate at the population level (i.e. the black line) is smaller than the local estimate for people with the same level of perfectionistic concerns (i.e. the grey perforated lines). More importantly, this local/partial effect should not be given interpretational primacy over a full network of associations. This nomological network follows a simplex pattern in which adjacent variables (i.e. perfectionistic standards and concerns; perfectionistic concerns and self-esteem) are more strongly associated with one another compared to non-adjacent variables (perfectionistic standards and self-esteem). The overall network of associations, which is characterized by a *negative indirect association*, should be seen as *the needed and sufficient evidence* for a theory in which perfectionism relates to lower self-esteem. If perfectionistic standards relate to higher perfectionistic concerns, on the one hand, while perfectionistic concerns relate to lower self-esteem, on the other hand, then we cannot accept that perfectionism is associated with more self-esteem. This position is not defendable. A defendable position considers the whole network of associations in which perfectionism is overall harmful and indirectly linked to lower self-esteem (i.e. an unhealthy outcome).

As showed in the Monte Carlo simulation of Gaudreau (2021), we can extend this model by including excellencism. This is important for at least two reasons. First, we need to estimate the effects of perfectionism with measures that neatly separate high standards and perfectionistic standards. Without this, it remains unclear if the observed effects are attributable to perfectionism, excellencism, or a mixture of both. Second, the MEP considers that the aiming and striving of perfection strivers extend beyond the pursuit of excellence. Controlling for excellencism is required to properly estimate the effects of perfectionism (and vice versa). To minimize the boosted positive direct effect between perfectionistic standards and self-esteem (see Figure 14.3, panels B and C), excellencism and perfectionism both need to be included in the same analysis. In several cases, excellencism (rather than perfectionistic standards) should be positively associated with a desirable outcome (i.e. low maladjustment and high adjustment). Future research in sport will benefit from this approach.

As you may note, the model avoids the methodological parlance of mediation. Theory elaboration and research designs often derive from the same epistemology but they are not obligatorily tied to one another. Assumptions of a simplex pattern (i.e. stronger links across adjacent compared to non-adjacent variables in a network) provides this flexibility because they do not inherently assume causality (e.g. Borsboom & Cramer, 2013; Hayduk, 1994; Howard et al., 2020). In contrast, mediation requires strong assumptions about causality (i.e. experimental designs), unidirectionality (i.e. recursive), and developmental precedence (e.g. Pirlott & MacKinnon, 2016; Rohrer et al., 2022). Inferences drawn from perfectionistic traits assume they are characteristics of the person and therefore unlikely candidates for experimental manipulations. Mental representations of perfectionism can potentially be primed or temporarily activated (e.g. Boone & Soenens, 2015; Hummel et al., 2023). Even when experimental effects match those observed in correlational studies, their isomorphism cannot be taken for granted. In other words, effects involved in naturally occurring traits or personality dispositions are those of the person whereas effects observed in experiments are those produced by a situation (Tracy et al., 2009). Intervention studies offer promising tests of causality because they more directly alter and try to permanently reshape the characteristics of the person. Here again, however, effects of within-person changes caused by an intervention are those attributable to a psychoeducational process rather than effects that naturally exist when someone already holds the optimal characteristics trained in our interventions. Research designs – spanning the entire spectrum of cross-sectional, longitudinal, experimental, and intervention – are all required to provide complementary information about the veracity, replicability, and robustness of the perfectionism effects. Greater efforts should nonetheless be made to closely align our interpretations with the underlying assumptions of our methodology.

Can We Decrease Perfectionism Without Inadvertently Decreasing Excellencism?

There is an increased need for effective and widely accessible intervention to reduce perfectionism. Children, adolescents, and emerging adults live in a society in which success and achievement are highly valued – so much that it can be experienced as social pressure (e.g. Curran & Hill, 2022; Luthar et al., 2020). Aiming at things such as fame, fortune, and glory are unfortunately downplaying our effort to live a happy and productive life (Bradshaw et al., 2022). Striving toward specific and difficult goals (Swann et al., 2022) and stretch goals (Kerr & LePelley, 2013) can backfire and fail to produce the promised behavioural outcomes. Nonetheless, many coaches, teachers, parents, and administrators will potentially resist and oppose to the idea that many children and adolescent should reduce their goals and standards in the hope of fully developing their athletic and academic potential (Wade, 2018). This idea is both counterintuitive (i.e. it defies what we learned) and countercultural (i.e. it defies social norms).

Novel research on the MEP offers a solution to this important challenge. Students (Gaudreau et al., 2022; Goulet-Pelletier et al., 2022) and athletes (Gaudreau et al., 2021) can earn just as good, if not better, achievement outcomes by aiming and striving toward excellence rather than perfection. Furthermore, excellence strivers less frequently experience the concerns, doubts, fears, and perceived social pressure that are more closely linked to the phenomenological experiences (the signature expressions) of being a perfectionist. Principles and research from the MEP provide valuable scientific arguments to persuade people about the need to transform perfectionism into excellencism.

Rapid progress has been made in the development and delivery of effective cognitive behavioural therapy for perfectionists (e.g. Egan et al., 2016). These programs usually target many of the signature expressions of perfectionism. As such, meta-analytical findings revealed that interventions delivered to perfectionists can significantly reduce their perfectionistic standards and perfectionistic concerns (e.g. Galloway et al., 2021; Iliakis & Masland, 2021; Robinson & Wade, 2021). What remains to be seen, however, is whether perfectionistic standards can be reduced without inadvertently reducing excellencism.

Grieve et al. (2022) conducted the first intervention study that measured both perfectionism and excellencism before and after an online cognitive behavioural intervention. A sample of 89 university students with elevated concern over mistakes were randomized into an experimental or a wait-list control group. Everyone completed the SCOPE (Gaudreau et al., 2022) at baseline and 8 weeks after the intervention. Results showed a larger decrease in both perfectionism and excellencism among those who received the intervention. The intervention was successful at reducing perfectionistic standards and concerns. However, the effects for excellencism were interpreted as unexpected but left with little interpretational guidance.

Gaudreau and Schellenberg (2022b) were inspired by the findings of Grieve et al. (2022) and proposed a framework to facilitate the interpretation of future intervention research. They reasoned that the decreases in perfectionism and excellencism should be interpreted together rather than in isolation. Different juxtapositions of effects hold different meanings to evaluate the effectiveness of an intervention. To clarify this rather abstract notion, the fictive cases of three competitive athletes (Avery, Bailey, and Cooper) are displayed in Figure 14.4. Before the intervention, the three athletes scored high on perfectionism and high on excellencism. They were perfection strivers. Avery benefited from the intervention with significant decrease in perfectionism and non-significant changes in excellence. Avery moved from being a perfection striver to an excellence striver. Bailey experienced a significant and comparable decrease in both perfectionism and excellencism. Bailey shifted from being a perfection striver to someone with low standards (i.e. nonexcellence/nonperfection striver). Finally, Cooper experienced a significantly stronger decrease in perfectionism compared to excellencism. Therefore, Cooper finished somewhere between a zone characterizing perfection, excellence, and nonexcellence/nonperfection strivers.

Although Grieve et al. (2022) found significant decreases in both perfectionism and excellencism, these effects can be reinterpreted in relative terms. More precisely, the decrease in perfectionism (raw difference = −1.04) was stronger than the decrease in excellencism (raw difference = −0.77). Based on these results, it can be concluded that students who initially were perfection strivers shifted into a zone between nonexcellence/nonperfection and excellence strivers after the intervention. This is comparable to the fictive case of Cooper in Figure 14.4. The intervention produced a *desirable juxtaposed effect* because it helped perfection strivers to move away from a zone of perfection striving. Other desirable juxtaposed effects could be seen when an intervention

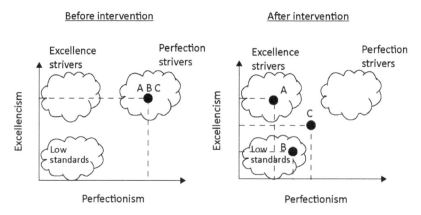

Figure 14.4 Juxtaposed effects of an intervention for Avery (A), Bailey (B), and Cooper (C).

either decreases perfectionism while not changing excellencism (i.e. the case of Avery) or if it decreases perfectionism while increasing excellencism. *Undesirable juxtaposed effects* would be seen when an intervention fails to reduce perfectionism or if it reduces perfectionism and excellencism to the same extent (i.e. the case of Bailey). Overall, the juxtaposition of effects provides a theory-driven principle that clarifies how intervention effects should be interpreted through the lens of the MEP.

A new generation of intervention research will be required to help members of the sport and dance communities. Cognitive behaviour therapies for perfectionists have included messages and exercises that mostly targeted the reduction of perfectionism. Some programs incorporated modules and some information about the need to replace perfectionism with a healthier pursuit of excellence (e.g. Vekas & Wade, 2017). To obtain desirable juxtaposed effects like the ones of Avery in Figure 14.3, new interventions will be needed to focus on transforming perfectionism into excellencism. We think that interventions that reduce perfectionism to a greater extent than excellencism (i.e. the case of Cooper) may be insufficient to significantly improve the mental health of athletes and dancers. This could explain why Grieve et al. (2022) did not find significant improvement in depression, stress, and anxiety.

Why is It Important to Understand Perfectionism Outside of Perfectionists?

Perfectionism at the Team Level

Perfectionism is generally studied at the level of the person. Recent advances have been made to study perfectionism at the team level (Hill & Grugan, 2020). This new line of research is important. Efforts to reduce personal standards (i.e. reshape perfectionism into excellencism) at the individual level will remain countercultural and less effective if we fail to account for how social norms contribute to the development and maintenance of perfectionism. Sport and dance are culture-defining social environments in which children, adolescents, and adults (both participants and coaches) frequently interact to shape and reshape each other. Modifying these complex social systems through the development and implementation of new policies, rules, and norms can have profound life-changing effects on athletes/dancers and coaches/teachers who participate in these highly competitive environments. Sport is a microcosm of life. Small changes in sport could inspire broader social changes to help schools and employers to reconsider and redefine their views of success and achievement. More research is needed at this broader level of analysis to understand perfectionism outside of perfectionists.

Two approaches have been used to study team-level perfectionism. The first approach taken by Hill et al. (2014) relied on a *team composition* framework. Each team may enrol none to many perfectionists. Having different compositions of non-perfectionists and perfectionists in a team may influence the feelings, behaviours, and performance of the individuals within the team and the team itself. A sample of 221 rowers from 36 boats were followed during four days of competition. Teams in which members had higher self-oriented perfectionism and perfectionistic expectations toward their teammates (i.e. team-oriented perfectionism) ranked better and improved their performance significantly more across the days of the competition. Having a high level of team perfectionism could mean that many athletes on a team are perfectionists or that a few athletes heavily contribute toward increasing their team's level of perfectionism. The effects of an athlete's perfectionism on the teammates may depend on the role, status (e.g. starter, seniority), leadership, and performance of that person. More research is needed to unpack these effects to better understand how perfectionism (compared to excellencism) impacts teams' dynamic and performance.

The second approach taken by Grugan et al. (2021) conceptualized team per-fectionism as an ambient phenomenon that emerges as a culture or a climate of perfectionism. The concept of *perfectionistic climate* was introduced to capture the idea that coaches, teachers, parents, leaders, and teammates can inculcate a percep-tion that doing good is never good enough. Through their use of language, feedback, advice, praise, and criticism, members of our social environments can create a culture or climate in which perfectionism is reinforced, valued, and imposed upon others. Five studies were conducted to create and validate the Perfectionistic Climate Questionnaire in Sport (PCQ-S). Results provided com-pelling evidence for a hierarchical model in which five characteristics can be neatly separated (i.e. unrealistic expectations, harsh criticism, control through rewards and punishments, recognition, and anxiousness) and regrouped into a broad dimension of perfectionistic climate. This conceptualization offers both precision and parsi-mony and should lead the way in examining different ways through which coa-ches can influence the development and maintenance of perfectionism of their trainees. Whether the PCQ-S can be tailored to study the influences of other social agents such as teachers, parents, and managers appears like a promising line of future investigations. Overall, it is commendable that items created to measure perfectionistic climate really focused on perfectionism. This contributes to con-ceptual clarifications promoted in the MEP and will facilitate empirical studies looking at the interplay between perfectionistic climate outside the person and both perfectionism and excellencism within the person.

The Hypothetical Role of the Motor Learning Environment

Beliefs of coaches and teachers can also shape their coaching and teaching in ways capable of influencing the perfectionism of their trainees. In this section, insights from motor learning and skill acquisition theories are highlighted. The ideas deli-neated here are hypothetical and meant to further our reflections about some coaching strategies potentially linked to perfectionism in sport and dance.

Many coaches still believe that a movement needs to be "perfected" in order to be automatized and optimally performed (e.g. Patterson & Lee, 2013). In their mind, a movement needs to be flawlessly rehearsed countless times in the exact same way in the hope of creating a so-called permanent "muscle memory". For example, golfers are instructed to produce the exact same movement (swing path, club speed) to grove their swing. Baseball pitchers are taught to perform the exact same movements to release the ball at a specific place to throw strikes. Deviations from "the perfect technique" are perceived as unacceptable and efforts are made to avoid and correct them. Research in motor learning clearly indicates that rigid reproduction of the same movement (without variations) can reduce exploration in the perceptual-motor space, slow down skill acquisition, and reduce their adaptability when performing in a changing environment (e.g. Gray, 2018; Silva et al., 2021). Contrary to the beliefs of many coaches, expert performers display more variability in their movements compared to less experienced performers (e.g. Preatoni et al., 2010; Seifert et al., 2013). Once internalized, the idea that a perfect technique exists and needs to be repeated the same way by everyone all the time can potentially aggravate one's predisposition toward perfectionism. This coaching myth can subtly create unrealistic and false expectations in coaches, athletes, and even parents. It can lead them to believe that a perfect movement exists, movement can be perfected, and is the only way to optimize one's performance. Nurturing these beliefs is a potentially devastating pathway that contributes to the development and maintenance of perfectionism in learners.

The science of learning has evolved over the last 20 years but many evidence-based principles have yet to influence how coaches and teachers design their practice (Soderstrom & Bjork, 2015; Weinstein et al., 2019). It is still common for a baseball coach to hit 10 consecutive ground balls at the exact same speed, with the same number of bounces in a highly predictable manner. Many golfers go to the driving range and hit 10 drivers without even aiming at a specific target. In highly repetitive environments (e.g. massed and blocked practice), athletes make mistakes during the first few trials, but their mistakes rapidly decrease across subsequent trials. Repeating the same thing in a massed learning design entertains the illusion that a movement has been properly learned, mastered, and perfected. This style of practice is often preferred by coaches and athletes because it minimizes errors and makes everyone feel good about their skills. This can be reassuring to perfectionistic coaches and athletes. However, such movements are acquired and rehearsed in a context that is not representative of the context in which the complete motor skill has to be performed in real life (e.g. Krause et al., 2018). As a result, mistakes will simply reappear after a break, when synchronizing a smaller movement into a complete routine, or performing in a game-like environment (e.g. Lee, 2012). This can also lead to the impression that an athlete is great in practice and mediocre during competition. Such unexpected variations in performance may be misattributed as "choking" and aggravate the tendency of perfectionist to avoid and negatively react to failures.

Alternative ways of practicing and rehearsing a movement (e.g. random, distributed/ spaced, and interleaved learning design) often yield deeper and more sustainable learning (e.g. Lee, 2012; Weinstein et al., 2019). For example, golfers could really improve their game by hitting their driver only once at the driving range before hitting a fairway wood or an iron as if they were hitting to a specific target on a golf course. A baseball coach could simulate a game by hitting different types of ground balls at different speed. Players will make mistakes. Their training will be ugly, but errors are a natural part of the learning process. Many alternative learning designs are often perceived as too difficult, discouraging, and frustrating (e.g. Benson et al., 2022) because they give the false impression that athletes are failing and not learning. As a result, coaches/athletes and teachers/students mostly rely on traditional and highly repetitive practice designs (Putnam et al., 2016), even if they are less effective for their learning. Optimal practice designs may be less enjoyable and more stressful for the perfectionistic coaches and athletes because they require a high tolerance for errors, mistakes, and novelty. Perfectionists are more likely to avoid exposing themselves to learning designs that could really help them optimize their skills. This could explain why perfectionists tend to underperform despite the incredible amount of time and effort they devote to their sport.

Many coaches talk too much to their athletes both during practices and games. In their mind, good coaching requires constant chatting to provide real-time corrective feedback. Evidence suggests that augmented feedback is indeed associated with improved learning of motor and sport-specific skills (Petancevski et al., 2022). However, augmented feedback interventions are meant to optimize the frequency, timing, duration, and quality of the feedback provided to athletes. Talking too much, highlighting each mistake made by an athlete, and being overly critical, cynical, and insulting are inconsistent with the underlying purposes of augmented feedback. Perfectionistic coaches are likely to provide too much of such feedback. The feedback provided has the potential to focus on errors and mistakes without paying consideration to strengths and improvements. Practicing and performing sport-specific skills can become extremely stressful and shaming when an athlete sustains the ever-ending yelling and non-verbal signs of anger and dissatisfaction of a perfectionistic coaches. Being under the constant scrutiny of a highly critical and insatiable coach could turn a confident athlete or dancer into a person who desperately starts to aim and pursue perfection to satisfy the unrealistic expectations of their coach.

Overall, studying perfectionism outside the perfectionists remains a largely unexplored area of the extant literature. Many aspects of the motor learning environment need to be studied as potential pathways in the development and maintenance of perfectionism. Addressing coaching myths and misconceptions through evidence-based coach education could help design learning environments capable of promoting excellencism (and preventing perfectionism) in sport, dance, exercise, and education.

Concluding Comments

In this chapter, we have tried to pull together and integrate recent theoretical (Gaudreau, 2019), conceptual (Gaudreau, 2021), empirical (Gaudreau et al., 2022), and intervention (Gaudreau & Schellenberg, 2022b) advances that followed the introduction of the MEP in the perfectionism literature. The MEP may look different, but it offers an integrative framework to clarify the conceptual domain of perfectionism. Perfectionism is reiterated as a multi-dimensional construct, but primacy is given to two fundamental distinctions: the difference between excellencism and perfectionism and the separation of the core definitional feature of perfectionism from its signature expression.

Perfectionism needs to be clearly separated from excellencism in our measurement instruments. The positive effects – generally attributed to perfectionistic standards – are potentially the effects of excellencism rather than the effects of perfectionism. This measurement artefact inadvertently increases the risk of erroneously concluding that perfectionism is desirable. This measurement practice must be stopped and replaced by a clear distinction between high standards (as in excellencism) and perfectionistic standards.

Perfectionism remains a broad and multifaceted construct in the MEP. The division between the definitional core (i.e. perfectionistic standards) and a host of signature expressions of perfectionism maintains all elements from previous research while organizing them in a novel nosology. This task is required to give precedence to an entire network of associations rather than to the partial and often suppressed effect of perfectionistic standards while accounting for perfectionistic concerns. Perfectionistic standards set the wheel in motion for unique, intense, and debilitative phenomenological experiences capable of explaining why perfectionists (compared to excellence strivers) are more likely to experience psychological difficulties.

Theory-driven interventions are needed to help perfectionistic athletes, dancers, exercisers, and students. Research on the MEP will be instrumental to develop scientific arguments to persuade the sport and dance communities of the need to help athletes and dancers reshape their personal standards, goals, and expectations. This will require a nuanced approach with well-crafted messages and psychoeducational activities designed to transform perfectionism into a healthier pursuit of excellence. Effects of interventions on both perfectionism and excellencism will need to be closely monitored and properly interpreted. The framework of Gaudreau and Schellenberg (2022b) offers needed guidance to align intervention with the underlying principles of the MEP.

Looking at one dependent variable at a time can provide a misleading picture of the healthiness of perfectionism. For example, Gaudreau et al. (2022) found that perfection strivers experience both elevated satisfaction and frustration of their need for competence. Perfection strivers will often make significant progress on their goals without savouring and reaping the full emotional benefits from their achievement. Thriving is only experienced when people feel successful, happy, and vivacious (e.g. Brown et al., 2017). A success that maintains or elevates pressure, stress, and distress cannot be considered as an adaptive outcome (Lazarus & Folkman, 1984). The complex antagonistic effects stemming from a desire to succeed and a fear to fail (e.g. Covington & Müeller, 2001) can only be captured if we measure and reconcile the positive and negative processes and outcomes associated with perfectionism.

Multivariable statistics are the main channel for empirical investigations on the MEP. In other words, bivariate correlations cannot be used to directly test the hypotheses of the MEP. We are currently designing a Shiny App (with R Studio) to help researchers visualize and compare the outcomes of nonexcellence/ nonperfection, excellence, and perfection strivers. Psychometric research is ongoing to create a brief SCOPE as well as translated versions in different languages. Research on perfectionism is flourishing and we hope that many researchers will contribute to the development of the MEP over the many years to come.

In conclusion, the difference between excellencism and perfectionism and the separation of the core definitional feature of perfectionism from its signature expressions can be seen as two related mini theories within the MEP. However proper investigations of the later require measures in which perfectionistic standards are no longer contaminated by high personal standards. The distinction between excellencism and perfectionism is pivotal not only in the MEP but across the entire perfectionism literature. It is our hope that researchers ten years from now will revisit our era and consider it as the decade of conceptual clarifications.

Acknowledgements

Preparation of this chapter was facilitated by a research grant from Social Sciences and Humanities Research Council of Canada (435-2022-0145) and a teaching release from the Faculty of Social Science awarded to Patrick Gaudreau. Antoine Benoit and Laurence Boileau played an equal role in the preparation of this chapter. Figures have been designed using the free and publicly accessible resources from Flaticon.com.

References

Benson, W. L., Dunning, J. P., & Barber, D. (2022). Using distributed practice to improve students' attitudes and performance in statistics. *Teaching of Psychology*, 49(1), 64–70. https://doi.org/10.1177/0098628320979680.

Besser, A., Flett, G. L., Guez, J., & Hewitt, P. L. (2008). Perfectionism, mood, and memory for positive, negative, and perfectionistic content. *Individual Differences Research*, 6(4), 211–244.

Blasberg, J. S., Hewitt, P. L., Flett, G. L., Sherry, S. B., & Chen, C. (2016). The importance of item wording: The distinction between measuring high standards versus measuring perfectionism and why it matters. *Journal of Psychoeducational Assessment*, 34, 702–717. https://doi.org/10.1177/0734282916653701.

Boone, L., & Soenens, B. (2015). In double trouble for eating pathology? An experimental study on the combined role of perfectionism and body dissatisfaction. *Journal of Behavior Therapy and Experimental Psychiatry*, 47, 77–83. https://doi.org/10.1016/j.jbtep.2014.11.005.

Borsboom, D., & Cramer, A. O. J. (2013). Network analysis: An integrative approach to the structure of psychopathology. *Annual Review of Clinical Psychology*, 9(1), 91–121. https://doi.org/10.1146/annurev-clinpsy-050212-185608.

Bradshaw, E. L., Conigrave, J. H., Steward, B. A., Ferber, K. A., Parker, P. D., & Ryan, R. M. (2022). A meta-analysis of the dark side of the American dream: Evidence for the universal wellness costs of prioritizing extrinsic over intrinsic goals. *Journal of Personality and Social Psychology*, online ahead of print. https://doi.org/10.1037/pspp0000431.

Brown, D. J., Arnold, R., Standage, M., & Fletcher, D. (2017). Thriving on pressure: A factor mixture analysis of sport performers' responses to competitive encounters. *Journal of Sport and Exercise Psychology*, 39(6), 423–437. https://doi.org/10.1123/jsep.2016-0293.

Covington, M. V., & Müeller, K. J. (2001). Intrinsic versus extrinsic motivation: An approach/avoidance reformulation. *Educational Psychology Review*, 13(2), 157–176. https://doi.org/10.1023/A:1009009219144.

Cox, B. J., McWilliams, L. A., Enns, M. W., & Clara, I. P. (2004). Broad and specific personality dimensions associated with major depression in a nationally representative sample. *Comprehensive Psychiatry*, 45(4), 246–253. https://doi.org/https://doi.org/10.1016/j.comppsych.2004.03.002.

Curran, T., & Hill, A. P. (2022). Young people's perceptions of their parents' expectations and criticism are increasing over time: Implications for perfectionism. *Psychological Bulletin*, 148, 107–128. https://doi.org/10.1037/bul0000347.

Egan, S. J., Wade, T. D., Shafran, R., & Antony, M. M. (2016). *Cognitive-behavioral treatment of perfectionism*. Guilford.

Flett, G. L., & Hewitt, P. L. (2019). Reflections on three decades of research on multidimensional perfectionism: An introduction to the special issue on further advances in the assessment of perfectionism. *Journal of Psychoeducational Assessment*, 38(1), 3–14. https://doi.org/10.1177/0734282919881928.

Flett, G. L., Hewitt, P. L., Nepon, T., & Besser, A. (2018). Perfectionism cognition theory: The cognitive side of perfectionism. In J. Stoeber (ed.), *The psychology of perfectionism: Theory, research, applications* (pp. 89–110). Routledge.

Frost, R. O., Marten, P., Lahart, C., & Rosenblate, R. (1990). The dimensions of perfectionism. *Cognitive Therapy and Research*, 14, 449–468. https://doi.org/10.1007/BF01172967.

Galloway, R., Watson, H., Greene, D., Shafran, R., & Egan, S. J. (2021). The efficacy of randomised controlled trials of cognitive behaviour therapy for perfectionism: A systematic review and meta-analysis. *Cognitive Behaviour Therapy*, 1–15. https://doi.org/10.1080/16506073.2021.1952302.

Gaudreau, P. (2019). On the distinction between personal standards perfectionism and excellencism: A theory elaboration and research agenda. *Perspectives on Psychological Science*, 14, 195–215. https://doi.org/10.1177/1745691618797940.

Gaudreau, P. (2021). Separating the core definitional feature and the signature expressions of dispositional perfectionism: Implications for theory, research, and practice. *Personality and Individual Differences*, 181, 110975. https://doi.org/10.1016/j.paid.2021.110975.

Gaudreau, P., Boileau, L., & Schellenberg, B. J. I. (2021). Peur de l'échec à l'école et dans les sports: Apport du modèle de l'excellencisme et du perfectionnisme [Fear of failure in sport and school: Contribution of the model of excellencism and perfectionism]. *Revue Québécoise de Psychologie*, 42(3), 173–194.

Gaudreau, P., & Schellenberg, B. J. I. (2022a). Attitudes of sport fans toward the electronic sign stealing scandal in Major League Baseball: Differing associations with perfectionism and excellencism. *Journal of Sport & Exercise Psychology*, 44(3), 220–229.

Gaudreau, P., & Schellenberg, B. J. I. (2022b). The impact of internet-based cognitive behavior therapy for perfectionism: A reinterpretation through the lens of the model of excellencism and perfectionism. Submitted for publication.

Gaudreau, P., Schellenberg, B. J. I., Gareau, A., Kljajic, K., & Manoni-Millar, S. (2022). Because excellencism is more than good enough: On the need to distinguish the pursuit of excellence from the pursuit of perfection. *Journal of Personality and Social Psychology*, 122, 1117–1145. https://doi.org/10.1037/pspp0000411.

Goulet-Pelletier, J.-C., Gaudreau, P., & Cousineau, D. (2022). Is perfectionism a killer of creative thinking? A test of the model of excellencism and perfectionism. *British Journal of Psychology*, 113, 176–207. https://doi.org/10.1111/bjop.12530.

Gray, R. (2018). Comparing cueing and constraints interventions for increasing launch angle in baseball batting. *Sport, Exercise, and Performance Psychology*, 7, 318–332.

Grieve, P., Egan, S. J., Andersson, G., Carlbring, P., Shafran, R., & Wade, T. D. (2022). The impact of internet-based cognitive behaviour therapy for perfectionism on different measures of perfectionism: a randomised controlled trial. *Cognitive Behaviour Therapy*, 51, 130–142. https://doi.org/10.1080/16506073.2021.1928276.

Grugan, M. C., Hill, A. P., Mallinson-Howard, S. H., Donachie, T. C., Olsson, L. F., Madigan, D. J., & Vaughan, R. S. (2021). Development and initial validation of the Perfectionistic Climate Questionnaire-Sport (PCQ-S). *Psychology of Sport and Exercise*, 56, 101997. https://doi.org/https://doi.org/10.1016/j.psychsport.2021.101997.

Hayduk, L. A. (1994). Personal space: Understanding the simplex model. *Journal of Nonverbal Behavior*, 18, 245–260. https://doi.org/10.1007/BF02170028.

Hewitt, P. L., Flett, G. L., & Mikail, S. F. (2017). *Perfectionism: A relational approach to conceptualization, assessment, and treatment*. Guilford.

Hill, A. P., & Curran, T. (2015). Multidimensional perfectionism and burnout: A meta-analysis. *Personality and Social Psychology Review*, 20, 269–288. https://doi.org/10.1177/1088868315596286.

Hill, A. P., & Grugan, M. (2020). Introducing perfectionistic climate. *Perspectives on Early Childhood Psychology and Education*, 4(2), 263–276.

Hill, A. P., Mallinson-Howard, S. H., & Jowett, G. E. (2018). Multidimensional perfectionism in sport: A meta-analytical review. *Sport, Exercise, and Performance Psychology*, 7(3), 235–270. https://doi.org/10.1037/spy0000125.

Hill, A. P., Stoeber, J., Brown, A., & Appleton, P. R. (2014). Team perfectionism and team performance: A prospective study. *Journal of Sport & Exercise Psychology*, 36, 303–315. https://doi.org/10.1123/jsep.2013-0206.

Hill, R. W., Huelsman, T. J., Furr, R. M., Kibler, J., Vicente, B. B., & Kennedy, C. (2004). A new measure of perfectionism: The Perfectionism Inventory. *Journal of Personality Assessment*, 82(1), 80–91. https://doi.org/10.1207/s15327752jpa8201_13.

Howard, J. L., Gagné, M., & Morin, A. J. S. (2020). Putting the pieces together: Reviewing the structural conceptualization of motivation within SDT. *Motivation and Emotion*. https://doi.org/10.1007/s11031-020-09838-2.

Hummel, J., Cludius, B., Woud, M. L., Holdenrieder, J., Mende, N., Huber, V., Limburg, K., & Takano, K. (2023). The causal relationship between perfectionism and negative affect: Two experimental studies. *Personality and Individual Differences*, 200, 111895. https://doi.org/https://doi.org/10.1016/j.paid.2022.111895.

Iliakis, E. A., & Masland, S. R. (2021). Internet interventions for perfectionism: A meta-analysis and proposals for the college setting. *Journal of American College Health*, 1–6. https://doi.org/10.1080/07448481.2021.1970559.

Jaccard, J., & Jacoby, J. (2010). *Theory construction and model-building skills*. Guilford.

Kerr, S., & LePelley, D. (2013). Stretch goals: Risks, possibilities, and best practices. In E. A. Locke & G. P. Latham (eds), *New developments in goal setting and task performance* (pp. 21–31). Routledge.

Krause, L., Farrow, D., Reid, M., Buszard, T., & Pinder, R. (2018). Helping coaches apply the principles of representative learning design: Validation of a tennis specific practice assessment tool. *Journal of Sports Sciences*, 36, 1277–1286. https://doi.org/10.1080/02640414.2017.1374684.

Lazarus, R. S., & Folkman, S. (1984). *Stress, appraisal, and coping*. Springer.

Lee, T. D. (2012). Contextual interference: Generalizability and limitations. In N. J. Hodges & M. A. Williams (eds), *Skill acquisition in sport: Research, theory, and practice* (pp. 79–93). Routledge.

Lin, S., & Muenks, K. (2022). Perfectionism profiles among college students: A person-centered approach to motivation, behavior, and emotion. *Contemporary Educational Psychology*, 71, 102110. https://doi.org/https://doi.org/10.1016/j.cedpsych.2022.102110.

Luthar, S., Kumar, N., & Zillmer, N. (2020). High-achieving schools connote risks for adolescents: Problems documented, processes implicated, and directions for interventions. *American Psychologist*, 75, 983–995. https://doi.org/10.1037/amp0000556.

McLaughlin, K. A., & Nolen-Hoeksema, S. (2011). Rumination as a transdiagnostic factor in depression and anxiety. *Behaviour Research and Therapy*, 49(3), 186–193. https://doi.org/https://doi.org/10.1016/j.brat.2010.12.006.

Osenk, I., Williamson, P., & Wade, T. D. (2020). Does perfectionism or pursuit of excellence contribute to successful learning? A meta-analytic review. *Psychological Assessment*, 32, 972–983. https://doi.org/10.1037/pas0000942.

Patterson, J. E., & Lee, T. D. (2013). Organizing practice: Effective practice is more than just reps. In D. Farrow, J. Baker, & C. MacMahon (eds), *Developing sport expertise: Researchers and coaches put theory into practice* (2nd ed., pp. 132–153). Routledge.

Petancevski, E. L., Inns, J., Fransen, J., & Impellizzeri, F. M. (2022). The effect of augmented feedback on the performance and learning of gross motor and sport-specific skills: A systematic review. *Psychology of Sport and Exercise*, 63, 102277. https://doi.org/https://doi.org/10.1016/j.psychsport.2022.102277.

Pirlott, A. G., & MacKinnon, D. P. (2016). Design approaches to experimental mediation. *Journal of Experimental Social Psychology*, 66, 29–38. https://doi.org/https://doi.org/10.1016/j.jesp.2015.09.012.

Preatoni, E., Ferrario, M., Donà, G., Hamill, J., & Rodano, R. (2010). Motor variability in sports: A non-linear analysis of race walking. *Journal of Sports Sciences*, 28, 1327–1336. https://doi.org/10.1080/02640414.2010.507250.

Putnam, A. L., Sungkhasettee, V. W., & Henry L.Roediger, I. (2016). Optimizing learning in college: Tips from cognitive psychology. *Perspectives on Psychological Science*, 11(5), 652–660. https://doi.org/10.1177/1745691616645770.

Robinson, K., & Wade, T. D. (2021). Perfectionism interventions targeting disordered eating: A systematic review and meta-analysis. *International Journal of Eating Disorders*, 54, 473–487. https://doi.org/https://doi.org/10.1002/eat.23483.

Rohrer, J. M., Hünermund, P., Arslan, R. C., & Elson, M. (2022). That's a lot to process! Pitfalls of popular path models. *Advances in Methods and Practices in Psychological Science*, 5(2), 25152459221095827. https://doi.org/10.1177/25152459221095827.

Sameroff, A. J. (2009). *The transactional model of development: How children and contexts shape each other*. American Psychological Association. https://doi.org/10.1037/11877-000.

Seifert, L., Button, C., & Davids, K. (2013). Key properties of expert movement systems in sport. *Sports Medicine*, 43(3), 167–178. https://doi.org/10.1007/s40279-012-0011-z.

Silva, A. F., Komar, J., & Seifert, L. (2021). Search of individually optimal movement solutions in sport: Learning between stability and flexibility [Editorial]. *Frontiers in Psychology*, 12. https://doi.org/10.3389/fpsyg.2021.728375.

Sirois, F. M., & Molnar, D. S. (2016). *Perfectionism, health, and well-being*. Springer.

Smith, M. M., Saklofske, D. H., Stoeber, J., & Sherry, S. B. (2016). The Big Three perfectionism scale: A new measure of perfectionism. *Journal of Psychoeducational Assessment*, 34, 670–687. https://doi.org/10.1177/0734282916651539.

Smith, M. M., Sherry, S. B., Ge, S. Y., Hewitt, P. L., Flett, G. L., & Baggley, D. L. (2021). Multidimensional perfectionism turns 30: A review of known knowns and known unknowns. *Canadian Psychology*, 63(1), 16–31. https://doi.org/10.1037/cap0000288

Soderstrom, N. C., & Bjork, R. A. (2015). Learning versus performance: An integrative review. *Perspectives on Psychological Science*, 10, 176–199. https://doi.org/10.1177/1745691615569000.

Stoeber, J. (2018a). The psychology of perfectionism: An introduction. In J. Stoeber (ed.), *The psychology of perfectionism: Theory, research, and applications* (pp. 3–16). Routledge.

Stoeber, J. (2018b). The psychology of perfectionism: Critical issues, open questions, and future directions. In J. Stoeber (ed.), *The psychology of perfectionism: Theory, research, and applications* (pp. 333–352). Routledge.

Stoeber, J., & Gaudreau, P. (2017). The advantages of partialling perfectionistic strivings and perfectionistic concerns: Critical issues and recommendations. *Personality and Individual Differences*, 104, 379–386. https://doi.org/10.1016/j.paid.2016.08.039.

Swann, C., Jackman, P. C., Lawrence, A., Hawkins, R. M., Goddard, S. G., Williamson, O., Schweickle, M. J., Vella, S. A., Rosenbaum, S., & Ekkekakis, P. (2022). The (over)use of SMART goals for physical activity promotion: A narrative review and critique. *Health Psychology Review*, online ahead of print. https://doi.org/10.1080/17437199.2021.2023608.

Thew, G. R., Gregory, J. D., Roberts, K., & Rimes, K. A. (2017). The phenomenology of self-critical thinking in people with depression, eating disorders, and in healthy individuals. *Psychology and Psychotherapy: Theory, Research and Practice*, 90(4), 751–769. https://doi.org/https://doi.org/10.1111/papt.12137.

Tracy, J. L., Robins, R. W., & Sherman, J. W. (2009). The practice of psychological science: Searching for Cronbach's two streams in social-personality psychology. *Journal of Personality and Social Psychology* 96, 1206–1225. https://doi.org/10.1037/a0015173.

Vekas, E., & Wade, T. D. (2017). The impact of a universal intervention targeting perfectionism in children: An exploratory controlled trial. *British Journal of Clinical Psychology*, 56, 458–473. https://doi.org/10.1111/bjc.12152.

Wade, T. D. (2018). Prevention of perfectionism in youth. In J. Stoeber (ed.), *The psychology of perfectionism: Theory, research, applications* (pp. 265–283). Routledge.

Weinstein, Y., Sumeracki, M., & Caviglioli, O. (2019). *Understanding how we learn: A visual guide*. Routledge.

Wysocki, A. C., Lawson, K. M., & Rhemtulla, M. (2022). Statistical control requires causal justification. *Advances in Methods and Practices in Psychological Science*, 5(2), 25152459221095823. https://doi.org/10.1177/25152459221095823.

15 Reflections on the Costs of Rigid Perfectionism and Perfectionistic Reactivity

The Core Significance of the Failure to Adapt in Sports and in Life

Gordon L. Flett and Paul L. Hewitt

> Pressure is a privilege and champions adapt or adjust. And I try to tell people, particularly young people, that champions in life, all we're doing is adapting. We adapt as we go through each day.
>
> – Billie Jean King (as reported in Gross, 2013)

Our work over the past three decades reflects the perspective that any benefits of perfectionism are far outweighed by its costs and consequences. This view reflects various realities. Case accounts have documented the trials and tribulations of perfectionists; sadly, in some instances, this includes mental health challenges have resulted in the deaths of perfectionists due to suicide. Unfortunately, when someone points to the many perfectionists who have been successful and achieved at elite levels, it is also easy to identify perfectionistic people who did quite well and achieved but nevertheless failed to reach their potential. One troubling aspect is the inability of extreme perfectionists to enjoy their successes; they seldom derive a lasting sense of satisfaction even when they are successful. This is especially the case when accomplished and acclaimed perfectionists engage in evaluative comparisons. In most instances, these comparisons are social comparisons with rivals. The perfectionistic athlete who does exceptionally well will nevertheless react strongly to being outperformed.

Other evaluative comparisons involve temporal self-comparisons. Canadian gold medal sprinter Donovan Bailey confessed 25 years later that it was still difficult for him to watch the video of his world record Olympic run because he would still focus years later on his slow start and the mistakes he made that precluded him from doing even better. Another form of comparison for elite athletes is the sense that others are comparing their current performances with the athlete's own flawless performances from the past. This concern was noted by tennis great Björn Borg who described the disquiet inherent in the sense that other people were unfavourably comparing him to his former self (see Adams, 2007). Borg provided this as one explanation for why he went into very early retirement after losing the US Open to John McEnroe in 1981.

DOI: 10.4324/9781003288015-20

We proposed in our chapter in the first edition of this book that perfectionistic reactivity is one reason why perfectionistic athletes are vulnerable and highly prone to difficulties (see Flett & Hewitt, 2016). That is, much of the vulnerability inherent in perfectionism stems from how perfectionists react to pressure, failures, mistakes, and losses. Perfectionistic reactivity is highly maladaptive and comes in many forms. This concept captures negative emotional reactions but also negative cognitive reactions and behavioral responses. Cognitive reactivity is particularly problematic for athletes. Cognitive tendencies including experiencing frequent automatic thoughts about needing to be perfect but not actually being perfect (see Flett et al., 1998), a failure to accept the past and rumination about past mistakes (Flett et al., 2020), and cognitive preoccupation with anticipated setbacks and related worries (see Frost & Henderson, 1991). Other forms of cognitive reactivity include ruminative brooding and triggering maladaptive beliefs and cognitive processes such as the overgeneralization of negative outcomes to the self (i.e. I did not do well so I am flawed and defective). Another form of cognitive vulnerability documented in recent research is clinging rigidly to extreme beliefs (see Klockare et al., 2022).

In the current chapter, we extend our analysis by arguing that limited adaptability is key aspect of perfectionistic reactivity that undermines performance and well-being. We focus on adaptability for three overarching reasons. First, adaptability is a topic that has largely neglected in the broader sports psychology field, even though it is a vital key to success. Overall, in psychology in general, there are countless research studies on resilience but relatively few on adaptability, and this is also true in the sports psychology field. We hope our emphasis on adaptability will provide the impetus for much more conceptualization and research with an explicit focus on self-reported or informant-reported individual differences in the ability to adapt.

Second, most previous analyses tend to focus on whether the perfectionist has the capability to be resilient and bounce back, but adaptability is arguably just as important, if not more important. Our focus on adaptability is an attempt to focus attention on a capacity that we believe is in short supply among driven perfectionists characterized by rigid perfectionism.

Finally, there have been extensive discussions of whether perfectionism has an adaptive element to it; this discussion in the sports field has focused on the proposed adaptiveness of perfectionistic striving (see Gotwals et al., 2012). We contend that any conclusions drawn are decidedly premature at this point given the lack of empirical attention on perfectionism and adaptability in sports, especially when we focus on the construct of rigid perfectionism described below and the inflexible, inexorable striving that accompanies it when rigid perfectionism is at an extreme level. The current chapter can be viewed as a reminder of the need to consider the notion of what is adaptive versus maladaptive from a broad, inclusive perspective that incorporates adaptability as a key criterion.

We return to the central role of adaptability and how it is vital to focus on the adaptability of perfectionists in a later segment of this chapter. First, however, we begin by revisiting previous articles and show how this focus on adaptability offers a unique perspective on past work in the perfectionism and sports literature. Specifically, we revisit the Flett and Hewitt (2005) article on the perils of perfectionism in sports and then the ground-breaking Frost and Henderson (1991) study that stands as the first extensive investigation of multidimensional perfectionism in sports.

The Perils of Perfectionism Revisited

Flett and Hewitt (2005) described the potential perils of perfectionism in sports from a variety of perspectives. The origin of this article was an invited keynote address from the first author to American Psychological Association Division 47: Society for Sport, Exercise, and Performance Psychology when the annual convention was held in Toronto in 2003. We began our article by highlighting what we described as "the perfectionism paradox". This refers to the fact that perfection is required to be successful in so many sports contexts, yet athletes who focus too much on needing to be perfect will succumb to pressures to be perfect and their performance will often falter. We also identified several debilitating aspects or correlates of perfectionism. A central focus was an ego orientation that results in self-consciousness rather than the presence of a positive task orientation. Although the concept of perfectionistic reactivity was not introduced formally until more than a decade later, several elements of perfectionistic reactivity were foreshadowed. Key elements included a hypersensitivity to mistakes and failures and associated forms of cognitive rumination following mistakes and failures. This aversion to failure in performance settings has been well-documented in experimental work (e.g. Curran & Hill, 2018).

Unfortunately, one aspect of our article is typically overlooked and this aspect is directly relevant to our current emphasis on the limited adaptability of perfectionists. Specifically, in a segment focused on intervening factors that mitigate the perils of perfectionism, we observed that protection from the perils of perfectionism will come if perfectionists "have developed a proactive, task-oriented approach to coping with difficulties and setbacks":

> A key aspect of the coping process for these athletes is to develop a sense of flexibility, so that they adjust their goals in accordance with situational demands and current levels of personal functioning.
>
> (Flett & Hewitt, 2005, p. 16)

We also discussed how perfectionists tend to be rely on emotion-oriented coping that reflects a defensiveness and preoccupation with the self, but the development of an adaptive problem-solving orientation could limit the destructiveness of perfectionism.

The observations fit very well with the notion of adaptability, as it is outlined below. Moreover, they also fit with a key element of the Frost and Henderson (1991) study that has similarly "flown under the radar" yet shines a light on the potential importance of adaptability.

Multidimensional Perfectionism in Sports

Frost and Henderson (1991) conducted a cross-sectional study. They described data from a sample of 40 women in varsity athletics. Participants completed the Frost Multidimensional Perfectionism Scale (FMPS; Frost et al., 1990), and measures assessing sports self-confidence, sports competition anxiety, thoughts before competition, specific reactions to mistakes during competition, a sports success orientation, and a sports failure orientation. Frost and Henderson (1991) reported that elevated scores on the FMPS concern over mistakes subscale were associated significantly with anxiety, low confidence, a failure orientation, and negative reactions to mistakes during competition. Moreover, self-oriented perfectionism (i.e. the high personal standards subscale) was associated with reports of difficulty concentrating while performing, and worries about the reactions of the audience.

We focus here on the results derived from reports from the coaches of these 40 athletes. Frost and Henderson (1991) placed great importance on the results derived from coach assessments because coaches were seen as relatively inde-pendent observers who view athletes across a range of situations and contexts over a prolonged time period. As part of their broader assessment, coaches provided ratings across three items that formed a subscale deemed to assess "reactions to mistakes and pressure". Inspection of the three items suggests that this subscale should have been titled "performance-related adaptability". Coaches rated the degree to which these athletes could: (1) adapt quickly to new and different competitive situations; (2) perform well under pressure; and (3) recover well from mistakes during competition. The overall alpha coefficient for this construct was an impressive .91. This level of internal consistency suggests that there were at least moderate to strong intercorrelations among the three items. Thus, we can infer that women athletes who were seen as adaptable also tended to be seen as having the tendency to handle pressure and recover well from mistakes. Of course, it can also be inferred from this part of the Frost and Henderson (1991) study that individual differences in athletes' adaptability were highly visible to their coaches.

How did scores on this measure relate to perfectionism? Frost and Hender-son (1991) reported a significant negative association between the athletes' perfectionism and the coach ratings of adaptability to pressure and mistakes. The correlation between coach-rated adaptability and total perfectionism scores was significant ($r = -.39$, $p < .05$). Subscale analyses indicated that adaptability ratings were associated negatively with concern over mistakes, doubts about actions, and parental criticism. The link with high standards also trended in the direction of lower adaptability but this correlation fell short of conventional standards for statistical significance, likely due to their only being 40 athletes in this study ($r = -.21$, $p < .05$). Unfortunately, this clear and early indication of the lower adaptability of perfectionistic athletes did not translate into pro-grammatic research on perfectionism-related deficits in athletes' adaptability. It remains an open question as to whether perfectionistic athletes are aware of their limitations in terms of the capacity to adapt; it is likely that some perfectionists are very much aware of these limitations while others are defensively oblivious to deficits in adaptability. The proposed link between perfectionism and reduced adaptability now needs to be studied in very challenging situations that takes contextual parameters into account. This research is clearly needed so that it can provide the impetus and support for adaptability training of perfectionistic athletes.

We now turn to a more general discussion of adaptability in sports. This discussion then leads into an extended analysis of how and why adaptability is especially antithetical to rigid perfectionism.

Adaptability in Sports: A Vital Extension of Resilience

Adaptability should be a highly salient theme right now as everyone continues to experience the trials and tribulations of the global COVID-19 pandemic. At present, we are in a prolonged period of things not being the way we anticipated. The pandemic has taught us many lessons, with perhaps the biggest lesson being that our lives can become dominated by unforeseeable life conditions that call for adaptability. If viewed from an adaptability perspective, behavioural tendencies such as the refusal to become vaccinated constitute a failure to adapt. Likewise, there are clear implications for modes of learning given evidence that students with lower levels of adaptability reported more difficult transitions to online learning (see Besser et al., 2022).

What is adaptability and how and when is it relevant in sports? Adaptability is the capacity to change positively to address and fit with new demands when confronted with new or uncertain circumstances. Erich Fromm (1941) discussed two types of adaptability. One type involves simply changing behaviour in the short-term to address a new situation or circumstance (e.g. learning to drive a car). Another type is more extensive and requires a transformation of the self and evolving in order to adjust to a new situation or circumstance. Both types apply to athletes when the focus becomes on their entire careers. Ultimately, athletes may be most challenged when they need to adapt their identities.

The conceptualization of adaptability advanced by Andrew Martin fits well with our emphasis on affective, behavioural and cognitive forms of perfectionistic reactivity. Martin focused on adaptability in academic contexts. He developed a nine-item scale that taps adaptability in terms of affect, behaviour, and cognition (see Martin et al., 2013). One affect-related item is, "When uncertainty arises, I am able to minimize frustration or irritation". Behaviour is tapped by the scale item, "To assist me in a new situation, I am able to change the way I do things if necessary." Finally, cognition is reflected by the adaptability item, "I am able to think through a number of possible options to assist me in a new situation".

The scale items listed above are worded in ways that reflect the fact that people who tend to high in adaptability tend to have a highly salient sense of self-efficacy. Research on individual differences also indicates that people who report higher levels of adaptability also tend to have a more hopeful outlook and feel a greater sense of connectedness and mattering to other people (see Besser et al., 2020; Besser et al., 2022). Similarly, interviews of 13 people with established track records of resilience and exceptional achievement identified one theme reflecting adaptability and flexibility and five other key themes (i.e. positive and proactive personality, experience and learning, sense of control, balance and perspective, and perceived social support; see Sarkar & Fletcher, 2014). One implication of acknowledging the other positive characteristics that typically accompany adaptability is that athletes who learn ways to adapt to new and uncertain circumstances should also have an array of other personal resources (e.g. hope, self-confidence, self-efficacy) to call on as needed. Adaptability combined with hope should be a powerful combination that serves most athletes well, but especially perfectionistic athletes, given evidence documenting the benefits of striving that is fuelled by hope and optimism (see Lizmore, Dunn, & Dunn, 2017).

We should note that Martin (2017) has emphasized that adaptability is not simply coping. Coping involves characteristic styles that may or may not fit depending on the situation (see Forsythe & Compas, 1987). In contrast, adaptability is the capability to read and interpret various situations and affectively, behaviourally, and cognitively approach the situation in ways that it can be managed and successfully negotiated. This ability to size up situations suggests that adaptability is more than the capacity to be flexible because it also involves a specific mindset and awareness.

When is Adaptability Needed in Sports?

All athletes experience failure and periods of little progress. Sometimes failure is a result of their own mistakes and failures, but in competition, failure can occur simply because an opponent is in the middle of an exceptional performance and there is not much an opponent can do in response. The immediate challenge for the athlete who is facing a competitor who is performing exceptionally is to adapt and find some way to transform the situation and combat the superior performance of the opponent (e.g. baseball batters working the count by not swinging at pitches to tire out a seemingly unbeatable starting pitcher). This process begins with non-defensively recognizing that there is a need to adapt.

Adaptability in sports is required most, if not all, of the time. Tamminen et al. (2014) observed that adaptation in sports entails continual adjustments as conditions change. They noted further that various types of functioning (i.e. physical, psychological, social, and emotional) are not static or fixed and, as such, this suggests the need for models of sports performance with a dynamic element. Just how relevant is adaptability? Collins and Macnamara (2017) proposed that self-driven adaptability should be the ultimate target in sports development.

There are numerous reasons to focus on adaptability in sports. Clearly, being successful to the point of becoming a champion requires an ability to adapt. Adaptability is needed by the baseball player who strikes out too much due to an inability to stop swinging at pitches that are low and outside. Adaptability is needed by the hockey goalie who realizes that opposing teams have learned that his glove hand is slow and is a way to score. The coach with a bad game plan also needs to adapt. Indeed, half-time intermissions during football games are recognized as a time for adjustments, but it was famously stated by acclaimed coach Bill Belichick in 2015 that delaying adjustments until half-time is waiting too long. The need to adapt is often immediate and can be conscious or reflect automatic tendencies. Adaptability is often needed in golf as well. The golfer who is able to adapt has a key advantage. One way to interpret the many swing alterations made by Tiger Woods over the years is that it reflected his sense of needing to find what works and what can be effective in the moment.

Adaptability is relevant during competition, but also while preparing for competition. Adaptability can involve learning to adjust to teammates or to opponents. It can involve all phases of athletics, including the orientation toward training and time management. The obsessed perfectionist who trains to an excessive degree is likely someone who is very low in adaptability. Adaptability is also essential when we take a person-focus and consider the life transitions experienced by athletes. The aging athlete must learn to adapt to compensate for physical changes. And finally, adaptability is essential when the athlete makes the transition to retirement and must cope with life after the playing career is over.

Given the presumed importance of adaptability in sports, personal narratives of successful athletes should reflect this key characteristic. Indeed, this is the case. For instance, a qualitative study by Herbison et al. (2019) involved interviewing 12 hockey players who played in the National Hockey League (NHL) despite never having been drafted. Their mean number of games of NHL experience was 153 games. Key factors they highlighted in terms of their journeys to making it into the NHL included past experiences with adversity and a host of personal characteristics (e.g. competitiveness, passion, and stable, enduring confidence). Adaptability was relevant in several respects. Specifically, players emphasized the importance of focusing their work on addressing their weaknesses. They attributed their ability to overcome weaknesses to the social support they received but also changes in goal setting strategies; adaptability here meant shifting from ego-oriented goals to task-oriented goals. This transition in goal setting strategies did not occur in a vacuum; it typically occurred after failure experiences and receiving social support, evaluation, and encouragement from credible hockey figures. Along similar lines, instead of becoming demoralized and just giving up, these players embraced deliberate practice techniques centred on addressing weaknesses such as needing to become a better skater. One goalie specifically noted that he emphasized paying greater attention to detail and finding ways to become a better player in every single practice.

Certain elements of the approach taken by these NHL players are reflected in a contemporary analysis of the mental toughness of Australian Rules Football players. This research by Clark et al. (2022) established that commitment, confidence and optimism were important and goals were set in accordance with these tendencies. Most notably, mental toughness was reflected in goal orientation and how goals are modified when this is needed. Specific examples that seem to reflect adaptability included being able to and willing to listen to others' opinions, seeking to learn new things every day, and having a routine "without becoming anal" about it. A central focus was being able to adjust goals and come up with alternative approaches, which would not be possible if decision-making was clouded by vulnerability and feelings of insecurity and inferiority.

Other evidence of adaptability in sports comes from the qualitative component of a study of school and sports burnout in adolescent athletes. Sorkkila et al. (2020) interviewed elite athletes deemed to be high or low in burnout risk. Several features and themes distinguished the nine athletes with a burnout risk profile from the seven athletes with the non-risk profile. The athletes with burnout tendencies had school-related stress, inadequate recovery, little social life, and coaching that was described as disempowering by the athletes. In contrast, athletes with little risk were differentiated by multiple resources (e.g. adaptability, social support, and intrinsic sports motivation). The composite description of the adaptable athlete relatively immune from burnout emphasized being able to implement adjustments in the amount of schoolwork taken out due to being cognizant of the times of year that required a greater focus on sports.

We now discuss adaptability within the context of the rigid perfectionism concept. Much can be learned about deficits in adaptability by studying an extreme personality linked with resistance to change. Therapists and counsellors are almost certainly very cognizant of this rigid resistance to change of inflexible perfectionists.

Rigid Perfectionism

Perfectionism is problematic in general, but this is especially the case with rigid perfectionism. We focus on rigid perfectionism in this segment of our chapter for two reasons. First, of course, there is obvious relevance in terms of our emphasis on adaptability. Second, to our knowledge, a comprehensive analysis of rigid perfectionism has not appeared in the published literature.

Rigid perfectionists are especially likely to have problematic forms of perfectionistic reactivity including an unwillingness or inability to respond well to novel and changing circumstances. Karen Horney (1937) alluded to this characteristic when she couched neurosis as a "certain rigidity in reaction" (p. 22). We alluded to a rigid form of perfectionism at the start of our 2014 article when we emphasized the "various costs and consequences that can result from the inflexible and rigid pursuit of perfection and associated ways of evaluating the self and other people" (Flett & Hewitt, 2014, p. 395). This reference to both the self and to other people is noteworthy. Rigid perfectionism is believed by most scholars to mostly involve self-oriented perfectionism as described by Hewitt and Flett (1991), but research with an emphasis on multidimensional perfectionism indicates that rigid perfectionism is associated significantly with self-oriented, other-oriented, and socially prescribed perfectionism (see Stoeber, 2014). Thus, just as it is the case with perfectionism in general, rigid perfectionism goes beyond the self and includes the self in relation to others.

We regard rigid perfectionism as one expression of perfectionism among other costly forms of perfectionism and it is problematic to view perfectionism that is less rigid as potentially adaptive. It remains for future investigators to determine whether rigid perfectionism is a discrete type of perfectionism that is qualitatively distinct or it is simply a more extreme and intense form of perfectionism according to a dimensional view. Research is also needed to determine the origins and antecedents of rigid perfectionism. Our sense is that rigid perfectionism is largely a reflection of feelings of insecurity and being defective and unmet interpersonal needs.

Analyses of rigid perfectionism are best informed by the broad literature on rigid personality. This research stretches across several decades and it indicates that personality rigidity is expressed in behaviour, but also in cognition and emotion. Rigidity can be reflected in terms of process and in terms of goals (see Cattell & Winder, 1952). Cognitive perseveration, repetition of thoughts, and a fixation on details can preclude a flexible approach to problem-solving (Cattell & Tiner, 1949) and undermine learning. Rigidity is reflected when a person seems capable of learning to problem solve and adapt to a particular situation but cannot or will not transfer this approach to other situations (see Forster et al., 1955). It involves a failure to shift to a strategy more likely to yield rewards (Wulfert et al., 1994), perhaps due to an inability or unwillingness to acknowledge the need for change. It can also involve a daily routinization that someone refuses to alter despite changing circumstances (e.g. running outside following an ice storm). Rigidity is further reflected in predictable decision-making and attitudinal inflexibility.

Taken to the extreme, personality rigidity is regarded as an indicator of personality dysfunction. This emphasis is a reflection of the longstanding interest in personality rigidity sparked by research and theory on inflexible authoritarians. It is generally recognized that personality disorder and dysfunction exist when personality rigidity "significantly, consistently, and chronically interferes with daily functioning, and/or causes significant distress" (Caligor et al., 2018, p. 27), either to the self or other people or to both the self and other people. By extension, it follows rigid perfectionism will linked inextricably with limitations in daily functioning and the generation and prolonging of significant distress and impairment.

Rigidity directed at others is likely to generate considerable stress and conflict but it is arguably even more problematic when rigidity is applied to the self. Personality rigidity here can entail neurotic inflexibility in terms of personal identity and associated defences (see Shapiro, 1965). Our approach to the treatment of perfectionists includes a strong emphasis on the relationship that the self has with the self (see Hewitt et al., 2017). The rigid perfectionist is someone who will both push and punish the self regardless of possible extenuating circumstances. This self-punitive stance stems from demanding perfection from the self. The rigid person will also harshly judge the self for deviations from personal dictates and there is little evidence of self-reinforcement and self-praise. Most notably, for extremely rigid perfectionists who are chronically dissatisfied, there is no escape from oneself.

Features of Rigid Perfectionism

To our knowledge, as mentioned above, a fulsome description of rigid perfectionism does not exist in the previously published literature despite attempts to characterize it and measure rigid perfectionism as a personality disorder symptom with obsessiveness-compulsive features (see Ayearst, Flett, & Hewitt, 2012). Moreover, the view taken here is that rigid perfectionism has elements that are broad and take it well beyond the tendency to equate rigid perfectionism with an obsession that details and things must be "just right", in keeping with our view that perfectionism is about perfecting the self and is largely achievement-based and a reflection of broad personal and interpersonal needs. Accordingly, rigid perfectionism continues to be poorly captured and under-represented in personality disorder frameworks that see it as a feature of obsessive-compulsive personality disorder. Moreover, extant measures of rigid perfectionism do not fully assess its elements.

What are the features of rigid perfectionism? We have summarized the various features in Table 15.1. Rigid perfectionism should be distinguishable in terms of affect, behaviour, cognition, and motivation.

Table 15.1 Characteristics and features of rigid perfectionism.

Characteristics and features
Relentless striving and an unabated need to be perfect and prove worth
Constant thoughts and images of being perfect and needing to be perfect
Inflexible, intense pursuit of perfection
Overarching sense of obligation and responsibility without exception
Hypercompetitive regardless of the situation
An irrational and overgeneralized importance to being perfect
Extreme commitment to and stubborn unwillingness to modify extreme goals and standards
Refusal to be satisfied with goal attainment and progress in achieving goals
Persistent insistence on the one right way to do things
Willingness to sacrifice timeliness if it leads to perfection
Impatience with the self and others
Activity-based self-worth that fuels tenacious striving
Fierce self-reliance to maintain freedom from social influence and control
Refusal to engage in self-care
Rigid beliefs about the weakness inherent in nurturing the self

We begin our analysis by noting that rigid perfectionism involves a form of perfectionistic striving that is not at all in keeping with characterizations of high levels of perfectionistic strivings that may be normal, health, and adaptive in a limited sense (see Stoeber & Otto, 2006). The attributes of rigid perfectionism are informed by classic descriptions of extreme and unremitting perfectionism provided by authors such as Burns (1980), Hamachek (1978), and Pacht (1984). It is also informed by the emphasis that Frost and DiBartolo (2002) placed on obsessive-compulsive features and "issues of control, security, and concern over criticism" (p. 380). The attributes in Table 15.1 describe the athlete who is a rigid perfectionist, but in keeping with the notion that it can go beyond the self, many attributes also apply to the extremely rigid other-oriented perfectionist who demands flawlessness and maximum effort from others.

We regard rigid perfectionism as a characterological form of inflexibility that is more evident when various trait perfectionism dimensions (e.g. self-oriented, other-oriented, and socially prescribed perfectionism) are already at an extreme level. People with high scores on our Multidimensional Perfectionism Scale (Hewitt & Flett, 1991, 2004) who are exceptionally rigid and insistent are far removed from an adaptive form of striving and conscientiousness. Indeed, this personality constellation shares features with the extreme hyper-conscientiousness documented by Carter et al. (2016). They showed that there is a level at which conscientiousness becomes maladaptive rather than advantageous due to features that result in a considerable overlap with obsessive-compulsive tendencies (e.g. single-minded rigid determination, excessive dutifulness, and ruminative deliberation as a form of over-thinking). This characterization fits with evidence suggesting that self-oriented perfectionism can be curvilinear and it becomes especially problematic at an extreme level (see Molnar et al., 2012).

What are other characteristics of rigid perfectionism? Flett and Hewitt (2006) emphasized an inflexible commitment to goals. The rigid perfectionist will not adjust goals downward, but it is possible that setbacks will result in raising the bar even higher in order to compensate for lost achievement opportunities. Frost and Henderson (1991) captured another feature of this goal orientation in performance situations with they asked their participants to respond to rating item, "My goals guide my every move during competition" (p. 326). It is bad when these goals are directed at the self but even worse when the rigid other-oriented perfectionist makes even greater demands of other people.

Ellis (2002) emphasized rigid thinking that involves absolute demands that the self and others must be perfect, but it is imperative to do perfectly well. This emphasis on imperatives and inflexible commitment suggests that rigid perfectionism captures the sense that the perfectionist has a duty to be perfect and is, in fact, obligated to be perfect. It translates into rigid, ceaseless striving at the behavioural level and a complete investment of the self. This emphasis on obligation, duty, and compulsion is in keeping with accounts of elevated perfectionism among runners who are obligatory exercisers (Coen & Ogles, 1993) and people who are consumed by an obsessive passion to be perfect. Perfectionism that is rigid moves beyond a harmonious form of passion; it instead becomes an obsessive, unrelenting passion and sense of being driven. This has been documented recently in qualitative research with adolescent perfectionists who admit that they know that perfectionism has its costs, but they cannot and will not stop trying to be perfect (see Molnar et al., 2022). Vallerand and Verner-Filion (2020) have described how obsessive passion typically entails rigid persistence towards an activity that limits the capacity to be flexible. They identified costs such as restricting creativity when it is needed and proneness to mounting life conflict when other components of the person's life have to put on hold when rigidly persisting with these activities. When it comes to rigidly perfectionistic athletes, goal pursuit sustained by obsessive passion may complicate their lives by adding to the interpersonal problems and the unmet interpersonal needs that we have identified as being central to understanding why so many people are so perfectionistic (see Hewitt et al., 2017).

Cognitive exhaustion is quite possible because this orientation not only includes perfectionistic thoughts and ruminations about being perfect and making mistakes, but also the work-related ruminative brooding that accompanies an excessive work orientation marked by an inability or unwillingness to relax. Some cognitive burnout may be due to the exhaustion that comes from feeling that the perfect front must be projected at all times.

An abiding sense of responsibility for everything may be at the root of this striving and unyielding sense of obligation. Frost et al. (1997) captured this element and how it can be a source of self-recrimination in crafting the scale items "I should not have allowed this to happen" and "I should have known better" (p. 214). This sense of personal responsibility is ever-present and unwavering, even when faced with uncontrollable and unmanageable circumstances.

The ceaseless striving outlined above is most evident when the rigid perfectionist is on familiar ground and is engaged in familiar activities. Millon (1969) reminded us that rigidity for those who become afraid of making mistakes comes in the form of avoiding the unfamiliar and operating within narrow life boundaries. He described people who fear the consequences of the unknown. Low adaptability here comes in the form of a refusal to try new activities due to chronic concerns about being negatively judged or revealed as incompetent.

As noted by Ayearst et al. (2012), rigid perfectionism is based on a conviction that there is only one right way to do things and a general belief in perfect solutions to problematic situations. There is a pervasive stubbornness and inflexibility reflected in goals, standards, and behaviour. As such, rigid perfectionism is the antithesis of adaptability and finding various ways of circumventing a challenge. Rigid perfectionism may also involve a willingness to sacrifice timelines in the quest for perfection, regardless of what this might entail, yet still experiencing an undercurrent of frustration and impatience with the self and others.

Smith et al. (2016) discussed rigid perfectionism as a "rigid insistence" that perfectionism must be obtained and developed a measure that assesses elements of rigid perfectionism. But how is rigid insistence expressed? Even miniscule mistakes are troubling for the rigid perfectionist because minor errors have great significance. However, rigid perfectionism as we see it likely goes further because it is also revealed by how the rigid perfectionist handles success. The rigid perfectionist is someone who seems driven by a sense of never being perfect enough. The notion of "relentless striving" refers in most instances to a relentless upward striving marked by an image of always being better or always doing better, perhaps due to the fear of being caught and surpassed by someone else. Missildine (1963) reflected this aspect when he sagely observed that most perfectionists are typically cognizant of their excessive striving but remain compelled to keep working excessively due to their self-critical nature but also an abiding sense that they can always do more and achieve more at a higher level.

Rigid perfectionism can also be viewed from a chronicity perspective. Does perfectionism require that the striving must never cease for these people? Rigid perfectionists will see reductions in striving as a form of weakness; these people always need to be perfect and this need never lessens, so they are unwilling to "pump the brakes" in life. The various tendencies linked with rigid perfectionism likely reflect the activity-based sense of self-worth described by DiBartolo and associates (see DiBartolo et al., 2004). People with an activity-based self-worth cannot feel good about themselves unless they are constantly active and goal-focused and this seems like it is a core contributor to burnout. The tendency to lighten up on striving may also be prohibited by the feared consequences of reducing effort and lowering standards.

The need to be perfect that is fuelling rigid perfectionism can seem addictive in the sense that being perfect or close to perfect may actually strengthen this need to be perfect. In such instances, the reality for elite performers is that success adds to pressure and raises expectations even higher and they feel like they have no choice but to keep striving and remain hypercompetitive. It involves a unidirectional drive upward that is akin to the unidirectional drive upward that fuels the social comparison of abilities described by Festinger (1954). In short, it feels like an upward spiral. Recently, we discussed similar tendencies by referring to the added pressure that can be experienced when someone high in socially prescribed perfectionism achieves success (see Flett et al., 2022).

Rigid perfectionism also entails a cognitive orientation that goes beyond typical descriptions of cognitive rigidity. The person who is a rigid perfectionist will be flooded with automatic thoughts we described that reflect the theme that perfection has not been attained and must be attained (see Flett et al., 1998). These thoughts can involve being consumed cognitively by self-recriminations. Rigidity also involves a chronic inability to shift attention and a tendency to be controlled by certain thoughts and images. We believe that Frost and Henderson (1991) were tapping into this element by asking their athletes about the degree to which their minds are flooded and controlled by associated images and thoughts, such as dreams of being the best and being perfect as well as images of mistakes. They alluded to these thoughts and images controlling the minds of perfectionistic athletes during competitions.

This rigidity extends to beliefs about the importance of being perfect and not making mistakes. Extreme perfectionists attach an irrational importance to being flawless. The intransigence here extends to an unwillingness to treat any situation as less important. Perhaps an unwillingness to downshift the importance level or been seen as doing this is fuelled by a fear that do so is an admission of inadequacy or it will be perceived as an admission of inadequacy.

The cognitive characteristics outlined above combine to undermine a healthy cognitive approach. Indeed, Flett and Hewitt (2022) emphasized how rigid perfectionism is antithetical to mindfulness and all it entails. The rigid perfectionist who is encouraged to become mindful, will, in all likelihood, regard mindfulness as the type of activity engaged in by people who simply don't measure up to expectations.

Rigid perfectionism also has an interpersonal element. Rigid perfectionists such as legendary golfer Ben Hogan are typically described as being fiercely independent and self-reliant as if they are rejecting social influence in ways that align with the dismissive attachment style. They are people who may seem remote even when in the presence of other people. Moreover, rigid perfectionists are typically unwilling to seek help and unable to admit a need for help from others. This inability to let other people know they are needed keeps people at a distance and adds to an image of aloofness that exacerbates the social disconnection they experience. The perfectionism social disconnection model is built around such tendencies and unmet interpersonal needs (see Hewitt et al., 2017).

Finally, rigidity extends to the approach to self-care and beliefs about self-care. The rigid perfectionist believes that the time to engage in self-care is a luxury that cannot be afforded. Efforts to rest, relax, and restore the self and the time taken to do so will likely elicit resistance, regret, and rumination about how competitors are not taking the time to slow down. Rigid beliefs are also involved such that self-care and self-compassion are seen as excuses that reflect weakness rather than strength.

As alluded to above, the driven perfectionist is highly persistent and tenacious in ways that clearly seem antithetical to the notion of adaptability. Flett and Hewitt (2014) focused on unhealthy, compulsive, and rigid striving when we pointed to perfectionists with exercise addictions who cannot relax in self-care and seem unable to relax despite the possibility that they are well beyond the point of exhaustion. This accords with qualitative accounts of driven athletes, dancers, and musicians as people with constantly increasing standards, obsessiveness, and rigid and dichotomous thinking and associated actions (see Hill et al., 2015). Consider, for instance, the retired American sprinter Michael Johnson. This extreme perfectionist has a lengthy list of exceptional accomplishments and was considered the world's greatest sprinter for several years. It was during his 2011 appearance on the BBC's *Desert Island Discs* that Johnson revealed that while competing, he trained every day for 10 years without ever taking a day off! Johnson went on to suffer a stroke; fortunately, he has recovered and is an accomplished broadcaster and commentator. This same approach to training and being unable or unwilling to tolerate any deviations from an excessively strict regimen is also an attribute displayed by English rugby player Johnny Wilkinson (see Hall et al., 2012).

Our description of rigid perfectionism and its facets paints a picture of an extreme form of perfectionism that is clearly differentiated from mild or moderate forms. The rigid perfectionist is someone who feels that perfection must be obtained and she or he absolutely has to be perfect, both in terms of the final outcome and in terms of the relentless pursuit of this outcome. This is a perfectionism driven by personal imperatives and imperatives directed at others. Our analysis refers to many elements that go well beyond the scale items that typically comprise existing measures of rigid perfectionism and it emphasizes the need to carefully assess and evaluate differences among people who all purport to be "perfectionists".

Perfectionism and Adaptability

We referred earlier to the legendary Ben Hogan. His life stands as a clear example of how perfectionism and perfectionists cannot ward off the unexpected. His almost fatal car accident in 1949 involved a head-on collision with a bus and resulted in physical injuries that meant he had no choice but to change virtually everything about himself and his approach. Ben Hogan's story is one of resilience but it is also a story of adaptability. Of course, the car accident experienced recently by Tiger Woods also has resulted in exceptional resilience and adaptability being required.

While there is extensive research on the coping styles of perfectionists, there has been little to no consideration thus far of what happens when perfectionists feel helplessness and hopeless to the point of paralysis and they have the urge to do nothing at all in response to adversity. It is at this precise moment that there is a need for adaptability and to believe that it is possible to evolve and adjust to such circumstances. Adaptability training that focuses on "finding a way" can make the difference between thriving versus perhaps not surviving unforeseeable adversities. This orientation is much more difficult to utilize when under pressure to not make a mistake or when burnout and cognitive exhaustion have made it very difficult to fathom constructive alternatives. The impact of being exposed to unrelenting pressure is important to underscore; a key question for elite athletes is whether they are able to not only cope with pressure, but also adapt to it.

It is useful here to consider the young athlete characterized by rigid perfectionism. This young person will often become self-preoccupied and defensive after failing to learn something or master something right away. This aspect of perfectionistic reactivity will be infused with anxiety and perhaps shame and embarrassment and these experiences will often preclude carefully considering alternative approaches to learning and task mastery. The limited capacity to adapt is on display when this athlete is consumed by a past mistake and is cognitively preoccupied with never making that same mistake again instead of trying out new solutions and strategies in the moment. They epitomize what Frost and DiBartolo (2002) meant when they referred to being preoccupied with mistakes during competition to the point that it interferes with task-relevant processing and adaptive reactions. Adaptability will be further limited when the young athlete is frustrated and inpatient and feels that deliberation and considering alternatives takes too much time and would reflect poorly on their ability or intelligence. Another limitation is the hypersensitivity to criticism and the tendency to anticipate negative reactions from other people. This image contrasts with other young athletes who are self-confident and who have learned to adapt because they trust themselves and their coaches and they know deep down inside that eventually they will master the task or overcome the challenge. The adaptability of these young athletes tends to be accompanied by openness to feedback and suggestions from coaches and mentors about constructive responses and alternative approaches to new and uncertain situations.

A case example featured in Flett and Hewitt (2022) seems especially relevant here. Gould et al. (1997) described the vulnerabilities of a junior tennis player named Jan. She experienced significant burnout and distress and ultimately stopped playing tennis. Her rigid perfectionism extended to an unwillingness to adapt by modifying her goals; she was unable or unwilling to adjust her training regime despite the burnout and a downward spiral of low self-esteem. Rigidity also precluded seeking help; she chose instead to hide her inner turmoil from others. This is a general reflection of how adolescent perfectionists hide behind "a perfect front" (see Molnar et al., 2022). But this case example also underscores how contextual factors can place limits on being adaptively flexible. In this instance, Jan was under enormous pressure from her demanding father and overly controlling coach. Clearly, developing and exercising the capacity to adapt is better served in highly supportive environments with people who model how to be adaptable rather than how to be rigid and inflexible.

What else does adaptability require from the perfectionist? We noted in a previous chapter that perfectionists differ in how they approach life and some perfectionists do considerably better than do others. Several key tendencies were noted in our analysis of perfectionists who are more or less able to flourish in life (see Flett & Hewitt, 2015). What distinguishes these people? Clearly, a flexible and growth-oriented mindset is preferred instead of a fixed mindset that roots failure in personal limitations. A general inability to be adaptable may be further exacerbated by the mental distress and burnout that is evident among so many perfectionists (for a discussion, see Flett & Hewitt, 2020). But another form of low adaptability involves an unwillingness to adjust the perceived importance of being perfect. We noted in a recent review article on the destructiveness of socially prescribed perfectionism that one key mediator is the degree to which socially prescribed perfectionism is all-consuming because it has been ascribed an extremely high level of importance (see Flett et al. 2022). Two decades earlier, Albert Ellis (2002) emphasized the irrational importance of needing to be perfect and saw it as central to the vulnerability of perfectionists. A key objective for the perfectionist is to learn when perfection and maximal effort are important and when they are simply not required.

This emphasis on the low adaptability of rigid perfectionists has some clear and obvious implications for the training and psycho-education of athletes and others who may struggle with perfectionism, including dancers and exercisers. It needs to be emphasized in coaching and training that it is important to develop a high level of adaptability and have this adaptability reflected in the approach to affect, behaviour, and cognition. It also seems evident that coaching and training needs to consider adaptability in terms developing the capability to proactively adapt to life and engage flexibly with problems, and perhaps how to read situations or anticipate them in advance to avoid becoming mired in unfavourable circumstances. Elite athletes in particular need to open to finding ways to adjust as their careers progress. The perfectionist with a strong sense of adaptability may be more open to the key distinction between striving for perfectionism versus striving for excellence (see Gaudreau, 2019; Gaudreau et al., 2022); realizing that perfection is not always needed or called for is likely a key to greater longevity.

A focus on training perfectionists to become higher in adaptability has the benefit of underscoring the importance of making adjustments to the athlete's mindset. A key overarching message is the need to counter the typical perfectionistic mindset with a mindset more in line with a focus on the notion of growth, change, learning, developing, and evolving rather than judging the self as a fixed entity and being a person who has what it takes or lacks what it takes. Another paradox that seems to apply to many perfectionists is that they recognize the need for improvement and embrace many self-improvement goals, yet they do so from a perspective that is dominated by fixed self-image goals and self-appraisals built too often on judging the self as a final product with little capability of growing and developing in positive ways.

This emphasis on a rigid perfectionism that restricts being adaptable can become an issue for anyone involved in elite sports and needing to make choices and decisions in high pressure circumstances. One overarching question from a coaching and management perspective is, "To what extent to which a rigid adherence to analytics results in poor decision-making?" Data-driven decisions to make a substitution for a tiring athlete who is still performing well need to consider whether the athlete's replacement has a comparable ability to handle and adapt to the pressure. Similarly, rigid perfectionism likely plays a role when coaches and managers adopt a rigid conceptualization of talent and an entrenched approach to player selection, evaluation, and development (for a discussion, see Baker, 2022).

It should be evident after even brief reflection that the dearth of research on perfectionism and adaptability means that there is much more still left to learn about perfectionism in general and perfectionism in sports in particular. Comparative research of perfectionists who are high versus low in adaptability should be illuminating and lead to new insights about how and when perfectionism is debilitating versus when it has fewer costs and consequences associated with it.

Summary

In summary, we continue to focus on the costs and consequences that await perfectionistic athletes. We chose to extend our analysis of perfectionistic reactivity by focusing on a neglected topic – perfectionism and adaptability – rather than revisiting the myriad themes found in our previous articles and chapters. Our current analysis focused on the notion of rigid perfectionism and how success for perfectionists will require them to learn how to adapt. Unfortunately, rigid perfectionists who recognize and acknowledge their need to adapt may view their need to adapt as yet another sign they have failed. It has been suggested that perfectionists are unwilling to change, but according to our perspective, many may simply be unable to change; indeed, they have little experience with adapting and changing to keep pace with changing circumstances.

We will close by noting that over 70 years ago, Karen Horney (1950) discussed perfectionism as reflecting "the tyranny of the shoulds" and she framed it in terms of people feeling they should be and must be the perfect parent, the perfect friend, or the perfect spouse. This tyranny extends to anyone who is invested in becoming the perfect athlete. Tyranny involves commanding the self and others to be absolutely flawless and never letting up. To us, rigid perfectionism seems to "ups the ante" in terms of this tyranny because it precludes adaptability and other functional ways of reacting to myriad challenges ahead.

References

Adams, T, (2007). "I can't explain except to say I wanted to play again. It was madness." *The Guardian*, 7 January. Retrieved from www.theguardian.com/sport/2007/jan/07/tennis.features2.

Ayearst, L., Flett, G. L., & Hewitt, P. L. (2012). Where is multidimensional perfectionism in DSM-5? A question posed to the DSM-5 Personality and Personality Disorders Work Group. *Personality Disorders: Theory, Research, and Treatment*, 3, 458–469.

Baker, J. (2022). *The tyranny of talent: How it compels and limits athletic achievement … and why you should ignore it.* Aberrant Press.

Besser, A., Flett, G. L., Nepon, T., & Zeigler-Hill, V. (2020). Personality, cognition, and adaptability to the covid-19 pandemic: Associations with loneliness, distress, and positive and negative mood states. *International Journal of Mental Health and Addiction*, online ahead of print. https://doi.org/10.1007/s11469-020-00421-x.

Besser, A., Flett, G. L., & Zeigler-Hill, V. (2022). Adaptability to a sudden transition to online learning during the COVID-19 pandemic: Understanding the challenges for students. *Scholarship of Teaching and Learning in Psychology*, 8(2), 85–105. https://doi.org/10.1037/stl0000198.

Burns, D. D. (1980). The perfectionist's script for self-defeat. *Psychology Today*, November, pp. 34–52.

Caligor, E., Kernberg, O. F., Clarkin, J. F., & Yeomans, F. E. (2018). *Psychodynamic therapy for personality pathology: Treating self and interpersonal functioning.* American Psychiatric Association Publishing.

Carter, N. T., Guan, L., Maples, J. L., Williamson, R. L., & Miller, J. D. (2016). The downsides of extreme conscientiousness for psychological well-being: The role of obsessive compulsive tendencies. *Journal of Personality*, 84(4), 510–522. https://doi.org/10.1111/jopy.12177.

Cattell, R. B., & Tiner, L. G. (1949). The varieties of structural rigidity. *Journal of Personality*, 17, 321–341. https://doi.org/10.1111/j.1467-6494.1949.tb01217.x.

Cattell, R. B., & Winder, A. E. (1952). Structural rigidity in relation to learning theory and clinical psychology. *Psychological Review*, 59(1), 23–39. https://doi.org/10.1037/h0055420.

Clark, J. D., Mallett, C. J., & Coulter, T. J. (2022). Personal strivings of mentally tough Australian Rules footballers. *Psychology of Sport and Exercise*, 58, 102090. https://doi.org/10.1016/j.psychsport.2021.102090.

Coen, S. P., & Ogles, B. M. (1993). Psychological characteristics of the obligatory runner: A critical examination of the anorexia analogue hypothesis. *Journal of Sport & Exercise Psychology*, 15(3), 338–354.

Collins, D. J., & Macnamara, A. (2017). Making champs and super-champs—Current views, contradictions, and future directions. *Frontiers in Psychology*, 8, article 823.

Curran, T., & Hill, A. P. (2018). A test of perfectionistic vulnerability following competitive failure among college athletes. *Journal of Sport & Exercise Psychology*, 40(5), 269–279. https://doi.org/10.1123/jsep.2018-0059.

DiBartolo, P. M., Frost, R. O., Chang, P., LaSota, M., & Grills, A. E. (2004). Shedding light on the relationship between personal standards and psychopathology: The case for contingent self-worth. *Journal of Rational-Emotive & Cognitive-Behavior Therapy*, 22(4), 237–250. https://doi.org/10.1023/B:JORE.0000047310.94044.ac.

Douglas, B. (2022). *McEnroe*. London, England: Sylver Entertainment.

Ellis, A. (2002). The role of irrational beliefs in perfectionism. In G. L. Flett & P. L. Hewitt (eds), *Perfectionism: Theory, research, and treatment* (pp. 217–229). American Psychological Association.

Festinger, L. (1954). A theory of social comparison processes. *Human Relations*, 7, 117–140. https://doi.org/10.1177/001872675400700202.

Flett, G. L., & Hewitt, P. L. (2005). The perils of perfectionism in sports and exercise. *Current Directions in Psychological Science*, 14, 14–18.

Flett, G. L., & Hewitt, P. L. (2006). Positive versus negative perfectionism in psychopathology: A comment on Slade and Owens's dual process model. *Behavior Modification*, 30(4), 472–495. https://doi.org/10.1177/0145445506288026.

Flett, G. L., & Hewitt, P. L. (2014) "The perils of perfectionism in sports" revisited: Toward a broader understanding of the pressure to be perfect and its impact on athletes and dancers. *International Journal of Sport Psychology*, 45, 395–407.

Flett, G. L., & Hewitt, P. L. (2015). Managing perfectionism and the excessive striving that undermines flourishing: Implications for leading the perfect life. In R. J. Burke, K. M. Page, & C. L. Cooper (eds), *Flourishing in life, work and careers: Individual wellbeing and career experiences* (pp. 45–66). Edward Elgar Publishing. https://doi.org/10.4337/9781783474103.00011.

Flett, G. L., & Hewitt, P. L. (2016). Reflections on perfection and the pressure to be perfect in athletes, dancers, and exercisers: A focus on perfectionistic reactivity in key situations and life contexts. In A. P.Hill (ed.), *The psychology of perfectionism in sport, dance, and exercise* (pp. 296–319). Routledge.

Flett, G. L., & Hewitt, P. L. (2020). The perfectionism pandemic meets COVID-19: Understanding the stress, distress, and problems in living for perfectionists during the global health crisis. *Journal of Concurrent Disorders*, 2(1), 80–105.

Flett, G. L., & Hewitt, P. L. (2022). *Perfectionism in childhood and adolescence: A developmental approach*. American Psychological Association. https://doi.org/10.1037/0000289-000.

Flett, G. L., Hewitt, P. L., Blankstein, K. R., & Gray, L. (1998). Psychological distress and the frequency of perfectionism thinking. *Journal of Personality and Social Psychology*, 75, 1363–1381.

Flett, G. L, Hewitt, P. L., Nepon, T., Sherry, S. B., & Smith, M. (2022). The destructiveness and public health significance of socially prescribed perfectionism: A review, analysis, and conceptual extension. *Clinical Psychology Review*, 93, 102130. https://doi.org/10.1016/j.cpr.2022.102130.

Flett, G. L., Nepon, T., Hewitt, P. L., Zaki-Azat, J., Rose, A. L., & Swiderski, K. (2020). The Mistake Rumination Scale: Development, validation, and utility of a measure of cognitive perfectionism. *Journal of Psychoeducational Assessment*, 38, 84–98.

Forster, N. C., Vinacke, W. E., & Digman, J. M. (1955). Flexibility and rigidity in a variety of problem situations. *The Journal of Abnormal and Social Psychology*, 50(2), 211–216. https://doi.org/10.1037/h0049230.

Forsythe, C. J., & Compas, B. E. (1987). Interaction of cognitive appraisals of stressful events and coping: Testing the goodness of fit hypothesis. *Cognitive Therapy and Research*, 11, 473–485.

Fromm. E. (1941). *Escape from freedom*. Holt and Company.

Frost, R. O., & DiBartolo, P. M. (2002). Perfectionism, anxiety, and obsessive-compulsive disorder. In G. L.Flett & P. L. Hewitt (eds), *Perfectionism: Theory, research, and treatment* (pp. 341–371). American Psychological Association. https://doi.org/10.1037/10458-014.

Frost, R. O., & Henderson, K. J. (1991). Perfectionism and reactions to athletic competition. *Journal of Sport and Exercise Psychology*, 13, 323–335.

Frost, R. O., Marten, P., Lahart, C., & Rosenblate, R. (1990). The dimensions of perfectionism. *Cognitive Therapy and Research*, 14, 449–468.

Frost, R. O., Trepanier, K. L., Brown, E. J., & Heimberg, R. G. (1997). Self-monitoring of mistakes among subjects high and low in perfectionistic concern over mistakes. *Cognitive Therapy and Research*, 21, 209–222.

Gaudreau, P. (2019). On the distinction between personal standards perfectionism and excellencism: A theory elaboration and research agenda. *Current Perspectives on Psychological Science*, 14, 197–215.

Gaudreau, P., Schellenberg, B. J. I., Gareau, A., Kljajic, K., & Manoni-Millar, S. (2022). Because excellencism is more than good enough: On the need to distinguish the pursuit of excellence from the pursuit of perfection. *Journal of Personality and Social Psychology*, 122(6), 1117–1145. https://doi.org/10.1037/pspp0000411.

Gotwals, J. K., J., Dunn, J. G. H., & Stoll, O. (2012). Are perfectionistic strivings in sports adaptive? A systematic review of confirmatory, contradictory, and mixed evidence. *Canadian Psychology*, 53, 263–279.

Gould, D., Tuffey, S., Udry, E., & Loehr, J. (1997). Burnout in competitive junior tennis players: III. Individual differences in the burnout experience. *The Sport Psychologist*, 11(3), 257–276.

Gross, T. (2013). Pioneer Billie Jean King moved the baseline for women's tennis. [Radio broadcast]. Retrieved from www.npr.org/transcripts/221362904.

Hall, H. K., Hill, A. P., & Appleton, P. R. (2012). Perfectionism: A foundation for sporting excellence or an uneasy pathway toward purgatory? In G. C. Roberts & D. Treasure (eds), *Advances in motivation in sport and exercise* (3rd ed., pp. 129–168). Human Kinetics.

Hamachek, D. E. (1978). Psychodynamics of normal and neurotic perfectionism. *Psychology*, 15, 27–33.

Herbison, J. D., Martin, L. J., & Sarkar, M. (2019). Achievement despite adversity: A qualitative investigation of undrafted national hockey league players. *Sport Psychologist*, 33, 285–294. doi:10.1123/tsp.2018-0037.

Hewitt, P. L., & Flett, G. L. (1991). Perfectionism in the self and social contexts: Conceptualization, assessment, and association with psychopathology. *Journal of Personality and Social Psychology*, 60, 456–470.

Hewitt, P. L., Flett, G. L., & Mikail, S. F. (2017). *Perfectionism: A relational approach to assessment, treatment, and conceptualization.* Guilford.

Hill, A. P., Hall, H. K., Duda, J. L., & Appleton, P. R. (2011). The cognitive, affective, and behavioural responses of self-oriented perfectionists following successful failure on a muscular endurance task. *International Journal of Sport and Exercise Psychology*, 9, 189–207.

Hill, A. P., Witcher, C. S. G., Gotwals, J. K., & Leyland, A. F. (2015). A qualitative study of perfectionism among self-identified perfectionists in sport and the performing arts. *Sport, Exercise, and Performance Psychology*, 4(4), 237–253. https://doi.org/10.1037/spy0000041.

Horney, K. (1937). *The neurotic personality of our time.* Norton.

Horney, K. (1950). *Neurosis and human growth.* Norton.

Klockare, E., Olffson, L. F., Gustafsson, H., Lundqvist, C., & Hill, A. P. (2022). Sports psychology consultants' view on working with perfectionistic elite athletes. *The Sport Psychologist*, 36, 219–227. https://doi.org/10.1123/tsp.2021-0055.

Lizmore, M. R., Dunn, J. G. H., & Dunn, J. C. (2017). Perfectionistic strivings, perfectionistic concerns, and reactions to poor personal performances among intercollegiate athletes. *Psychology of Sport and Exercise*, 33, 75–84. https://doi.org/10.1016/j.psychsport.2017.07.010.

Martin, A. J. (2017). Adaptability—what it is and what it is not: comment on Chandra and Leong (2016). *American Psychologist*, 72, 696–698.

Martin, A. J., Nejad, H. G., Colmar, S., & Liem, G. A. D. (2013). Adaptability: how students' responses to uncertainty and novelty predict their academic and non-academic outcomes. *Journal of Educational Psychology*, 105, 728–746. https://doi.org/10.1037/a0032794.

Millon, T. (1969). *Modern psychopathology: A biosocial approach to maladaptive learning and functioning.* W. B. Saunders Company.

Missildine, W. H. (1963). *Your inner child of the past.* Simon & Schuster.

Molnar, D. S., Flett, G. L., Sadava, S. W., & Colautti, J. (2012). Perfectionism and health functioning in women with fibromyalgia. *Journal of Psychosomatic Research*, 73(4), 295–300. https://doi.org/10.1016/j.jpsychores.2012.08.001.

Molnar, D. S., Blackburn, M., Tacuri, N., Zinga, D., Flett, G. L., & Hewitt, P. L. (2023). "I need to be perfect or else the world's gonna end": A qualitative analysis of adolescent perfectionists' expression and understanding of their perfectionism. Canadian Psychology. https://doi.org/10.1037/cap0000357.

Pacht, A. R. (1984). Reflections on perfection. *American Psychologist*, 39, 386–390.

Sarkar, M., & Fletcher, D. (2014). Ordinary magic, extraordinary performance: Psychological resilience and thriving in high achievers. *Sports, Exercise, and Performance Psychology*, 3, 46–60.

Shapiro, D. (1965). *Neurotic styles.* Basic Books.

Smith, M. M., Saklofske, D. H., Stoeber, J., & Sherry, S. B. (2016). The Big Three Perfectionism Scale: A new measure of perfectionism. *Journal of Psychoeducational Assessment*, 34(7), 670–687. https://doi.org/10.1177/0734282916651539.

Sorkkila, M., Ryba, T. V., Selänne, H., & Aunola, K. (2020). Development of school and sport burnout in adolescent student-athletes: A longitudinal mixed-methods study. *Journal of Research on Adolescence*, 30(Suppl 1), 115–133. https://doi.org/10.1111/jora.12453.

Stoeber, J. (2014). Multidimensional perfectionism and the DSM-5 personality traits. *Personality and Individual Differences*, 64, 115–120. https://doi.org/10.1016/j.paid.2014.02.031.

Stoeber, J., & Otto, K. (2006). Positive conceptions of perfectionism: Approaches, evidence, challenges. *Personality and Social Psychology Review*, 10(4), 295–319. https://doi.org/10.1207/s15327957pspr1004_2.

Tamminen, K. A., Crocker, P. R. E., & McEwen, C. E. (2014). Emotional experiences and coping in sport: How to promote positive adaptational outcomes in sport. In A. R. Gomes, R. Resende, & A. Albuquerque (eds), *Positive human functioning from a multidimensional perspective, Vol. 1. Promoting stress adaptation* (pp. 143–162). Nova Science Publishers.

Vallerand, R. J., & Verner-Filion, J. (2020). Theory and research in passion for sport and exercise. In G. Tenenbaum, & R. Eklund (eds), *Handbook of sport psychology* (4th edition, pp. 206–229). Wiley. https://doi.org/10.1002/9781119568124.ch11.

Wulfert, E., Greenway, D. E., Farkas, P., & Hayes, S. C. (1994). Correlation between self-reported rigidity and rule-governed insensitivity to operant contingencies. *Journal of Applied Behavior Analysis*, 27(4), 659–671. https://doi.org/10.1901/jaba.1994.27-659.

Index